MS Project 2016 Instructions in *Contemporary Project Management 4e*

Chapter	MS Project
3	MS Project 2016 Introduction

3   MS Project 2016 Introduction

       Ribbon, Quick Access Toolbar, view panes, Zoom Slider, Shortcuts, Scheduling Mode Selector

    Setting Up Your First Project

       Auto schedule, start date, identifying information, summary row

    Create Milestone Schedule

       Key milestones, zero duration, must finish on, information

7   Set Up a Work Breakdown Structure (WBS)

       Understand the WBS definitions and displays

       Enter WBS Elements (tasks), Create the outline,

       Insert WBS Code Identifier column, Hide or show subtasks detail

8   Using MS Project for Critical Path Schedules

    Set Up the Project Schedule

       Set or update the project start date, Define organization's working and nonworking time

    Build the Network Diagram and Identify the Critical Path

       Enter tasks and milestones, edit the timescale, understand and define task dependencies, assign task duration estimates, identify the critical path, understand the network diagram view

    Display and Print Schedules

9   Define Resources

       Resource views, max units, resource calendars

    Assigning Resources

       Basic assignment, modify an assignment

    Identify Overallocated Resources

       Resource usage and Detailed Gantt views together

    Overallocated Resources

       Finding overallocated resources, dealing with overallocations

    Crashing a Critical Path Activity

10   Develop Bottom-up Project Budget

       Assignment costs, task costs, various cost perspectives

    Develop Summary Project Budget

12   Baseline the Project Plan

       First time baseline, subsequent baselines, viewing variances

14   Using MS Project to Monitor and Control Projects

    What Makes a Schedule Useful?

    How MS Project recalculates based on reported actuals, current and future impacts of variances, define the performance update process (who, what, when)

    Steps to Update the Project Schedule

       Acquire performance data, set and display status date, Enter duration-based performance data, reschedule remaining work, revise future estimates

15   Close Project

       Creating project progress reports, sharing reports, export a report to MS Excel, archive project work, capture and publish lessons learned

PMBOK® Guide 6e Coverage in *Contemporary Project Management 4e*

The numbers refer to the text page where the process is defined.

Project management (PM) processes and knowledge areas 10–11
Projects and strategic planning 33–37
Portfolio and program management 37–42

Project life cycle 7–10, 62–64
Organizational influences 102–110

		PMBOK® Guide, 6th ed. Coverage			
Knowledge Areas	Initiating Process Group	Planning Process Group	Executing Process Group	Monitoring & Controlling Process Group	Closing Process Group
Project Integration Management	Develop Project Charter 60–79	Develop Project Management Plan 409–410	Direct and Manage Project Work 459–460 Manage Project Knowledge 192–193, 504–508	Monitor and Control Project Work 460–462 Perform Integrated Change Control 229–232, 462–463	Close Project or Phase 503, 508–511
Project Scope Management		Plan Scope Management 211–212 Collect Requirements 212–216 Define Scope 216–220 Create WBS 220–229		Validate Scope 500–501 Control Scope 475–476	
Project Schedule Management		Plan Schedule Management 246 Define Activities 249–253 Sequence Activities 253–255 Estimate Activity Durations 255–258 Develop Schedule 259–267		Control Schedule 476–480	
Project Cost Management		Plan Cost Management 329–330 Estimate Costs 330–341 Determine Budget 342–344		Control Costs 345, 476–480	
Project Quality Management		Plan Quality Management 401–404	Manage Quality 404–406, 469–474	Control Quality 406–409, 469–474	
Project Resources Management		Plan Resource Management 290–295 Estimate Activity Resources 290	Aquire Resources 138–141 Develop Team 141–157 Manage Team 157–161	Control Resources 476	
Project Communications Management		Plan Communications Management 188–192	Manage Communications 193–199, 465–467	Monitor Communications 467–468	
Project Risk Management		Plan Risk Management 360–366 Identify Risks 75, 366–368 Perform Qualitative Risk Analysis 75, 368–372 Perform Quantitative Risk Analysis 372–373 Plan Risk Responses 75, 373–377	Implement Risk Responses 464–465	Monitor Risks 463–464	
Project Procurement Management		Plan Procurement Management 431–433, 438–441	Conduct Procurements 434–438	Control Procurments 441	
Project Stakeholder Management	Identify Stakeholders 75–77, 178–184	Plan Stakeholder Engagement 184–186	Manage Stakeholder Engagement 187–188	Monitor Stakeholder Engagement 188	

Source: Adapted from *A Guide to the Project Management Body of Knowledge (PMBOK® Guide), 6th ed.* (Newtown Square, PA: Project Management Institute, Inc., 2017): 31.

Contemporary Project Management

ORGANIZE · LEAD · PLAN · PERFORM

FOURTH EDITION

TIMOTHY J. KLOPPENBORG
Xavier University

VITTAL ANANTATMULA
Western Carolina University

KATHRYN N. WELLS
Keller Williams Real Estate

CENGAGE

Australia · Brazil · Mexico · Singapore · United Kingdom · United States

Contemporary Project Management, Fourth Edition

Timothy J. Kloppenborg

Vice President, Business and Economics: Mike Schenk

Sr. Product Manager: Aaron Arnsparger

Content Developer: Conor Allen

Product Assistant: Renee Schnee

Sr. Marketing Manager: Nate Anderson

Digital Content Specialist: Jennifer Chinn

Manufacturing Planner: Ron Montgomery

Sr. Art Director: Michelle Kunkler

Cover Image: iStockphoto.com/PeopleImages

Intellectual Property Analyst: Brittani Morgan

Intellectual Property Project Manager: Nick Barrows

Production Service: Lumina Datamatics, Inc.

For product information and technology assistance, contact us at
Cengage Learning Customer & Sales Support, 1-800-354-9706

For permission to use material from this text or product, submit all requests online at **www.cengage.com/permissions**
Further permissions questions can be emailed to
permissionrequest@cengage.com

Library of Congress Control Number: 2017947974

ISBN: 978-1-337-40645-1

Cengage Learning
20 Channel Center Street
Boston, MA 02210
USA

Cengage Learning is a leading provider of customized learning solutions with employees residing in nearly 40 different countries and sales in more than 125 countries around the world. Find your local representative at **www.cengage.com.**

Cengage Learning products are represented in Canada by Nelson Education, Ltd.

To learn more about Cengage Learning Solutions, visit **www.cengage.com**

Purchase any of our products at your local college store or at our preferred online store **www.cengagebrain.com**

Printed in Mexico
Print Number: 07   Print Year: 2020

MS Project 2016 Instructions in *Contemporary Project Management 4e*

Chapter	MS Project

3   MS Project 2016 Introduction

         Ribbon, Quick Access Toolbar, view panes, Zoom Slider, Shortcuts, Scheduling Mode Selector

         Setting Up Your First Project

                 Auto schedule, start date, identifying information, summary row

         Create Milestone Schedule

                 Key milestones, zero duration, must finish on, information

7   Set Up a Work Breakdown Structure (WBS)

                 Understand the WBS definitions and displays

                 Enter WBS Elements (tasks), Create the outline,

                 Insert WBS Code Identifier column, Hide or show subtasks detail

8   Using MS Project for Critical Path Schedules

         Set Up the Project Schedule

                 Set or update the project start date, Define organization's working and nonworking time

         Build the Network Diagram and Identify the Critical Path

                 Enter tasks and milestones, edit the timescale, understand and define task dependencies, assign task duration estimates, identify the critical path, understand the network diagram view

         Display and Print Schedules

9   Define Resources

                 Resource views, max units, resource calendars

         Assigning Resources

                 Basic assignment, modify an assignment

         Identify Overallocated Resources

                 Resource usage and Detailed Gantt views together

         Overallocated Resources

                 Finding overallocated resources, dealing with overallocations

         Crashing a Critical Path Activity

10   Develop Bottom-up Project Budget

                 Assignment costs, task costs, various cost perspectives

         Develop Summary Project Budget

12   Baseline the Project Plan

                 First time baseline, subsequent baselines, viewing variances

14   Using MS Project to Monitor and Control Projects

         What Makes a Schedule Useful?

         How MS Project recalculates based on reported actuals, current and future impacts of variances, define the performance update process (who, what, when)

         Steps to Update the Project Schedule

                 Acquire performance data, set and display status date, Enter duration-based performance data, reschedule remaining work, revise future estimates

15   Close Project

                 Creating project progress reports, sharing reports, export a report to MS Excel, archive project work, capture and publish lessons learned

PMBOK® Guide 6e Coverage in *Contemporary Project Management 4e*

The numbers refer to the text page where the process is defined.

Project management (PM) processes and knowledge areas 10–11
Projects and strategic planning 33–37
Portfolio and program management 37–42

Project life cycle 7–10, 62–64
Organizational influences 102–110

		PMBOK® Guide, 6th ed. Coverage			
Knowledge Areas	Initiating Process Group	Planning Process Group	Executing Process Group	Monitoring & Controlling Process Group	Closing Process Group
Project Integration Management	Develop Project Charter 60–79	Develop Project Management Plan 409–410	Direct and Manage Project Work 459–460 Manage Project Knowledge 192–193, 504–508	Monitor and Control Project Work 460–462 Perform Integrated Change Control 229–232, 462–463	Close Project or Phase 503, 508–511
Project Scope Management		Plan Scope Management 211–212 Collect Requirements 212–216 Define Scope 216–220 Create WBS 220–229		Validate Scope 500–501 Control Scope 475–476	
Project Schedule Management		Plan Schedule Management 246 Define Activities 249–253 Sequence Activities 253–255 Estimate Activity Durations 255–258 Develop Schedule 259–267		Control Schedule 476–480	
Project Cost Management		Plan Cost Management 329–330 Estimate Costs 330–341 Determine Budget 342–344		Control Costs 345, 476–480	
Project Quality Management		Plan Quality Management 401–404	Manage Quality 404–406, 469–474	Control Quality 406–409, 469–474	
Project Resources Management		Plan Resource Management 290–295 Estimate Activity Resources 290	Aquire Resources 138–141 Develop Team 141–157 Manage Team 157–161	Control Resources 476	
Project Communications Management		Plan Communications Management 188–192	Manage Communications 193–199, 465–467	Monitor Communications 467–468	
Project Risk Management		Plan Risk Management 360–366 Identify Risks 75, 366–368 Perform Qualitative Risk Analysis 75, 368–372 Perform Quantitative Risk Analysis 372–373 Plan Risk Responses 75, 373–377	Implement Risk Responses 464–465	Monitor Risks 463–464	
Project Procurement Management		Plan Procurement Management 431–433, 438–441	Conduct Procurements 434–438	Control Procurments 441	
Project Stakeholder Management	Identify Stakeholders 75–77, 178–184	Plan Stakeholder Engagement 184–186	Manage Stakeholder Engagement 187–188	Monitor Stakeholder Engagement 188	

Source: Adapted from *A Guide to the Project Management Body of Knowledge (PMBOK® Guide), 6th ed.* (Newtown Square, PA: Project Management Institute, Inc., 2017): 31.

Brief Contents

Flowchart of PMBOK Processes

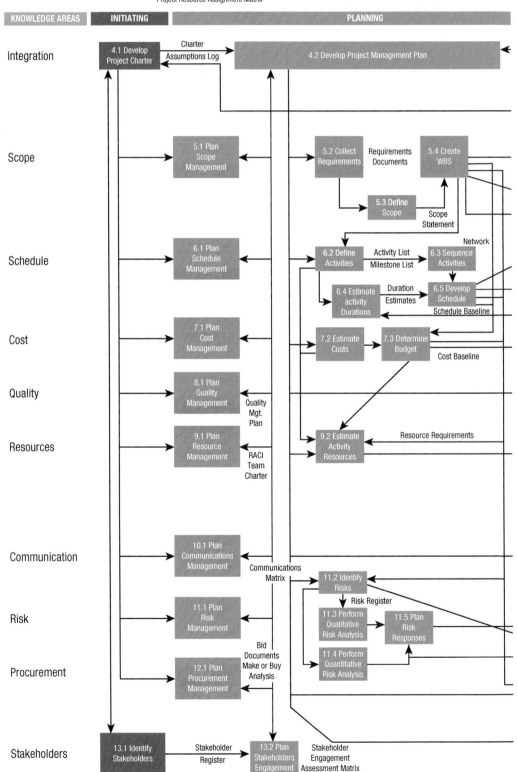

KNOWLEDGE AREAS	INITIATING	PLANNING

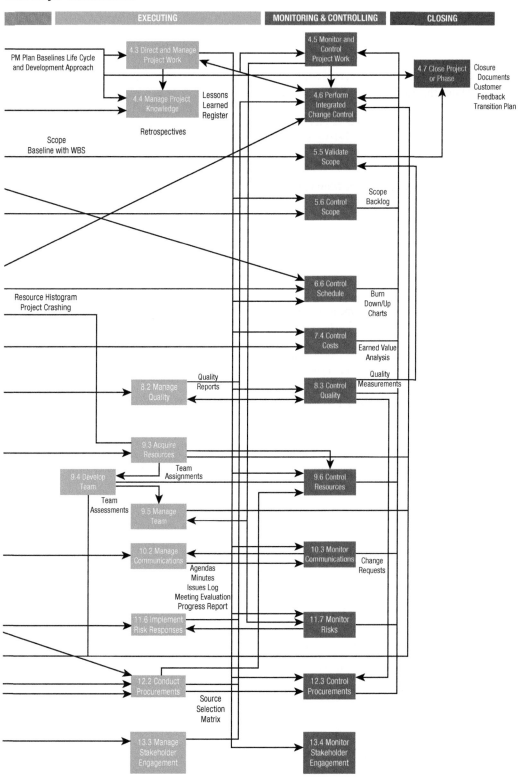

and Major Deliverables

Realizing **Benefits**

Benefits Analysis

EXECUTING | **MONITORING & CONTROLLING** | **CLOSING**

PM Plan Baselines Life Cycle and Development Approach

4.3 Direct and Manage Project Work

4.4 Manage Project Knowledge

Lessons Learned Register

Retrospectives

Scope Baseline with WBS

4.5 Monitor and Control Project Work

4.6 Perform Integrated Change Control

4.7 Close Project or Phase

Closure Documents Customer Feedback Transition Plan

5.5 Validate Scope

5.6 Control Scope

Scope Backlog

6.6 Control Schedule

Burn Down/Up Charts

Resource Histogram Project Crashing

7.4 Control Costs

Earned Value Analysis

Quality Reports

8.2 Manage Quality

8.3 Control Quality

Quality Measurements

9.3 Acquire Resources

9.4 Develop Team

Team Assignments

9.6 Control Resources

Team Assessments

9.5 Manage Team

10.2 Manage Communications

10.3 Monitor Communications

Change Requests

Agendas Minutes Issues Log Meeting Evaluation Progress Report

11.6 Implement Risk Responses

11.7 Monitor Risks

12.2 Conduct Procurements

12.3 Control Procurements

Source Selection Matrix

13.3 Manage Stakeholder Engagement

13.4 Monitor Stakeholder Engagement

Contents

PART 1   Organizing Projects

PART **2**   Leading Projects

CHAPTER **4**

Organizational Capability: Structure, Culture, and Roles 100

PART 4   Performing Projects

CHAPTER **13**

Project Supply Chain Management 426

Preface

While project managers today still need to use many techniques that have stood the test of several decades, they increasingly also must recognize the business need for a project, sort through multiple conflicting stakeholder demands. They must know how to deal with rapid change, a myriad of communication issues, global and virtual project teams, modern approaches to quality improvement, when to tailor their project management approach to include methods and behaviors from Agile, and many other issues that are more challenging than those in projects of the past.

Contemporary project management utilizes the tried-and-true project management techniques along with modern improvements such as the most current versions of Microsoft® Project Professional 2016, the sixth edition of the *Guide to the Project Management Body of Knowledge (PMBOK® Guide),* and many approaches derived from adaptive (Agile) project management. Contemporary project management also uses many tools and understandings that come from modern approaches to quality and communications, expanded role definitions, leadership principles, human strengths, and many other sources. Contemporary project management is scalable, using simple versions of important techniques on small projects and more involved versions on more complex projects.

Distinctive Approach

This book covers contemporary project management topics using contemporary project management methods. For example, when considering the topic of dealing with multiple stakeholders, every chapter was reviewed by students, practitioners, and academics. This allowed simultaneous consideration of student learning, practitioner realism, and academic research and teaching perspectives.

The practical examples and practitioner reviewers came from a variety of industries, different parts of the world, and from many sizes and types of projects in order to emphasize the scalability and universality of contemporary project management techniques.

New to This Edition

- *Core, behavioral, and technical learning objectives.* We have expanded the number of learning objectives and classified them as core, behavioral, or technical. About half of the objectives are core: what we believe every student of project management should learn. A professor could teach a solid project management introductory class by deeply using only the core objectives. On the other hand, there are measurable student objectives for either a behavioral or a technical approach. All suggested student assignments and questions are tied specifically to one of the learning objectives. A professor could use this text for a two-semester sequence that emphasizes both in-depth behavioral and technical approaches.
- *Videos.* Exclusively available to those using the MindTap product for this book, we have created dozens of short (average time, five minutes) videos to show the art of many of the techniques. These demonstrate the use of many of the techniques in a by-hand or spreadsheet fashion as well as using Microsoft Project 2016. Several questions that can be assigned to students are included with the videos that

demonstrate how to use Microsoft Project to complement learning. Answers (sometimes definitive, sometimes representative, depending on the nature of the technique) are included in the instructor's manual (IM).

- *Extensive flowchart to help the sixth edition of the* **PMBOK®** Guide *come to life*.
  All sixth edition *PMBOK® Guide* knowledge areas, processes, and process groups,
  plus major deliverables from each process and the primary workflows between
  them, are specifically included in an interactive, color-coded flowchart that is
  included in full inside the back cover of the text. We also start each chapter by
  showing the portion of the flowchart that is covered in that chapter. We now use
  definitions both from the *PMBOK® Guide, Sixth Edition* and also from more than
  a dozen Project Management Institute specialized Practice Guides and Standards.
  The end of each chapter contains specific suggestions for PMP® and CAPM® test
  preparation pertaining to the chapter's topics plus ten *PMBOK® Guide*-type questions that are typical of what would be seen on PMP® and CAPM® exams.
  Appendix A gives general study suggestions for the CAPM® and PMP® exams.

- *Project deliverables*. A list of 38 project deliverables that can be used as assignments
  for students and in-class exercises are included in Appendix D. Each deliverable is
  specifically tied to a student learning objective and shown on the *PMBOK® Guide*
  flowchart. About half of these are core, while the others are behavioral or technical.
  Examples of completed deliverables are included in the text. Teaching suggestions
  and grading rubrics are included in the IM. Appendix D identifies the type of objective, chapter covered, and *PMBOK® Guide* process, knowledge area, and process
  group in which the deliverable is typically created on a real project.

- *Substantial increase in Agile coverage*. Agile techniques and methods are considered much more often than even three years ago. As such, many experienced project
  managers who have also become Agile proponents have contributed to the increased
  Agile coverage in this book. At multiple points in most chapters, if Agile methods or
  suggested behaviors are different from traditional project management, these variations are noted. We use an Agile icon to draw attention to these. We also have created Appendix B, which is a bulleted list of the approximately 180 differences
  between Agile and traditional project management that are discussed in the book.
  This extensive coverage allows a professor to teach project management emphasizing
  an Agile approach, if desired. It also allows a professor to develop an Agile project
  management course.

- *Two new continuing project examples*. We have created two project examples that
  are included in all 15 chapters of the text. One project is a construction project by a
  for-profit company that is planned and managed in a traditional fashion. The other
  is a development project at a nonprofit that is planned and managed in a more (but
  not exclusively) Agile fashion. In Chapter 1, we introduce both these case studies.
  After that, we alternate chapters, with each chapter showing what one project did
  using the concepts and techniques of a chapter and posing questions for the students to answer about the other project. Answers to the questions are in the IM.
  This can be another useful vehicle for students to practice their skills and to generate
  class discussion.

Distinctive Features

- **PMBOK® Guide, Sixth Edition** *approach*. This consistency with the current standard gives students a significant leg up if they decide to become certified Project
  Management Professionals (PMPs®) or Certified Associates in Project Management

(CAPMs®). This text includes an color-coded *PMBOK® Guide, Sixth Edition* flow-chart, all definitions consistent with PMI guides and standards, CAPM and PMP test preparation suggestions, and test practice questions.

- *Actual project as learning vehicle.* A section at the end of each chapter lists deliverables for students to create (in teams or individually) for a real project. These assignments have been refined over the last two decades while working with the local PMI® chapter, which provided a panel of PMP® judges to evaluate projects from a practical point of view. Included in the IM are extensive tools and suggestions developed over the last 20 years for instructors, guiding them as they have students learn in the best possible way—with real projects. Students are encouraged to keep clean copies of all deliverables so they can demonstrate their project skills in job interviews. A listing of these deliverables is included in Appendix D.
- *Student-oriented, measurable learning objectives.* Each chapter begins with a list of the core objectives for the chapter along with more in-depth behavioral and/or technical objectives for most chapters. The chapter also starts with showing the PMBOK® topics covered in the chapter. The chapter material, end-of-chapter questions and problems, PowerPoint® slides, all deliverables, and test questions have all been updated to correlate to specific objectives.
- *Microsoft® Project Professional 2016 fully integrated into the fabric of eight chapters.* Microsoft® Project Professional 2016 is shown in a step-by-step manner with numerous screen captures. On all screen captures, critical path activities are shown in contrasting color for emphasis. We have created videos to demonstrate these techniques and developed questions tied to specific learning objectives that can be assigned to the videos to test student learning.
- *Blend of traditional and modern methods.* Proven methods developed over the past half century are combined with exciting new methods, including Agile, that are emerging from both industry and research. This book covers the responsibilities of many individuals who can have an impact on projects both as they are practiced in traditional and in Agile environments, so aspiring project managers can understand not only their own roles, but also those of people with whom they need to interact.
- *Integrated example projects.* A variety of experienced project leaders from around the world have contributed examples to demonstrate many of the techniques and concepts throughout the book. These highly experienced and credentialed managers have worked closely with the authors to ensure that the examples demonstrate ideas discussed in the chapter. The variety of industries, locations, and sizes of the projects help the students to visualize both how universal project management is and how to appropriately scale the planning and management activities.

Organization of Topics

The book is divided into four major parts. Part 1, **Organizing Projects,** deals with getting a project officially approved.

- Chapter 1 introduces contemporary project management by first tracing the history of project management and then discussing what makes a project different from an ongoing operation. Various frameworks that help one understand projects—such as the *PMBOK® Guide* and Agile—are introduced, as well as the executive-, managerial-, and associate-level roles in managing projects.
- Chapter 2 discusses how projects support and are an outgrowth of strategic planning, how a portfolio of projects is selected and prioritized, how a client company

selects a contractor company to conduct a project, and how a contractor company secures project opportunities from client companies.

- Chapter 3 presents project charters in a step-by-step fashion. Short, powerful charters help all key participants to develop a common understanding of key project issues and components at a high level and then to formally commit to the project. Charters have become nearly universal in initiating projects in recent years. Microsoft® Project Professional 2016 is utilized to show milestone schedules within charters.

Part 2, **Leading Projects**, deals with understanding the project environment and roles and dealing effectively with team members and stakeholders.

- Chapter 4 deals with organizational capability issues of structure, life cycle, culture, and roles. The choices parent organizations make in each of these provide both opportunities and limitations to how projects can be conducted.
- Chapter 5 deals with leading and managing the project team. It includes acquiring and developing the project team, assessing both potential and actual performance of team members and the team as a whole, various types of power a project manager can use, and how to deal productively with project conflict.
- Chapter 6 introduces methods for understanding and prioritizing various stakeholder demands and for building constructive relationships with stakeholders. Since many projects are less successful due to poor communications, detailed communication planning techniques are introduced along with suggestions for managing meetings, an important channel of communication.

Part 3, **Planning Projects,** deals with all aspects of project planning as defined in the *PMBOK® Guide*. It proceeds in the most logical order possible to maximize effectiveness and stress continuity, so that each chapter builds on the previous ones, and students can appreciate the interplay between the various knowledge areas and processes.

- Chapter 7 helps students understand how to determine the amount of work the project entails. Specifically covered are methods for determining the scope of both the project work and outputs, the work breakdown structure (WBS) that is used to ensure nothing is left out, and how the WBS is portrayed using Microsoft® Project Professional 2016.
- Chapter 8 is the first scheduling chapter. It shows how to schedule project activities by identifying, sequencing, and estimating the durations for each activity. Then, critical path project schedules are developed, and methods are shown for dealing with uncertainty in time estimates, Gantt charts are introduced for easier communications, and Microsoft® Project Professional 2016 is used to automate the schedule development and communications.
- Chapter 9 is the second scheduling chapter. Once the critical path schedule is determined, staff management plans are developed, project team composition issues are considered, resources are assigned to activities, and resource overloads are identified and handled. Schedule compression techniques of crashing and fast tracking are demonstrated, and multiple alternative scheduling techniques including Agile are introduced. Resource scheduling is demonstrated with Microsoft® Project Professional 2016.
- Chapter 10 deals with project budgeting. Estimating cost, budgeting cost, and establishing cost controls are demonstrated. Microsoft® Project Professional 2016 is used for developing both bottom-up and summary project budgets.
- Chapter 11 demonstrates project risk planning. It includes risk management planning methods for identifying risks, establishing a risk register, qualitatively analyzing

risks for probability and impact, quantitatively analyzing risks if needed, and deciding how to respond to each risk with contingency plans for major risks and awareness for minor risks.

- Chapter 12 starts by covering project quality planning. This includes explaining the development of modern quality concepts and how they distill into core project quality demands. Next, the chapter covers how to develop a project quality plan. It then ties all of the planning chapters together with discussions of a project kickoff meeting, a baselined project plan, and the ways Microsoft® Project Professional 2016 can be used to establish and maintain the baseline.

Part 4, **Performing Projects,** discusses the various aspects that must be managed simultaneously while the project is being conducted.

- Chapter 13 deals with project supply chain management issues. Some of these issues, such as developing the procurement management plan, qualifying and selecting vendors, and determining the type of contract to use are planning issues, but for simplicity, they are covered in one chapter with sections on how to conduct and control procurements and to improve the project supply chain.
- Chapter 14 is concerned with determining project results. This chapter starts with a balanced scorecard approach to controlling projects. Internal project issues covered include risk, change, and communication. Quality is also covered, with an emphasis on achieving client satisfaction. Financial issues discussed are scope, cost, and schedule, including how to use Microsoft® Project Professional 2016 for control.
- Chapter 15 deals with how to end a project—either early or on time. This includes validating to ensure all scope is complete, formally closing procurements and the project, knowledge management, and ensuring the project participants are rewarded and the clients have the support they need to realize intended benefits when using the project deliverables.

MindTap

MindTap is a complete digital solution for your project management course. It has enhancements that take students from learning basic concepts to actively engaging in critical thinking applications, while learning Project 2016 skills for their future careers.

The MindTap product for this book features videos from the authors that explain tricky concepts, videos that explain the finer points of what you can do with Project 2016, and quizzes and homework assignments with detailed feedback so that students will have a better understanding of why an answer is right or wrong.

Instructor Resources

To access the instructor resources, go to www.cengage.com/login, log in with your SSO account username and password, and search this book's ISBN (9781337406451) to add instructor resources to your account. Key support materials—instructor's manual with solutions, test bank in Word and Blackboard formats, data set solutions, and PowerPoint® presentations—provide instructors with a comprehensive capability for customizing their classroom experience. All student resources are also available on the instructor companion site.

- ***Instructor's Manual with Solutions***. Prepared by Tim Kloppenborg and updated by Kate Wells, based on their years of experience facilitating the student learning experience in their own project management classes (undergraduate, MBA, Masters in

Health Informatics, and continuing education on six continents), with teaching in classroom, hybrid, and online formats, each chapter of the instructor's manual includes an overview of core, behavioral, and technical learning objectives, detailed chapter outlines, teaching recommendations for both classroom and online, and many specific suggestions for implementing community-based projects into your project management class. Solutions are also provided for all of the end-of-chapter content.

- *Microsoft® Word Test Bank.* Prepared for this edition by Joyce D. Brown, PMP® and Thomas F. McCabe, PMP® of the University of Connecticut, this comprehensive test bank builds upon the original test bank created by Kevin Grant of the University of Texas at San Antonio. The test bank is organized around each chapter's learning objectives. All test questions are consistent with the PMBOK®. Every test item is labeled according to its difficulty level, the learning objective within the textbook to which it relates, and its Blooms Taxonomy level, allowing instructors to quickly construct effective tests that emphasize the concepts most significant for their courses. The test bank includes true/false, multiple choice, essay, and quantitative problems for each chapter.
- *Cognero™ Test Bank.* Cengage Learning Testing Powered by Cognero™ is a flexible, online system that allows you to author, edit, and manage test bank content from multiple Cengage Learning solutions; create multiple test versions in an instant; and deliver tests from your LMS, your classroom, or wherever you want. The Cognero™ test bank contains the same questions that are in the Microsoft® Word test bank.
- *PowerPoint Presentations.* Prepared by Kate Wells, the PowerPoint presentations provide comprehensive coverage of each chapter's essential concepts in a clean, concise format. Instructors can easily customize the PowerPoint presentations to better fit the needs of their classroom.
- *Templates.* Electronic templates for many of the techniques (student deliverables) are available on the textbook companion website. These Microsoft® Word and Excel documents can be downloaded and filled in for ease of student learning and for consistency of instructor grading.

Student Resources

Students can access the following resources by going to www.cengagebrain.com and searching 9781337406451. The companion website for this book has Excel and Word Project templates, data sets for selected chapters, and instructions for how to get access to a trial version of Microsoft Online Professional Trial. (Note that while we are happy to provide instructions for accessing this trial, Microsoft controls that access and we are not responsible for it being removed in the future.)

Acknowledgments

A book-writing project depends on many people. Through the last three decades of project work, we have been privileged to learn from thousands of people, including students, faculty members, co-trainers, co-consultants, co-judges, clients, research partners, trade book authors, and others. Hundreds of individuals who have provided help in research and developing teaching methods are co-members of the following:

- PMI's undergraduate curriculum guidelines development team,
- PMI's Global Accreditation Center,

- Multiple chapters of the Project Management Institute,
- The Cincinnati and Louisville sections of the Center for Quality of Management,
- Project Management Executive Forum, and
- Agile Cincinnati.

We also want to acknowledge the wonderful help of various professionals at Cengage Learning, including Aaron Arnsparger (Sr. Product Manager) and Conor Allen (Content Developer). We also want to thank Charles McCormick, Jr., retired Senior Acquisitions Editor, for his extensive help and guidance on the first and second editions of *Contemporary Project Management*.

Other individuals who have provided significant content are Nathan Johnson of Western Carolina University, who provided the Microsoft® Project 2016 material, Joyce D. Brown, PMP® and Thomas F. McCabe, PMP® of University of Connecticut, who revised the test bank and provided additional PMBOK® questions to each chapter, Jim King, who professionally taped and edited videos, and Kathryn N. Wells, Independent Consultant, PMP®, CAPM®, who provided the PowerPoint presentations.

Special thanks are also due to all the people whose feedback and suggestions have shaped this edition of *Contemporary Project Management* as well as the previous two editions:

Carol Abbott,
Fusion Alliance, Inc.

Stephen Allen,
Truman State University

Siti Arshad-Snyder,
Clarkson College

Loretta Beavers,
Southwest Virginia
Community College

Shari Bleure,
Skyline Chili

Neil Burgess,
Albertus Magnus College

Reynold Byers,
Arizona State University

John Cain,
Viox Services

Robert Clarkson,
Davenport University

Nancy Cornell,
Northeastern University

Steve Creason,
Metropolitan State
University

Jacob J. Dell,
University of Texas at
San Antonio

Scott Dellana,
East Carolina University

Maling Ebrahimpour,
Roger Williams
University

Jeff Flynn,
ILSCO Corporation

Jim Ford,
University of Delaware

Lynn Frock,
Lynn Frock & Company

Lei Fu,
Hefei University of
Technology

Patricia Galdeen,
Lourdes University

Kathleen Gallon,
Christ Hospital

Paul Gentine,
Bethany College

Kevin P. Grant,
University of Texas–San
Antonio

Joseph Griffin,
Northeastern University

Raye Guye,
ILSCO Corporation

William M. Hayden Jr.,
State University of
New York at Buffalo

Sarai Hedges,
University of Cincinnati

Marco Hernandez,
Dantes Canadian

Stephen Holoviak,
Pennsylvania State
University

Bill Holt,
North Seattle Community
College

Morris Hsi,
Lawrence Tech
University

Sonya Hsu,
University of Louisiana
Lafayette

Paul Hudec,
Milwaukee School of
Engineering

Anil B. Jambekar,
Michigan Technological
University

Dana Johnson,
Michigan Technological
University

Robert Judge,
San Diego State
University

David L. Keeney,
Stevens Institute of
Technology

George Kenyon,
Lamar University

Naomi Kinney,
MultiLingual Learning
Services

Paul Kling,
Duke Energy

Matthew Korpusik,
Six Sigma Black Belt

Sal Kukalis,
California State
University–Long Beach

Young Hoon Kwak,
George Washington
University

Laurence J. Laning,
Procter & Gamble

Dick Larkin,
Central Washington
University

Lydia Lavigne,
Ball Aerospace

Jon Lazarus,
Willamette University

James Leaman,
Eastern Mennonite
University

Linda LeSage,
Davenport University

Claudia Levi,
Edmonds Community
College

Marvette Limon,
University of Houston
Downtown

John S. Loucks,
St. Edward's University

Diane Lucas,
Penn State University–
DuBois Campus

Clayton Maas,
Davenport University

S. G. Marlow,
California State
Polytechnic University

Daniel S. Marrone,
SUNY Farmingdale State
College

Chris McCale,
Regis University

Abe Meilich,
Walden University

Bruce Miller,
Xavier Leadership Center

Ali Mir,
William Paterson
University

William Moylan,
Eastern Michigan
University

Merlin Nuss,
MidAmerica Nazarene
University

Warren Opfer,
Life Science Services
International

Peerasit Patanakul,
Stevens Institute of
Technology

Joseph Petrick,
Wright State University

Kenneth R. Pflieger,
Potomac College

Charles K. Pickar,
Johns Hopkins University

Connie Plowman,
Portland Community
College

Mark Poore,
Roanoke College

Antonios Printezis,
Arizona State University

Joshua Ramirez,
PMP,
MSM-PM, Columbia
Basin College

Chris Rawlings,
Bob Jones University

Natalee Regal,
Procter & Gamble

Pedro Reyes,
Baylor University

Linda Ridlon,
Center for Quality of
Management,
Division of GOAL/QPC

Kim Roberts,
Athens State University

David Schmitz,
Milwaukee School of
Engineering

Sheryl R. Schoenacher,
SUNY Farmingdale State
College

Jan Sepate,
Kimberly Clark

Patrick Sepate,
Summitqwest Inc.

William R. Sherrard,
San Diego State
University

Brian M. Smith,
Eastern University

Kimberlee D. Snyder,
Winona State University

Tony Taylor,
MidAmerica Nazarene
University

Rachana Thariani,
Atos-Origin

Dawn Tolonen,
Xavier University

Nate Tucker,
Lee University

Guy Turner,
Castellini Company

Jayashree Venkatraman,
Microsoft Corporation

Nathan Washington,
Southwest Tennessee
Community College

Scott Wright,
University of Wisconsin–
Platteville

And we especially want to thank our family members for their love and support: Bet, Nick, Jill, Andy, Cadence, and Ellie

—Timothy J. Kloppenborg

About the Authors

Timothy J. Kloppenborg is an Emeritus Professor of Management at Williams College of Business, Xavier University. He previously held faculty positions at University of North Carolina Charlotte and Air Force Institute of Technology and has worked temporarily at Southern Cross University and Tecnológico de Monterrey. He has authored over 100 publications, including 10 books, such as *Strategic Leadership of Portfolio and Project Management, Project Leadership,* and *Managing Project Quality.* His articles have appeared in *MIT Sloan Management Review, Project Management Journal, Journal of Management Education, Journal of General Management, SAM Advanced Management Journal, Information Systems Education Journal, Journal of Managerial Issues, Quality Progress, Management Research News,* and *Journal of Small Business Strategy.* In his capacity as the founding collection editor of portfolio and project management books for Business Expert Press, he has edited 14 books with more in the pipeline. Tim has been active with the Project Management Institute for over 30 years and a PMP® since 1991. He is a retired U.S. Air Force Reserve officer who served in transportation, procurement, and quality assurance. Dr. Kloppenborg has worked with over 150 volunteer organizations, many directly and others through supervising student projects. He has hands-on and consulting project management experience on six continents in construction, information systems, research and development, and quality improvement projects with organizations such Duke Energy, Ernst and Young LLP, Greater Cincinnati Water Works, Kroger, Procter & Gamble, Tri-Health, and Texas Children's Hospital. Dr. Kloppenborg has developed and delivered innovative corporate training, undergraduate, MBA, and Executive MBA classes in project management, leadership, teamwork, and quality improvement and he teaches PMP Prep classes. He holds a BS in business administration from Benedictine College, an MBA from Western Illinois University, and a PhD in Operations Management from University of Cincinnati.

Dr. Vittal Anantatmula is a professor in the College of Business, Western Carolina University and a campus of University of North Carolina. He is also the Director of Graduate Programs in Project Management and was a recipient of excellence in teaching and research awards. Dr. Anantatmula is a Global Guest Professor at Keio University, Yokohama, Japan. He is a director and board member of the Project Management Institute Global Accreditation Center (PMI-GAC). He serves on the editorial board of several scholarly journals. At Western Carolina University, he was recognized with the University Scholar Award in 2017. He has won several other awards for excellence in both research and teaching.

Prior to joining Western Carolina University, he taught at The George Washington University. He worked in the petroleum and power industries for several years as an electrical engineer and project manager and as a consultant in several international organizations, including the World Bank. Dr. Anantatmula has authored more than 60 publications, five books, and about 50 conference papers. Two of his conference papers received the best paper award. His work has been published in scholarly journals, including *Project Management Journal, Journal of Knowledge Management, Journal of Management in Engineering, Journal of Information and Knowledge Management Systems,* and

Engineering Management Journal. He received his PhD from The George Washington University and is a certified project management professional.

Kathryn N. Wells holds a master's degree in Education, as well as degrees in Organizational Communication and Spanish. Kate has a passion for teaching, in both academic and corporate settings. In addition to over a decade's experience in project management education, Kate is a top-producing real estate agent with Keller Williams. Her blend of experience in real estate—including working with many investors—and classroom teaching gives her a unique perspective and insights into many components of project management, including Planning, Communication, Stakeholder Management, and Project Control.

In addition to her work on *Contemporary Project Management,* Kate is the lead author of *Project Management Essentials* (2015) and co-author of *Project Management for Archaeology* (2017), both published by Business Expert Press. She has trained and consulted with several organizations around the world and has occasionally been contracted to provide translations of project management educational materials (Spanish to English). Some of her clients include the University of Cincinnati, Children's Hospital of Cincinnati, Givaudan International, and Tec de Monterrey University—where Kate has repeatedly served as visiting faculty at multiple campuses in Mexico. Kate is a certified project management professional (PMP).

ORGANIZING PROJECTS

Organizing for success in project management includes several basic frameworks for understanding projects and tools to select, prioritize, resource, and initiate projects. Basic frameworks described in Chapter 1 include how the work of project management can be categorized by knowledge area and process group, how project success is determined, and how both plan-driven and adaptive approaches are frequently used. Chapter 2 describes how projects are investments meant to help achieve organizational goals. Tools are demonstrated to select, prioritize, and resource projects. Chapter 3 describes how charters are essential to initiating projects and then demonstrates how to construct each portion of a charter.

CHAPTER 1

Introduction to Project Management

frantic00/Shutterstock.com

I have returned from a successful climb of Mount Aconcagua in Argentina; at 22,841 feet, it is the highest peak in the world outside of the Himalayas. While there, seven other climbers died; we not only survived, but our experience was so positive that we have partnered to climb together again.

During the three decades that I've been climbing mountains, I've also been managing projects. An element has emerged as essential for success in both of these activities: the element of discipline. By discipline, I am referring to doing what I already know needs to be done. Without this attribute, even the most knowledgeable and experienced will have difficulty avoiding failure.

The deaths on Aconcagua are an extreme example of the consequences associated with a lack of discipline. The unfortunate climbers, who knew that the predicted storms would produce very hazardous conditions, decided to attempt the summit instead of waiting. They did not have the discipline that we demonstrated to act on our earlier decision to curtail summit attempts after the agreed-to turn-around time or in severe weather.

PMBOK® 6E COVERAGE	
PMBOK® 6E	**OUTPUTS**
1.2 Foundational Elements	Project Customer Trade-off Matrix
2.4 Organizational Systems	Project Success Definition
3.3 The Project Manager's Sphere of Influence	
3.4 Project Manager Competencies	
3.5 Performing Integration	

PMBOK® GUIDE

Topics:
- Project management introduction
- Project life cycle
- Stakeholders
- Project management process
- Project integration management

CHAPTER OUTPUTS
- Customer Trade-off Matrix
- Project Success Definition

I've experienced similar circumstances in project management. Often I have found myself under pressure to cast aside or shortcut project management practices that I have come to rely on. For me, these practices have become the pillars of my own project management discipline. One of these pillars, planning, seems to be particularly susceptible to challenge. Managing projects at the Central Intelligence Agency for three decades, I adjusted to the annual cycle for obtaining funding. This cycle occasionally involved being given relatively short notice near the end of the year that funds unspent by some other department were up for grabs to whoever could quickly make a convincing business case. While some may interpret this as a circumstance requiring shortcutting the necessary amount of planning in order to capture some of the briefly available funds, I understood that my discipline required me to find a way to do the needed planning and to act quickly. I understood that to do otherwise would likely propel me toward becoming one of the two-thirds of the projects identified by the Standish Group in their 2009 CHAOS report as not successful. I understood that the top 2 percent of project managers, referred to as Alpha Project Managers in a 2006 book of the same name, spend twice as much time planning as the other 98 percent of project managers. The approach that I took allowed me to maintain the discipline for my planning pillar. I preplanned a couple of projects and had them ready at the end of the year to be submitted should a momentary funding opportunity arise.

A key to success in project management, as well as in mountain climbing, is to identify the pillars that will be practiced with discipline. This book offers an excellent set of project management methods from which we can identify those pillars that we will decide to practice with the required levels of discipline. I believe that project management is about applying common sense with uncommon discipline.

—Michael O'Brochta, PMP, founder of Zozer Inc. and previously senior project manager at the Central Intelligence Agency

1-1 What Is a Project?

Frequently, a business is faced with making a change, such as improving an existing work process, constructing a building, installing a new computer system, merging with another company, moving to a new location, developing a new product, entering a new market, and so on. These changes are best planned and managed as projects.

Often, these changes are initiated due to operational necessity or to meet strategic goals, such as the following:

- Market demand
- Customer request

- Technological advance
- Legal requirements or regulatory compliance
- Replace obsolete equipment, technology, system, or physical facility
- Crisis situation
- Social need

So, what is a project?

A **project** is a new, time-bound effort that has a definite beginning and a definite ending with several related and/or interdependent tasks to create a unique product or service. The word *temporary* is used to denote project duration; however, it does not mean that project duration is short; in fact, it can range from a few weeks to several years. Temporary also does not apply to the project deliverable, although project teams are certainly temporary.

A project requires an organized set of work efforts that are planned with a level of detail that is progressively elaborated on as more information is discovered. Projects are subject to limitations of time and resources such as money and people. Projects should follow a planned and organized approach with a defined beginning and ending. Project plans and goals become more specific as early work is completed. The project output often is a collection of a primary deliverable along with supporting deliverables such as a house as the primary deliverable and warrantees and instructions for use as supporting deliverables.

Taking all these issues into consideration, a project can be defined as "*a time-bound effort constrained by performance specifications, resources, and budget to create a unique product or service.*"

Each project typically has a unique combination of stakeholders. **Stakeholders** are people and groups who can impact the project or might be impacted by either the work or results of the project. Projects often require a variety of people to work together for a limited time, and all participants need to understand that completing the project will require effort in addition to their other assigned work. These people become members of the project team and usually represent diverse functions and disciplines.

Project management is the art and science of using knowledge, skills, tools, and techniques efficiently and effectively to meet stakeholder needs and expectations. This includes work processes that initiate, plan, execute, control, and close work. During these processes, trade-offs must be made among the following factors:

- Scope (size and features)
- Quality (acceptability of the results)
- Cost
- Schedule
- Resources
- Risks

When project managers successfully make these trade-offs, the project results meet the agreed-upon requirements, are useful to the customers, and promote the organization. Project management includes both administrative tasks for planning, documenting, and controlling work and leadership tasks for visioning, motivating, and promoting work associates. The underlying principle of project management discipline is to make effective and efficient use of all resources and it is this principle that influences some of these trade-off decisions. Project management knowledge, skills, and methods can be applied and modified for most projects regardless of size or application.

1-2 History of Project Management

Projects of all sizes have been undertaken throughout history. Early construction projects included the ancient pyramids, medieval cathedrals, Indian cities, and Native American pueblos. Other large early projects involved waging wars and building empires. In the development of the United States, projects included laying railroads, developing farms, and building cities. Many smaller projects consisted of building houses and starting businesses. Projects were conducted throughout most of the world's history, but there was very little documentation. Therefore, there is no evidence of systematic planning and control. It is known that some early projects were accomplished at great human and financial cost and that others took exceedingly long periods of time to complete. For example, the Panama Canal was started in 1881 and completed in 1914.

Project management eventually emerged as a formal discipline to be studied and practiced. In the 1950s and 1960s, techniques for planning and controlling schedules and costs were developed, primarily on huge aerospace and construction projects. During this time, project management was primarily involved in determining project schedules based on understanding the order in which work activities had to be completed. Many large manufacturing, research and development, government, and construction projects used and refined management techniques. In the 1980s and 1990s, several software companies offered ever more powerful and easier ways to plan and control project costs and schedules. Risk management techniques that were originally developed on complex projects have increasingly been applied in a simplified form to less complex projects.

In the last few years, people have realized more and more that communication and leadership play major roles in project success. Rapid growth and changes in the information technology and telecommunications industries especially have fueled massive growth in the use of project management in the 1990s and early 2000s. Simultaneously, systems and processes were developed for electronic documentation of the historical data of projects using information systems (IS) and knowledge management tools.

People who are engaged in a wide variety of industries, including banking, insurance, retailing, hospital administration, healthcare, and many other service industries, are now turning to project management to help them plan and manage efforts to meet their unique demands. Project planning and management techniques that were originally developed for large, complex projects can be modified and used to better plan and manage even smaller projects. Now, project management is commonly used on projects of many sizes and types in a wide variety of manufacturing, government, service, and non-profit organizations.

Further, in today's global economy, geographically dispersed virtual project teams are becoming a familiar entity in many organizations. Managing a project is challenging in the current global economy due to the exponential growth of information technology and ever-increasing market demand that organizations offer products and services efficiently and quickly. Understanding the characteristics of global projects for improving global project performance is of critical importance.

The use of project management has grown quite rapidly and is likely to continue growing. With increased international competition and a borderless global economy, customers want their products and services developed and delivered better, faster, and cheaper. Because project management techniques are designed to manage scope, quality, cost, and schedule, they are ideally suited to this purpose.

 AGILE

Throughout this book, we will present concepts and techniques that are either unique to Agile projects or are emphasized more on Agile projects. Many of these ideas can be used to improve practice on traditional projects.

In 2001, a group of thought leaders became frustrated with the use of traditional, plan-driven project management for software projects and as a result, they wrote a document called *The Agile Manifesto*.[1] The four core values of Agile as shown below are completely consistent with our approach to Contemporary Project Management. *Agile* will be defined in Chapter 3, but throughout the book, a margin icon will indicate ideas from Agile, and the text will be in color.

- Value individuals more than processes.
- Value working software more than documentation.
- Value customer collaboration more than negotiation.
- Value response to change over following a plan.

1-3 How Can Project Work Be Described?

Project work can be described in the following ways:

- Projects are temporary and unique, while other work, commonly called operations, is more continuous.
- Project managers need certain "soft skills" and "hard skills" to be effective.
- Project managers frequently have more responsibility than authority.
- Projects go through predictable stages called a life cycle.

Managing a project requires identifying requirements, establishing clear and achievable objectives, balancing competing demands of quality, scope, cost, and time, and meeting customer expectations by making adjustments to all aspects of the project. Due to uniqueness, projects are often associated with uncertainties and unknowns that present many challenges to managing project work.

1-3a Projects versus Operations

All work can be described as fitting into one of two types: projects or operations. Projects as stated above are temporary, and no two are identical. Some projects may be extremely different from any other work an organization has performed up to that time, such as planning a merger with another company. Other projects may have both routine and unique aspects, for example, building a house; such projects can be termed process oriented. These projects are associated with fewer unknowns and uncertainties.

Operations, on the other hand, consist of the ongoing work needed to ensure that an organization continues to function effectively. Operations managers can often use checklists to guide much of their work. Project managers can use project management methods to help determine what to do, but they rarely have checklists that identify all the activities they need to accomplish. Some work may be difficult to classify as totally project or totally operations. However, if project management methods and concepts help one to better plan and manage work, it does not really matter how the work is classified.

Both the projects and the operations are associated with processes. A process is described as a series of actions designed to bring about the consistent and similar result or service. A process is usually designed to improve productivity. Thus, processes are repetitive and produce consistent and similar results, whereas projects are unique: each project delivers results that are distinct from other projects. However, one must remember that project management discipline includes various processes (planning, risk management, communication management, etc.) that facilitate managing projects and product- or service-oriented processes such as scope definition, scope management, and quality management.

1-3b Soft Skills and Hard Skills

To effectively manage and lead in a project environment, a person needs to develop both "soft" and "hard" skills. **Soft skills** include the ability to work in teams, interpersonal skills, communication, conflict resolution, negotiation, and leadership activities. **Hard skills** can include risk analysis, quality control, scheduling, budgeting, change control, planning other related activities, and project execution. Soft and hard skills go hand in hand. Some people have a stronger natural ability and a better comfort level in one or the other, but to be successful as a project manager, a person needs to develop both, along with the judgment about when each is needed. A wise project manager may purposefully recruit an assistant who excels in his area of weakness. Training, experience, and mentoring can also be instrumental in developing necessary skills.

Soft skills such as interpersonal relations, conflict resolution, and communication are of critical importance in managing people. As such, of all the resources, managing human resources presents more challenges. Managing and leading people are the most challenging aspects of a managing a project and the project team. These challenges underline the importance of soft skills.

1-3c Authority and Responsibility

A project manager will frequently be held accountable for work that she cannot order people to perform. Projects are most effectively managed with one person being assigned accountability. However, that person often needs to negotiate with a **functional manager**, who is "someone with management authority over an organizational unit."[2] Functional managers negotiate for workers to perform the project work in a timely fashion. Since the workers know their regular manager often has other tasks for them and will be their primary rater, they are tempted to concentrate first on the work that will earn rewards. Hence, a project manager needs to develop strong communication and leadership skills to extract cooperation from functional managers and to persuade project team members to focus on the project when other work also beckons. Often, it is the project manager's responsibility that the work be performed, but at the same time, he or she has no formal authority over the project team members.

1-3d Project Life Cycle

All projects go through predictable stages called a project life cycle. A **project life cycle** is "the series of phases that a project goes through from its initiation to its closure."[3] An organization needs the assurance that the work of the project is proceeding in a satisfactory manner, that the results are aligned with the original plan, and they are likely to serve the customer's intended purpose. The project customer is the person or organization that will use the project's product, service, or result. Customers can be internal to the organization (that is, part of the company performing the project) or external to the organization.

Many different project life cycle models are used for different types of projects, such as information systems, improvement, research and development, and construction. The variations these pose will be explored in Chapter 4. In this book, we will use the following project stages:

- *Selecting and initiating*—starts when an idea for a project first emerges and the project is selected and planned at a high level, and ends when key participants commit to it in broad terms.

- *Planning*—starts after the initial commitment, includes detailed planning, and ends when all stakeholders accept the entire detailed plan.
- *Executing*—starts when the plan is accepted, and includes authorizing, executing, monitoring, and controlling work until the customer accepts the project deliverables.
- *Closing and realizing*—includes all activities after customer acceptance to ensure the project is completed, lessons are learned, resources are reassigned, contributions are recognized, and benefits are realized.

The pace of work and amount of money spent may vary considerably from one life cycle stage to another. Often, the selecting is performed periodically for all projects at a division or corporate level, and then initiating is rather quick—just enough to ensure that a project makes sense and key participants will commit to it. The planning stage can become rather detailed and will normally require quite a bit more work. The execution stage or stages are the time when the majority of the hands-on project tasks are accomplished. This tends to be a time of considerable work. Closing is a time when loose ends are tied up and the work level decreases significantly, but realizing benefits from the project occurs over time, may be measured months after project completion, and may be done by people other than those who performed the project. Occasionally, some of these phases overlap with each other, depending on the project complexity, urgency of the deliverable, and ambiguity associated with the project scope.

 See Exhibit 1.1 for a predictive or plan-driven project life cycle and Exhibit 1.2 for an adaptive or change-driven project life cycle. The primary difference is that in the first, the product is well understood and all planning precedes all executing, while in the second, early results lead into planning later work. The extreme of predictive is sometimes called *waterfall* and the extreme of adaptive is sometimes called *Agile*.

EXHIBIT 1.1

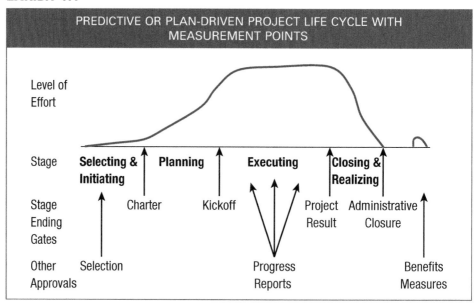

PREDICTIVE OR PLAN-DRIVEN PROJECT LIFE CYCLE WITH MEASUREMENT POINTS

EXHIBIT 1.2

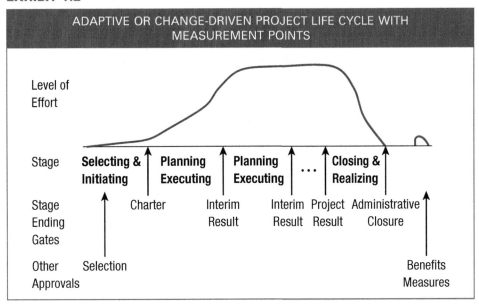

ADAPTIVE OR CHANGE-DRIVEN PROJECT LIFE CYCLE WITH MEASUREMENT POINTS

Three other points should be made concerning the project life cycle. First, most companies with well-developed project management systems insist that a project must pass an approval of some kind to move from one stage to the next.[4] In both exhibits, the approval to move from selecting and initiating to planning, for instance, is the approval of a charter. Second, in some industries, the project life cycle is highly formalized and very specific. For example, in the construction industry, the executing stage is often described as the three stages of design, erection, and finishing. Third, many companies even have their own project life cycle model, such as the one Midland Insurance Company has developed for quality improvement projects, as shown in Exhibit 1.3.

EXHIBIT 1.3

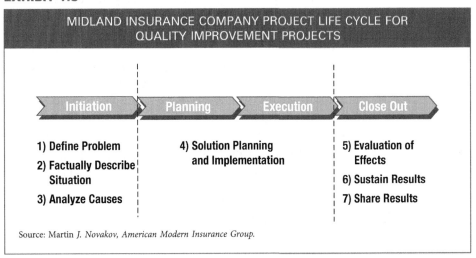

MIDLAND INSURANCE COMPANY PROJECT LIFE CYCLE FOR QUALITY IMPROVEMENT PROJECTS

Source: Martin *J. Novakov, American Modern Insurance Group.*

This book will present examples of company-specific life cycle models, but for clarity will use the predictive or plan-driven model shown in Exhibit 1.1 when describing concepts, except when we discuss Agile with the adaptive or change-driven model. In addition to stage-ending approvals, frequently projects are measured at additional points such as selection, progress reporting, and benefits realization, as shown in Exhibit 1.1.

1-4 Understanding Projects

Several frameworks that can help a person better understand project management are described below: the Project Management Institute (PMI); the *Project Management Body of Knowledge (PMBOK® Guide);* methods of selecting and prioritizing projects, project goals and constraints; project success and failure; use of Microsoft Project to help plan and measure projects, and various ways to classify projects.

1-4a Project Management Institute

Project management has professional organizations just as do many other professions and industry groups. The biggest of these by far is the Project Management Institute.

The Project Management Institute was founded in 1969, grew at a modest pace until the early 1990s, and has grown quite rapidly since then. As of February 2017, PMI had well over 475,000 members. PMI publishes and regularly updates over a dozen extensions, guides, and standards. The best known is A *Guide to the Project Management Body of Knowledge (PMBOK® Guide).* Definitions in this book that have specific nuances come from the most current edition of PMI standards and guides. Those definitions that are common knowledge are defined in typical terms. PMI has established eight professional certifications, with the most popular being Project Management Professional (PMP)®. Currently, over 650,000 people hold the PMP® certification. To be certified as a PMP®, a person needs to have the required experience and education, pass an examination on the *PMBOK® Guide,* and sign and be bound by a code of professional conduct. PMI has also established a second certification—Certified Associate in Project Management (CAPM)—that is geared toward junior people working on projects before they are eligible to become PMPs. PMI also has established six additional credentials plus multiple practice standards and extensions to the *PMBOK® Guide* in areas such as program management, Agile, risk, scheduling, resource estimating, work breakdown structures, earned value management, construction, and government.[5]

1-4b Project Management Body of Knowledge (PMBOK®)

A *Guide to the Project Management Body of Knowledge®,* known as *PMBOK®,* consists of three introductory chapters covered collectively in Chapters 1, 2, and 3 of this book; five process groups; 10 knowledge areas; and 49 processes. A **project management process group** is "a logical grouping of the project management processes to achieve specific project objectives."[6] The five process groups, paraphrased from the *PMBOK® Guide,* are as follows:

1. **Initiating**—"define a project or a new phase by obtaining authorization"
2. **Planning**—"establish the project scope, refine objectives, and define plans and actions to attain objectives"
3. **Executing**—"complete the work defined to satisfy project specifications"
4. **Monitoring and controlling**—"track, review, and regulate progress and performance, identify changes required, and initiate changes"
5. **Closing**—"formally complete or close project or phase"[7]

The 10 knowledge areas, paraphrased from the *PMBOK® Guide,* are as follows:

1. **Integration management**—"processes and activities to identify, define, combine, unify, and coordinate the various processes and project management activities"
2. **Scope management**—"processes to ensure that the project includes all the work required, and only the work required, to complete the project successfully"
3. **Schedule management**—"processes to manage timely completion of the project"
4. **Cost management**—"processes involved in planning, estimating, budgeting, financing, funding, managing, and controlling costs so that the project can be completed within the approved budget"
5. **Quality management**—"processes to incorporate the organization's quality policy regarding planning, managing, and controlling quality requirements to meet stakeholder expectations"
6. **Resource management**—"processes to identify, acquire, and manage resources needed to successfully complete the project"
7. **Communications management**—"processes to ensure timely and appropriate planning, collection, creation, distribution, storage, retrieval, management, control, monitoring, and ultimate disposition of project information"
8. **Risk management**—"processes of conducting risk management planning, identification, analysis, response planning, response implementation, and monitoring risk on a project"
9. **Procurement management**—"processes to purchase or acquire products, services, or results from outside the project team"
10. **Stakeholder management**—"processes to identify the people, groups, or organizations, that could impact or be impacted by the project, analyze their expectations and impact, and develop strategies for engaging them in project decisions and execution"[8]

Project Processes There are 49 individual project work processes that are each in a process group and a knowledge area. Exhibit 1.4 shows the general flow of when each process occurs during a project if one reads the chart from left to right. For example, the first two processes are to develop the project charter and identify stakeholders. Both occur during project initiation. The charter development is part of integration management, while stakeholder identification is part of stakeholder management. These processes flow from one into another, as shown in the more complete flowchart in the inside back cover of the text. These processes use inputs and create outputs. Many of the outputs are project charts and tools that are used to plan and control the project, as also shown on that complete flowchart. Other outputs are deliverables. A **deliverable** is any unique and verifiable product, result, or capability to perform a service that is produced to complete a process, phase, or project.[9]

One should remember that all these processes might not be required for all projects. These PMBOK processes are designed to be all-inclusive and are meant for large and complex projects.

1-4c The PMI Talent Triangle

PMI research shows that to be a successful project manager, a person needs to develop knowledge and skills in technical areas, leadership, and strategic business management. The objectives in this book are grouped first with those core skills and knowledge that all project management classes would typically cover. Core objectives are those the authors firmly believe anyone who takes a course in project management should master. The core objectives include those that the Talent Triangle classifies as technical,

EXHIBIT 1.4

FLOWCHART OF PMBOK PROCESSES AND MAJOR OUTPUTS

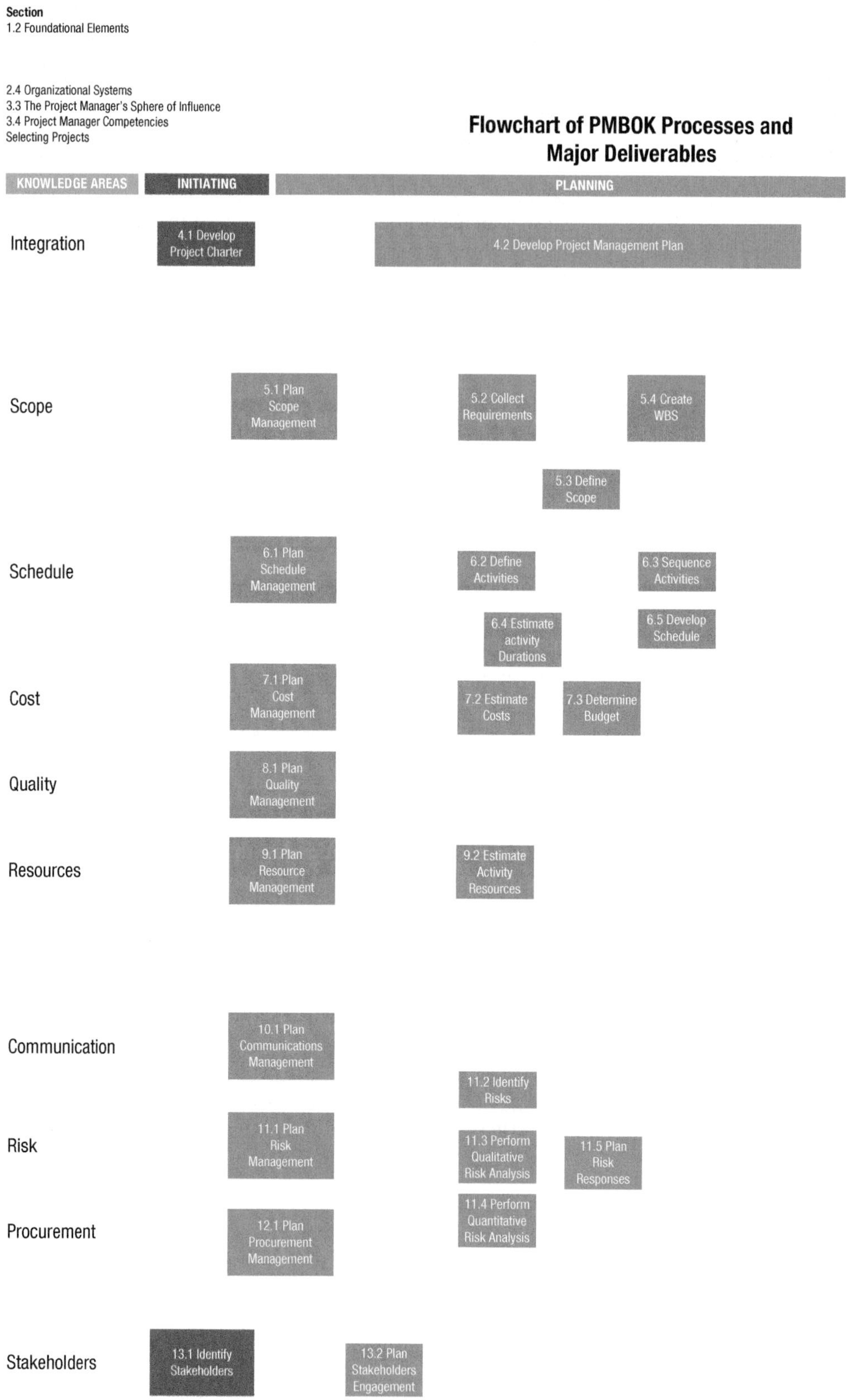

Section
1.2 Foundational Elements

2.4 Organizational Systems
3.3 The Project Manager's Sphere of Influence
3.4 Project Manager Competencies
Selecting Projects

Flowchart of PMBOK Processes and Major Deliverables

KNOWLEDGE AREAS	INITIATING	PLANNING		
Integration	4.1 Develop Project Charter	4.2 Develop Project Management Plan		
Scope		5.1 Plan Scope Management	5.2 Collect Requirements	5.4 Create WBS
			5.3 Define Scope	
Schedule		6.1 Plan Schedule Management	6.2 Define Activities	6.3 Sequence Activities
			6.4 Estimate activity Durations	6.5 Develop Schedule
Cost		7.1 Plan Cost Management	7.2 Estimate Costs	7.3 Determine Budget
Quality		8.1 Plan Quality Management		
Resources		9.1 Plan Resource Management	9.2 Estimate Activity Resources	
Communication		10.1 Plan Communications Management		
Risk		11.1 Plan Risk Management	11.2 Identify Risks	
			11.3 Perform Qualitative Risk Analysis	11.5 Plan Risk Responses
Procurement		12.1 Plan Procurement Management	11.4 Perform Quantitative Risk Analysis	
Stakeholders	13.1 Identify Stakeholders	13.2 Plan Stakeholders Engagement		

EXECUTING	MONITORING & CONTROLLING	CLOSING	KNOWLEDGE AREAS
4.3 Direct and Manage Project Work	4.5 Monitor and Control Project Work	4.7 Close Project or Phase	Integration
4.4 Manage Project Knowledge	4.6 Perform Integrated Change Control		
	5.5 Validate Scope		Scope
	5.6 Control Scope		
			Schedule
	6.6 Control Schedule		
	7.4 Control Costs		Cost
8.2 Manage Quality	8.3 Control Quality		Quality
9.3 Acquire Resources			Resources
9.4 Develop Team	9.6 Control Resources		
9.5 Manage Team			
10.2 Manage Communications	10.3 Monitor Communications		Communication
11.6 Implement Risk Responses	11.7 Monitor Risks		Risk
12.2 Conduct Procurements	12.3 Control Procurements		Procurement
13.3 Manage Stakeholder Engagement	13.4 Monitor Stakeholder Engagement		Stakeholders

behavioral, and strategic. More advanced technical objectives appear in some chapters for professors who wish to teach with a technical approach. More advanced behavioral objectives are also included in some chapters for professors who wish to emphasize the behavioral/leadership aspects of project management.

1-4d Selecting and Prioritizing Projects

During the selecting and initiating stage of a project, one of the first tasks leaders must do is to identify potential projects. Ideally, this is accomplished in a systematic manner—not just by chance. Some opportunities will present themselves. Other good opportunities need to be discovered. All parts of the organization should be involved. For example, salespeople can uncover opportunities through open discussions with existing and potential customers. Operations staff members may identify potential productivity-enhancing projects. Everyone in the firm should be aware of industry trends and use this knowledge to identify potential projects.

Potential projects are identified based on business needs such as capability enhancement, new business opportunities, contractual obligations, changes in strategic direction, innovative business ideas, replacing obsolete equipment, or adopting new technology.

Once identified, organizations need to prioritize among the potential projects. The best way to do this is to determine which projects align best with the major goals of the firm. The executives in charge of selecting projects need to ensure overall organizational priorities are understood, communicated, and accepted. Once this common understanding is in place, it is easier to prioritize among the potential projects. The degree of formality used in selecting projects varies widely. Regardless of the company's size and the level of formality used, the prioritization efforts should include asking the following questions:

- What value does each potential project bring to the organization?
- Are the demands of performing each project understood?
- Are the resources needed to perform the project available?
- Is there enthusiastic support both from the external customers and from one or more internal champions?
- Which projects will best help the organization achieve its goals?

One of the popular decision tools used to select projects is an evaluation model based on selection criteria; these selection criteria, in turn, are based on project attributes, organizational indices, financial performance attributes, and strategic goals. More sophisticated tools like decision trees, analytical hierarchical process (AHP), expected net present value, and other economic evaluation models are sometimes used for project selection.

1-4e Project Goals and Constraints

All projects should be undertaken to accomplish specific goals. Those goals can be described both by **scope** and by **quality**. **Scope** is a combination of product scope and project scope. **Product scope** is the entirety of what will be present in the actual project deliverables. **Project scope** is the entirety of what will and will not be done to meet the specified requirements. **Quality** is "the characteristics of a product or service that bear on its ability to satisfy stated or implied needs."[10] Taken together, scope and quality are often called *performance* and should result in outputs that customers can be satisfied with as they use them to effectively do their job. From a client perspective, projects generally have time and cost constraints. Thus, a project manager needs to be concerned with achieving desired scope and quality, subject to constraints of time and cost. If the project were to proceed exactly according to plan, it would be on time, on budget, and with the agreed-upon scope and the agreed-upon quality.

EXHIBIT 1.5

PROJECT CUSTOMER TRADE-OFF MATRIX			
	ENHANCE	MEET	SACRIFICE
Cost			Pay up to $5,000 extra if it saves 10 days
Schedule	Save up to 10 days		
Quality		Must meet	
Scope		Must meet	

Source: Adapted from Timothy J. Kloppenborg and Joseph A. Petrick, *Managing Project Qualify* (Vienna, VA: Management Concepts, 2002): 46.

However, many things can happen as a project is conducted. Obstacles or challenges that may limit the ability to perform often arise, as do opportunities to exceed original expectations. A project manager needs to understand which of these four goals and constraints (scope, quality, time, budget) should take precedence and which can be sacrificed. The project manager needs to help the customer articulate how much he wants to enhance achievement of one of these four dimensions. The customer must also state which dimension he is willing to sacrifice, by how much, and under what circumstances to receive better achievement of the other one. For example, on a research and development (R&D) project, a customer may be willing to pay an extra $5,000 to finish the project 10 days early. On a church construction project, a customer may be willing to give up five extra light switches in exchange for greater confidence that the light system will work properly. Understanding the customer's desires in this manner enables a project manager to make good project decisions. A project manager can use a project customer trade-off matrix such as the one in Exhibit 1.5 to reflect the research and development project trade-offs discussed above.

In addition, project plans undergo changes due to uncertainties and unknowns associated with the project. These changes must be assessed for their impact on cost and duration of the project before implementing them.

From an internal perspective, a project manager also needs to consider two more constraints: the amount of resources available and the decision maker's risk tolerance.

 From an Agile perspective, in a given iteration, resources (including cost) and schedule are considered fixed and what can vary is value to the customer.

1-4f Defining Project Success and Failure

Project success is creating deliverables that include all of the agreed-upon features (meet scope goals). The outputs should satisfy all specifications and please the project's customers. The customers need to be able to use the outputs effectively as they do their work (meet quality goals). The project should be completed on schedule and on budget (meet time and cost constraints).

Project success also includes other considerations. A successful project is one that is completed without heroics—that is, people should not burn themselves out to complete the project. Those people who work on the project should learn new skills and/or refine existing skills. Organizational learning should take place and be captured for future projects. Finally, the performing organization should reap business-level benefits such as development of

EXHIBIT 1.6

PROJECT SUCCESS

- **Meeting Agreements**
  —Cost, schedule, and specifications met
- **Customer's Success**
  —Needs met, deliverables used, customer satisfied
- **Performing Organization's Success**
  —Market share, new products, new technology
- **Project Team's Success**
  —Loyalty, development, satisfaction

Source: Adapted from Timothy J. Kloppenborg, Debbie Tesch, and Ravi Chinta, "21st Century Project Success Measures: Evolution, Interpretation, and Direction," Proceedings, PMI Research and Education Conference 2012 (Limerick, Ireland, July 2012).

new products, increased market share, increased profitability, decreased cost, and so on. A contemporary and complete view of project success is shown in Exhibit 1.6.

Project failure can be described as not meeting the success criteria listed in Exhibit 1.6. Many projects are fully successful in some ways but less successful in other aspects. The goal of excellent project management is to reach high levels of success on all measures on all projects. Serious project failure—when some of the success criteria are missed by a large amount and/or when several of the success criteria are missed—can be attributed to numerous causes. In each chapter of this textbook, more specific possible failure causes will be covered, along with how to avoid them, but some basic causes of failure are as follows:

- Incomplete or unclear requirements
- Inadequate user involvement
- Inadequate resources
- Unrealistic time demands
- Unclear or unrealistic expectations
- Inadequate executive support
- Changing requirements
- Inadequate planning

1-4g Using Microsoft Project to Help Plan and Measure Projects

A useful tool to capture and conveniently display a variety of important project data is Microsoft® (MS) Project. MS Project is demonstrated in a step-by-step fashion using screen shots from a single integrated project throughout the book. If you're using the MindTap product for this book, you have access to short videos demonstrating how to use the software.

1-4h Types of Projects

Four ways to classify projects that help people understand the unique needs of each are by industry, size, understanding of project scope, and application.

CLASSIFYING BY INDUSTRY   Projects can be classified in a variety of ways. One method is by industry, which is useful in that projects in different industries often have unique requirements. Several industry-specific project life cycle models are in use, and various trade groups and special interest groups can provide guidance.

CLASSIFYING BY SIZE   Another method of classifying projects is by size. Large projects often require more detailed planning and control. Typically, most of the processes outlined in PMBOK are relevant and applicable for large projects that require a few years and hundreds of project team members for execution. However, even the smallest projects still need to use planning and control—just in a more simplified manner. For example, construction of a multistory building in China would require a highly detailed construction schedule, but even a much simpler construction project of building a one-car garage also needs to follow a schedule.

CLASSIFYING BY TIMING OF PROJECT SCOPE CLARITY   A third method of classifying projects deals with how early in the project the project manager and team are likely to be able to determine with a high degree of certainty what the project scope will be. For example, it may be rather simple to calculate the cubic feet of concrete that are required to pour a parking lot and, therefore, how much work is involved. At the opposite end of the spectrum, when developing a new pharmaceutical or developing a new technology, very little may be determined in the project until the results of some early experiments are reported. Only after analyzing these early experiment results is it possible to begin estimating cost and determining the schedule with confidence. For such projects, change is constant and is caused by uncertainty and unknowns associated with these projects. Consequently, it is important to manage project risks. The planning becomes iterative, with more detail as it becomes available. In the first case, predictive or plan-driven project techniques may work well. In the second case, adaptive or change-driven methods to iteratively determine the scope and plan for risks may be more important.

 Agile methods are increasingly being used when scope clarity emerges slowly.

CLASSIFYING BY APPLICATION   For the purpose of this book, we will discuss many types of projects, such as those dealing with organizational change, quality and productivity improvement, research and development, information systems, and construction. Many of these projects include extensive cross-functional work, which contributes to the challenges associated with managing project teams and the triple constraints of scope, duration, and cost. Remember, all projects require planning and control. Part of the art of project management is determining when to use certain techniques, how much detail to use, and how to tailor the techniques to the needs of a specific project.

1-4i Scalability of Project Tools

Projects range tremendously in size and complexity. In considering construction projects, think of the range from building a simple carport to building an office tower. In both cases, one would need to determine the wants and needs of the customer(s), understand the amount of work involved, determine a budget and schedule, decide what workers are available and who will do which tasks, and then manage the construction until the owner accepts the project results. It should be easy to see that while both projects require planning and control, the level of detail for the carport is a tiny fraction of that for the office tower. In this book, we first demonstrate concepts and techniques at a middle level and then use a variety of project examples to demonstrate how to scale the complexity of the techniques up or down.

1-5 Project Roles

To successfully initiate, plan, and execute projects, a variety of executive, management, and associate roles must be accomplished. Traditional project roles are shown in Exhibit 1.7.

EXHIBIT 1.7

TRADITIONAL PROJECT ROLES		
EXECUTIVE ROLES	MANAGERIAL ROLES	ASSOCIATE ROLES
Sponsor	Project Manager	Core Team Member
Customer	Functional Manager	Subject Matter Expert (SME)
Steering Team	Facilitator	
Project Management Office		

In a large organization, a person often fills only one of these roles; sometimes, more than one person fills a particular role. In small organizations, the same person may fill more than one role. The names of the roles also vary by organization. The work of each role must be accomplished by someone. Project managers are successful when they build strong working relationships with the individuals who execute each of these roles.

1-5a Project Executive-Level Roles

The four traditional project executive-level roles are the sponsor, customer, steering team, and the project management office. The first executive-level project role is that of sponsor. A modern definition of executive **sponsor** is "a senior manager serving in a formal role given authority and responsibility for successful completion of a project deemed strategic to an organization's success."[11] This textbook expands the sponsor's role to include taking an active role in chartering the project, reviewing progress reports, playing a behind-the-scenes role in mentoring, and assisting the project manager throughout the project life, specifically in making critical decisions and supporting the project team.

The second executive-level project role is that of the customer. The **customer** needs to ensure that a good contractor for external projects or project manager for internal projects is selected, make sure requirements are clear, and maintain communications throughout the project. In many traditional projects, the sponsor carries out the role of customer. On many Agile projects, the customer role is quite significant.

The third executive role is the **steering or leadership team** for an organization. This is often the top leader (CEO or other officer) and his or her direct reports. From a project standpoint, the important role for this team is to select, prioritize, and resource projects in accordance with the organization's strategic planning and to ensure that accurate progress is reported and necessary adjustments are made. Another important function of this executive role is midstream evaluation of projects and portfolios to ensure that they stay on track and produce expected results.

The fourth executive-level project role is that of **project management office (PMO)**, which is defined as "a management structure that standardizes the project-related governance processes and facilitates the sharing of resources, methodologies, tools and techniques."[12] The PMO work can range from supporting project managers to controlling them by requiring compliance to directives in actually managing projects. The PMO supports projects by mentoring, training, and assisting project teams and promotes enterprise functions such as developing and augmenting processes, creating and maintaining historical information, and advocating for project management discipline.

EXHIBIT 1.8

AGILE PROJECT ROLES		
EXECUTIVE ROLES	MANAGERIAL ROLES	ASSOCIATE ROLES
Customer (product owner)	Customer (product owner)	Team Member
Sponsor (product manager)	Scrum Master	
Portfolio Team	Functional Manager	
Project Management/Scrum Office	Coach	

Agile project management roles are shown in Exhibit 1.8. Most of the same work still needs to be accomplished in organizations using Agile methods. Some of the work is performed by different people because of the emphasis on empowering teams, and some is performed at different times as requirements and scope emerge gradually instead of just at the project start. Collaborative effort and communication, specifically with the client, are common features of Agile project teams.

On Agile projects, arguably the most essential role is the customer representative—sometimes called the product owner. This person ensures that the needs and wants of the various constituents in the customer's organization are identified and prioritized and that project progress and decisions continually support the customer's desires.

In Agile projects, the customer representative role is so continuous and active that we show it as both an executive- and managerial-level role. The customer representative does much of what a sponsor might in traditional projects, but there also may be a designated sponsor (sometimes known as a product manager) who controls the budget. A portfolio team often performs much of the work of a traditional steering team, and a similar office that may be titled differently such as Scrum office performs much of the work of a project office.

1-5b Project Management-Level Roles

The most obvious management-level role is the project manager. The **project manager** is "the person assigned by the performing organization to lead the team that is responsible for achieving the project objectives."[13] The project manager is normally directly accountable for the project results, schedule, and budget. This person is the main communicator, is responsible for the planning and execution of the project, and works on the project from start to finish. The project manager often must get things done through the power of influence since his or her formal power may be limited. The contemporary approach to project management is to lead in a facilitating manner to the extent possible.

Another key management role is the functional manager (sometimes called a resource manager). Functional managers are the department or division heads—the ongoing managers of the organization. They normally determine how the work of the project is to be accomplished, often supervise that work, and often negotiate with the project manager regarding which workers are assigned to the project.

The third managerial role is that of facilitator. If the project is complex and/or controversial, it sometimes makes sense to have another person help the project manager with the process of running meetings and making decisions.

 On Agile projects, the customer representative or product owner works with the team on a continuous basis, often performing some of the work a project manager might on a traditional project. The Scrum Master serves and leads in a facilitating and collaborative manner. This is a more limited, yet more empowering role than the traditional project manager. The functional manager has a similar, but sometimes more limited, role than the traditional department head. Many organizations using Agile also have a coach who acts as a facilitator and trainer.

1-5c Project Associate-Level Roles

The **project team** is composed of "*a selected group of individuals with complimentary skills and disciplines who are required to work together on interdependent and interrelated tasks for a predetermined period to meet a specific purpose or goal.*"[14] In this book, these individuals are called core team members. The core team, with the project manager, does most of the planning and makes most of the project-level decisions.

The temporary members who are brought on board as needed are called subject matter experts.

 The team members in Agile projects are assigned fulltime as much as possible, so there are few subject matter experts. The teams are self-governing, so they perform many of the planning and coordinating activities that a project manager would typically perform. Small and co-located teams often characterize Agile projects, and they work closely together.

1-6 Overview of the Book

Contemporary project management blends traditional, plan-driven, and contemporary Agile approaches. It is integrative, iterative, and collaborative. Project management is integrative since it consists of the 10 knowledge areas and the 5 process groups described in the *PMBOK® Guide,* and one must integrate all of them into one coherent and ethical whole. Project management is iterative in that one starts by planning at a high level and then repeats the planning in greater detail as more information becomes available and the date for the work performance approaches. Project managers need to balance planning, control, and agility. Project management is collaborative since there are many stakeholders to be satisfied and a team of workers with various skills and ideas who need to work together to plan and complete the project. With these thoughts of integration, iteration, and collaboration in mind, this book has four major parts: Organizing and Initiating Projects, Leading Projects, Planning Projects, and Performing Projects.

1-6a Part 1: Organizing and Initiating Projects

Part 1 consists of three chapters that deal with organizing for and initiating projects.

CHAPTER 2   Chapter 2 covers project selection and prioritization. This includes both internal projects, which should be selected in a manner consistent with the strategic planning of the organization, and external projects. It also explains how to respond to requests for proposals.

CHAPTER 3   Chapter 3 discusses chartering projects. The **project charter** is "a document issued by the project initiator or sponsor that formally authorizes the existence of a project and provides the project manager with the authority to apply organizational resources to project activities."[15] The charter can further be considered an agreement by which the project sponsor and project manager (and often the project core team) agree at a high level what the project is, why it is important, key milestone points in the schedule, major risks, and possibly a few other items. It allows the project manager and core team to understand and agree to what is expected of them.

Finally, Microsoft Project, a tool that facilitates effective project planning, controlling, and communicating, is introduced. Microsoft Project is utilized in eight chapters to demonstrate how to automate various project planning and control techniques. The examples and illustrations in this book use Microsoft Project 2016. If a person is using an earlier version of Microsoft Project, there are slight differences. If a person is using a competing project scheduling package, the intent remains the same, but the mechanics of how to create certain documents may differ.

1-6b Part 2: Leading Projects

Part 2 consists of three chapters on leadership aspects of projects.

CHAPTER 4   Chapter 4 focuses on organizational structure, organizational culture, project life cycle, and project management roles of the parent organization. The organizational structure section describes ways an organization can be configured and the advantages and disadvantages of each in regard to managing projects. Next covered is the culture of the parent organization and the impact it has on the ability to effectively plan and manage projects. The industry and type of project often encourage managers to select or customize a project life cycle model. The roles covered include executive-, managerial-, and associate-level responsibilities that must be performed. The demands of each role are explained, along with suggestions for how to select and develop people to effectively fill each role, considering both the role and the unique abilities and interests of each person.

CHAPTER 5   Chapter 5 describes how to carry out the project work with a project team in order to accomplish the project objectives. The project manager needs to simultaneously champion the needs of the project, the team, and the parent organization. The project manager manages the people side of the project by effectively using the stages of project team development, assessing and building the team members' capability, supervising their work, managing and improving their decision making, and helping them maintain enthusiasm and effective time management. Project managers guide their team in managing and controlling stakeholder engagement.

CHAPTER 6   Chapter 6 begins by identifying the various project stakeholders, their wants and needs, and how to prioritize decisions among them. Chapter 5 also includes communications planning for the project because poor communication can doom an otherwise well-planned and well-managed project. The information needs of each stakeholder group should be included in the communications plan.

1-6c Part 3: Planning Projects

Part 3 includes six chapters dealing with various aspects of project planning.

CHAPTER 7   Chapter 7 shows how to determine the project scope and outline it in the **work breakdown structure (WBS)**. The WBS is "deliverable-oriented hierarchical decomposition of the work to be executed by the project team to accomplish the project objectives and create the required *deliverables*."[16]

The WBS is a document that progressively breaks the project down into its components so that each piece can be described as a deliverable for which one person can plan, estimate the costs, estimate the time, assign resources, manage, and be held accountable for the results. This is a critical document since it is the foundation for most of the other planning and control activities. The chapter ends with instructions on putting a WBS into Microsoft Project.

CHAPTER 8 Chapter 8 deals with scheduling projects. The **project schedule** is "an output of a schedule model instance that presents the time-based information required by the communication plan, including activities with planned dates, durations, milestone dates, and resource allocation.[17] This chapter starts with background information on project scheduling and then covers construction of schedules by defining activities, determining the order in which they need to be accomplished, estimating the duration for each, and then calculating the schedule. Chapter 8 also includes instructions on how to interpret a project schedule; clearly communicate it using a bar chart called a Gantt chart; and use Microsoft Project to construct, interpret, and communicate project schedules.

CHAPTER 9 Chapter 9 demonstrates how to schedule resources on projects: determining the need for workers, understanding who is available, and assigning people. All of the techniques of resourcing projects are integrated with the behavioral aspects of how to deal effectively and ethically with the people involved. Resource needs are shown on a Gantt chart developed in Chapter 8, the responsibilities are shown as they change over time, conflicts and overloads are identified, and methods for resolving conflicts are introduced. Alternative approaches for creating and compressing schedules are shown. Many of the techniques in this chapter are also shown with MS Project.

CHAPTER 10 Chapter 10 discusses the project budget, which is dependent on both the schedule and the resource needs developed in the previous two chapters. The **project budget** is "The sum of work package cost estimates, contingency reserve, and management reserve.[18] Cost planning, estimating, budgeting, establishing cost control, and using MS Project for project budgets are all included.

CHAPTER 11 Chapter 11 starts with establishing a risk management plan. It covers methods for identifying potential risks and for determining which risks are big enough to justify specific plans for either preventing the risk event from happening or dealing effectively with risk events that do happen. Finally, in risk response planning, strategies for dealing with both positive risks (opportunities) and negative risks (threats) are discussed.

CHAPTER 12 Chapter 12 begins with a discussion of how modern project quality concepts have evolved. Then it deals with core project quality demands of stakeholder satisfaction, empowered performance, fact-based management, and process management. The third topic of this chapter is developing the project quality plan. Next, the chapter describes various quality improvement tools for projects.

Since Chapter 12 is the last planning chapter, it concludes with a method of integrating the various sections developed in the previous chapters into a single, coherent project plan. Conflicts that are discovered should be resolved, judgment needs to be applied to ensure that the overall plan really makes sense, and one or more kickoff meetings are normally held to inform all of the project stakeholders and to solicit their enthusiastic acceptance of the plan. At this point, the project schedule and budget can be baselined in MS Project.

While bits of the project that might have caused delays if they were not started early may already be in progress, the formal kickoff is the signal that the project is under way!

1-6d Part 4: Performing Projects

Part 3 includes three chapters that deal with performing the project.

CHAPTER 13   Chapter 13 begins by introducing relevant supply chain concepts such as a supply chain view of projects, the components that form a supply chain, factors to consider when dealing with a supply chain, and methods of improving the performance of a supply chain. Make-or-buy analysis and contract types lead the reader through procurement planning. Identifying and selecting sellers lead into managing contracts to assure receipt of promised supplies and services according to contractual terms. The chapter ends with advantages and requirements of effective project partnering.

CHAPTER 14   While the project work is being performed, the project manager needs to determine that the desired results are achieved—the subject of Chapter 14. **Monitor and control project work** is defined as "the process of tracking, reviewing, and reporting the progress to meet the performance objectives defined in the project management plan."[19] This starts with gathering performance data already identified during project initiating and planning. The actual performance data are then compared to the desired performance data so that both corrective and preventive actions can be used to ensure that the amount and quality of the project work meet expectations. MS Project can be used for this progress reporting and for making adjustments. Earned value analysis is used to determine exactly how actual cost and schedule progress are compared with planned progress. Overcoming obstacles, managing changes, resolving conflicts, reprioritizing work, and creating a transition plan all lead up to customer acceptance of the project deliverables.

CHAPTER 15   Chapter 15 deals with finishing projects and realizing benefits. **Close project or phase** is defined as all the work needed to formally close a project or phase. This chapter includes a section on terminating projects early, in case either the project is not doing well or conditions have changed and the project results are no longer needed, and a section on timely termination of successful projects. Topics include how to secure customer feedback and use it along with the team's experiences to create lessons learned for the organization; reassign workers and reward those participants who deserve recognition; celebrate success; perform a variety of closure activities; and provide ongoing support for the organization that is using the results of the project. Finally, after the project deliverables have been used for some time, an assessment should determine if the promised benefits are being realized.

PMP/CAPM Study Ideas

Everything in this book is designed to mirror and explain the content in the latest edition—the sixth—of the *Guide to the Project Management Body of Knowledge (PMBOK)*, the international standard produced by the Project Management Institute (PMI). Not only will the content and questions in this book help you learn the best practices for managing and executing projects, but they will also help you prepare for one of the licensing exams if you choose to pursue a project management credential such as the CAPM or PMP. More information on these and other PMI certifications can be found at www.pmi.org/certifications/types.

While either of these credentials can open doors for you professionally, the effort needed to acquire them should not be underestimated. In addition to work and education requirements (specified at the website noted above), you will need to pass an online test consisting of 150 (CAPM) or 200 (PMP) questions, respectively. PMI does not publish the exact pass rates of either of these tests, but they are designed to be difficult. It will not be enough for you to just memorize knowledge areas, process groups, and inputs and outputs; rather, you will need a solid understanding of each of these in order to answer higher-level thinking questions of a wide variety. In this book, we will provide dozens of questions in each chapter for you to use as a guide.

Summary

A project is an organized set of work efforts undertaken to produce a unique output subject to limitations of time and resources such as materials, equipment, tools, and people. Since the world is changing more rapidly than in the past, many people spend an increasing amount of their working time on projects. Project management includes work processes that initiate, plan, execute, monitor, control, and close project work. During these processes, trade-offs must be made among the scope, quality, cost, and schedule, so that the project results meet the agreed-upon requirements, are useful to the customers, and promote the organization.

All projects, regardless of size, complexity, or application, need to be planned and managed. While the level of detail and specific methods vary widely, all projects need to follow generally accepted methods. PMI is a large professional organization devoted to promoting and standardizing project management understanding and methods. One of PMI's standards, *A Guide to the Project Management Body of Knowledge (PMBOK® Guide)*, is composed of five process groups: initiating,

planning, executing, monitoring and controlling, and closing; along with ten knowledge areas: integration, scope, schedule, cost, quality, resources, communications, risk, procurement, and stakeholders.

To successfully initiate, plan, and execute projects, two more things are needed. One is to understand what project success is and what drives it, along with what project failure is and its major causes. The other is an understanding of the various executive-, managerial-, and associate-level roles in project management. This book is organized to be useful to students who will enter a variety of industries and be assigned to projects of all sizes and levels of complexity. Students will learn how to understand and effectively manage each of these process groups and knowledge areas. Microsoft Project 2016 is used in eight chapters to illustrate how to automate various planning, scheduling, resourcing, budgeting, and controlling activities. All definitions used are from the *PMBOK Guide*, sixth edition. This book follows a chronological approach throughout a project's life cycle, emphasizing knowledge and skills that lead to project success.

Key Terms Consistent with PMI Standards and Guides

The glossary in this book uses terms as defined in various Project Management Institute guides and standards where they are distinct. The glossary also uses commonly understood definitions where terms are standard.

project, 4
stakeholders, 4
project management, 4
soft skills, 7
hard skills, 7
functional manager, 7
project life cycle, 7
project management process group, 10
initiating processes, 10
planning processes, 10

executing processes, 10
monitoring and controlling processes, 10
closing processes, 10
integration management, 11
scope management, 11
schedule management, 11
cost management, 11
quality management, 11
resources management, 11
communications management, 11

Chapter Review Questions

1. What is a project?
2. What is project management?
3. How are projects different from ongoing operations?
4. What types of constraints are common to most projects?
5. What are the three components of the Talent Triangle?
6. At what stage of a project life cycle are the majority of the "hands-on" tasks completed?
7. During which stage of the project life cycle are loose ends tied up?
8. What are the five process groups of project management?
9. Which process group defines a new project or phase by obtaining authorization?
10. What are the 10 project management knowledge areas?
11. What two project dimensions are components of project performance?
12. How do you define project success?
13. How do you define project failure?
14. List four common causes of project failure.
15. What are three common ways of classifying projects?
16. What is predictive or plan-driven planning, and when should it be used?
17. What is adaptive or change-driven planning, and when should it be used?
18. What makes someone a project stakeholder?
19. What are the three project executive-level roles?
20. List and describe each of the managerial and associate project roles.

Discussion Questions

1. Using an example of your own, describe a project in terms that are common to most projects.
2. Why are more organizations using project management? If you were an executive, how would you justify your decision to use project management to the board of trustees?
3. Explain how to scale up or down the complexity of project planning and management tools and what effect, if any, this might have on the project life cycle.
4. List and describe several issues that pertain to each stage of the project life cycle.
5. Put the five project management process groups in order from the one that generally requires the least work to the one that requires the most.
6. Name the 10 project management knowledge areas, and briefly summarize each.
7. Discuss how a project could be successful in terms of some measures yet unsuccessful by others.
8. What does project failure mean? What are some examples?
9. Compare and contrast advantages and disadvantages of predictive/plan-driven and adaptive/change-driven project life cycle approaches.
10. You are given a project to manage. How do you decide whether to use a predictive or adaptive approach?
11. Contrast project managers and functional managers.
12. List as many project roles as you can, and identify what each one is responsible for in terms of the project.

PMBOK® Guide Questions

The purpose of these questions is to help visualize the type of questions on PMP and CAPM exams.

1. Which project role provides resources or support for the project, promotes and protects the project at higher levels of management, and takes an active role in the project from the chartering stage through project closure?
   a. functional manager
   b. project manager
   c. project team member
   d. project sponsor

2. Which PMBOK® Guide Knowledge Area includes those processes required to ensure that the project includes all the work required, and only the work required, to complete the project successfully?
   a. cost management
   b. scope management
   c. risk management
   d. quality management

3. In order to be successful, the project team must be able to assess the needs of stakeholders and manage their expectations through effective communications. At the same time, they must balance competing demands among project scope, schedule, budget, risk, quality, and resources, which are also known as project _____.
   a. plan elements
   b. deliverables
   c. constraints
   d. targets

4. Projects pass through a series of phases as they move from initiation to project closure. The names and number of these phases can vary significantly depending on the organization, the type of application, industry, or technology employed. These phases create the framework for the project, and are referred to collectively as the _____.
   a. project life cycle
   b. project management information system (PMIS)
   c. product life cycle
   d. Talent Triangle

5. Based on PMI's definition, which of these is a good example of a project?
   a. manufacturing a standard commodity
   b. following policies and procedures for procuring an item
   c. designing and launching a new website
   d. using a checklist to perform quality control

6. When would a predictive project life cycle be the preferred approach?
   a. when the high-level vision has been developed, but the product scope is not well defined
   b. when the environment is changing rapidly
   c. when the product to be delivered is well understood
   d. when the product will be created through a series of repeated cycles

7. To be effective, a project manager needs to possess all of the following competencies except _____.
   a. personal effectiveness—attitudes, core personality traits, leadership
   b. authority—power or right granted by the organization
   c. performance—what project managers can accomplish while applying their project management knowledge
   d. knowledge of project management—understanding of project management tools and techniques

8. In Adaptive Life Cycles (change-driven or Agile methods), _____.
   a. the overall scope of the project is fixed, and the time and cost are developed incrementally
   b. the overall cost is fixed, and the project scope and schedule are developed iteratively
   c. the time and cost are fixed, but the scope is developed iteratively
   d. change control is very important

9. The two traditional project management associate-level roles are different in each of the following ways *except* _____.
   a. duration of time spent on project
   b. ability to work within project constraints
   c. degree of input contributed to project planning
   d. skill set

10. A freelance project manager is brought in by Company X to lead a large, expensive project. This project manager has excellent leadership skills and a strong technical understanding of the project. In order for her to optimize every component of the Talent Triangle, what might be a good activity for the project manager at the start of her time with Company X?

   a. familiarize herself with the long-term objectives of Company X
   b. host an icebreaker for all team members
   c. attend a seminar on advanced leadership techniques
   d. send an email including her résumé to all SMEs to ensure they are aware of her technical background

---

INTEGRATED EXAMPLE PROJECTS

We will use two example projects throughout all 15 chapters of this book. One will be a construction project suited to mostly traditional project planning and management. The other will be a development project suited more toward Agile project planning and management. In this chapter, we will introduce both of them. In subsequent chapters, we will choose one to demonstrate techniques and concepts from the chapter and ask leading questions of the other one. We will alternate chapters so professors can choose to use the questions as assignments if they wish.

SUBURBAN HOMES CONSTRUCTION PROJECT

Purchasing a new home is the single largest investment most of us will make in our lifetime. You can either purchase the home from a reputed real estate building company or manage the construction of your home using project management principles that you have mastered. The latter approach can save significant amounts of money over the life of a typical 30-year mortgage. Additionally, it is likely to provide you with one of the most satisfying experiences in your life because you will get an opportunity to see the results of choices you made in building your home.[1] However, on the downside, if you manage the project poorly, it also has the potential on many levels to be a disaster.

The experience of managing the construction of a single-family home provides a coherent account of costs, benefits, other considerations related to construction, risks, hazards, and critical decisions. The experience also has the potential for joy if the project is a successful endeavor.

Suburban Homes is a medium-sized, fast-growing construction company in the Midwest region of the United States. Due to its significant growth and good reputation for building quality single-family homes and townhomes, the company decided to expand its business to several Southern states in the United States. However, Suburban Homes recognized the scope for managing resources effectively and efficiently to increase profits. It has decided to formalize project management practices by developing and implementing standard and promising processes, tools, and techniques. For this purpose, the company was looking for a competent project manager to manage its projects. They hired Adam Smith as their new project manager.

Adam Smith had worked for several years in the construction industry and supplemented his experience with project management education. Consequently, he gained considerable experience and developed expertise in managing construction projects. Adam believes in managing projects by adhering to various project management processes, tools, and techniques. In his new position as the project manager, Adam's primary task is to improve the performance of project management and increase the project success rate.

What advice would you offer to Adam Smith?

---
[1]Suprick J. and Anantatmula V. (2010).

CASA DE PAZ DEVELOPMENT PROJECT

Casa de Paz is an intentional community supporting the transformative journey of recovery for Latina women and their children. It is a 501(c)(3) nonprofit organization that is just starting. The vision is to create a communal living space for multiple Latina women and their children. The women and their children also would have access to a variety of service providers in the form of graduate students living in the same building. Two possible buildings have been identified. Some of the many things that need to take place for this vision to become a reality are board and working group structuring, fundraising, accountancy, promotion, website development, community relations development, building purchase and renovation, program development, legal services, educational advocacy, and English as a Second Language (ESL) tutoring, among others. While every project has trade-offs, success on this project will be measured more on the creation of a safe environment with needed services than on cost and schedule.

Casadepazcinci.org

Why Is This Project So Important?

Hundreds of thousands of people are fleeing violence in their home countries. In the United States, many of them come from Latin America. Often, they lack communities for support and integration as they transition from their countries of origin. In addition, many face many obstacles to stability and flourishing. How would you put your life back together if you were a mother fleeing violence in your country of origin, and once in a new country, that same violence continues in your new home? Few spaces offer stability and encouragement in such circumstances, much less cultural sensitivies and professional services to facilitate the transformation to self-sufficiency and success. Casa de Paz/House of Peace is an intentional community that encourages and draws out women's resilience both by meeting them where they are and providing time and space to heal, recover, and grow. Most shelters for women and children are temporary; the average stay is seven to twelve days. Casa de Paz provides up to six months of stability, community, and professional services to support women's growth along a continuum of self-sufficiency matrixes. It is a community that recognizes women's dignity and celebrates each step toward the realization of their gifts as human beings.

Semester Project Instructions

This book is designed to give your professors the option to have you practice the concepts and techniques from each chapter on a real project. Often, the project chosen will be for a nonprofit group of some kind such as a United Way agency, a church, or a school. The project could, however, be for a company or a part of the university. The semester project can often be one that several students will be assigned to work on as a team.

Each chapter provides suggested assignments to practice project management skills on the real or potential project you are using. Depending on the emphasis your professor chooses, you may need to perform some, most, or all of these assignments. At a minimum, your professor will probably assign the charter, work breakdown structure, and schedule.

In any case, each of the following chapters prompts you to perform various activities to plan and execute the project. At some point in the first couple of weeks, your professor will probably invite at least one representative from each organization to your class to introduce their project and to meet you. We will call these

persons *sponsors* and define their role more fully in Chapter 3. Since this first chapter is a broad introduction to project management, your task for the Chapter 1 sample project may be just to familiarize yourself with your new student team, your sponsor, your sponsor's organization, and the overall direction of your project. If you have enough input from your sponsor, your professor may also ask you to create a customer trade-off matrix, as shown in Exhibit 1.6 and/or a definition of success for your project, as in Exhibit 1.7. Your professor also may ask you to answer certain specific and/or open-ended questions concerning your newly assigned project.

Subsequent chapters give you more in-depth tools to acclimate you to your project, the organization you will be working for, and the various stakeholders who have an interest in the project. For example, in the next chapter, you learn how project selection flows from an organization's strategic planning, and you should seek to learn why this project was chosen and how it supports the strategic goals of the organization.

PROJECT MANAGEMENT *IN ACTION*
Using Appreciative Inquiry to Understand Project Management

Each project creates a unique product, service, or result that certain stakeholders desire. Project success requires understanding stakeholder requirements, clarifying project expectations, and agreeing upon project scope. As such, it is imperative to identify relevant stakeholders and to have a constructive engagement with them. One tool that is helpful for allowing such engagement and for navigating through complexities is appreciative inquiry (AI).

What Is Appreciative Inquiry?

The principles: Appreciative inquiry (AI) is a positive philosophy for change, wherein whole systems convene to inquire for change (Cooperrider, 2003). AI recognizes the power of the whole and builds on conversational learning that emerges out of the whole. It operates on the belief that human systems move in the direction of their shared image and idea of the future, and that change is based on intentional and positive inquiry into what has worked best in the past. In this sense, AI suggests that human organizing and change are a relational process of inquiry that is grounded in affirmation and appreciation. Typically, the process works its way through the four phases of Discovery, Dream, Design, and Delivery (Conklin, 2009).

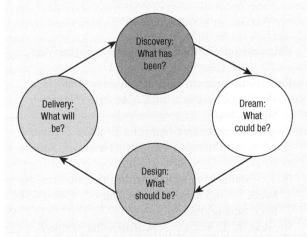

Implications of AI on Defining Project Scope

Project success partially depends upon identifying key stakeholders: eliciting their true wants and needs to determine project scope; and keeping them appropriately engaged throughout the entire project. The early involvement is critical because it lays out clear goals and boundaries of project scope. However, eliciting accurate responses may be difficult, especially since many projects may be planned and conducted in an atmosphere of uncertainty. The ongoing involvement helps to ensure stakeholders know what they will get from the project and will be pleased.

Appreciative inquiry is a tool that may assist project stakeholders to navigate through their inquiries via positive conversations. For example, a typical process may look like this:

Discovery (What has been?): This phase inquires into and discovers the positive capacity of a group, organization, or community. People are encouraged to use stories to describe their strengths, assets, peak experiences, and successes to understand the unique conditions that made their moments of excellence possible. In this step, stakeholders reflect on the past to recollect instances when they believed they could clearly articulate their true needs and wants; and when their needs and wants were folded into the project scope. Through storytelling, they collectively discover the process of project selection and prioritization and articulate a gauge of project success. As they discuss, they start generating a dense web of understanding—an understanding and an appreciation of all their capacities that make moments of excellence possible. Agile projects use a similar method of storytelling to understand user requirements and ultimately define project scope.

Dreaming (What could be?): Building on the moments of excellence of the participants, this phase encourages the participants to imagine what would happen if their moments of excellence were to become a norm. Participants dream for the ideal conditions and build hope and possibility of an ideal future. As people share their stories, the focus of the process now shifts to dreaming of a perfect, desirable state for the stakeholders. Through this journey, the goal should be to enable the participants to build positive energy around their strengths and also to dream about the direction in which they feel comfortable moving.

Designing (What should be?): This phase creates design principles that will help the participants realize their dream. Participants are encouraged to stretch their imagination to move the system from where it currently is to where the participants want it to be. At this stage, the participants should be encouraged to imagine a perfect world without any constraints. Therefore, if there were no resource constraints, what would the scope of the project look like?

Delivery (What will be?): In this phase, participants are encouraged to think of the various subsystems that should take the responsibility of the design phase to "sustain the design from the dream that it discovered" (Cooperrider et al., 2003, p. 182). In this phase, various stakeholders are encouraged to decide what they will be committing themselves to.

Key Outcome

Going through this entire process allows stakeholders to elicit and articulate their expectations from the project. Stakeholders also have a better understanding of how their needs and wants link to and lead them to a desirable future state. Finally, in order to sustain their dream, their commitment is clearly articulated. As stakeholders commit themselves to specific endeavors on the project, they will implicitly revisit the opportunities and cost that lay ahead of them, which allows stakeholders to draw a realistic boundary around their commitment to the project.

Projects are temporary and unique and may have shifting boundaries over time. The process of engaging stakeholders via appreciative inquiry (AI) is an effective way to address the ambiguity and uncertainty in project management.

Source: Rashmi Assudani, Associate Professor and Chair, Department of Management and Entrepreneurship, Williams College of Business, Xavier University. Adapted from Conklin, T. A., "Creating Classrooms of Preference: An Exercise in Appreciative Inquiry." *Journal of Management Education* 33 (6) (2009): 772–792. Cooperrider, D. L., D. Whitney, and J. M. Stavros, *Appreciative Inquiry Handbook* (Bedford Heights, OH: Lakeshore, 2003).

References

A *Guide to the Project Management Body of Knowledge (PMBOK® Guide)*, 6th ed. Exposure Draft (Newtown Square, PA: Project Management Institute, 2017).

Anantatmula, Vittal S., *Project Teams: A Structured Developmental Approach*, 2016, New York: Business Expert Press.

Chandler, Dawne E., and Payson Hall, *Improving Executive Sponsorship of Projects: A Holistic Approach*, 2017, New York: Business Expert Press.

Cooper, Robert G., "Winning at New Products: Pathways to Profitable Innovation," *Proceedings, PMI Research Conference 2006* (Montreal, July 2006).

Crowe, Andy, Alpha Project Managers: What the Top 2% Know That Everyone Else Does Not (Atlanta: Velociteach, 2006).

Kloppenborg, Timothy J., and Warren A. Opfer, "The Current State of Project Management Research: Trends, Interpretations, and Predictions," *Project Management Journal* 33 (2) (June 2002): 5–18.

Kloppenborg, Timothy J., Debbie Tesch, and Broderick King, "21st Century Project Success Measures: Evolution, Interpretation, and Direction," *Proceedings,*

PMI Research and Education Conference 2012 (Dublin, Ireland, July 2012).

Muller, R., and R. Turner, "The Influence of Project Managers on Project Success Criteria by Type of Project," *European Management Journal* 25 (4) (2007): 298–309.

PMI Lexicon of Project Management Terms Version 3.0, 2015 (Newtown Square, PA).

Project Management Institute, *Business Analysis for Practitioners: A Practice Guide*, 2015 (Newtown Square, PA).

Project Management Institute, *Practice Standard for Scheduling 2nd ed.*, 2011 Newtown Square, PA).

Project Management Institute, Practice Standard for Work Breakdown Structures 2nd ed., 2006 (Newtown Square, PA).

Shenhar, A. J., and D. Dvir, *Reinventing Project Management* (Boston: Harvard Business School Press, 2007).

https://asq.org/quality-resources/quality-glossary/q, accessed February 6, 2017.

Endnotes

1. https://www.smartsheet.com/comprehensive-guide-values-principles-agile-manifesto, accessed December 1, 2016.

2. Wikipedia https://en.wikipedia.org/wiki/Functional_manager, accessed February 6, 2017.

3. PMI Lexicon of Project Management Terms Version 3.0, 2015 (Newtown Square, PA): 9.

4. Robert G. Cooper, "Winning at New Products: Pathways to Profitable Innovation," *Proceedings* (2006).

5. http://www.pmi.org/pmbok-guide-standards/foundational, accessed February 6, 2017.

6. Project Management Institute, *A Guide to the Project Management Body of Knowledge (PMBOK® Guide),* 6th ed. Exposure Draft. (Newtown Square, PA: Project Management Institute, 2017): 15.

7. Ibid.

8. PMI Lexicon of Project Management Terms Version 3.0, 2015 (Newtown Square, PA): 7.

9. PMI Lexicon of Project Management Terms Version 3.0, 2015 (Newtown Square, PA): 7.

10. https://asq.org/quality-resources/quality-glossary/q, accessed February 6, 2017.

11. Dawne E. Chandler and Payson Hall, *Improving Executive Sponsorship of Projects: A Holistic Approach,* 2017 (New York: Business Expert Press): 1.

12. PMI Lexicon of Project Management Terms Version 3.0, 2015 (Newtown Square, PA): 13.

13. Ibid.

14. Vittal S. Anantatmula, *Project Teams: A Structured Developmental Approach,* 2016, New York: Business Expert Press, 9.

15. PMI Lexicon of Project Management Terms Version 3.0, 2015 (Newtown Square, PA): 5.

16. Project Management Institute, Practice Standard for Work Breakdown Structures 2nd ed., 2006 (Newtown Square, PA): 121.

17. Project Management Institute, *Practice Standard for Scheduling 2nd ed., 2011* (Newtown Square, PA): 138.

18. PMI Lexicon of Project Management Terms Version 3.0, 2015 (Newtown Square, PA): 8.

19. Project Management Institute, *A Guide to the Project Management Body of Knowledge (PMBOK® Guide),* 6th ed. Exposure Draft. (Newtown Square, PA: Project Management Institute, 2017): 15.

CHAPTER 2

Project Selection and Prioritization

Monkey Business Images/Shutterstock.com

CHAPTER OBJECTIVES

After completing this chapter, you should be able to:

CORE OBJECTIVES:

- Explain in your own words the strategic planning and portfolio management processes.
- Describe how to select, prioritize, and resource projects as an outgrowth of strategic planning.
- From a contractor's viewpoint, describe how to secure projects.

TECHNICAL OBJECTIVES:

- Compare the strengths and weaknesses of using financial and scoring models to select projects.
- Given organizational priorities and several projects, demonstrate how to select and prioritize projects using a scoring model.

BEHAVIORAL OBJECTIVES:

- Explain the strengths an organization might possess that could improve its ability to perform projects.

With the development of a new five-year strategic plan, significant financial growth, and a major reorganization, Living Arrangements for the Developmentally Disabled (LADD) found itself overwhelmed with tasks and at a point that required the thoughtful selection and prioritization of projects. Prior strategic plans were largely dictated by the former executive director, created in a silo of sorts. It was through the introduction of a new executive director to LADD and complete new leadership at the management level that an opportunity presented itself for new, cross-department collaboration, innovative methods to carry out established practices, and the ability to identify and draw on the strengths of the individual members of the team.

LADD is a medium-sized nonprofit corporation that is mission focused and considered a leader in the field of supporting individuals with developmental disabilities. Its efforts reach beyond day-to-day functions and extend in large part to awareness, advocacy, and action. With the sponsorship of a national film festival focused on disabilities and its work in the civic and government sectors at local and national levels, LADD has been able to influence positive change in legislation and the inclusion of people with disabilities at all levels of society.

PMBOK® GUIDE

Topics:

- 1.2 Foundational Elements
- Selecting Projects

CHAPTER OUTPUTS

- Elevator Pitch
- Project Selection and Prioritization Matrix
- Project Resource Assignment Matrix

Project selection and prioritization were exactly what LADD needed because they were trying to maintain pace with a large program and revenue growth curve, new leadership at the helm, and federal changes in the way services were to be delivered to those with developmental disabilities. Projects from the strategic plan were scored based on established value sets that included criteria such as if the project met the mission, was financially feasible, or strengthened personal or community relationships.

LADD's strategic plan contains 32 primary goals and many more objectives. The project selection and prioritization process was a key tool to build a framework that would inspire agency success over the next five years. It is also anticipated to be a method to reduce program competition and increase understanding within the management team as occasions for team development and departmental collaboration occur. In the end, each step of the process will lead the agency to achieve its vision of propelling the inclusion and success of people with disabilities forward with a positive impact throughout the community.

—Amy Harpenau, Vice President, Living Arrangements
for the Developmentally Disabled.

2-1 Strategic Planning Process

One of the tasks of a company's senior leadership is to set the firm's strategic direction. Some of this direction setting occurs when an organization is young or is being revamped, but some needs to occur repeatedly. Exhibit 2.1 depicts the steps in strategic planning and how portfolio management should be an integral part.

2-1a Strategic Analysis

The first part of setting strategic direction is to analyze both the external and internal environments and determine how they will enhance or limit the organization's ability to perform. This strategic analysis is often called strengths, weaknesses, opportunities, and threats (SWOT). The internal analysis (elements within the project team's control) consists of asking what strengths and weaknesses the organization possesses. The external analysis (elements over which the project team has little or no control) consists of asking what opportunities and threats are posed by competitors, suppliers, customers, regulatory agencies, technologies, and so on. The leaders of an organization often need to be humble and open to ideas that are unpleasant and contradictory to their beliefs when conducting this analysis. Performed correctly, a strategic analysis can be very illuminating and can suggest direction for an organization. An example of SWOT analysis

EXHIBIT 2.1

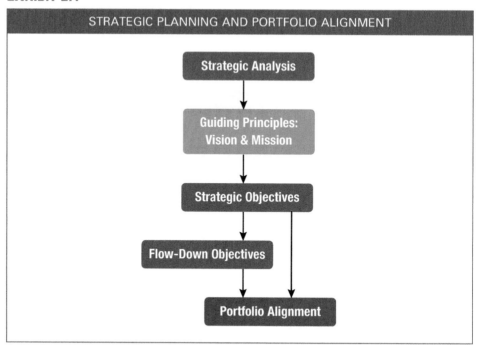

STRATEGIC PLANNING AND PORTFOLIO ALIGNMENT

- Strategic Analysis
- Guiding Principles: Vision & Mission
- Strategic Objectives
- Flow-Down Objectives
- Portfolio Alignment

for the Built Green Home at Suncadia is shown in Exhibit 2.2. The Built Green Home at Suncadia, Washington, was developed using advanced sustainability concepts and a large degree of stakeholder involvement.

2-1b Guiding Principles

Once the SWOT analysis is complete, the organization's leadership should establish guiding principles such as the vision and mission. Some organizations break this step into more parts by adding separate statements concerning purpose and/or values. Often, these sections are included in the mission. For simplicity's sake, they will be treated as part of the mission in this book. It is more important to understand the intent of each portion and achieve it rather than worry about the exact format or names of individual portions.

VISION   The **vision** is a one-sentence statement describing the clear and inspirational long-term, desired change resulting from an organization or program's work.[1] A clear and compelling vision will help all members and all stakeholders of an organization understand and desire to achieve it. Visions often require extra effort to achieve but are considered to be worth the effort. Visions are often multiyear goals that, once achieved, suggest the need for a new vision.

One of the visions most often cited, because it was so clear and compelling, was President John F. Kennedy's goal of placing a man on the moon before the end of the 1960s. Kennedy set this goal after Russia launched Sputnik and the United States found itself behind in the space race. His vision was very effective in mobilizing people to achieve it; further, it rapidly transformed a huge suburban area near Houston into a developed and sustainable economic and technology zone.

EXHIBIT 2.2

SWOT ANALYSIS FOR THE BUILT GREEN HOME AT SUNCADIA	
STRENGTHS	WEAKNESSES
Green building has a buzz	Green building has not reached mainstream
Seattle has a strong green building community support	Limited project resources community Distance away from Seattle Green building is perceived to be costly
Strong community support	High cost of green projects
Growth in green building projects that demonstrate value	
Need to provide numbers on green building value	
Committed developer and builder	
OPPORTUNITIES	THREATS
Uniqueness of product	Existing thinking on green building and its niche focus
Location	Building schedule
Community surrounding house	Community (location)
Lack of data on green building (wealth) value	Rumors

Source: Brenda Nunes, developer, Built Green Home at Suncadia.

A more recent example was in 2009 when hundreds of community leaders in Cleveland, Ohio, decided to use a systems approach to guide many interrelated social and economic efforts in their region. The vision they stated is, "Cleveland and other cities throughout Northeast Ohio should be green cities on a blue lake...."[2] They continue to use this vision to guide regional leaders as they choose where to invest their time and resources in bettering the region and life for its residents. They also are currently planning their 2019 Sustainable Cleveland Summit.[3]

Increasingly, companies are incorporating the triple bottom line into their vision statements. This approach emphasizes the social, environmental, and economic health of the company's stakeholders rather than a narrow emphasis only on the economic return for shareholders. This stated desire to be a good corporate citizen with a long-term view of the world can motivate efforts that achieve both economic return for shareholders and other positive benefits for many other stakeholders.

MISSION STATEMENT   The vision should lead into the **mission statement**, which is a way to accomplish the vision. The mission statement includes the "organization's core purpose, core values, beliefs, culture, primary business, and primary customers."[3] Several of these sections may flow together in the mission statement and, sometimes, an overall statement is formed with expanded definitions of portions for illustration. The rationale for including each section (either as one unified statement or as separate statements) is as follows:

- By including the organization's purpose, the mission statement communicates why the organization exists.
- By including the organization's core values, a mission statement communicates how decisions will be made and the way people will be treated. True organizational

EXHIBIT 2.3

CINCINNATI CHILDREN'S HOSPITAL MEDICAL CENTER VISION AND MISSION

Vision

Cincinnati Children's Hospital Medical Center will be the leader in improving child health.

Mission Statement

Cincinnati Children's will improve child health and transform delivery of care through fully integrated, globally recognized research, education, and innovation. For patients from our community, the nation and the world, the care we provide will achieve the best:

- Medical and quality of life **outcomes**
- Patient and family **experiences** and
- **Value**

today and in the future.

Source: Cincinnati Children's Hospital Medical Center, http://www.cincinnatichildrens.org/about/mission/, accessed January 9, 2017.

values describe deeply held views concerning how everyone should act—especially when adhering to those values is difficult.

- By including beliefs, a mission statement communicates the ideals for which its leaders and members are expected to stand. Beliefs are deeply held and slow to change, so it is quite useful to recognize them, as they can either help or hinder an organization's attempt to achieve its vision.
- By including the organization's culture, the mission statement instructs and expects members to act in the desired manner.
- By including the primary business areas, everyone will know in what business the organization wishes to engage.
- By identifying the primary customers, everyone will understand which groups of people need to be satisfied and who is counting on the organization. The mission needs to be specific enough in describing the business areas and customers to set direction, but not so specific that the organization lacks imagination.

An example of a vision and mission statement from Cincinnati Children's Hospital Medical Center is shown in Exhibit 2.3.

2-1c Strategic Objectives

With the strategic analysis, mission, and vision in place, leaders turn to setting **strategic objectives**, which should be the means of achieving the mission and vision. For most organizations, this strategic alignment of objective setting occurs annually, but some organizations may review objectives and make minor revisions at three- or six-month intervals. While the planning is normally performed annually, many of the strategic objectives identified will take well over one year to achieve. The objectives describe both short- and long-term results that are desired, along with measures to determine achievement. Organizations that embrace a triple bottom line in their guiding values will have objectives promoting each bottom line, and projects that are selected will contribute toward each. These objectives should provide focus on decisions regarding which

EXHIBIT 2.4

INTERNET SOCIETY STRATEGIC OBJECTIVES FOR 2012–2014 PLANNING CYCLE

1. **Facilitate** and **promote** policy environments that enable the continued evolution of an open and trusted Internet.
2. **Increase** the global **relevance** of collaborative, bottom-up, technical, consensus-based, open standards development.
3. **Strengthen** Internet Society **leadership** in Internet Development.
4. **Build** the **visibility** and **influence** of the Internet Society as the trusted source on global Internet issues.

Source: http://www.internetsociety.org/who-we-are/organization-reports-and-policies/internet-society-2015-action-plan, accessed February 7, 2017.

projects to select and how to prioritize them, since they are an expression of the organizational focus. Many writers have stated that for objectives to be effective, they should be "SMART—that is, specific, measurable, achievable, results based, and time specific."[4] An example of strategic objectives from The Internet Society is shown in Exhibit 2.4.

2-1d Flow-Down Objectives

Once an organization's strategic objectives are identified, they must be enforced. Some objectives may be implemented by work in ongoing operations. However, projects tend to be the primary method for implementing many objectives. If the organization is relatively small, leaders may proceed directly to selecting projects at this point. Larger organizations may elect a different route. If the organization is so large that it is impractical for the overall leaders to make all project selection decisions, they might delegate those decisions to various divisions or functions with the stipulation that the decisions should be aligned with the organization's strategic planning that has taken place to this point. Regardless of whether the organization is small and the top leaders make all project selection decisions or whether the organization is large and some of the decisions are cascaded one or more levels down, several methods of project selection may be used.

2-2 Portfolio Management

Companies that use a strategic project selection process to carefully align projects with their organizational goals will find they tend to be more successful at completing their projects and deriving the expected benefits from them. **Portfolio management** is the centralized management of one or more portfolios to achieve strategic objectives.[5] "The goal of portfolio management is to achieve the maximum benefit toward the strategic goals of the company. To accomplish this, executives need to identify, select, prioritize, resource, and govern an appropriate portfolio of projects and other work."[6] Governing will be covered in Chapter 14, and all other portfolio management topics will be covered here. Project success at these companies is measured by how much the project contributes to the organization's objectives (business needs) as well as the traditional measures of staying within budget and schedule and achieving the specific technical goals promised at the start of the project to obtain a desired return on investment.

For ease of understanding how various work is related, many organizations utilize an approach of classifying portfolios, programs, projects, and subprojects. Not all companies use all four classifications, but understanding how they are related helps one see where any particular portion of work fits in the organization.

PORTFOLIO EXAMPLE   We are a major national health insurance company. Our planning approach starts with creating an inventory of project initiatives, which has been identified by the key business areas. We separate the projects into foundational pillars

EXHIBIT 2.5

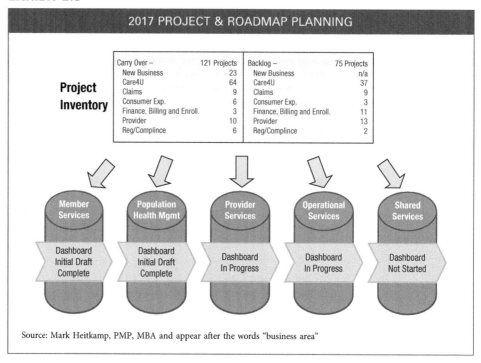

2017 PROJECT & ROADMAP PLANNING

Project Inventory

Carry Over –	121 Projects	Backlog –	75 Projects
New Business	23	New Business	n/a
Care4U	64	Care4U	37
Claims	9	Claims	9
Consumer Exp.	6	Consumer Exp.	3
Finance, Billing and Enroll.	3	Finance, Billing and Enroll.	11
Provider	10	Provider	13
Reg/Complince	6	Reg/Complince	2

Member Services — Dashboard Initial Draft Complete

Population Health Mgmt — Dashboard Initial Draft Complete

Provider Services — Dashboard In Progress

Operational Services — Dashboard In Progress

Shared Services — Dashboard Not Started

Source: Mark Heitkamp, PMP, MBA and appear after the words "business area"

(operation functions) and develop roadmaps of activities going out six quarters (18 months) as can be seen in Exhibit 2.5. Priority and timing of business need determine which quarter(s) the project initiatives are developed and implemented. The roadmaps also include smaller activities called capabilities that are integrated with the project activities. Each of these foundational pillars aligns with the supporting agile sprint teams and the backlog of activities gets translated into stories within the sprints. A key role is the Product Owner who represents the business area and determines which activities (stories) go into each sprint. There is one Product Owner for each pillar and they are at a Director level within the organization. The product owner must have a complete understanding of the organizations strategy and short-term goals of their respective business area.

2-2a Portfolios

Organizations require many work activities to be performed, including both ongoing operational work and temporary project work. Large organizations often have many projects underway at the same time. A **portfolio** is "projects, programs, subportfolios, and operations managed as a group to achieve strategic business objectives."[7] Project portfolios are similar to financial portfolios. In a financial portfolio, efforts are made to diversify investments as a means of limiting risk. However, every investment is selected with the hope that it will yield a positive return. The returns on each investment are evaluated individually, and the entire portfolio is evaluated as a whole.

Each project in the portfolio should have a direct impact on the organization. Put another way, an organization's leaders should identify the organization's future direction through strategic planning. Then multiple possible initiatives (or projects) can be identified that might help further the organization's goals. The leaders need to sort through the various possible projects and prioritize them. Projects with the highest priority should be undertaken first. Organizations typically try to have a sense of balance in their portfolios; that is, an organization includes in its portfolio:

- Some large and some small projects
- Some high-risk, high-reward projects, and some low-risk projects
- Some projects that can be completed quickly and some that take substantial time to finish
- Some projects that serve as efforts to enter new markets and new products or services and some to improve current products

2-2b Programs

A **program** is "a group of related projects, subprograms, and program activities managed in a coordinated way to obtain benefits not available from managing them individually."[8] This group of related projects or the program often shares the same goal and requires similar resources.

Program management is defined as applying knowledge, skills, tools, and techniques to meet requirements and to obtain predetermined benefits. It is a systematic approach of aligning multiple components of the program to achieve the program goals while optimizing the integrated cost, schedule, and effort required to execute the program. Programs and program management are of great importance, specifically for the government and large and multinational corporations.

Programs often last as long as the organization lasts, even though specific projects within a program are of limited duration. For example, the U.S. Air Force has an engine procurement program. As long as the Air Force intends to fly aircraft, it will need to acquire engines. Within the engine program are many individual projects. Some of these projects are for basic research, some are for development of engines, some are for purchasing engines, and a few others are for maintaining and improving the performance of engines in use. Each project has a project manager, and the entire program has a program manager. While the project managers are primarily concerned with the trade-offs associated with cost, schedule, scope, and quality on their individual projects, the program manager is concerned with making trade-offs between projects for the maximum benefit of the entire program. To avoid confusion, programs deal with a specific group of related projects, while a portfolio deals with all of an organization's projects. A portfolio can include multiple programs as well as multiple projects.

A program may include components such as portfolios, projects, and subprograms. It is important to understand comparative analysis of projects, programs, and portfolios.

While the leadership group of a company may make portfolio decisions and delegate the program management decisions to a program manager, both portfolios and programs are managed at a level above the typical project manager. For practical purposes, project managers should attempt to understand how both portfolio and program decisions impact their projects and then spend most of their efforts focused on their project.

Some of the unique responsibilities of a program manager are leading program activities in a coordinated way, communicating with internal and external stakeholders, resolving cost, scope, schedule, risk, and quality across all projects with shared governance, and managing external and internal factors such as culture and socioeconomic issues. See Exhibit 2.6 for a comparison of projects, programs and portfolios.

2-2c Projects and Subprojects

Just as a program is made up of multiple projects, a large project may be composed of multiple subprojects. A **subproject** is a part of a larger project organized as a project

EXHIBIT 2.6

COMPARISON OF PROJECTS, PROGRAMS, AND PORTFOLIOS

	PROJECTS	PROGRAMS	PORTFOLIOS
Scope	• Defined scope • Progressive elaboration	• Larger scope • Significant benefits	• Organizational scope • Changes with strategic goals
Change	• Change is norm • Change management	• Internal and external changes	• Changes due to external and internal environment
Plan	• Detailed plans	• High-level program plan • Detailed component plan	• Create processes • Maintain processes
Monitor	• Project deliverables	• Progress of program components	• Strategic changes, risk • Resource allocation
Success	• Scope quality, cost, time • Customer satisfaction	• Needs and benefits of the program	• Investment performance • Benefit realization
Manage	• Project deliverables • Project team	• Program staff and PM • Vision and leadership	• Portfolio staff

Adopted from PMI, *Standard for Program Management,* 3rd ed. (2013): p. 8.

itself to make it easier to plan and manage. If the project is quite large, individuals may be assigned as subproject managers and asked to manage their subproject as a project. Some of those subproject managers may even work for another company. The project manager needs to coordinate the various subprojects and make decisions that are best for the overall project. Sometimes this may require that a particular subproject be sacrificed for the greater good of the project. The relationships among a portfolio, programs, projects, and subprojects are illustrated in Exhibit 2.7.

EXHIBIT 2.7

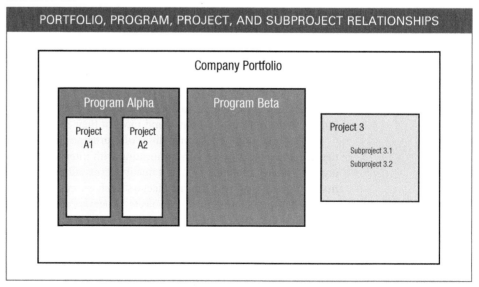

PORTFOLIO, PROGRAM, PROJECT, AND SUBPROJECT RELATIONSHIPS

Company Portfolio

Program Alpha

Project A1   Project A2

Program Beta

Project 3

Subproject 3.1
Subproject 3.2

Because projects are frequently performed in a fast-paced environment, it is helpful if they can be guided by organizational priorities.

The first step is to carefully align potential projects with the parent organization's goals. While many companies are motivated to align projects with organizational goals for these benefits, an additional reason for companies that sell to the government is that the Federal CIO Roadmap states, "CIOs are responsible for ... maintaining and facilitating the implementation of a sound and integrated IT architecture; monitoring performance of IT programs; using metrics to evaluate the performance of those programs; and modifying or terminating programs or projects."[9] This was introduced in the Sarbanes-Oxley requirements. All publicly traded companies must now follow certain guidelines that require some sort of financial decision model for selecting projects for execution.

When managers assess the organization's ability to perform projects and then identify, select, prioritize, resource, and govern a portfolio of projects and other work that they believe will help the organization achieve its strategic goals, they are performing portfolio management. While a team of senior executives may conduct many of the portfolio management activities, project managers should understand how their specific projects are aligned with the organization's objectives since they will need to either make or provide input on many decisions.

When organizations consider their entire portfolio of work, they sometimes envision projects as means of developing knowledge that can be capitalized upon in ongoing work processes to provide profit, as shown in Exhibit 2.8. Furthermore, new knowledge encourages organizations to be creative and develop new project ideas and knowledge-building projects.

In times when the economy is poor, many companies struggle to get enough business. In such an environment, some firms might accept almost any work they can get. Even during bleak economic times, however, one should be careful how internal projects are selected, since selecting one project limits resources (money, people, etc.) available to other projects.

EXHIBIT 2.8

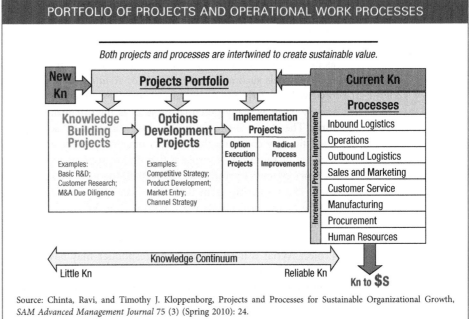

Source: Chinta, Ravi, and Timothy J. Kloppenborg, Projects and Processes for Sustainable Organizational Growth, *SAM Advanced Management Journal* 75 (3) (Spring 2010): 24.

During good or bad economic times, people should take the same care and prudence with external projects and ensure that they are consistent with the organization's goals.

2-2d Assessing an Organization's Ability to Perform Projects

Assessing an organization's strengths and weaknesses is an essential part of aligning projects with the organization. If an organization does not have the right capabilities, a project that may otherwise support organizational goals may be too difficult to successfully complete. Some questions to ask regarding a firm's ability to support projects are as follows:

- Do we have the right skills, capabilities, technical knowledge, and resources that are required for potential projects? If we do not have them, can we acquire them easily?
- Do we have a teamwork attitude, free and open communication, creativity, and empowered decision making?
- Do we have a clearly defined project management process?
- Do our associates have the right attitudes, skills, and competencies to use the project management process?
- Are our leaders at each level willing to take appropriate personal risk?
- Does senior leadership establish a strong leadership foundation?
- Do individuals and teams exhibit leadership at their respective levels?
- Do we monitor and understand our external environment?

2-2e Identifying Potential Projects

The second part of aligning projects with the firm's goals is to identify potential projects. In general, some potential projects can be to capitalize upon a strategic opportunity or technological advance. Others may serve a social need, an environmental consideration, a customer request, or a legal requirement. Ideally, this is accomplished in a systematic manner—not just by chance. Some opportunities will present themselves to the organization. Other good opportunities will need to be discovered. All divisions of the organization should be involved. This means people at all levels, from frontline workers to senior executives and people from all functional areas need to help identify potential projects. For example, salespeople can uncover many opportunities by maintaining open discussions with existing and potential customers, and operations staff may identify potential productivity-enhancing opportunities as projects. Everyone in the firm should be aware of industry trends. Many industries have trade journals such as *Elevator World* or *Aviation Week and Space Technology* that can be reviewed regularly for potential project ideas. One reasonable goal is to identify approximately twice as many potential projects as the organization has time and resources to perform. The reason is simple: under close examination, some potential projects may not be a good fit. Any company that accepts practically every potential project will probably waste some of its resources on projects that do not support its organizational goals.

Once potential projects are identified, the next step is to develop a brief description of each. The leadership team that will select and prioritize projects needs to understand the nature of the projects they are considering. While the level of documentation different firms require varies greatly, a bare minimum can be called the elevator pitch. This is when a person meets another waiting for an elevator and asks, "I hear you are on XYZ Project. What is it all about?" The responder may have only a brief time to give a reply before the elevator arrives and must be prepared to answer quickly with simple statements about the project work and why it is important to the organization.

The work is often summarized in a brief **statement of work**, which is a "narrative description of products, services, or results to be supplied."[10] Why the project is important is often summarized as a **business case**, which is "the benefits of a selected component … used as a basis for the authorization of further project management activities."[11]

The business case generally includes both why the project is needed and, if the firm uses financial justification as part of project selection, an estimate of costs and benefits. Armed with this elevator pitch, the series of processes that collectively are used to select, prioritize, and initiate projects begins. Selecting and prioritizing are covered next, and chartering is covered in Chapter 3.

METHODS FOR SELECTING PROJECTS   The people in charge of selecting projects need to ensure overall organizational priorities are understood, agreed upon, and communicated. Once this common understanding is in place, it is much easier to prioritize potential projects. The degree of formality used in selecting projects varies widely. In a smaller organization, it can be straightforward. The prioritization should consider criteria derived from project management, finance, and strategic aspects and should include asking questions such as these:

- What value does each potential project bring to the organization?
- Are the demands of performing each project understood?
- Are the resources needed to perform the project available?
- Is it feasible to complete the project within the expected time and at the projected cost while managing associated risks?
- Is the project financially beneficial and compatible with other investment decisions?
- Is there enthusiastic support both from external customers and from one or more internal champions?
- Which projects will best help the organization achieve its strategic goals?

There are several different methods of systematically selecting projects. The methods include both financial and scoring models. The primary reason for including financial analysis—either to make the project selection decisions directly or to at least assist in the decision making—is that, from management's perspective, projects are investments. Therefore, proper selection should yield a portfolio of projects that collectively contribute to organizational success.

Three different approaches are commonly used to ensure both financial and nonfinancial factors are considered when selecting projects. First, some organizations use financial analysis as the primary means of determining which projects are selected, and management merely tempers this with informal inclusion of nonfinancial factors. Second, some organizations use financial models as screening devices to qualify projects or even just to offer perspective; qualified projects then go through a selection process using a scoring model. Third, at still other organizations, financial justification is one factor used in a multifactor scoring model. The common thread in all three of these approaches is that both financial and nonfinancial factors are considered when selecting projects. Let us consider both financial and scoring models. Financial models will be covered in concept, but the calculations will not be shown since they are explained in depth in most required finance courses. Scoring models will be covered in both concept and calculation since many students might not have them in another course.

2-2f Using a Cost-Benefit Analysis Model to Select Projects

Cost-benefit analysis is "a financial analysis tool used to determine the benefits provided by a project against its costs."[12] These models compare expected project costs to expected project benefits. Several models can be used in making project selection decisions.

EXHIBIT 2.9

	NET PRESENT VALUE (NPV)	BENEFIT-COST RATIO (BCR)	INTERNAL RATE OF RETURN (IRR)	PAYBACK PERIOD (PP)
Calculation	PV revenue–PV cost	Cash flow/Project investment	Percentage return on project investment	Project costs/Annual cash flows
Neutral Result	NPV = $0	Ratio = 1.0	IRR = Cost of capital	Payback period = Accepted length
If used to screen projects or to select projects outright	NPV > Acceptable amount	Ratio > Acceptable amount	IRR > Acceptable amount	Payback period < Acceptable length
If used to compare projects	Higher NPV better	Higher ratio better	Higher IRR better	Shorter payback period better

FINANCIAL MODELS FOR PROJECT SELECTION

NET PRESENT VALUE (NPV)   Net present value (NPV) is the most widely accepted model and will be covered first. When using net present value, the analyst first discounts the expected future value of both the project costs and benefits, recognizing that a dollar in the future is worth less than a dollar today. Then the analyst subtracts the stream of discounted project costs from the stream of discounted project benefits. The result is the net present value of the potential project. If the net present value is positive, then the organization can expect to make money from the project. Higher net present values predict higher profits. See the summary in Exhibit 2.9.

BENEFIT-COST RATIO (BCR)   A second financial model sometimes used is benefit-cost ratio (BCR). The ratio is obtained by dividing the cash flow by the initial cash outlay. A ratio above 1.0 means the project expects to make a profit, and a higher ratio than 1.0 is better. The cash flow can be determined for the life of the project using net present or discounted value principles.

INTERNAL RATE OF RETURN (IRR)   The third financial model is internal rate of return (IRR). In this model, the analyst calculates the percentage return expected on the project investment. A ratio above the current cost of capital is considered positive, and a higher expected return is more favorable.

PAYBACK PERIOD (PP)   The fourth financial model that is sometimes used is the payback period (PP). In this analysis, a person calculates how many years would be required to pay back or recover the initial project investment. The organization would normally have a stated period that projects should be paid back within, and shorter payback periods are more desirable.

ADVANTAGES AND DISADVANTAGES OF EACH METHOD   Financial models are useful in ensuring that selected projects make sense from both cost and return-on-investment perspectives. These models have weaknesses that need to be understood before they are used. For example, payback period models do not consider the amount of profit that may be generated after the costs are paid. Thus, two projects with a similar payback period could look equal, but if one has substantially higher revenue after the payback period, it would clearly be superior. BCR would not be acceptable unless all costs and benefits were calculated in present dollars (in which case it is similar to NPV except it is a ratio of benefits to cost instead of the difference between revenue and cost). However, there are benefits and costs that are intangible and cannot be determined in financial terms. IRR and BCRs have problems if used for choosing between mutually exclusive projects because they can favor smaller projects that create less total value for the firm but have high percentage returns. For example, a huge project with a medium rate of return would create a lot of value for a firm but might not be chosen over a smaller project with a higher return if only one can be chosen. Additionally, it is sometimes quite difficult to calculate an IRR if a project has nonconventional cash flows. For the most part, the finance discipline recommends using net present value. The other measures can be calculated to provide perspective on whether a project meets a minimum financial return threshold or to communicate with people who might not understand NPV.

However, none of the financial models ensure alignment with an organization's strategic goals. Therefore, financial analysis, while very useful, is normally not enough.

2-2g Using a Scoring Model to Select Projects

In addition to ensuring that selected projects make sense financially, other criteria often need to be considered. A tool called a scoring model helps to select and prioritize potential projects. It is useful whenever there are multiple projects and several criteria to be considered. A few organizations use more complex models such as analytical hierarchy process (AHP) to compare projects, but since many more organizations keep things simple with variations of scoring models, that is what we will cover.

IDENTIFYING POTENTIAL CRITERIA   These criteria should include how well each potential project fits with the organization's strategic planning. The criteria may also include such items as risk, timing, resources needed, and so on. A normal practice is for the company's leadership team to jointly determine what criteria will be used to select projects. A list of questions executives may use to develop their list of criteria is shown in Exhibit 2.10.

DETERMINING MANDATORY CRITERIA   Once the leadership team agrees on a list of criteria that are important, the next step is to determine whether any of the criteria are mandatory. That is, are there any situations that dictate a project must be chosen regardless of any other considerations? Examples of this include government mandates and clear safety or

EXHIBIT 2.10

EXAMPLES OF PROJECT SELECTION CRITERIA
How well does this project fit with at least one organizational objective?
How many customers are there for the expected results?
How competitively can the company price the project results?
What unique advantages will this project provide?
Does the company have the resources needed?
What is the probability of success?
Are the data needed to perform the project available or easily collected?
Do the key stakeholders agree that the project is needed?
What is the expected return on investment?
How sustainable will the project results be?
How does this project promote (or hinder) our corporate social responsibility?
What risks are there if we do not perform this project?

EXHIBIT 2.11

PROJECT SELECTION AND PRIORITIZATION MATRIX					
Project/Criteria & Weight	New Products 10	Customer Relations 8	Supplier Relations 5	Success Probability 5	Weighted Total Score
Project A					
Project B					
Project C					
Project D					

security situations. This list of "must-do" projects should be kept as small as possible since these projects automatically get selected and can crowd out other worthwhile projects.

WEIGHTING CRITERIA   Next, the leadership team determines the relative importance or weight of each decision criteria. While more complex methods of determining criteria weights and project evaluations have been used in the past, many firms now use the simple methods described here for determining criteria weights. See Exhibit 2.11 for an example of project evaluations. First, executives determine which criterion is most important and give that a weight of 10. Then they ask how important in comparison each of the other criteria is. For example, if the executives in a consumer products company thought development of new products was most important, it would be assigned a weight of 10. If the customer relations factor was deemed almost as important as new product development, maybe it would be assigned 8. If the factors of supplier relations and probability of project success were each deemed to be half as important as new product development, each would be assigned 5. Perhaps other criteria such as cost reduction, safely, and so forth were also considered but determined to not be as important. The resulting criteria with weights are shown in Exhibit 2.11 in the top row of the selection and prioritization matrix. Most organizations will decide to use about three to five criteria. Lesser-rated criteria can be used as tiebreakers if needed.

EVALUATING PROJECTS BASED ON CRITERIA   Now the leadership team evaluates each project on each criterion. The most efficient and accurate method is to concentrate on one criterion at a time, going down each column in turn. An easy method for this is to rate each project on that specific criterion, with scores ranging from 1 (potential project has very little or even negative impact on this criterion) to 5 (project has excellent impact on this criterion). The upper-left portion of each cell in the matrix can display the rating, representing how well that project satisfies that criterion.

Once a project has been rated on a specific criterion, that rating should be multiplied by the weight assigned to that criterion and displayed as the weighted score in the main body of each cell. The total for each project should be added across the row. The highest-scoring projects would ordinarily be selected. If several projects have close scores (virtual ties), other criteria or discussion can be used to break the tie. For example, in Exhibit 2.12, there is a virtual tie between Projects A and B.

EXHIBIT 2.12

COMPLETED PROJECT SELECTION AND PRIORITIZATION MATRIX					
Project/Criteria & Weight	New Products 10	Customer Relations 8	Supplier Relations 5	Success Probability 5	Total
Project A	5 / 50	3 / 24	5 / 25	2 / 10	109
Project B	5 / 50	2 / 16	3 / 15	5 / 25	106
Project C	1 / 10	5 / 40	3 / 15	3 / 15	80
Project D	2 / 20	4 / 32	1 / 5	2 / 10	67

SENSITIVITY ANALYSES   Scoring models allow leadership teams to perform sensitivity analyses—that is, to examine what would happen to the decision if factors affecting it were to change. Selection criteria may be added or altered. Participants may decide that some criteria are more important than others and weight them accordingly. Missing criteria or new alternatives can be added and the decision revisited. For example, if the executive team evaluating the projects in Exhibit 2.12 had a bad experience with an unsuccessful project and decided to reevaluate their decisions with success probability now weighted a 9 for very important, the new project selection and priority matrix would be calculated as shown in Exhibit 2.14.

Decision makers can ensure that they use very solid ratings for each potential project. For example, if one criterion was the number of customers, the marketing department could interview some potential customers to gauge their level of interest.

A company might want to select several projects. If so, the scores from the selection matrix could serve as one method of prioritizing the projects.

EXHIBIT 2.13

REVISED PROJECT SELECTION AND PRIORITIZATION MATRIX					
Project\Criteria & Weight	New Products 10	Customer Relations 8	Supplier Relations 5	Success Probability 9	Total
Project B	5 / 50	2 / 16	3 / 15	5 / 45	126
Project A	5 / 50	3 / 24	5 / 25	2 / 18	117
Project C	1 / 10	5 / 40	3 / 15	3 / 27	92
Project D	2 / 20	4 / 32	1 / 5	2 / 18	75

Source: Chris Bridges.

Selection of projects based on certain criteria is a decision-making process that varies geographically as priorities and thinking styles tend to be different.

Due to cultural differences, learning, and education principles, people think and approach a problem differently; therefore, they also adopt different decision-making styles. This aspect assumes importance due to increased diversity in workplaces that provides an opportunity to work with people from different cultures and countries. Due to these factors, someone might rely more on inductive, deductive, or a combination of these approaches in making decisions. This diversity would influence how people look at a scoring model or any other decision-making tool in selecting projects and making project portfolio management decisions. These issues are discussed further in Chapter 15.

2-2h Prioritizing Projects

Once all projects have been selected, they will need to be prioritized—that is, the decision makers will need to determine which ones will get assigned resources and be scheduled to begin first. If a company selects several projects for a year (or even for a fiscal quarter), it cannot expect to start all of them at the same time. The scoring models are useful in providing input into the starting order of projects. Most leadership teams will consider the weighted scores of each project as a starting point in assigning resources to projects and determining their start dates. The leadership team members, however, also generally discuss other issues, such as:

- The urgency of each project
- The cost of delaying the expected benefits from various projects
- Practical details concerning the timing
- Opportunity costs associated with the project

For example, an important process improvement project may be far less disruptive to perform when the factory is shut down for routine maintenance. One more discussion frequently occurs in the prioritizing process—if there is a conflict between resource needs for two projects, which one gets the needed resources first? Often, this is left to the project sponsors to iron out; especially for important projects, it may be formally decided by the leadership team. In that way, the probability of the critical project being held up by a misunderstanding is greatly decreased.

Exhibit 2.14 shows how the Alternative Breaks (AB) planning committee at a university ranked spring break projects. This exhibit shows four of the twenty-six projects that were selected for trips. This book will include multiple examples of the AB project to illustrate how various project-planning tools work together. Each trip is a small or subproject, while the combination of all twenty-six trips forms the overall project.

2-2i Resourcing Projects

Once all projects have been prioritized, it is time to assign resources to each. Resources can include key personnel such as sponsors, project managers, core team members, and subject matter experts. Resources can also include space, materials, equipment that may be in short supply, and the funds necessary to acquire these resources. The easiest way is to use a resource assignment matrix and begin by assigning resources to the highest-priority projects. Once an individual resource is no longer available, the organization is limited in the number of projects that it can take on during a particular time.

Assigning resources like this requires a prioritized project list such as shown in Exhibit 2.13, a list of resources and how much of each is available, and an estimate of how much of each key resource each project will need. For simplicity's sake, organizations often plan for a fiscal quarter. Exhibit 2.15 shows the same four projects and choices of project

EXHIBIT 2.14

ALTERNATIVE BREAKS PROJECT SELECTION AND PRIORITIZATION MATRIX					
PROJECT/SELECTION CRITERIA	ACTIVE SERVICE OPPORTUNITY	ISSUE ITSELF	ORGANIZATION TO WORK WITH	COST	
	9	10	6	5	Total
New York Vegan Farm	5 45	4 40	3 18	4 20	123
West Virginia Sustainability	4 36	3 30	4 24	5 25	115
Chicago Halfway House	2 18	4 40	4 24	4 20	102
El Salvador Cultural Immersion	1 9	5 50	5 30	1 5	94

managers, team members, and the budget for each. Note that while there is enough project manager time to start all four projects, there is neither enough team member time nor enough cash. Therefore, only three projects can be started.

2-3 Securing Projects

The discussion above pertains to projects that are internal to an organization. This section deals with projects a company (called the client) wants performed, but for which it may hire external resources (called contractors) to execute significant parts or all of the work. External projects can be viewed either from the perspective of the client company that wants the project to be executed or from the perspective of the contractor company that wants to perform the

EXHIBIT 2.15

RESOURCE ASSIGNMENT MATRIX							
PROJECT/RESOURCE	PM/DEJI	PM/BUD	PM/CORY	TEAM/ BRADLEY	TEAM/ RAJEEV	TEAM/ LARRY	MONEY
Maximum Availability	200	400	300	300	150	150	$30 million
Project List							
Project B: PM 240, Team 200, $5M		240		200			$5M
Project A: PM 200, Team 150, $10M	200				150		$10M
Project C: PM 300, Team 150, $14M			300			150	$14M
Project D: PM 150, Team 180, $4M							
Remaining Availability	0	160	0	100	0	0	$1M

work. Client companies may first put prospective external projects through a selection and prioritization process as described above and, if selected, then decide whether to perform the work internally (make) or hire the project to be performed by others (buy). If the decision is to buy, then the client company needs to plan and conduct the procurement.

Contractor companies need to identify potential project opportunities, determine which they will pursue, submit proposals, and be prepared to either bid or negotiate to secure the work. We consider the client company's perspective in Chapter 12, Project Supply Chain Management. We consider the contractor's perspective next.

2-3a Identify Potential Project Opportunities

Contractors seeking external projects to perform should pursue this in a fashion similar to that of any company considering internal projects, as described earlier in this chapter in the portfolio alignment section on identifying potential projects. Additionally, since they need to look for projects externally, contractor companies should have representatives at trade shows, professional conferences, and anywhere information on the intentions of potential customers and competitors may surface. Contractor companies should also actively practice customer relationship management by establishing and nurturing personal contacts at various levels and functions. Contractor companies can also practice customer relationship management by linking information systems to the extent practical so as to identify any useful information concerning potential future projects and improve management of current projects.

2-3b Determine Which Opportunities to Pursue

Just as all companies should decide which internal projects to select, as previously described in the methods for selecting projects, most contractor companies are best served by targeting the projects they wish to pursue. Some companies have a policy that they will bid on every potential project, knowing that if they do not bid, they will not be awarded the project. More companies find that if they target their opportunities, their "hit rate" or probability of securing the work on any given proposal increases. It takes time and resources to put together a good proposal, so it makes sense to increase the acceptance rate by developing a bid/no-bid decision strategy.

Each company has strengths and weaknesses compared to its competitors. Hence, a quick SWOT analysis could be used to decide whether to pursue a potential project,

Nappiness/pixabay.com

just as a more involved version of SWOT analysis was described earlier and depicted in Exhibit 2.2. Decision makers can also ask how well a potential project will help achieve their objectives. If they determine a project will help achieve their objectives, the next considerations are the cost to pursue the work and the probability of successfully securing the project given the likely competition. A company frequently considers risks both of pursuing and not pursuing a potential project[13] Finally, does the company have the capability to perform the work if it is awarded?

2-3c Prepare and Submit a Project Proposal

When a firm prepares to submit a proposal, it is really conducting a small project with the primary deliverable of the project being a compelling and complete proposal. The contractor should understand the project's **source selection criteria**, the "basic minimum criteria the sellers have to be fulfilled to get shortlisted."[14] While criteria will vary extensively from one project to another, generally a client will likely want to be convinced that the potential contractor is technically, managerially, financially, and operationally competent. Successful project managers try hard to convince potential clients that they are capable on all four dimensions. A short list of these factors is shown in Exhibit 2.16.

2-3d Negotiate to Secure the Project

Negotiation is an approach to redefine an old relationship that is not working effectively or to establish a new relationship. Negotiations should aim at a win-win solution, and the outcome must benefit both the parties involved in negotiations.

Once all proposals have been delivered and evaluated, the client company may elect to either award the project or enter into negotiations with one or more potential contractors. On more routine projects, the contract may be awarded at this point. Further clarifications and negotiations may follow for complex projects.

A client company and a contractor company may negotiate the amount of money to be paid for a project. They may also negotiate the contractual terms, schedule, specific personnel to be assigned to work on the contract, quality standards, reporting mechanisms, and various other items. A project manager may need to make arrangements with potential suppliers to secure the products and services needed to perform the project. All these considerations will be covered in subsequent chapters.

Successful project managers understand that they need to prepare well for negotiations. This starts with a clear understanding of what is most important to their management. Often, it includes fact finding with the client company to understand its needs and abilities. Armed with an understanding of both perspectives, a project manager attempts to find a solution that allows the organization to secure the project work with enough profit potential and with the start of a good working relationship with the client. In the end, the client company will select the contractor(s) and award the contract(s).

EXHIBIT 2.16

TYPICAL SOURCE SELECTION CRITERIA			
TECHNICAL	MANAGEMENT	FINANCIAL	OPERATIONAL
Technical experience	Management experience	Financial capacity	Production capacity
Needs understanding	Project charter	Life cycle cost	Business size and type
Technical approach	Planning and scheduling	Cost basis and assumptions	Past performance
Risk mitigation	Project control	Warranties	References

PMP/CAPM Study Ideas

You won't see a whole lot of questions on either of these tests pertaining to portfolio or program management, since these happen at an executive level, beyond the purview of individual projects or project managers. At the same time, it is imperative that you understand the interrelationship of portfolio and project management, as well as how they relate to an organization's mission: the mission leads to strategic objectives, and projects are the primary vehicle through which these objectives are achieved.

As with other chapters, make sure you are familiar with the PMBOK terms—especially *statement of work* and *business case*—and be prepared to put them into context with real projects. You will ultimately need to know how to calculate net present value. Finally, be familiar with the common causes of project failure and how to prevent them.

Summary

Project selection does not occur in isolation. Ideally, it begins with the organization's strategic planning. This planning begins with a strategic analysis of the organization's internal strengths and weaknesses as well as the external threats and opportunities it faces. The organization should then develop its guiding principles such as mission and vision statements. Most companies will have an annual planning session in which strategic objectives are developed. Larger organizations will continue this effort with one or more levels of planning in which the overall objectives are flowed down to determine objectives that are appropriate for each organizational level.

Once the strategic planning is accomplished, the organization's leadership team engages in portfolio management. The first part is an open and honest assessment of the organization's ability to perform projects. The decision makers need to understand how many resources are available, the organization's overall capabilities, and the capabilities of the individuals who will be assigned to projects. An ongoing portfolio management activity is for everyone in the firm to identify possible opportunities that they feel might help the organization achieve its goals. Each potential project should be described at least by stating in a sentence or two what work is involved and

how it would help the organization achieve one or more of its goals.

Once potential projects are identified and briefly described with statements of work and business cases, they should be put through a process to determine which will be selected and what their relative priorities are. Both financial and scoring models are frequently used to evaluate potential projects. Net present value is the preferred financial method, although others are sometimes used. Financial analysis tells the leadership team how much each potential project is worth from a benefits-versus-cost comparison, but it does not tell how each potential project may help to achieve the organization's goals. Scoring models can incorporate various goals and should also be used. Once a project list is selected, the projects need to be prioritized so some can start right away and others can start later.

Contractor companies need to be constantly on the lookout for potential project opportunities. Once potential projects are identified, companies need to decide which ones they pursue. Just as for internal projects, some external projects will be better at helping an organization reach its goals because they are a better fit. The contractor needs to prepare and submit proposals for desired projects and be prepared to follow up and often negotiate in order to secure them.

Key Terms Consistent with PMI Standards and Guides

portfolio management, 38
portfolio, 38
program, 38
vision, 38
mission statement, 38
strategic objectives, 38

program management, 38
cost benefit analysis, 38
subproject, 39
statement of work, 42
business case, 42
source selection criteria, 50

Chapter Review Questions

1. List and describe each step in the strategic planning process.
2. Name at least four things that a mission statement should include.
3. What does the strategic analysis acronym SWOT stand for?
4. What is the most widely accepted financial model for selecting projects?
5. What are some advantages and disadvantages of using a financial model for selecting projects?
6. What are some advantages and disadvantages of using a scoring model for selecting projects?
7. What are some common reasons for project failure?
8. Who should be involved in identifying potential projects?
9. If there is a conflict between resource needs for two projects, who decides which one gets the needed resources first?
10. In a project scoring model, why is each decision criteria given a weight?
11. What purpose do sensitivity analyses serve in using scoring models to choose projects?
12. If several projects have close scores as the result of a scoring model, what can be done to break the virtual tie?
13. Why might a contractor company perform a SWOT analysis prior to bidding on a potential project?
14. Why is it important for a contractor to understand the source selection criteria a client uses to decide to whom they will award a project?
15. Name five things that may be negotiated between a client company and a contractor company.

Discussion Questions

1. How might the internal and external parts of a SWOT analysis affect one another?
2. Describe the interaction between vision and mission statements.
3. How is a company's portfolio similar to and different from a financial portfolio?
4. What is the best way for an organization to prioritize among selected projects? Does it vary among organizations?
5. Why is aligning potential projects with the parent organization's goals the first step in avoiding project failure?
6. Why is it a good practice for organizations to identify twice as many potential projects as they plan to implement?
7. Suppose you are purchasing a new car, and you decide to use a scoring model to decide among four options. What would be your top three criteria, and what would be each criterion's relative weight?
8. Under what circumstances should a selected project take precedence over other selected projects?
9. If you are a contractor looking for project work, why might you decide not to pursue a particular project opportunity?
10. What are the four main areas of competency a client company is looking for in a project manager? How can you best demonstrate these competencies to a potential client?

PMBOK® Guide Questions

1. A collection of projects, programs, and operations managed as a group to achieve strategic objectives is called a:
   a. process
   b. portfolio
   c. subprogram
   d. life cycle
2. Projects may be undertaken as a result of any of the following strategic reasons *except:*
   a. social need
   b. market demand
   c. need to keep workers busy during slow times
   d. environmental considerations
3. A narrative description of products, services, or results to be delivered by the project is a/an:
   a. request for information
   b. business case
   c. project statement of work
   d. elevator pitch
4. All of the following statements are true *except:*
   a. A portfolio may contain multiple programs and projects.

b. A project manager has the discretion to make trade-offs in regard to which programs to pursue.

c. A program manager has the discretion to make trade-offs in regard to which projects to pursue.

d. Projects have a finite timeline, while programs may exist as long as the parent organization does.

5. Which of the following is a financial analysis tool that an organization may use to determine the cost-value of potential projects?
   a. Payback period (PP)
   b. Internal rate of return (IRR)
   c. Net present value (NPV)
   d. All of the above

6. All projects should be aligned with their organization's strategic plan, which includes the organization's vision, goals, and objectives. Which of these describes an organization's vision?
   a. Conveys a larger sense of organizational purpose, and is both inspiring and guiding
   b. Describes short- and long-term results along with measures to determine if they have been achieved
   c. Includes the organization's core purpose, core values, beliefs, culture, primary business, and primary customers
   d. Is SMART: specific, measurable, achievable, results-based, and time-specific

7. The _____ best describe(s) *why* a project is being undertaken.
   a. statement of work
   b. business case
   c. subprojects
   d. source selection criteria

8. The document that includes the necessary information to determine whether a project is worth the required investment, and is used for decision making by upper management, is called the:
   a. project scope statement
   b. project charter
   c. business case
   d. case study

9. An organization's vision often includes reference to its social, environmental, and economic health, collectively referred to as the:
   a. triple bottom line
   b. business case
   c. statement of work (SOW)
   d. net present value (NPV)

10. A business case typically contains information regarding the business need and a financial analysis. Which model divides the cash flow by the initial cash outlay?
    a. Benefit-cost ratio (BCR)
    b. Internal rate of return (IRR)
    c. Net present value (NPV)
    d. Payback period (PP)

Exercises

1. Complete the following scoring model. Show all your work. Tell which project you would pick first, second, third, and last. How confident are you with each choice? If you lack confidence regarding any of your choices, what would you prefer to do about it?

Project\ Criteria & Weight	Criteria 1 10	Criteria 2 6	Criteria 3 4	Weighted Total Score
Project A	4	3	5	
Project B	3	2	3	
Project C	2	4	3	
Project D	1	3	4	

2. Complete the following scoring model. Show all your work. Tell which project you would pick first, second, third, and last. How confident are you with each choice? If you lack confidence regarding any of your choices, what would you prefer to do about it?

Project\ Criteria & Weight	Criteria 1 10	Criteria 2 7	Criteria 3 3	Weighted Total Score
Project A	1	3	4	
Project B	3	5	3	
Project C	5	4	3	
Project D	2	3	1	

3. Pretend you are on the leadership team for a pharmaceutical company that is in a difficult financial situation due to patents that have expired on two of your most profitable drugs. Brainstorm a list of criteria by which you would select and prioritize projects. Weight the criteria.

4. Pretend you are on the leadership team of a manufacturing company that is currently challenged by low-cost competition. Brainstorm a list of criteria by which you would select and prioritize projects. Weight the criteria.

INTEGRATED EXAMPLE PROJECTS
SUBURBAN HOMES CONSTRUCTION PROJECT

Suburban Homes, like any other real estate company, has many strategic directions to pursue to expand the company operation and increase revenue and profits. To explore and pursue various investment opportunities that would eventually translate into projects, the company developed strategic directions to successfully invest in real estate. It identified six options for portfolio project management. They are investments in purchasing land for future development, communities for single-family homes, multifamily properties, small-scale apartment buildings, large-scale apartment complexes, and commercial investments.

1. Purchasing land in areas that have potential for future growth makes sense, as the cost of land tends to be substantially cheaper 10–20 years before it is turned into a developed suburban area. At an appropriate opportunity, the land can be improved to add value, or it can be leased or rented to create cash flow. Further, the land can be divided and parts of it can be sold for a profit. However, this option requires a vision for future growth and development and consequently, risks are also associated with this strategic direction.

2. Building single-family homes in suburban areas is one of the best and most popular strategic directions for growth for companies like Suburban Homes. Most of the clients who are interested in a quality life and view their home as an investment prefer buying single-family homes. Clients realize that it is easy to rent, sell, and finance.

3. Small multifamily properties usually consist of two to four units. They also present similar advantages that are associated with a single-family home such as easy financing and being a wise investment option for clients while providing a good residence for their family.

4. Small apartment buildings usually consist of 5 to 50 units for clients to reside in. They are more popular among those who prefer urban areas and a busy social life.

Clients are usually unmarried or married with no children. These properties can be more difficult to finance because they rely on commercial lending standards. For this investment option, Suburban Homes must look for investment opportunities closer to densely populated areas, and the investor must provide parking areas.

5. Large apartment complexes require that you include pools, a gym, tennis courts, and parking facilities, in addition to other attractions that lure people to choose the complex as a residence. Such a complex requires full-time staff to manage the property, provide safety and security, and provide good customer service. These properties can be very expensive to purchase. However, this investment option provides steady revenue flow.

6. Commercial investment, in its truest sense, is an investment for growth and diversity in a portfolio. The aim of this investment is to lease the property for business. Size, style, and purpose also vary. Clients could range from small business owners to large malls and mega office complexes. This investment option offers a consistent cash flow. However, occupancy would depend largely on the local economy and could prove to be risky. Further, investments are of higher magnitude and Suburban Homes is seriously considering this option after establishing steady growth in the residential market and improving their financial stability and growth.

Given these six options, Suburban Homes has approached you to develop a project selection model to maintain a balanced portfolio.

Reference

https://www.biggerpockets.com/real-estate-investing/strategies-niches

CASA DE PAZ DEVELOPMENT PROJECT

Casa de Paz is an ambitious project with several dimensions to it. There is a shelter that provides six-month housing for families, along with professional services to support a process of healing and transformation. There is a support group for women that serves residents and nonresidents alike.

The early meetings for Casa de Paz include seeking volunteers to serve on the board and the three main working groups. Then a facilitated meeting is being held to determine the minimal viable product (MVP) to build. This is an open and operating facility. Some of the features that are needed include a director, staff, a building, remodeling the building, funding, a website, programming, and volunteers. Organizational responsibilities also must be defined. An important question is: What can Casa de Paz do quickly without waiting for other things to happen? What are some of the things they need to do concurrently? How many projects can each of the groups (the board and the three working groups) realistically begin right away?

Armed with the answers to these questions, each of the probable projects should have an elevator pitch: What is included and why is it important? Then the most critical few projects can be selected, resourced, and chartered.

An example of an elevator pitch is: There is a need to acquire a building and there is competition for both buildings under consideration. One building is more attractive than the other as the cost is considerably less—although the number of families served would be less.

Another elevator pitch is the need for website development. A fledgling website exists, but there are so many communication, fundraising, volunteer soliciting, and other possible uses of the website that early development is attractive. The elevator pitch could answer the following questions:

- Why is enhancing the website so important?
- How can the website help us do other work we desire to perform?
- Where are we now?
- What do we want?

Semester Project Instructions

Your instructor may bring example projects to class and facilitate the assignment of students to the various project teams. Alternatively, your instructor may ask you to identify potential projects. Therefore, you may or may not be involved in project selection. If your instructor has each student bring in a project idea, you will first need to create your elevator pitch to describe tersely what work is involved in your project and why it is important. Then you and a small team will likely need to select one of the potential projects using a scoring model. Unlike the criteria for selecting among projects in a typical organization, for your class, you may use criteria that will help you learn. You may want to include size and complexity criteria so the project is involved enough for you to benefit by using many of the techniques in this book, but small enough so you can do the work in a reasonable amount of time. Finally, you may need to identify resources to accomplish the project using a resource matrix.

Regardless of whether your project is student or faculty generated, one of the first things you should do when assigned to a project is to learn about the company or other organization that wants the project to be completed. Why did they select this project? Is it a "must-do" project or did it get chosen over other competing projects? By understanding what makes the project so important, you will make better decisions and will be more motivated through the term. If your project is a "must-do" project, explain why. If it is not a "must-do" project, explain how it was selected. Explain where it fits in priority with other work of the organization.

PROJECT MANAGEMENT *IN ACTION*

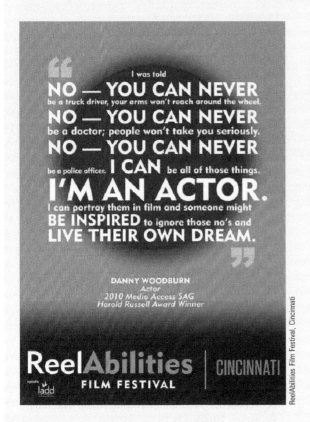

ReelAbilities Film Festival, Cincinnati

Prioritizing Projects at LADD

LADD's project prioritization process introduced at the start of this chapter brought along a few surprises. It was not a clean and quick process. With a staff of seven directors in the room, all with varying levels of experience and understanding, many conversations transpired requesting clarification and explanation on why peers used criteria to rank projects higher or lower than the overall average. The wall of the board room was covered with paper that contained projects, numbers, and many markings that could be deciphered only by those involved in the process. Some directors provided unsolicited advice as to why their program's project deserved higher marks. Such requests were generally met with equal banter, advocacy for one's own project, and

ultimately ended in a fruitful discussion that resolved any discord.

As projects were scored and then ranked, the outcomes were not always predictable. A project such as the film festival emerged as the top priority because it was so closely linked with the scored criteria of generating revenue and having a large community impact. Creating an infrastructure for IT needs was last because it would cost a significant amount of money and have no direct return for the individuals LADD supports. From the process, it was evident that a small handful of projects were nonnegotiable and would require completion in order to establish a base for other larger, more impactful projects.

Ultimately, the leadership team was able to create a plan of action that is scheduled to accomplish all of the objectives outlined in the strategic plan in a deliberate, organized manner within the five-year timeline. LADD's leadership team members assumed the title of project manager for the majority of projects. They will work across departments, employing the strengths of many and be held accountable to their peers weekly when the prioritization plan is reviewed at the director's meeting.

Although in its infancy, LADD has taken the top-ranked 12 projects and broken down quarterly expected outcomes for each. The outcomes may be revenue based and focused on generating income for the organization or task based with a method of planning and implementation. Whatever the method, program managers are held responsible for the project being supervised, and project progress will be reported directly to LADD's board of directors. Such a framework allows for accountability all the way through the organizational structure and a conclusively better service provision for those who LADD supports.Exhibit 2.16 illustrates the prioritization process with the highest ranked projects selected by LADD and shows the five criteria used to do so.

EXHIBIT 2.16

LADD PROJECT SELECTION AND PRIORITIZATION MATRIX						
PROJECT	MISSION (10)	FINANCE (9)	WORKFORCE (8)	RELATIONSHIPS (8)	COMMUNITY (7)	TOTAL
Film Festival	40	36	32	32	35	175
Expand meaningful community-inclusion activities	50	27	32	40	21	170
Develop Victory Parkway site	50	36	16	40	28	170
Implement vacation/ respite services	40	36	24	24	35	168
Health and Wellness Program	50	18	40	32	21	161

References

A Guide to the Project Management Body of Knowledge (PMBOK® Guide), 6th ed. (Newtown Square, PA: Project Management Institute, 2017).

Barclay, Colane, and Kweku-Muata Osei-Bryson, "Toward a More Practical Approach to Evaluating Programs: The Multi-Objective Realization Approach," *Project Management Journal* 40 (4) (December 2009): 74–93.

Brache, Alan P., and Sam Bodley-Scott, "Which Imperatives Should You Implement?" *Harvard Management Update,* Article reprint no. U0904B (2009).

Cannella, Cara, "Sustainability: A Green Formula," 2008 *Leadership in Project Management* 4: 34–40.

Caron, Franco, Mauro Fumagalli, and Alvaro Rigamonti, "Engineering and Contracting Projects: A Value at Risk Based Approach to Portfolio Balancing," *International Journal of Project Management* 25 (2007): 569–578.

Chinta, Ravi, and Timothy J. Kloppenborg, "Projects and Processes for Sustainable Organizational Growth," *SAM Advanced Management Journal* 75 (2) (Spring 2010): 22–28.

Cooper, Robert G., "Winning at New Products: Pathways to Profitable Innovation," *Proceedings of PMl Research Conference 2006* (Newtown Square, PA: Project Management Institute, 2006).

Daft, Richard L., *Management,* 9th ed. (Mason, OH: South-Western Cengage Learning, 2010).

Eager, Amanda, "Designing a Best-in-Class Innovation Scoreboard," *Technology Management* (January–February 2010): 11–13.

Evans, R. James, and William M. Lindsay, *Managing for Quality and Performance Excellence,* 8th ed. (Mason, OH: South-Western Cengage Learning, 2011).

State of Federal Information Technology, https://cio.gov/wp-content/uploads/filebase/cio_document_library/CIO-Council-State-of-Federal-IT-Report-January-2017(12).pdf, accessed April 14, 2017.

Kenny, John, "Effective Project Management for Strategic Innovation and Change in an Organizational Context," *Project Management Journal* 34 (1) (March 2003): 43–53.

Kloppenborg, Timothy J., Arthur Shriberg, and Jayashree Venkatraman, *Project Leadership* (Vienna, VA: Management Concepts, 2003).

Kloppenborg, Timothy J., and Laurence J. Laning, *Strategic Leadership of Portfolio and Project Management* (New York: Business Expert Press, 2012).

Labuschagne, Les, and Carl Marnewick, "A Structured Approach to Derive Projects from the Organizational Vision," *Proceedings of PMI Research*

Conference 2006 (Newtown Square, PA: Project Management Institute, 2006).

Milosevic, Dragan Z., and Sabin Srivinnaboon, "A Theoretical Framework for Aligning Project Management with Business Strategy," *Project Management Journal* 37 (3) (August 2006): 98–110.

Organizational Project Management Maturity Model Knowledge Foundation, 2nd ed. (Newtown Square, PA: Project Management Institute, 2008).

PMI Requirements Management: A Practice Guide (Newtown Square, PA: Project Management Institute 2016).

Practice Standard for Work Breakdown Structures, 2nd ed. (Newtown Square, PA: Project Management Institute, 2006).

Reginato, Justin, and C. William Ibbs, "Employing Business Models for Making Project Go/No Go Decisions," *Proceedings of PMI Research Conference 2006* (Newtown Square, PA: Project Management Institute, 2006).

Senge, Peter, Bryan Smith, Nina Kruschwitz, Joe Laur, and Sara Schley, *The Necessary Revolution: How Individuals and Organizations Are Working Together to Create a Sustainable World* (New York: Broadway Books, 2008).

Smallwood, Deb, and Karen Furtado, "Strategy Meets the Right Projects at the Right Time," *Bank Systems & Technology* 46 (4) (June–July 2009): 34.

The Standard for Portfolio Management, 3rd ed. (Newtown Square, PA: Project Management Institute, 2013).

The Standard for Program Management, 3rd ed. (Newtown Square, PA: Project Management Institute, 2013).

Steffey W. R., and V. Anantatmula, "International Projects Proposal Analysis: Risk Assessment Using Radial Maps," *Project Management Journal* 42 (3) (2011): 62–74.

Wheatley, Malcolm, "Beyond the Numbers" *PMNetwork* 23 (8) (August 2009): 38–43.

Zhang, Weiyong, Arthur V. Hill, Roger G. Schroeder, and Keyin W. Linderman, "Project Management Infrastructure: The Key to Operational Performance Improvement," *Operations Management Research* 1 (1) (September 2008): 40–52.

http://en.wikipedia.org/wiki/Triple_bottom_line, accessed February 2, 2010.

http://www.gcbl.org/about, accessed March 12, 2013.

http://www.bia.ca/vision.htm, accessed March 5, 2013.

http://ocio.os.doc.gov/s/groups/public/@doc/@os/ accessed February 7, 2017.

@ocio/@oitpp/documents/content/prod01_002082.pdf, accessed March 6, 2013.

https://topnonprofits.com/examples/vision-statements/, accessed January 9, 2017.

http://www.sustainablecleveland.org accessed February 7, 2017.

http://www.ecowatch.com/cleveland-a-green-city-on-a-blue-lake-1882095827.html, accessed January 9, 2017.

http://www.internetsociety.org/who-we-are/organization-reports-and-policies/internet-society-2015-action-plan, accessed February 7, 2017.

http://pmzilla.com/proposal-evaluation-techniques-source-selection-criteria accessed February 7, 2017.

Endnotes

1. https://topnonprofits.com/examples/vision-statements/, accessed January 9, 2017.

2. http://www.sustainablecleveland.org accessed February 7, 2017.

3. http://www.ecowatch.com/cleveland-a-green-city-on-a-blue-lake-1882095827.html, accessed January 9, 2017.

4. Lussier, Robert N., and Christopher F. Achua, *Leadership: Theory, Application, Skill Development,* 4th ed. (Mason, OH: Thomson South-Western, 2010): 425.

5. PMI Standard for Portfolio Management, 3rd ed. (2013): 190.

6. Kloppenborg, Timothy J., and Laurence J. Laning, *Strategic Leadership of Portfolio and Project Management* (New York: Business Expert Press, 2012): 21.

7. *PMI Standard for Portfolio Management,* 3rd ed. (2013): 190.

8. *PMI Standard for Program Management*, 3rd ed. (2013): 178.

9. *Federal_CIO_Roadmap-[2010.07.02].pdf,* p. 4, accessed February 7, 2017.

10. *PMI Practice Standard for Work Breakdown Structures,* 2nd ed. (2006): 121.

11. *PMI Requirements Management: A Practice Guide* (2016): 77.

12. *PMI Business Analysis for Practitioners: A Practice Guide* (2015): 207.

13. Steffey, W. R., and V. Anantatmula, "International Projects Proposal Analysis: Risk Assessment Using Radial Maps," *Project Management Journal* 42 (3) (2011): 62–74.

14. http://pmzilla.com/proposal-evaluation-techniques-source-selection-criteria, accessed February 7, 2017.

CHAPTER 3

Chartering Projects

A Lot Of People/Shutterstock.com

Planning a project is similar to putting together a large puzzle. If you were to dump a 1,000-piece puzzle on a table, you would probably not start the detailed "planning" right away by comparing two pieces randomly to see if they fit. You would likely take several preliminary steps. Some of these steps might include turning the pieces so the picture side was visible on each, sorting outside pieces so you could form the boundaries, studying the picture on the box, and sorting by color so you could match pieces more easily. (A few more-organized people may like to count and make sure that there are, indeed, 1,000 pieces.) These preliminary steps make the detailed planning of the puzzle much easier and more efficient. If completing projects is analogous to putting puzzles together, then project charters are the initial steps. Initiating a project requires some preliminary actions, including understanding the needs and concerns of stakeholders, most critically the project sponsor.

Ball Aerospace & Technologies Corp., Systems Engineering Solutions provides a wide range of air, space, and counterspace engineering and professional analytic services. At Ball, we increase stakeholder buy-in by addressing and thinking about things up front; with an agreed-upon charter, this gives the project team

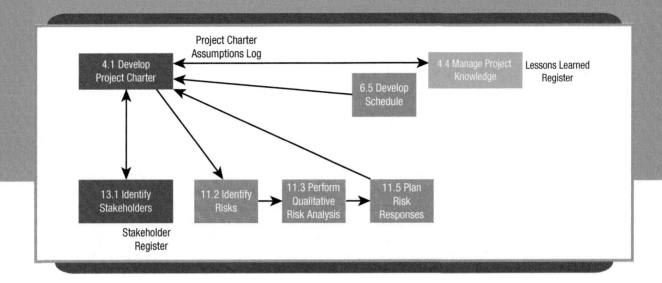

some guidance to effectively plan and execute the effort. In addition, by going through the chartering process, stakeholders take ownership in the project.

At Ball, our project sponsors are typically U.S. government customers, and we provide work for them on a contractual basis. They provide funding and broad direction for our efforts, and we go through a formal proposal process for all our projects. Project sponsors provide initial statements of work or objectives defining their goals for the task and then select among several proposals from interested companies such as Ball to fulfill their requirements. The chosen company is then under an official formal contract to complete the project. This is, in effect, a pre-chartering process.

Typically, after an effort is under contract, a kickoff meeting is scheduled to review the objectives of the project between the project sponsor and the chosen company. This is part of the initiating stage, where stakeholders review and approve the following as part of the project's charter:

- Overall project objectives
- Contrast between technical approach as written in the company's proposal for execution and sponsor expectations
- Milestones, checkpoints, and potential payment plans
- Success criteria and schedule
- Identification of key stakeholders and risks
- Processes for executing, monitoring, controlling, and overall management of the project

There are a number of things to consider when initiating a project and generating a project charter. These serve as pieces of the overall puzzle of managing and executing a project. A little pre-work in initiating the project goes a long way, with increased goodwill and understanding from the project sponsor, clear tasks and goals for the project team, and a single way forward toward achieving the products and services of the project.

—*Lydia Lavigne, Ball Aerospace*

This chapter describes what a project sponsor, manager, and team need to understand to quickly initiate a project. The project then proceeds into planning, and the elements of a charter are planned in as much detail as needed. Chapters 5 through 11 describe project planning.

3-1 What Is a Project Charter?

For a project manager, team member, or project sponsor, one of the first and most important project management concerns is a project charter. This short document (usually about three pages) serves as an informal contract between the project team and the sponsor (who represents both senior management of the organization and the outside customer, if there is one).

From a behavioral perspective, the project charter reflects a common understanding and collaboration between the project sponsor and the project manager. Negotiation skills of the project manager also play an important role in developing the project charter.

Since a charter is like a contract, it is helpful to remember what a contract is. First, it is an agreement entered into freely by two or more parties. Second, one party cannot arbitrarily change it. Third, there is something of value in it for each party. Finally, it is a living document that can evolve with changing conditions if both parties agree and receive something of value for making the change. The charter signing represents the transition from the high-level project initiation stage into the more detailed project planning stage. See Exhibit 3.1 for a review of the project life cycle.

The project charter is the deliverable that grants a project manager the right to continue into the more detailed planning stage of a project. This may include *only* permission to plan the project, permission to make decisions that would slow the project if delayed (such as ordering long-lead materials or hiring special workers), or permission to plan and perform the entire project in the case of a small, simple project. Officially, a charter is drafted by either project manager or sponsor and then negotiated; however, as projects are often conducted in a more collaborative fashion, some organizations are assigning core team members early enough that they can help draft the charter. Also, early input from key stakeholders may be considered.

While either party (the sponsor or the project manager) can write the rough draft, more often than not, the project manager writes the draft charter. Ideally, then, the project manager and the sponsor candidly discuss each part of the charter. Like a contract, the people who sign a charter are wise to ensure that they understand and agree to all of it. Unlike a contract, however, both parties feel obligated to the spirit (as opposed to the letter) of the charter since the project details have not yet been worked out and specifics will certainly change.

Thinking of a charter like a contract means that both the project manager and the sponsor sign the charter willingly and strive to make the project successful. When core team members have helped write the charter rough draft, they may also sign the charter. If the project manager feels bullied into making a change, it is not a free choice. However, the sponsor may legitimately need to insist on receiving the project results more quickly or make some other

EXHIBIT 3.1

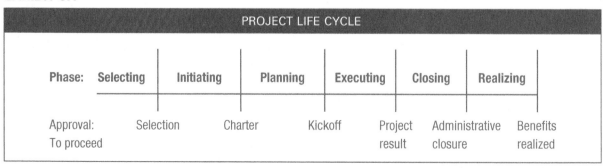

	PROJECT LIFE CYCLE					
Phase:	**Selecting**	**Initiating**	**Planning**	**Executing**	**Closing**	**Realizing**
Approval: To proceed	Selection	Charter	Kickoff	Project result	Administrative closure	Benefits realized

change to the project. In the spirit that one party cannot arbitrarily change a contract, the sponsor would not just tell the project team, "I need the project a month sooner and you get no more resources and no relief from any other work responsibilities." Rather, if the project must change, the sponsor needs to consider herself or himself to be a partner with the project team in determining how to accomplish the change.

3-2 Why Is a Project Charter Used?

The four major purposes for a charter are to:

1. Authorize the project manager to proceed
2. Help the project manager, sponsor, and team members, if any are already assigned, develop a common understanding
3. Help the project manager, sponsor, and team members commit to the spirit of the project
4. Quickly screen out obviously poor projects

First, a **project charter** is "a document that formally authorizes the existence of a project and provides the project manager with the authority to apply organizational resources to project activities."[1] Many project managers do not have the authority to commit resources without a charter. This gives the project and the project manager official status within the parent organization.

Second, everyone involved in the upcoming project needs to develop a common understanding of what the project entails. This includes at least the broad justification for the project, how it aligns with the goals of the parent organization, determination of what is included and excluded in the project scope, rough schedule, success measures, major risks, rough estimate of resource needs, and stakeholders. On larger and more complex projects, additional understanding may be required at this point. Small, simple projects may use a simplified single-page charter. Once everyone has a common understanding of clear project goals, several additional benefits occur:

- Teamwork develops.
- Agreement, trust, communication, collaboration, and commitment among the sponsor, project manager, and project team develop.
- The project team does not worry if management will accept a decision and can focus on the project plan.
- The sponsor is less likely to unilaterally change the original agreement.[2]

Third, each person needs to personally and formally commit to doing their level best to achieve the agreed-upon project results—even when things do not go as planned. It is a moral duty of all the project team members to commit to the shared goals articulated in the charter. This formal commitment often helps a person decide to keep working hard on a project when things are not going well.

Fourth, a charter is used to quickly screen potential projects to determine which appear to be poor choices. Needless to say, a charter is much quicker to put together than a full, detailed project plan and schedule. If by constructing a charter it is determined that the project is likely to fail, much planning time (and therefore money) will be saved.

Remember, the charter helps all project stakeholders. Charters are often publicly shown to many individuals beyond the project team and sponsor for communication. The culture of some companies is more trusting, competitive, focused on time, preoccupied with details, and so on than at other companies. Therefore, charters used in different industries and companies have somewhat different elements and formats.

3-3 When Is a Charter Needed?

Project methods can be scaled from very simple to very detailed. Consequently, a project charter can vary in its length from one-page to multiple pages. A project manager wants to use details that are adequate enough to develop a common understanding and agreement between the project manager and the project sponsor.

TriHealth has developed both full and mini charters, for large and small projects, respectively. They have also developed the decision matrix shown in Exhibit 3.2 to help people determine if a full charter, mini charter, or no charter is needed.

EXHIBIT 3.2

PROJECT CHARTER DECISION MATRIX						

Project Name

Date

When an improvement, change, or new program is going to be implemented, it is important to first determine whether or not it is a project. If it is a project, TriHealth has specific tools that should be used to guide the planning and implementation.

In general, a project is "a temporary endeavor undertaken to create a unique product, service, or result." If your project impacts more than one department, requires expertise or resources beyond your own department, or could affect the operations in another area, the standardized templates should be used. Answering the questions below with a check will help you determine what types of tools are needed for your project. Evaluate where the majority of your checks lie and use the most appropriate tool.

Resources	☐	Little or no monies, supplies, or change in resources	☐	Requires moderate resources	☐	Requires significant and/or additional FTEs
Multidisciplinary	☐	1 discipline involved/impacted	☐	2–3 disciplines involved/impacted or more than one site	☐	More than 3 disciplines involved/impacted
Complexity	☐	Little complexity	☐	Moderate complexity; affects care delivery	☐	Very complex
Technology Involvement	☐	No technology changes	☐	IS consult needed	☐	IS resources assigned
Approvals	☐	None needed	☐	Approval by immediate supervisor	☐	Executive-level approval
Potential Risk Level	☐	Minimal impact on customer	☐	Moderate impact on customer	☐	Significant impact on customer
Staff Commitment	☐	Involvement of 2–3 people for solution	☐	Small team needed to generate solutions	☐	Requires large team of multiple departments for improvement
Communication and Education	☐	Simple communication plan or unit-based education only	☐	Moderate communication plan; requires education across departments	☐	Complex communication/education plan with various media
Metrics	☐	Requires at least a one-time follow-up check	☐	Improvement will be tracked	☐	Baseline and ongoing tracking of data
If the majority of your checks lie in this area:		⬇		⬇		⬇
	☐	No charter needed	☐	Complete a mini charter	☐	Complete a full project charter

Source: TriHealth.

3-4 Typical Elements in a Project Charter

The following sections list some of the typical key elements in a project charter. While the intent of most of these sections is included in many charters, some project teams combine sections or leave out a few of them. Furthermore, while the term *charter* is a widely used standard, some organizations use other names such as *project request, project submission form,* or *project preplanning form.* As long as the four purposes of a charter (authorization, understanding, commitment, and screening) are accomplished, the exact format and title are negotiable. Typical charter elements and the question each element answers are shown in Exhibit 3.3.

The charter should be short enough so that the project team and sponsor (and any other interested stakeholder) can examine it carefully to ensure they understand and agree. One to four pages in total is generally about the right length.

3-4a Title

The existence of a meaningful project title is critical. In an organization with a number of projects, the title can be used to quickly identify which project is being referenced.

3-4b Scope Overview

The scope overview and business case sections are the high-level "what and why" of the project. They are sometimes considered to be the "elevator speech" that a person would use if given a very short amount of time, such as a one-floor elevator ride, to describe their project. Sometimes, an additional background statement is helpful.

The scope overview is the project in a nutshell: a high-level description of what needs to be accomplished and how it will be done. What needs to be accomplished can be described as the product scope, all the characteristics that must be present in the actual project deliverables or as **requirements**, each of which is an attribute that needs to be present in order to satisfy a contract, client, or other stakeholder. How it will be done is the project scope, the entirety of what will and will not be done to meet the specified

EXHIBIT 3.3

CHARTER ELEMENTS AND QUESTIONS ANSWERED	
CHARTER ELEMENT	ANSWERS THE QUESTION
Scope overview	What?
Business case	Why?
Background	Why?
Milestone schedule	When?
Success criteria	What?
Risks, assumptions, and constraints	Whoa!
Resources	How much?
Stakeholders	Who?
Team operating principles	How?
Lessons learned	How?
Signatures and commitment	Who?

requirements. The scope overview quickly describes the project work and results. The scope overview is used to distinguish between what the project will and will not do. It is used to help prevent **scope creep**, which is an incremental increase in the work of a project without corresponding adjustments to resources, budget, or schedule. The scope overview can be considered to define project boundaries. It states what is included and what is not—at least at a fairly high level.

Quantifying the scope, such as "15 touch points will be included," helps everyone to better understand the project's size. If a project could be compared to an animal, the scope overview briefly describes both the size and features so one can tell if it is a rabbit or an elephant. By understanding what is included and what is not, the project team is more likely to accurately estimate cost, resource, and schedule needs and to understand and handle project risks.

3-4c Business Case

The business case is the project purpose or justification statement. It answers the question "why?" and helps all parties understand the purpose of the project. A business case is used to justify the necessity of the project. It should clearly tie the project to the organization's strategy and explain the benefits the organization hopes to achieve by authorizing the project or the strategic goals it meets.

Depending on the organization, a business case can either be just the rationale for the project, or it can also include high-level estimates of the costs and benefits of the project. A business case may also include emotional and ethical reasons for performing the project. A well-written business case should persuade decision makers to support the project and inspire the project team members and key stakeholders to work hard toward successful completion of the project.

3-4d Background

Many people are quite busy and prefer short statements that can be quickly reviewed. Key project stakeholders should know enough about the project after reviewing the short scope overview and business case statements, as these statements will provide all of the information they need to know. Some other stakeholders may need more details to understand the rationale and purpose behind these statements. A more detailed background statement may be helpful in these cases.

Unlike the first two statements, which should be limited to about two to four sentences each, the background statement can be any length. The background statement is purely optional—develop one only when it is necessary.

3-4e Milestone Schedule with Acceptance Criteria

The **milestone schedule** is a high-level plan that indicates a few significant accomplishments that are anticipated over the life of the project. It divides the project into a few (about three to eight) intermediate points or milestones whose completion can be verified. The team estimates a date when they expect to complete each milestone. A milestone schedule should list major milestones and deliverables that the project team especially wants to ensure are completed both on time and to the satisfaction of key decision makers. The milestone schedule is considered very useful for communicating with the key stakeholders who are not actively involved with the project.

A deliverable as defined in Chapter 1 is a "unique and verifiable product, result, or capability to perform a service that is required to be produced to complete a process, phase, or project."[3] Requirements of a deliverable are often translated into specifications so that the deliverable can be validated, qualified by measurable conditions, and bounded by constraints.

Sometimes, milestones occur right before the approval of a large expenditure. At other times, they occur at completion of a critical design, a key deliverable, or a major

EXHIBIT 3.4

MILESTONE SCHEDULE EXAMPLE			
MILESTONE	DATE	WHO JUDGES	ACCEPTANCE
1. Existing facility	9-19-16		
2. Site visit/audit	9-22-16	PM/Customer	Site data verified
3. Design and approval	10-22-16	Customer	Customer approval
4. Equipment deliverables	12-2-16	Engineering & Manufacturing	B.O.M. check
5. Project execution	1-6-17	Installation & Customer	Commissioned
6. System turnover	1-13-17	Customer	System throughout of 35,000 cases per day

accomplishment of the scope. It is helpful to identify the relatively few milestones and key deliverables in the project that the team and sponsor wish to check closely.

Adding a column for acceptance criteria factors to the milestone schedule helps the project team understand who will judge the quality of the deliverable associated with each milestone and what criteria will be used for that determination. **Acceptance criteria** stipulate which conditions must be met in order for the deliverables to be approved.

Acceptance criteria are like the project's vital signs. A paramedic would check pulse, breathing, maybe skin color, and body temperature immediately when answering a 911 call. Other tests are not as critical and may be performed, just not immediately. It is important to identify the vital signs for the project. Project success is easy to measure after the project is complete. The equally important, but often more challenging, decision is how to measure success while the project is progressing so there is still time to make changes if necessary.

Another way to understand acceptance criteria is to understand how a key stakeholder such as the sponsor, customer, or end-user is going to determine if the deliverables created are of good enough quality to accept. Since some of the milestones are often preliminary (drafts, prototypes, concepts, outlines, etc.), it is helpful to have the same person who will judge the final project deliverables judge them at the intermediate milestones. By doing this, the decision maker is much less likely to state at the end of the project, "No, that is not what I meant." Including advance understanding of criteria is similar to the old saying that a trial lawyer never asks a question without knowing how the witness will answer. An astute project manager never turns in a deliverable without knowing how it will be judged. An example of a milestone schedule is shown in Exhibit 3.4.

 One key concept in Agile projects is that something of value will be delivered at each iteration. Something of value for IT projects means working software. For other projects, it still refers to something the user can use—not just documentation. An agreement is reached during iteration planning on the "definition of done"—meaning exactly how each feature and function must perform. This is comparable to deliverables with acceptance criteria for each milestone as just described.

3-4f Risks, Assumptions, and Constraints

A **risk** is an uncertain situation that could negatively *or positively* affect the project if it occurs. **Assumptions** are suppositions made during project planning that are treated as correct or factual, though they have not been proven. Project teams frequently identify, document, and validate assumptions as part of their planning process. Assumptions

wavebreakmedia/Shutterstock.com

generally involve a degree of risk. A **constraint** is anything that limits the implementation of a project.

Taken together, assumptions and constraints are what could cause project problems. They are included with risks so that all of the key participants—sponsor, project manager, and core team—are aware in advance of what could prevent them from successfully completing the project. While it is unrealistic to believe that the team can think of every single thing that could go wrong, the more comprehensive this section is, the more likely the team is to uncover problems before they occur and while there is time to easily deal with them.

If an assumption turns out to be false, it becomes a risk. A constraint that limits the amount of money, time, or resources needed to successfully complete a project is also a risk. Some organizations, especially for small projects, group all risks, assumptions, and constraints together, while others handle each as a separate charter section. The most important point is not how each is managed, but that each *is* managed.

Project managers and teams should look at risks for three reasons. First, any negative risk that is a threat that may inhibit successful project completion (to the satisfaction of stakeholders, on time, and on budget) needs to be identified. And, if it is a major risk, a plan must be developed to overcome it. Second, a positive risk is an opportunity to complete the project better, faster, and/or at lower cost or to capitalize upon the project in additional ways, and a plan should be developed to capitalize upon it. Third, sometimes there is more risk to the organization if the project is not undertaken—and this provides additional rationale for doing the project.

For each major negative risk identified, an "owner" is assigned responsibility. Then one or more response plans are normally developed to either lessen the probability of the risk event from happening in the first place and/or to reduce the impact if the risk event should materialize. Sometimes, transferring the risk to a third party makes sense. The goal is not to eliminate all risk, but to reduce the risk to a level that decision makers deem acceptable.

3-4g Resource Estimates

Remember that executives consider projects to be investments. The scope overview and business case sections of the charter describe the return expected, while the resources section describes what will be invested. These sections collectively help decision makers determine if the project is worth approving. **Resources** include the workers, tools, equipment, and anything else needed in order to execute your project. Since executives consider projects to be investments of resources, they will want a rough estimate. This can be an estimate of the amount of staff time, equipment, or materials that are in short supply, and/or the amount of money that is required. Since there is only very general understanding of the project at this point, any budget will also be approximate and should be stated as such by calling it a preliminary budget and including the level of confidence one has in the estimate; this is often expressed in percentage terms (such as plus or minus 50 percent) regarding the accuracy of the estimate.

On some internal projects, the pay for the associates who work on the project often comprises much of the expense. Frequently, however, at least a few expenses are incurred. It is helpful to identify which expenses the project manager can authorize and which the sponsor needs to control.

3-4h Stakeholder List

Project success is partially dictated by identifying and prioritizing stakeholders, managing robust relationships with them, and making decisions that satisfy stakeholder objectives. Therefore, it is good practice to identify and prioritize stakeholders early in a project.

3-4i Team Operating Principles

Team operating rules or principles are sometimes established to enhance team performance. The goal is to increase team effectiveness and ensure that all parties are aware of what is expected. Team operating principles that are especially useful are those that

The key players of a project show their commitment to the project by signing the commitment section of the charter.

deal with conducting meetings, making decisions, accomplishing work, and treating each other with respect. This concept is further elaborated on as a Team Charter in Chapter 5 because some organizations will choose to create a separate team charter instead of including team operating principles in their project charter.

3-4j Lessons Learned

While every project is unique, a great deal can be learned from the successes and failures of previous projects and turned into practical advice. **Lessons learned** represent the knowledge acquired by the project team throughout the project planning and execution, including things that should be replicated and things that should be avoided on future projects. To ensure that lessons learned are used, a sponsor should only sign a charter authorizing the project to begin when at least one or two good, specific lessons from the successes and/or failures of recently completed projects are included. This essentially forces the new project manager and team to look at the organization's lessons learned repository to find applicable learnings. A **lessons learned register** is an accumulation of the knowledge gained during previous projects' selection, planning, and executing that can be easily referenced to help with planning and executing future projects. These lessons could be stored in a dedicated database, on a shared drive, or in a less formal manner. The database should be intuitive to use, and it should be easy to retrieve relevant information. It is important for new project teams to learn together; otherwise, they risk repeating mistakes from previous projects.

3-4k Signatures and Commitment

The commitment section of the charter lists who is involved and sometimes describes the extent to which each person can make decisions and/or the expected time commitment for each person. This is where the project sponsor, project manager, and perhaps core team members publicly and personally show their commitment to the project by signing the charter. By formally committing to the project, the key players are more likely to keep working hard during difficult periods and see the project through to a successful conclusion.

3-5 Constructing a Project Charter

It is wonderful if the sponsor can work with the project manager and possibly core team members who have been preassigned to construct the charter. The sponsor, however, as a busy executive, often does not have time to be present for the entire chartering period. In those cases, it is very helpful if the sponsor can create the first draft—however crude—of the scope overview and business case. A sponsor's ability to tell the project manager and core team concisely what the project is and why it is important gets the team off to a good start. If the sponsor wants the team to consider any important constraints, assumptions, risks, or other factors, she can help the team by pointing that out up front.

Sometimes, on an especially important project, the organization's leadership team may draft more than just the business case and scope overview statements. If the leadership team feels something is very important, they can save everyone time by just stating it up front. Likewise, if the sponsor knows he or she will only approve a charter with one of the elements written a particular way, he or she should tell the team that up front. Otherwise, the project manager, possibly with the core team, most frequently writes much of the rough draft.

3-5a Scope Overview and Business Case Instructions

When possible, the first draft of these two sections should be provided by the sponsor or the leadership team. One to four sentences for each is enough—but it needs to be in writing. Many teams find that, because these are the "what and why" of the project, it is easier to work on them at the same time. Teams often brainstorm key ideas and then craft the parts on which they agree into smooth-flowing statements. If the sponsor provides a first draft of these sections, the project manager and core team carefully dissect it to ensure they both understand and agree. The project manager and team frequently propose refinements on the original draft.

Scope overview and business case examples are depicted in Exhibit 3.5.

3-5b Background Instructions

The project manager and team decide whether this optional section is necessary for their project as they construct the scope overview and business case. If the scope overview and

EXHIBIT 3.5

SCOPE OVERVIEW AND BUSINESS CASE EXAMPLES

PHASE II MULTICENTER TRIAL SCOPE OVERVIEW

This project will initiate a Phase II multicenter clinical trial at Cincinnati Children's Hospital Medical Center (CCHMC). The trial will be conducted at five medical centers in the United States to investigate the safety and efficacy of an investigational drug's ability to improve cognitive functioning and quality of life in pediatric patients with Tuberous Sclerosis Complex. The project is a follow-up study of a Phase I clinical trial conducted at CCHMC.

ONLINE TUITION REIMBURSEMENT PROJECT SCOPE OVERVIEW

This project will design, develop, and implement an online tuition reimbursement system that will provide employees with a self-service tool to submit a request for tuition reimbursement payment. This project will incorporate a workflow process that will do the following:

- Move the request to the appropriate personnel for approval.
- Alert the employee of any additional items necessary for processing the request/
- Upon approval, send the request to payroll for final processing.
- Notify the employee of payment processing.

DEVELOPMENT OF A BIOLOGICAL RESEARCH SPECIMEN SHIPPING CENTER PROJECT BUSINESS CASE

The purpose of this shipping center is to provide professional shipping services and supplies for CCHMC employees who are responsible for shipping biological specimens as part of research. This shipping center will improve compliance, streamline shipping processes, enhance research productivity, reduce time and money invested in employee training, and reduce potential liability for noncompliance.

ESTABLISHING A SECOND PULMONARY FUNCTION TESTING (PTF) LAB PROJECT BUSINESS CASE

An additional PTF lab will *enhance patient access* by:

> Decreasing wait times and
> Providing a convenient location close to primary care appointments.

It will also *improve patient outcomes* by assisting in:

> Diagnosis,
> Accurate assessment, and
> Chronic management of pediatric lung disease.

In addition, establishing a PFT lab will increase revenue by:

> Increasing availability of PTF and
> Increasing community referrals for PFT.

Source: Cincinnati Children's Hospital Medical Center.

EXHIBIT 3.6

BACKGROUND SECTION EXAMPLE

Interfaith Business Builders is an organization of diverse Cincinnatians that develops and promotes community-based, employee-owned and -operated cooperative businesses (co-ops). Our co-ops create new jobs and ownership opportunities for low-income people in sustainable local businesses. Members of IBB come from a variety of faith and social backgrounds, share a passion for social justice and the empowerment of people, and value community, cooperation, opportunity, and solidarity. Our cooperatives are businesses that follow these seven principles: voluntary and open membership; democratic member control; members' economic participation; autonomy and independence; education, training, and information; cooperation among cooperatives; and concern for community.

business case seem detailed enough for all important stakeholders, an extra background section may not be needed. If necessary, the team probably brainstorms ideas and then combines them into a single smooth statement. An example of a background statement for a project to start a new co-op business is shown in Exhibit 3.6.

3-5c Milestone Schedule with Acceptance Criteria Instructions

The first step in the iterative process of developing a project schedule is to define major milestones. This section of the charter can be developed most effectively by focusing on why you are doing a project before diving into all of the details. A method of depicting all of this information so it is simple to understand is to set up a four-column table with *Milestone, Completion Date, Stakeholder Judge,* and *Acceptance Criteria* heading the columns. An example of a milestone schedule with acceptance criteria for a project converting to a centralized electronic record system for a major research hospital is shown in Exhibit 3.7.

SIX STEPS IN CONSTRUCTING A MILESTONE SCHEDULE   The most effective way to construct the milestone schedule with acceptance criteria is to use the six-step procedure described below. Identifying the end points first (Steps 1 and 2) helps project teams avoid the problem of sinking into too much detail too quickly. Note that dates are the final item to be identified. It is unethical for a project manager to agree to unrealistic dates. Even though the milestone schedule is not very detailed, it is the first time a team thinks through how the project will be performed and how long it will take at each point. This allows a bit of realism in the schedule.

Step 1 The first task is to briefly describe (in three or four words) the current situation that requires the project and place this description in the first row of the milestone column. The current state may be a shortened version of the business case. The starting point for many projects is either something that exists, but does not work as well as desired, or a desire exists for something completely new. However, the starting point for some projects is the ending point of a previous project. Keep the description very short, and it will form an effective starting place. In Exhibit 3.7, the problem was paper records that were not centralized.

Step 2 Once the current state is agreed upon by the project manager and team, skip to the desired future state. Describe the project (or phase if there will be future phases) at its successful completion in three or four words. Put this description in the last row of the milestone column. It is hard for many core teams to distill this to the ideal three or four words, but keeping it concise helps the team develop a better understanding of what is

EXHIBIT 3.7

MILESTONE SCHEDULE WITH ACCEPTANCE CRITERIA EXAMPLE			
COMPLETION DATE	MILESTONE	STAKEHOLDER JUDGE	ACCEPTANCE CRITERIA
Current state: Paper, noncentralized records			
Needs assessment	28-Feb	Ops management	List of needed features
Hardware selection	15-Apr	Ops management, CIO	Hardware choice with contract
Vendor selection	30-May	Ops management	Vendor choice with contract
Installation and configuration	15-Jul	Application specialist, IS department head	Functional software in test environment
Conversion	31-Aug	Application specialist, IS department head	All files converted
Testing	15-Oct	Application specialist, IS department head	Sign off on test
Training	30-Nov	Ops management, HR	Sign off on training
Future state: Electronic, centralized records	30-Nov	Sponsor	Ability to enter and retrieve information from all departments
↓ ┊ ↓			
Ultimate goal Seamless information flow throughout organization			

truly most important. If the current project is a phase of a larger project, also write briefly what the final successful result of the last future stage will be. In Exhibit 3.7, the desired future state is to have records centralized and available in electronic form, and the ultimate goal is for seamless information flow throughout the organization. More work will need to be completed beyond this project to reach that ultimate goal. Since contemporary project management is often iterative, many projects are part of a larger goal.

Step 3 Next, describe the acceptance criteria for the final project deliverables (at the future state). What stakeholder(s) will judge the deliverables, and on what basis? Exactly how will they become confident that the project results will work as desired? These stakeholders will almost always demand a demonstration of project results. The project team wants to understand what that demonstration will be at this early point so they can plan to achieve it. Note that there very well could be multiple stakeholders and multiple methods of ensuring the project results are satisfactory. At this point, strive to identify the most important stakeholders and acceptance criteria. Place these in the bottom row of the third and fourth columns. In Exhibit 3.7, the sponsor wants a representative from each department to show they can enter and retrieve pertinent data.

Step 4 Now, go back to the milestone column. Determine the few key points where quality needs to be verified. On most small to medium-sized projects, approximately three to eight intermediate points are satisfactory. Start by identifying the three most important intermediate points, and add more if necessary. If you need to identify considerably more major deliverables at this point, you might consider splitting your project into phases and concentrate on the first phase for now. Satisfactory completion of each milestone will be determined by how the sponsor and other stakeholders will judge your performance. They should be in enough detail so stakeholders are comfortable with your progress, yet not so detailed that you feel micromanaged. The project in Exhibit 3.7 has seven milestones.

On Agile projects, the first iteration is planned as a milestone with acceptance criteria just as described above. Rather than have a defined set of milestones, an agile charter after the first milestone is more of a general roadmap of the product. Subsequent milestones and acceptance criteria are determined on a just-in-time (JIT) basis.

Step 5 Now, for each milestone, determine who the primary stakeholder(s) is and how he or she will judge the resulting deliverable. Remember, these are intermediate deliverables, and often it is not as easy to determine desired performance. One idea to keep in mind: if practical, ask the person who will judge the overall project results at the end to judge the intermediate deliverables also to make sure you are on the right track. Quite a few different stakeholders will judge various milestones in the project in Exhibit 3.7.

Step 6 Finally, determine expected completion dates for each milestone. Do not be overly optimistic or pessimistic. You will be at approximately the right level of detail if you have a milestone somewhere between every one and six weeks on many projects. Obviously, there will be exceptions for especially large or small projects. Most of the milestones in the project in Exhibit 3.7 are about six weeks apart.

Some companies that perform many projects use templates to guide their project teams through chartering and other activities. An example of a template for the milestone schedule and acceptance criteria for a Six Sigma project is shown in Exhibit 3.8.

EXHIBIT 3.8

SIX SIGMA MILESTONE SCHEDULE AND ACCEPTANCE CRITERIA TEMPLATE			
Milestone	**Completion Date**	**Stakeholder**	**Acceptance Criteria**
Current Situation Define	_____	_____	Problem in operational terms Customers and metrics identified Project schedule and assignments
Measure	_____	_____	Causal relationships defined Data gathering procedures approved Sufficient data gathered
Analyze	_____	_____	Potential variables identified; Root causes statistically proven
Improve	_____	_____	Problem resolution ideas gathered Solution evaluated and confirmed Solution implemented
Control Future State	_____	_____	Standards, procedures, training in place

3-5d Risks, Assumptions, and Constraints Instructions

First, the project manager (possibly with core team members, sponsor, and/or key stakeholders if available) should brainstorm all the things that could pose a risk to the project schedule, budget, usefulness of any project deliverables, or satisfaction of any project stakeholder. This is the process of risk identification. All of the risk processes will be covered in more detail in the risk planning chapter. Constraints that limit choices and unproven assumptions can be identified. Assumptions are especially important when a cross-functional team is performing the project because some team members may make vastly different assumptions based upon the manner in which work is normally accomplished in their respective departments. The brainstorming often works very well with each team member writing one risk, constraint, or assumption per Post-it Note. On large, complicated projects, risks, assumptions, and constraints may form separate sections of a charter. An **assumptions log** is often created as a living document to record all assumptions and the findings of whether they proved to be true or false. However, in this book, we deal with them together. From this point forward, all risks, assumptions, and constraints are simply referred to as *risks*.

Either the project manager or one of the team members can then act as a facilitator and assess one risk at a time. Risks can be assessed on probability of occurring and impact if realized. Both dimensions can be shown with a simple continuum of low to high using a flip chart or marker board. The team can agree to assess each risk at any point on the continuum. It works best if one dimension is considered at a time. For example, first ask how likely the risk event is to occur. Only after this is answered, ask how big the impact will be if it happens.

After all risks are assessed, the team needs to decide which of the risks should be considered major risks. That is, which are important enough to require a formal response plan with someone assigned responsibility? The other, more minor risks are not formally considered further in the charter, but they very well may get more attention in the planning and executing stages. This is the process of qualitative risk analysis.

The project team constructs a table depicting each major risk, with its contingency plan and "owner." This is the process of planning risk responses.

Examples of risk assessment and major risk response planning for a hardware upgrade project in an Irish factory are shown in Exhibits 3.9 and 3.10, respectively.

3-5e Resources Needed Instructions

Armed with the milestone schedule, the project manager and team may be prepared to make crude estimates of the project budget and other resource needs—such as people, equipment, or space. It is imperative to describe how the estimates were developed and the level of confidence the team has in them, such as "this is a rough order of magnitude estimate only based upon the milestones, and the true project cost could range from 25 percent below this to 75 percent above it." On many projects, especially those with customers internal to the organization, a budget is not established. However, a limit of spending authority for the project manager is often developed. An example of resources needed for a project is shown in Exhibit 3.11.

3-5f Stakeholder List Instructions

Stakeholders are all the people who have an interest in a project. They can be internal or external to the organization, be for or against the project, and have an interest in the project process and/or the project results. The project manager and team begin by identifying all stakeholders and determining which are most important. They next ask what

EXHIBIT 3.9

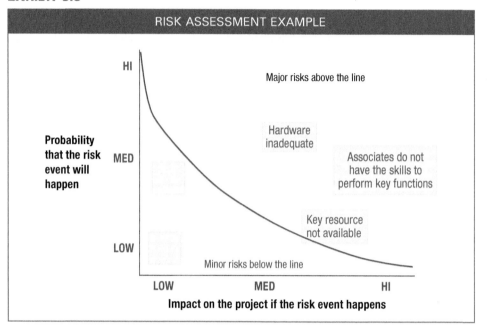

RISK ASSESSMENT EXAMPLE

Major risks above the line

Hardware inadequate

Associates do not have the skills to perform key functions

Key resource not available

Minor risks below the line

Probability that the risk event will happen

HI
MED
LOW

LOW   MED   HI

Impact on the project if the risk event happens

EXHIBIT 3.10

RISK RESPONSE PLANNING EXAMPLE		
RISK EVENT	RISK OWNER	RISK RESPONSE PLAN(S)
Hardware inadequate	Edie	1. Techs revise existing hardware 2. Replace hardware
Associates do not have skills to perform key functions	Padraig	1. Train existing associates 2. Hire additional people
Key resource not available	Ute	1. Identify external resources to fill need

EXHIBIT 3.11

RESOURCES NEEDED ESTIMATE		
MONEY	PEOPLE	OTHER
Marketing $10,000	Project Manager, 250 hours	1 Dedicated Conference Room
	Core Team Members, 500 hours	
AV and Communications $5,000	Internal Consultant, 100 hours	
Miscellaneous $5,000	Data Analyst, 100 hours	
	Focus Group Participants, 50 hours	
Total = $20,000	Total = 1,000 hours	**1 Room**

interest each stakeholder has in the project. A stakeholder list example for a clinical research project is shown in Exhibit 3.12. This is the process of identifying stakeholders, and the resulting list is the start of a stakeholder register. Both will be described in more detail in the stakeholder chapter.

3-5g Team Operating Principles Instructions

The project manager and team will decide what project team operating principles they will use. The operating principles establish how meetings will be conducted, how decisions will be made, how work will get done, and how everyone will treat each other with respect. Exhibit 3.13 is an example of team operating principles.

3-5h Lessons Learned Instructions

Each project by definition is at least somewhat different from any other project. That said, there are many commonalities in how projects can be planned and managed. A project manager and team need to consider what has worked well and what has worked

EXHIBIT 3.12

STAKEHOLDER LIST EXAMPLE		
STAKEHOLDER	PRIORITY	INTEREST IN PROJECT
Institutional Review Board	Key	Unexpected problems, progress
Food and Drug Administration	Key	Serious adverse events, progress
Site Principal Investigators	Key	Protocol, safety reports, changes
Pharmaceutical Company (Customer)	Other	Serious adverse events, progress
Research Subjects (Patients)	Other	Purpose of study, risks and benefits, protocol

EXHIBIT 3.13

TEAM OPERATING PRINCIPLES EXAMPLE

ABC Project Team Operating Principles

1. Team members will be prepared with minutes from previous meeting, agenda, and project updates.
2. Meetings will normally last for up to 90 minutes.
3. Team members will rotate the role of recorder.
4. Each team member will be responsible for setting his or her own deadline.
5. In the event that a team member cannot have his or her assignment complete by the expected date, he or she must notify the team leader prior to the due date.
6. The team leader will be responsible for drafting the minutes from the previous meeting and the agenda for the next meeting within 48 hours.
7. Decisions will be made by:
   Team leader on _____ issues.
   Consensus on _____ issues.
   Delegation on _____ issues.

poorly on previous projects when starting a new one. A sponsor is wise not to sign a project charter authorizing work until the project manager and team show they have learned lessons from recently completed projects. One easy way to accomplish this is to have each project report lessons learned at key reviews and at project completion and to have the lessons available to all in a lessons learned knowledge base. The project manager and team can then look at the lessons until they find at least a couple that can help them on their project. These lessons are included in the charter. The more specific the lessons, the more likely the team will find them useful. Exhibit 3.14 is an example of project lessons learned.

3-5i Signatures and Commitment Instructions

The project sponsor, manager, and team members sign the charter to publicly acknowledge their commitment. Sometimes other key stakeholders also sign. An example of a charter signature section is shown in Exhibit 3.15.

EXHIBIT 3.14

PROJECT LESSONS LEARNED EXAMPLE
All parties are responsible for defining and following the project scope to avoid scope creep.
All parties should share good and bad previous experiences.
Aligning team roles to sponsor expectations is critical.
Keep sponsor informed so sponsor stays committed.
Identify any possible changes as soon as possible.
Use weekly updates on project progress to avoid unpleasant schedule surprises. Review previous events for specific lessons.

EXHIBIT 3.15

CHARTER SIGNATURE EXAMPLE		
Anne E., Sponsor		
	Signature	Date
Karen H., Project Leader		
	Signature	Date
Jim B., Team Member		
	Signature	Date
Charlie H., Team Member		
	Signature	Date
Mitch N., Team Member		
	Signature	Date
Katie S., Team Member		
	Signature	Date

3-6 Ratifying the Project Charter

The project manager and team formally present the project charter to the sponsor for approval. In some organizations, the leadership team is also present for this meeting. The sponsor (and leadership team members, if present) ideally is supportive, but also ready to ask questions regarding any part of the charter. These questions are for both clarification and agreement. Once all questions are satisfactorily answered—including any agreements regarding changes—the sponsor, project manager, and core team all sign the project charter and feel bound by it.

Project managers are generally held more accountable for performance than they have the responsibility to direct people to perform. Because of this, project managers must negotiate. Here, we discuss how they need to negotiate a project charter with their sponsor. Later in the book, we discuss how they often need to negotiate with functional managers for the particular people they wish to have work on the project; with customers concerning schedule, budget, scope, and a myriad of details; and with sponsors, suppliers, SMEs, and core team members.

Nobody loves a project as much as the project manager does. However, a project manager must remember that negotiations will be smoother if she realizes that everyone with whom she negotiates has their own set of issues and goals.

Regardless of the negotiation size or complexity, the six-step process shown in Exhibit 3.16 can serve as a guide.

The negotiation process is based on the project manager and the sponsor attempting in good faith to reach a solution that benefits both—useful deliverables for the sponsor and a manageable process for the project manager.

Step 1 involves advance fact finding to determine what is needed from the negotiation. This includes seeking to understand both what the sponsor is likely to want and how he or she may act during the negotiations.

Step 2 is for the project manager to understand the bottom line. What is the minimum acceptable result? Just as when buying a car, a project manager needs to understand when to walk away. This can vary a great deal depending on how much power each party has. The sponsor is likely to have more power. However, project managers need to understand that if they have the power and take advantage of their negotiation partner, that partner may not work with them on a future project. Therefore, the goal is not to always drive the hardest bargain, but to drive a fair bargain.

Step 3 is for the project manager to understand the underlying needs of the sponsor and to share his or her own needs. This is not a 10-second political sound bite that says "take it or leave it." This is developing a real understanding of each other's needs. Once both parties understand what the other really needs, various creative solutions can be developed. This is the essence of Step 4.

Step 5 consists of the process and strategies of the negotiation itself. It is helpful to keep in mind the ultimate goal while focusing on the many details of information sharing, trading of concessions, and exploring possible solutions. Step 6 is actually a reminder to reach an agreement and then to document that agreement.

3-7 Starting a Project Using Microsoft Project

Microsoft (MS) Project is a software application designed to aid project managers in the planning, execution, and assessment of projects. It allows the project manager to track project tasks, set milestones, create corresponding schedules, and administer resources and budgets. Throughout the text (Exhibit 3.16), various MS Project processes will be demonstrated in a series of tutorials using the textbook's running *Suburban Homes*

EXHIBIT 3.16

NEGOTIATION PROCESS	
STEP	EXPLANATION
1. Prepare for negotiation.	Know what you want and who you will negotiate with.
2. Know your walk-away point.	Determine in advance the minimum you need from the negotiation.
3. Clarify both parties' interests.	Learn what the other party really wants and share your true interests to determine a common goal.
4. Consider multiple options.	Brainstorm multiple approaches—even approaches that solve only part of the issue.
5. Work toward a common goal.	Keep the common goal in mind: seek and share information, make concessions, and search for possible settlements.
6. Clarify and confirm agreements.	Agree on key points, summarize, and record all agreements.

Source: Adapted from Aldag, Ramon J., and Loren W. Kuzuhara, *Mastering Management Skills: A Manager's Toolkit* (Mason, OH: Thomson South-Western, 2005): 129–132; and Baldwin, Timothy T., William H. Bommer, and Robert S. Rubin, *Developing Management Skills: What Great Managers Know and Do* (Boston: McGraw-Hill, 2008): 307–318.

Construction Project as a basis. A fully functioning demonstration version of MS Project 2016 is available for download from Microsoft.

3-7a MS Project 2016 Introduction

MS Project 2016 is part of the Microsoft Office family; therefore, much of the basic interface and interaction with the software should seem familiar. You will find the unique aspects of the application in the project-specific tools and visuals the software provides the project manager. When you first open MS Project, you have the option to create a new (blank) plan, open a recently used or saved plan, or start a plan based on a template. The following overview showcases the visible features of the main MS Project interface once a "blank" project has been created.

1. Ribbon—As with other Microsoft Office applications, the "ribbon bar" along the top of the interface contains the controls (or access to controls) used to develop and manipulate your project data. Controls are logically grouped in the following tabs:
   - **FILE** includes familiar commands such as Open, Save, Print, and Options.
   - **TASK**, **RESOURCE**, and **PROJECT** tabs allow task, resource, and project data entry and adjustment.
   - **REPORT** offers a variety of customizable visual and print reports of project data.
   - **VIEW** offers multiple ways to visualize your project data, including Calendar, Gantt Chart, Network Diagram, Resources, and Teams. A "split" (or "combination") view is also available, providing two different types of data displays at once.
   - **FORMAT** displays formatting controls that apply to the current *active* view. The Format tab header (above the tab) identifies the currently active view (e.g., Gantt Chart).

2. Quick Access Toolbar—As with other Microsoft Office applications, this customizable area allows you to create shortcuts to regularly used commands.

3. Project Schedule Details View Pane(s)—Below the ribbon is the project data "view" pane that displays information about the project. MS Project offers several different views, but the default setting is a split, dual display of the project Timeline and Gantt

EXHIBIT 3.17

CHAPTER	CHAPTER TITLE	MS PROJECT PROCESS
3	Chartering Projects	Introduce MS Project 2016; Set up a project; Create a milestone schedule
7	Scope Planning	Set up a work breakdown structure (WBS)
8	Scheduling Projects	Set up schedule; Build logical network diagram; Understand the critical path; Display and print schedules
9	Resourcing Projects	Define resources with calendars; Assign resources, including modifications; Find and resolve over-allocations
10	Budgeting Projects	Develop project budget
12	Project Quality Planning and Project Kickoff	Baseline the project plan
14	Determining Project Progress and Results	Update and report on project schedule
15	Finishing Projects and Realizing Benefits	Close projects

Chart views in an upper and lower pane. Although both are visible, only one view is active (indicated by a colored view name label on the far-left end of the view pane). The active view can be changed in the View tab or with the View Shortcut buttons.

- Timeline View: The Timeline View shows you the "big picture" of your project schedule. Milestones or other key activities can be marked and highlighted in the timeline to help better visualize the project.
- Gantt Chart View: The Gantt Chart is a commonly used tool to represent a project schedule. Once a list of project task details is inputted into the table on the left-hand side of the view, horizontal bars populate the right side to graphically represent each task against a calendar along the top of the view.

4. Zoom Slider—The zoom slider is useful in any view that contains calendar data. It quickly changes the timescale by sliding left or right.
5. View Shortcuts—View Shortcuts provides a quick switch from the active view to five different views: Gantt Chart, Task Usage, Team Planner, Resource Sheet, and Report.
6. Scheduling Mode selector—Scheduling Mode reports the default scheduling mode (manual or automatic) for each new task. To change it, click Control and choose the desired setting from the list (a change only applies to the active schedule). See the next section for more on Scheduling Mode.

3-7b Setting up Your First Project

There are two scheduling modes in MS Project 2016: Auto Scheduled and Manually Scheduled. Auto scheduling calculates the project's running schedule based on task start and finish dates, as well as other changes you might make in the future. Manually Scheduled is the default setting, but we will change that immediately to take advantage of the program's automatic scheduling powers. To change the scheduling mode, do the following (Exhibit 3.18):

7. With a blank, new project open, click **File tab**>>**Options**>>**Schedule**.
8. In the "Scheduling options for this project" section:
    • Change the dropdown to "**All New Projects**"
    • Change the "New tasks created" option to "**Auto Scheduled**"
9. Click **OK**.

Note: This action sets all future projects you may start in MS Project to Auto Scheduled. These options allow you to change this setting on a project-by-project basis, or you can simply click the "Scheduling Mode Selector" shortcut on the left-hand side of the bottom status bar and choose your desired scheduling method.

3-7c Define Your Project

Next, you need to define your project by entering the following information:

1. Set the project start date (Exhibit 3.19)
    • Click **Project tab**>>**Project Information**
    • In the dialog box, enter your project's start date (e.g., Mon 10/16/17)
    • Click **OK**; you'll notice Timeline View has updated with your start date!
2. Enter identifying information about the project (Exhibit 3.20).
    • Click **File tab**

EXHIBIT 3.18

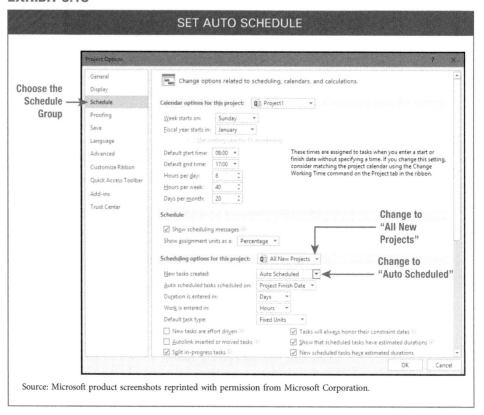

Source: Microsoft product screenshots reprinted with permission from Microsoft Corporation.

EXHIBIT 3.19

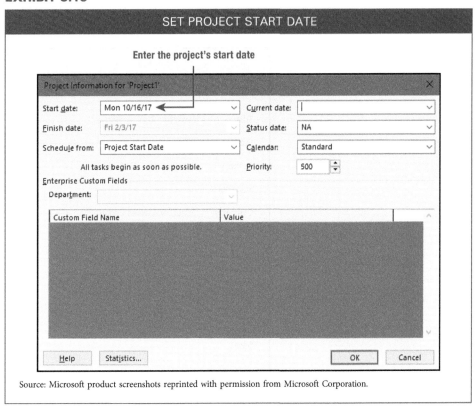

Source: Microsoft product screenshots reprinted with permission from Microsoft Corporation.

- On the right-hand side of the screen, click **Project Information>>Advanced Properties**.
- In the **Summary tab**, enter "Suburban Park Homes" in the Title box
- Add other information as needed for future reports
- Click **OK**

3. Generate a "Project Summary" task row (Exhibit 3.21)

Creating a Project Summary task row gives you another overview of the entire project in the top row of the Gantt Chart view

- Click **File tab>>Options>>Advanced**
- On the Advanced page, scroll to the "Display options for this project" section
- Click the checkbox for "**Show project summary task**"
- Click **OK**; you'll notice a new summary row at the top of the Gantt Chart table!

3-7d Create a Milestone Schedule

You will now create a milestone schedule that will capture significant deliverable completion dates and be viewable in your Gantt Chart view.

- Click the Gantt Chart view to make it active
- Enter the milestone names from the *Suburban Park Homes* project in the "Task Name" cells below the Project Summary row (You can find milestone information from the project on page 91.)
- In the Duration cells, use the up/down arrows to set each milestone's value to zero

EXHIBIT 3.20

ENTER IDENTIFYING INFORMATION

Suburban Park Homes Properties   ?   ✕

General   Summary   Statistics   Contents   Custom

Title: Suburban Park Homes ◄─────────────────

Subject: Building Project ◄──────────────────

Author: Art Vandelay, PMP ◄─────────────────

Manager:

Company: Suburban Homes Construction ◄────────

Category:

Keywords:

Comments:

Hyperlink
base:

Template:

☐ Save preview picture

                            OK   Cancel

Source: Microsoft product screenshots reprinted with permission from Microsoft Corporation.

- For each milestone row:
    a.   Double-click the milestone name to activate the "Task Information" dialog box (Exhibit 3.22)
    b.   Click the **Advanced tab**; change the Constraint type to "**Must Finish On**"
    c.   In the Constraint date box, enter the milestone date
    d.   Click **OK**

Your milestone schedule in the Gantt Chart view should now look like the example in Exhibit 3.23.

Now, we will add milestone markers to the summary row so the key project dates will remain easily visible as the Gantt Chart task list expands.

- Right-click the **Suburban Park Homes summary task row>>Information**
- On the **General tab**, check the "Hide Bar" and "Rollup" boxes
- Click **OK** (Exhibit 3.24)
- Hold the **Shift** key and click your first task row>>click the last task row
- Now all tasks should be selected
- **Right-click** on the selected group>>**Information**
- On the **General tab**, check the "Rollup" box until a checkmark appears
- Click **OK** (Exhibit 3.25)

EXHIBIT 3.21

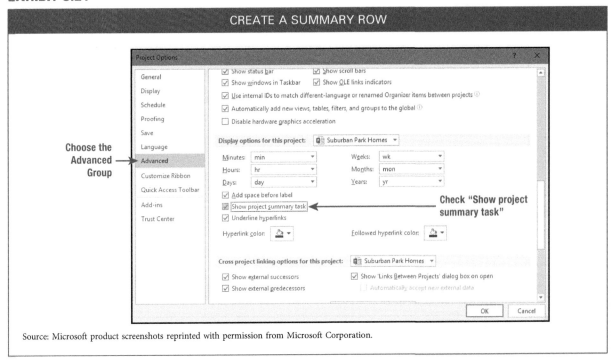

Source: Microsoft product screenshots reprinted with permission from Microsoft Corporation.

EXHIBIT 3.22

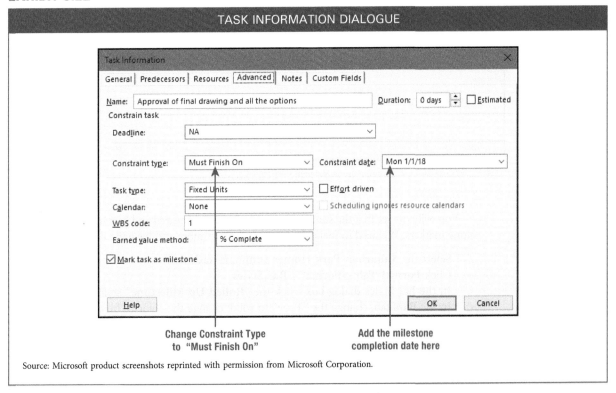

Source: Microsoft product screenshots reprinted with permission from Microsoft Corporation.

EXHIBIT 3.23

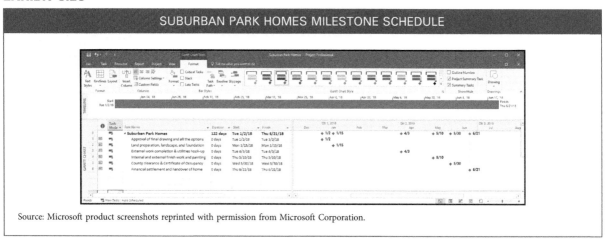

SUBURBAN PARK HOMES MILESTONE SCHEDULE

Source: Microsoft product screenshots reprinted with permission from Microsoft Corporation.

EXHIBIT 3.24

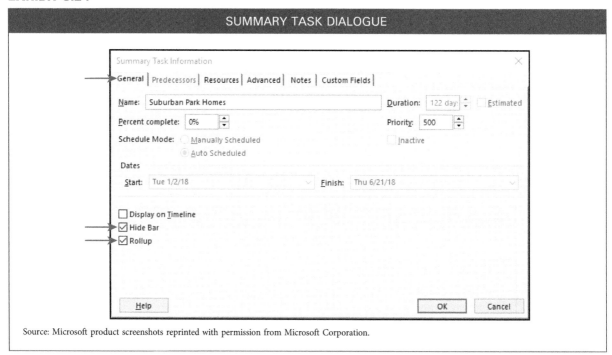

SUMMARY TASK DIALOGUE

Source: Microsoft product screenshots reprinted with permission from Microsoft Corporation.

You will now see that the summary row "bar" has disappeared and been replaced with milestone markers. We need to make them stand out a bit more and have the date (Exhibit 3.26).

- Select the **Suburban Park Homes summary task row**
- Click **Format Tab>>Format>>Bar Styles**
- In the Bar Styles dialog box, click the "**Rolled Up Milestone**" style
- In the **Bars** tab, change the "Type" to solid; change the color to blue (or your choice!)
- Click the **Text** tab, click "**Right**" (or Left if you prefer!), choose "**Finish**" from the drop-down
- Click **OK**

EXHIBIT 3.25

MULTIPLE TASK INFORMATION DIALOGUE

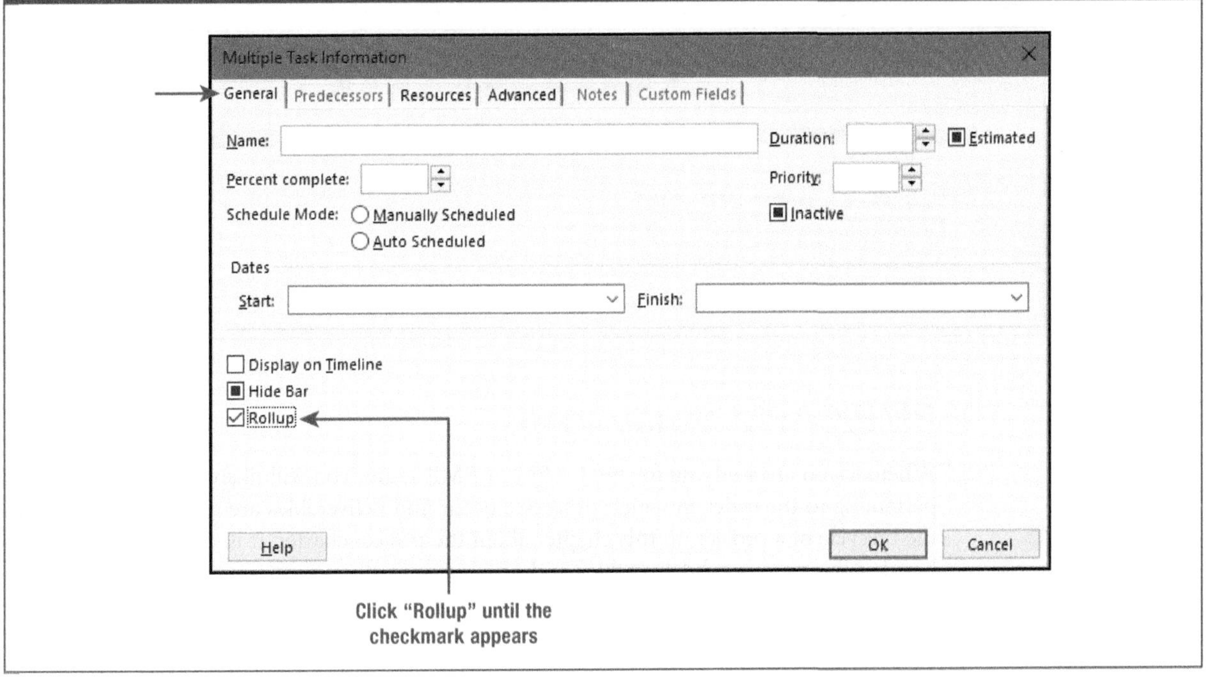

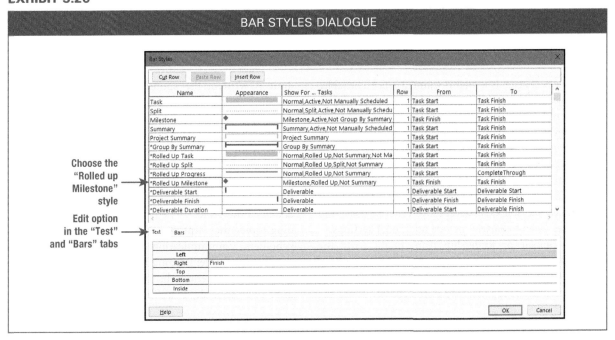

Click "Rollup" until the
checkmark appears

EXHIBIT 3.26

BAR STYLES DIALOGUE

Choose the
"Rolled up
Milestone"
style

Edit option
in the "Test"
and "Bars" tabs

Your milestone schedule in the Gantt Chart view should now look like the example in Exhibit 3.27.

EXHIBIT 3.27

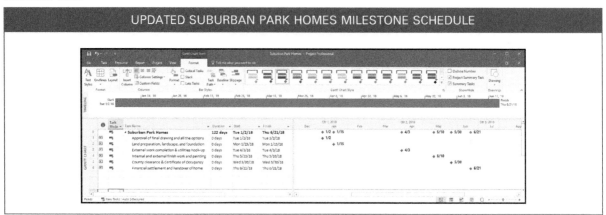

UPDATED SUBURBAN PARK HOMES MILESTONE SCHEDULE

PMP/CAPM Study Ideas

Whether you are studying for the CAPM or PMP exam, you will likely see many questions pertaining to the order in which processes occur and deliverables are produced throughout the lifecycle of a project. In this chapter about the project charter, it is important to remember that the various subdeliverables and processes are all encompassed within the *Initiating* phase. In fact, it is the ratification of the project charter that allows us to proceed from the *Initiating* to the *Planning* phase.

In other words, even though the charter and its components represent a high-level project plan, you should think of this as the "preplanning" because it is still in rough-draft form and will be significantly expanded upon during the *Planning* phase. So, if you plan to sit for one of these tests, make sure you know the logical order of the steps involved in creating a charter, but also keep in mind that every single one of these precedes the more-detailed processes to come.

Summary

The project charter is a vital document since it enables the project sponsor and project manager to reach mutual understanding and agreement on the project at a high level. Often, core team members who have been preassigned and sometimes a key stakeholder or two sign also sign the charter. All parties can commit to the intent of the charter with confidence. Charters typically include sections such as a scope overview, business case, milestone schedule, acceptance criteria, risks, and signatures. Many charters include additional sections.

The sponsor or leadership team might write the rough draft of the business case and scope overview, but the project manager and core team typically write the rough draft of the majority of the charter. Once the

draft is written, the sponsor meets with the project manager and core team to go over the charter in detail both to ensure understanding and to reach agreement.

The charter, by signaling commitment on the part of the team and authorization on the part of the sponsor, is the document that completes the project initiating stage. Once the charter is complete, the project team can usually turn their attention to planning the details of the project. The first detailed behavioral planning topics that deal with the project team, other stakeholders, communication, and leadership form the next book module: Leading Projects. The other detailed planning topics tend to be more technical and form the third book module: Planning Projects.

Key Terms Consistent with PMI Standards and Guides

project charter, 63
requirements, 65
scope creep, 66

milestone schedule, 66
acceptance criteria, 67
risk, 68

Chapter Review Questions

1. What is a charter?
2. Describe what an effective charter should accomplish.
3. How is a charter like a contract? How is it different from a contract?
4. How long should a typical charter be?
5. Signing the charter marks the transition between which two project stages?
6. Who generally writes the rough draft of a charter?
7. Give three reasons for using a charter.
8. What are some typical elements of a charter?
9. What is scope creep and how can it be prevented?
10. When would a background section be helpful?
11. On most small to medium-sized projects, how many intermediate milestones should be identified in the charter?
12. What types of resources might be included in a resources-needed section of a charter?
13. Name three reasons project managers and teams should look at risk.
14. Why should each contingency plan have an "owner" who is responsible for it?
15. What are the four columns of the milestone schedule?
16. With whom might the project manager and project team need to negotiate when creating the charter?
17. What is the primary difference between "Auto" and "Manually" scheduled settings in Microsoft Project?

Discussion Questions

1. Identify the purpose of each element in a project charter.
2. Explain how a charter helps secure both formal and informal commitment.
3. How are risks, assumptions, and constraints related?
4. If you are a project manager and have the choice of forming your core team before or after charter approval, which would you do and why?
5. List and describe at least four lessons you have learned from previous projects. Relate how each is valuable in planning a new project.
6. In your opinion, what are the three most important items in your project charter? How did each help you initiate your project better?
7. Give an example of how an incorrect assumption could become a risk.
8. Briefly summarize the process of creating a milestone schedule.
9. How are *project* scope and *product* scope similar and different?
10. Upon seeing the rough draft of your charter, your project sponsor asks you to move the finish date up by two months. What do you do?
11. What are the greatest advantages to using a computerized scheduling program like Microsoft Project?

PMBOK® Guide Questions

1. Which of the following is *not* a purpose of an approved project charter?
   a. formally authorizes the existence of a project
   b. provides detailed information about financial resources
   c. helps the team and sponsor develop a foundational understanding of project requirements
   d. provides project manager with authority to apply organizational resources to the project
2. Adding to the project after it has already begun without making adjustments to time, cost, or resources, is known as:
   a. scope creep
   b. risk
   c. milestones
   d. acceptance criteria
3. "It is inconvenient and time consuming for employees to walk across campus every day to

eat lunch, which is why we need an employee lunchroom in our building" is an example of:
a. project scope
b. business case
c. milestone schedule
d. constraint

4. What information does the project charter contain that signifies how the customer or user of the final product, service, or result will judge the deliverables, in order to determine that they have been completed satisfactorily?
a. high-level project risks
b. measurable objectives and acceptance criteria
c. high-level project boundaries
d. project assumptions

5. The project charter should include "factors that are considered to be true, real, or certain without proof or demonstration." These are known as _____.
a. risks
b. assumptions
c. high-level requirements
d. objectives

6. The signing of the project charter represents all of these *except*:
a. a formal acknowledgment of the sponsor's commitment to the project
b. the formal approval of the detailed project schedule
c. authorization to transition from the high-level project initiation stage into the more detailed project planning stage
d. the organization's commitment to apply resources to the project

7. What project charter component documents significant points or events in the project and, per the author, may be developed most effectively when combined with other information such as acceptance criteria?
a. network diagram
b. Gantt chart

c. stakeholder management strategy
d. summary milestone schedule

8. You are the project manager. Upon presenting your charter to your sponsor, she requests several changes. What do you do?
a. Agree to all the changes in order to make your sponsor happy.
b. Refuse to change the charter, since that would be unfair to your team.
c. Have your team vote on whether or not to make the changes and go with the will of the majority.
d. Negotiate with your sponsor to see how you can best accommodate her requests without agreeing to unreasonable expectations.

9. The charter is the primary deliverable of a project's _____ phase.
a. Selecting
b. Initiating
c. Planning
d. Executing

10. According to the PMBOK, the rough order of magnitude for the summary budget within the project charter is _____.
a. −100% to 200% accuracy
b. −25% to +75% accuracy
c. −5% to +10% accuracy
d. none of the above

11. After identifying potential project risks, the project team should then _____.
a. develop risk response plans for all identified risks.
b. wait for the sponsor to conduct a risk assessment.
c. move on to other components of the charter, since identifying risks is the only risk-related activity in the *initiating* phase.
d. assess each risk based on probability and likely impact, and then create a risk response plan for each major risk.

Exercises

1. Consider a major team project for a class. Write the scope overview and business case sections of a charter.

2. Write the business case and scope overview sections of a project charter for a project in which your company is considering buying out another company.

3. You are part of a student team that is going to host a picnic-style party as a fundraiser event for a deserving local nonprofit. Develop a milestone schedule with acceptance criteria for this event. Include between four and eight milestones.

4. You are part of a student team that has volunteered to host an alumni event at a recently reopened museum in the downtown part of your city. The event has the twin purposes of establishing contacts with long-lost alumni and raising awareness of the newly reopened museum. Brainstorm the potential risks for this, quantify them both according to probability and impact, assign responsibility for each major risk, and create one or more contingency plans for each major risk.

5. You are part of a student team that is hosting a number of inner-city junior high and high school students from several nearby cities at your campus for a weekend. The primary purpose is to encourage them to attend college and, second, to attend

your college. Identify as many stakeholders as possible for this project, prioritize them, and list the interests each has in your project.

6. You have started a project working with your peers at your rival college to create a "crosstown help-out." You want to encourage many people in the community to contribute a day's work on a Saturday for various community projects. You have a rather heated rivalry with this other college. Create a comprehensive set of team operating principles to use on this project. Which of these principles is most important and why? Do you expect any of them to be difficult to enforce and why? What do you plan to do if some of them do not work?

INTEGRATED EXAMPLE PROJECTS
SUBURBAN HOMES CONSTRUCTION PROJECT

Scope Overview

Building a single-family, partially custom-designed home as required by Mrs. and Mr. John Thomas on Strath Dr., Alpharetta, Georgia. The single-family home will have the following features:

- 3,200 square-feet home with 4 bedrooms and 2.5 bathrooms
- Flooring—hard wood in the first floor, tiles in the kitchen and bathrooms, carpet in bedrooms
- Granite kitchen countertops, GE appliances in the kitchen
- 3-car garage and external landscaping
- Ceiling—10′ in first floor and vaulted 9′ ceilings in bedrooms

Business Case

Suburban Homes is in the business of constructing high-quality homes at an affordable cost with luxury options to provide quality of life for families. The business strategy is to use the best construction technologies and practices to enhance productivity and increase profits, while offering cost-effective and best-value homes for all its customers simultaneously. The current project, "Suburban Park Homes," is aimed to expand business operations in Georgia.

Milestone Schedule and Deliverables

CM–Construction Manager; PM–Project Manager

Milestone	Completion Date	Stakeholder Judge	Acceptance Criteria
Approval of final drawing and all the options	2nd January	Client	PM and the client to approve
Land preparation, landscape, and foundation	15th January	CM	PM and CM approval
External work completion and utilities hookup	3rd April	CM	PM and CM approval
Internal and external finish work and painting	10th May	CM	PM and CM approval
County clearance and Certificate of Occupancy	30th May	CM	County Inspectors and PM
Financial settlement and handover of home	21st June	PM, Client	Design Specifications–approval by PM and the client

Risks

Project Risks	Risk Owner	Contingency Plans
County approval and permissions	Suburban Homes, PM	None
County Property Taxes hike	Client, Suburban Homes	Document as contract clause
Traffic congestion	Client, County, DMV	None

Resources Required

- Funding: the client, underwriters, and Suburban Homes
- People: Suburban project management team, contractors, subcontractors, and skilled labor
- Equipment: construction equipment, tools, and machinery
- Material: building materials, appliances, landscaping, shrubs, and trees

Stakeholders

Stakeholders	Interest in Project
Primary: The client Suburban Homes County Officers	Overall project cost, time, quality Overall project cost, time, quality, success criteria Adherence to the county standards
Others: Contractors Suppliers Utility companies	Timely payment of invoices Business expansion, profits Adherence to laws, business expansion

Team Operating Principles

- Commitment to project schedule: Project team and contractors will complete their assigned work as per schedule.
- Progress Meetings: Construction team meetings scheduled on Mondays at 8 a.m. every week and as demanded by work progress. Members should prepare for these meetings with information required for review.
- Communication: Regular updates of status, reporting issues, and weekly progress reports.

Lessons Learned

- Team participation in developing project schedule is critical.
- Transparent communication is encouraged for resolving issues.
- Conflicts must be reported to the construction manager immediately.
- County laws and utility standards must not be compromised.

Commitment

Sponsor	Department/Organization	Signature

Project Manager	Department/Organization	Signature

Core Team Members	Department/Organization	Signature

CASA DE PAZ DEVELOPMENT PROJECT

Questions for Students to Answer:

1. Given the information provided in Chapter 2 on how this project was selected, create scope overview and business case sections for a charter.

2. If you were the project manager, what expertise would you like from the sponsor, stakeholders, or core team members to create a milestone schedule with acceptance criteria?

3. Work with at least two other people and brainstorm pertinent risks. Assess them to determine which you believe are major risks, and develop at least one response for each major risk.

4. Who are the key stakeholders for this project and what is the interest of each? Which stakeholders have the most power?

Semester Project Instructions

Determine one member of your student project team to be the primary contact with the project sponsor (the manager or executive who came to class when projects were announced). The sponsor is also the customer representative. This sponsor was encouraged by your professor to come with a draft of the business case and scope overview sections of the charter, but some sponsors probably did a better job than others. You need to ensure that you understand these statements and how they fit with the organization's goals.

Then, your student team needs to draft the remainder of the charter with as much help as you can get from the sponsor and/or other people at the organization.

Once the charter is in rough-draft form, submit it for comments to your professor. Armed with the professor's suggestions, you can present it to your sponsor and any other people your sponsor chooses. Often, this may involve a leadership team, department heads (functional managers), and/or project team members. One difference on this project is that your student team will likely do most of the planning and only part of the execution, while members of the organization for whom you are planning the project will need to complete the execution. Therefore, you need to consider how you will transition responsibility over to the parent organization near the end of the class.

PROJECT MANAGEMENT *IN ACTION*

Information Systems Enhancement Project Charter

The following charter was used when a nonprofit agency formed a project team to upgrade its information systems. Comments on the left side give advice

from a communications perspective regarding how to write a project charter, and comments on the right side offer suggestions regarding the content of each section.

DESIGN PRINCIPLES

Headings:

Headings facilitate *scanning* by identifying information covered in each section.

Heading descriptions should accurately indicate the information that follows.

Lists:

Listing techniques help readers remember key details of a message.

Numbers, bullets, and other ordering devices promote retention and improve visual design.

Lists are best limited to five points so they do not look overwhelming to readers.

Lists are written in parallel structure, with the first word of each item having the same grammatical form, such as all nouns, all verbs, or all *-ing* words.

PROJECT CHARTER: INFORMATION SYSTEMS ENHANCEMENT PLAN

Scope Overview

This team will implement a new information system based on a needs assessment of personnel of the agency. The project team will detail technological issues, as well as upward, downward, and lateral communications issues within each department and recommend software package options for each program area. The sponsor will select a vendor, and the project team will oversee implementation.

Business Case—Objective

The agency needs to overhaul its information systems to increase productivity for staff, and create additional learning opportunities for clients. It is estimated that 20 percent more clients will be served with the new system.

MILESTONE	COMPLETION DATE	STAKEHOLDER JUDGE	ACCEPTANCE CRITERIA
Outdated facility, poor productivity	Start 1/6/18		
Staff survey	1/31/18	Sponsor	Discussion with department heads
Software recommendations	3/14/18	Operations Manager	All areas included, pilot results
Vendor selected	3/28/18	Sponsor	Best meets qualifications
Technology in place	5/9/18	Project Manager	System test demonstration
Updated facility, productivity improved	5/30/18	Sponsor	Two-week data reports from department heads

CONTENT PRINCIPLES

Scope Overview:

The scope overview defines the major deliverables. It sets project boundaries by clarifying what is included and, sometimes, what is not included.

Business Case:

The business case defines project objectives and why they are important to the parent organization.

Milestone Schedule:

The milestone schedule shows the project starting point, a few major milestones, and the ending point.

Acceptance Criteria Factors:

These identify which stakeholder will judge the acceptability of each milestone and what criteria they will use.

DESIGN PRINCIPLES

Tables:

Use tables to organize complex information into an easy-to-follow column and row format.

Design tables so they make sense when read independently of the text.

Use table headings that reflect logical groupings of information.

Phrase column language so it is in parallel structure.

Character Formatting:

Use character formatting, including boldface, italics, underlines, and centering to highlight headings.

Use character formatting hierarchically. Boldface, underlines, and all caps are best for major headings. Use fewer or less dramatic techniques for subheadings.

Type Size and Face:

Use 10-, 11-, or 12-point type for most documents. People who have poor vision often prefer larger type.

Use a conventional typeface, such as Arial, Times Roman, or Palatino.

White Space:

Use white space to separate document sections attractively and to improve readability.

Page Breaks:

When possible, complete entire sections on the same page. Redesign documents where one or two lines of text from a section run onto the next page.

Major Risks

RISK	RISK OWNER	RESPONSE PLANS
System may not work properly	Technical lead	Define top defect and focus on it exclusively until fixed.
Implementation may cost too much	Accountant	Identify areas of cost reduction and added funding.
Lack of sponsor buy-in	Project Manager	1. Conduct staff survey to identify most-needed capabilities. 2. Understand sponsor requirements.

Resources Needed

This project will require the project manager to spend 50% of her time and the lead user and 3 core team members 25% of their time for 5 months. The budget estimate is $45,000.

Stakeholder List

STAKEHOLDER	INTEREST IN PROJECT
Board Sponsor Department Heads	Overall cost and overall project success Overall project success, resource needs; Impact on their department, resource needs
Lead user	New work methods, productivity increases

CONTENT PRINCIPLES

Project Risks and Assumptions:

This section identifies major risks and how the team will either reduce their probability of happening and/or their impact if they do occur. One person is assigned responsibility for each risk.

Resources Needed:

This is an estimate of the money, personnel, and other resources expected to be needed.

Stakeholder List:

Identifies those individuals and groups who have an interest in either the project process and/or results.

DESIGN PRINCIPLES

Sentences:

To express complex ideas effectively and to make ideas easy for readers to understand, compose most sentences to be 15–25 words long.

Simple Language:

So all readers understand your language easily, substitute short, action-oriented, easily understood words for long, unfamiliar, and unpronounceable words.

Team Operating Principles

- Commitment to timetable. The project management team members will complete their assigned work on time.
- Regularly scheduled project team and sponsorship meetings. Project team meetings will be held every Saturday at 4:15 p.m. The team will also communicate via e-mail as required. Sponsorship meetings with the agency staff will be held bimonthly and as-needed.
- Timely communication. The project management team will communicate status, issues, and questions with agency via e-mail or conference call weekly. Project actions will be distributed to the team every Monday.
- Majority rule. The project management team will negotiate and resolve issues on a majority-rule basis.

Lessons Learned

- Agreeing on project scope is a key preliminary project planning activity.
- Maintaining project goals and timeline requires open communication and quick issue resolution.
- Understanding roles and responsibilities facilitates smooth teamwork and timely project completion.

Commitment

Sponsor	Projec Manager
Lead User	Core ˉeam Member
Core Team Member	Core ˉeam Member

CONTENT PRINCIPLES

Operating Principles:

Operating principles indicate agreement on deadlines, meetings, decision making, and how participants will treat each other with respect.

Lessons Learned:

This section highlights specific learnings from previous similar projects that will help the team copy good practices and avoid problems.

Commitment:

Project principals signal agreement in principle to the project, recognizing that some of the specifics will probably change when the detailed planning is complete.

References

A Guide to the Project Management Body of Knowledge (PMBOK® Guide), 6th ed. (Newtown Square, PA: Project Management Institute, Inc., 2017).

Altwies, Diane, and Frank Reynolds, *Achieve CAPM Exam Success: A Concise Study Guide and Desk Reference* (Ft. Lauderdale, FL: J. Ross Publishing, 2010).

Assudani, Rashmi, and Timothy J. Kloppenborg, "Managing Stakeholders for Project Management Success: An Emergent Model of Stakeholders," *Journal of General Management* 35 (3) (Spring 2010): 67–80.

Evans, James R., and William M. Lindsay, *The Management and Control of Quality*, 8th ed. (Mason, OH: Cengage, 2011).

Johnson, Craig E., *Meeting the Ethical Challenges of Leadership* (Los Angeles: Sage, 2009).

Kloppenborg, Timothy J., and Laurence J. Laning, *Strategic Leadership of Portfolio and Project Management* (New York: Business Expert Press, 2012).

Kloppenborg, Timothy J., and Joseph A. Petrick, *Managing Project Quality* (Vienna, VA: Management Concepts, Inc., 2002).

PMI Lexicon of Project Management Terms–Version 3.0 (Newtown Square, PA: Project Management Institute, Inc., 2015).

Skilton, Paul F., and Kevin J. Dooley, "The Effects of Repeat Collaboration on Creative Abrasion," *Academy of Management Review* 35 (1) (2010): 118–134.

Endnotes

1. *PMI Lexicon of Project Management Terms–Version 3.0*, 2015: 13.

2. Kloppenborg, Timothy J., and Joseph A. Petrick, *Managing Project Quality* (Vienna, VA: Management Concepts, Inc., 2002): 39.

3. PMI Lexicon of Project Management Terms Version 3.0 (Newtown Square, PA, 2015): 7.

PART 2

LEADING PROJECTS

ORGANIZE **LEAD** PLAN PERFORM

Leading for success in project management includes leading the parent organization that is conducting the project, leading the project team, and leading the various stakeholders who care about the project in one way or another. Chapter 4 deals with the parent organization giving ideas about how the organizational structure, organizational culture, project life cycle model, and roles of various players impact a project. Chapter 5 includes acquiring, developing, and leading the project team. Chapter 6 includes engaging stakeholders, managing communications, and running project meetings.

CHAPTER 4

Organizational Capability: Structure, Culture, and Roles

After completing this chapter, you should be able to:

CORE OBJECTIVES:

- Compare and contrast the advantages and disadvantages of the functional, project, strong matrix, balanced matrix, and weak matrix methods of organization; describe how each operates and when to use each.
- Relate how an organization's structure influences the implementation of its strategic plan.
- Describe organizational culture elements that are helpful in planning and managing projects and demonstrate how to overcome organizational culture elements that hinder project success.
- Describe different project life cycle models and distinguish when each is appropriate.

BEHAVIORAL OBJECTIVES:

- Describe the duties, motivations, and challenges of each of the executive, managerial, and team roles in projects and list important attributes for selecting each.
- Given a project situation, explain ethical behavior consistent with PMI's Code of Ethics and Professional Conduct.
- Predict the impact of organizational structure and associated culture on individual and team behaviors.
- Predict the impact of organizational structure and associated culture on individual and team performance.

Monkey Business Images/Shutterstock.com

We implement project management best practices for the purpose of increasing the likelihood for project success. Formerly, as an executive, I was responsible for establishing, operating, and evolving a national project management office (PMO) for one of the nation's largest print/mail and electronic outsourcing firms. **Organizational structure, culture, roles** and responsibilities of project participants, and **project life cycle standard processes and tools** were critical influencers to achieving project success. As there is no single way to implement project management, how we chose to address each influencer shaped the way projects were managed. A snapshot of our approach follows:

From an operations perspective, there was a strategic need to implement a centralized approach to project management. Through a number of mergers and acquisitions, 10 geographically dispersed operation centers were servicing a broad range of expanding customer needs. As a result, two key factors were at play. One: the customer base was growing from regionally based to nationally based customers. Two: the best-of-the-best operations technology needed to be leveraged across all centers. Structurally, the decision was made to consolidate

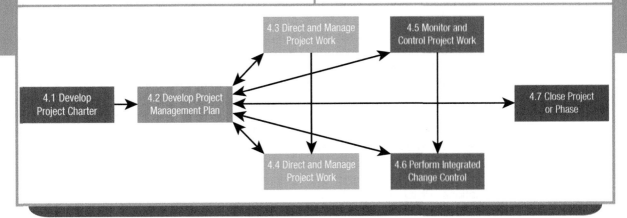

PMBOK® 6E	PRIMARY OUTPUTS
1.2 Foundational elements	Life Cycle and Development Approach
2.4 Organizational systems	
3.4 Project manager competencies	Leader Roles and Responsibilities

operation centers to three, geographically in the East, Central, and West. This meant that internal and external projects that applied nationally could no longer be managed at a regional level using only regional resources. A new type of project manager was needed to manage national resources using a standardized set of practices. Creating a matrixed project organization to serve the functional organization was the first phase.

Monkey Business Images/Shutterstock.com

Ensuring the culture would accept and support these changes was critical to success as change is not easy and resistance was anticipated. Senior management buy-in was essential and plans were implemented to dialogue, collaborate, and communicate the benefits of a PMO throughout the organization. The PMO's first mission was to establish national project management standards and manage a select few strategic national projects with a limited set of project managers. Proof of concept was key to continued buy-in. Clear roles and responsibilities for executive sponsors, project managers, and project team members were collaboratively established. Standard processes and tools used by the project teams were jointly developed. Training occurred from the executive suite to project managers and project team members. As time progressed, project success rates increased and the PMO responsibilities were expanded to include the project management of all strategic operational projects and new customer implementations. Career paths for regional project managers were established. Selected regional project managers were promoted and trained to be national project managers. The organizational structure changed with selected regional project managers reporting to the national PMO. The executive sponsorship roles continued to evolve along with standard processes and practices to facilitate new responsibilities. In *Improving Executive Sponsorship of Projects: A Holistic Approach,* additional insight on each influencer, considerations, pitfalls, and tips for project management implementation approaches can be found.[1]

—*Dawne E. Chandler, PhD, PMP*

Chapter 2 dealt with organizational issues of strategic planning, selecting, and resourcing projects. Chapter 3 details how to initiate a project—usually by composing and ratifying a charter. This chapter introduces both project leadership and project planning. Leadership in this chapter includes organizational structure and culture along with roles of all key project participants. Planning is introduced in the selection of the project life cycle approach and introduction to the concept of a project plan. Both project leadership and planning lead to project success, as shown in Exhibit 4.1. Effectively leading project team members and other stakeholders leads to a foundation of respect and trust, which, in turn leads to project success. Effective project planning lays the groundwork for effective project execution, monitoring, control, and closeout, which also lead to project success.

EXHIBIT 4.1

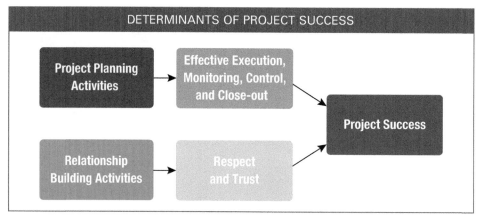

4-1 Types of Organizational Structures

Contemporary companies choose among various methods for establishing their organizational structure. Organization structure is often developed by grouping people together based on criteria such as functional or technical skills or long-term activities. The structure size and complexity increase with the increase in the number of employees. The structure is the way in which an organization divides its people into distinct tasks to achieve coordination among all these groups. Organizational structure can be considered to include work assignments, reporting relationships, and decision-making responsibility. Each method of structuring organizations has strengths and weaknesses. In this section, we will investigate various organizational methods and the impact of each on managing projects. The advantages and disadvantages of each organizational form are discussed in the following sections and then summarized in Exhibit 4.5.

4-1a Functional

A **functional organization** is "an organizational structure in which staff is grouped by areas of specialization and the project manager has limited authority to assign work and apply resources."[2] This is the traditional approach in which there are clear lines of authority according to type of work. For example, all accountants might report to a head of accounting, all marketers report to a head of marketing, and so on. An organizational chart for a functional organization is shown in Exhibit 4.2. Note that everyone in the organization reports up through one and only one supervisor. That supervisor is the head of a discipline or function (such as marketing).

The functional manager generally controls the project budget, makes most project decisions, and is the primary person who coordinates project communications outside the functional areas by contacting his or her peer functional managers.

ADVANTAGES   One advantage of the functional form of organization is called *unity of command*—all workers understand clearly what they need to do because only one "boss" is

EXHIBIT 4.2

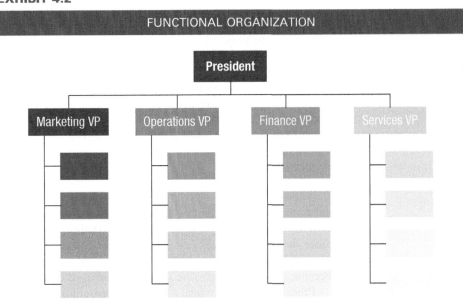

giving them instructions. Communication is vertical and clearly established. Another advantage is that since all workers in a discipline report to the same supervisor, they will have an opportunity to interact frequently and can learn readily from each other and keep their technical skills sharp. Having the same supervisor also acts as a motivating factor for several employees to maintain and improve their technical expertise. A third advantage is that workers know that when they finish work on a project, they will still have a job because they will continue to report to the same functional manager. For small projects that require most of the work from one department, the functional organization often works well, both because of the advantages already stated and because the functional manager can share resources among various small projects and centrally control the work.

DISADVANTAGES   That said, the functional form of organization can slow down communications when multiple functions need to have input. It also can be challenging from a technical standpoint if input is required from multiple disciplines. The functional manager is probably quite good within his or her domain, but may have less understanding of other disciplines. However, in small organizations where most people have been forced to understand multiple areas, this may be less of an issue. Coordination between departments is frequently conducted at the manager level as the functional managers have a great deal of decision-making authority. This often means communication needs to first travel up from an employee at a low level in the structure to the manager, then across from one functional manager to another manager, and then down from the manager to an employee at a low level who will be working on it. This can become more complex when organizations have multiple levels of hierarchy within functional divisions and a chain of command must be followed. In short, coordination in a functional organization is complex and time consuming. These long communication channels often make for slow decision making and slow response to change. Integration becomes difficult and it may lead to frustration and a decrease in motivation and innovation. Also, decisions will tend to favor the strongest functional group or division. For these reasons, some organizations choose other forms of organization.

4-1b Projectized

The exact opposite form of functional organization is the **projectized organization**, which is defined as "group employees, collocated or not, by activities on a particular project. The project manager in a projectized structure may have complete, or very close to complete, power over the project team."[3] In this organizational form, the larger organization is broken down into self-contained units that support large projects, geographies, or customers. Most people in the organization are assigned to a project and report upward through the project manager, as can be seen in Exhibit 4.3. While the structure of the two organizational charts appears similar, the reporting manager is a project manager instead of a functional manager. The project manager has extensive authority for budgets, personnel, and other decision-making issues in this organizational structure. This provides adequate time for the project manager to make decisions. Projectized organization structure provides an opportunity to maintain expertise on a given project.

ADVANTAGES   The advantages of the projectized organizational form are very different from the advantages of the functional form. Because people from different functions now report to the same project manager, traditional department barriers are reduced. Since the project manager is responsible for communications, response times and decision making tend to be swift. All workers understand clearly what they need to do because only one "boss"—the project manager—is giving them instructions.

Projectized organizational structures often utilize the technique of **co-location**, which is "an organizational technique in which the project team members are moved to

EXHIBIT 4.3

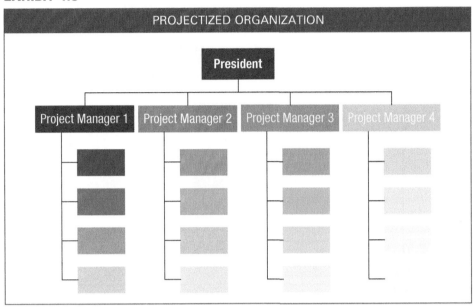

alternate locations (either full time or only for parts of days) to allow them to better work with one another, and on the project in general."[4] This co-location often results in enhanced project team identity as well as trust, collaboration, coordination, strong customer focus, and effective integration of effort on the project.

DISADVANTAGES   However, this organizational form also has disadvantages. Team members are often assigned to just one project, even if the project only needs part of their time, which leads to idle time. This can be costly because project team members are retained during and even after completing the project. Since the project manager is in charge and the team may be physically located on-site rather than with the rest of the organization, some projects tend to develop their own work methods and disregard those of the parent organization. While some of the new methods may be quite useful, project teams not watched closely can fail to practice important organizational cultural norms, or accepted practices, and they sometimes fail to pass the lessons they learn on to other project teams. Team members who are co-located, while learning more about the broader project issues, often do not keep up their discipline-specific competence as well. Team members sometimes worry about what they will do when the project is completed, which leads to adverse motivational, morale, and security issues. In short, motivating people could become a challenge.

4-1c Matrix

Each of the extreme strategies already described (extreme in the sense that either the functional manager or the project manager has a great deal of authority) has strong advantages, but also significant weaknesses. In an attempt to capture many of the advantages of both, and to hopefully not have too many of the weaknesses of either, many organizations use an intermediate organizational strategy in which both the project manager and the functional manager have some authority and share other authority.

This intermediate strategy is the **matrix organization**, which is "any organization in which the project manager or project team leader actually shares responsibility for the project with a number of individual functional managers."[5] A matrix organization is shown in Exhibit 4.4. Note that project team members report to both functional and

EXHIBIT 4.4

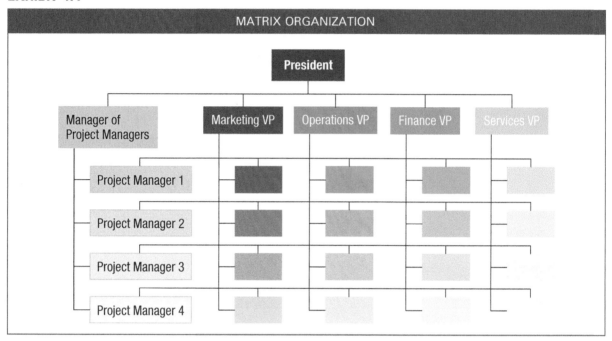

project managers. This is a clear violation of the unity-of-command principle; however, it is necessary to enjoy the benefits of a matrix organization. In short, the hoped-for benefit of a matrix structure is a combination of the task focus of the projectized organizational structure with the technical capability of the functional structure.

ADVANTAGES   Matrix organizations have many advantages, which is why an increasing number of companies are using some variation of them today. One advantage is that because both project and functional managers are involved, there is good visibility into who is working where, and resources can be shared between departments and projects. This reduces possible duplication—a major advantage in this age of lean thinking in business. Since both types of managers are involved, cooperation between departments can be quite good. There is more input, so decisions tend to be high quality and are better accepted. This is a major issue since enthusiastic support for controversial decisions often helps a project team work through challenges. Since people still report to their functional manager, they are able to develop and retain discipline-specific knowledge. Since the various disciplines report to the same project manager, effective integration is still possible. Because people report to both the project manager, who is responsible for capturing lessons learned, and to the functional manager, who is responsible for how the work in a function is performed, lessons learned can be shared effectively between projects. Furthermore, policies and procedures for each project can be set separately. The project manager can commit resources and respond to changes, conflicts, and project needs quickly.

Yet another advantage of the matrix form is its flexibility. The amount of decision-making authority can be shared in whatever manner is desired. When the functional managers have relatively more power, it is almost like a functional organization. This is the way many organizations start evolving—by giving project managers a bit more decision-making authority. This is called a weak matrix since the project managers have less authority than the functional managers. The next step in the progression is a balanced matrix in which project managers and functional managers have about equal

EXHIBIT 4.5

PROGRESSION OF ORGANIZATIONAL FORMS					
ORGANIZATIONAL FORM	FUNCTIONAL	WEAK MATRIX	BALANCED MATRIX	STRONG MATRIX	PROJECTIZED
Who has power?	FM almost all	FM more	Equally shared	PM more	PM almost all

power. Finally, a strong matrix is one where the project managers have more power than functional managers. This is more similar to a projectized organizational form. The progression of forms is shown in Exhibit 4.5.

DISADVANTAGES   The matrix organizational form has drawbacks as well. Some people claim that having two bosses (both a functional manager and a project manager) is a disadvantage. This problem certainly needs to be managed because the two managers may each try to do what they think is best for their project or department and may give conflicting advice. Dual responsibility and accountability can be demotivating for some people. However, this is common territory for most people. Most students take multiple classes per term. Most companies have multiple customers. Having to balance competing demands can be difficult, but it is often the norm. Since more people are providing the necessary input, there are more sources of conflict, more meetings, and more challenges to control. Decisions may not get made as fast. Also, priorities are likely to change routinely.

Firms need to consider which organizational structure is best for them so they can capitalize on its advantages and mitigate its disadvantages. These decisions can change over time. Exhibit 4.6 summarizes a comparison of organizational structures.

Note that in a matrix organization, a new role is inserted in the organizational chart—that of manager of project managers. Sometimes this person leads an office called the project management office (PMO). This does not mean that other organizations cannot have a PMO. In some organizations, an additional manager will be in the reporting chain between the project managers and the person in charge (shown as the president). In other matrix organizations, the project managers report directly to the person in charge. For simplicity, this chart shows each function with four workers and each project with four team members. In reality, some functions may have more workers than others, and some projects may have more team members than others. In fact, some people may only report to a functional manager since they are not currently assigned to a project, and others may report to more than one project manager since they are assigned on a part-time basis to multiple projects. Those people will have more than two supervisors.

While both project managers and functional managers have certain authority in any matrix organization, the extent of this authority can vary substantially. Often, the project manager has authority to determine what work needs to be accomplished and by when. The functional manager often retains authority to determine how the work is accomplished. Sometimes, the two managers will negotiate to determine which workers will be assigned to the project. While both hopefully want the best for the overall organization, each has specific responsibilities. For example, the functional manager with several workers reporting to her wants each employee to have enough work but not be overloaded. She also wants all workers to grow in expertise. The project manager, on the other hand, wants the best workers for the project so she can be more assured of delivering good results. In a case like this, when they negotiate, the project manager may want the best resource (who is already busy), but the functional manager may offer the least experienced resource (who is available).

EXHIBIT 4.6

	FUNCTIONAL	MATRIX	PROJECTIZED
ORGANIZATIONAL STRUCTURE COMPARISON			
Who makes most project decisions?	Functional manager	Shared	Project manager
Advantages	• Good discipline-specific knowledge • Easy for central control • Effective for shared resources • One "boss" • Clear career path for professionals	• Flexible • Easy to share resources • Good cooperation between departments • More input for decisions • Wide acceptance of decisions • Good discipline-specific knowledge • Effective integration on project • Increased knowledge transfer between projects	• Break down department barriers • Shorter response time • Quicker decisions • One "boss" • Enhanced project team identity • Customer focus • Effective integration on project
Disadvantages	• Slow communication between departments • Slow response to change • Slow decision making	• Two "bosses" • Many sources of conflict • More meetings • Slow reaction time • Hard to monitor and control	• Duplication of resources • Rules not always respected • Potential lessons learned can be lost • Discipline-specific knowledge can slip • Less career continuity for project team members

Source: Adapted from Richard L. Daft, *Management,* 9th ed. (Mason, OH: South-Western Cengage Learning, 2010): 250–255; and PMBOK® *Guide,* 21–26.

One other source of potential conflict between the project and functional managers deals with performance reviews. Often, the functional manager is tasked with writing performance reviews, yet some workers may spend a great deal of their time on projects. If the project managers are not allowed to provide input into the performance reviews, some project team members will work harder to please their functional managers and the projects can suffer. One project manager offers ideas regarding performance reviews in Exhibit 4.7.

Closely related to the organizational structure is another organizational decision that needs to be made—that of organizational culture. Project managers are not often part of the executive group that decides on organizational structure or organizational culture,

EXHIBIT 4.7

360-DEGREE PERFORMANCE REVIEWS

In some organizations, the functional manager performs a 360-degree evaluation. This appraisal style requires that the functional manager seek feedback from a representative sample of the staff who have worked with that project team member to provide feedback on a 360-degree form. Being appraised by your peers or team members on a given project is considered best practice because they've observed the individual in action "in the trenches." Many large organizations use this appraisal technique, since in large and/or complex organizations some staff rarely see their direct supervisor or manager, depending upon their function in that organization.

Source: Naomi J. Kinney, CPLP, principle consultant, Multilingual Learning Services.

but they certainly need to understand how these decisions impact reporting relationships, decision-making methods, and commitment for their projects.

4-2 Organizational Culture and Its Impact on Projects

Just as project managers need to understand the structure of the parent organization, they also need to understand the culture of the parent organization if they are to communicate effectively. Organizational culture consists of values, social rituals, symbols, work ethics, organizational behavior, beliefs, and practices that are shared among members of the organization and are taught to new members. "Values serve as a moral compass to guide us and provide a frame of reference to set priorities and determine right or wrong."[6] Values are implemented through social rituals such as meetings, training, and ceremonies, along with symbols such as work layout and dress code.[7] Collectively, these can informally:

- Motivate the ethical actions and communications of managers and subordinates;
- Determine how people are treated, controlled, and rewarded;
- Establish how cooperation, coordination, collaboration, competition, conflict, and decision making are handled; and
- Encourage personal commitment to the organization and justification for its behavior.[8]

Once a project manager understands the culture of the parent organization, he can determine how to best foster the culture within his project. Many projects are completed cooperatively between two or more parent organizations, or one organization (a contractor) will perform the project for the other organization (a client). Whenever more than one parent organization is involved, the project manager needs to understand the culture of each well enough to facilitate effective project communications and decision making.

4-2a Culture of the Parent Organization

When a project manager studies the culture of the parent organization, she needs to ask the following questions:

- What is the corporate culture in general?
- What are the ascribed values?
- Are there standard project management practices and policies?
- How is the organization viewed by others in terms of being true to its values?
- How does the organization like to communicate internally and externally?
- How well does the organization support project management specifically?

TYPES OF POWER   One framework that is helpful in understanding a corporate culture distinguishes the following four types of culture according to what is the most powerful motivator:

1. Power culture
2. Role culture
3. Task culture
4. Personal culture

Power cultures exist when the supervisor exerts a great deal of economic and political power and everyone tries to please the boss. Those in formal authority control competition, conflict resolution, and communication.

Role cultures motivate everyone to understand and closely follow their appointed roles. Reliable workers follow formal designations of responsibility with utmost respect for regulations and laws.

In task cultures, it is more important to get the job done than to worry about who does the work or who gets credit. Hallmarks of task cultures are skill-based assignments, self-motivated workers, and more deference paid to knowledge than to formal authority.

In personal cultures, people show genuine interest in the needs of workers, consider worker development as critical to the organization's success, and display an attitude that collaboration is satisfying and stimulating.[9]

Many organizations will have one dominant culture modified by at least one of the other types. An astute person will look not only for what people say when trying to understand the culture but also will look for actions, decisions, symbols, and stories that guide behavior.

A variety of organizational culture characteristics make project success more likely. These characteristics include appreciation for project management; formal recognition for project management; collaboration to meet organizational goals; engagement of stakeholders; desire to provide value to customers; teamwork across cultures; integrity; trust; transparency; insistence on continual learning; knowledge management practices that are tied to individual and organization learning; and provision of appropriate rewards and recognition. Recent research has added the following organizational culture themes as helpful in achieving project success: vision-led, egalitarian, goal-oriented, timely and effective communication, and flexible leadership with rapid decision making.[10]

MIDLAND INSURANCE COMPANY   Midland Insurance Company espouses its values by giving every employee the "One Pager" that lists the organization's mission, strategic imperatives, and core values. The CEO will often pull his "One Pager" out at meetings and expects everyone else to do likewise. In talk and in action, Midland tries to live out the core values that comprise its organizational culture. Exhibit 4.8 shows Midland's culture.

EXHIBIT 4.8

MIDLAND INSURANCE COMPANY VALUES	
• Integrity Win/Win	• Creativity
• Team	• Propriety
• Humility	• Sharing/Caring
• Strong Work Ethic	• Personal Growth

Source: Martin J. Novakov, American Modern Insurance Group.

4-2b Project Cultural Norms

While some of the project team's culture is dictated by that of the parent organization, effective sponsors and project managers can do many things to promote good working cultural norms within the project. Many times, participants on a project might not have worked together previously and may even come from parts of the organization (or outside organizations) that have historically been rivals. The sponsor and project manager need to understand organizational politics and work to develop cooperation both within the core project team and among the various groups of project stakeholders. A project team charter helps to formalize this process and set expectations specifically for existing team members and inducting new team members.

When the project sponsor and manager are determining how to create the project culture, ethics should be an important consideration. One aspect of an ethical project culture is to determine how people should act. Project sponsors and managers learn that they need to act in the best interests of three constituencies: (1) the project itself—attempting to deliver what is promised, (2) the project team—encouraging and developing all team members, and (3) the other project stakeholders—satisfying their needs and wants. Ethical project managers make decisions so that one of the three constituencies does not suffer unfairly when satisfying the other two. One list of behaviors adapted from the *PMI Code of Ethics and Professional Conduct* tells project managers to exhibit the following:

- Responsibility—take ownership for decisions.
- Respect—show high regard for ourselves, others, and resources.
- Fairness—make decisions and act impartially.
- Honesty—understand the truth and act in a truthful manner.[11]

The other aspect of an ethical culture is how people actually act. Every project has difficult periods, and the measure of project ethics is how people act at those times. The project manager needs to show courage both in personally making the right decisions and in creating an atmosphere in which others are encouraged to make the right decisions. An ethical project culture in which people know how to act and have the courage to do so yields better ideas; when a spirit of mutual trust prevails, everyone participates with their ideas and effective partnering relationships within and beyond the project team.

4-3 Project Life Cycles

All projects go through a predictable pattern of activity, or project management life cycle, which we refer to as project life cycle. Project planning teams use project life cycle models because various types of projects have differing demands. A research and development (R&D) project may require a certain test to be performed before management approves the expenditure of large amounts of cash, while the manager of a quality improvement project may need to document how the work is currently performed before

EXHIBIT 4.9

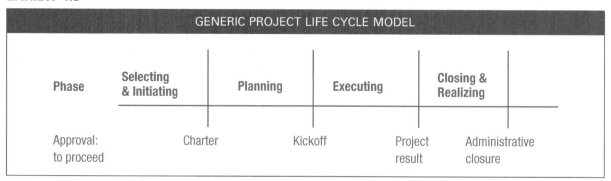

GENERIC PROJECT LIFE CYCLE MODEL					
Phase	**Selecting & Initiating**	**Planning**	**Executing**	**Closing & Realizing**	
Approval: to proceed	Charter	Kickoff	Project result	Administrative closure	

it makes sense to experiment with a new method. The major types of project life cycle models, while differing in details, have some things in common:

- They all have definite starting and ending points.
- They involve a series of phases that need to be completed and approved before proceeding to the next phase.
- The phases generally include at least one initiating, one planning, one closing, and one or more executing phases.
- The various life cycle models are all frequently adapted based on how they align with the organizational culture and language.

We will now look at several models that represent those used in improvement, research, construction, and Agile projects. We introduce the Agile approach to project management immediately after its life cycle model. In the remainder of the book, we will deal with the generic, plan-driven model that includes selecting and initiating, planning, executing, and closing and realizing benefits, as shown in Exhibit 4.9. We will post an Agile icon in the margin wherever we highlight how the Agile or adaptive approach is different.

4-3a Define-Measure-Analyze-Improve-Control (DMAIC) Model

Many firms use projects to plan and manage quality and productivity improvement efforts. Various models are used for these improvement efforts. While these models appear to be somewhat different, they all strive to use facts to make logical decisions and to ensure that the results are as desired. The Six Sigma approach to quality improvement (a popular current approach explained in Chapter 11) uses the DMAIC model. A simple version of this model is shown in Exhibit 4.10.

EXHIBIT 4.10

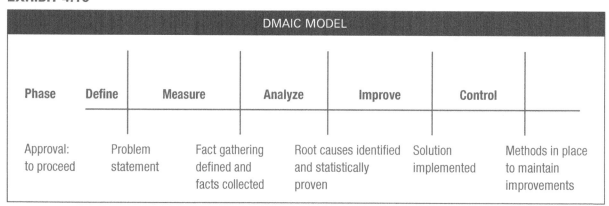

DMAIC MODEL					
Phase	**Define**	**Measure**	**Analyze**	**Improve**	**Control**
Approval: to proceed	Problem statement	Fact gathering defined and facts collected	Root causes identified and statistically proven	Solution implemented	Methods in place to maintain improvements

EXHIBIT 4.11

R&D PROJECT LIFE CYCLE MODEL					
Phase	**Idea Generation**	**Idea Screening**	**Concept Development**	**Validation**	**Transition**
Approval: to proceed		Opportunity analysis	Business case	Proven concept	Prototype	First lot and hand off

4-3b Research and Development (R&D) Project Life Cycle Model

Many organizations use project management techniques to organize, plan, and manage research and development efforts. These can vary in length from as much as a decade for taking a new pharmaceutical product from idea to successful market introduction to as little as a few weeks to reformat an existing food product and deliver it to a client. Some R&D project models are complex and have many phases because of huge risks and demanding oversight; yet some are much simpler. One simple R&D model adapted from defense development projects is shown in Exhibit 4.11.

4-3c Construction Project Life Cycle Model

Just as in other project applications, since construction projects differ greatly in size and complexity, a variety of project life cycle models are in use. A generic construction project life cycle model used for design build projects is shown in Exhibit 4.12.

4-3d Agile Project Life Cycle Model

One type of model increasingly used in information systems and some other projects allows for incremental plans and benefits. These approaches have been variously called iterative, incremental, adaptive, or change driven. While *Agile* is the umbrella name, some of the specific approaches are called *SCRUM, XP, Crystal, EVO, phased delivery, rapid prototyping,* and *evolutionary.* While these models may start like other project life cycle models, they provide short bursts of planning and delivery of benefits in multiple increments during project execution. A generic Agile project life cycle model is shown in Exhibit 4.13.

EXHIBIT 4.12

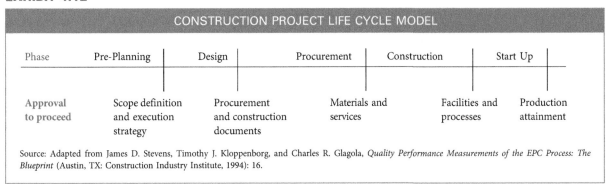

CONSTRUCTION PROJECT LIFE CYCLE MODEL					
Phase	Pre-Planning	Design	Procurement	Construction	Start Up
Approval to proceed	Scope definition and execution strategy	Procurement and construction documents	Materials and services	Facilities and processes	Production attainment

Source: Adapted from James D. Stevens, Timothy J. Kloppenborg, and Charles R. Glagola, *Quality Performance Measurements of the EPC Process: The Blueprint* (Austin, TX: Construction Industry Institute, 1994): 16.

EXHIBIT 4.13

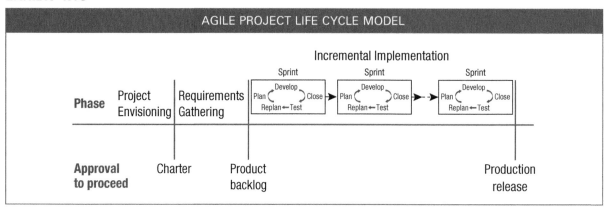

4-4 Agile Project Management

In this section, we introduce several basic ideas from Agile. In subsequent chapters, we will explain some of them in more detail. In many situations, project managers find the most useful method takes good practices from both plan-driven and change-driven approaches, just as the matrix form of organizing takes good ideas from both functional and projectized organizations.

4-4a What Is Agile?

Agile is a form of adaptive or change-driven project management largely reacting to what has happened in the early stages of a project rather than planning everything in detail from the start. Documentation is minimal early in the project but becomes progressively more complete. To understand Agile, one needs to know both the methods and the mindset of Agile practice. For the methods, a project vision is developed and shared early—often as part of a charter. Project teams plan in short bursts (generally of one to four weeks), often called sprints or iterations. The details are planned for the upcoming iteration and very little change is allowed during it. Products are defined and delivered one iteration at a time with an output that has business value successfully delivered at the end of each iteration. Then the next iteration is planned. The mindset is empowering, engaging, and openly communicating as detailed as follows.

4-4b Why Use Agile?

Traditional plan-driven project management works well in many situations, but if the scope is hard to define early in the project and/or when much change is expected, an Agile approach often works better. For these ill-defined and rapidly changing projects, Agile proponents claim to decrease time, cost, and risk while increasing visibility and innovation.

4-4c What Is an Agile Mindset?

While much has been written about Agile, starting with the Agile Manifesto, a simplified version of the mindset needed to successfully plan and manage Agile projects boils down to four key ideas:

1. Satisfy the customer by placing emphasis on outputs that fulfill their needs.
2. Engage all participants through empowerment, cooperation, and knowledge sharing.

3. Facilitate that engagement through servant leadership and visible and continual communication.
4. Keep things simple with a sustainable pace or cadence and emphasis on process improvement.

4-4d What Are the Key Roles in Agile Projects?

All Agile roles are more collaborative than confrontational. Arguably the most essential role is the customer representative—sometimes called the product owner. This person ensures that the needs and wants of the various constituents in the customer's organization are identified and prioritized and that project progress and decisions continually support the customer's desires. The customer representative does much of what a sponsor might in traditional projects and also works with the team on a continuous basis, often performing some of the work a project manager might on a traditional project.

The scrum master serves and leads in a facilitating and collaborative manner, emphasizing the need to facilitate and remove obstacles. The scrum master is a more limited, yet more empowering role than that of a traditional project manager. The team members in Agile projects are assigned full time and co-located as much as possible. The teams are self-governing, so the team now accomplishes many of the planning and coordinating activities a project manager would typically perform.

4-4e How Do You Start an Agile Project?

An Agile project should start with a charter, as any other project should. This high-level agreement between the product owner, scrum master, and empowered team will help share the compelling project vision, create commitment, uncover risks, identify stakeholders, ensure common understanding of success criteria, and establish working agreements and ground rules as needed. Often, the first iteration is used to determine the product to be built and prioritize the most valuable work for the next iteration.

4-4f How Do You Continue an Agile Project?

Perhaps the easiest way to understand the process of running an Agile project is to visualize the four types of meetings (often called ceremonies) used:

1. **Iteration planning meetings** have the product owner share the highest value-added output he or she would like the team to work on next, along with a definition of what "done" or quality completion is. The project team then commits to how much output it can deliver in the iteration. This meeting may include backlog grooming, which is reprioritizing the work, or backlog grooming may be conducted in a separate meeting.
2. **Daily stand-up meetings** are often held for 15 minutes early in the morning and each team member shares the previous day's accomplishments, the plans for the current day, and any issues. Problem solving is not done in these team meetings, but if one teammate can help another, the two talk off-line afterward.
3. **Demonstration meetings** are held at least once per iteration where the team demonstrates usable product. Only a completed, usable product is shown.
4. **Retrospective meetings** are held at the end of each iteration where the project team, scrum master, product owner, and possibly other key stakeholders openly share what worked well and what could work better by making a change of some sort. The goal is to improve the work processes.

4-4g What Is Needed for Agile to Be Successful?

Experienced and motivated team members are needed because one hallmark of Agile is self-managed teams. Without experience and willingness to be a cross-functional team member, the teams would likely flounder. A key stakeholder, often called the **product owner or customer**, needs to commit to frequent and detailed meetings, as described above, with the development team both for initial chartering and requirements gathering, but also for ongoing prioritization and evaluation. **Trust** between the client and contractor (or user and developer) is needed because the details of the requirements and scope are initially unknown. Trust is also needed as the client needs to prioritize to get maximum value, given time and resource constraints, and the project team needs to commit to creating certain working output during each iteration.

4-5 Traditional Project Executive Roles

Projects do not exist in a vacuum. They exist in organizations where they require resources and executive attention. Projects are the primary method that organizations use to reach their strategic goals. As such, a variety of players need to be involved at the executive, managerial, and associate levels, as shown in Exhibit 4.14. Especially in small organizations, one person may perform more than one role. For example, a sponsor may perform some or all of the activities normally expected from the customer. The four project executive roles are the steering team (ST), the sponsor, the customer, and the chief projects officer (CPO), often known as the project management office (PMO).

4-5a Steering Team

In small to medium-sized organizations, the steering team (sometimes known as the executive team, management team, leadership team, operating team, or other titles) often consists of the top person in the organization and his or her direct reports. They should collectively represent all of the major functions of the organization. In larger organizations, there may be steering teams at more than one level. When that occurs, the steering teams at lower levels are directed and constrained by decisions the top-level steering team makes. Some organizations divide the duties of the steering team by creating project review committees and delegating tasks to them. In any event, the duties of the steering team revolve around the following five activities:

1. Overall priority setting
2. Project selection and prioritization
3. Sponsor selection
4. General guidance
5. Encouragement

EXHIBIT 4.14

TRADITIONAL PROJECT EXECUTIVE, MANAGERIAL, AND ASSOCIATE ROLES		
EXECUTIVE LEVEL	MANAGERIAL LEVEL	ASSOCIATE LEVEL
Steering Team (ST)	Functional Manager (FM)	Core Team Member
Sponsor	Project Manager (PM)	Subject Matter Expert (SME)
Customer	Scrum master	
Chief Projects Officer (CPO)	Facilitator	

The steering team generally sets overall organizational priorities with the CEO. This is a normal part of strategic planning, as described in Chapter 2. Once the overall organizational goals have been set, the steering team agrees on the criteria for selecting projects and then selects the projects the organization plans to execute during the year. Once the overall project list is complete, they determine the relative priorities of the projects to determine which will start first.

Simultaneously, the steering team often helps the CEO decide who will sponsor potential upcoming projects. In turn, the steering team often helps the sponsor select the project manager. In some cases, the steering team even gets involved in deciding which critical team members will be on the project. This is especially true if very few people in the organization have highly demanded skills. The steering team can decide which project these people will work on as part of the prioritizing effort.

Guidance from the steering team includes feedback during formal reviews as well as informal suggestions at other times. Since steering teams understand how important project success is in achieving organizational objectives, they normally demand to have formal project reviews. These can occur either at set calendar times or at a project **milestone**, which is "a significant point or event in the project."[12] At these formal reviews, the steering team can tell the project team to continue as is, to redirect their efforts in a specific manner, or to stop the project altogether.

In terms of informal suggestions, it is very empowering to project participants if the steering team members ask how the project is going and offer encouragement when they run into each other in the normal course of work. It shows project participants that their work is important and has high visibility in the organization.

4-5b Sponsor

We defined a sponsor in Chapter 1 as "a senior manager serving in a formal role given authority and responsibility for successful completion of a project deemed strategic to an organization's success."[13] In this sense, the sponsor is normally an individual who has a major stake in the project outcome. Sponsors often perform a variety of different tasks that help a project, both in public and behind the scenes. Major sponsor responsibilities are shown by project stage in Exhibit 4.15. The sponsor for major projects is often a member of the steering team. On smaller projects, the sponsor may hold a lower position in the organization. The interaction—indeed, the partnership—of the sponsor and project manager is critical to project success.

As a member of the steering team, the sponsor should understand the corporate strategy and be prepared to help with project selection and prioritization to link each project explicitly with organizational strategy.[14] Sponsors should pick the project manager and core team (sometimes with help from the project manager and/or others). Sponsors should mentor the project manager to ensure that person understands his role and has the skills, information, and desire to successfully manage the project.

In the previous chapter, we discussed chartering. Sponsors ideally take an active role in chartering the project by creating a first draft of the business case and scope overview statements for the project. If a sponsor does not take time for this, the project manager needs to ask questions to elicit this business case and scope overview information. Then the sponsor should insist that a milestone schedule, preliminary budget, risk identification, assessment criteria, communication plan, and lessons learned be developed by the project manager and team. In this way, the sponsor sets performance goals and establishes priorities.[15] The sponsor then either personally approves the charter or takes the charter to the steering team for approval.

As the project progresses, the sponsor helps behind the scenes by obtaining resources, removing roadblocks, making high-level decisions, and interfacing between the project core team and the executive team. Sponsors often share their vision for the project with

EXHIBIT 4.15

SPONSOR RESPONSIBILITIES BY STAGE	
STAGE	SPONSOR RESPONSIBILITIES
Overarching	Provide resources, manage stakeholder relationships, deliver results
Selecting	Identify, select, prioritize projects
Initiating	Select and mentor project manager, charter project
Planning	Meet key stakeholders, ensure planning
Executing	Nurture key stakeholders, ensure communications, ensure quality
Closing	Ensure stakeholder satisfaction, closure, and knowledge management
Realizing	Ensure benefits are achieved and capability is increased

Source: Adapted from Timothy J. Kloppenborg and Laurend J. Laning, *Strategic Leadership of Portfolio and Project Management* (Business Expert Press, New York 2012): 47; Timothy J. Kloppenborg, Debbie Tesch, and Chris Manolis, "Project Success and Executive Sponsor Behaviors: Empirical Life Cycle Stage Investigations," *Project Management Journal* (February/March, 2014): 15–17; and Timothy J. Kloppenborg and Debbie Tesch, "How Effective Sponsors Influence Project Success," *MIT Sloan Management Review* (Spring 2015): 28–30.

various stakeholders. When providing staff, sponsors ensure they are adequate in number and skill. This may include training. It may also include negotiating for staff. Sponsors often let their project managers arrange this training and negotiate for resources. However, the sponsor needs to make sure that both are satisfactorily completed.

Once again, sponsors with experienced project managers may merely need to ensure their project managers have the means in place to monitor and control their projects. Large projects with many stakeholders often have formal kickoff meetings. The sponsor's presence demonstrates corporate commitment. Sponsors represent the customer to the project team. The sponsor must ensure that several important customer-related tasks are performed as follows:

- All customers (stakeholders) have been identified.
- Their desires have been uncovered and prioritized.
- The project delivers what the customers need.
- The customers accept the project deliverables.

Again, the project manager should do much of this, but the sponsor is also responsible for its completion. While sponsors represent their projects, they also represent the larger organization. As such, they often should be one of the first persons to determine the need to stop a project that is no longer needed or is not performing adequately. Finally, after the project results have been used for a period of time, the sponsor should make sure the expected results have been achieved.

So, who makes a great sponsor? In addition to having a major stake in the project outcome and fulfilling the responsibilities described above, the following general behaviors and temperaments are desirable:

- Excellent communication and listening skills
- Ability to handle ambiguity
- Ability to self-manage
- Approachability
- Collaborative attitude
- Responsiveness[16]

Nejron Photo/Shutterstock.com

4-5c Customer

While the specific demands of the customer role are spelled out here, understand that some or all of this role may be carried out by the sponsor—particularly for projects internal to a company. When a busy customer buys something, it may be tempting to just place an order and have it delivered. That process is fine for an off-the-shelf item or for a transactional service. However, when it is a one-of-a-kind project, hands-off ordering does not work. The question then becomes: What does a customer need to do to ensure the desired results? Exhibit 4.16 shows a list of seven tasks a customer can do before and during a project to enhance the probability of success. The customer performs three of these tasks independently and the other four jointly with the project manager. The three customer-only project tasks are prioritizing the project need, carefully selecting a good contractor, and killing the project if necessary. The four joint tasks are writing and signing the project charter, developing clear and detailed requirements, setting up and using project control systems, and conducting a great project kickoff meeting.

INDEPENDENT TASKS   The first requirement is to prioritize each project. The knowledge that one particular project is the highest priority for a company should be

EXHIBIT 4.16

CUSTOMER TASKS ON PROJECTS	
INDEPENDENT TASKS	JOINT TASKS WITH PROJECT MANAGER
1. Prioritize project 2. Select good contractor 3. Kill project if needed	1. Write and sign charter 2. Develop clear requirements 3. Use control system 4. Conduct kickoff meeting

communicated, and that project should be tackled by the "A team." A related prioritization question is: Do we need this project so badly right now that we are willing to start it even without the skilled personnel, resources, or technology on hand that would improve the probability of successful completion? If so, ensure this particular project gets top billing. If not, consider delaying it. A third prioritizing decision that needs to be made repeatedly is what project requirements must be satisfied first so the project team is working on what matters most to the customer.

The second customer task is to carefully select a competent and honest contractor to perform the project. All of the important joint tasks are much easier with the right contractor, the probability of success goes up, and everyone's stress level goes down.

The third customer task is to determine whether to pull the plug on a troubled project. This could happen right at the start if the project appears to be impractical. It could happen during detailed planning when the requirements, schedule, budget, risks, or other aspects indicate trouble. More often, it occurs during project execution when the project progress does not live up to the plan. A customer needs to decide when to stop throwing good money after bad.

JOINT TASKS WITH PROJECT MANAGER   The first joint task for customers and project managers is to create and ratify the project charter. The charter is a broad agreement concerning the project goals, rationale, risks, timeline, budget, approach, and roles—even though all of the details have yet to be determined. The charter should help to identify projects that appear risky or otherwise impractical from the outset. These projects should either be scrapped, or a different approach should be used. If the project looks promising, both the contractor and the customer normally sign the charter and feel morally bound to its spirit.

Once the charter is signed, the contractor and customer need to develop detailed requirements. Some of the challenges many customer companies face are differing project expectations among the members of the organization. Somehow, the conflicting desires of multiple people in the customer's organization must be combined into one set of requirements that will be provided to the people who will perform the project work. Senior customer representatives and project managers frequently work together to determine the requirements.

The customer and the contractor often collaborate on the setup and use of several project control systems. One of these is a communications plan (which is explained in Chapter 6). Since the customer is often the recipient of communications, he needs to tell the contractor what he needs to know, when he needs to know it, and what format will be most convenient. This should include regular progress reports. Second is a change control system (explained in Chapter 7). Most projects will have multiple changes. A method must be created to approve potential changes, document their impact, and ensure that they are carried out as agreed. Third is a risk management system (explained in Chapter 11). Customers should work with developers to brainstorm possible risks, consider how likely each risk is to occur, measure a risk's impact should it happen, and develop contingency plans. The customer needs to ensure that effective communications, change management, and risk management systems are used.

Customers must help plan and participate in a project kickoff meeting. This meeting should be widely attended, give everyone involved in the project a chance to ask questions, and be used to build excitement for the project.

Customers get what they pay for on projects, but only when actively involved in key activities. Customers have the sole responsibility of prioritizing their own needs, selecting a contractor to perform their project, and terminating a project that is not working. Customers and contractors share the responsibility for crafting and agreeing to a project charter, articulating requirements, developing and using project control systems, and conducting an informative and energetic project kickoff.

4-5d Chief Projects Officer/Project Management Office

Organizations need to have one person who "owns" their project management system and is responsible for all the people who work on projects. While different companies use different titles for this position (such as project director or manager of project managers), we will use the title chief projects officer (CPO). Just as companies' size and complexity vary greatly, so does the role of CPO. Large companies frequently have a project management office (PMO). The PMO performs the CPO role. At small companies, the CPO role may be performed informally by the CEO, who also juggles many other time demands. Companies in the medium-size range may find it useful to appoint an executive who already has other responsibilities as the CPO. Ensuring projects are planned and managed well is so central to the success of most companies that a highly capable individual is normally assigned this responsibility.

To be effective, the CPO must consider organizational enablers for project success: these include standardized supporting processes such as approvals and appointments; standardized execution guidance such as performance assessment criteria and templates; well-defined responsibility systems such as sponsor and project team roles; and a mature organizational structure that fosters cooperation and joint problem solving.[17]

So, what are the responsibilities of the chief projects officer? They include ensuring that the company's steering team:

- Identifies potential projects during strategic planning
- Selects a manageable set of projects to be implemented
- Prioritizes effectively within that set
- Ensures enough resources (people, money, and other resources) are available to perform the projects
- Selects appropriate project sponsors and teams
- Charters the project teams
- Monitors and controls the implementation of the projects
- Rewards the participants
- Celebrates the results of successful projects!

If that is not enough, the CPO also ensures that each individual serving on a project:

- Receives the training he or she needs
- Captures lessons learned from completed projects
- Uses lessons learned from previous projects on new projects
- Uses templates and standards when appropriate

4-6 Traditional Project Management Roles

The manager-level roles in traditional projects include the functional manager, project manager, and facilitator.

4-6a Functional Manager

Functional managers are often department heads. Projects come and go, but departments generally remain. Functional managers have a large role in deciding how the project work in their functional area is done. Functional managers and project managers may negotiate who will be assigned to work on the project.

Generally, top management in an organization needs to decide how the relative decision-making power in the organization is divided between project managers and functional managers. Organizations that are new to formalized project management often start with functional managers having more power. Often, this changes over time until project managers for big projects have relatively more power.

4-6b Project Manager

The project manager is the focal point of the project. He or she spends a large amount of time communicating with everyone who is interested in the project. The project manager leads the planning, execution, and closing of the project. This person ideally should be a flexible, facilitating leader. Since project managers are responsible for the project schedule, they have a large role in deciding when project activities need to be accomplished. Project managers are trusted with delivering project results needed by their parent organizations. As such, project managers need to be worthy of that trust by possessing both integrity and necessary skills.

DESIRED BEHAVIORS   Exhibit 4.17 shows a few of the behaviors project managers can develop first in regard to integrity and then in regard to each of the 10 project management knowledge areas needed to successfully plan and manage projects. This book describes some of the factual knowledge project managers need to acquire to become proficient. Project managers also need to acquire experiential knowledge by practicing

EXHIBIT 4.17

DESIRED PROJECT MANAGER BEHAVIORS

INTEGRITY: A PM demonstrates integrity by making honest decisions, protecting people, defending core values, leading major change, honoring trust, showing respect, establishing a culture of honesty, and displaying total commitment to project and people.

INTEGRATION: A PM is an effective integrator by leading the chartering process, coordinating assembly of a detailed and unified project plan, balancing the needs of all stakeholders, making logical trade-off decisions, and keeping focus on primary objectives.

SCOPE: A PM deftly handles project scope by obtaining a deep understanding of stakeholder wants and needs, determining true requirements, learning if proposed changes are essential, stopping unnecessary scope creep, and demonstrating needed flexibility.

TIME: A PM is an effective scheduler by leading schedule development, understanding resource and logic limitations, understanding the project life cycle, focusing on key milestones, and making schedule decisions while being aware of cost and scope issues.

COST: A PM maintains cost control by developing an accurate understanding of project scope, determining reliable cost estimates, controlling all project costs, and calculating and honestly reporting all variances in a timely and transparent manner.

QUALITY: A PM achieves project quality by learning customer expectations and how they relate to organizational objectives, insisting project decisions are based upon facts, utilizing lessons learned, ensuring effective work processes are used, and leading testing.

HUMAN RESOURCES: A PM effectively handles human resource issues by leading in a facilitating manner when possible and forcefully when needed, attracting and retaining good workers, developing a self-directed project team, and creating a sense of urgency.

COMMUNICATIONS: A PM displays good communications by listening and speaking well, advocating the project vision, maintaining enthusiasm, focusing attention on key issues, establishing order, working through conflict, seeking support, and openly sharing.

RISK: A PM effectively deals with project risk by openly identifying risks and opportunities, honestly evaluating each, developing avoidance strategies when practical and mitigation strategies when needed, and courageously recommending needed actions.

PROCUREMENT: A PM effectively procures needed goods and services by accurately documenting all requirements, identifying and fairly considering all potential sellers, proactively managing contracts and relationships, and ensuring all deliveries.

STAKEHOLDER: A PM deals effectively with stakeholders by robustly identifying all who are interested in the project, asking probing questions to understand their desires, and ensuring someone on the project team maintains effective relationships with each.

EXHIBIT 4.18

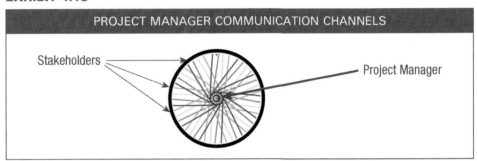

PROJECT MANAGER COMMUNICATION CHANNELS

Stakeholders — Project Manager

these behaviors on projects. Not all project managers will become equally adept at each behavior, but an understanding of the behaviors exhibited by excellent project managers is a great way to start. Remaining chapters in this book elaborate on these behaviors. Collectively, all of these skills make for a great, well-rounded project manager.

COMMUNICATION CHANNELS   Envision a bicycle wheel, as shown in Exhibit 4.18. The project manager is like the hub, and the spokes are like the many communication channels the project manager needs to establish and use with project stakeholders. While there are many project manager requirements, some of the technical needs can probably be delegated, but every project manager needs integrity, leadership, and communications skills.

CHALLENGES   Project managers deal with several challenges. One is that they often have more responsibility than authority. This means they need to persuade people to accomplish some tasks rather than order them to do so. Project managers can create interesting and challenging work assignments for their team members. Many people find this stimulating. Project managers can more effectively attract followers when they display high integrity and the ability to get the job done. This includes both technical ability and communications ability. Project managers primarily deal with networks of people both within and outside their parent company. An effective project manager knows how to get to the source of the networks. A challenge for project managers is determining how networks function within certain organizational cultures. This is why organizational culture is so important. What are the networks within the organization? How do people work, communicate, and problem solve beneath the function of their job titles?

A rookie project sponsor and rookie project manager should not be assigned to the same project. While the sponsor normally mentors the project manager, when a sponsor is new, some of the mentoring may go the other way—just as a master sergeant may help a new lieutenant learn about leading troops.

JUDGMENT CALLS   Due to the very nature of projects—each one having a unique set of stakeholders, output, and project team—project managers cannot always follow a cookbook approach in how they manage. They must develop judgment. Exhibit 4.19 lists some judgment calls that project managers need to be prepared to make on a frequent basis.

COMPETENCIES BY PROJECT STAGE   Just as sponsor demands vary by project life cycle stage, so do those of project managers, as shown in Exhibit 4.20.

PROJECT LEADERSHIP   Many people have become convinced that project managers need to provide leadership in various ways. Knowing the tools and techniques of project management and even knowing the content of the *PMBOK Guide* is useful, but not enough to be a great project manager. A dozen of the more common leadership challenges faced by project managers are shown in Exhibit 4.21. Anther way to understand

EXHIBIT 4.19

PROJECT MANAGER JUDGMENT CALLS

A few general questions project managers need to ask themselves is when to:

- Act versus analyze
- Lead versus follow
- Lead versus administer
- Repeat versus change
- Change expectations versus accept them
- Take over versus let the team perform
- Focus on the big picture versus focus on details
- Focus on technical versus focus on behavioral
- Focus on short term versus focus on long term
- Promote order (control) versus promote innovation (freedom)
- Allow (constructive) conflict versus discourage (destructive) conflict
- Focus communications inside the project versus focus communications outside
- Demonstrate optimism versus demonstrate pessimism
- Advocate for the project versus accept termination
- Focus on project goals versus organizational, personal, or team member goals
- Enhance, maintain, or accept changes in scope, quality, cost, and schedule

leadership demands of project managers is to consider the core competencies at a glance shown in Exhibit 4.22.

4-6c Facilitator

Some project management situations require facilitation because the situation is so complex and/or because the opinions are so varied. Sometimes, the workers on a project need to expand their thinking by considering the many possibilities (possible projects, approaches, risks, personnel, and other issues). Other times, the workers on the project

EXHIBIT 4.20

PROJECT MANAGER COMPETENCIES BY PROJECT LIFE CYCLE STAGE	
STAGE	COMPETENCY
Initiation	Effective questioning/generating feedback Persuasiveness/Marketing/Selling Listening skills Vision oriented/articulate the business problem Consensus building
Planning	Project management skills and knowledge Consensus building Technical skills/theoretical knowledge
Implementation	Ability to get along/team player Results oriented Truthful/honest
Close	Writing skills Share information and credit Pride in workmanship/qualitytruthful/honest

Source: Gregory J. Skulmoski and Francis T. Hartman, "Information Systems Project Manager Soft Competencies: A Project-Phase Investigation," *Project Management Journal* (March 2010): 61–77.

EXHIBIT 4.21

A DOZEN PROJECT LEADERSHIP CHALLENGES

General Project Leadership

- Provide situational and shared leadership
- Develop trust
- Manage and negotiate conflicts
- Manage political, social, cultural, and ethical issues

Team Leadership

- Develop high-performing project teams
- Participate in self-organizing project teams
- Overcome team-building obstacles
- Facilitate team decision making

Stakeholder Leadership

- Engage all stakeholders
- Influence stakeholder behavior
- Maintain effective multidirectional communications
- Deal with changes in the environment and within the project

Source: Adapted from unpublished discussion of Project Management Executive Forum meeting, October 10, 2106, Cincinnati, OH.

EXHIBIT 4.22

AGILE PROJECT LIFE CYCLE MODEL

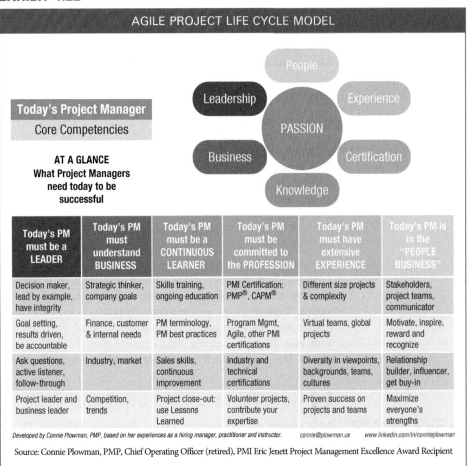

Today's Project Manager
Core Competencies

AT A GLANCE
What Project Managers
need today to be
successful

Today's PM must be a LEADER	Today's PM must understand BUSINESS	Today's PM must be a CONTINUOUS LEARNER	Today's PM must be committed to the PROFESSION	Today's PM must have extensive EXPERIENCE	Today's PM is in the "PEOPLE BUSINESS"
Decision maker, lead by example, have integrity	Strategic thinker, company goals	Skills training, ongoing education	PMI Certification: PMP®, CAPM®	Different size projects & complexity	Stakeholders, project teams, communicator
Goal setting, results driven, be accountable	Finance, customer & internal needs	PM terminology, PM best practices	Program Mgmt, Agile, other PMI certifications	Virtual teams, global projects	Motivate, inspire, reward and recognize
Ask questions, active listener, follow-through	Industry, market	Sales skills, continuous improvement	Industry and technical certifications	Diversity in viewpoints, backgrounds, teams, cultures	Relationship builder, influencer, get buy-in
Project leader and business leader	Competition, trends	Project close-out: use Lessons Learned	Volunteer projects, contribute your expertise	Proven success on projects and teams	Maximize everyone's strengths

Developed by Connie Plowman, PMP, based on her experiences as a hiring manager, practitioner and instructor.   *connie@plowman.us*   *www.linkedin.com/in/connieplowman*

Source: Connie Plowman, PMP, Chief Operating Officer (retired), PMI Eric Jenett Project Management Excellence Award Recipient

need to focus their thinking by selecting from many options (a project, an approach, a contractor, or a mitigation strategy). Most project managers and sponsors can and do facilitate many meetings. However, the project manager may prefer to focus on the content of a meeting and enlist a facilitator to help focus on the process of the meeting. In these situations, an outside facilitator may be useful. Often, a disinterested sponsor or project manager (one who works on other projects, but not on this one) is used when a facilitator is needed. Sometimes, the chief projects officer or an outside consultant is used to facilitate.

4-7 Traditional Project Team Roles

The team- or associate-level roles in projects are core team members and subject matter experts (SMEs).

4-7a Core Team Members

Core team members are the small group of people who are on the project from start to finish and who jointly with the project manager make many decisions and carry out many project activities. If the project work expands for a period of time, the core team members may supervise the work of SMEs who are brought in on an as-needed basis. Ideally, the core team is as small as practical. It collectively represents and understands the entire range of project stakeholders and the technologies the project will use. It is generally neither necessary nor useful to have every single function represented on the core team, since that would make communication and scheduling meetings more difficult. Also, if every function is represented directly, team members tend to fight for turf.

The ideal type of core team member is one who is more concerned with completing the project (on time, with good quality, and on budget, if possible) than with either personal glory or with only doing work in his or her own discipline. He or she does what it takes to get the project done.

4-7b Subject Matter Experts

While core team members are typically assigned to the project from start to finish, many projects also have a specific and temporary need for additional help. The necessary help may be an expert who can help make a decision. It may be extra workers who are needed at a busy time during the life of the project. Some extra help may be needed for as little as one meeting; other extra help may be needed for weeks or months. These extra helpers are often called subject matter experts (SMEs) since they are usually needed for their specific expertise.

SMEs are brought in for meetings and for performing specific project activities when necessary. A project could have almost any number of SMEs, depending on its size and complexity. SMEs are not on the core team but still are essential to the project. SMEs may be on a project for a long time and thus be almost indistinguishable from core team members.

However, SMEs may spend only a little time on a particular project and, therefore, may not relate strongly to it. At times, it is a struggle to get them scheduled and committed. Typically, a project manager would have a newly assigned SME read the project charter and the minutes from the last couple of meetings before discussing the project with him. It is a balancing act to ensure that the SME understands what she needs to do and how important it is, without spending a great deal of time in the process.

4-8 Role Differences on Agile Projects

Agile project management roles are shown in Exhibit 4.23. Most of the same work still needs to be accomplished in organizations using Agile methods. Some of the work is

EXHIBIT 4.23

AGILE PROJECT ROLES		
EXECUTIVE ROLES	MANAGERIAL ROLES	ASSOCIATE ROLES
Customer (product owner)	Customer (product owner)	Team Member
Sponsor (product manager)	Scrum Master	
Portfolio Team	Functional Manager	
Project Management/Scrum Office	Coach	

performed by different people as there is an emphasis on empowering teams, and some is performed at different times as requirements and scope emerge gradually instead of just at the project start. Collaborative effort and communication specifically with the client are common features of Agile project teams.

On Agile projects, arguably the most essential role is the customer representative—sometimes called the product owner. This person is responsible for the return on investment earned by the project and accepting or rejecting acceptance of deliverables at the end of each iteration. The customer representative ensures that the needs and wants of the various constituents in the customer's organization are identified and prioritized and that project progress and decisions continually support the customer's desires. In Agile projects, the customer representative role is so continuous and active that we show it as both an executive- and managerial-level role. The customer representative does much of what a sponsor might in traditional projects, but there also may be a designated sponsor (sometimes known as a product manager) who controls the budget. The customer representative or product owner works with the team on a continuous basis, often performing some of the work a project manager might on a traditional project.

A portfolio team often performs much of the work of a traditional steering team and a similar office that may be titled differently, such as scrum office, performs much of the work of a project office.

The scrum master serves and leads in a facilitating and collaborative manner. In effect, this is a project manager who serves and leads in a collaborative, facilitating manner. This is totally consistent with contemporary project management since many individuals do much better work when they actively plan rather than have work assigned to them. The scrum master guides team members as they prioritize tasks and removes obstacles to their progress. This is a more limited, yet more empowering role than the traditional project manager. In this book, we consider the scrum master to be the project manager.

The functional manager (sometimes called a resource manager) has a similar, but sometimes more limited, role than the traditional department head. Many organizations using Agile also have a coach—acting as a facilitator and trainer.

The team members in Agile projects are assigned full time as much as possible, so there are very few subject matter experts. The teams are self-governing, so the team now accomplishes many of the planning and coordinating activities a project manager would typically perform. Small and co-located teams often characterize Agile projects and they work closely together. They organize themselves and exhibit significant maturity. They create their own estimates and report to each other daily. The same members should be on the team for the entire project or at least for an entire iteration, although the team can change from one iteration to the next. The members should be co-located and assigned to the project full time for the duration of the iteration.

PMP/CAPM Study Ideas

When it comes to studying for the CAPM or PMP exams, make sure you know the Project Management Code of Ethics & Professional Conduct (referenced on p. 111 of this chapter) inside and out. This is one of the few things *not* found in the *PMBOK® Guide* itself but can be accessed directly from the PMI website. While only eight pages long, this code generally shows up multiple times on either test, thus providing a great deal of "bang for your buck" in terms of studying.

In this chapter, we highlight the fact that a project's life cycle is often industry-specific or even unique to an organization. Regardless, PMI has identified five generic Process Groups, representing the stages that are typical of most projects. These include *Initiation, Planning, Executing, Monitoring & Controlling, and Closing.* You will be expected to know these in a great deal of detail, including inputs and outputs of each stage; into which process group and knowledge area each of the 49 individual processes fit; and how these processes interact with one another. This flow is shown graphically in the inside back cover of this book to help you visualize it. This will require a tremendous amount of studying and should not be underestimated.

Summary

Projects are accomplished either within an organization or between multiple organizations when different firms work together. Project managers are more effective if they understand the impact the organization has on the project. In contemporary society, different organizations choose different organizational structures because they feel there is an advantage in their unique circumstances. While many are still officially organized in a traditional functional manner, an increasing number of organizations have at least informal matrix relationships. The days of having only one boss are gone for many workers—and especially for many project managers. Each form of organization has strengths and challenges with respect to projects.

Organizations also have a culture—the formal and informal manner in which people relate to each other and decisions are made. The hierarchical approach with the boss having supreme authority has long vanished in many places. Many organizations today use a more collaborative approach—some much more than others. Whatever the approach, project managers need to

understand it and the impact it creates on their project. Project managers and sponsors need to create a culture in their project that is consistent with, or at least can work effectively with, that of the parent organization. Both organizational structure and culture can become more complicated if more than one organization is involved in the project and if they differ in these respects.

Projects follow a predictable pattern or project life cycle. Many industries have typical project life cycles, but they vary greatly. A project manager needs to at least understand what project life cycle model is used at her organization and often needs to select or modify the project life cycle to the specific demands of the project.

Multiple executive-, managerial-, and associate-level roles need to be performed in projects. The project manager is a central role and the subject of this book. Project managers need to understand the other roles and relate effectively to them, regardless of whether their project is being conducted using a traditional, Agile, or hybrid approach.

Key Terms Consistent with PMI Standards and Guides

functional organization, 102
projectized organization, 104
co-location, 105

matrix organization, 105
agile, 114
milestone, 117

Chapter Review Questions

1. Describe how a strong (project) matrix is different from a weak (functional) matrix.
2. Which organizational structure is often used for small projects that require most of their work from a single department?
3. List advantages and disadvantages of functional, projectized, and matrix forms of organization.
4. What is co-location, and why is it used?
5. What are organizational values, and why should a project manager be aware of them?
6. List and describe four different types of corporate culture.
7. If more than one parent company is involved in a project, why is it important for the project manager to understand the culture of each?
8. The project manager and sponsor need to act in the best interest of which three constituencies?
9. According to the *PMI Code of Ethics and Professional Conduct,* project managers need to exhibit which four behaviors?
10. In your own words, describe an ethical project culture.
11. What are some characteristics of almost all project life cycles?
12. What does the DMAIC model acronym stand for? When is this type of model used?
13. What distinguishes an Agile project life cycle model from other types of life cycle models?
14. For what five activities is the project steering team responsible?
15. Who should select the project manager and the core team?
16. Who is responsible for ensuring that the steering team completes its tasks?
17. What types of control systems should a customer and contractor work together to set up and utilize?

Discussion Questions

1. Marissa Mayer, former CEO of Yahoo!, sparked a national debate when she insisted that all her employees be physically present for work. Debate the merits of co-location, including its advantages and disadvantages.
2. Identify each of the four organizational culture types with respect to power, and the strongest motivator for each type. In which organizational cultures do you feel most and least comfortable working? Why?
3. List and describe at least four organizational culture characteristics that increase the likelihood of project success. Why is each characteristic helpful?
4. Explain multiple methods through which project managers can lead by example.
5. Define your personal project code of ethics.
6. Brainstorm techniques that effective project leaders can use to resolve ethical conflicts on projects.
7. You work for a software company. What benefits do you achieve by utilizing an Information Systems project life cycle model as opposed to other project life cycle models?
8. If a project will be divided into many phases, which life cycle model would you recommend using to plan it? Why?
9. Describe a possible imbalance between a project manager's authority and responsibility. What impact might it have on a project?
10. Is it important to choose a member from every impacted function of a project for the core team? Explain why or why not.

PMBOK® *Guide* Questions

1. All of the following are characteristics of a projectized organization *except:*
   a. Decision making is streamlined.
   b. Coordination is the responsibility of project managers.
   c. Functional managers have the majority of authority.
   d. Focus is on the customer.
2. Characteristics of an organizational culture can have a major impact on a project's success. All of these are attributes of an organizational culture *except:*
   a. motivation and reward systems
   b. risk tolerance
   c. code of conduct
   d. financial control procedures

3. _____ organization structures can be classified as weak, balanced, or strong, depending on the relative level of influence between the functional manager and the project manager.
   a. Silo
   b. Matrix
   c. Composite
   d. Projectized

4. A hierarchical organization where each employee has one clear superior, and staff are grouped by areas of specialization and managed by a person with expertise in that area is known as a:
   a. composite organization
   b. functional organization
   c. projectized organization
   d. weak matrix organization

5. In an Agile life cycle model, _____.
   a. the scrum master controls the team
   b. detailed planning precedes execution
   c. customer requirements are gathered early in the project
   d. the team is self-directed

6. The project sponsor's responsibilities during the executing stage include:
   a. reviewing and signing the project charter
   b. signing off on the detailed project plan
   c. ensuring communications with key stakeholders
   d. producing project status reports

7. Group phenomena that evolve over time and include established approaches to initiating and planning projects, the acceptable means for getting the work done, and recognized decision-making authorities are referred to as:
   a. organization structures
   b. roles and responsibilities
   c. project culture (norms)
   d. vision and mission

8. Customer responsibilities on a project might include all of the following *except:*
   a. perform the work of the project to achieve its objectives
   b. advise on project requirements
   c. review and accept project deliverables
   d. participate in status or kickoff meetings

9. The Chief Projects Officer's or PMO's responsibilities might include:
   a. signing the project charter
   b. ensuring enough resources are available to perform the project
   c. working with the team to create a project schedule and budget
   d. promoting the project at the executive level of the organization

10. PMI's *Code of Ethics and Professional Conduct* is a guide for project management practitioners that describes the expectations that they should hold for themselves and others. Which of these is *not* one of the desired behaviors and basic obligations referenced by the code of conduct?
    a. fairness
    b. honesty
    c. authority
    d. respect

Exercises

1. Given a scenario, select a preferred organizational structure and justify your selection.

2. Describe examples of ethical (or nonethical) behavior as outlined in PMI's Code of Ethics and Professional Conduct exhibited on a project in the news.

3. Describe, with examples, how a project manager on a project you have observed did or did not exhibit desirable project manager behaviors as described in Exhibit 4.17.

4. Briefly describe how the sponsor of your project is or is not displaying appropriate life cycle-specific behaviors as described in Exhibit 4.15.

INTEGRATED EXAMPLE PROJECTS
SUBURBAN HOMES CONSTRUCTION PROJECT

Suburban Homes, once a medium-sized company, is rapidly expanding its business to southern states and is focused on maintaining its status as the fastest-growing construction company in the Midwest region of the United States. Its significant growth and good reputation for building quality single-family homes and townhomes presents both challenges and opportunities.

Suburban Homes is considering various options to expand its operations while retaining its focus on managing resources effectively and efficiently to increase profits:

- Given the nature of its projects, Suburban Homes is considering either a projectized or matrix organization structure. However, a functional organization structure has not been ruled out.
- With its focus on maintaining high quality in its construction tasks and end-product (home for the customer) as well as quality assurance in implementing project management processes, the company is actively considering a combination of the DMAIC model with a traditional project life-cycle approach.
- Organization culture plays an important role in sustaining and promoting efficiency. The culture, in turn, is influenced by the organization structure. Suburban Homes is highly committed to employee development and functional expertise through training, mentoring, and collaborative learning.

Which type of organization structure is more suitable as Suburban Homes opens new offices in other states? What is your advice to the company to address all these issues comprehensively and coherently?

CASA DE PAZ DEVELOPMENT PROJECT

First, the organizational structure for Casa de Paz is in a separate document. We still need names of individuals who are volunteering for each working group. For this book, we will list names by first name and initial of last name to protect privacy.

How do you envision this organization operating? Casa de Paz has a strong ethos of community, rooted in values of human dignity and a recognition that all of us thrive better in an atmosphere of mutual respect and care. Every subset of the community, from board members to staff to volunteers and affiliates to residents, communicates care and respect in their interactions with one another. Other behavioral norms stem from both these values and the vulnerability of the population we serve. Given the need, at times, for the organization to respond rapidly to serious, stressful, even life-threatening situations, board members, working group members, and even volunteers need to maintain confidentiality, think carefully, use discretion, and behave in a trustworthy manner.

For each project selected, we will have one person from the board serve as sponsor (product owner) and one person from the respective working group serve as project manager (scrum master). The product owner for multiple products is sometimes referred to as a product manager. This person is Gillian A. The chair of the board and the scrum master for the entire effort is ___.

Since Casa de Paz is a 501(c)(3) nonprofit organization, part of the culture is voluntary. One challenge from a project management perspective is to get people to commit to completing certain work according to schedule when many have other full-time jobs. Helping the project teams make team decisions may be relatively easy. The pillars of PMI's Code of Ethics and Professional Conduct of responsibility, respect, fairness, and honesty should be very well accepted and valued.

An Agile approach makes the most sense for this project as many of the requirements are poorly understood at the start and many things are changing rapidly—such as having two buildings to consider with competition for both such that a third building might need to be found. Also, in Agile, we ask for commitment. If the team cannot commit to the body of work for the iteration, the plan is changed. The commitment is made at the team level at the start of the iteration.

Semester Project Instructions

For your example project, describe the organizational structure of the agency or company for which you are planning the project. Describe as many of the organizational culture attributes as you can. List, by name, as many of the project executive, management, and team roles as you can identify. Be sure to assign roles to yourself and your classmates if you are doing the project as a team. How do you anticipate that the organizational structure, culture, and role assignments help or hurt your ability to successfully plan this project? Describe the project life cycle model that is used in the organization—and if one is not currently used, describe the life cycle model you plan to use and tell why it is appropriate.

PROJECT MANAGEMENT *IN ACTION*

Project Leadership Roles at TriHealth

TriHealth is a company that manages several large hospitals and a variety of other health organizations, such as physical fitness facilities and nursing services. Due to the company's increasing size and complexity, TriHealth leadership decided they needed to formally define roles of project executive sponsor, project leader, performance improvement consultant, core team member, and subject matter expert. These roles are shown as follows.

Project Executive Sponsor Initiating Stage

- Empower Project Leader with well-defined charter, which is the overarching guide
- Clearly define expected outcomes
- Demonstrate commitment to and prioritization of project
- Define decision-making methods and responsibility—sponsor/project leader/team
- Partner with Project Leader to identify obstacles, barriers, and silos to overcome

Planning Stage

- Ensure Project Leader understands business context for organization
- Ensure Project Leader develops overall project plan
- Assist Project Leader in developing vertical and horizontal communication plan
- Demonstrate personal interest in project by investing time and energy needed
- Secure necessary resources and organizational support

Executing Stage

- Communicate and manage organizational politics
- Visibly empower and support Project Leader vertically and horizontally
- Build relationships with key stakeholders
- Actively listen to and promote team and project to stakeholders
- Remove obstacles and ensure progress of project
- Ensure goals are met and stakeholders are satisfied

Closing Stage

- Ensure closure; planned completion or termination
- Ensure results and lessons learned are captured and shared
- Ensure assessment of related applications or opportunities
- Ensure any necessary next steps are assigned and resourced
- Recognize contributions and celebrate completion
- Negotiate follow-up date(s) to assess project status

Project Leader

All of the roles listed are the ultimate responsibility of the Project Leader. However, in the development of the charter, the Sponsor and the Project Leader will have a discussion about the Project Leader role. At that time, the individuals will determine if the Project Leader needs additional assistance or skills to facilitate the project success and which of these responsibilities need to be delegated to others with expertise in those areas.

- Leads negotiation with Sponsor for charter definition.
- Collaborates with Sponsor to clarify expectations.
- Provides direction to the team with integrity, leadership, and communication skills.
- Facilitates productive meetings and supports the team's decisions.
- Prepares the high-level work plan and timeline.
- Champions the project on the management level and with the staff.
- Leads the implementation of the project.
- Manages project flow, including agenda setting, meeting documentation, and coordination of team assignments.
- Develops implementation, education, and communication plans for the project.
- Responsible for the team and project progress and proactively intervenes to promote team and project success.
- Identifies, communicates, and facilitates the removal of barriers to enable successful project completion.

- Supports the team with tools and methodologies to accomplish goals.
- Facilitates collection and analysis of data.
- Leads the team in developing a plan to sustain the change and monitor effectiveness.
- Leads the team in developing recommended next steps.
- Closes project with Sponsor and ensures lessons learned are captured.
- Establishes with Sponsor the dates for post-project checkup and overall measurable effectiveness of project.

Performance Improvement Consultant

If the Sponsor and the Project Leader determine additional support/expertise is needed, a Performance Improvement Consultant can provide the following expertise:

- Provides direction to the Project Leader in establishing targets and a measurement and monitoring system.
- Mentors the Project Leader on leading the team through the project management process.
- Collaborates with the Project Leader to prepare a work plan and timeline for the project.
- Proactively intervenes to promote team and project success based on teamwork and interactions.
- Assists the Project Leader in identifying, communicating, and removing barriers to enable successful project completion.
- Assists in the researching, best practices, and benchmarking.
- Coaches the Project Leader on the development and implementation of a comprehensive communication, education, and change management plan.
- Provides the Project Leader support in ensuring regular communication with the Sponsor and Stakeholders.
- Offers expertise to the team with tools and methodologies to accomplish goals.

- Collaborates with the Project Leader on the collection and analysis of data.
- Ensures a system-wide perspective is considered and downstream effects analyzed.
- Provides change management education and assists the Project Leader in developing key strategies for successful change management.
- Provides coaching to the Project Leader on key strategies for successful planning, implementation, and sustainability of the project.

Core Team Member

- Takes responsibility for the success of the team.
- Attends meetings for duration of the project.
- Actively participates in team meetings.
- Understands the entire range of the project.
- Actively participates in the decision-making process.
- Supports the team's decisions.
- Completes outside assignments.
- Carries out many of the project activities; produces deliverables on time.
- Provides testing or validation of decisions being made by the team.
- Provides data collection and reporting.
- Participates in the communication, education, implementation, and evaluation of the project.
- Gathers input from the areas they represent, if appropriate.
- Shares team decisions and plans throughout the project.
- May work directly with Stakeholders or Subject Matter Experts.

Subject Matter Expert

- Not a core team member of the team.
- Participates in demonstrations/presentations and/or team meetings, as needed.
- Carries out project activities as assigned; produces deliverables.
- Responsible for supplying requirements.
- Provides input to the team or complete activities based on a specific expertise he or she possesses that is essential to the project.

Source: TriHealth.

References

A Guide to the Project Management Body of Knowledge (PMBOK® Guide), 6th ed. (Newtown Square, PA: Project Management Institute, 2017).

Ahsan, Kamrul, Marcus Ho, and Sabik Khan, "Recruiting Project Managers: A Comparative Analysis of Competencies and Recruitment Signals from Job Advertisements," *Project Management Journal* (December 2013): 36–54.

Aldag, Ramon J., and Loren W. Kuzuhara, *Mastering Management Skills* (Mason, OH: Thomson South-Western, 2005).

Andersen, Erling S., "Understand Your Project's Character," *Project Management Journal* (December 2003): 4–11.

Aronson, Zvi H., Aaron J. Shenhar, and Peerasit Patanakul, "Managing the Intangible Aspects of a Project: The Affect of Vision, Artifacts, and Leader Values on Project Spirit and Success in Technology-Driven Projects," *Project Management Journal* (February 2013): 35–58.

Blomquist, Tomas, and Ralph Muller, "Practices, Roles and Responsibilities of Middle Managers in Program and Portfolio Management," *Project Management Journal* (March 2006): 52–66.

Chandler, Dawne, and Payson Hall, *Improving Executive Sponsorship of Projects: A Holistic Approach* (New York, NY: Business Expert Press, 2016).

Chandler, Dawne E., and Janice L. Thomas, "Does Executive Sponsorship Matter for Realizing Project Management Value?" *Project Management Journal* (October/November 2015): 46–61.

Cobb, Charles G., "At Odds?" *PMNetwork* (May 2012): 26–27.

Collyer, Simon, "Culture, Communication, and Leadership for Projects in Dynamic Environments," *Project Management Journal* (December/January 2017): 111–125.

Collyer, Simon, Clive Warren, Bronwyn Hemsley, and Chris Stevens, "Aim, Fire, Aim—Project Planning Styles in Dynamic Environments," *Project Management Journal* (September 2010): 106–121.

Crawford, Lynn, "Developing Organizational Project Management Capability: Theory and Practice," *Project Management Journal* (August 2006): 74–86.

Daft, Richard L., *Management*, 9th ed. (Mason, OH: South-Western Cengage Learning, 2010).

Gale, Sarah F. "The Evolution of Agile," *PMNetwork* (January 2012): 28–33.

Johnson, Craig E., *Meeting the Ethical Challenges of Leadership: Casting Light or Shadow*, 3rd ed. (Thousand Oaks, CA: Sage Publications, Inc., 2009).

Kloppenborg, Timothy J., and Debbie Tesch, "How Executive Sponsors Influence Project Success," *MIT Sloan Management Review* (Spring 2015): 27–30.

Kloppenborg, Timothy J., and Laurence J. Laning, *Strategic Leadership of Portfolio and Project Management* (New York: Business Expert Press, 2012).

Kloppenborg, Timothy J., Deborah Tesch, and Chris Manolis, "Project Success and Executive Sponsor Behaviors: Empirical Life Cycle Stage Investigations" *Project Management Journal* (February/March 2014): 9–20.

Laufer, Alexander, et al., "What Successful Project Managers Do," *MIT Sloan Management Review* (Spring 2015): 43–51.

Lussier, Robert N., and Christopher F. Achua, *Leadership: Theory, Application, and Skill Development*, 4th ed. (Mason, OH: South-Western Cengage Learning, 2010).

Millhollan, Chuck, and Michelle Kaarst-Brown, "Lessons for IT Project Manager Efficacy: A Review of the Literature Associated with Project Success," *Project Management Journal* (October/November 2016): 89–106.

Ortiz-Marcos, Isabel, et al., "Competency Training for Managing International Cooperation Engineering Projects," *Project Management Journal* (April 2013): 88–97.

Practice Standard for Scheduling, 2nd ed. (Newtown Square, PA: Project Management Institute, 2011).

Rath, Tom, and Barry Conchie, Strengths-Based Leadership: Great Leaders, Teams, and Why People Follow (New York: Gallup Press, 2008).

Skulmoski, Gregory J., and Francis T. Hartman, "Information Systems Project Manager Soft Competencies: A Project-Phase Investigation," *Project Management Journal* (March 2010): 61–77.

Stevens, James D., Timothy J. Kloppenborg, and Charles R Glagola, *Quality Performance Measurements of the EPC Process: The Blueprint* (Austin, TX: Construction Industry Institute, 1994): 16.

Wikipedia, http://en.wikipedia.org/wiki/New_product_development, accessed May 28, 2010.

Wen, Qi, and Maoshan Qiang, "Enablers for Organizational Project Management in the Chinese Context," *Project Management Journal* (February/March 2016): 113–126.

http://www.pmi.org/About-Us/Ethics/~/media/PDF/ Ethics/ap_pmicodeofethics.ashx, Project Management Institute Code of Ethics and Professional Conduct, accessed May 22, 2013.

Agile Project Management For PMPs – VersionOne http://www.versionone.com/Webcasts/Agile_PM_ for_PMPs.asp, accessed May 22, 2013.

http://www.internetsociety.org/who-we-are/mission/ strategic-objectives, Internet Society: Who We Are, accessed May 22, 2013.

http://www.slideshare.net/bkappe/agile-requirements-writing, Slideshare Agile, accessed April 14, 2017.

http://agilemanifesto.org/principles.html, accessed January 13, 2017.

https://www.atlassian.com/agile/ceremonies, accessed January 13, 2017.

Atlassian, Have we met: Four Agile Ceremonies Demystified, accessed April 14, 2017.

http://www.whizlabs.com/blog/projectized-organization/, accessed April 14, 2017.

http://project-management-knowledge.com/definitions/c/co-location/, accessed February 7, 2017.

http://project-management-knowledge.com/definitions/m/matrix-organization/, accessed February 7, 2017.

Endnotes

1. Chandler, Dawne, and Payson Hall. *Improving Executive Sponsorship of Projects: A Holistic Approach* (New York, NY: Business Expert Press, 2016).

2. PMI Lexicon of Project Terms, 2015, 4.

3. http://www.whizlabs.com/blog/projectized-organization/, accessed February 7, 2017.

4. http://project-management-knowledge.com/definitions/c/co-location/, accessed February 7, 2017.

5. http://project-management-knowledge.com/definitions/m/matrix-organization/, accessed February 7, 2017.

6. Johnson, Craig E., *Meeting the Ethical Challenges of Leadership: Casting Light or Shadow*, 3rd ed. (Thousand Oaks, CA: Sage Publications, Inc., 2009): 89.

7. Aronson, Zvi H., Aaron J. Shenhar, and Peerasit Patanakul, "Managing the Intangible Aspects of a Project: The Affect of Vision, Artifacts, and Leader Values on Project Spirit and Success in Technology-Driven Projects," *Project Management Journal* (February 2013): 51.

8. Adapted from Erling S. Andersen, "Understand Your Project's Character," *Project Management Journal* (December 2003): 4–11; and Ramon J. Aldag and Loren W. Kuzuhara, *Mastering Management Skills* (Mason, OH: Thomson South-Western, 2005).

9. Adapted from Erling S. Andersen, "Understand Your Project's Character," *Project Management Journal* (December 2003): 4–11.

10. Collyer, Simon, "Culture, Communication, and Leadership for Projects in Dynamic Environments," *Project Management Journal* (December/January 2017): 111.

11. *PM1 Code of Ethics and Professional Conduct*, http://www.pmi.org/-/media/pmi/documents/public/pdf/ethics/pmi-code-of-ethics.pdf, accessed January 23, 2017.

12. *Practice Standard for Scheduling*, 2nd ed. (Newtown Square, PA: Project Management Institute, 2011): 134.

13. Chandler, Dawne E., and Payson Hall, *Improving Executive Sponsorship of Projects: A Holistic Approach* (New York: Business Expert Press, 2017): 1.

14. Chandler, Dawne E., and Janice L. Thomas, "Does Executive Sponsorship Matter for Realizing Project Management Value?" *Project Management Journal* (October/November 2015): 47.

15. Kloppenborg, Timothy J., and Debbie Tesch, "How Executive Sponsors Influence Project Success," *MIT Sloan Management Review* (Spring 2015): 28–29.

16. Chandler, Dawne E., and Payson Hall, *Improving Executive Sponsorship of Projects: A Holistic Approach* (New York, NY: Business Expert Press, 2016): 83–88.

17. Wen, Qi, and Maoshan Qiang, "Enablers for Organizational Project Management in the Chinese Context," *Project Management Journal* (February/March 2016): 121.

Leading and Managing Project Teams

CHAPTER OBJECTIVES

After completing this chapter, you should be able to:

CORE OBJECTIVES:

- Describe stages of team development and strategies to move teams through the project life cycle.
- Describe characteristics of a high-performing project team; assess your individual and team capability; and describe how your team can improve.
- Describe methods of project team decision making and the circumstances in which each is likely to be most effective.

BEHAVIORAL OBJECTIVES:

- Explain how to utilize the project team relationship and process ground rules to improve it.
- Describe types of project manager power and when each is appropriate.
- Describe typical sources of project conflict along with the steps in a conflict-resolution process, styles of handling conflict, and steps in a negotiation process.
- Summarize how to develop high-performance traditional and virtual teams.

Gallup Consulting is a global research-based consultancy, specializing in employee and customer management. Our goal is to take discoveries in behavioral economics and apply them to management and business problems. Every organization has an enormous, but largely untapped, potential for breakthrough improvements in productivity through leveraging how human nature drives business performance. This unrealized potential can be measured and managed to improve performance.

Our consulting work is managed as a series of projects. At the start of each client engagement, project leaders gather the high-level information required to identify the client's problems and possible remedies, while understanding any constraints that will affect project success over the long term. The resulting project charter is a business case for the project and a description of how Gallup will add value to the client's organization. Codifying these commitments also helps in enumerating the roles and responsibilities of the project team members.

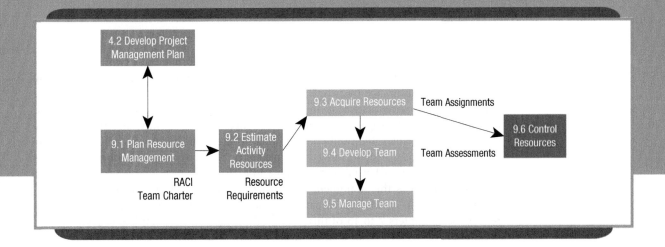

Staffing a team is critical to project success. Our research shows that there are three keys to being an effective project leader:

1. Knowing and investing in your own strengths and the strengths of your project team.
2. Getting people with the right talents on your team.
3. Satisfying the four basic needs of those who follow your leadership: trust, compassion, stability, and hope.

By "strength," I mean an ability to provide consistent, near-perfect performance in a specific activity. The first step to building strength is to identify your greatest talents—the ways in which you most naturally think, feel, or behave. Strengths are created when your naturally powerful talents are combined with learnable skills, such as how to put together a project budget. Gallup has studied more than 6 million people, and we have found that individuals have much more potential for growth and productivity in areas of great talent than areas of weakness.

A strengths-based approach improves team cohesion and generates better results. We have found that high-performing teams are more likely to match individuals' talents to assigned tasks and emphasize individual strengths versus seniority in making personnel decisions. High-performing teams also have leaders who meet the needs of trust, compassion, hope, and stability.

We have found that while each team member has his or her own unique strengths, the most successful and cohesive teams possess a broader array of strengths. A tool like the Clifton StrengthsFinder® is useful for helping team members identify the ways they can best contribute to the team's goals. Our research shows that the 34 StrengthsFinder themes naturally cluster into these four groups:

1. Executing—making things happen
2. Influencing—reaching a broader audience
3. Relationship building—holding the team together
4. Strategic thinking—focusing on all the possibilities

The student website describes these strengths from a project management perspective and tells you how to discover your own unique strengths.

—Jim Asplund, Gallup Consulting

An experienced project manager envisions project performance as two related activities. First, people must perform their roles in completing work activities according to the plan. Performance by people is the topic of this chapter. Second, data must be collected and used to determine the project progress and results. Data collection and determining project progress as measured in schedule, cost, quality, and risk terms are the subject of Chapter 14. While determining progress and results is conducted largely in parallel with people performing the project, the two are covered in separate chapters to emphasize exactly what needs to be done in each.

"**Management** is the attainment of organizational goals in an effective and efficient manner through planning, organizing, leading, and controlling organizational resources."[1] Chapters 7 to 15 of this book deal primarily with planning, organizing, and executing the project. This chapter deals mostly with managing and leading project teams. While certain aspects of both management and leadership are necessary in dealing with project teams, in the contemporary approach to projects, the project manager works collaboratively with the project team to the extent possible while continually pushing to reach project goals. "**Leadership** is the influencing process of leaders and followers to achieve organizational objectives through change."[2]

To further elaborate on the focus of this chapter, management is generally focused on traditional functions such as planning, organizing, and controlling. In this chapter, management is concerned with making decisions and working in teams to improve operational efficiency and effectiveness. Leadership, on the other hand, is about providing direction, motivating, and guiding people and teams to realize their potential and achieve challenging organizational goals.

This chapter starts with acquiring the project team up to the point that team members have been successfully brought on board to the project. The second section deals with various activities needed to develop the project team's capability—many of which require leadership from the project manager. The third section includes several considerations for the project manager when managing the performance of the project team. The fourth section covers how to develop effective relationships within the core project team. The fifth section presents issues about conflict and resolution that occur when dealing with both team members and stakeholders. Finally, the concluding section details actions to develop virtual teams.

5-1 Acquire Project Team

Acquire project team is "the process of confirming human resource availability and obtaining the team necessary to complete project assignments."[3] Chances are the core team has already been assembled, as it is very helpful to have the core team together for planning—and even earlier, for chartering a project. However, on some projects, some core team members may be added later. Also, on many large projects, subject matter experts (SMEs) may be added during the early stages. This section deals with the timing of assigning a project team member (preassignment), securing the needed and desired team members (negotiation), and successfully adding them to the project team (onboarding).

It is not necessary for the project manager to always have an opportunity to select the project team members. However, she is still responsible for their performance. Likewise, in certain organizational settings, the project manager may not have total authority over the team member, but she still is accountable for all individuals' and the team's performances.

5-1a Preassignment of Project Team Members

Generally, it is helpful for a project to assign both core team members and SMEs as early as possible for various reasons. One reason is that people often do not like to be told what they must do, but are usually enthusiastic if they get a chance to help in creating a project plan. Therefore, it is good for motivational purposes to include the implementers in planning. A second reason is that when the people who will perform the work help to plan it, many more details may be considered and the resulting plans are often more realistic. Yet another reason to assign project team members early is to be sure they will be dedicated and be available when needed. For external projects, it is a common practice to list specific workers who will be assigned to a project team in the proposal, and occasionally they must be approved by the client. If the project is secured, it is helpful to bring the workers onto the project as quickly as possible.

The downside to bringing SMEs on board before they need to complete project activities is that it could be expensive. For a highly paid expert, this decision can be substantial and impractical. Another problem with bringing people on board early is that they may first be committed to finishing work on a previous project and may not devote the necessary attention to the new project. Regardless of how early you bring a person on a project, it is helpful to keep communications open with the prospective team member and his or her boss so they understand when the person is needed. This is especially critical if the project has a tight deadline and/or if the organization is using critical chain project management.

5-1b Negotiation for Project Team Members

Depending on the norms of the organization, a project manager may need to negotiate with the functional manager and/or a prospective team member directly to secure his or her services for a project. The functional manager (perhaps called a department head or line manager) has the responsibility of running his or her department. For example, the head of accounting is responsible for how the accounting function is performed. She wants to keep all of her workers busy, but not too busy, and wants all of her workers to progress in their capability.

The functional manager may see this project as a good opportunity for some on-the-job training to help a newer employee gain experience. The project manager, on the other hand, wants the "best" resource for his or her project. The best resource may already be busy. Wise project managers often develop good relationships with functional managers to have leverage in negotiating for a good worker. Functional and project managers may look at the situation from the perspective of the department or project, respectively, and have different ideas of who is the appropriate person to work on the project.

A project manager cannot expect to have the best resource from every department (unless perhaps the project is the highest priority project for the company). The functional manager may sometimes need to agree to a different resource from what he or she prefers. In short, most projects have a combination of experienced and inexperienced resources. If a project manager finds all functional managers are only offering inexperienced people, he should probably ask his sponsor for support.

In many organizations, project managers also need to persuade workers to work on their project. For experienced project managers, reputation goes a long way. A project manager can earn a reputation of being a good boss by caring for team members, helping people develop, and assisting them in securing interesting work and promotions at the end of a project. It is important to align individual aspirations and goals with project goals to get the best results from everyone on the project team.

Many employees campaign hard to work for a great project manager and avoid a poor project manager. When negotiating with a potential team member, a project manager wants to sell the project to the person. Of course, strong technical skills are important for SMEs and are helpful for core team members. However, especially for core team members, it may be more critical to be an excellent generalist and skilled at communication and making decisions. Many core team members need to deal with a variety of issues beyond their discipline and focus on making trade-offs that key stakeholders demand.

Sometimes, it is necessary to recruit project team members from outside of the parent organization. Tatro, Inc., uses this strategy, as described in Exhibit 5.1.

5-1c On-Boarding Project Team Members

The ideal time to bring team members and even a few SMEs on board, is when the project charter is being written. When that is not possible, the first thing a project manager might do is share the charter and the meeting minutes with the new member and then have a one-on-one discussion with that person. There are several purposes for this discussion. The first is to ensure that the new person understands the project at a high level and is enthusiastic about being part of it. The second is to learn about the person's personal and professional aspirations. The most effective and happy workers are those who understand how their personal goals and project goals are aligned. Does he or she want to experience the joy of working on something new, travel, training, new coworkers, and so on? What unique strengths does he or she already bring to the project, and what strengths does he or she want to further develop? At this point, the project manager can accomplish the third purpose of the talk, which is to assign the new team member to specific activities and develop a plan for personal improvement. Exhibit 5.2 illustrates how one consulting company that has many projects acquires and on-boards resources.

EXHIBIT 5.1

TATRO, INC., STRATEGY FOR RECRUITING PROJECT TEAM MEMBERS

Tatro, Inc., is a designer and builder of high-end landscape projects. Its strategy is to retain its core strengths of securing contracts, designing exceptional landscapes, and managing projects with demanding clients. It subcontracts most other work, but wants to be very careful that the work is done as well as possible. Tatro understands it needs to have self-motivated workers who are very presentable to discriminating clients. Tatro primarily relies on recommendations to identify potential workers. To screen potential workers, Tatro performs extensive background checks. It examines previous work performed by the worker, talks to previous clients, and attempts to ensure the worker's finances will allow him or her to be stable.

At that point, it attempts to recruit these proven workers. Chris Tetrault, president of Tatro, Inc., states that he uses a combination of four strategies to recruit, as follows:

1. Pay well.
2. Pay quickly.
3. Provide signature projects for the workers to showcase their skills.
4. Try to get them to like me.

Source: Chris Tetrault, President, Tatro, Inc. Reprinted with permission.

EXHIBIT 5.2

ACQUIRING AND ON-BOARDING RESOURCES AT ATOS-ORIGIN

Resources are the most important assets of a consulting company. It becomes very important to nurture them, utilize them effectively, and at the same time make money for the company. At Atos-Origin (a leading IT consulting company), a structured process is followed to manage resources. Resource skills, credentials, and travel preferences; the business unit to which the resource belongs; a summary of projects worked on; and so forth are maintained in a searchable database. Utilization (amount of time a resource is used on projects) is tracked on at least a weekly basis. Resource availability (amount of time each resource is idle or is available for client projects) is also tracked and published to a large group of managers to keep in mind for upcoming assignments.

A central resource manager is responsible for tracking and managing resource utilization. If any member of the management team has an open requirement, the resource manager is first notified of the requirement, so that work can begin on tracking the right person for the role. Resource managers from each business unit meet regularly to discuss staff availability and open positions.

Weekly meetings are held with senior management teams to understand the open staffing requirements. As a first fit, internal available resources are aligned (based on the skills required, time frame of the project, and whether the role aligns with a person's career preferences) with open positions. Since Atos-Origin is a global organization, this helps the company to increase utilization of the individual resource and of the group as a whole. If existing resources are not available or do not fit into the assignment, a requisition to hire new resources is completed, and the job is posted for recruitment.

Atos-Origin considers three different types of external hires: full-time employees (the preferred option), hourly employees (work on an hourly basis; the option used when the project is for a short period of time or when the right resource does not want to accept a full-time offer), and subcontractors (contracting with other companies; the option used sometimes to mitigate resource risks).

The new resource who is hired is on-boarded to the company in a structured fashion, and the same process for managing the person's utilization and availability is followed. This structured process has helped reduce attrition, increased internal transfer of resources, helped individual resource growth, and increased the company's profitability.

Source: Rachana Thariani, PMP, Atos-Origin.

5-2 Develop Project Team

Develop project team is "the process of improving the competencies, team member interaction, and overall team environment to enhance project performance."[4] Developing a highly effective project team requires the following six activities from the project manager. Note these six activities build upon each other and are overlapping.

5-2.1.1 Understand stages of project team development.

5-2.1.2 Understand characteristics of high-performing project teams.

5-2.1.3 Assess individual member capability.

5-2.1.4 Assess project team capability.

5-2.1.5 Build both individual and team capability.

5-2.1.6 Establish team ground rules (team charter).

5-2a Stages of Project Team Development

Project teams typically go through a predictable set of stages as they work together. By effectively using project tools and developing trust and understanding within their teams, project managers can greatly diminish some of the negative aspects of project team development stages. While almost all teams go through these stages, the duration of each stage varies for each team, based on various factors such as familiarity among the team members, corporate culture, uncertainties and unknowns associated with the project, and the urgency of the project. Consequently, some teams get "stalled" in an early stage and do not progress. Some get further along and then have a setback. Setbacks for project teams can also come from losing or gaining core team members or SMEs, changes in project requirements, quality problems with project deliverables, or other reasons. The good news for a team that suffers a setback is that because they worked through the team development stages once, they can probably work through the stages more quickly the second time. The bad news is that they do need to work their way through.

Each stage of team development has its own challenges. For a project manager to successfully help a team develop, he or she should be aware of how team members feel and what behaviors they frequently attempt at each stage. People have a tendency to be friendly with people who have similar values, while differences are often seen as a threat that may affect collaboration and lead to undesirable attitudes and behaviors. This behavioral issue presents challenges in managing teams, specifically global project teams, where diversity and cultural differences are the norm.

Exhibit 5.3 presents information about behavioral characteristics of the team during each stage of team development and ideas for managing them.

In learning about and using some of the project management tools that are described throughout this book, one can implement quite a few of the strategies for team

EXHIBIT 5.3

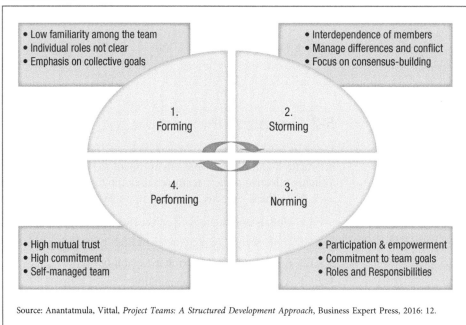

Source: Anantatmula, Vittal, *Project Teams: A Structured Development Approach*, Business Expert Press, 2016: 12.

development. For example, when a team works together to create a good charter, they rapidly work through the project-forming stage and often begin to develop the openness, understanding, and trust that help make their storming stage faster and easier. Information regarding the issues, behaviors, and strategies associated with each stage is displayed in Exhibit 5.4.

Understanding the stages of development that project teams typically progress through is a basis for project goal attainment and project team development. For example, if a project manager of a new team wants to help his or her team progress through the stages without too much trouble, he or she can look at the top and bottom rows of Exhibit 5.4. New members often feel a combination of excitement about being picked for the new team and concern that the work may be difficult. The project manager can help the new team develop team-operating methods early—when they construct the project charter. Having the team decide how they will work together helps establish workable methods and simultaneously helps the team members start to know and trust each

EXHIBIT 5.4

PROJECT TEAM PROGRESSION THROUGH DEVELOPMENT STAGES					
	FORMING	STORMING	NORMING	PERFORMING	ADJOURNING
Team member relationship issues	Feel excitement, yet skepticism	Feel resistance, yet longing to commit to project	Feel part of team and believe project will succeed	Feel close to teammates and understand teammates	Feel strong attachment to team and feel loss when team disbands
Team members attempt to	Understand expectations, activities needed, and power structures	Jockey for power, ask many questions, and establish dubious goals	Accept team members, hold open discussions, and establish team norms	Improve self, prevent and solve problems, and expand beyond official role	Complete project on high note, maintain relationships with teammates, and seek next challenge
PM strategies to promote organization needs	Develop business case and acceptance criteria in charter	Develop stakeholder analysis, communication plan, budget, and quality plan	Manage trade-offs per stakeholder desires, include sponsor in talks, and conduct audit	Share applied learnings with organization and report progress to stakeholders	Secure customer acceptance of deliverables, honestly appraise team members, and provide ongoing support to users
PM strategies to promote project needs	Develop scope overview, milestone schedule, risks, and learnings in charter	Develop scope statement, WBS, schedule, and risk register	Add SMEs as needed, authorize work, and improve work processes	Monitor and control project according to plan and update plans as needed	Test project deliverables and secure team member endorsement of them
PM strategies to promote team member needs	Develop team operating methods and commitment in charter, and help members build relationships	Clarify each member's role, encourage all to participate, and determine team ground rules	Personalize each member's role, collaborate when possible, and assess and build members and team capability	Capture applied learnings and improve meeting and time management	Celebrate success, reward team members, and help team members secure follow-on work

Source: Adapted from Barbara J. Streibel, Peter R. Sholtes, and Brian L. Joiner, *The Team Handbook*, 3rd ed. (Madison, WI: Oriel Incorporated, 2005): 6–8.

other. Once the initial forming is over, it is common for teams to "storm"—that is, to feel more stress as they begin to understand how big and difficult the project appears upon closer scrutiny. Some of the team members may want to participate in the project performance yet may resist committing fully. The project manager may work with the team to help ensure that everyone understands and accepts their respective roles. Further, when each team member understands the other members' roles, they can see how the project will be accomplished. The project manager can continue to encourage all team members to actively participate and to refine the team operating methods into ground rules if necessary.

Once a project team weathers the storming period, the members often are relieved because they start to believe they will be successful. Continued team building can help a team to refine its ability to perform. As team members are encouraged to collaborate and build capability, the team moves to a higher level, which is often called the performing stage. Not every team reaches this level. However, it is very satisfying for the teams that do because the team members realize and increase their potential. Also, this level is a valuable milestone at which lessons learned can be realized and used to help improve other project teams. Finally, project teams disband when the project is over. If the project has been successful, team members often feel both excited about facing new challenges and sad about leaving a satisfying experience and good friends. Project managers should use celebration, rewards, and appropriate follow-on work to guide the team through this last stretch.

5-2b Characteristics of High-Performing Project Teams

Once a project manager understands the typical stages of team development, it is time to understand the characteristics of high-performing project teams. These characteristics, which are an elaborate expansion of the performing column in Exhibit 5.4, reflect the ideals toward which a project manager tries to guide his or her team.

Teams eager to become high performing often create and use a team charter to enhance their effectiveness. A team charter presents information about how members are expected to collaborate in the activities of the project and participate in making decisions. Specifically, team members work in concert with one another. The team charter also specifies professional performance and the personal behavior of the team members to achieve harmony, teamwork, team spirit, and dedication.

Developing a team charter promotes collaboration and synergy among the team members and leads to better team performance. The team charter describes group norms, which are either written or unwritten rules that dictate behaviors and expectations of the team members. The charter guides team members regarding work ethics, honesty, integrity, respect, conflict management, decision making, and communication protocols. It is preferred for a project team to develop a team charter to improve its performance by defining norms for common understanding and agreement, as shown in Exhibit 5.5.

This chain of high-performing project team characteristics is shown in Exhibit 5.6. Remember, this is the ideal. Many project teams perform well and exhibit some, but not all, of these characteristics. Nevertheless, a conscientious project manager keeps these characteristics in mind and strives to help his team develop each one.

The characteristics of high-performing project teams start with the *personal values* of individual team members. While a project manager can and should strive to improve upon these values, it is far easier if team members are recruited with a good start on the following values:

EXHIBIT 5.5

PROJECT TEAM CHARTER

Basic Performance
- Reporting/Processes
- Elemental Data Reporting
- Responsibilities and Assignments
- Set Consequences of Nonconformance
- Timeliness (Attendance as Well as Delivery)
- Work Hours

Specify
- Time Spent
- Obligations
- Reporting
- Deliverables
- Knowledge Sharing
- Tracking (Plan vs. Actual)

Personal Behavior Expectations
- Civility
- Meeting Protocols
- Social Graces
- Decision Protocol
- Receiving/Offering Assistance

Attitudinal Expectations
- Cooperative Stance
- Honest Communication
- Conflict Recognition
- Negotiations
- Teamwork

Desirable Norms
- Demeanor
- Communication
- Conflict management
- Negotiation

Expected Outcomes
- Trust
- Team Spirit
- Harmony
- Cohesiveness
- Rare major conflicts
- Commitment

Source: Anantatmula, Vittal, *Project Teams: A Structured Development Approach*, Business Expert Press, 2016: 136–139.

- High need for achievement
- Understanding and acceptance of personal responsibility
- Commitment to self-development and self-directed behavior
- Ability to put project needs before their own needs within reason
- Willingness to consider alternative views and to change
- Personal commitment to the project

EXHIBIT 5.6

CHARACTERISTICS OF HIGH-PERFORMING PROJECT TEAMS

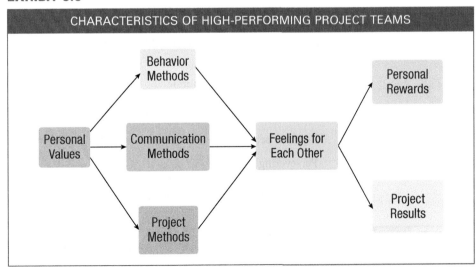

The personal values can be enhanced by utilizing the following effective team behavior methods:

- Team members are selected to represent the right skill mix.
- Team members help each other.
- Team members demonstrate a constant focus on improvement.
- Team members use effective time management, including for meetings.
- Team members strive for innovation with few formal procedures.
- Team members capture, share, and use lessons learned.

The personal values can be further improved by practicing the following beneficial communications methods:

- Information is freely and widely shared within and beyond the team.
- All important topics are openly discussed.
- Conflict over approaches is valued, but personal conflict is discouraged.
- Potential problems are proactively reported.
- Teams conduct frequent debriefings and reflect to collectively learn.
- Barriers to communication are overcome.

Project managers can certainly use some of the following project management methods to further the team development:

- Agree on common goals and objectives for the project.
- Jointly plan the project.
- Use the charter to guide joint decision making.
- Work together to accomplish activities.
- Proactively identify and solve problems.
- Hold each other mutually accountable with individualized feedback.

Using effective team, communications, and project management methods leads to development of the following appropriate feelings that team members can begin to hold toward one another:

- Recognizing how interdependent they are
- Being flexible on how each contributes to the project
- Being willing to share risks with teammates and having tolerance for minor mistakes
- Understanding, appreciating, liking, and trusting each other
- Sharing in strong project leadership

This chain leads to two favorable outcomes. The first set of outcomes is personal rewards that each team member is likely to receive such as the following:

- Enjoyment of their work
- High spirit and team morale
- Pride in being part of the team
- Satisfaction in project accomplishments

The other set of favorable outcomes includes the following strong project results:

- Persevering despite challenges
- Producing high-quality results
- Consistently meeting or exceeding stakeholder expectations.[5]

In addition to these characteristics, agile teams are often described as being self-managed, focused on project goals, strong communicators, able to decide quickly, more responsible, and willing to trust their instincts once they understand their sponsor. The result is that these team members are more satisfied, flexible, and accommodating.

Traditional projects use distributed work teams and more specialists and adopt a process-oriented approach. On the other hand, teams on agile project typically employ co-located teams to manage rapid changes and increments. However, agile teams can be in multiple locations. Further, agile teams require motivated members with a higher level of commitment. Agile teams have these seven desirable traits:

- Question everything
- Focus on innovation
- Fail their way to success
- Communicate thoughts and ideas
- Deliver value
- Change incrementally
- Connect with their purpose[6]

The Agile project team members are also responsible for regularly checking for deviations and should be capable of detecting aspects of the project that violate the specifications.

5-2c Assessing Individual Member Capability

Synergy results in a team having a collective capability that exceeds the sum of individual capabilities. Conversely, if team synergy is absent, the collective capability would fall short of individual capabilities put together. More often than not, individual team members with high capability can effectively be developed into a strong team. So, what capabilities should project team members possess? Five types of useful project team member capabilities are as follows:

1. Activity-specific knowledge and skills
2. Personal planning and control
3. Personal learning
4. Organizational understanding
5. Interpersonal skills and sensitivity

The first three capabilities are necessary for a person to be a strong individual performer, and the last two capabilities help a person become a valuable team player. While all five are useful, if a project manager wants to develop a strong project team, the last two capabilities may be more important. Too many teams have not achieved the expected success because team members were content with their individual performance.

The first type is activity-specific capability. If a team member is responsible for a specific function such as managing the construction of a stone wall, he or she should understand in detail what needs to be accomplished to create a desirable stone wall. If she will personally build the wall, she also needs the skills to do so. A second desirable capability is personal planning and control, for example, setting personal goals, accomplishing work as planned, and managing time wisely. Regarding the third capability, project team members should desire to continually improve and invest effort in their personal improvement. Learning should never stop.

The fourth useful capability is understanding the organizational structure, culture, and roles and using that knowledge to support the project manager in accomplishing project activities. This involves knowing the informal methods and networks within the parent organization. If the project is being performed for a client, it can also include knowing how things work within the client's organization. The last useful team member capability is interpersonal skills and sensitivity. This includes skills such as active listening, effective speaking, and conflict management. It also includes possessing emotional intelligence and having sensitivity toward others who have different personalities or backgrounds.

5-2d Assessing Project Team Capability

When assessing project team capability, the project manager should remember that his or her responsibilities are to simultaneously support the parent organization, the project, and the project team. These three are intertwined in many ways. While much has been written concerning teams, Exhibit 5.7 summarizes the success factors of project teams. Note the related chapter number and specific topic where this book gives guidance to help achieve each success factor. Many practices of good project management (and good organizational management) help a project team to excel, just as many team success factors help a project team deliver desired project and organizational results.

For example, the project charter covered in Chapter 3 is helpful in achieving many of the project team success factors. The entire project charter is a basis for more detailed project planning and for understanding project objectives. Working together to develop, sign, and distribute the charter greatly aids in communications and commitment. Specific sections of the charter also help teams develop successfully as they realize shared goals and challenges. The team operating methods section helps guide team member behaviors as they resolve conflicts, the applied learnings help create a stimulating work environment, and the acceptance criteria help team members understand when they satisfy project stakeholders.

Following is a brief description of why each project team success factor listed in Exhibit 5.7 is useful:

1. Project teams with strong leadership are more likely to be successful. Leadership can occur at every level within a project team. Each member performs better by understanding both his or her own role and those of all the other executives, managers, and associates that are part of the team. Part of project team leadership is the project culture nurtured by the sponsor and project manager.
2. Effective team leadership can lead to mutual trust, respect, and credibility among all parties.
3. This, in turn, can lead to the cross-functional cooperation and support that help guide a project through turbulent situations.

4–5. Project managers have many project tools to guide a team—charters, stakeholder analysis, communications plans, scope statements, WBSs, schedules, and kickoff meetings. Collectively, they help to create clarity and active support for the project. It is difficult to overestimate the impact that effective communication has on project teams. When people are not given information, they must guess. Proactive project managers realize that developing and implementing an effective two-way communication plan is a major key to their teams' success.

6–8. The next three project team success factors—skills, objectives, and behaviors—apply specifically to the team. Assembling the right blend of skills and experience for the project team can be quite challenging. This is especially true in the current work environment of cost-control measures. One option for project managers is to staff the project with a combination of experienced and inexperienced members because it often costs less to include an inexperienced person in the project team. An expectation

EXHIBIT 5.7

	PROJECT TEAM SUCCESS FACTORS		
	PROJECT TEAM SUCCESS FACTORS	CPM CHAPTER	TOPIC
1	Team leadership in setting direction and project culture	4	Project management roles, organization, and project cultures
2	Mutual trust, respect, and credibility among team members and leaders	4	Project management roles
		6	Build relationships
		5	Develop project team
3	Cross-functional cooperation, communication, and support	3	Project charter
		6	Communications planning
4	Clear project plans created by team and supported by organization	3	Project charter
		6	Stakeholder analysis
		7	Scope and WBS
		8	Activity schedule
		12	Kick off project
5	Effective communications including feedback on performance	6	Communications planning
		6	Information distribution
		14	Report progress
		15	Secure customer acceptance
6	Team skills and experience appropriate and adequate	9	Resource projects
		5	Acquire and develop project team
		14	Manage overloads and resolve resource conflicts
7	Clearly defined and pursued project and team objectives	3	Project charter
		14	Direct and manage project execution
8	Use of task and relationship behaviors to resolve conflicts and problems	3	Team operating methods
		6	Build relationships, meeting management
		11	Risk planning
9	Stimulating work environment with opportunities for improvement and learning	3	Applied learnings
		14	Process improvement
		15	Capture and share applied learnings
10	Opportunity for team and personal recognition when project satisfies stakeholders	3	Acceptance criteria
		15	Celebrate success

Source: Adapted from Hans J. Thamhain, "Team Leadership Effectiveness in Technology-Based Project Environments," *Project Management Journal* 35 (4) (December 2004): 38–39; and Roy C. Herrenkohl, *Becoming a Team: Achieving a Goal* (Mason, OH: Thomson South-Western, 2004): 9, 25.

can be set for the more experienced person to mentor the junior person. This promotes organizational learning as well as achieving the project's goals at a lower cost. Many project teams include a section in their charter on team operating methods. This section often spells out methods of decision making, meeting management, and demonstrating professionalism. While working through staffing decisions, an astute project manager may recognize people in two categories: task oriented or people oriented (relations). Both types are necessary, and the project manager will have to manage a balance by developing or recruiting team members.

9–10. When the first eight project team success factors are adequately accomplished, the last two are often realized. These last two—stimulating work and opportunity for recognition—have shown the strongest correlation to successful project performance as perceived by senior managers.[6] People work hard and enthusiastically if they find their work stimulating and believe they will be rewarded for it. Appropriate and sincere recognition can often be at least as powerful a motivation as monetary rewards. Project managers can use their creativity to reward all who merit it.

All 10 of these project team success factors can be influenced by a project manager. Many of the success factors require some early work, such as the project charter, and some require continuing work as the project progresses. A new project manager can ask questions to determine to what extent his project team currently displays each of these success factors. Then he will be ready to build the team's capacity upon this base.

5-2e Building Individual and Project Team Capability

Project managers have many tools at their disposal for developing individuals and teams. Many of the methods can be used together and reinforce each other. Seven methods that many project managers find useful are as follows:

1. Demonstrate personal leadership.
2. Utilize project management tools.
3. Demand situational leadership.
4. Create a desirable team identity.
5. Teach personal responsibility.
6. Develop understanding and respect.
7. Use a learning cycle.

PERSONAL LEADERSHIP   A good way for project managers to build the capability of their team is to start by being an effective leader. An effective leader creates and shares a strong vision for the project. Leading by example gives team members a model to follow. A project manager leads by balancing the demands of the parent organization, the project, and the team members. In this context, the project manager is a team member—but one who treats herself and all the other team members in a respectful manner. The project manager must use the highest levels of honesty and ethics. This includes never stating anything that is false, but also not giving any false impressions. This can cause a bit of extra work or conflict in the short term, but it is the only appropriate behavior and pays great dividends in the long run by encouraging (and even demanding) everyone else to do what is right. Transparency in communication and action and aligning both are critical and will set an example for the rest of the team and instill trust among all team members.

PROJECT MANAGEMENT TOOLS   Project managers can use project management tools to develop focus and cohesion among team members. For example, the charter helps a team to start quickly and collectively. The WBS, schedule, and other project management tools each help to focus the team in explicit ways. Specifically, the WBS is the best tool for project integration and assimilation of the project team to work toward specific goals and shared outcomes.

SITUATIONAL LEADERSHIP   Depending on the team's initial capability, a project manager may need to start as a strong individual leader, but the goal is to develop multiple leaders on the project team. In fact, in a great project team, leadership is situational; that is, each member may have a leadership role in certain circumstances and follower roles in other situations. In areas in which a junior team member has specific knowledge, he or she should ensure that everyone understands the situation. Even a junior team member is often expected to lead in certain situations. Furthermore, during the initial stages of team development, the project manager assumes the roles of directing and monitoring team activities, but those change to supporting and facilitating roles once the team moves to the performing stage.

DESIRABLE TEAM IDENTITY   Another way to build team capacity is to create a desirable team identity. Frequently, the project manager and sponsor start thinking about this even before they recruit the first team members. People want to be associated with a winner. If people believe that a project is vital to the organization and that the work is professionally stimulating, they want to be part of the team. Depending on the organization, some teams give detailed thought to the project name and "brand." Military organizations and sports teams often do well in developing and maintaining team identity by associating themselves with pride and prestige. Uniforms demonstrate this identity externally.

RESPONSIBILITY   Project team members need to understand they all have three responsibilities. The first is to complete their individual work on time, on budget, and correctly as specified in the WBS dictionary. Second, they must complete their joint work responsibilities with teammates on time, on budget, and according to the plan. Third, each team member is responsible for improving work methods. Everyone needs to improve his or her personal work and work with the team to jointly improve the project team's capabilities.

UNDERSTANDING AND RESPECT   Project team members need to develop understanding and trust in each other to develop team capability. Understanding other team members starts with understanding oneself. A self-aware individual is more effective in establishing relationships by better appreciating and valuing the contributions of others and being willing to learn from them. One method of understanding both oneself and others better is to use StrengthsFinder and to realize how each individual strength can be productively applied on projects, as shown on the student website. As team members understand one another and develop interdependence, they are naturally able to understand and develop interdependence beyond the project team. Since most projects have multiple stakeholders, this ability to connect at many levels is vital to team development.

LEARNING CYCLE   Building project team capability can be envisioned as a learning cycle in which the team uses creativity to jointly develop and consider alternative approaches while striving to learn at each point in the process. This learning cycle can be easily understood using the plan-do-check-act (PDCA) model. The project team capability building cycle is shown in Exhibit 5.8.

Project team capacity building is performed in the context of planning and executing project work. Project teams can pass through this capability-building cycle repeatedly as

EXHIBIT 5.8

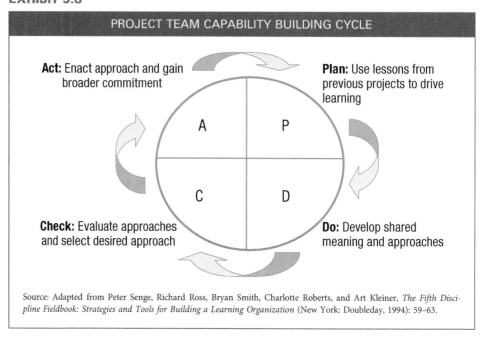

PROJECT TEAM CAPABILITY BUILDING CYCLE

Act: Enact approach and gain broader commitment

Plan: Use lessons from previous projects to drive learning

Check: Evaluate approaches and select desired approach

Do: Develop shared meaning and approaches

A   P

C   D

Source: Adapted from Peter Senge, Richard Ross, Bryan Smith, Charlotte Roberts, and Art Kleiner, *The Fifth Discipline Fieldbook: Strategies and Tools for Building a Learning Organization* (New York: Doubleday, 1994): 59–63.

they progressively learn how to work better together to reach their project goals. Free and open communications along with a willingness to challenge each other are important because the project team may need to unlearn or give up past behaviors in favor of new approaches that might be more effective.

In the "plan" step, project teams are challenged with using lessons learned from previous projects to drive their improvement efforts. These lessons need to be compared to the emerging requirements for the project that the team learns from methods such as gathering requirements, meeting with customers, brainstorming risks, and holding design reviews. Further, historical data from Earned Value Management (EVM) of previously executed projects, which provide actual and realistic data, can improve accuracy of cost and time estimates of the current project, specifically for similar or identical WBS elements.

In the "do" step, the project team then uses this knowledge to develop shared meaning and potential approaches that they may use. The team uncovers assumptions, brainstorms alternative approaches, and often develops rolling wave plans so the results of early work will give the information needed to create good plans for later work.

In the "check" step, the project team evaluates the potential approaches and selects one. They can use techniques such as piloting new technology, creating a subject matter expert panel for recommendations, conducting feasibility studies, and reviewing the problem with key stakeholders to obtain a clear decision.

In the "act" step, the project team finishes the planning, carries it out, and gathers data regarding it. This data can be verified with the planned data for continuous improvement of the planning process of scope, cost, and time. Simultaneously, the team seeks acceptance beyond their team through articulating the project's business case, involving key stakeholders, proactively communicating according to plans, and not acting until enough support is in place.

The cycle then repeats. Project teams that are serious about improving their capability repeat this cycle quickly within project stages, at key milestones, and from project to

Select team members with a variety of strengths to ensure balanced participation.

moodboard/Alamy Stock Photo

project. The improved capacity of one project team can be shared with other projects through lessons learned and sharing core team members and SMEs with other projects.

5-2f Establishing Project Team Ground Rules

Project teams often create a brief set of operating principles in their charter as described in Chapter 3. For small teams performing simple projects, these principles are enough to guide their behavior. This is especially true if the company has a track record of success with teams. However, many managers understand that more specific ground rules can help prevent many potential problems that some project teams encounter. Ground rules are acceptable behaviors adopted by a project team to improve working relationships, effectiveness, and communication. Therefore, many times, the simple set of operating principles is expanded into a broader set of ground rules.

Exhibit 5.9 lists a dozen of the most frequent topics that project teams choose to create ground rules to cover. Note the topics are classified as either dealing primarily with process issues or primarily with relationship issues. Note also that there is more than one way to implement each ground rule. Also listed in Exhibit 5.9 are two strengths from the student website that might be used in very different ways to accomplish each ground rule—and other strengths could be applied as well—each in its own unique manner.

RELATIONSHIP TOPICS   The relationship topics both help the team make better decisions and help project team members feel valued. People who feel valued often work with much more enthusiasm and commitment.

Encourage Participation   The first relationship topic is to encourage balanced participation. This balance can include drawing out an introverted person and asking a

EXHIBIT 5.9

A DOZEN GROUND RULE TOPICS FOR PROJECT TEAMS	
RELATIONSHIP TOPICS	PROCESS TOPICS
1. Encourage participation. Consistency Includer	**1. Manage meetings.** Achiever Discipline
2. Discuss openly. Communication Intellection	**2. Establish roles.** Arranger Individualization
3. Protect confidentiality. Deliberative Relator	**3. Maintain focus.** Command Focus
4. Avoid misunderstandings. Connectedness Harmony	**4. Consider alternatives.** Analytical Strategic
5. Develop trust. Belief Responsibility	**5. Use data.** Context Input
6. Handle conflict. Adaptability Empathy	**6. Make decisions.** Activator Restorative

talkative person to let another individual speak. Balance can mean ensuring that all functions are given the opportunity to provide input. Balanced participation can also mean sharing leadership roles. The project manager certainly needs to be a leader, but each project team member can provide leadership in certain situations.

Discuss Openly and Protect Confidentiality   The second relationship topic is to encourage open discussion. When some topics are off limits for discussion, sometimes important issues are not raised, and poor decisions are made. Closely related to open discussion is the issue of protecting confidentiality. People should have trust that a sensitive issue will not be repeated outside of the project team. It is hard to work effectively together if team members are concerned that important issues could be shared inappropriately.

Avoid Misunderstandings   Since projects are often staffed by people from different functions and even different companies, there is a strong potential for misunderstandings. Both the person stating something and the person listening have a responsibility to avoid potential misunderstandings. Many active listening techniques are useful for this purpose, such as summarizing what was said, asking the listener to restate what was conveyed, or asking for an example.

Develop Trust   The fifth relationship topic is to develop trust. Each project team member has two responsibilities to establish trust. First, one should always be worthy of the trust of his or her teammates. This means accomplishing work as promised, communicating transparently, and being completely truthful always. Part of being truthful may be expressing in advance a concern about the ability to do certain work due to reasons such as skills, knowledge, or time constraints. The second responsibility is to trust his or her teammates unless and until one proves unworthy of trust. Many people live up to the expectations of others.

By practicing the highest ethical standards and expecting the same from other team members, a project manager can expect most team members to demonstrate their trustworthiness. That does not mean that you trust an inexperienced person naively to figure out how to perform a complex task independently. Common sense must be exercised in assigning work and determining the level of support required for everyone in the team.

Handle Conflict   The final relationship ground rule topic is how to handle conflict. Conflict can bring out creative discussion and lead to better methods and solutions if the conflict is confined to a technical or task issue. However, conflict that becomes personal can be destructive and demotivating. Therefore, conflict over ideas is often encouraged (up to a point), while personal conflict is often settled by the concerned individuals off the project. The project manager may get involved and/or may bring in a neutral third party if necessary to resolve people-related conflicts. Conflict management is covered later in this chapter.

PROCESS TOPICS   Process topics include how a project team works together as they gather data, meet, and make important project decisions.

Manage Meetings   The process topic regarding meeting management is introduced in Chapter 6 in the context of improving and documenting meetings. Special applications of meeting management are covered in Chapter 12 for kickoff meetings and Chapter 14 for progress reporting meetings.

Establish Roles   The second process topic is to establish roles. People are usually assigned to a project team in the role of project manager, core team member, or subject matter expert. Within the team, however, it is often helpful to assign roles regarding items such as who plans a meeting, who watches the time, and who records the minutes. One important principle with these role assignments is to try to help everyone feel valued. A person who is constantly assigned to perform unpleasant tasks may not feel as important or as motivated to contribute. Another part of assigning roles is to assign tasks to project team members between meetings. Each worker is then responsible for completing their assignments and to report if these assignments are not completed as planned. However, it is good practice to follow up with the members between meetings to ensure that project tasks are completed as planned.

Maintain Focus   Project managers and the team are often under pressure to complete the project below the budget and ahead of schedule. Therefore, project managers need to ensure that the team stays focused. A periodic review of actual progress using the project plan and project documents to resolve disagreements regarding decisions can help greatly. The project charter and the plan remind the team what they are trying to accomplish and why. Another means of maintaining focus is referring to the stakeholder analysis and the trade-off decisions that the key stakeholders have indicated. The key with focus is to spend the most time and energy on important issues and to delegate, postpone, or ignore less important issues.

Consider Alternatives   The fourth process-oriented ground rule topic is to always consider at least two alternative approaches before proceeding. It is amazing how many project teams simply agree with the first suggestion that someone makes. A team that invests as little as a couple of minutes of time can ensure that they have considered alternative approaches. Quite often, a much better idea emerges from a second or third suggestion than from the first one. Also, many times a project team decides to combine the better parts of two alternatives. This consideration of alternatives not only often yields a better approach, but it also often results in better commitment because more people's ideas were considered.

For example, in a project to install a suite of equipment at a customer's site, a final site investigation revealed that a major piece of equipment was not functional. One answer was to expedite the shipment of a duplicate piece of equipment, while a competing alternative was to use overtime labor and consultants to refurbish the onsite equipment. Both alternatives were expensive, and neither looked very promising. However, upon further discussion, it was determined that one section of the equipment was the primary concern, so a new section could be airfreighted in and the workers onsite could install it. This hybrid alternative proved to be far less expensive and more practical than either alternative that the panicked team first considered.

Use Data   The fifth process-oriented ground rule topic is to always use data when possible. Gather the facts instead of arguing over opinions. In meetings, make the data visible to everyone on the team so that all can use it to help make informed decisions. It is possible that a team will generate more alternatives if the data is presented in meetings because it promotes constructive discussions and synergy. Many of the quality tools listed in Exhibit 14.9 help the project team to gather, organize, prioritize, and analyze data for making informed decisions.

Make Decisions   The final process-related topic is decision making. Project decisions can be made in several different ways. Adherence to the other ground rule topics will help regardless of which decision-making method is chosen. Methods that project teams often use to make decisions include the following:

- The project manager or sponsor makes the decision.
- One or two team members recommend or make the decision.
- The project team uses consensus to make the decision.
- The project team votes to make the decision.

On some issues, the project sponsor or project manager retains the right to make a decision. Sometimes, this is because a decision needs to be made quickly or it takes higher authority. A sponsor or project manager may also ask for input from the team and then make the decision. While this is often a good idea, that person should be very careful to tell the team up front that he or she still intends to make the decision. Otherwise, the team members who provided input may feel that their ideas were not considered.

Project managers may choose to delegate a decision to one or two team members—either members of the core team or SMEs. This strategy works well when not enough information or time is available at the current meeting and the decision needs to be made before the following meeting. Decisions that primarily impact one or two members rather than the entire project team are ripe for delegation. Delegating to two team members has the secondary benefit of their getting to know each other better and working well together for the rest of the project duration. A variation on this delegation strategy is to ask one or two team members to investigate and recommend a solution on which the team can decide at the next meeting. Over the course of a project, most team members will probably get the chance to make certain decisions.

Consensus is wonderful, but reaching it requires a time-consuming technique. True consensus means each person actively supports the decision—even if it is not his or her first choice. The team tells stakeholders that after discussion they understand the decision that was made is the best one for the project. To reach this true consensus, each person needs to be able to articulate what he or she believes is important in the decision and why. Creative approaches may need to be developed when none of the original ideas pleases everyone. Consensus is helpful when significant commitment is necessary to implement the decision. Consensus also might involve cultural issues, so it is important to include everyone in making decisions.

One final method that project teams might use to make decisions is to vote. This is often a poor choice since the losers of the vote may not be very enthusiastic and may not support implementation of the choice wholeheartedly. Another method may be better than standard voting. A straw vote—that is, a test for agreement—is a method by which a team may take a nonbinding vote. If most of the team agrees, then it may not take long to drive toward consensus. If many members do not agree, then delaying the decision, gathering more data, or agreeing to let one person make the decision may be in order.

5-3 Manage Project Team

Manage project team is "the process of tracking team member performance, providing feedback, resolving issues, and coordinating changes to optimize project performance."[7] When managing the project team, a project manager uses various forms of power to get team members to prioritize and commit to project work. Project managers are often called upon to either assess members' performance or to at least provide input for the performance assessments.

5-3a Project Manager Power and Leadership

Since project managers often rely on people who do not report directly to them to perform some of the project work, they need to use various forms of power to encourage people to perform. Types of power available to project managers are shown in Exhibit 5.10.

EXHIBIT 5.10

TYPES OF PROJECT MANAGER POWER		
TYPE OF POWER	BRIEF DESCRIPTION	WHEN USED
Legitimate	Formal authority based upon user's position	Asking people to perform within their job description
Reward	Persuading others based upon giving them something	If team members perform well and if negotiating for resources
Coercive	Punishing others for not performing	Only when needed to maintain discipline or enforce rules
Referent	Persuading others based upon personal relationship	Frequent since project managers often lack legitimate power based upon position
Expert	Persuading others based upon your own knowledge and skills	When others respect your opinions
Information	Control of information	Frequent, as a large part of a project manager's role is to convey information
Connection	Informal based upon user's relationships with influential people	When working with project sponsors and when negotiating for resources

Source: Adapted from Robert N. Lussier and Christopher F. Achua, *Leadership: Theory, Application, Skill Development,* 4th ed. Mason, OH: South-Western Cengage Learning, 2010: 110–117.

LEGITIMATE POWER   Project managers often may not have authority over the project team members, although they are responsible and accountable for their performance. Therefore, project managers often have less legitimate power than other managers. However, to the extent that project managers can ask team members to perform certain activities, they should do so. In contemporary project management, a project manager often has a core team to help plan and manage major parts of the project. These core team members are probably the people the project manager can instruct to perform certain activities, but he or she would be better served when it is possible to ask them to plan the activities. The old axiom is true: people tend to support the things they helped to create.

REWARD AND COERCIVE POWER   Reward and coercive power are opposites of each other. Not all rewards cost money. In fact, stimulating work is one of the most powerful rewards. Enticing people to perform well so they can be assigned to more interesting and/or challenging work helps the team member, the immediate project, and the organization. While reward power is the preferred method, there are times when a person is not performing and a threat, or coercion, may be necessary. This is especially true if most members of the project team are performing and one or two members are not. People who work hard value teammates who also work hard and are often upset when some members do not contribute their share.

REFERENT POWER   Referent power is when a project team member works for the project manager out of personal desire. Project managers sow the seeds for referent power when interviewing candidates for their project team. If the project manager takes the time to understand the personal motives of each team member, he or she can create desirable opportunities for each. Individual project managers who remember the adage "no one loves your project as much as you do" use their referent power by continuing to describe their project's purpose in ways that appeal to each individual worker's desires. Many successful project managers work hard to develop both friendships and respect with their team members. Loyalty must go both ways. If a team member believes a project manager has his or her best interests at heart and will advocate for him or her, then that team member is more likely to demonstrate loyalty to the project manager by working hard.

EXPERT POWER   Generally, people want to succeed in whatever they do. Project managers can tap into this desire by using expert power. If a project manager has a reputation for success and can convince others that he or she understands enough of the project management technology and politics to successfully guide the project, then people will be more inclined to work hard on the project. They will be convinced that their efforts will pay off and that they will have a chance to learn and grow professionally.

INFORMATION POWER   Information power is something that project managers want to use, but not in a coercive manner. While information is power, withholding or distorting information is unethical. A project manager's responsibility is to ensure that whoever needs certain information receives it in a timely manner, in a form they can understand, and with complete honesty and accuracy. That does not mean sharing confidential information inappropriately. It does mean empowering the core team to distribute information promptly and accurately according to the communication plan. This gives the core team more knowledge power.

CONNECTION POWER   The very reason for having executives sponsor projects is because the sponsor frequently has more legitimate power than the project manager. Project managers can use the power of the sponsor when necessary. A project manager who frequently asks the sponsor to intervene looks weak. On the other hand, a project manager who does not ask for the sponsor's help when it is really needed lacks judgment. Project managers can create many champions for their project by continuing to expand their contacts with important people and by continuing to talk about the importance of their project.

5-3b Assessing Performance of Individuals and Project Teams

The second aspect of managing project teams is assessing the performance of both individuals and the project team. Goals of performance assessments include administrative uses such as rewards and promotions and professional development such as determining areas for improvement and training. In many organizations, a large percentage of people dread performance assessments. Many people do not enjoy giving honest feedback— particularly about shortcomings. Also, many people do not like to receive constructive feedback. However, for both reward purposes and to improve performance, honest assessments are needed. Performance assessment can be both informal and formal. Project managers often perform informal assessments by observing, asking questions, and providing suggestions. This improves performance if it is done regularly, as timely and specific feedback is most effective.

Formal performance assessments are often the primary responsibility of the manager toward people who directly report to him. In many organizations, this is a functional manager. However, because many project team members spend significant time on a project, the project manager is often asked to provide input for the formal performance assessment. The ideal situation for this input is when the team member helped participate in the project planning and is judged by how his or her work corresponds to the planned work. Many project team members may work on several projects during the formal assessment period. When that is the case, the projects where they spent the greatest time would ideally count the most toward their performance rating. On some large projects, a project manager may seek input from other team members regarding the team member's performance.

5-3c Project Team Management Outcomes

A variety of outcomes may result from managing the project team, such as the following:

- Morale changes
- "Quarter-mile stones" to "inch stones"
- Staff changes
- Training needs
- Discipline
- Role clarification
- Issues
- Lessons learned

MORALE CHANGES   Many projects have periods that are difficult, when work demands are high and milestones to celebrate are few. During these times, the project manager needs to remember that the way he or she wields power, communicates, appraises progress, and generally manages can enhance or detract from the morale of all involved. Continuing to reinforce the project's purpose, encouraging and supporting workers, and trying hard to understand their concerns can go a long way toward boosting morale.

QUARTER-MILE STONES TO INCH STONES   When constructing the project charter, the team developed a list of milestones that could be used to measure progress. On some projects, that is enough detail against which performance can be measured. On other projects, however, more details are needed. Perhaps these greater details could be considered "quarter-mile stones"—giving the ability to check progress more frequently. When assessing the performance of individual workers, if one individual worker consistently does not perform well, the project manager may decide that more detailed oversight is necessary. This could result in "yard, foot, or inch stones," depending on the level of oversight deemed necessary. Hopefully, for most projects and most workers, this additional oversight will not be necessary. It takes time and effort that could be spent on other productive activities. However, a wise project manager is not going to let a project get derailed because of one worker who is not performing well.

STAFF CHANGES   Poor appraisals, insufficient progress, conflict, necessary reassignments, or other causes may warrant staff changes on a project. When this occurs, wise project managers treat everyone with respect and recognize that changes are happening. When new people are added, they are given a formal introduction to the team and provided information about the project.

TRAINING NEEDS   In the course of performance appraisals, training needs are sometimes identified. Project managers should keep the immediate project needs along with the training needs in mind as they approve training.

DISCIPLINE   Performance on some projects is so poor that employees need to be disciplined. While coercive power is often considered a last resort, it should be used at times. Project managers must ensure that prior warnings of poor performance are issued to a struggling team member so that person has an opportunity to make amends. Specific behaviors or lack of progress are documented, the need for the discipline is explained clearly, and specific improvement strategies are developed to reduce the chance that further discipline will be needed.

ROLE CLARIFICATION   Sometimes, progress may be lacking because of misunderstandings in responsibilities or miscommunication. In those cases, the project manager can clarify roles of all impacted employees by detailing their roles in completing WBS tasks, responsibilities toward other team members and the project, and what is expected of them in terms of project tasks and professional behavior.

ISSUES AND LESSONS LEARNED   Many project managers keep issue logs. These serve as living documents of issues that arise while managing the project and the project team. As issues are raised, they are added to the log, and once they are resolved, they are deleted. The resolved issues sometimes make good lessons learned if they can help future project teams avoid similar problems. These lessons can be documented and stored for easy retrieval in a lessons-learned knowledge base.

5-4 Relationship Building Within the Core Team

Project sponsors and managers who wish to create highly productive workplaces ensure that core team members understand what is expected of them, have the chance to do work they are well suited to perform, receive appropriate recognition, have good coworkers, have their opinions considered, and have opportunities to grow and develop.[8] The sponsor and the project manager ideally begin by asking one another about personal expectations regarding the project and project goals such as specific capabilities of the project deliverables. Both the project manager and sponsor may have *individual motives* also. It is helpful to disclose and acknowledge these personal goals to each other.

The project manager, in turn, asks each core team member what he or she personally wants from being involved in the project. These conversations not only help the project manager understand priorities but also understand motivations. For example, core team members may want to participate in a stimulating experience, gain new skills, or earn a promotion. Understanding these motivations will make it easier for the project manager to address them. Aligning individual aspirations with project goals in determining individual roles and responsibilities is desirable and productive.

The project manager can encourage *open and transparent communication* such as keeping people informed, demonstrating that everyone's input is valued, personally sharing feelings, and respecting confidentiality. She should set the expectation that all team members practice these habits.

Joint establishment of project meeting agendas helps in building relations because all team members feel their concerns are addressed, and they develop a greater sense of ownership in meetings. When members get to *share in meaningful project learning*, they feel their insight is valued. *Frequent celebration of small successes* helps project team members *share the enjoyment* of working on a project, which in turn helps them stay committed to successful project completion.

One other key relationship-building activity that needs to start early and continue throughout the project is concerned with *appropriate decision making and problem solving*. The project manager and core team need to understand who makes each type of project decision and how those decisions are made. One consideration is that people involved in making decisions tend to support them. Decisions made by groups tend to take longer, and projects are often pushed for time. Some decisions are best made by a single expert, while others are best made by a group that represents various points of view. Each project team will need to determine who will make which types of decisions. Exhibit 5.11 gives general advice that can be applied in making this determination.

5-5 Managing Project Conflicts

Projects create unique outputs, work with diverse stakeholders, are represented by team members from various functions and even different companies, and frequently operate in a matrix environment. These factors, along with scope, time, and cost constraints, contribute to potential conflicts. Many project management initiating and planning tools exist to reduce destructive aspects of conflict, at least partly. This section discusses different ways to view conflict, along with various styles and approaches for dealing with it. This section also introduces a project conflict-resolution process model.

In dealing with task-related conflicts, project charters are meant to help the project core team, project manager, and sponsor understand many aspects of the project at a high level and head off potential conflict between individuals. Several components included in charters,

EXHIBIT 5.11

PROJECT DECISION-MAKING GUIDE	
PERSON/METHOD	WHEN
Sponsor decides	Critical decision, large monetary stake, "big picture" needed
Project manager decides	Time is critical, no need for other input
Functional manager decides	"How" functional work is done
Core team discusses and project manager decides	Team input is useful
Core team consensus	Buy-in is critical
Delegated to one or two team members to recommend	Needs to be investigated, team input useful
Delegated to one or two team members to decide	Needs to be investigated, team input not needed

Neale Cousland/Shutterstock.com

for example, assumptions, risks, roles, responsibilities, and acceptance criteria are examples of potential sources of conflict. Stakeholder analysis and communications planning can identify needs and desires of many others who will be impacted by either the process of performing the project or a deliverable of the project. These tools help to identify and deal with potential sources of conflict among the broader stakeholders. The more-detailed planning tools such as the WBS, schedule, and budget help to identify other conflict sources.

People-related conflicts can be effectively addressed by developing a team charter, as discussed in Section 5-2b of this chapter. Everyone comes with unique experience, knowledge, IQ, and personality type and these differences can be a source of conflict. A team charter helps to define norms, attitudinal preferences, work ethics, and responsibilities for all team members. Adherence to team charter elements promotes mutual understanding and conflict resolution.

5-5a Sources of Project Conflict

Some conflicts on projects are useful; other conflicts can be destructive. Conflict over ideas on how to proceed with a project can lead to more creative approaches. Conflict over how to complete a project with a tight schedule can also be positive. Competition for ideas on how to best handle a project activity has the potential for generating more innovative and successful approaches and can be highly stimulating work. However, when conflict becomes personal, it can often become negative. These types of conflict need to be handled with care. A few typical sources of project conflict are shown in Exhibit 5.12. Generally, it is better to deal with conflict on projects promptly—or even proactively. Conflicts do not get better with time! This is especially true for projects with significant pressure to stay on schedule or on budget (in other words, many projects).

EXHIBIT 5.12

TYPICAL SOURCES OF PROJECT CONFLICT	
RELATIONSHIP SOURCES	TASK SOURCES
Roles and responsibilities	Stakeholder expectations
Lack of commitment	Unique project demands
Communications failure	Money and other resources
Different personalities	Technical approach
Stakeholder relationships	Priorities
Personal motives of participants	Differing goals of stakeholders
Energy and motivation	Task interdependencies
Next project assignment	Schedule
Individual rewards	Risks

Virtually all studies have determined that relationship conflict can be detrimental to project team success. When people spend time and emotional energy arguing, they have less energy to work on the project. Also, when people have personal conflicts to the point where they really do not like each other, they often feel less committed to the project and to their team.

Task conflict is a bit more complicated. A certain amount of task conflict can encourage people to consider alternative approaches and to better justify decisions. Up to that point, task conflict can be useful. However, beyond a certain point, when people spend a great deal of time arguing over task-type issues, conflict takes away from the project team's progress and camaraderie. The timing of task conflict can also make a difference on whether it helps or hurts the project. The best times to discuss different options are during the initiating stage, when high-level approaches are being decided, and during the planning stage, when more detailed decisions are being made. However, once the plans are made, a project team needs to be a bit more careful because prolonged discussions during the executing periods of the project can lead to schedule slippage and cost overruns.

In general, conflict occurs due to incompatible goals and differences in thoughts or emotions among the team members. It is a common experience with any team or a group of highly skilled and exceptionally creative individuals to interpret facts and events differently. The project manager must capitalize on this intellectual diversity using effective communication techniques and debates to identify the most appropriate resolution.

5-5b Conflict-Resolution Process and Styles

Once a project manager recognizes that a conflict exists, if it is a task conflict, he or she tries to utilize it to develop a better solution. If it is a relationship conflict, he or she tries to resolve it before it escalates. A project manager can use the six-step project conflict-resolution process, making sure to pay attention both to the tasks and relationships needed at each step.

Six-Step Project Conflict-Resolution Process

1. Understand the conflict.
2. Agree on conflict-resolution goals.
3. Identify causes of the conflict.
4. Identify potential solutions for the conflict.
5. Pick the desired conflict solution.
6. Implement the chosen solution.

First, the project manager and the team investigate the situation: What are the signs of the conflict? Is it specific to a certain stage in the project? Does each party in the conflict understand it the same way? If not, they need to ask clarifying questions, summarize how the other person has stated the problem, and confirm that they have a common understanding.

Next, ensure that all parties agree on what a successful conflict resolution would be. While there are often conflicting goals on projects, all stakeholders typically want useful deliverables on time and on budget. Use the project goals as a basis for what the solution needs to cover.

Many conflicts have multiple causes, such as those shown in Exhibit 5.12. Identify potential causes and then verify which cause(s) are contributing to the conflict.

The next step is to identify potential solutions to the conflict. This is clearly a time where creativity and mutual trust are helpful. It is important to focus on the conflict issue and not the person. Also, potential solutions should be considered based on their value and should not be evaluated based on the person who suggests a solution.

The fifth step is deciding how to resolve the conflict. There are five general styles for resolving project conflict, as depicted in Exhibit 5.13.

The collaborative style is preferred for important decisions that require both parties to actively support the final decision. However, collaboration requires both parties to develop trust in each other and, therefore, often takes longer than the other styles. Therefore, each style in 5.13 has its value in dealing with project conflicts.

The final step is to implement the chosen solution. For a major conflict, this could be almost like a mini-project plan with activities identified and responsibility assigned. It is vital to include communication of the solution to all concerned parties.

5-5c Negotiation

Negotiation is about redefining an old relationship that is not working effectively or establishing a new relationship.[9] Negotiation is the most commonly used process and the first step to resolve a dispute, a difference, or a conflict.

Project managers are generally held accountable for more performance issues than they have responsibility to direct people to perform. Because of this, project managers must negotiate. As stated earlier in this chapter, they often need to negotiate with functional managers for the people they wish to have on the project team. Project managers

EXHIBIT 5.13

			STYLES OF HANDLING PROJECT CONFLICT
STYLE	CONCERN FOR SELF	CONCERN FOR OTHERS	WHEN APPROPRIATE FOR PROJECTS
Forcing/ Competing	High	Low	Only when quick decision is necessary, we are sure we are right, and buy-in from others is not needed
Withdrawing/ Avoiding	Low	Low	Only when conflict is minor, there is no chance to win, or it is helpful to secure needed information or let tempers cool
Smoothing/ Accommodating	Low	High	Only when we know we are wrong, it is more important to other party, or we are after something bigger later
Compromising	Medium	Medium	Only when an agreement is unlikely, both sides have equal power, and each is willing to get part of what they want without taking more time
Collaborating/ Problem Solving	High	High	Whenever there is enough time, trust can be established, the issue is important to both sides, and buy-in is needed

Source: Adapted from Richard L. Daft, *Management*, 9th ed. (Mason, OH: Southwestern Cengage Learning, 2010): 519–520; Ramon J. Aldag and Loren W. Kuzuhara, *Mastering Management Skills: A Manager's Toolkit* (Mason, OH: Thomson South-Western, 2005): 416–419; and *PMBOK® Guide* 240.

often need to negotiate with customers and other key stakeholders concerning schedule, budget, scope, and a myriad of details. They also often need to negotiate with sponsors, suppliers, SMEs, and core team members.

Nobody is as committed to or involved with a project as much as the project manager. However, a project manager must remember that negotiations will be smoother if she realizes that everyone she negotiates with has their own set of issues and goals.

Many of the project management tools discussed thus far in this book, such as charters, stakeholder analysis, communication plans, schedules, budgets, and change control, make negotiations easier. Several of the soft skills discussed in this book, such as involving your team in planning, treating everyone with respect, keeping communications open, and establishing trust, also simplify negotiations. The issues project managers need to negotiate can greatly vary in size and complexity. For example, many small issues can involve day-to-day scheduling issues. On the other hand, the entire set of project deliverables with accompanying schedule and budget are often negotiated.

Regardless of the negotiation size or complexity, the six-step process shown in Exhibit 5.14 can serve as a guide.

The negotiation process is based on the project manager and the other party attempting in good faith to reach a solution that benefits both—in other words, a win-win solution. Project managers need to be vigilant, however, because not everyone they must negotiate with takes that same attitude. Smart project managers recognize that their reputation is based on how they act in all situations. Therefore, even when negotiating against someone who plays hardball, it is still wise to stay ethical and keep emotions in check.

Step 1 involves advance fact-finding to determine what is needed from the negotiation. This may include checking with the sponsor and/or other stakeholders and determining the impact that various settlements may have on the project. It also includes seeking to understand both what the other party is likely to want and how he or she may act during the negotiations.

Step 2 is for the project manager to understand the bottom line. What is the minimum acceptable result? Just as when buying a car, a project manager needs to understand when to walk away. This can vary a great deal depending on how much power each party has. Project

EXHIBIT 5.14

NEGOTIATION PROCESS	
STEP	EXPLANATION
1. Prepare for negotiation	Know what you want and who you will negotiate with.
2. Know your walk-away point	Determine in advance the minimum you need from the negotiation.
3. Clarify both parties' interests	Learn what the other party really wants and share your true interests to determine a common goal.
4. Consider multiple options	Brainstorm multiple approaches—even approaches that only solve part of the issue.
5. Work toward a common goal	Keep the common goal in mind: seek and share information, make concessions, and search for possible settlements.
6. Clarify and confirm agreements	Agree on key points, summarize, and record all agreements.

Source: Adapted from Ramon J. Aldag and Loren W. Kuzuhara, *Mastering Management Skills: A Manager's Toolkit* (Mason, OH: Thomson South-Western, 2005): 129–132; and Timothy T. Baldwin, William H. Bommer, and Robert S. Rubin, *Developing Management Skills: What Great Managers Know and Do* (Boston: McGraw-Hill, 2008): 307–318.

managers need to understand that if they have the power and take advantage of their negotiation partner, that partner may not work with them on a future project. Therefore, the goal is not to always drive the hardest bargain, but to drive a fair bargain. It is worth mentioning that if one party has more power than the other party, even if it is only a perception, negotiation may not be the right option until the inequality issue is addressed.

Step 3 is for the project manager to understand the underlying needs of the other party and to share his or her own needs. This is not a 10-second political sound bite that says, "Take it or leave it." This is developing a real understanding of each other's needs.

Step 4 is to create multiple options. This is easy once both parties understand what the other party really needs because various creative solutions can then be developed that help to satisfy those underlying needs.

Step 5 consists of the process and strategies of the negotiation itself. It is helpful to keep in mind the ultimate goal while focusing on the many details of information sharing, trading of concessions, and exploring possible solutions.

Step 6 is actually a reminder to reach an agreement and then to document that agreement. A consultant friend of mine often says: we have reached a violent agreement" when people essentially have agreed, but keep talking. Clarify and document your agreement.

5-6 Communication Needs of Global and Virtual Teams

As organizations change more rapidly, more projects are conducted with member from various parts of the larger organization, various organizations, and even various parts of the world. These teams draw from a wider pool of talent, but can pose added challenges.

5-6a Virtual Teams

In contemporary project management, project managers use less-onerous command and control than they might have a few years ago. This trend is even more pronounced with global and virtual teams. A **virtual team** is also sometimes known as a distributed team. They rarely meet in person, but rely on communications technology. When project teams operate in a virtual mode, many of the following characteristics are present:

- Team members are physically dispersed.
- Time boundaries are crossed.
- Communication technologies are used.
- Cultural, organizational, age, gender, and functional diversity are present.[10]

5-6b Cultural Differences

Cultural patterns differ in various parts of the world, so project team members need to be more sensitive as to how their actions are interpreted. For example, in some cultures, making eye contact signifies that you are paying close attention. In other parts of the world, however, eye contact is considered rude; in these cultures, people may look slightly downward in deference to authority. When people do not have face-to-face contact, they do not have the opportunity to see and learn from a person's body language. Project managers working with global and virtual project teams need to be especially mindful of the increased need for communications using methods other than face to face. Reading comprehension and listening skills are valuable for virtual teams.

Cultural differences make communication challenges more difficult. The various methods regarding charter development described in Chapter 4, along with stakeholder analysis and communications planning in this chapter, are even more critical on virtual and global

EXHIBIT 5.15

INCREASED CHALLENGES FOR VIRTUAL AND GLOBAL PROJECT TEAM	
PROJECT MANAGEMENT NEED	INCREASED CHALLENGES
1. Initiate project	1. More unique project needs
2. Understand stakeholders	2. More difficult to understand
3. Build relationships	3. Needs more time
4. Determine communications needs and methods	4. More unique needs, more reliance on electronic means
5. Establish change control	5. More facilitating than directing
6. Manage the meeting process	6. Less nonverbal clues, interest may wander
7. Control issues	7. With less group interaction, harder to identify

teams partially due to cultural differences. The more unusual a team is, the more critical charters and communications vehicles become. Exhibit 5.15 lists some of the extra communications challenges posed by virtual and global project teams. Note that each project management need has a specific and increased challenge—for example, the third need, relationship building, needs more time since people do not have the advantage of full face-to-face communication. Project managers and teams can enhance stakeholder satisfaction by learning the cultural ethics and values of all their stakeholders, working hard to establish trust, and ensuring that they use fast and reliable information systems.

5-6c Countries and Project Communication Preferences

It is helpful if the project team members can meet each other face to face, even one time. While this can be expensive, it may be much less expensive than poor performance on the project. Sometimes, the core project team is assembled to write and approve the project charter. The core team members then get to know each other and are inclined to give each other the benefit of doubt in case of any misunderstandings. Another method that is frequently used is to confirm meetings and calls with quick meeting minutes or e-mail follow-ups. By documenting any decisions, it is easier to remember what happened and to uncover lessons learned when the project is complete.

While abundant differences exist among people from various countries, the method and timing of project communications are of interest here. For example, Ralf Mueller and J. Rodney Turner studied how cultural differences impact preferred modes of project management communication.[11] They examined how collectivism versus individualism, along with the extent individuals in various cultures accept unequal power and ambiguity, impact project communications preferences. The results show that country preferences can be shown in four categories with common preferences on frequency and type of communications for each group.

PMP/CAPM Study Ideas

While PMI absolutely recognizes the importance of the "soft skills" regarding management and communication, you shouldn't expect to see many—if any—questions directly from the lists in this chapter. Rather, you will be expected to understand the best practices we describe and to apply them to mock situations. One type of question you will see in many guises has to do with change requests. Whether a customer, sponsor, or team member requests a change, if you have already completed your project management plan, *any change must go through a change request process.* In other words, it may be your natural instinct to want to please the person making the request—especially if the change seems small—but the best practice/correct answer will always be to go through the change control process (more information on this is provided in Chapters 7 and 14).

Other test questions you may see from this chapter include the stages of team development—forming, storming, norming, performing, and adjourning—and both capturing and utilizing lessons learned.

Summary

While the project core team is ideally assembled early in the project to participate in chartering and planning the project, SMEs are commonly assigned as needed. Project managers try to secure the services of these important people as early in the project as possible. This often involves negotiating with the functional managers to whom the SMEs report. When new project team members arrive, they need to be on-boarded; that is, they need to understand the project and start to develop working relationships with their new team members. Experienced project managers ensure that the new members understand project goals but also share their personal goals so that both can simultaneously be achieved.

Teams progress through typical stages of development. High-performing project teams share a number of characteristics. Project managers can use understanding of these stages and characteristics to guide their team to better performance. They do this by assessing individual and team capabilities and developing strategies to improve both. The project team often develops team operating principles in the charter. Many teams expand upon these with more specific team ground rules. The ground rules are tailored to the unique needs of the project situation, but generally include both rules for improving relationships among team members as well as improving the process of how the team works.

The project manager must manage the human side of his project. This involves utilizing appropriate forms of power in managing the project team to obtain desired results. Project teams also need to manage and control stakeholder engagements through understanding their expectations, delivering on those expectations, and communicating effectively. Projects are ripe for many kinds of conflict. Constructive conflict over ideas often yields better approaches, but destructive conflict that gets personal needs to be headed off when possible and dealt with when it occurs. Many good project management practices and techniques are helpful in channeling conflict in constructive directions. Project managers also need to utilize many general conflict reduction techniques not only within the project team, but also with and between various stakeholders.

Key Terms Consistent with PMI Standards and Guides

management, 138
leadership, 138
acquire project team, 138
develop project team, 141

manage project team, 157
negotiation, 164
virtual teams, 166

Chapter Review Questions

1. What is the potential downside to bringing in project workers too early in the project?
2. Why is it often necessary for project managers to persuade workers to be part of the project team?
3. When is the best time to on-board core team members?
4. What are the five stages of team development?
5. During which stage do team members often feel close to one another and have a good understanding of how to work together?
6. List two *personal values of individual team members* that contribute to a high-performing team. List two *team behaviors* that can enhance these personal values.
7. What are the two favorable outcomes of fostering a high-performing project team?
8. During all five stages of team development, is it important that the project manager keep in mind the needs of which three groups?

9. Why might it be helpful to bring out the charter when people are arguing over a decision?

10. What is meant by the term *ground rules?* Give examples.

11. Under which circumstances might a project manager or sponsor retain the right to make a project decision?

12. What are the benefits of delegating a decision to one or two team members?

13. When might consensus be the best decision-making strategy?

14. _____ power is the ability to persuade others based upon the project manager's personal knowledge and skills.

15. _____ power should be used by a project manager when she is asking her team members to perform a task within their job description.

16. _____ power should only be used in instances in which it is necessary to maintain discipline.

17. In order to manage stakeholders' expectations, a project manager needs to understand the stakeholders' assumptions. Which document(s) can help with this?

18. The collaborative style for handling conflict has a(n) _____ concern for self and a(n) _____ concern for others.

19. Why is it important for project managers to have one-on-one discussions with their core team members?

20. What is a virtual team?

21. Name three increased challenges for a global and/or virtual team.

22. Why is it helpful for a virtual team to meet in person at least once?

Discussion Questions

1. You are a project manager leading an IT development project. Halfway through your project, you realize you need to hire an additional worker in order to complete the project on time. How will you convince your project sponsors to authorize the hire? How will you on-board your new worker?

2. Describe how to use project documents to help a team progress through the stages of development.

3. How can a project manager promote the needs of the organization during the norming phase?

4. How can a project manager promote the team members' needs during the forming stage?

5. Describe in your own words what a high-performing project team can do.

6. Describe, in your own words, what you believe are the four most important characteristics of high-performing project teams. Tell why you believe each is so critical, explain how they are related to each other, and give at least two specific suggestions for each.

7. Assess your individual capability for project teamwork. Tell why you feel you are strong in certain capabilities, and give strategies for improving in areas you feel you need to develop.

8. What is meant by the term *situational leadership?* How can you apply this as a project manager?

9. Describe the three responsibilities of project team members.

10. Pick the four ground rule topics for project teams that you believe are the most important. Tell why you believe each is so critical, explain how they are related to each other, and give at least two specific suggestions for each.

11. Using examples, describe how a project manager can use active listening. Why is this useful?

12. Describe each method of decision making a project team may use. Using examples, tell when each is most appropriate.

13. In your opinion, why is it necessary for the project manager to assess the performance of both individual team members and the project team as a whole?

14. List several characteristics of a project that can often result in creating conflict.

15. Give an example of when a conflict would be beneficial to a project and an example of when conflict would be harmful to a project.

16. You are working for a multinational organization and need to relay information to Japan. Which communication method would you choose to use and why?

17. Give as many examples of cultural differences as you can, using information from this text and your own experiences.

PMBOK® *Guide* Questions

1. _____ is the process of "confirming human resource availability and obtaining the team necessary to complete project activities."
   a. Plan Human Resource Management
   b. Acquire Project Team
   c. Develop Project Team
   d. Manage Project Team

2. All of these are stages of team development *except:*
   a. adjourning
   b. storming
   c. learning
   d. performing

3. _____ establish(es) clear expectations regarding acceptable behavior by project team members, and may cover topics such as protecting confidentiality, establishing trust, and handling conflict.
   a. The employee handbook
   b. Ground rules
   c. Management by objectives
   d. Personnel directives

4. The objective of the _____ process is to improve competencies, team member interaction, and overall team environment to enhance project performance.
   a. Plan Human Resource Management
   b. Acquire Project Team
   c. Develop Project Team
   d. Manage Project Team

5. All of these are techniques for managing project conflicts *except:*
   a. smooth/accommodate
   b. withdraw/avoid
   c. collaborate/problem solve
   d. none of the above

6. A document used to manage points of discussion or dispute that arise during projects, in order to monitor them and ensure that they are eventually resolved and added to lessons learned, is called a(n) _____.
   a. risk register
   b. stakeholder register
   c. SWOT analysis
   d. issue log

7. Which of these is *not* a challenge of working on global and virtual teams?
   a. competencies
   b. language
   c. time zones
   d. culture

8. An output of the process Develop Project Team, an evaluation of the team's success in achieving project objectives for schedule, budget and quality levels, is called team _____.
   a. project performance review
   b. performance assessments
   c. annual review
   d. work performance reporting

9. Which of the following steps is *not* part of the six-step project conflict-resolution process?
   a. Identify causes of conflict
   b. Identify potential solutions
   c. Determine which teammate was in the wrong
   d. Understand the conflict

10. The sources of most project conflicts can be grouped into those related to _____ and those related to _____.
    a. relationships; tasks
    b. technical skills; budget
    c. personalities; deadlines
    d. schedule; risks

INTEGRATED EXAMPLE PROJECTS
SUBURBAN HOMES CONSTRUCTION PROJECT

Suburban Homes, a medium-sized, fast-growing construction company, has an ambitious plan to expand its business to several southern states in the United States as a result of its significant growth and good reputation for building quality single-family homes and townhomes.

As a project manager, Adam Smith worked for several years in the construction industry and supplemented his experience with project management education. From his initial realization that managing projects successfully requires implementation of various project management processes, tools, and techniques, Adam recognized the importance of building project teams composed of well-trained staff. From his experience managing a few projects in the Midwest and based on the lessons learned from these projects, it was evident to Adam that Suburban Homes did not place a strong emphasis on people-related factors and team development. Adam recognized the scope for improvement in managing and developing high-performance teams and decided to act on this knowledge immediately.

Adam's primary task was to improve the performance of project management and increase the project success rate, so he wanted to address project team selection and the team development processes. Further, he realized that employee turnover and the expansion of the business in southern states led Suburban Homes to recruit more employees. Many of these new recruits have prior experience in the construction industry. In addition, the workforce now represents different work cultures, attitudes, commitment, and work ethics.

Adam recognized the immediate need to manage human resources effectively and efficiently. He decided to formalize project team selection, development, and management so that all the locations in the Midwest and South will have similar team management philosophy and practices. To achieve these purposes, Adam has considered the following:

1. Train project managers as leaders. Also, project managers must be trained to identify talent, select project team members, and nurture their growth.
2. Develop a team charter so that all the team members are aware of performance expectations, professional behavior, and other team norms. The charter should also help in training newly recruited employees to improve productivity, collaboration, coordination, communications, and conflict resolution.
3. Develop a conflict management plan and prepare guidelines for all employees to identify and manage conflicts.
4. Design and implement a decision-making protocol for all the projects and in all locations.
5. Develop norms for high-performing teams.

You are hired as a consultant to develop the above five deliverables.

CASA DE PAZ DEVELOPMENT PROJECT

Questions for students to answer:
1. What actions do you suggest to help the project team through the stages of team development?
2. What would you want to see in a team charter for this development project?
3. Construct a RACI chart with major tasks you see and the type of person you feel should do each.
4. List types of decisions that will need to be made and the appropriate person, group, or method for each, for example, individual team member, team collectively, scrum master, and product owner.

Semester Project Instructions

Assess your project team's capability. Develop a strategy to improve your team's capability. Develop ground rules to use on your project.

As a team, audit one of the other project teams in your class and have them audit your team. Develop an improvement strategy for that team based on the audit results.

Brainstorm situations for your project for which each source of power makes sense.

Identify what you have done to manage and control stakeholder engagement and how you know the current level of satisfaction that your stakeholders feel. Identify issues you may need to negotiate and determine the style you will use to handle the conflict and your expectations at each step of the negotiation process.

PROJECT MANAGEMENT *IN ACTION*
Centralizing Planning and Control in a Large Company after Many Acquisitions

The restaurant chain where I work was founded over 50 years ago. Through internal growth and external acquisitions, this company has become a Fortune 500 company. The company recently decided to centralize merchandizing, retail operations control, advertising, and sales planning for the enterprise.

Human resources (HR) and other support organizations needed to improve their performance to support this massive change. Cycle times were too long, service quality was too low, and internal customers frequently complained about corporate functions. HR started its transformation by creating a process improvement team to lead toward a process-driven structure with work drivers identified to establish staffing levels. A new HR vice president had a vision for the operation, and her leadership was critical to make anything happen.

Up to this point, process engineering had only been applied to manufacturing and distribution operations. The culture for process engineering, project management, and change management was generally immature in the company. This was declared to be the biggest change to our HR function in 35 years. A vice president was assigned to make the HR transition happen.

The project manager assigned to this project immediately interviewed the various management members of the HR organization and the retail operations transition team. He created a project charter to define the scope, objectives, problem statement, outcomes expected, benefits, team members, and inputs for this project. This project manager interviewed all senior staff members for their insights.

A communications plan was drafted because this change directly touched several hundred persons and indirectly many tens of thousands. The company is a very large distributed organization with many global operations. Therefore, a great deal of collaboration was required to create the buy-in needed. A conference was held for all HR leaders to begin developing this needed buy-in.

In preparation for the conference, the project manager created the following high-level WBS:

1. Planning the HR Transformation
2. Initiating the Project
3. Planning the Workshops
4. Stakeholder Analysis
5. Communications Plan
6. Planning the Project
7. Executing the Plan
8. Holding the Workshops
9. Identifying Opportunities for Improvements
10. Obtaining the VOC (Voice of Customer)
11. Creating the Foundational Communications
12. Initial Launch
13. Executing the Implementation Plan
14. Sustaining the Transformation

A schedule was created that reflected all the WBS elements needed to perform this massive organizational change initiative, driven by process analysis and by meeting all the relevant PMI PMBOK® guidelines for project management good practices. This project schedule covered the elements of a plan to gather Voice of the Customer information and perform workshops for the identified Centers of Excellence:

1. The business processing center
2. Total reward systems
3. Administration systems
4. Workforce planning systems
5. Talent management systems
6. Systems and data management
7. Training and development

The project schedule included all the communications needed to create synergy toward an agreed-upon solution. At the end of the first conference, we had a core team meeting of five leaders. The job of the core team was to define a vision for the organization, a mission statement for the operation, and an elevator speech that defined the project's objectives and could be repeated in less than 45 seconds to a novice on the topic. This team's efforts gave us great clarity regarding what we were trying to accomplish.

Next, we brought in over 100 HR professionals from around the company for a series of workshops. An agenda and handouts were created to drive the workshops. During the workshops, artifacts were created to define the "as is" and "to be" process states. These models were built in Supplier, Input, Process, Output, Customer (SIPOC), and organization deployment process maps. In addition, we created organization structures to support the future-state process maps. Once we designed structures, we built job description documents and measurement plans for the new and old processes. The processes modeled impacted all HR operations. We needed to know where the work would be accomplished. We started the detailed organization chart reviews. We needed to know where the work was done, and by how many persons, today. Then we could start to estimate how many resources might be needed in a future state by location and by element of work.

We evolved a framework of principles to drive the project forward, which included:

- Streamline every process using the lean Six Sigma tools.
- Focus on quality, speed, and cost while delivering improved value.
- Take transactions out to a service center where a lower cost is achieved.
- Drive all outside agreements toward negotiated service level agreements.
- Consider multiple alternatives for the sourcing of needed services.
- Improve the client-facing organization.
- Build Centers of Excellence that deliver improved value.
- Push employee support closer to them while leveraging consolidated service center capabilities.

Monthly HR leader conference calls, weekly status reports, preliminary design sessions, corporate staff design sessions, and follow-up conferences for leaders were all part of the high-touch, high-communications approach to this project. We expect the many automation initiatives, headcount reductions, vendor outsourcing efforts, and in-sourcing of transactions to a wholly owned service center to deliver millions of dollars of cost reductions across the company. We promoted lean and improvement ideas continually to the leadership. We have collected field-based best practices and have moved into a phase to validate these practices. Once validated, these best practices will be rolled out to all operations. We communicate by posting everything to a SharePoint site for all to see. We also use e-mail communications and have many one-on-one telephone calls.

We are now presenting the new design for implementation and are getting buy-in. We continue to involve others and to learn what will meet their needs—and so far we are spot on with high acceptance. At one time, we thought all regions were different, and they are, but their processes and structures are nearly 80 percent the same. We have reached agreement that one common process is acceptable to all regions asked. This is a major breakthrough. We also have had concessions from labor relations regarding its role and from those regions that were already down the road on a couple key position implementations.

The team concepts that were applicable to this project were as follows:

- Recognize the Forming, Storming, Norming, and Performing stages.
- Create a strong vision to rally the team.
- Ask the customers of the process for requirements.
- Have consistent sponsorship of the project.
- Respect, empower, and engage everyone in a change initiative.
- Respect differences and leverage the value of diversity.
- You cannot overcommunicate—so communicate.
- Make everything an open book.

Source: William Charles (Charlie) Slaven, PMP.

References

A Guide to the Project Management Body of Knowledge (PMBOK® Guide), 6th ed. (Newtown Square, PA: Project Management Institute, 2017).

Aldag, Ramon J., and Loren W. Kuzuhara, *Mastering Management Skills: A Manager's Toolkit*, 1st ed. (Mason, OH: Thomson South-Western, 2005).

V. Anantatmula, *Project Teams: A Structured Development Approach* (Business Expert Press: New York, NY, 2016).

Baldwin, Timothy T., William H. Bommer, and Robert S. Rubin, *Developing Management Skills: What Great Managers Know and Do* (Boston: McGraw-Hill, 2008).

Chen, Hua Chen, and Hong Tau Lee, "Performance Evaluation Model for Project Managers Using Managerial Practices," *International Journal of Project Management* 25 (6) (2007): 543–551.

Daft, Richard L., *Management*, 9th ed. (Mason, OH: Cengage South-Western, 2010).

Dayan, Mumin, and Said Elbanna, "Antecedents of Team Intuition and Its Impact on the Success of New Product Development Projects," *Journal of Product Innovation Management* 28 (S1) (2011): 159–174.

Fleming, John H., and Jim Asplund, *Human Sigma* (New York: Gallup Press, 2007).

Herrenkohl, Roy C., *Becoming a Team: Achieving a Goal*, 1st ed. (Mason, OH: Thomson South-Western, 2004).

Herzog, Valerie Lynn, "Trust Building on Corporate Project Teams," *Project Management Journal* 32 (1) (March 2001): 28–35.

Kloppenborg, Timothy J., and Joseph A. Petrick, "Leadership in Project Life Cycles and Team Character Development," *Project Management Journal* 30 (2) (June 1999): 8–13.

Kloppenborg, Timothy J., Arthur Shriberg, and Jayashree Venkatraman, *Project Leadership* (Vienna, VA: Management Concepts, Inc., 2003).

Lee-Kelley, Liz, and Tim Sankey, "Global Virtual Teams for Value Creation and Project Success," *International Journal of Project Management* 26 (1) (2008): 51–62.

Liu, Li, and David Leitner, "The Antecedents and Effect of Ambidexterity in the Management of Complex Engineering Projects," Proceedings Project Management Institute Research and Education Conference 2012, July 2012, Limerick, Ireland.

Lussier, Robert N., and Christopher F. Achua, *Leadership: Theory, Application, Skill Development*, 4th ed. (Mason, OH: South-Western Cengage Learning, 2010).

Melkonian, Tessa, and Thierry Picq, "Opening the Black Box of Collective Competence in Extreme Projects: Lessons from the French Special Forces," *Project Management Journal* 41 (3) (June 2010): 79–90.

Merla, E., The Agile Minded Professional: 7 Habits to Agility Success, Project Management Institute, 2011.

Mueller, Ralf, and J. Rodney Turner, "Cultural Differences in Project Owner–Project Manager Communications," *Innovations Project Management Research 2004* (Newtown Square, PA: Project Management Institute, 2004): 403–418.

Opfer, Warren, "Building a High-Performance Project Team," in David I. Cleland, ed., *Field Guide to Project Management*, 2nd ed. (Hoboken, NJ: John Wiley & Sons, 2004): 325–342.

Owen, Jill, et al., "The Role of Leadership in Complex Projects," Proceedings Project Management Institute Research and Education Conference 2012, July 2012 Limerick, Ireland.

Pellerin, Charles J., How NASA Builds Teams: Mission Critical Soft Skills for Scientists, Engineers, and Project Teams (Hoboken, NJ: John Wiley & Sons, 2009).

PMI Code of Ethics and Professional Responsibility, http://www.pmi.org/About-Us/Ethics/~/media/PDF/Ethics/ap_pmicodeofethics.ashx, accessed June 12, 2013.

Rath, T., and B. Conchie, Strengths-Based Leadership: Great Leaders, Teams, and Why People Follow (New York: Gallup Press, 2008).

Senge, Peter, Richard Ross, Bryan Smith, Charlotte Roberts, and Art Kleiner, *The Fifth Discipline Fieldbook: Strategies and Tools for Building a Learning Organization* (New York: Doubleday, 1994).

Schlenkrich, Lara, and Christopher Upfold, "A Guideline for Virtual Team Managers: The Key to Effective Social Interaction and Communication," *Electronic Journal Information Systems Evaluation* 12 (1) (2009): 109–118.

Streibel, Barbara J., Peter R. Sholtes, and Brian L. Joiner, *The Team Handbook*, 3rd ed. (Madison, WI: Oriel Incorporated, 2005).

Thamhain, Hans J., "Team Leadership Effectiveness in Technology-Based Project Environments," *Project Management Journal* 35 (4) (December 2004): 35–46.

_____, "Influences of Environment and Leadership on Team Performance in Complex Project Environments," Proceedings, Project Management Institute Research and Education Conference 2010.

Wagner, Rodd, and Gale Muller, Power of 2: How to Make the Most of Your Partnerships at Work and in Life (New York: Gallup Press, 2009).

Endnotes

1. Daft, Richard L., *Management,* 9th ed. (Mason, OH: Southwestern Cengage Learning, 2010): 5.

2. Lussier, Robert N., and Christopher F. Achua, *Leadership: Theory, Application, Skill Development,* 4th ed. (Mason, OH: South-Western Cengage Learning, 2010): 6.

3. *PMBOX® Guide* 526.

4. *PMBOK® Guide* 537.

5. Adapted from Herrenkohl, Roy C., *Becoming a Team: Achieving a Goal* (Mason, OH: Thomson Southwestern, 2004): 185 and 216–217; Opfer, Warren, "Building a High-Performance Project Team," in David I. Cleland, ed., *Field Guide to Project Management,* 2nd ed. (Hoboken, NJ: John Wiley & Sons, 2004): 326–327; and Melkonian, Tessa, and Thierry Picq, "Opening the Black Box of Collective Competence in Extreme Projects: Lessons from the French Special Forces," *Project Management Journal* 41 (3) (June 2010): 79–90.

6. Merla, E., The Agile Minded Professional: 7 Habits to Agility Success, Project Management Institute, 2011.

7. Thamhain, Hans J., "Team Leadership Effectiveness in Technology-Based Project Environments," *Project Management Journal* 35 (4) (December 2004): 39.

8. Adapted from Herzog, Valerie Lynn, "Trust Building on Corporate Project Teams," *Project Management Journal* 32 (1) (March 2001): 33–34; and Kloppenborg, Timothy J., and Joseph A. Petrick, "Leadership in Project Life Cycles and Team Character Development," *Project Management Journal* 30 (2) (June 1999): 11.

9. Anantatmula, Vittal, *Project Teams: A Structured Development Approach* (Business Expert Press: New York, NY, 2016).

10. Adapted from Schlenkrich, Lara, and Christopher Upfold, "A Guideline for Virtual Team Managers: The Key to Effective Social Interaction and Communication," *Electronic Journal of Information Systems Evaluation* 12 (1) (2009): 110.

11. Mueller, Ralf, and J. Rodney Turner, "Cultural Differences in Project Owner–Project Manager Communications," *Innovations Project Management Research 2004* (Newtown Square, PA: Project Management Institute, 2004): 403–418.

CHAPTER 6

Stakeholder Analysis and Communication Planning

amophoto_au/Shutterstock.com

Humans are social animals who engage with each other in complex ways, especially in artificial environments such as organizations and projects. Inexperienced project managers can become buried in the control of the project plan's tactical aspects and miss the more strategic components like stakeholder engagement and effective communication. Ultimately, successful delivery of a project is about *both* managing the tangible outputs (which are generally easily and objectively measured (time, cost, and project deliverables) *and* leading others through the more strategic and intangible outcomes (relations, power, influence, motivation, interests, etc.). Traditionally, measures of success focus on scope, time, cost, and quality to determine the success of the project as an entity. However, a more accurate measure of success also considers the longer-term outcomes delivered by what your project stimulated to happen after it was complete.

For example, the Sydney Opera House was a disaster as a project, but it made highly significant contributions to the culture, identity, meaning, and belonging of the Australian nation well beyond being a failed project, and there are many other examples like this in human history. Equally, there are project successes that

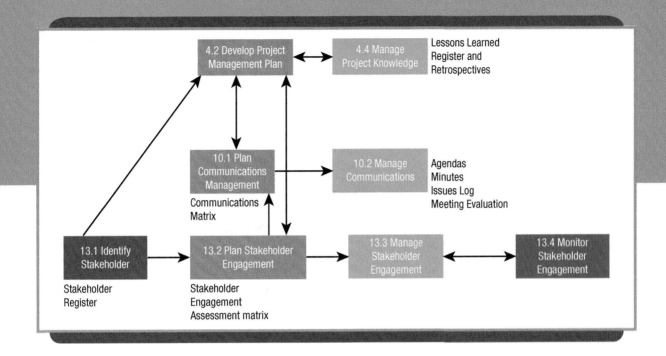

PMBOK® GUIDE

Topics:

- Identify stakeholders
- Plan stakeholder engagement
- Manage stakeholder engagement
- Monitor stakeholder engagement
- Plan communications management
- Manage communications

CHAPTER OUTPUTS

- Stakeholder register
- Stakeholder engagement assessment matrix
- Strategies for managing different stakeholders
- Communications matrix
- Meeting agenda
- Meeting minutes
- Issues log
- Meeting evaluation

only make negative contributions to society. This is because your stakeholders have varying perceptions of the worth of the project.

Stakeholders and your communications with them are highly subjective aspects of projects and more difficult to manage than some of the hard skills discussed in earlier chapters. As such, these aspects are often not managed with anywhere near the time and thought investment of the tangible aspects of a project. And while not every project manager (PM) needs to be a skilled wordsmith or a psychologist (though these would, in fact, be very useful skills for a PM to have), the *PMBOK®* is now starting to build more content around these aspects of leading and managing projects, and there is increasing literature acknowledging the importance of the "soft skills" required to be a successful project manager. Capable project managers invest effort to create and maintain informed stakeholder engagement matrices and insightful communications plans. They know whom to engage at what stage of the project (including critical stakeholders *before* the project starts, at times), at what frequency, and through what medium to secure optimal results. They then implement this plan and adjust as circumstances change. In essence, this is the art of project management.

One effective and fun way a PM can accelerate the development of their stakeholder engagement and communication skills is to use metaphor reflections developed by Arthur Shelley. This approach uses animals to represent behaviors and stimulate constructive conversations about interactions between people. The Organizational Zoo describes a set of 27 characters that collectively represent the most common behaviors in the Zoo (that is, your team, project, organization, or community). They are easy to remember (one for each letter of the alphabet, plus one "double"), and the cartoon characters help to make the conversation fun. Team members profile themselves and their stakeholders in order to understand what they are like and how they should engage with them. Because we all have considerable prior knowledge of animals, understanding is intuitive, and the tool makes it easy to quickly assess our behavioral environments. It is clear a

© Arthur Shelley

mouse does not approach a lion in the same way it would approach a dog, and a lion leader is different from an eagle.

In projects, the use of creative tools such as metaphor and reflective conversations is becoming more common and makes a significant contribution to success and the learning experiences of those involved. The free online profiler can be used for project team activities and to discover more about your own inner animals.

www.organizationalzoo.com/profiler
Copyright Arthur Shelley, 2013
Image artist John Szabo

6-1 Identify Stakeholders

Projects are undertaken because someone needs the project's output. A project must satisfy its users and their needs to be successful. Several things can complicate this goal. First, there may be multiple users, and each may have different wants and needs. Second, often end-users may not fully understand what they want because they do not know what alternatives may be available. Third, the customer who pays for the project may not be the actual person or group who uses the project deliverable or outcome, and the customer may not fully understand the end-users' needs. Fourth, when someone else is paying for the project, some users will ask for many project outcomes that are expensive or time consuming to deliver. Finally, many stakeholders, in addition to the users of a project's outcomes, have an interest in the project. Project managers need to first understand their stakeholders, build relationships with them, and then develop a communications management plan for managing them.

6-1a Find Stakeholders

One way to understand who stakeholders are is to ask, "Who will use, will be affected by, or could impact this project?" The answer includes users of the project results and others who may have some changes forced upon them by the project outcomes. It also includes people and groups who might choose to influence the project in some way. We use the **identify stakeholders** process to determine the people, and groups, who might impact or be impacted by some aspect of our project. Stakeholders include people who:

- Work on the project
- Provide people or resources for the project
- Have their routines disrupted by the project
- Monitor regulations, laws, and standards of practice at local, county, state, and federal levels

Another way to identify stakeholders is to determine whether they are internal to the organization performing the project or external to it. Examples of project stakeholders based on these categories are shown in Exhibit 6.1. Note that there are potentially more types of stakeholders affected by the process of performing the project than by the project results and more external than internal stakeholders.

Project managers and project core teams (often in consultation with the project sponsor) can use the examples in Exhibit 6.1 to find possible project stakeholders. This can be done using a brainstorming technique. Classic rules of brainstorming apply—initially, the emphasis is on generating a long list of potential stakeholders in the first column of a

EXHIBIT 6.1

EXAMPLES OF PROJECT STAKEHOLDERS		
	INTERNAL	EXTERNAL
Affected by Project Process	Owner Sponsor Project Manager Functional Managers Competing Projects Financing SourceProject Core Team Subject Matter Experts Employees Stockholders	Suppliers Partners Creditors Government Agencies Special Interest Groups Neighbors Client Professional Groups Media Taxpayers Union Competitors
Affected by Project Result	Internal Customer Sponsor Users	Client Public Special Interest Groups

chart without evaluating and analyzing them. It may be easy to construct this chart on a large work surface such as a whiteboard or flip chart. Another suggestion is to be specific; identify stakeholders by name when possible.

For each potential stakeholder, list the various project processes and results in which he or she might have an interest. Consider financial, legal, and emotional interests of potential stakeholders. The project charter can be useful here. Many stakeholders have an interest in multiple aspects of a project. Once the stakeholders and their interests have been listed, they may be combined into like groups with the same interests.

6-1b Analyze Stakeholders

Stakeholder analysis is a stakeholder identification technique composed of gathering and evaluating information to determine whose interests should be emphasized throughout the project. The first part of stakeholder analysis is to prioritize the stakeholders. Prioritization is important because on many projects, there are too many stakeholders to spend a great deal of time with each. While it is important not to ignore any stakeholder, it also makes sense to concentrate on those who are most vital. Stakeholders are frequently prioritized based upon level of:

1. Power—ability to get others to do something
2. Legitimacy—perception that their actions are appropriate
3. Urgency—time sensitivity and legitimacy of claim[1]

Some organizations use additional criteria such as interest, influence, and impact. Some organizations only use two or three criteria; others may use up to six. Each aspect used can be rated on a simple scale of 1 to 3, with 3 representing the highest priority. For the first aspect, *power*, a stakeholder who could order the project shut down or changed in a major way would be a 3, and a stakeholder who could not change the project much would be a 1. The other aspects can be analyzed in a similar fashion. The scores from the aspects are added to form a total prioritization score.

We will use an example of an African university that changed its entire curriculum to a modular approach—a major change project. This large university was in danger of closure because of failed quality ratings and public criticism of its performance. Major improvements were required. The newly appointed vice chancellor decided to modularize all the courses offered by the university, which allowed the students to "pick and mix" topics and create courses that better suited their needs. This change impacted every part of the university, and it was not a popular decision. The appropriate engagement of stakeholders was crucial. One of the major challenges to the modularization program was the shift in power base from academic management (the deans of faculty) to the academic registry. In Exhibit 6.2, you can see that the academic registrar scores highly in every line. This shift in power was always going to meet resistance, and the program manager would need to carefully consider the positions of the three key stakeholder groups to find an appropriate strategy.

By determining who the stakeholders are and what each group wants, project managers effectively:

- Set clear direction for further project planning, negotiating, and execution
- Prioritize among competing objectives
- Learn to recognize complex trade-offs and the consequences of each
- Make and facilitate necessary decisions
- Develop a shared sense of risk
- Build a strong relationship with their customers

EXHIBIT 6.2

MODULAR COURSES: STAKEHOLDER IDENTIFICATION AND PRIORITIZATION MATRIX						
	VICE CHANCELLOR	DEANS OF FACULTY (*)	ACADEMIC REGISTRAR:	LECTURERS: (*)	STUDENT SUPPORT	STUDENTS
What Is Important to This Stakeholder						
Power	3	3	3	2	1	1
Interest	3	1	2	1	2	2
Influence	1	3	2	2	1	1
Impact	3	2	3	1	1	1
Urgency	2	1	2	1	1	1
Legitimacy	2	1	3	3	1	3
Total:	14	11	15	9	7	6
Priority (Key or Other):	Key	Key	Key	Secondary	Other	Other

(*) Lecturers and the deans are unlikely to be homogeneous in their views—more information is needed to identify groupings and interest areas. For this case, we have kept it simple. Source: Louise Worsley.

- Lead associates, customers, and suppliers with empowering style and principles
- Serve as good stewards of the resources of both the parent and customer organizations

The project team should next select the top 10 to 15 stakeholders for emphasis in the remainder of their planning. The stakeholders with the highest total scores are often considered to be key influencers for the project. The project manager and the core team should also plan to periodically review this prioritized list of stakeholders, as the relative importance may change as the project progresses, especially if the project goals are not clear at the outset. While from a practical standpoint, project managers need to be especially attentive to the top stakeholders, the enlightened "management for stakeholders" approach also encourages project managers to ensure that interests of all the stakeholders, including less powerful ones, are considered.[2] This approach of giving preference to the most important stakeholders while recognizing needs of all stakeholders requires judgment, and the advice of the sponsor is often helpful.

One additional consideration is that various stakeholders often have competing interests. For example, the client may want the work done quickly, while the accountant is worried about cash flow. Exhibit 6.3 itemizes how different types of stakeholders frequently define project success. Another consideration is that each project was selected to support a specific business purpose and that purpose should help determine the relative importance of various stakeholders.

It is not necessary that all stakeholders favor the project. Competitors in the business, public interest groups, voluntary organizations that promote environmental sustainability and, occasionally, a segment of end-users may oppose the project and its execution. The project manager must identify them and monitor their actions closely.

EXHIBIT 6.3

SUCCESS CRITERIA FOR VARIOUS STAKEHOLDERS

STAKEHOLDER/ SUCCESS CRITERIA	ON TIME	ON BUDGET	MEET REQUIREMENTS	PART-NER SHIP	PROFIT REALIZED	FOLLOW-ON WORK	MINIMAL OVERTIME	RECOGNITION	CHALLENGE	WELL-PAID	QUALITY
Customer	X	X	X	X							X
End-user	X		X	X			X				X
Customer management	X	X	X	X			X	X			X
Project manager	X	X	X	X	X	X	X	X		X	X
Contractor management	X	X	X	X	X	X	X				X
Project team member	X		X	X		X	X	X	X	X	X
Subcontractor	X	X		X	X	X	X			X	X

Source: Adapted from Ralph R. Young, Steven M. Brady, and Dennis C. Nagle, Jr., *How to Save a Failing Project: Chaos to Control* (Vienna, VA: Management Concepts, 2009): 14. www.managementconcepts.com/pubs.

If the project team developed the stakeholder identification and prioritization matrix without their sponsor, now would be a good time to share it with the sponsor and ask for feedback. Chances are good the sponsor will want to make some adjustments before the team continues with the stakeholder management plan. Sponsors are especially useful in helping to sort out conflicting priorities. Typically, when a conflict exists, external paying customers and top management are considered to be highly important stakeholders. The project team primarily considers these top stakeholders while they:

- Develop a communications plan (later in this chapter)
- Define the scope of the project (see Chapter 7)
- Identify threats and opportunities (see Chapter 11)
- Determine quality standards (see Chapter 12)
- Prioritize among cost, schedule, scope, and quality objectives (see Chapter 12)

6-1c Document Stakeholders

The primary output of the "identify stakeholders" process is a stakeholder register. The **stakeholder register** is a repository of information regarding all project stakeholders. Teams use it to develop strategies to either capitalize upon stakeholder support or to mitigate the impact of their resistance. The stakeholder register provides input to relationship building with the various stakeholders and helps determine their requirements. In turn, these requirements serve as the basis of developing project scope. The stakeholder register is a living document that changes as needed. A stakeholder register often is in the format of a matrix. In the stakeholder register shown in Exhibit 6.4, we start to evaluate the interests of the different stakeholder groups. Sometimes referred to as the WIIFT

EXHIBIT 6.4

MODULAR COURSES: PROJECT STAKEHOLDER MATRIX			
STAKEHOLDER	INTEREST IN PROJECT	PRIORITY	SUPPORT/MITIGATION STRATEGIES
Vice Chancellor	Make major improvements in university services and avoid government intervention.	Key	Consult on target improvement areas—use his power to support key and difficult changes.
Deans of Faculty	Protect against changes that could influence their power base. Reduce detrimental impact on faculty activities.	Key	Work with nominated representatives to identify and seek out solutions to barriers to change. Establish and communicate wins for faculties.
Academic Registrar (AR)	Develop the power base of AR—demand and obtain quality improvements on courses across the university.	Key	Increase visibility and power of AR. Increased visible support for AR regarding resources and political support from senior management.
Lecturers	Be kept informed of impacts upon them. Reduce or resist changes that are considered negative to them.	Secondary	Identify supportive champions. Create, test, and deliver carefully considered communication strategy.
Student support	Be able to prepare and train staff on how to roll out new schemes to current and prospective students.	Other	Help student support guide staff through process—develop training programs and online web support.
Students	University shows signs of improvement and ensures students' needs are considered.	Other	Set up consultation and communication groups. Keep informed.

Source: Louise Worsley.

(what's-in-it-for-them), this analysis can be used to help identify where there may be common areas of interest between the groups, and note that what made this particular program complex was the absence of common ground. Strategies would need to be sought to change positions or reduce the impact of the behaviors of some of the groups.

6-2 Plan Stakeholder Engagement

Project teams **plan stakeholder engagement** both by creating a tool called a stakeholder engagement assessment matrix and by planning to build relationships with the stakeholders.

6-2a Creating a Stakeholder Engagement Assessment Matrix

Project teams create a **stakeholder engagement plan** to define how they will effectively engage stakeholders in planning and performing the project based on the analysis of the stakeholders' needs, wants, and impacts. A primary tool used in this plan is the **stakeholder engagement assessment matrix.** This matrix typically includes a first column showing the stakeholders. For each stakeholder, additional columns may represent how much they are currently supporting or opposing the project, where you would like them to be, barriers to their changing, and strategies you may employ to move them. Strategies for powerful and supporting stakeholders may include accepting their ideas, compromising, or offering them trade-offs, while strategies for opponents might entail doing the minimum possible or fighting their demnds.[3] It is not uncommon to think that the best one can do with opposing stakeholders is to help move them to a neutral position, while those who are unaware of or neutral toward the project may be turned into supporters.

EXHIBIT 6.5

MODULAR COURSES—STAKEHOLDER ENGAGEMENT ASSESSMENT MATRIX				
STAKEHOLDER	CURRENT POSITION	TARGET POSITION	BARRIERS TO CHANGE	STRATEGY
Vice Chancellor	Leading	Leading	Competing day-to-day priorities	Ensure engagement is 'efficient' and effective. Consider extending role of deputy Chancellor to cover for some day-to-day activities.
Deans of Faculty	Resistant	Neutral, Supportive, or Leading	Some Deans more powerful than others (relates to student numbers and academic ratings). 'Power owners' are very influential.	Consider each Dean's WIIFT individually. Consider strategies for individuals as well as the group.
Academic Registrar (AR)	Supportive	Leading	Competing day-to-day priorities—lack of leadership skills.	Engage deputy, provide skills and mentorship.
Lecturers	Unaware to neutral	Neutral or supportive	Very large group with veto power through unionized actions.	Involve HR and legal department to evaluate all changes that may impact lecturers. Identify supportive champions and stakeholder groupings for engagement.
Student support	Neutral	Leading	Not considered important by academic staff—services currently limited and not highly rated.	Provide consultancy support to team to redesign and promote new services (including student website).
Students	Unaware	Neutral	Very large group. Student representative council not well resourced or highly valued by students.	Set up consultation and communication groups. Keep informed. Consider use of social media.

Exhibit 6.5 identifies both the current and target positions of the stakeholder groups. The greater the change in position, the greater the risk and the greater the engagement effort required. Student Services had a relatively unimportant position in the old system but would be critical to the new modularized operation. Significant expenditure was anticipated in this area. It is of interest to note that the initial analysis (see Exhibit 6.4) had identified this group as "other stakeholder." As the nature and impact of changes become clearer, they can alter the relative importance of different groups. Stakeholder positions and stakeholder strategies must be reevaluated throughout the project.

6-2b Planning to Build Relationships with Stakeholders

Project managers and teams seek to develop strong working relationships with important stakeholders. This is an ongoing process throughout the life of the project. In fact, the project manager normally continues to nurture the relationship even after the project is completed to increase the chances of securing future project work and to maintain good will with the external stakeholders. In building relationships both within the project core team and with other stakeholders, project managers need to remember that mutual respect and trust greatly enhance the prospect of project success. Therefore, relationship-building activities that lead to respect and trust should be planned and carried out carefully.

 A principal idea in Agile is that relationships with stakeholders need to be based upon collaboration, communication, and trust. Analyzing stakeholder information helps the Agile team understand them better and leads to effective relationship building. It makes more sense for Agile as client interaction is continuous and desirable throughout the project life cycle.

Typically, relationship-building activities are most effective when they are used in the process of planning a project. Project relationship-building activities (described more fully below) that are especially useful include the following:

- Share individual motives.
- Encourage open communication.
- Jointly establish agenda.
- Use shared learning.
- Regularly celebrate success.
- Share enjoyment of project.
- Use appropriate decision-making and problem solving.[4]

Establishing a positive relationship early with all key stakeholders is vital for two reasons. First, it helps create a desire on the part of stakeholders to give positive support to the project—or at least refrain from disrupting the project. This early building of a coalition of supporters and engagement of opposition can help to positively shape the social and political context of the project and lead to success.[5] Second, it serves as the communications foundation for the project. The remainder of the project planning and execution are greatly enhanced by effective communication channels with key project stakeholders.

The sponsor, project manager, and core team can establish powerful and meaningful relationships with key stakeholders by delivering on all promises, always providing fair treatment, creating a sense of pride by association, and even helping the stakeholder develop a passion for the project.[6] This starts by learning what motivates each stakeholder. The old saying "What is in it for me?" describes what each stakeholder wants, and that is what the project team needs to understand. Stakeholders who feel threatened can disrupt a project during its process and are less likely to perceive that they receive project benefits in the end. Unhappy stakeholders are a sign of project failure. On the other hand, stakeholders can be treated as partners right from the start of planning by speaking their language and providing them opportunities to participate. Here are some things that customers (one of the primary stakeholders) value most from a contractor who is performing the project:

- A sincere invitation to early and continued involvement
- Responsiveness
- Transparency
- Reliability[7]

These stakeholders are more likely to take ownership in the project by educating the project team about their needs and making timely project decisions. Consequently, stakeholders are more likely to feel that their expectations are in line with the project team's plans. They are more likely to go beyond merely inspecting results and writing checks. Further, they may participate early and often when their input is meaningful and they feel that the project is successful. The important thing for project managers to remember is that developing respect and trust among all project stakeholders is a goal that must be started early and continued throughout the project. Stakeholder relations and engagement are just as critical to project success as the more technical planning and should demand equal attention from project managers.

6-3 Manage Stakeholder Engagement

Manage stakeholder engagement is a process of the project team communicating and working with stakeholders to satisfy their needs (and additional desires, when possible), handle issues quickly, and encourage active stakeholder participation throughout. This process can be visualized as shown in Exhibit 6.6, with managing on the left and monitoring on the right.

The first part of managing stakeholder engagement—understanding stakeholder assumptions—was performed while creating the charter (Chapter 3), along with the stakeholder register and stakeholder engagement assessment matrix discussed earlier in this chapter. The requirements matrix, which will be developed in the following chapter, is also helpful in understanding stakeholder assumptions. Different stakeholders may hold very different assumptions concerning the project at the outset, and these assumptions form the basis of their expectations. Therefore, the project manager clarifies the assumptions, challenges and negotiates some of them, and uses them in project planning.

These clarified assumptions are then stated as expectations regarding project deliverables, features of the product, timelines, costs, quality measures, and generally how the project manager and team will act. Next, the stakeholders have a chance to agree or challenge the expectations before committing to them. The expectations are then documented.

EXHIBIT 6.6

MANAGING AND MONITORING STAKEHOLDER ENGAGEMENT

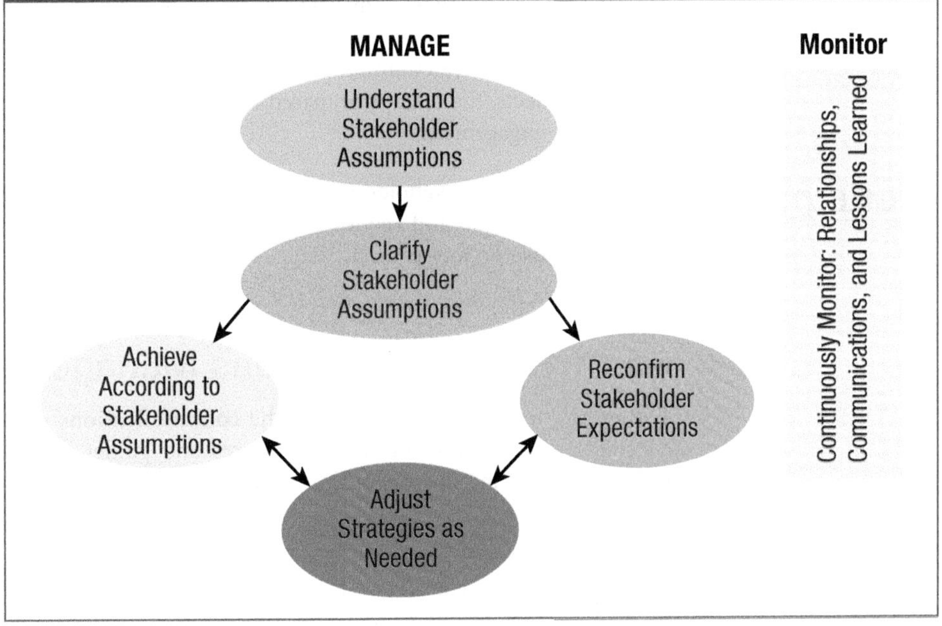

During project execution, the team works toward satisfying these expectations. This involves work between project meetings to complete assigned activities and to quickly resolve problems that have surfaced. Concurrent with the achievement of expectations is the continual recommitment to the expectations. One method that project teams can use to reconfirm expectations is to share planning documents, such as schedules, with stakeholders. The team informs the stakeholders that all the planning documents reflect the team's understanding of what has been asked to do. It is what the team is expected to achieve and be judged against.

Some stakeholders may identify further expectations when they see everything spelled out. Project managers often hold informal conversations with various stakeholders to ensure that they fully understand and agree with all of the planning details. Finally, as project teams report progress to stakeholders, additional expectations emerge. When additional expectations emerge, they need to be considered in terms of the project's formal change control process and, if accepted, the project plan will be revised and these additional expectations would become additional project activities to be performed. All of the activities related to managing engagement increase support from those stakeholders who favor the project and decrease resistance from other stakeholders.

6-4 Monitor Stakeholder Engagement

Monitor stakeholder engagement is the process of engaging stakeholders and managing relations with them effectively. The vertical box on the right in Exhibit 6.6 shows three things a project manager must monitor throughout the process of managing stakeholder expectations: relationships, communications, and lessons learned. Through honest and ethical behavior, the project manager and project team must build trust with all project stakeholders. They need to continually manage effective two-way communications with all stakeholders as described in the communications plan. This includes a true willingness to encourage stakeholders to ask probing questions, as that is an effective way to develop confidence with some stakeholders. Finally, they should use lessons learned from previous projects and previous phases of the current project. Armed with trusting relationships, effective communications, and methods to overcome some problems from previous projects, the team is prepared to adjust strategies and plans as needed to control stakeholder engagement.

On Agile projects, stakeholders need to be educated about their roles; alerted in advance concerning changes; and request early and continuous feedback. These are all excellent methods to use on any project.

6-5 Plan Communications Management

The project team should next create the **communications management plan.** This plan considers stakeholders' information desires and guides the project communications. It needs to be a living document that adapts to changing project needs.

6-5a Purposes of a Project Communications Plan

Projects face many challenges, including technical, cost, and schedule difficulties. Failure to manage any of them well can throw off a project. Perhaps the most common challenge to project success is communication. Many projects require a group of people to work together who have not done so before. Projects may involve people from various functional areas that all have their own unique challenges. Sometimes, people from multiple companies may end up working together on projects. All projects are unique and therefore they have a different set of stakeholders. "Communication leads to cooperation, which leads to coordination, which leads to project harmony, which leads to project success."[8]

6-5b Communications Plan Considerations

A myriad of considerations must be kept in mind when creating a communications plan. A project team can develop a workable communications plan, use it, and improve it as the project progresses. Some factors that Fiesta® San Antonio organizers considered when creating a project communication plan are shown in Exhibit 6.7. These factors apply to all project communications. Therefore, we discuss these factors first and then explain who provides information needs to the project team and to whom the team needs to supply information.

PURPOSE COLUMN   The first column in Exhibit 6.8 instructs a project team to consider the *purpose* for each communication. Without good use for the communication, it makes no sense to develop it. A project manager must use effective communications to set and manage expectations of all stakeholders as well as to ensure that project work is completed properly and on time. Communications *from* stakeholders are necessary in

EXHIBIT 6.7

FIESTA SAN ANTONIO COMMUNICATION PLAN NEEDS

In August 2012, the Institute of Texan Cultures, a museum specializing in Texas culture and diversity, forged a partnership with the Fiesta® San Antonio Commission to produce a series of exhibitions showcasing the traditions of Fiesta®, San Antonio's premiere festival. Fiesta® is an annual 10-day festival of over 100 events and 5 large parades. The festival draws 3.5 million visitors. It is tradition for Fiesta® events to commission new medals each year to give to event-goers to wear and trade throughout the festival.

The museum's leadership team convened with the Fiesta® San Antonio Commission's executive director at the end of August to assemble a project management plan. The parties identified stakeholders who would be impacted by the project. They prioritized stakeholders by influence, and divided responsibilities for developing and maintaining relationships with each of those stakeholders.

The following challenges were anticipated:

- It would take time for the 120 Participating Member Organizations (PMOs) to reach their members and assemble a full collection of medals to loan to the museum.
- Some PMOs might be offended if their medals were not displayed more prominently than other PMOs.
- The museum would be engaging the same PMOs to support future exhibitions, so it was critical to maintain positive relationships.

It was clear that a comprehensive communications plan would need to be implemented to establish lines of communication, nurture relationships, and manage the flow of information between stakeholders.

Source: Aaron Parks, Institute of Texan Cultures

EXHIBIT 6.8

PROJECT COMMUNICATIONS PLAN CONSIDERATIONS			
PURPOSES	STRUCTURES	METHODS	TIMING
Authorization	Existing organizational forms (reuse)	Push methods:	Project life cycle
Direction setting		Instant messaging	Charter
Information seeking	Project specific:	E-mail	Project plan
Status reporting:	Templates (adapt)	Voice mail	Milestones
Schedule	Unique (create)	Text	Output acceptance
Cost		Pull methods:	Project close-out
People		Shared document repositories	Routine time
Risk		Intranet	Daily—member
Issues		Blog (repository)	Weekly—core team
Quality		Bulletin boards	Monthly—sponsor
Change control		Interactive methods:	As needed—others
Approval of project outputs		Telephone—teleconferencing	
Escalation		Wikis	
Lessons learned		VOIP/videoconferencing	
		Groupware	

authorizing work, determining requirements, uncovering and resolving issues and assumptions, and receiving feedback on project progress and results. Different stakeholders often have conflicting desires; effective communications are necessary to understand and resolve these differences. Communications *to* stakeholders are necessary to help them make good decisions (by understanding options and risks), assure them of adequate understanding and project progress, enable them to fully commit to the project, and be ready to accept project deliverables. Yet another communication purpose is to plan and manage escalation of issues that cannot be handled in a timely manner by the project manager. Wise project managers determine in advance how soon an issue will be escalated to the sponsor and/or other decision makers. Finally, communications plans ensure that at project conclusion, meaningful lessons can be documented to benefit future projects.

A project manager develops trust with her core team and other stakeholders partly by using open and transparent communications to the extent possible. However, she needs to respect all promises of confidentiality and to use good judgment on what is or is not appropriate to share.

STRUCTURES COLUMN   The second column suggests that when an organization has adequate existing communication *structures,* it should use them! There is no need to reinvent every document and, indeed, it would be confusing and costly to do so. Many stakeholders in organizations are accustomed to a particular method of communications, and using that method will make it easier for them to understand you. When no exact organizational model is available for a specific communication, one can use a template, which is still easier than creating an entirely new type of document.

Using any of the three choices, project teams need to maintain version control on all of their communications. One easy method is to end the file name of every document with six numbers representing year, year, month, month, and day, day. For example, an early version of this chapter was saved on February 1, 2017, and the file name given was "Chapter 6 Stakeholder Analysis and Communication Planning 170201." The advantage of a simple system is that the files can still be easily found by their descriptive named titles, but they can also be sorted easily by the last date they were updated.

METHODS COLUMN   The third column in Exhibit 6.8 deals with *methods* of communicating. Projects rely on "push" methods in which communications are sent or pushed; "pull" methods where communications are posted either on paper or in electronic form and interested stakeholders need to take the initiative to receive the communication; and interactive methods in which communications flow in multiple directions. A typical project communication plan will utilize a variety of these methods.

TIMING COLUMN   The fourth column is a reminder that a project team needs to consider *timing* issues when developing a project communications plan. Communications typically are delivered according to one of three types of timing schedules. First is the project life cycle, with communications typically needed at the end of each major stage in the project and upon completion of each major project deliverable. The second timing schedule follows a more formal organizational structure. Project progress is often reported at regularly scheduled meetings. Meetings at the frontline level are usually more frequent than reports to higher levels within the organization. The third timing scheme is on an as-needed basis. Many times, a stakeholder wants to know a certain fact about a project and cannot wait until the next formal meeting or report. Project teams need to keep themselves up to date so they can handle the as-needed requests.

6-5c Communications Matrix

At this point, project teams will normally assemble a project **communications matrix**. This matrix lists the following information:

Who	does the project team need to learn from?
What	does the team need to learn from this stakeholder?
Who	does the project team need to share with?
What	does this stakeholder need to know?
When	do they need to know it?
What	is the most effective communications method for this stakeholder to understand?
Who	on the project team is responsible for this communication? (the owner)

The communications needs of each project are unique and, therefore, the assignment of communications responsibilities will vary widely from project to project. A partially completed project communications matrix for the Modular courses program is shown in Exhibit 6.9. This identifies the information needs of the program team and the stakeholders. Various methods of communication are proposed, depending on the purpose of the communication and the constraints within which the stakeholder engagement must take place. It won't be possible to meet with the program board every day, so weekly meetings, supplemented by short one-on-one stand-ups with the Vice Chancellor are planned. It was decided to create a program board made up of key decision makers—to

EXHIBIT 6.9

MODULAR COURSES - PROJECT COMMUNICATIONS MATRIX				
STAKEHOLDER	PROJECT INFO. NEEDS	STAKEHOLDER INFO. NEEDS	METHODS	TIMING
Program Board (Vice Chancellor)	Direction, strategy, budget, authorizations	Status—progress and SH positions	Scheduled board meetings, circulated minutes, one-on-ones with Vice Chancellor	Weekly and as needed Daily 15-min. stand-up with Vice Chancellor
Deans of Faculty	Concerns, WIIFT	Plans, changes to practices affecting their staff	Program newsletter, across-faculty workshops, informal one-on-ones consultation	Every 2-3 weeks depending upon concerns.
Academic Registrar (AR)	Requirements	Resource commitments, status	Workshops with team, e-mails	Frequent in early stages then timed to delivery points.
Lecturers	Concerns	Plans, changes to practices affecting them	Program newsletter, presentations, e-mails	Monthly
Student support	Requirements	Resource commitments, status	Workshops with team, e-mails	Frequent in early stages then timed to delivery points
Students	Concerns	Changes to enrollment procedures	Social media, e-mails, presentations	E-mail and meetings

serve as an important communication and decision-making conduit for the program. The actual communication plans impact the scope of the project. For example, having a program newsletter adds to the scope—the effort and costs of the project. In complex projects, the communications plan can form a major proportion of the project scope.

Stakeholders want to know how much work has been successfully delivered (acceptance tests passed) and how much work is remaining. Project team members use the information to motivate and improve their performance. Sponsors use the information to strategically understand if the project team will complete all work on time and within budget. Other stakeholders may share the sponsors' overall concern but want details of work that concerns their functions. While these communication needs are common on all projects, Agile projects have unique reports such as velocity, burn-down charts, running tested features, and earned business value.[9]

6-5d Manage Project Knowledge

If a company does extensive project work and uses project management capability as an organizational strength, it is important to keep developing expertise in it. One way to develop and expand expertise is to capture and reuse the knowledge developed. **Knowledge** can be defined as insights derived from information and experience. Knowledge also is "a conclusion drawn from information after it is linked to other information and compared to what is already known."[10] Ironically, knowledge will remain dormant, and not very useful, until it is reflected in future actions. **Manage project knowledge** is the process of using and developing knowledge to help improve both the current project and the capability of the organization.

To increase knowledge and the successful use and reapplication of it, organizations often create a lessons learned knowledge base. For this database to be useful, it is important to communicate project successes and failures from all aspects of the project process. Captured throughout the life of the project, recommendations to improve future performance can be based on technical, managerial, and process aspects of the project. In addition, part of the project closeout process should include facilitating a lessons learned session for the entire project, *especially on unsuccessful projects*. Remember, "people learn, not organizations. ... Knowledge is created and exchanged through trusted relationships and social interaction."[11]

6-6 Manage Communications

Manage communications includes all the work associated with the project communications plan, starting with planning for it; generating it; organizing and sharing it; and, finally, storing and disposing of it. In order to successfully communicate the right project information to the right stakeholders, in the right format, at the right time, several things must happen. First, all of the information required to develop the project communications management plan should be assessed and obtained. Then, while the project is under way, the project manager and team need to determine any additional information needs not already uncovered, establish an information retrieval and distribution system, collect information on executed work and work in progress, and then report progress to all stakeholders.

6-6a Determine Project Information Needs

Many stakeholder information needs were identified during communications planning, such as authorization to proceed, direction setting, status reporting, and approval of outputs. Often, other information needs arise during project execution. All needs must be handled accurately, promptly, and in a manner that balances effectiveness with cost and effort.

- Communicate accurately—Accurate communications means not only being factually honest but also presenting information in a manner that people are likely to interpret correctly.
- Communicate promptly—"Promptly" means providing the information soon enough so that it is useful to the recipient to facilitate timely decisions.
- Communicate effectively—Effectiveness is the extent to which the receiver opens, understands, and acts appropriately upon the communication.

It is very easy to just copy everyone on an e-mail, but that is neither convenient nor effective for some people. Face-to-face communication tends to be the most effective, the telephone less so, and e-mail and formal reports even less. It is in the project manager's best interest to communicate effectively since the information provided allows stakeholders to make decisions, understand real challenges, remain motivated, and believe that the project is in control.

6-6b Establish Information Retrieval and Distribution System

Project information can be retrieved from many different sources. It can also be distributed via many systems. Project management software such as MS Project is frequently used for schedule information and sometimes for cost and human resource information. Project managers use many methods of communicating. In this information age, project managers need to keep three things in mind with communications:

1. Target the communications. More is not better when people are already overloaded.
2. Many methods are available, and the choices change rapidly. Use new methods if useful, but do not discard proven methods just for the sake of change.

3. Projects often have many stakeholders who need specific information. Use your communications plan and always keep asking if there is any other stakeholder in need of upward, downward, or sideways communications.

Tatro, Inc., uses a hosted project management page on its website that clients can access with a password to witness project progress from anywhere in the world on a 24/7 basis. It displays photos that show actual progress for the client to view.

One specific and important skill that project managers can use to retrieve information is active listening. Active listening requires focus on what the person is saying. The active listener can ask clarifying questions and paraphrase to ensure that he or she understands exactly what is meant. Making eye contact and using body language that shows eagerness encourage the speaker to continue. An effort to simultaneously understand both the meaning of the message and the hidden emotions helps the receiver to understand the full message. Recognize that many speakers are not especially skilled in communications, so paying more attention to their message than their style of delivery also helps. Often, a project manager can successfully end the conversation by orally confirming what he or she just heard and by following up with an e-mail for documentation.

6-6c Project Meeting Management

Planning and conducting projects require a variety of meetings, such as meetings to:

- Establish project plans
- Conduct the project activities
- Verify progress
- Make decisions
- Accept deliverables
- Close out projects

Meetings are an important process on projects since many important decisions are made at meetings and much time of expensive project personnel is invested in meetings.

One common feature of Agile projects is the "stand-up meeting." These short (15 minute or less) meetings are often held at the start of each day with no comforts such as coffee or chairs. Each project team member briefly states what she accomplished the previous day, what she plans to accomplish this day, and what obstacles may challenge her.

Project meetings should be conducted as efficiently and effectively as possible. One way to improve the project meeting process is to apply the simple and effective plan-do-check-act (PDCA) model.

PDCA MODEL   The idea behind process improvement with the PDCA is that any process practiced repeatedly, focusing on reusing and adapting things that worked well and avoiding things that did not work well, improves over time. Exhibit 6.10 depicts the PDCA model as it is applied to project meetings. Each of the four sections will be explained in more detail in the following sections, but, in short, this model gives advice on how to do the following for meetings:

P   **Plan:** prepare an advanced agenda to guide the meeting

D   **Do:** conduct the meeting and write meeting minutes

C   **Check:** evaluate the meeting and

A   **Act:** perform in-between meeting tasks.

PROJECT MEETING AGENDA TEMPLATE When applying the PDCA improvement model specifically to improving project meetings, the first step is planning the project meeting in advance. The project manager assures that the agenda is prepared and distributed ahead of time. If a project team is meeting often, this advance agenda

EXHIBIT 6.10

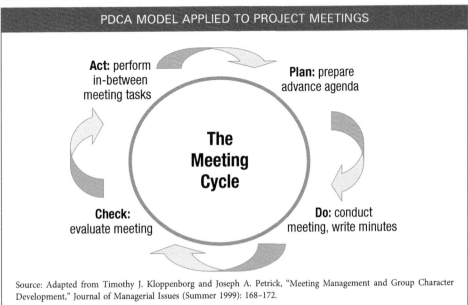

Source: Adapted from Timothy J. Kloppenborg and Joseph A. Petrick, "Meeting Management and Group Character Development," *Journal of Managerial Issues* (Summer 1999): 168–172.

preparation may be done at the end of the meeting for the next meeting. That way, everyone understands beforehand what will be covered in the upcoming meeting and will have the opportunity to prepare for the meeting. The agenda also can be helpful in deciding whether to invite a particular subject matter expert (SME) or other guest to the meeting. A project meeting agenda template is shown in Exhibit 6.11.

The top part of the agenda contains meeting logistics. The second item on the template is the meeting purpose. If a project manager cannot state in a sentence why he wants to conduct a meeting, perhaps the meeting is not necessary. The main body of the agenda has three columns. First is a list of the topics. This starts with a quick review of the agenda, because projects often move quickly, and this provides an opportunity to add or delete an item from the agenda. Also, it helps busy people rushing from another meeting to manage their time and focus on relevant agenda items. The major topics of the meeting are listed next in the order in which they will be covered. Often, remaining items from previous meetings or other urgent matters top the list. However, a project manager wants to be sure to cover the most important matters, even if they may not have the same sense of urgency. The second-to-the-last item on the standard agenda is the meeting summary. The project manager summarizes major decisions that were made as well as work assignments that were distributed. This helps people remember what they agreed to do. The final item on the agenda is an evaluation of the meeting. This is explained in the check step of the PDCA model.

The second column lists the person responsible for each topic on the agenda. Typically, the project manager takes care of the meeting start and close, but individual project team members may be assigned specific action items. When people know in advance that they are responsible for an action item, they are more likely to be prepared. Additionally, if the advance agenda is available for key stakeholders to see, some of the stakeholders may contact the responsible person in advance to provide input. This is a good way to keep stakeholders engaged.

The third column is a time estimate for each item. While the project manager does not need to be a slave to the clock, recognition of how long team members are in

EXHIBIT 6.11

PROJECT MEETING AGENDA TEMPLATE		
Project Team _____ Date _____ Time _____ Place _____		
PURPOSE:		
Topic	**Person**	**Time**
Review agenda	_____	2 min
Topic 1	_____	____
Topic 2	_____	____
Topic 3	_____	____
Summary	_____	5 min
Meeting evaluation	_____	2 min

meetings and how many items are accomplished goes a long way. People are more likely to attend a meeting if they are sure it will end on time.

PROJECT MEETING MINUTES TEMPLATE   The second step in the PDCA process—"do"—means to conduct the meeting and to capture minutes as the meeting is conducted. Many project teams rotate the role of minutes taker so each team member feels equal. A template for taking project minutes is shown in Exhibit 6.12.

6-6d Issues Management

The project minutes mirror the agenda to the extent that both refer to the same meeting. The top part of the minutes form is logistics, just as in the agenda. The four primary types of information captured in a project meeting are:

1. Decisions made
2. New issues surfaced and old issues resolved
3. Action items agreed to
4. An evaluation of the meeting

DECISIONS AND ISSUES   First, any decisions that were made should be documented. Second, any new issues that surfaced or existing issues that were resolved should be recorded. An **issue** is a situation that requires a decision to be made, but one that the team cannot make now, usually either due to needing information or more time. An **issues log** is a dynamic repository of information regarding both open issues and those that have been resolved. Issues logs benefit a project in at least two ways. First, when an important issue—but not one that can be solved in the immediate meeting—is introduced, the project manager can add it to the open issues and not spend time on it in the

EXHIBIT 6.12

PROJECT MEETING MINUTES TEMPLATE

Project Team _____ Date _____ Time _____

Members present:

_____

_____

Decisions Made:

_____

Issues Log:

Resolved Issues _____

New Issues _____

Action Item	**Person Responsible**	**Completion Date**

Meeting Evaluation

EXHIBIT 6.13

PROJECT ISSUES LOG				
OPEN ISSUES				
NAME	DATE OPENED	ORIGINATOR	POTENTIAL IMPACT	PROGRESS
CLOSED ISSUES				
NAME	DATE OPENED	ORIGINATOR	HOW RESOLVED	DATE CLOSED

current meeting when more pressing matters need to be settled. Second, the issues log ensures that important issues are not forgotten. An issues log template is shown in Exhibit 6.13.

ACTION ITEMS   The third type of project information is action items. Each of these is a task that one or more members of the project team agree to perform by a specific date. These are recorded, and the project manager reminds the team at the end of each meeting what each member agreed to do.

EVALUATION   The final item to be recorded on the project meeting minutes is an evaluation of both good points from the project meeting that the team would like to repeat or at least adapt and poor points from the meeting that the team would like to avoid or perform in a different manner in the future. An experienced team can collect these points in a minute or two; the time they save in future meetings often pays great dividends. An easy way to capture these evaluations is a Plus-Delta template, as shown in Exhibit 6.14.

 On Agile projects, this evaluation is called retrospectives.

When assessing the project meeting with a Plus-Delta method, a project manager can simply draw the form on a flip chart or marker board. Then, each person is asked to offer his opinion on at least one aspect of the meeting that either was good (+) that she would like to see repeated or one thing that was poor (Δ) and could be overcome in future meetings. The key to making this work for the project manager is how she responds to any deltas. If the project manager responds defensively, the team members may not want to offer further suggestions.

EXHIBIT 6.14

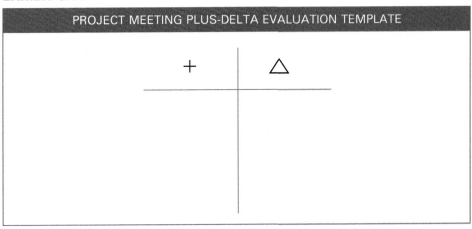

Finally, the "act" part of the PDCA cycle for project meetings is for every team member to complete the action items they promised and for the project manager to communicate with the team members to make sure nothing is holding them back from their commitments. Wise project managers keep active but informal contact with team members between meetings to ensure action items are completed on time. When all steps of the PDCA cycle are applied to project meetings, the meetings improve; the team members gain satisfaction; and the project makes better progress.

PMP/CAPM Study Ideas

There is a great deal of overlap between Project Communications Management and Project Stakeholders Management. Each edition of the PMBOK makes changes with and between these two groups, so be sure you are using the sixth edition if you are studying for one of the PMI certification tests. Besides developing the project charter—which is like a mini pre-plan that gives the project manager and team the authority to begin planning in more detail—the only other activity that takes place during the Initiating Process Phase is Identify Stakeholders.

The main work of the next phase—the Planning Process Group—is creating the Project Management Plan. The project management plan is the aggregate of plans from each of the ten knowledge areas, including the Communications management plan and Stakeholders Management Plan. As always, you will need to be familiar with the inputs, tools and techniques, and outputs that go into each.

Summary

Projects frequently have many diverse stakeholders. Some stakeholders do not know exactly what they want, and different stakeholders sometimes want different things. The project manager and sponsor need to build effective working relationships with the project team and stakeholders. When good relationships are built and maintained, the project team can enjoy the trust that is so helpful in successfully completing the project.

Armed with the stakeholder analysis and the project charter, a project team is ready to create a communications management plan. One important component of this plan is the communications matrix. This is the document that answers these questions:

- Who needs to know something about the project?
- What does each need to know?
- When do they need to know it?
- What format is easiest for them to receive and understand the information?
- Who is responsible for sending it?

Other important aspects of a project communications management plan include managing and improving meetings; managing and escalating issues; and capturing and using lessons learned.

Once stakeholders have been analyzed and communications are planned, the project team can get into more detailed planning of scope, schedule, resources, budget, risks, and quality—the topics of the next six chapters.

Key Terms Consistent with PMI Standards and Guides

identify stakeholders, 179
stakeholder analysis, 180
stakeholder register, 183
plan stakeholder engagement, 184
stakeholder engagement plan, 184
stakeholder engagement assessment matrix, 184
manage stakeholder engagement, 186
monitor stakeholder engagement, 197

plan communications management, 188
communications matrix, 191
knowledge, 192
manage project knowledge, 192
manage communication, 193
issue, 197
issues log, 197

Chapter Review Questions

1. List three reasons why understanding stakeholders is important to successful project management.
2. What is the difference between an internal and external stakeholder?
3. Which three criteria should you consider when prioritizing stakeholders?
4. When should relationship building between the project manager/other core team members and important stakeholders occur?
5. What are some ways to build relationships within the core team?
6. What are some ways to build relationships with key stakeholders?
7. What are some important functions of communication *from* stakeholders?
8. What are some important functions of communication *to* stakeholders?

9. In order to manage stakeholders' expectations, a project manager needs to understand the stakeholders' assumptions. Which document(s) can help with this?
10. What is the difference between "push" and "pull" methods of communication? Give examples of each.
11. What are three types of project communications timing schedules?
12. What six columns should a communications matrix contain?
13. Why is it so important to capture lessons learned in a knowledge database?
14. List the items that go into a project team meeting agenda and tell the purpose of each.
15. Describe an Agile "stand-up" meeting.

Discussion Questions

1. A new grocery store is being erected that will demolish a neighborhood basketball court. Who would be some internal stakeholders? Who would be some external stakeholders?
2. With a few of your classmates, conduct an Agile stand-up meeting and briefly discuss the three meeting components mentioned in this chapter.

3. Think of a recent project you completed and choose three stakeholders. Prioritize them, using the six-criteria model.
4. In your opinion, what is the single most important component of building relationships within a project team? Why?

5. In your opinion, what is the greatest benefit of having good communication between the project team and project stakeholders? Why?

6. Imagine you are the project manager of a team tasked with building a new hotel. When brainstorming project communication plan considerations, what would you list under "purposes"?

7. Using the same scenario as question 6, which timing schedule would you choose to use for each communication? Why?

8. Create a project meeting agenda for an upcoming project (or class) meeting you have.

9. Give an example of a time you have used push, pull, and interactive communication methods. Why did you choose the method you did based on the circumstances?

10. Betty, a project manager, sent out agendas before an upcoming meeting to everyone involved. During the meeting, she got a team member to take minutes. After the meeting, Betty followed up with team members to check on their progress. Evaluate Betty's actions using the PDCA model. What, if anything, could she have done better?

PMBOK® Guide Questions

1. The "component of the project management plan that describes how project communications will be planned, structured, and monitored" is the:
   a. communication model
   b. communications management plan
   c. stakeholder register
   d. organizational breakdown structure

2. In order for a new grocery store to be erected, a neighborhood basketball court located on the building site will have to be demolished. The neighborhood children who liked to play basketball there could be considered _____.
   a. subject matter experts
   b. internal stakeholders
   c. external stakeholders
   d. customers

3. A common method of prioritizing stakholders is based on the stakeholders':
   a. legitimacy
   b. power
   c. urgency
   d. all of the above

4. The components of a project communications management plan should typically include the purpose of the communication, structure (format, content, etc.), methods or technologies to be used, and _____:
   a. work performance data
   b. time frame and frequency
   c. stakeholder priorities
   d. lessons learned

5. Most project meetings are formal, planned events between project stakeholders. Effective meetings typically have a purpose, a prearranged time and place, a list of attendees and their roles, and an agenda with topics and issues to be discussed. After the meeting, _____ are circulated.
   a. refreshments
   b. business cards
   c. meeting minutes
   d. lessons learned

6. The "project document that includes the identification, assessment, and classification of project stakeholders" is called the _____.
   a. stakeholder engagement matrix
   b. organizational breakdown structure
   c. stakeholder register
   d. weighted scoring model

7. A document used to manage points of discussion or dispute that arise during projects, in order to monitor them and ensure that they are eventually resolved and added to lessons learned, is called a(n) _____.
   a. risk register
   b. stakeholder register
   c. SWOT analysis
   d. issue log

8. One of the key responsibilities of a project manager is to manage stakeholder expectations. It is important for the project manager to have interpersonal or "soft" skills that include: overcoming resistance to change, resolving conflict, active listening, and _____.
   a. displaying confidence
   b. subject matter expertise
   c. ability to command and control
   d. building trust

9. The process of communicating with stakeholders and working with them to meet their expectations, address issues as they occur, and obtain their continued commitment to the success of the project is called _____.
   a. Manage Stakeholder Engagement
   b. Monitor Stakeholder Engagement
   c. Monitor Communications
   d. Manage Project Team

10. The communication method that is used for large audiences or large volumes of information and requires recipients to access the content at their own discretion, is called _____ communication.
    a. push
    b. pull
    c. synchronous
    d. interactive

INTEGRATED EXAMPLE PROJECTS
SUBURBAN HOMES CONSTRUCTION PROJECT

Suburban Homes realizes the importance of maintaining excellent relations with all its key stakeholders. Among the stakeholders are clients who purchase homes, local law enforcement agencies, potential buyers, county and state agencies for real estate development, environmental regulatory agencies, both local and federal, community leaders, contractors, subcontractors, local construction material suppliers, and the list goes on.

Suburban Homes decided to build a new community of 120 homes in a suburb of Atlanta. It has acquired 15 acres of land for this purpose. It also has submitted a preliminary plan to the local county government for approval.

Suburban Homes is thinking of hiring a consultant for developing a stakeholder management plan and communication plan. For its stakeholder management plan, they would like to identify all the stakeholders and develop a stakeholder register. Further, it is considering selection of at least six key stakeholders for a detailed analysis of a prioritization matrix, as shown Exhibit 6.2, and to develop a stakeholder matrix, as shown in Exhibit 6.4.

As a consultant to Suburban Homes, you are asked to develop a stakeholder engagement plan (Exhibit 6.5) and a comprehensive stakeholder management plan after developing the stakeholder prioritization matrix and stakeholder matrix, as shown in Exhibits 6.2 and 6.4, respectively.

Using the stakeholder management plan, the company has also requested you to develop a communication plan that makes use of Exhibits 6.8 and 6.9.

CASA DE PAZ DEVELOPMENT PROJECT

In this chapter, the first thing we need to do is understand who our stakeholders are and the importance of each set of stakeholders. The initial look at stakeholders is shown in the matrix below.

Once we have our stakeholder priority matrix, we will ask each stakeholder what they want from this project. We will then use that information to develop a communications matrix showing for each stakeholder what they need to know from the project team and what they need to share with the project team, along with the most effective methods and times for these communications to take place and who on the project team is responsible for each communication. We will also develop meeting agendas, minutes, issues logs, and meeting evaluations.

In Agile, the role of communication with stakeholders is much more formalized to enable the team to focus on the work. The product owner is the primary contact for all stakeholders and acts as a buffer between stakeholders and team members while the iteration is under way. The ceremonies in some Agile approaches act as a time for the stakeholders to see the progress and make comments.

Stakeholder Prioritization
Project: Casa de Paz

Stakeholder	Power	Legitimacy	Urgency	Total
Parish Council	5	5	4	14
Casa de Paz Staff	5	5	4	14
Board Members	5	5	3	13
Community Council	3	5	4	12
Casa de Paz Volunteers	2	4	4	10
Residents/Future Residents of Casa de Paz	1	5	4	10
Members of Phoenix Support Group	1	5	4	10
Donors	2	3	4	9
Student Interns	2	4	2	8
Su Casa (who also serves sme community	1	5	1	7
YWCA	1	5	1	7
Protective Services	1	5	1	7
	1	5	1	7

Semester Project Instructions

Do each of the following for your project:

- Develop a stakeholder analysis. Identify as many stakeholders as you can using Exhibit 6.1. List stakeholders by name and title where possible.
- Prioritize the listed stakeholders, as shown in Exhibit 6.2.
- Specifically identify each stakeholder's interests, as shown in Exhibit 6.4. Recognize that some stakeholders may have an interest in multiple aspects of the project process or results.
- Describe the activities you are using to build relationships with your stakeholders.

- Create a stakeholder engagement matrix like Exhibit 6.5.
- Develop a communications matrix like Exhibit 6.9. Be sure to use considerations in Exhibit 6.8 for ideas regarding purpose, structures, methods, and timing for each communications need.
- Document a project meeting with an advance agenda, meeting minutes, issues log, and Plus-Delta form of evaluation like Exhibits 6.11 through 6.14.

PROJECT MANAGEMENT *IN ACTION*

Project Communication Planning for a Distributed Project

During an IT rollout of servers, clients, networking equipment, and a central data center involving a range of subcontractors at each of the roughly 50 regional schools, **the original communication plan** showed:

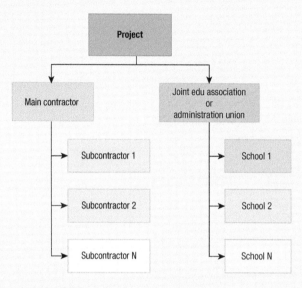

Original communication plan

After being appointed PM for rollout and implementation, I noticed that this was far from enough and needed to be amended.

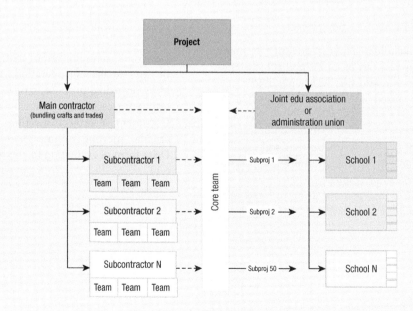

Revised communication plan

First of all, **two on-site visits at each location** were introduced in order to

1. **get to know** the location and the people involved and
2. **make sure** all environmental preconditions agreed upon had been properly set up.

For each location, there were between 5 and 20 people involved who all needed special information (depending on their role), thus multiplying the planned effort of communication considerably. However, the still early discovery of the complex stakeholder situation also facilitated a degree of fast-tracking and intensifying the cooperation, which was essential to finalize the project in quality, time, and budget, despite several buffer-consuming events, with very favorable media coverage and proper project close, which otherwise would have been impossible.

Apart from the headmaster and IT teacher, **what other roles** did we "discover"?

- All teachers whose classrooms were involved (receiving equipment, have to move/exchange furniture, rearrange the room).
- Caretaker (usually the one who knew about walls, wires, changes to the building, and the construction history where there were no drawings available).
- Owner of the building (community, private owner, society).
- Sponsor for each individual school (who had to agree to a detailed plan and a float sum of money. This was quite a topic since originally it was thought that a float lump sum of money could be spent on the whole project moving money between sites according to need. The need differed greatly since a newly build school (concrete/steel) poses a whole different range of tasks as compared to 150-year-old converted castle schools with thick walls (think of wireless LAN, think of "protection of historical monuments" = no drilling of holes anywhere and a long analysis and certificates for every little change to the building, think of moist or even wet intended server locations).
- The schools all had preferred local partners for electricity (dedicated electrical phases for 19" server, power supply and network equipment, ideally dry

and ventilated and cool, usually a small moist place with no air flow at all like a broom closet of the Harry Potter type in Privet Drive).
- Structural fire protection authority (they had serious words for the people who suggested drilling through a bulkhead firewall).
- Regional politicians who support the improvement of learning environments.
- Media who supported the project in terms of regional development and marketing the initiative to improve education and bring up-to date learning facilities also to the more rural areas.
- And not to forget the neighborhood and especially the parents (in particular, the ones less IT enthusiastic) who needed a good portion of convincing that this was something big and essential to their kids' development and future chances.

What finally saved the project?

1. Initial core team brainstorming and **proper stakeholder analysis** (no matter whether according to PMI, IPMA, or PRINCE2, list them all, check their expectation, interests, influence, power, degree of potential support, and involvement).
2. Two alternative Meetings **informing all interested parties** (obligatory to certain stakeholders and open to the public and invited media), so everyone KNEW, everyone received a roughly 50-page handout with detailed plans and intentions, involvement of all relevant parties, order of steps, phases of progress, ways of communication, etc.
3. A short **pilot** consisting of 8 schools, 2 schools **of every one of the 4 different types** (primary/small, secondary/middle, gymnasium/large, special needs) helped us group the remaining location in mixed regional groups for each rollout team. Scheduling the whole procedure was a challenge because due to different sizes and varying numbers of equipment, totally different buildings, etc., there was no chance to cut everything into weekly time boxes à la "sprints" in Agile scrum. Instead, every team had their own stream of tasks, consisting of nearly the same steps, however, with independent underlying amounts of effort.
4. At virtually every first on-site visit, **someone unexpected played a vital role** (relevant for interdependency of activities, e.g., schedule, cost, resources, communication, risks, basically the whole range of

PM topics), we (the project core team on "whistle-stop tour," usually four to five people) explained everything we said at the two kickoff meetings again, answered more questions, and made clear that local support according to schedule was vital, and deliberately failing to meet deadlines meant moving down the list and along the time line.

5. During the second on-site meeting, we checked the **"preconditions ready"** and **if so** delivery and setup of IT equipment were approved, **if not** another school from further down the list was invited to move up if they met the criteria.

6. Every piece of equipment had a checklist, all functions were tested and ticked off by a technician and a school representative reporting status "green,"

Source: Martin Kontressowitz.

which automatically approved the final steps including training of staff on-site by the same technicians who worked on-site the 1–2 weeks beforehand.

Bear in Mind:

1. Have a **plan**. You need to follow a systematic approach throughout the project.
2. Employ **structured Information**.
3. **Pilot** what you do.
4. Communicate **face to face** on site.
5. Have **clear rules**.
6. Have a **realistic time line, including buffers** for all sorts of risks and additional stakeholder involvement wherever necessary.

References

A *Guide to the Project Management Body of Knowledge (PMBOK® Guide)*, 6th ed. (Newtown Square, PA: Project Management Institute, 2017).

Aaltonen, Kirsi, et al., "Stakeholder Dynamics During the Project Front-End: The Case of Nuclear Waste Repository Projects," *Project Management Journal* 46 (6): 15–41.

Alderton, Matt, "What's Your Number?" *PMNetwork* 26 (12) (December 2012): 48–53.

Anantatmula, Vittal, and Michael Thomas, "Managing Global Projects: A Structured Approach for Better Performance," *Project Management Journal* 41 (2) (April 2010): 60–72.

Assudani, Rashmi, and Timothy J. Kloppenborg, "Managing Stakeholders for Project Management Success: An Emergent Model of Stakeholders," *Journal of General Management* 35 (3) (Spring 2010): 67–80.

Badiru, Adedeji B., Triple C Model of Project Management: Communication, Cooperation, and Coordination (Boca Raton, FL: CRC Press, 2008).

Basten, Dirk, Georgios Stavrou, and Oleg Pankratz, "Closing the Stakeholder Expectation Gap: Managing Customer Expectations Toward the Process of Developing Information Systems," *Project Management Journal* 46 (6): 70–88.

Bourne, Lynda, and Derek H. T. Walker, "Visualizing Stakeholder Influence: Two Australian Examples," *Project Management Journal* 37 (1) (March 2006): 5–21.

Daft, Richard L., *Management*, 9th ed. (Mason, OH: South-Western Cengage Learning, 2010).

Eskerod, Pernille, Martina Huemann, and Claudia Ringhofer, "Stakeholder Inclusiveness: Enriching Project Management with General Stakeholder Theory," *Project Management Journal* 46 (6): 42–53.

Fleming, John H., and Jim Asplund, *Human Sigma* (New York: Gallup Press, 2007).

Goodpasture, John C., *Project Management the Agile Way: Making It Work in the Enterprise* (Fort Lauderdale, FL: J. Ross Publishing, 2010).

Kloppenborg, Timothy J., and Joseph A. Petrick, "Leadership in Project Life Cycles and Team Character Development," *Project Management Journal* 30 (2) (June 1999): 8–13.

Kloppenborg, Timothy J., and Joseph A. Petrick, "Meeting Management and Group Character Development," *Journal of Managerial Issues* (Summer 1999): 140–159.

Montoya, Mitzi M., Anne P. Massey, Yu-Ting Caisy Hung, and C. Brad Crisp, "Can You Hear Me Now? Communication in Virtual Product Development Teams," *Journal of Product Innovation Management* 26 (2009): 139–155.

Montoya, Mitzi M., Anne P. Massey, and Vijay Khatri, "Connecting IT Services Operations to Services Marketing Practices," *Journal of Management Information Systems* 26 (4) (Spring 2010): 65–85.

Mueller, Ralf, and J. Rodney Turner, "Cultural Differences in Project Owner–Project Manager Communications," *Innovations Project Management Research 2004* (Newtown Square, PA: Project Management Institute, 2004): 403–418.

Patanakul, Peerasit, Bookiart Iewwongcharien, and Dragan Milosevic, "An Empirical Study of the Use of Project Management Tools and Techniques across Project Life-Cycle and Their Impact on Project Success," *Journal of General Management* 35 (3) (Spring 2010): 41–65.

Shelley, Arthur, KNOWledge SUCCESSion: Sustained Performance and Capability Growth Through Strategic Knowledge Projects (New York: Business Expert Press, 2016).

The Standard for Program Management, 3rd ed. (Newtown Square, PA: Project Management Institute, 2013).

Turkulainen, Virpi, Kirsi Aaltonen, and Paivi Lohikoski, "Managing Project Stakeholder Communication: The Qstock Festival Case," *Project Management Journal* 46 (6) (December 2015/January 2016): 74–91.

Yang, Rebecca, Yaowu Wang, and Xiao-Hua Jin, "Stakeholder's Attributes, Behaviors, and Decision-Making Strategies in Construction Projects: Importance and Correlations in Practice," *Project Management Journal* 46 (6): 74–90.

Young, R. Ralph, Steven M. Brady, and Dennis C. Nagle, Jr., *How to Save a Failing Project: Chaos to Control* (Vienna, VA: Management Concepts, 2009).

Endnotes

1. Turkulainen, Virpi, Kirsi Aaltonen, and Paivi Lohikoski, "Managing Project Stakeholder Communication: The Qstock Festival Case," *Project Management Journal* 46 (6) (December 2015/January 2016): 76.

2. Eskerod, Pernille, Martina Huemann, and Claudia Ringhofer, "Stakeholder Inclusiveness: Enriching Project Management with General Stakeholder Theory," *Project Management Journal* 46 (6): 45.

3. Yang, Rebecca, Yaowu Wang, and Xiao-Hua Jin, "Stakeholder's Attributes, Behaviors, and Decision-Making Strategies in Construction Projects: Importance and Correlations in Practice," *Project Management Journal* 46 (6): 78–79.

4. Bourne, Lynda, and Derek H. T. Walker, "Visualizing Stakeholder Influence: Two Australian Examples," *Project Management Journal* 37 (1) (March 2006): 5–21.

5. Aaltonen, Kirsi, et al., "Stakeholder Dynamics During the Project Front-End: The Case of Nuclear Waste Repository Projects," *Project Management Journal* 46 (6): 28.

6. Adapted from John H. Fleming and Jim Asplund, *Human Sigma* (New York: Gallup Press, 2007): 97.

7. Basten, Dirk, Georgios Stavrou, and Oleg Pankratz, "Closing the Stakeholder Expectation Gap: Managing Customer Expectations Toward the Process of Developing Information Systems," *Project Management Journal* 46 (6): 76.

8. Badiru, Adedeji B., *Triple C Model of Project Management: Communication, Cooperation, and Coordination* (Boca Raton, FL: CRC Press, 2008): 29.

9. Alderton, Matt, "What's Your Number?" *PMNetwork* 26 (12) (December 2012): 48–53.

10. Daft, Richard L., *Management*, 9th ed. (Mason, OH: South-Western Cengage Learning, 2010): 631.

11. Shelley, Arthur, *KNOWledge SUCCESSion: Sustained Performance and Capability Growth Through Strategic Knowledge Projects* (New York: Business Expert Press, 2016): 18.

PART 3

PLANNING PROJECTS

ORGANIZE   LEAD   PLAN   PERFORM

Planning is a large and critical part of project management. Planning may be largely completed before much executing work begins in traditional project management, in a completely iterative fashion using Agile, or somewhere in between in a hybrid environment. Project planning tends to be collaborative with many people involved and integrative in that many factors need to be considered. That said, we cover the various aspects of planning in distinct chapters to clarify what needs to be done in each. Chapter 7 shows how to plan the scope by collecting requirements and creating work breakdown structures. Chapter 8 shows how to create and communicate project schedules. Chapter 9 follows closely by resourcing projects and dealing with overloaded workers and the frequent need to compress schedules.

Chapter 10 shows how to create a time-phased project budget that will be used for control. Chapter 11 covers details of identifying, assessing, and dealing with a myriad of project risks. Finally, Chapter 12 deals with quality planning and with integrating all parts of the schedule into a single coherent whole.

Scope Planning

After completing this chapter, you should be able to:

CORE OBJECTIVES:

- Describe the planning of scope management, collecting requirements, and defining scope processes.
- Create a requirements traceability matrix, project scope statement, and change request form.
- Describe a work breakdown structure (WBS) and its importance to project planning and control.
- Compare different methods of developing a WBS.

TECHNICAL OBJECTIVE:

- Create a WBS, including work packages and a numbering system for the code of accounts, both by hand and using MS Project.

Rawpixel.com/Shutterstock.com

You're browsing a favorite retailer's website and you notice the onscreen recommendations are just right for you. The site seems to know what you've bought before. This great customer service is enabled by the retailer's web intelligence solution from Teradata.

Teradata is the world's largest company focused solely on enterprise data warehousing and analytic solutions. The simple web-shopping scenario is just one example of how our customers use information to improve their relationship with you.

So what does this have to do with project scope management? In this example, the retailer purchased a Teradata solution that included hardware, software, and a consulting project for the implementation. Teradata implemented this project based on our experience and a methodology built upon a foundation of scope management.

We can manage scope in various ways—ranging from traditional waterfall to Agile approaches—to deliver the right solution in an effective manner.

The first step in project scope management is to mutually agree on what the project will deliver, or in the case of Agile, what we will focus on. In our example, the retailer needed to integrate data from their web analytics software, an in-house customer relationship system, and other sources. They also had requirements for reports and the technical integration with their IT infrastructure. The

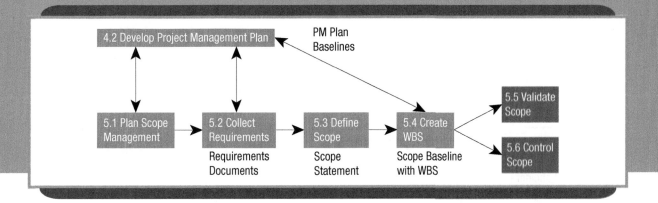

PMBOK® GUIDE

Topics:

- Plan scope management
- Collect requirements
- Define scope
- Create WBS

CHAPTER OUTPUTS

- Requirements documents
- Scope statement
- Scope baseline with WBS

Teradata team elicited requirements in a way that uncovered what the customer really needed.

Projects often use a statement of work (SOW) or similar document to outline the high-level scope. In a Teradata project, this is part of our customer contract. We then elaborate on more detailed requirements in a traceability matrix. This ensures all requirements tie "end to end" from the contract through project testing and customer acceptance. The time spent up front in requirements management pays dividends during project testing and customer acceptance, where discovering unknown requirements is much more time consuming and expensive.

Teradata follows traditional project management practice to develop a work breakdown structure (WBS) as the basis for a detailed project schedule and resource plan. We typically use Microsoft Project as a scheduling tool; a plan based on the WBS makes it easy to track and communicate the status of each deliverable.

Finally, the entire set of requirements is managed under change control. This is an important process, because the team must balance control and flexibility. We also must meet (or agree to change) the project cost and schedule parameters. Our project manager facilitates an analysis of the technical, schedule, and cost impact, and then all parties reach an agreement on how to proceed.

This simple example illustrates how the Teradata project methodology builds upon a foundation of scope management to deliver exactly what the customer needs in the most efficient manner. An effective scope management approach fosters open communications and sound decision making to ensure all parties get the business value expected from the project.

—*Mike Van Horn, Teradata*

7-1 Plan Scope Management

Once all the stakeholders for a project have been identified, the project team members develop a scope management plan, assess project requirements, develop the project's scope, and create a work breakdown structure (WBS). These are the scope planning processes that will be covered in this chapter. When planning scope, it is also wise to plan for changes. While this is not technically part of scope planning, it will also be covered in this chapter because accurate assessment of the client's requirements can minimize scope changes, and, to that extent, scope planning is an effective means to control changes to the project.

The flow of scope planning is illustrated in Exhibit 7.1. The boxes represent the project work processes involved, and the documents shown before and after the boxes represent major inputs needed to perform the processes as well as major outputs created by the work processes. Documents covered in previous chapters (Charter in Chapter 3 and Stakeholder Register in Chapter 6) are needed inputs for the first two processes.

EXHIBIT 7.1

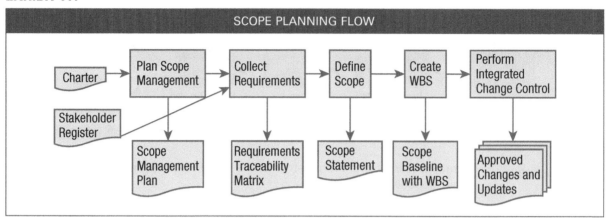

The first scope process, **plan scope management**, is the process of developing a plan that includes the total scope of what needs to be done and what is excluded from the project, implementation and validation of the scope, and control deviations from the scope statement. The product scope describes features and functions of a project outcome such as product, and, in some cases, service or result. The project team also needs to determine the project scope, which is the work required to be performed for delivering a product, service, or result with the required features and functions. Together, the product scope (the outputs the team will deliver to its customers) and the project scope (the work they need to perform to create the project's outputs) form the total scope. In other words, the project team members determine what they will do to ensure they have identified and organized all the project work so they can use it as the basis of all other planning activities and then as the basis for executing and controlling the project work. For many projects, the client or the end user may not be concerned about the project scope and may be interested only in the product scope.

 The priority of the product in Agile is more significant than in traditional project management. The outcome, or the product, will drive the elaboration of the project. The end state of the product is not predetermined. In Agile, we flip the 80/20 proposition on its head and focus on the product 80 percent of the time and the project 20 percent. While this model will not work in all project scenarios, it does work in projects in which the main product is a creative, virtual result. Agile aligns to the needs of the customer. However, if an intermediary is managing scope and cost, the project manager needs to maintain alignment and remain focused on delivering value through the product.

7-2 Collect Requirements

A **requirement** is a condition or capability needed by a user to solve a problem or achieve an objective that satisfies a standard, a specification, or any other formally documented need.

Collect requirements is a systematic effort to understand and analyze stakeholder needs to define and document these needs and requirements with a focus on meeting project objectives. The first step in collecting requirements is to ensure that the project team is clear on the project objectives. This could be accomplished by reviewing the project charter—particularly the "why" section that justifies the project. The project team members then may describe in more depth what each believes the expected project benefits are and/or what problems the project is attempting to overcome. On simple projects, this may not take a lot of time. On complex projects, a project manager may choose to use idea generation, grouping, and/or cause-and-effect techniques to make sure that everyone on the project team understands why the project is being conducted. Understanding broad project objectives will help in making more-detailed decisions later. This also reinforces the project's importance and may help motivate team members and other stakeholders during challenging periods in project execution. It is especially useful with multifunctional, virtual, and global project teams. Finally, a clear understanding of the project's objectives helps if the project plan needs to be revised at some point.

Collecting requirements is the same no matter what type of project approach you undertake; however, in more iterative projects, the documentation of the requirement is normally much less formal. Agile leverages the progressive elaboration mindset that allows for the project to unfold before the implementation team. This works best when the expected outcome is unclear or customers may change their mind once they see the initial product.

7-2a Gather Stakeholder Input and Needs

The second step is to gather input from the various project stakeholders. Needs assessment begins with a high level of understanding of the client needs during the project inception. A project manager is assigned and more detailed requirements assessment is done after a project's core team is selected. This core team size would depend on the nature of the project and the number of disciplines required to plan and execute the project.

When a project manager and team listen closely to both internal and external customers, they understand better both what their needs are and what risks and issues may confront them during the project. Successful project managers know that for a project outcome to be useful to the project's customers, the customers need to be able to use the output to better serve their own customers in turn. In other words, end-users of the project deliverable, the product of the project, and their needs must be integral to the list of requirements.

The methods of developing deep understanding of customers and their needs vary extensively from one industry to another. The traditional methods of obtaining and documenting requirements are many, such as:

- Meetings with key stakeholders
- Interviews
- Focus groups
- Questionnaires
- Surveys
- Observations
- Prototypes
- Industry standards
- Reference documents,
- Market analysis
- Competitive analysis
- Requests from the client
- Standard specifications

For example, in new product development projects, teams often use voice of the customer (VOC) techniques to elicit the benefits and features the customers want out of the project expressed in the customer's language. Teams using VOC try to understand the customer by not only asking questions but also by placing themselves in the customer's situation. If a project team is designing a new system that is to be used in the field, the team member should get down in the mud with the mechanic and hand the mechanic repair tools to see from the mechanic's point of view how the new system will be used.

Requirements can be classified as functional/technical and nonfunctional. The first category is usually the focus of needs assessment exercises and is centered on performance of the deliverable—such as the mechanic's needs just described. The second category includes requirements such as scalability, reliability, maintainability, and testability.

Once captured, these customer wants and needs are then stated in operational terms that the people performing the project work can use to plan that work. If the customer wants blue food coloring in a food item, the project team developing the item needs to know the precise desired shade of blue, the quality grade, the tolerance for color variation, and how the blue color may interact with other ingredients.

The project manager wants to understand how a project's success will be determined from the customer's perspective. The best way to gain this understanding (and to begin building a strong relationship with customers) is to directly ask customers. The project leaders can ask the customer(s) to specify how they will judge the quality of the project based on both functional and nonfunctional requirements.

On an information systems project, the team may use a joint application design (JAD) session to elicit customer requirements. This is often a facilitated session in which users of the software should articulate their preferences regarding how the software should work. The project manager and the team often send their understanding of the project objectives and deliverables in advance to all the users so that they are better prepared to discuss their needs and provide clarifications. Only one group of users is normally in this meeting at a time, while the project manager and the technical workers are in the session for its duration. Each possible feature of the system should be discussed. If the system is large and complicated, the amount of time that can be spent per item may be scheduled. Users often wish to talk in depth about how they want to use the system, while developers often want a detailed discussion about how they plan to create the feature. To avoid sinking into too much detail, the project manger can ask the users to start with only a high-level description of their reasons for the requested feature and then guide the discussion with the following five questions:

1. What do we not understand about the feature?
2. What is the business reason for the feature?
3. What is the impact of not providing this feature?
4. What action items need to be accomplished if we do this?
5. What impact will this have on other features of the project or elsewhere?

Exhibit 7.2 lists requirement along with other related information such as acceptance criteria for each requirement, which can be either high level or very detailed (using specification in measurable terms). The requirement type suggests whether the requirement is functional, nonfunctional, or needed by a particular stakeholder. The traceability matrix also includes the status of the requirement, its priority, and who is responsible for the requirement.

On some types of projects, the customers can provide their ideas using one of the techniques above, and the project team can be confident that the customers' wants and needs have been captured. On other projects, once the customers' viewpoint is captured, it makes sense to create a model or prototype of some sort so the customers can decide if their wishes have been fully and accurately captured. Often, this extra step helps the

EXHIBIT 7.2

REQUIREMENTS TRACEABILITY MATRIX							
ID	REQUIREMENT	ACCEPTANCE CRITERIA	TYPE	STATUS	STAKE-HOLDER GROUP(S)	PRIORITY	OBJECTIVES
1	The BA must be able to customize the information collected for requirements		Stakeholder	Approved	BA	Must	PO#1
1.1	The system shall allow for renaming of requirement attributes	1. BA can rename an existing field 2. Field displays new name on input forms 3. Field dispalys new name on reports	Functional	Approved	BA	Must	PO#1
1.2	The system shall allow new requirement fields to be identified	1. BA can add a new field 2. BA can set field attributes 3. BA can indicate field lookup values 4. Custom field available for input 5. Custom field available for reports	Functional	Approved	BA	Should	PO#1
1.3	The system shall allow for lookup of allowable fields for a requirements attribute	1. BA can enter custom list of lookup value 2. Lookup fields can be provided from an external system through data interface	Functional	Approved	BA	Should	PO#1
2	The BA must be able to provide different reports for different audiences		Stakeholder	Approved	BA, Team, Sponsor, Stakeholders	Must	PO#1
2.1	The system shall include a base set of standard reports.	Reports include 1. Requirements Traceabilty Matrix 2. Business Requirements Documents	Functional	Approved	BA, Team, Sponsor, Stakeholders	Must	PO#1
2.2	The system shall allow a business analyst to filter reports based on various requirement attributes	1. BA can filter report based on a. Type b. Stakeholder c. Status d. Priority e. Objective	Functional	Approved	BA	Must	PO#1
2.3	The system shall provide an option to download data to an Excel supported file so the BA can customize	1. BA can select to extract data to an Excel supported file 2. Extracted data is formatted as a tabular data set with no row breaks	Functional	Proposed	BA	Should	PO#1
2.4	The system shall allow for customization of reports to include filtering and displayed fields.	1. BA can selected fields to include or exclude in resulting report 2. BA can filter report (see 2.2.1)	Functional	Approved	BA	Should	PO#1

PO#1 - Project Objective #1 - "record, manage, communicate, and update requirements so that requirements can be captured once and then managed and communicated efficiently"

Priority uses MoSCoW - **M**ust be include in release (mandatory), **S**hould be included in release (highly desired), **C**ould be included in release (nice to have), **W**on't be included in release (out of scope)

Source: Vicki James, PMP, CBAP, PMI-PBA, CSM.

customers become more fully vested in the project and creates a strong working relationship that is helpful when difficulties arise during project execution.

It is helpful to list requirements and their supporting information in a requirements traceability matrix such as that shown in Exhibit 7.2.

When requirements are complete, each requirement needs to be:

- Traceable back to the business reason for it
- Identified with the stakeholder(s) who need it
- Unambiguous
- Qualified by measurable conditions
- Validated for its value and completion
- Bounded by constraints
- Prioritized according to value, cost, time risk, or mandate so trade-off decisions can be made if needed

Once these requirements are developed, they are translated into specifications, as shown in Exhibit 7.3.

 There are several differences in gathering stakeholder input in Agile. In an Agile project, the Product Owner is the interface to the product stakeholders and is responsible for aligning stakeholders to priorities and capabilities. Agile focuses on delivering value to the customer quickly, so feedback can get to the development team quickly. This eliminates waste. Agile further assumes that the people doing the work know how to do the work, and requirement writers are not qualified to tell them how to do that work. At every iteration, the delivered product should be ready for use, if the customer would choose to do so. As you can see, this would not work for a building that does not have windows, so the type of project in which you engage will start to take shape as you see the outcome being requested. In Agile, we are more likely to produce a color of blue that seems to make sense to the team and get feedback. The goal is not to be right: it is to get feedback. In a more Agile environment, there is only the judgment of how well the product works. The customer ideally would not get involved in how the product is created. Creating a model or prototype described above is analogous to Agile delivering working software every few weeks to get feedback. If all is well, we keep going; if not, we pivot and deliver more. In Agile, the requirements are captured in a product backlog. The product manager prioritizes them on an ongoing basis. They are delivered in short iterations and reviewed with the stakeholders on a normal cadence.

EXHIBIT 7.3

REQUIREMENTS TRANSLATED INTO SPECIFICATIONS	
REQUIREMENTS	SPECIFICATIONS
• Unambiguous—not subject to interpretation • Complete—nothing left out • Consistent—no conflicts, which also means no duplication • Modifiable—amenable to change • Traceable—to a customer need • Verifiable—means provided to verify the requirement	• Unique set—each stated only once • Normalized—should not overlap • Linked set—shows relationships • Complete—nothing left out • Consistent—no conflicts • Bounded—specifies nonnegotiable constraints • Modifiable—amenable to change • Configurable—traceable changes • Granular—right level of abstraction

Adopted from: IEEE 1233

7-3 Define Scope

Define scope is the process of translating stakeholder needs and requirements into detailed specifications of the project outcomes and products. Essentially, the project scope statement includes three things regarding the total scope. First, the team needs to determine both what they will deliver to the project stakeholders at the end of the project and what they need to deliver along the way to ensure they will be successful in the end. These are the deliverables—the *product scope*. For example, if a final project deliverable is a new computer program, intermediate deliverables may include an outline of what will be included and a prototype. Second, the team should decide what work needs to be accomplished to create the deliverables. This is the project work statement—the *project scope*. Third, the team needs to determine what will limit or influence the project work—such as exclusions, constraints, and assumptions.

7-3a Reasons to Define Scope

Scope definition is an important part of project planning because all other planning is based on the project scope. While the requirements collected represent the customers' statement of what they need, the defined scope is the project team's response—asking the customer, "If we provide this, will it solve your problem?" It is impossible to estimate how much a project will cost, how many (and what type of) workers will be needed, how long a project will take, what risks are involved, or what quality standards will be invoked without first understanding what work is included in the project.

Scope definition also is vital in preventing scope creep. Scope creep happens for two common reasons. First, if the scope is not clearly defined and agreed upon, it is easy to add additional work (scope creep) to the project with or without realizing that more time and resources (additional cost) will be required. Second, sometimes when a project is going as planned, a customer is so excited that he or she asks an innocent-sounding question: "Can the project output also do … ?" The person performing the project work is often flattered and agrees without understanding the implications of making this change. In contemporary business, pleasing the customer is desirable. However, the best time to gain customer understanding is when the project team is defining the scope—not while executing the project scope work.

7-3b How to Define Scope

Scope definition can vary greatly from one project to another. For a small, routine construction project, it may be quite simple to determine what project outputs will be created and what work is involved in creating them. On other projects, such as one large company acquiring another, it may be very difficult to determine the total amount of work that needs to be accomplished. Regardless of how easy or difficult it may be to define scope and despite industry-specific methods that may be helpful in doing so, all project teams need to complete each part of this process.

LIST DELIVERABLES AND ACCEPTANCE CRITERIA   The first step is to list project deliverables. The requirements elicited from the customer often lead to some of the final deliverables. Project teams need to understand that there are often multiple deliverables. For example, if a project entails constructing a house, the homeowners probably want not only the house but also documentation on systems within it, perhaps an explanation (training) on how to use certain items such as an innovative thermostat, and a warranty procedure. The project team also needs to list intermediate deliverables—those things that need to be developed while making progress to complete the project. Some of these were probably listed in the charter, but others may not yet be identified. Then the project team needs to determine the acceptance criteria for each deliverable.

ESTABLISH PROJECT BOUNDARIES   The second step in defining scope is to establish the project boundaries. Think of the project boundaries as the sidelines on an athletic field. By understanding what is in play and what is not, athletes know clearly when to play and when to stop. Likewise, project team members need to know which tasks should be executed and which tasks need not be executed.

The first part of the boundary definition is to decide which features and work elements are included (in scope) and which are excluded (out of scope). Collectively, clients and end users often request far more features and work than a project is originally planning to deliver or can deliver. Therefore, the team needs to know and decide what is included and what is not. Usually, the sponsor makes decisions regarding larger scope decisions, but the project manager and team still have many detailed scope decisions to make.

The second part is to manage expectations regarding any project. The project team members need to understand the constraints imposed on the project. If the work must be delivered by a certain date or if only limited resources are available, the project may be constrained, and the team should be careful to promise only what it can deliver. In planning, people make assumptions about dates, times, and availability of resources; for example, a shipment of required materials will arrive by the date the supplier promised. These assumptions should be stated. If an assumption proves to be false, it frequently increases the project risk and may also limit the project scope.

CREATE A SCOPE DESCRIPTION   The final step is to create a **scope description**. This description briefly states the work that needs to be accomplished to create the project deliverables.

A project scope statement guides the project team during subsequent planning and execution. For some very small projects, a well-developed project charter could also serve as a scope statement. On most projects, a scope statement needs to be developed prior to development of the WBS. An example scope statement for the Alternative Breaks project is shown in Exhibit 7.4.

7-3c Defining Scope in Agile Projects

Agile strives to use smaller iterations to get feedback because understanding the desired outcome tends to evolve as the customers see the work being done by the team.

Humans tend to be poor estimators, and the more unique the project, where volumes of reliable data are not available for making estimates, the harder it is to be predictable. In construction, for example, there are software packages that help estimate how long it will take to hang drywall or run electrical wire. However, in more creative endeavors like creating software, there is little documented knowledge of how long a project will take. This is where the adage to underpromise and overdeliver becomes words to the wise.

With Agile projects, the project manager is challenged with conflicting aspirations and actions between finalizing the scope specifications and maintaining flexibility to modify them to meet changing business needs or adding new requirements of stakeholders. Agile scope definition is a complex process as the scope is not clear to either the project team or the client. The project manager and the project team must demonstrate greater adaptability to frequently changing scope and employ iterative or phased planning of scope. Consequently, Agile projects present more flexibility.

On Agile projects, the scope definition starts with large chunks of work; for example, we want to be able to take credit card payments on a website. This large feature, and

EXHIBIT 7.4

SCOPE STATEMENT

ALTERNATIVE BREAKS PROJECT SCOPE STATEMENT

Scope Description: This project will educate groups of 12 students on social justice issues, send them out to perform direct service on the issues, and provide reflective opportunities throughout the process. **Key deliverables with acceptance criteria (product scope):**

KEY DELIVERABLES	ACCEPTANCE CRITERIA
Project plan	Secured housing, Agreement with organization
Fundraising	Adequate money
Education	Syllabus
Reorientation	Digital archives
Trip itself	Return safely, pre- and post-evaluation

Exclusions: No alcohol, drugs, or romances; ratio number of trips to student population

Constraints: Van holds only 12 people—11 students and one faculty or staff; number of highly qualified site leaders

Assumptions: Service builds active citizens; international trips add more value than expense; a trip is better with a staff or faculty member.

Source: Chris Bridges.

there will be many of them for a fully functioning website, will be broken down into stories and prioritized later. The team creates "personas," which are fictional people who represent user types. These personas provide information about what they will do with the project deliverables and how they will benefit. These user stories define scope and functionality. Acceptance tests will also be agreed upon during the scope definition phase by describing the way project deliverables will be tested and how they should prove workable. At the project outset, the overall scope is only defined at a high level, and a backlog of possible work is identified. The customer representative (sometimes called the owner) prioritizes the scope based upon business need, value, cost, and risk. The team then commits to the amount of work they can perform in the first iteration. As the project progresses, the scope is described more specifically and is documented more closely. The level of documentation is less important and takes a secondary role. The primary measure of success in an Agile project is working software. The Agile method for defining scope is primarily applicable when the project scope is unclear or poorly defined.

7-4 Work Breakdown Structure (WBS)

After scope definition is complete, the project manager will have a greater clarity about project work and milestones as compared to the high-level understanding of the project when the project charter is defined (discussed in Chapter 3). The milestones defined in the project charter are not necessarily accurate due to lack of complete understanding of the total project work. It is important to note that the project charter must be seen as an authorization document with accuracy of estimates (cost and time) in the range of + 50 percent. With the definition of scope, more details about the project are available to develop WBS and new milestones.

A detailed understanding of the project scope and work to be performed must be simplified for execution, and it is essential to divide the total work into smaller and manageable elements. A tool that is used on virtually all traditional projects is the WBS. To understand this tool, we will first define it, tell why it is important, show several common formats to use when constructing one, and then demonstrate the steps required to construct a WBS.

7-4a What Is the WBS?

The WBS is, or should be, a uniform, consistent, and logical method for dividing the project into small, manageable components to manage project scope and for planning, estimating, and monitoring (Rad and Anantatmula, 2009). It is a project planning tool that is defined as the concept of hierarchical decomposition for transforming the project scope into deliverable work elements at the highest level. Its composition continues until it facilitates managing these work elements effectively. The WBS helps develop an optimum project schedule and cost estimates at the work element level.

The WBS is a tool that project teams use to progressively divide the deliverables of a project into smaller and smaller pieces. The project team members start by identifying the major deliverables to be created and by continuously asking: "What are the components of this deliverable?" The WBS is *not* a list of work activities, an organizational chart, or a schedule. The WBS *is* a framework that is used as a basis for further planning, execution, and control.

The WBS also is an important project planning tool that uses the concept of hierarchical decomposition for transforming the scope into deliverable work elements. Typically, the WBS is created after the scope is defined on large projects. In contemporary project management, particularly on small and middle-sized projects, the WBS may be created concurrently with the scope statement.

The WBS is normally developed by listing deliverables—major deliverables first and then progressively smaller ones until the team feels that every deliverable has been identified. Managers of smaller projects sometimes perform another process concurrent with WBS development: defining activities and milestones. **Define activity** is a project planning process that identifies and determines specific actions to develop and deliver the project outcomes, such as products, services, or results. Many people find that work activities can be easily defined once the various deliverables are itemized. To clearly distinguish between the work processes of WBS development and activity development, WBS development is covered in this chapter, and activity development is covered as part of project scheduling in the next chapter. Developing the WBS and defining the activities form an example of how two separate work processes are sometimes performed together (especially on small or simple projects) and sometimes separately (especially on large or complex projects).

7-4b Why Use a WBS?

The reasons for using a WBS are many. Planning projects requires discipline and visibility. A properly developed WBS encourages a systematic planning process, reduces the possibility of omission of key project elements, and simplifies the project by dividing it into manageable units (Rad and Anantatmula, 2009).

A WBS can be used as a pictorial representation of project deliverables. By using a systematic process for creating a WBS, project team members can ensure that they

Framing a house is a major deliverable in a house project.

wavebreakmedia/Shutterstock.com

include all deliverables that are required to be created. Deliverables that are not planned, but need to be, often add to schedule delays and budget overruns.

The WBS provides a framework of common reference for all project elements, for specific tasks within the project, and ultimately for better schedules and better estimates. It is the basis for all subsequent planning of such important functions as schedule, resources, cost, quality, and risk. It also serves as an outline for integrating all these planning elements. The WBS is easily modified and thus can handle the changes that often occur on projects. The impact of these changes is then shown in the schedule, budget, and other control documents. If a problem occurs during project execution, the WBS is helpful in understanding exactly where and why the problem occurred. This helps to diagnose problems, manage the quality of the project deliverables, and keep all the other facets of the project on schedule while the isolated problem is fixed.

The WBS is also helpful in project communications. Typically, many stakeholders contribute to developing the WBS, and this effort helps them understand the project. Further, it clearly shows the importance of each work element, why it is required, and how it is integrated with project deliverables. In a nutshell, the WBS presents the entire scope of the project and serves as an excellent communication and integration tool. Software such as Microsoft Project enables a WBS to be shown in its entirety to people who need to understand the details, but it also allows project details to be hidden so that others can see the big picture.

7-4c WBS Formats

There are various formats for constructing a WBS, but they all have the same purpose. The overall project is considered the first level, as shown in Exhibit 7.5. In this example, a WBS for a house is presented in the indented outline format.

The second level in this example depicts major deliverables from the house project, namely the house in its framed state, when it is wired, and when it is drywalled. This second level is indented one tab. Note that a section is included for the work of planning and managing the project.

A WBS usually has one or more intermediate levels, which generally represent items that need to be created to produce the final deliverables, such as drafts, prototypes, and designs. These are frequently called interim deliverables. All levels of the WBS with at least one level

EXHIBIT 7.5

HOUSE WBS IN INDENTED OUTLINE FORMAT

HOUSE
- Project Management
- Framed House
  - Framing Contractor
  - Wood
  - Assembled Frame
- Wired House
  - Wiring Contractor
  - Wiring
  - Installed Wiring
- Drywalled House
  - Drywall Contractor
  - Drywall
  - Hung Drywall

EXHIBIT 7.6

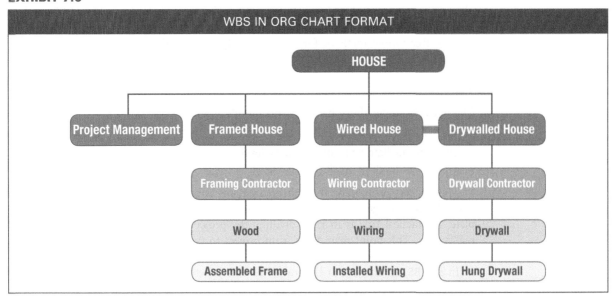

WBS IN ORG CHART FORMAT

below are considered summary levels. The completion of summary-level elements is based upon completion of all levels underneath. For example, in Exhibit 7.5, the house would not be framed until the framing contractor, wood, and assembled frame interim deliverables were complete.

Exhibit 7.5 used the indented outline format for the WBS method, but other methods are sometimes used. Another method is the hierarchical or "org chart" (short for *organizational chart,* which it resembles) method. A third method is called free format because the facilitator is free to draw it in any manner. The same house project shown in Exhibit 7.5 in indented outline format is shown in Exhibit 7.6 in org chart format and in Exhibit 7.7 in free format.

EXHIBIT 7.7

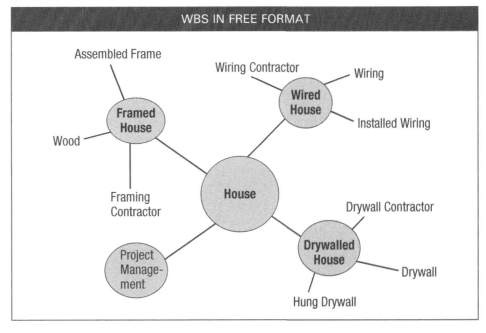

WBS IN FREE FORMAT

A marker board or flip chart can be used to develop all these methods and also offers plenty of room to add additional elements as the scope is revised. The WBS method using indented outlines can easily be imported into MS Project. Teams using the org chart or free format methods for WBS generally translate them into the indented outline format for input into software.

7-4d Work Packages

The house example above has only three levels as follows:

1. The first level, or project title level
2. One intermediate level, or summary level
3. The lowest level, or work package level

This process of dividing the deliverable items is continued until the project has been divided into manageable, discrete, and identifiable items requiring simple tasks to complete. A practical rule is to keep dividing the project until it no longer can be divided realistically. This point may differ from project to project. The lowest level is known as a work package.

In a WBS, an element at the lowest level is called a **work package**, which is usually the work component at the lowest level of the WBS for which cost and duration can be estimated and managed. Work packages are the basis for all subsequent planning and control activities. Exhibit 7.8 shows a WBS in org chart format with work packages in solid boxes.

One frequently asked question when breaking the deliverables into work packages is how small is small enough. The answer is, "It depends." In Exhibit 7.8, work packages occur at levels 3, 4, and 5. The work package is the point from which:

- Work activities are defined
- The schedule is formed

EXHIBIT 7.8

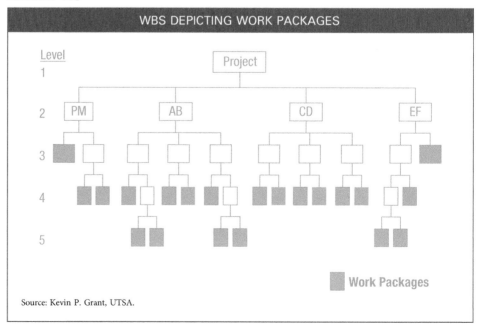

WBS DEPICTING WORK PACKAGES

Source: Kevin P. Grant, UTSA.

- Resources are assigned
- Many of the control features are developed

Work packages need to be detailed enough to facilitate further planning and control. If they are too detailed, the burden of tracking increases. The project manager needs to feel confident that the work to create the work package can be assigned to one person who can estimate the schedule and cost and can be held responsible for its completion. However, the work package may require multiple resources (including more than one person) to complete it.

If the work is composed of a single deliverable that is well understood, it is clear how the deliverable will be judged for quality and completeness, and the assigned workers have proven credentials, then the work package may not have to be too detailed. On the other hand, if the deliverable and/or how it will be judged for its completion are poorly understood, and the assigned worker or workers are yet to be proven reliable, a more detailed work package may make sense.

For ease of communication and comprehension, work packages and other components of a WBS are usually stated in very few words; one should avoid verbs and instead use adjectives to describe WBS elements at all levels. A **WBS component** is a work element that is part of the WBS at any level. The phrases or words to describe WBS elements should not be repeated. However, because the names are typically short, there is still the potential to get confused by exactly what is included in a work package or WBS component. Therefore, WBS components are often defined further using a WBS dictionary. A **WBS dictionary** is a document that provides detailed information about each work package by providing details about the associated deliverable, activity, scheduling information, predecessor, successor, person responsible for it, resources required, and associated risks. An example of a WBS dictionary entry with detailed information for a work package is shown in Exhibit 7.9. Note that some of this additional information such as activities, resource assignments, effort, and cost will be described in subsequent chapters.

EXHIBIT 7.9

WORK PACKAGE DETAIL			
Project: Expansion to Full Scale Production	**Work Package: Assembly Hardware Test**		
Description: Plan, conduct, evaluate, and report results of tests to ensure proper function of the assembly hardware.	**Deliverable(s):** Test results summary. **Input(s):** Assembly hardware prototype		
Activities	**Resource**	**Expected Duration**	**Cost**
Prepare test plan	Production Analyst	**8h**	$ 720
Conduct test	Production Analyst	**16h**	1,440
Evaluate test results	Production Analyst	**6h**	540
Prepare test results summary	Production Analyst	**8h**	720
			$3,420

Source: Kevin P. Grant, UTSA.

7-4e How to Construct a WBS

The information for a WBS is drawn primarily from the project objectives statement, and from historical files containing planning information of past projects. When a project team needs to construct a WBS, it needs to include in its planning team a subject matter expert (SME) who understands how each segment of the work will be accomplished. Teams approach this task in two ways. The first approach is that teams include only the core team members and plan the WBS as in as much detail as they can. At that point, different core team members are assigned to identify and seek the SMEs to plan the remaining details. In the second approach, teams invite the SMEs to the WBS planning meeting right from the start and utilize their input throughout the WBS development. Often, the choice of how to include SMEs is determined by the size and complexity of the project and by the cultural norms of the company.

The planning team uses a top-down approach in creating the WBS. This is easy to start when the type of project is familiar and at least some members of the planning team are likely to understand the general flow of work. If the project is similar to past projects, either a template or the WBS from a previous project can be used as a starting point. Then, using this template or WBS, the project team would identify additional project needs for inclusion and irrelevant elements of the previous project for deletion. Templates and previous examples can save teams a great deal of time, but caution must be exercised because each project is unique.

Sometimes, however, a project is so unique and different from previous projects that the team finds it useful to jump-start the WBS construction by brainstorming to identify a list of project deliverables to help to understand and develop the overall structure of the project WBS. However, once the overall structure is understood, the team proceeds with the typical top-down approach for the remainder of the WBS development.

IDENTIFY MAJOR DELIVERABLES   The team defines the project deliverables by reviewing the project planning completed thus far. The team members review the project charter, requirements traceability matrix, and scope statement to define the project's major deliverables. Remember that while many projects may have a primary deliverable such as a house, almost all projects have additional deliverables such as documentation and customer support. These could include training, service, or other means of helping the customer use the project's products effectively.

One of the first decisions is how to organize the second level of the WBS. (Remember, the first level is the overall project.) As defined earlier, the WBS is, or should be, a uniform, consistent, and logical method for dividing the project into small manageable components. WBS development is viewed as the process of grouping all project elements into several major categories, normally referred to as level one; each of these categories will itself contain several subcategories, normally referred to as level two. Alternately, and more accurately, development of a WBS involves dividing the project into many parts that, when combined, would constitute the project deliverable. This process of dividing the deliverable items is continued until the project has been divided into manageable, discrete, and identifiable items requiring simple tasks to complete.

Three methods are shown in Exhibit 7.10. One method is by project phase, with the second level being the signing of a contract, building the foundation, and framing the house. Alternatively, the second level can be organized by design components (deliverable-basis), such as kitchen, bedrooms, and bathrooms. Finally, the second level can be organized by work function (resource-basis). A house project organized this way might have carpentry, plumbing, and electrical as second-level elements.

EXHIBIT 7.10

WBS ORGANIZATION EXAMPLES		
PROJECT PHASE	DESIGN COMPONENTS/ DELIVERABLES	WORK FUNCTION/ SUBPROJECT
Project Management	Project Management	Project Management
Contract	Kitchen	Carpentry
Foundation	Bedrooms	Plumbing
Framed House	Bathrooms	Electrical
…	…	…

Organizing by project phase (schedule-basis) has the advantage of using the milestones in the project charter as an organizing principle. It also facilitates rolling wave planning. **Rolling wave planning** is a planning technique of identifying and defining the work to be completely accomplished in the near term and planning the future work at a higher level. In other words, once the near-term work is complete, the next phase of the project is planned in detail. In essence, it is an iterative process. If the planners of the project in Exhibit 7.10 used rolling wave planning, the work associated with the contract would be planned in detail immediately, and work for the foundation and framing might only be planned at a high level at first with more detail worked out as the project team worked on the contract. Rolling wave planning allows a team to get a quick start on a project—especially one in which details of later phases may depend on the results of work performed during early phases. Rolling wave planning helps a project team avoid either of two extremes. One extreme is to never start doing anything because the plan is not yet complete, which is also known as *analysis paralysis*. The opposite extreme is not planning at all because of fear that planning will take too long; this is known as *ready, fire, aim*.

Organizing by either phase or design components/deliverables helps to focus communications on project deliverables and their interactions. Organizing by work function allows the functions to focus on their specific activities, but often does not promote cross-functional discussion. Handoffs of work from one group to another are not always as smooth. Therefore, if a project manager decides to organize the WBS by work function, extra care needs to be taken in establishing interfunctional communications.

Of the three approaches, the most generally useful, and the most difficult, method for developing a WBS is to use design components/deliverables as the basis of the breakdown of the project. It is also known as a deliverable-based WBS. The deliverable-basis, or design-basis, is developed by looking at the project from the client's perspective and not from the project execution perspective. Further, it makes sense to all key stakeholders and facilitates easy communication.

In this deliverable-basis or design-basis mode, the project is divided into individual distinct components that ultimately comprise the project, such as hardware, software, physical structure, concrete foundation, or steel roof. This deliverable-based WBS division can be based on product, function, or physical location of the deliverable (Rad and Anantatmula, 2009). The deliverable basis of WBS development is far superior to the other bases because it is customer focused and easy to facilitate during project execution.

Note that one additional second-level item is shown on all three methods—that of project management. This includes the work of planning and managing the effort and includes preparing documents, attending meetings, integrating diverse portions of the project, handling communications, and so on. Since much of the work involved in project management is the level of effort, this section may not be decomposed. If the work of managing the project is left out, it is more likely that the project will not be completed on time and within the budget.

It is very important to understand that, in many cases, the client is not concerned about the intricacies of project execution or project management activities. From a client's perspective, the focus is only on what is delivered as the project outcome. So, project management is not typically included in a deliverable-based WBS. However, there are exceptions to this rule. For large and mega projects, programs, and federal government contracts, it is possible that the client is interested in project management activities and project progress reports. In such cases, including project management in the WBS may be sensible, even in a deliverable-based WBS.

DECOMPOSE DELIVERABLES   Once the major deliverables have been defined, it is time to break them into smaller deliverables or components. This is called **decomposition**, a method of dividing the project scope into many parts that, when combined, would constitute the project deliverable. It is the process of breaking down the project scope until it has been divided into manageable, discrete, and identifiable components requiring simple tasks to complete.

The team members can use the top-down approach, asking what all the components of each major deliverable are. Alternatively, the team members may use a bottom-up approach by brainstorming a list of both interim and final deliverables that they feel need to be created. Each deliverable can be written on an individual Post-it Note. These deliverables are then assembled on a large work space where team members group the smaller deliverables either under the major deliverables that have been previously identified or into additional related groups that are then headed by major deliverables.

CONTINUE UNTIL DELIVERABLES ARE THE RIGHT SIZE   At this point, the WBS has been formed and can be reviewed for completeness. Once it is determined to be complete, the team can ask if the deliverables at the lowest level need to be divided further for planning and control as described above. For example, in the new car development project in Exhibit 7.11, level-two components, such as product design, are at too high of a level to plan and control. Therefore, at least one more level should be included. If some of those components, such as Product Goals, are still too broad, yet another level would need to be developed.

REVIEW   At this point, several things should be considered to ensure that the WBS is structured properly. One consideration with WBS construction is the parent-child concept. The higher level is considered the parent and the lower-level elements are considered children. For example, in Exhibits 7.5, through 7.7, "Framed House" is a parent to the children: "framing contractor," "wood," and "assembled frame." "Framed House," in turn, is a child to "HOUSE." The framed house component is not complete until all of its children components are complete. The team asks if, once these elements are complete, the framing is complete. In an effort to simplify the WBS, where only one child element for a parent exists, you would not break it down. In fact, a good rule of thumb is to have somewhere between three and nine child elements for each parent. The fewer levels a WBS has, the easier it is to understand.

To avoid confusion, each component in the WBS needs to have a unique name. Therefore, two similar components may be *"draft* report" and *"final* report," instead of merely calling each "report." The team also assigns a unique number to each component.

EXHIBIT 7.11

PARTIAL WBS OF CAR DEVELOPMENT PROJECT

Car Development Project
    Project Management
    Product Design
        Product Goals
        Concept Design
        Modeling Design
        Vehicle Integration
        Engineering Feasibility
        Detailed Engineering Design
        Performance Development
        Regulatory Certification
  Process Development
  Prototype
  Production Materials Procurement
  General Materials Procurement
  Trial Manufacture

In one common numbering system, the number for a child item starts with the number assigned to its parent and adds a digit. An example of a WBS with components numbered is shown in Exhibit 7.12.

Different organizations sometimes develop their own unique variations of project planning and control techniques. Exhibit 7.13 describes the manner in which a large, complex organization (the U.S. Central Intelligence Agency) combines stakeholder analysis with WBS.

7-5 Establish Change Control

A **baseline** is the approved project plan mainly consisting of scope, schedule, and cost. It is not normally altered unless a formal change control request is approved for modifying these plans. The project team looks at the scope statement and WBS to ensure completeness and seeks to validate the scope by verifying it with the sponsor, customers, and/or other stakeholders. Simultaneously, the project team can be planning other aspects of the project such as schedule, resources, budget, risks, and quality. Once all these plans are complete and any impacts to scope have been accounted for, it is time to baseline the scope statement and the entire project plan. This is discussed in more detail at the end of the planning stage (Chapter 12).

Most projects are planned and conducted in an environment of uncertainty. Projects are planned with assumptions based upon the best information available to the project team, but many things can change during the course of a project. Therefore, project teams deal with change by establishing and using a **change control system** that entails processes to receive and review change proposals and accept or reject them after evaluating their impact on project scope, cost, and schedule. In essence, it is a system of managing and controlling changes and modification to the project plan and

EXHIBIT 7.12

LIBRARY PROJECT WBS WITH COMPONENTS NUMBERED

LIBRARY PROJECT

1. **Project Management**
2. **Facility Needs**
   2.1 VISION STATEMENT
   2.2 STAKEHOLDER INPUT
   2.3 OPTIONS
3. **Building Proposal**
   3.1 RECOMMENDED SIZE AND SCOPE
   3.2 SITING
   3.3 COST RATIONALE
4. **Building Approval**
   4.1 VP OF FINANCE APPROVAL
   4.2 PRESIDENT APPROVAL
   4.3 BOARD APPROVAL
5. **Staff Education**
   5.1 LITERATURE REVIEW
   5.2 LIBRARY VISITS
   5.3 SUPPLIER INPUT, PROCESS, OUTPUT, CUSTOMER ANALYSIS
   5.4 TRAINING
6. **Fundraising**
   6.1 POTENTIAL DONOR LIST
   6.2 RELATIONSHIP BUILDING WITH POTENTIAL DONORS
   6.3 EDUCATION OF POTENTIAL DONORS
   6.4 DONATIONS
   6.5 FOLLOW-UP WITH DONORS
7. **Building Documents**
   7.1 FACILITY AND SITE SPECIFICATIONS
   7.2 SCHEMATIC DESIGNS
   7.3 DEVELOPMENT PLANS
   7.4 CONTRACT DOCUMENTS
8. **Building Construction**
   8.1 ARCHITECT
   8.2 CONTRACTORS
   8.3 CONSTRUCTION
   8.4 FURNISHINGS
9. **Building Acceptance**
   9.1 BUILDING AND GROUNDS ACCEPTANCE
   9.2 BUILDING OCCUPANCY
   9.3 BUILDING DEDICATION
   9.4 WARRANTY CORRECTIONS

EXHIBIT 7.13

STAKEHOLDER ANALYSIS AND WBS AT THE CIA

At the CIA, where I created and run our agency-wide project management training and certification program, I come in contact with large numbers of dedicated project managers. With enrollment averaging about 2,500 students per year, I encounter a work-force with a broad spectrum of experiences, skills, and expectations. One of the more prevalent expectations is associated with stakeholder analysis and communication; employees invariably feel that they pretty much know most or all they need to know in this area and may even begrudge somewhat the three days associated with our Project Communications Management course. What they discover are the shortcomings in their appreciation for and knowledge about project communications. Using a five-point Likert scale, we have every student perform a self-assessment of their communications proficiency prior to and after the class. To the students' surprise, proficiency increases average a full point; student feedback virtually always includes statements to the effect that they didn't realize just how much more effective they can be in project management by investing more in the project communications area.

The organizational chart plays a central role in how the CIA approaches the analysis of stakeholders. Employees learn through classroom exercises to use the organizational chart as a roadmap for identifying the stakeholders. As they march through the branches in this chart, they make conscious decisions about whether the function represented by the title or box on the chart or whether the individual performing that function is a stakeholder. Once they have identified the stakeholders and performed the associated stakeholder analysis, they then turn to the WBS to help with the planning and implementation of the communications tasks that follow. In fact, communications for the types of projects undertaken at the CIA have taken on such importance that we advocate it be placed at the first level of WBS decomposition alongside equally important components such as project management. For projects of sufficient size, a full-time leader is often assigned to the communications component; the scope of their duties includes communications within the project as well as communications outside the project.

Source: Michael O'Brochta, PMP, director, PPMC Program, CIA.

project deliverables. Uncontrolled change is known as scope creep. Sometimes, the effects of scope creep are so bad that a well-started project can run into serious trouble.

The critical aspect of a change control system is the method of documenting changes. Each potential change to a project is normally documented by some sort of **change request**, which is a written request or a formal proposal to propose changes to any project planning component such as a document, project deliverable, or baseline (scope, cost, and time).

This means every change to a project needs to be formally proposed. The potential change is then either accepted or not. If it is accepted, the project plans are changed to reflect the impact of the change. Most people quickly understand the need to document major changes, but some resist the effort it takes to document small changes. The impact of many small changes is like the old saying, "killed by a thousand small cuts." Many small changes individually have small impacts on a project, but collectively they have a major impact. Project managers need to create an expectation that all changes be formally documented using a simple change request form so all team members will document proposed changes. A simple change request form is shown in Exhibit 7.14.

Change request forms typically include several sections. The top section lists basic information to track the change request to the project and to the person who submitted it. The second section contains two simple statements describing the change and why the change is needed. The third section details the impact expected from the potential change. This can vary in length from a simple check and comment section, as in Exhibit 7.14, to an extremely involved description of potential impact on complex system projects such as designing an aircraft. In complex projects, small changes can

EXHIBIT 7.14

CHANGE REQUEST FORM

ORIGINATOR: PROJECT #:

Date

Description of Change:

Why needed:

Impact on project scope:

Impact on deadline dates:

Impact on budget:

Impact on quality:

Impact on risk:

Impact on team:

Date approved:

Project manager   Sponsor   Customer

_____   _____   _____

sometimes have catastrophic impacts. Finally, there should be a space for the change to be approved. Regardless of the complexity and format, the most important consideration is that potential changes must be submitted and documented whether they are approved or not.

7-6 Using MS Project for Work Breakdown Structures (WBS)

As you have likely realized, the WBS is one of the most important and powerful project planning tools available to the project manager. It is one of the key building blocks on which all further project activities are based. By creating a WBS in MS Project, the project manager lays the foundation for automating many other planning and communication tools the software has to offer. Complete the following steps to set up a WBS in MS Project.

7-6a Set Up a WBS in MS Project

Setting up a WBS in MS Project has five basic steps:

1. Understand the WBS definitions and displays.
2. Enter project deliverable and work package elements.

3. Create the outline of your WBS.
4. Insert a WBS code identification column.
5. Hide (or show) the desired amount of detail in the WBS.

STEP 1: UNDERSTAND THE WBS DEFINITIONS AND DISPLAYS   MS Project refers to WBS task elements as summary tasks, tasks, and subtasks and displays them in an indented outline table format:

- Summary tasks are the main or interim WBS deliverables and are displayed in bold font.
- Subtasks are all the tasks that make up the deliverables (work packages) and are indented below their parent summary task.
- WBS tasks can also be viewed in Gantt views with different graphical shapes:
  - For instance, a summary task might also be a milestone that you would want to denote graphically in your Gantt chart (typically a diamond in MS Project).
  - You will see these graphical representations in future tutorials.

Exhibit 7.15 shows a Gantt table view of a WBS in MS Project. Note that MS Project codes the overall project (Suburban Park Homes) as level zero, not level one. The task durations have not been defined at this point and show "1 day?" for all tasks. If you are following along in MS Project, you will notice "Start" and "Finish" columns to the right of the Duration column that also have not been defined. The Start and Finish columns are not shown in the following exhibits for clarity's sake.

STEP 2: ENTER WBS ELEMENTS (TASKS)   In Exhibit 7.16, you will see WBS task elements added to the existing Suburban Park Homes project milestone list (from Chapter 3). In this WBS example, the existing milestones will double as the main deliverables (summary tasks). Enter these WBS elements to your project as follows:

1. In the Task Name field, select the row *below* where you want the new row to be (after making your selection, holding the **SHIFT** key and selecting a different row will highlight all rows between the two selections and result in that number of blank rows being inserted in the next step).
2. Click **Task Tab>>Insert Group>>Task**.
   a.   Alternatively, you can **Right-Click>>Insert Task**.
3. You will see a new row (or rows if you added multiple) with the words **<New Task>** in the Task Name field. Click on **<New Task>** and enter the name of the desired WBS element (you may have to delete <New Task> before typing in your new task name).
4. Repeat these processes as needed to enter additional tasks between the Suburban Park Homes milestones until your WBS looks like Exhibit 7.16.

STEP 3: CREATE THE OUTLINE FOR YOUR WBS   You now need to set up the outline structure of the WBS to show summary tasks and subtasks (deliverables, interim deliverables, and work packages). To do this, use the Indent and Outdent controls shown in Exhibit 7.17 (**Task Tab>>Schedule Group>>Green Arrows**).

1. Click the Task Name field of the row to be indented.
2. **Task Tab>>Schedule Group>>Indent Task (right Green Arrow)**.
   a.   The task element above the indented task(s) becomes a summary row as indicated by a bold font.

EXHIBIT 7.15

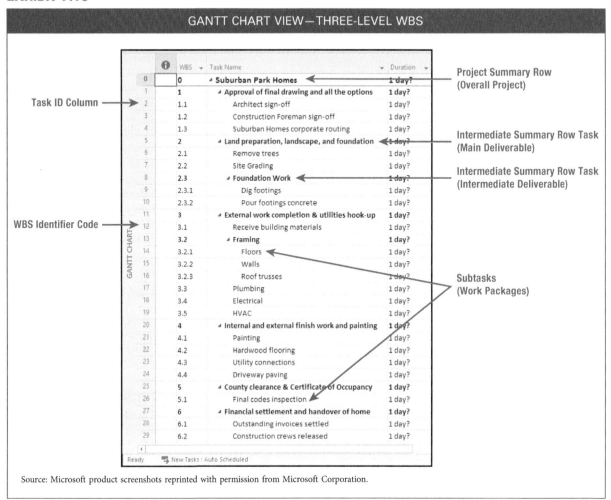

    b.   Indenting a summary row will also indent its lower-level items.

    c.   Multiple rows under a summary row can be indented (or outdented) at the same time by **Shift-Click** selecting all of them before clicking the Indent control.

3. Clicking **Task Tab>>Schedule Group>>Outdent Task (left Green Arrow)** will similarly *decrease* indentation of the selected row(s) or summary task.

4. Indent to create deliverables, interim deliverables, and work packages until your WBS resembles the outline shown in Exhibit 7.15.

STEP 4: INSERT WBS CODE IDENTIFIER COLUMN MS Project can automatically assign identifier codes to all your WBS tasks. WBS codes allow the Project Team to easily categorize and communicate information about project tasks in the WBS. In this example, WBS codes will be assigned in a new column to the left of the Task Name column:

1. **Right-click** the Task Name column heading and click **Insert Column**.
2. A drop-down list appears in a new column.

EXHIBIT 7.16

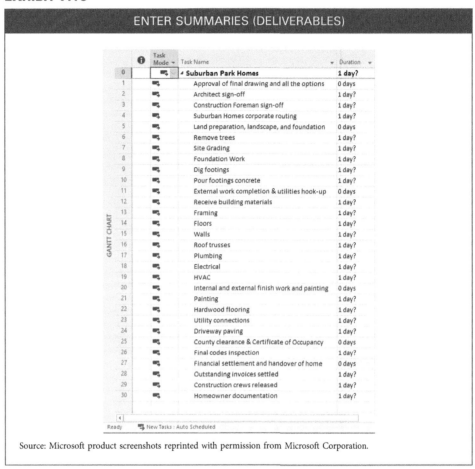

		Task Mode ▼	Task Name ▼	Duration ▼
0		◢ Suburban Park Homes	**1 day?**
1		Approval of final drawing and all the options	0 days
2		Architect sign-off	1 day?
3		Construction Foreman sign-off	1 day?
4		Suburban Homes corporate routing	1 day?
5		Land preparation, landscape, and foundation	0 days
6		Remove trees	1 day?
7		Site Grading	1 day?
8		Foundation Work	1 day?
9		Dig footings	1 day?
10		Pour footings concrete	1 day?
11		External work completion & utilities hook-up	0 days
12		Receive building materials	1 day?
13		Framing	1 day?
14		Floors	1 day?
15		Walls	1 day?
16		Roof trusses	1 day?
17		Plumbing	1 day?
18		Electrical	1 day?
19		HVAC	1 day?
20		Internal and external finish work and painting	0 days
21		Painting	1 day?
22		Hardwood flooring	1 day?
23		Utility connections	1 day?
24		Driveway paving	1 day?
25		County clearance & Certificate of Occupancy	0 days
26		Final codes inspection	1 day?
27		Financial settlement and handover of home	0 days
28		Outstanding invoices settled	1 day?
29		Construction crews released	1 day?
30		Homeowner documentation	1 day?

Ready   New Tasks : Auto Scheduled

Source: Microsoft product screenshots reprinted with permission from Microsoft Corporation.

3. From the drop-down list, choose **WBS**, as shown in Exhibit 7.18.
   a.   A WBS code column is now in place.
   b.   Resize the column to conserve space.
4. **Right-click** the Task Mode column heading and click **Hide Column**.
5. Your result should look like Exhibit 7.19.

EXHIBIT 7.17

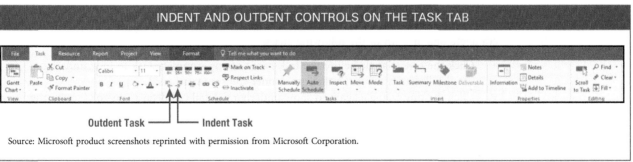

INDENT AND OUTDENT CONTROLS ON THE TASK TAB

Outdent Task ——— └— Indent Task

Source: Microsoft product screenshots reprinted with permission from Microsoft Corporation.

EXHIBIT 7.18

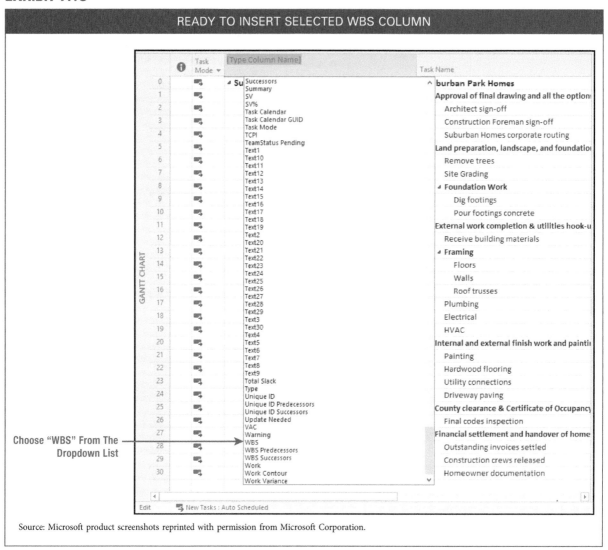

> READY TO INSERT SELECTED WBS COLUMN

Choose "WBS" From The Dropdown List

STEP 5: HIDE (OR SHOW) SUBTASKS DETAIL   Some stakeholders will not want or need to see the lower levels of WBS detail (particularly in large, complex projects with lots of WBS detail). You can easily "roll-up" (or "un-roll") subtasks underneath their parent summary task to hide (or show) detail. To display the appropriate level of detail, complete one or both of the following steps:

- Click the tiny triangle before the task name of any summary task to hide underlying detail (all details will be "rolled-up" under the summary task).
- Click the tiny triangle again to show underlying detail (all details "un-roll" under the summary task and are again visible).

In Exhibit 7.20, the underlying detail for the "**Land preparation, landscape, and foundation**" deliverable and the "**Framing**" interim deliverable summaries has been hidden.

EXHIBIT 7.19

		WBS ⌄	Task Name ⌄	Duration ⌄
			WBS COLUMN INSERTED	
0		0	⌄ **Suburban Park Homes**	**1 day?**
1		1	⌄ **Approval of final drawing and all the options**	1 day?
2		1.1	Architect sign-off	1 day?
3		1.2	Construction Foreman sign-off	1 day?
4		1.3	Suburban Homes corporate routing	1 day?
5		2	⌄ **Land preparation, landscape, and foundation**	1 day?
6		2.1	Remove trees	1 day?
7		2.2	Site Grading	1 day?
8		2.3	⌄ **Foundation Work**	1 day?
9		2.3.1	Dig footings	1 day?
10		2.3.2	Pour footings concrete	1 day?
11		3	⌄ **External work completion & utilities hook-up**	1 day?
12		3.1	Receive building materials	1 day?
13		3.2	⌄ **Framing**	1 day?
14		3.2.1	Floors	1 day?
15		3.2.2	Walls	1 day?
16		3.2.3	Roof trusses	1 day?
17		3.3	Plumbing	1 day?
18		3.4	Electrical	1 day?
19		3.5	HVAC	1 day?
20		4	⌄ **Internal and external finish work and painting**	1 day?
21		4.1	Painting	1 day?
22		4.2	Hardwood flooring	1 day?
23		4.3	Utility connections	1 day?
24		4.4	Driveway paving	1 day?
25		5	⌄ **County clearance & Certificate of Occupancy**	1 day?
26		5.1	Final codes inspection	1 day?
27		6	⌄ **Financial settlement and handover of home**	1 day?
28		6.1	Outstanding invoices settled	1 day?
29		6.2	Construction crews released	1 day?
30		6.3	Homeowner documentation	1 day?

Ready   New Tasks : Auto Scheduled

Source: Microsoft product screenshots reprinted with permission from Microsoft Corporation.

PMP/CAPM Study Ideas

It has been said that the discipline of project management lends structure to common sense. Nowhere is this more true than with scope planning. If you can remember to conduct your planning with the end goal in mind, many of the processes and activities in this chapter will seem intuitive. Another way of saying this is that you will work backward from the outcome you desire (a successful product and/or project).

Begin by identifying what it would take for your product—and your project—to be successful. Be sure to include your customers and end users in making this determination ("Collect requirements"), as well as subject matter experts who can speak to the technical expertise needed and the feasibility of the project plan. Identify the final deliverables, as well as any important interim deliverables.

EXHIBIT 7.20

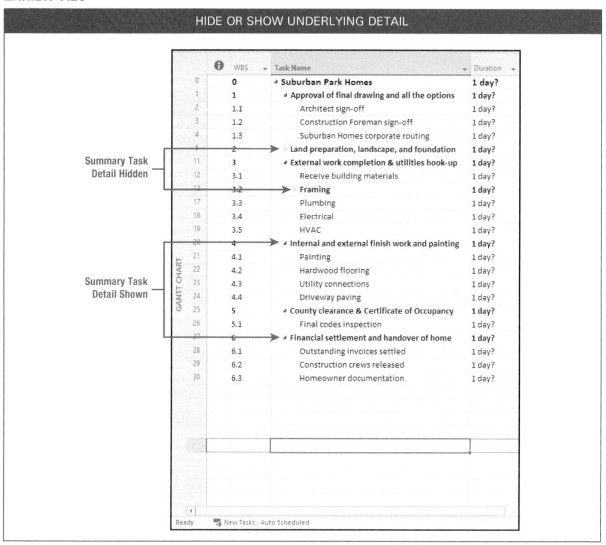

HIDE OR SHOW UNDERLYING DETAIL

Discussing these deliverables and what it will take to produce them is a good chance for the team to further "define scope," or determine what is included—and *not* included—in your project.

Once you have the main deliverables, you will use the process of decomposition to break them down into smaller pieces, thus creating a Work Breakdown Structure. It is important to remember that the WBS deals with *things,* not activities (though on a very small project, these may be planned concurrently). The lowest level of the WBS is the "work package," which is small enough that it can be easily planned and overseen by one person.

To be sure, this is an oversimplification of everything that goes into planning scope, and you will need to be fluent in all the activities and processes in this chapter in order to pass a CAPM or PMP test. But it can be helpful to remember that there is an organizing structure to all this work—one that begins with the end result in mind.

Summary

Once a project is formally approved by a sponsor ratifying its charter, it is time for detailed planning. While project planning is iterative, normally the first steps are to identify stakeholders, plan communications, and determine what will be created on the project. Project teams start this process by asking customers what end-of-project deliverables they want. From the customers' response, the planning team can determine both what interim deliverables need to be created and what work needs to be performed to create all of the deliverables. Just as important as determining what will be produced during the project is determining what will *not* be produced. These boundaries of what will and will not be included constitute the project's scope.

Once the scope is defined, it can be organized into a work breakdown structure (WBS). A WBS is used to progressively decompose the project into smaller and smaller pieces until each can be assigned to one person for planning and control. The WBS serves as a basis for determining the project schedule, budget, personnel assignments, quality requirements, and risks. As those other functions are planned, items are commonly identified that should be added to the WBS.

Some teams create their WBS by hand using the org chart or free format methods, while others directly type their WBS into project scheduling software such as Microsoft Project.

Key Terms Consistent with PMI Standards and Guides

plan scope management, 212
requirement, 212
collect requirements, 212
define scope, 217
define activity, 221
work package, 224
WBS component, 225

WBS dictionary, 225
rolling wave planning, 227
baseline, 229
decomposition, 228
change control system, 229
change request, 231

Chapter Review Questions

1. What is the first step in developing a project scope management plan?
2. What three tasks comprise the "define scope" process?
3. For a construction project, the house is the _____ deliverable, and how-to instruction sheets are _____ deliverables.
4. Why is scope definition important?
5. What are two common causes of scope creep?
6. What does the acronym WBS stand for?
7. What are the advantages of using a WBS?
8. List three ways of organizing a WBS.
9. The lowest level of the WBS is known as a(n) _____.
10. What is a WBS dictionary used for?
11. What is rolling wave planning?
12. What is uncontrolled change known as?
13. Why do project teams use change control systems?
14. List the major sections that should be included in a change request form, and tell why each is important.
15. What is a project baseline?

Discussion Questions

1. Are the product scope and project scope ever the same? Cite examples to support your answer.
2. Create a template of a change request form. What sections did you include and why?

3. Compare the strengths and weaknesses of the three formats of constructing a WBS: indented outline, organizational chart, and free format.

4. Give an example of scope creep from one of your own projects or from a project that has made the news in recent years.

5. What are the advantages of completing the "define activity" process *after* creating the WBS?

6. Describe the roles various executives, managers, and associates play in scope planning.

7. You are the project manager in charge of expanding a popular restaurant. How could you use voice of the customer (VOC) techniques to gain insight into your stakeholders?

8. Identify two projects your company or school will be performing in the future. Which one do you think will have a more detailed WBS? Why?

9. The sponsor for a project you have been managing sends you an e-mail that he would like to make a small change to the project. What is your response and why?

10. A potential client wants you to be project manager for the construction of a new house, but she is vague about the details. List a few questions you could ask her to gain a better understanding of the scope of the project.

PMBOK® Guide Questions

1. The process where project deliverables and project work are subdivided into smaller and smaller pieces is called _____.
    a. collect requirements
    b. define scope
    c. plan scope management
    d. create WBS

2. The project scope baseline consists of the approved versions of three of the four documents listed below. Which of these documents is *not* included in the project scope baseline?
    a. project scope statement
    b. project charter
    c. work breakdown structure (WBS)
    d. WBS dictionary

3. Which of the following statements about a work package is true?
    a. It requires the work of the entire project team.
    b. It is the responsibility of the project manager.
    c. It is the lowest level of the WBS.
    d. It consists of a single activity.

4. During WBS creation on a large, complex project, the product and project deliverables are broken down into progressively lower levels of detail. Once the WBS has been defined at the second or third level of detail, whose input is essential in order to break down the work further?
    a. sponsor
    b. subject matter experts

    c. internal stakeholders
    d. external stakeholders

5. Which of the following is *not* a common method for organizing a WBS?
    a. free format
    b. indented outline
    c. hierarchical
    d. cross-functional

6. A "component of the project management plan that describes how the scope will be defined, developed, monitored, controlled, and verified" is the _____.
    a. project statement of work
    b. requirements management plan
    c. scope management plan
    d. WBS dictionary

7. A grid that links product requirements from their origins (e.g., business reason needed, stakeholder who requested them) to the deliverables that satisfy them is referred to as a _____.
    a. network diagram
    b. Gantt chart
    c. requirements traceability matrix
    d. stakeholder register

8. Which of these is *not* a component of a Project Scope Statement?
    a. summary budget
    b. project deliverables
    c. acceptance criteria
    d. project exclusions or boundaries

9. The key output of the scope planning process is an approved version of the scope baseline. After this baseline is established, it can be referenced during project execution in order to _____.
   a. staff the project properly with the right skill sets
   b. link requirements back to their origins
   c. communicate with stakeholders effectively
   d. identify changes in scope that will go through formal change control procedures
10. The process of breaking the WBS into smaller and smaller deliverables is called:
    a. decomposition
    b. functional design
    c. detailed specifications
    d. value engineering

Exercises

1. Create a requirements traceability matrix like Exhibit 7.2 for a project in which you plan an event on your campus.
2. Create a scope statement like Exhibit 7.3 for a project in which you plan an event on your campus.
3. Construct a WBS in indented outline format like Exhibit 7.11 for a project in which you plan an event on your campus. Be sure to number each row. Also, construct the same WBS in MS Project like Exhibit 7.18.

INTEGRATED EXAMPLE PROJECTS
SUBURBAN HOMES CONSTRUCTION PROJECT

Refer to the project charter from Chapter 3. The initial scope as identified in the project charter is mentioned below:

Building a single-family, partially custom-designed home as required by Mrs. and Mr. John Thomas on Strath Dr., Alpharetta, Georgia. The single-family home will have the following features:

- 3,200 square-feet home with 4 bedrooms and 2.5 bathrooms
- Flooring—hard wood in the first floor, tiles in the kitchen and bathrooms, carpet in bedrooms
- Granite kitchen countertops, GE appliances in the kitchen
- 3-car garage and external landscaping
- Ceiling—10' in first floor and vaulted 9' ceilings in bedrooms

Summary Milestone Schedule
- Approval of final drawing and all the options: 02 January 2017
- Land preparation, landscape, and foundation: 15 January 2017
- External work completion and utilities hookup: 03 April 2017
- Internal and external finish work, appliances, and painting: 10 May 2017
- County clearance and Certificate of Occupancy: 30 May 2017
- Financial settlement and handover of the property: 21 June 2017

High-Level Assumptions and Constraints
- List of options are limited and cost of the house would vary based on options selected
- Client must choose one model among the models offered
- Seven-year warranty for structure and two-year warranty for finishing components

When this charter was developed, Suburban Homes did not have complete information on all the customer requirements and needs and complete understanding of the project. The company realizes that the milestone schedule is not accurate and will be subject to changes.

Tasks to Complete
- You are asked to obtain requirements from the client. To do so, Suburban Homes requests that you develop a **Requirements Template** that will capture all the needs of the client. Then, Suburban Homes will have complete information to develop a scope plan.
- Develop a scope statement along with inclusions, exclusions, assumptions, and constraints.
- Develop a deliverable-based (design-focused) Work Breakdown Structure (WBS) for this project.

CASA DE PAZ DEVELOPMENT PROJECT

Note that this is a larger project and from this point forward in the book, we will focus on the features and the work for the Promotion and Community Relations Working Group only. The Development and Fundraising Working Group and the Program Development Working Groups are concurrently performing similar planning and executing of the project. The work within each group is planned and executed primarily by the team members with the project manager (scrum manager) removing roadblocks and coordinating between groups.

The Promotion and Community Relations Working Group needs to:

1. Document the requirements needed by the users of the project deliverables.
2. Determine what work will be included and what will be excluded.
3. Organize everything into a product backlog that can be used for all subsequent planning.

These three actions can be accomplished in a facilitated meeting by first asking the question: "To open on time on October 1, what are the three to five most important things that need to be created? To make it easier for your practice, the project team chose the following five features of the project:

Features of the Project:

Website

Location/building

Partnerships/sponsors

Communication methods

Joint venture (between university and Casa de Paz)

Now, for each feature, what details do you believe need to be accomplished to create the features? These are the stories. The features and supporting stories form the scope of this project and will be in the backlog until selected for work in a given iteration.

Semester Project Instructions

For your example project, create the following:

1. Scope management plan to direct your efforts
2. Requirements traceability matrix like Exhibit 7.2 to understand customer desires
3. Scope statement like Exhibit 7.3
4. Change request form like Exhibit 7.13
5. WBS first using either the free format or the org chart format like Exhibits 7.5 and 7.6
6. WBS in MS Project like Exhibit 7.18

PROJECT MANAGEMENT *IN ACTION*

Work Breakdown Structure Template

This WBS for an industrial complex presents a deliverable-oriented approach to developing it by employing a consistency in the division basis for each level of the WBS. Usually, we can develop a deliverable WBS using function, product, or physical location.

However, within a level of WBS, we must employ only one of these to develop WBS into the next level. The first-level division basis is physical as an industrial complex is divided into a powerhouse, factory, office, and grounds. The division basis for the second level of the "Powerhouse" is a functional basis as it is divided into a steam-generation system, electrical-generation system, and electrical-transmission system. The division basis for the second level of the "Factory" is a product basis as it is divided into receiving equipment, processing equipment, and packaging equipment. The second level of WBS for the "Office" is a physical basis as it is divided into first floor, second floor, and third floor. Finally, the division basis for "Grounds" is again a product-basis division as it is divided into shrubs and trees, lawn, walkways, and a parking lot. This WBS is focused on the "what" aspect of the project and not on "how" we execute the project. Essentially, this WBS is developed from the client's perspective and not from the project team's perspective, which is focused on how the project is likely to be executed (schedule-oriented WBS).

Vittal Anantatmula, PMP, PhD.

References

1233-1998 - IEEE Guide for Developing System Requirements Specifications, http://ieeexplore.ieee.org/document/741940/.

A Guide to the Project Management Body of Knowledge (PMBOK® Guide), 5th ed. (Newtown Square, PA: Project Management Institute, 2013).

Caudle, Gerrie, *Streamlining Business Requirements: The XCellR8™ Approach* (Vienna, VA: Management Concepts, Inc., 2009).

Collyer, Simon, Clive Warren, Bronwyn Hemsley, and Chris Stevens , "Aim, Fire, Aim—Project Planning Styles in Dynamic Environments," *Project Management Journal* (September 2010): 41 (4): 106–121.

Fister Gale, Sarah, "The Evolution of Agile," *PMNetwork* 26 (1) (January 2012): 28–33.

Hass, Kathleen B., Don Wessels, and Kevin Brennan, *Getting It Right: Business Requirement Analysis Tools and Techniques Structures* (Vienna, VA: Management Concepts, Inc., 2008).

Haugan, Gregory T., *Effective Work Breakdown Structures* (Vienna, VA: Management Concepts, Inc., 2002).

Howard, Dale, and Gary Chefetz, What's New Study Guide Microsoft Project 2010 (New York: Chefetz LLC dba MSProjectExperts, 2010).

Hunsberger, Kelley, "Change Is Good: For Agile Projects, Redefining Scope Isn't Such a Creepy Thing," *PMNetwork* (February 2011) 25 (2): 48–53.

Miller, Dennis P. *Building a Project Work Breakdown Structure: Visualizing Objectives, Deliverables, Activities, and Schedules* (Boca Raton, FL: CRC Press, 2009).

Project Management Institute Practice Standard for Work Breakdown Structures, 2nd ed. (Newtown Square, PA: Project Management Institute, 2006).

Rad, Parviz, and Vittal Anantatmula, *Integrated Project Planning* (Berkeley Heights, NJ: Project Management Excellence, 2009).

Rad, Parviz, and Vittal Anantatmula, *Project Planning Techniques* (Vienna, VA: Management Concepts, Inc., 2005).

Turk, Wayne, "Scope Creep Horror: It's Scarier than Movie Monsters," *Defense AT&L* (March–April 2010): 53–55.

Warner, Paul, and Paul Cassar, "Putting Together a Work Breakdown Structure," in David I. Cleland, *Field Guide to Project Management*, 2nd ed. (Hoboken, NJ: John Wiley & Sons, 2004).

CHAPTER 8

Scheduling Projects

Raywoo/Shutterstock.com

Scheduling and Agile

The need to comply with government regulations by mandated deadlines does not change when a company switches from waterfall to Agile. And Agile organizations still suffer by not having enough time to deliver what's been requested at a reasonable cost. But I've worked with people who mistakenly think Agile makes project management principles irrelevant. Or that the Agile methodology is incompatible with concepts like Schedule, Scope, and Cost. Communicating with team members and sponsors with those beliefs has been quite challenging for me as a project manager.

One of my colleagues tells organizations they have these options for managing a project's "triple constraint" no matter what methodology is used—Agile, waterfall, or hybrid:

- <u>Scope</u>-driven: deliver what is requested no matter how long it takes (**Schedule**) or how much it **Costs**
- <u>Schedule</u>-driven: meet the deadline by
- Delivering whatever **Scope** you can within the budget (**Cost**)

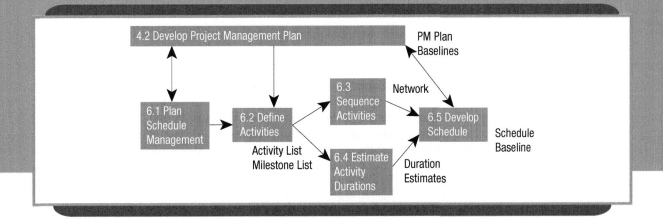

- Investing as many resources as needed (**Cost**) to deliver the **Scope**
- <u>Cost</u>-driven: deliver whatever **Scope** you can until the budget is exhausted. Your **Schedule** ends when the money runs out.

I've been on projects companies decided should be schedule-driven, but team members delivered as though they were scope-driven and sponsors monitored like they were cost-driven. In these circumstances, I've had to keep reminding people what option was chosen for the project, and why, throughout its duration, sometimes years. And this communication has been vitally important to managing the schedule.

Agile has made some of my projects easier to schedule and others a lot more difficult! With a software manufacturer using a single team for each of its products, the developers themselves took more ownership of the schedule. On the job, they learned how to estimate activities better and apply dependencies, leads, lags, and float within their daily stand-ups. The teams were on the same iteration cycles, so ceremonies like sprint retrospectives naturally became milestones in the project schedule, on cadences familiar to the folks doing the work.

But I've also been on projects where Agile, waterfall, and hybrid teams from different organizations were dependent on one another to deliver results. Not only did the varying methodologies and terminologies hamper scheduling but our Agile teams' iteration cycles also were completely different. So once we'd identified activities, sequenced them, identified mandatory dependencies and figured out whether they were FS, FF, SS, or SF, there were gaps caused by teams' varying iterations that extended schedule duration with no corresponding benefits. And that was just in the planning stage: different geographic locations, vocabulary, iterations, and systems made the schedule virtually unmanageable because communicating changes to it was nearly impossible. Luckily, everyone decided to align on a common iteration cycle, which went a long way toward solving our problems. But that is not always possible.

Investing team members in a project's schedule beyond just completing their own activities has always been a challenge for me, but Agile has made that even tougher. People feel they are succeeding as long as they make incremental progress every day, but they can do that while our team still fails to meet the schedule. That's why continuing to study this chapter, and discussing its content with other project managers, is important to me.

—*Carol A. Abbott, PMP*

8-1 Plan Schedule Management

As is true of other project planning knowledge areas, planning for time is iterative. A project manager and team usually develop as much of the schedule as they can based upon the information in the work breakdown structure (WBS). The communication plan, requirements traceability matrix, and scope statement are often either complete or at least in draft form at this point. Once a project is scheduled, the budget can be formulated, resource needs can be identified and resources assigned, risks can be identified and plans developed to deal with the identified risks, and a quality management plan can be created. In many projects, these are not all treated as discrete activities, and some of them may be performed together. However, for clarity, each of these planning processes will be described individually.

The building blocks of a project schedule are activities. An **activity** is "a component of project scope work performed during the course of a project."[1] For activities to be useful as schedule building blocks, they should have the following characteristics:

- Clear starting and ending points
- Tangible output that can be verified
- Scope small enough to understand and control without micromanaging
- Resources, other costs, and schedule that can be estimated and controlled
- A single person who can be held accountable for each activity (Often more than one person is required to complete the work; however, one person should be responsible.)[2]

Since activities represent work that needs to be performed, they should be listed in a verb-noun format, such as "prepare budget," "build frame," "test code," "transmit information," "analyze data," and "develop plan." Each activity should be clearly differentiated from other activities, so it is often helpful to write the activities in verb-adjective-noun format, such as "write draft report" and "write final report."

The Project Management Institute (PMI) has divided project time management into the following seven work processes.

1. **Plan schedule management**—arranging how to develop, manage, execute, and control the project schedule
2. **Define activities**—a project planning process that identifies and determines specific actions to develop and deliver the project outcomes, such as products, services, or results
3. **Sequence activities**—determining the predecessor and successor relationships among the project activities
4. **Estimate activity durations**—the process of approximating the number of work periods needed to complete individual activities with estimated resources[3]
5. **Develop schedule**—the process of analyzing activity sequences, durations, resource requirements, and schedule constraints to create the project schedule[4]
6. **Control schedule**—the process of regulating changes to the project schedule[5]

Planning schedule management, defining activities, sequencing activities, estimating activity durations, and part of developing schedules will be covered in this chapter. The remainder of developing schedules will be discussed in Chapter 9 (Resourcing Project Activities). Chapter 14 (Determining Project Progress and Results) will focus on controlling the schedule.

8-2 Purposes of a Project Schedule

Projects are undertaken to accomplish important business purposes, and people often want to use the project results as quickly as possible. Many specific questions such as the following can be answered by having a complete and workable schedule:

- When will the project be complete?
- What is the earliest date a particular activity can start, and when will it end?
- What activity must begin before which other activities can take place?
- What would happen if a delivery of material were one week late?
- Can a key worker take a week of vacation the first week of March?
- If one worker is assigned to do two activities, which one must go first?
- How many hours do we need from each worker next week or month?
- Which worker or other resource is a bottleneck, limiting the speed of our project?
- What will the impact be if the client wants to add another module?
- If I am willing to spend an extra $10,000, how much faster can the project be completed?
- Are all of the activities completed that should be by now?
- How many resource types are required, and are they available?
- How much time and effort are required from each resource?
- What time constraints is the project likely to encounter?

8-3 Historical Development of Project Schedules

Throughout history, projects have been performed, but many early projects such as cathedrals in Europe took decades or longer to complete. As competition drove the need for more rapid completion, systematic methods were developed for scheduling projects.

In the 1950s, two project scheduling methods were developed: program evaluation and review technique (PERT) and critical path method. The **critical path method (CPM)** is "A technique used to determine the amount of scheduling flexibility (float) on various logical network paths in the project schedule network, and to determine the minimum total project duration."[6]

Both CPM and PERT were founded on the concepts still in place today of identifying activities, determining their logical order, and estimating the duration for each. Networks representing the activities were developed and the schedule calculated. Each of the techniques also boasted a capability the other did not possess.

PERT was developed in the Navy's Special Program Office because the Navy was developing the large and complex Polaris Weapons System. To complete it as quickly as possible, many activities needed to be worked on simultaneously. Furthermore, many aspects of the Polaris used unproven technology. There was considerable uncertainty regarding how long some of the new technology would take to develop. PERT enabled project managers to estimate the most likely amount of time needed to complete a project, and the level of confidence in completing it in a particular time. This has proven to be useful in research and development projects involving individual activities that are hard to estimate precisely. How uncertainty in project schedules is handled by PERT will be discussed more in Section 8.9.

CPM was developed in the Engineering Services Division of DuPont. DuPont needed to plan large projects when it built and refurbished enormous plants. Planners using CPM estimated the time for each individual work activity using a single time estimate. The focus was on understanding the longest sequence of activities, which determined how long the project would take. CPM enabled project managers to ask what-if questions such as "If the project needs to be finished three weeks early, which activities should be speeded up and how much will it cost?" This proved to be useful in the

EXHIBIT 8.1

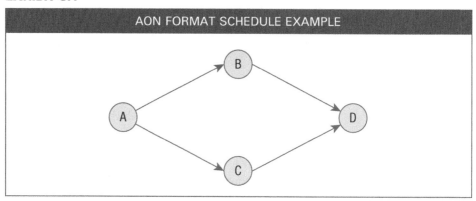

AON FORMAT SCHEDULE EXAMPLE

construction industry where delays such as rain and other weather-related issues often necessitate the acceleration of a project.

PERT and CPM originally used a method for displaying the work activities called activity on arrow (AOA) or arrow diagramming method (ADM), in which schedule activities are represented by arrows and connected at points called nodes. Because it is often confusing to draw an accurate AOA network, this method is rarely used today. The more common method used today is called activity on node (AON) or the **precedence diagramming method (PDM)**. AON or PDM is "a technique in which the scheduled activities are represented by nodes and are graphically linked by one or more logical relationships to show the sequence in which the activities are performed."[7] A small project schedule is shown in Exhibit 8.1 with work activities A through D connected by arrows showing logical relationships (A must be complete before B and C can begin and both B and C must finish before D can begin).

The basic logic of these techniques still serves as the backbone of many project schedules today. However, other advances have added to scheduling capability, and since computers have become much more powerful and easier to use, they've allowed many additional features to be added to project schedules. Another trend is that with many organizations operating in a "lean" mode, resource limitations rather than just the logical order of activities are a major determinant of project schedules.

8-4 How Project Schedules Are Limited and Created

There is generally a trade-off among the three constraints—scope, cost, and schedule—and the project should have flexibility to manipulate at least one of these three constraints. Project schedules sometimes get higher priority over scope and cost when it is a time-constrained project. In addition to these constraints, the project schedule is constraints by other factors. One way to understand project schedules and how they are constructed is to understand that five factors may limit how fast a project can be completed:

1. Logical order
2. Activity duration
3. Resource availability
4. Imposed dates
5. Cash flow

- The first factor is the logical order in which activities need to be completed. For example, one needs to dig a hole before cement can be poured in it. This is covered in the section on sequencing activities.

- The second factor is how long each individual activity will take to complete. This is discussed in the section on estimating activity duration. It includes methods for estimating durations, problems with estimates, and remedies to those problems.
- The third factor is how many key resources are available at specific times in the project. For example, if six rooms were available to be painted at the same time, and fewer than six painters were available, progress would be slower. This is discussed in Chapter 9 in the section on resource availability.
- The fourth factor is imposed dates. For example, a project working on a government contract may not be able to start until the government's new fiscal year, which starts on October 1.
- The fifth and final factor is cash flow. Projects may not start until the budget is approved, but progress may also be slowed until enough revenue arrives to cover expenses. This is covered in Chapter 10.

Because project schedules are limited by these five factors, creating a realistic schedule is an iterative process. A common method of developing the schedule is to do the following:

1. First, identify all of the activities and then determine the logical order by creating a network diagram.
2. Once the order is determined, make an estimate of the time required for that activity.
3. Then assign resources to each activity, and if an assigned resource is not available when the activity is scheduled, make an adjustment of some type. The schedule can be computed with all of this information.
4. Next, it is time to compare the emerging schedule with any imposed dates and cash flow estimates.

Any inconsistencies may cause the team to adjust the schedule. Other factors often need to be considered, such as quality demands and risk factors. When all of these have been planned, the final schedule can be approved.

The pressure to complete a project as quickly as possible is often great. The sponsor or customer may try to dictate a schedule before anyone knows whether it is feasible or not. Before agreeing, the project manager must first understand what makes sense in terms of a schedule before she is in a position to know whether to accept a sponsor's suggestions or to argue about why it may be impractical. A project manager has the ethical responsibility to determine a schedule that is possible to achieve, persuade all stakeholders that the schedule makes sense, and then see to it that the project is delivered according to that agreed-upon schedule.

The remainder of this chapter and the other planning chapters describe in detail how to plan for each of these, culminating in an approved schedule and project plan that all stakeholders believe is reasonable. The project manager is then accountable to deliver the project on schedule. That project delivery is the essence of the final three chapters of this book.

 In Agile projects, schedules are created by first considering the product backlog to be accomplished. The overall project schedule may be developed only at a high level. Within an iteration, the team will consider how much uncertainty and complexity exist in the outputs they plan to create. At this detailed level, the number of team members as resources is often the primary limitation to the schedule, but logical order may also be considered.

8-5 Define Activities

The first process in developing a project schedule is to define all of the work activities. The last row or the lowest level of a WBS represents the work packages or the lowest-level deliverables. Now is the time to ask: "What work activities must be completed to create each of the project deliverables?" Exhibit 8.2 shows a WBS with the deliverables identified by numbers 1 through 9, and Exhibit 8.3 shows the same project with the activities required to create the deliverables listed. Notice that project management is the first section of the WBS and that each row in both exhibits has a unique number. The number of each activity shows the deliverable it helps to create. For example, activity 4.2, *contact local bands*, is needed for higher-level deliverable 4. *entertainment*.

As teams define activities, they need to be careful not to omit any work elements. It is a good idea to have someone on your project team play devil's advocate to challenge the team to identify additional activities. It is better to identify activities that need not be accomplished than to forget activities that will need to be added later. The team may think all of the activities have been identified; however, when the next process is performed—activity sequencing—it may become obvious that some activities have been forgotten. Another activity can always be added later. Remember, the schedule will not be approved until all of the related planning is in place. It is better to discover a missing activity in the later stages of planning than after the schedule is approved. Activities that need to be added after the final schedule is approved will add time and money to the project, perhaps driving it over budget and causing it to fall behind schedule.

If the project being planned is similar to previous projects, the team can look at those projects both for defining activities and for other planning that follows. Some organizations have templates or checklists for certain types of projects or certain project deliverables that can be used as a starting point in defining activities. Regardless of the starting point, team members should keep on asking how the project at hand is different from previous ones. Often, a new project includes a few unique activities that need to be included.

In addition to the activity list, the project milestones should be listed. A milestone is an important point in a project schedule that the project sponsor and manager want to use as a checkpoint. A few major milestones are often identified in the project charter, but quite commonly more milestones are identified during project schedule planning. Common milestones include completion of a major deliverable, completion of a critical activity, or the time just before a large amount of money needs to be committed to the project. A team may also decide to put a milestone at a merging point in the project schedule where multiple activities need to be complete before any further progress can be made. The common denominator in each of these decisions is to identify a few key points in the life of a project at which management can determine if the project is progressing as planned.

A milestone list is shown in Exhibit 8.4. Note that the line numbers assigned to the milestones are one greater than the line numbers of the activities that must be completed

EXHIBIT 8.2

WORK BREAKDOWN STRUCTURE WITH DELIVERABLES ONLY

COLLEGE FUNDRAISER PROJECT

1. Project Management
2. Location
3. Information
4. Entertainment
5. Safety
6. Parking
7. Food
8. Sanitation
9. Volunteers

EXHIBIT 8.3

WORK BREAKDOWN STRUCTURE WITH ACTIVITY LIST ADDED

COLLEGE FUNDRAISER PROJECT

1. **Project Management**
2. **Location**
   - 2.1 CONTACT UNIVERSITY FOR PERMISSION
   - 2.2 DETERMINE IDEAL LOCATION TO MEET CAPACITY
   - 2.3 DETERMINE ALTERNATIVE LOCATION IN CASE OF INCLEMENT WEATHER
3. **Information**
   - 3.1 PROVIDE TEAM INFORMATION
   - 3.2 PRODUCE PRE-EVENT ADVERTISEMENTS
   - 3.3 DISPLAY WELCOME SIGNS AT ALL ENTRANCES
   - 3.4 SET UP SIGN-IN TABLE
   - 3.5 DISPLAY SIGNS WITH RULES
4. **Entertainment**
   - 4.1 FIND INFORMATION ABOUT LOCAL NOISE ORDINANCES
   - 4.2 CONTACT LOCAL BANDS
   - 4.3 SET UP STAGE, SPEAKERS, FUN BOOTHS
5. **Safety**
   - 5.1 DETERMINE LIGHTING NEEDS
   - 5.2 CONTACT LOCAL FIRE DEPARTMENT (EMS)
   - 5.3 CONTACT LOCAL POLICE DEPARTMENT
   - 5.4 OBTAIN PERMISSION TO USE WALKIE-TALKIES
   - 5.5 COORDINATE FIRST AID BOOTH
6. **Parking**
   - 6.1 FIND ADEQUATE LOTS TO ACCOMMODATE CAPACITY
   - 6.2 COORDINATE SHUTTLE SERVICE FROM LOTS TO SITE
   - 6.3 RESERVE SPECIAL PLACES FOR HANDICAPPED
7. **Food**
   - 7.1 CONTACT FOOD/BEVERAGE VENDORS FOR CONCESSIONS
   - 7.2 MAKE GOODIE BAGS FOR CHILDREN
   - 7.3 ORDER SUFFICIENT WATER
8. **Sanitation**
   - 8.1 PROVIDE TRASH RECEPTACLES
   - 8.2 PROVIDE ADEQUATE NUMBER OF PORTA-JOHNS
   - 8.3 COORDINATE POST-EVENT CLEAN-UP
   - 8.4 PURCHASE PAPER PRODUCTS AND SOAP
9. **Volunteers**
   - 9.1 RECRUIT VOLUNTEERS
   - 9.2 PRODUCE A MASTER VOLUNTEER ASSIGNMENT LIST
   - 9.3 MAKE NAMETAGS FOR ALL VOLUNTEERS

for each milestone. For example, the milestone "Information needs finalized" (item 3.6) represents the point in time that all of the information-related activities (items 3.1 through 3.5) are completed. For clarity, items 3.1 through 3.5 have been imported from Exhibit 8.3 and set in a lighter font. Notice also that the verb choice on the milestones is past tense, such as "confirmed," "finalized," and so on. This indicates that the activities leading up to each milestone must be complete.

EXHIBIT 8.4

WORK BREAKDOWN STRUCTURE WITH MILESTONE LIST

COLLEGE FUNDRAISER PROJECT

1. **Project Management**
2. **Location**
   - 2.4 LOCATION CONFIRMED
3. **Information**
   - 3.1 PROVIDE TEAM INFORMATION
   - 3.2 PRODUCE PRE-EVENT ADVERTISEMENTS
   - 3.3 DISPLAY WELCOME SIGNS AT ALL ENTRANCES
   - 3.4 SET UP SIGN-IN TABLE
   - 3.5 DISPLAY SIGNS WITH RULES
   - 3.6 INFORMATION NEEDS FINALIZED
4. **Entertainment**
   - 4.4 BAND CONTRACT SIGNED
   - 4.5 ENTERTAINMENT ARRANGED
5. **Safety**
   - 5.6 SAFETY REQUIREMENTS COMPLETED
6. **Parking**
   - 6.4 ALL PARKING NEEDS ARRANGED
7. **Food**
   - 7.4 FOOD AND BEVERAGES READIED
8. **Sanitation**
   - 8.5 ALL SANITATION NEEDS IN PLACE
9. **Volunteers**
   - 9.4 VOLUNTEERS PREPARED

On Agile projects, typically the product owner and the team agree on what work will be completed in an iteration, and the team then identifies all of the work activities for that iteration. The team commits to the body of work for the iteration, without having the how worked out in detail yet.

8-6 Sequence Activities

Once the activities have been identified, it is time to determine the logical order in which they can be accomplished. This process is called **sequence activities** and it entails determining the predecessor and successor relationships among the project activities. This sequencing activity is routinely performed for traditional (waterfall) projects and performed for each iteration of Agile projects. A common method of determining this sequence is to put each defined activity on a Post-it Note and to display them on a large work space (whiteboard, several flip chart sheets on a wall, etc.). The activities that are expected to be accomplished early in the project can be placed on the left portion of the work surface, those activities expected to be accomplished midway in the project near the middle, and those expected to be last on the right. Then, one person can serve as a facilitator by asking, "What activity or activities can be started right away and do not depend on any others?" Once one or more of these initial activities have been identified, the facilitator asks, "What activity or activities can we start now?" The initial activity is called a **predecessor activity**, which is "The schedule activity that determines when the logical successor activity can begin or end."[8] The following activity is called a **successor activity**, which is "the schedule activity that follows a predecessor activity, as determined by their logical relationship."[9] The facilitator then places the successor activity after its predecessor and draws an arrow to show the relationship, such as finish-to-start. Four types of relations are possible, and the default relation is finish-to-start. The team continues with this analysis until all activities have been placed on the work surface with arrows showing the predecessor–successor relationships. At that time, the team should mentally go through the network to ensure that no "dead-ends" are present where the chain of arrows from the project start to end is broken.

Exhibits 8.5 and 8.6 illustrate sequencing activities with the simple example of upgrading a product. The activities are identified in Exhibit 8.5, and their sequence is shown in Exhibit 8.6. The first activity is to determine the product features. As soon as that is done, two other activities can be performed.

This product upgrade example illustrates the basic logic of showing predecessor–successor dependency relationships. Dependencies can be either mandatory or discretionary. A **mandatory dependency** is "a logical relationship between activities that that must happen—usually due to a physical or legal demand." A **discretionary dependency** is "a logical relationship between activities that is considered desirable, usually based upon experience or best practice." A mandatory example is "the hole must be dug before concrete

EXHIBIT 8.5

ACTIVITY LIST FOR PRODUCT UPGRADE PROJECT
• Determine product features
• Acquire prototype materials
• Produce prototype
• Design marketing campaign
• Design graphics
• Conduct marketing
• Perform sales calls

EXHIBIT 8.6

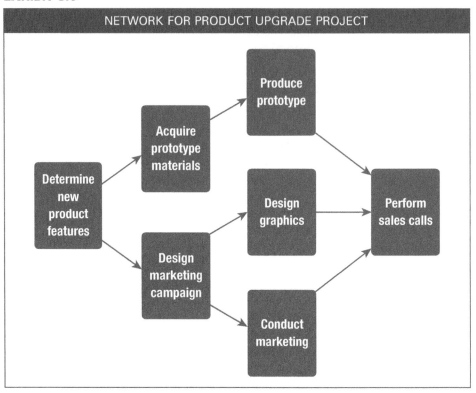

NETWORK FOR PRODUCT UPGRADE PROJECT

can be poured into it," and a discretionary example is "past experience tells us it is better to delay designing product graphics until the marketing plan is complete." The team needs to include all of the mandatory dependencies and use its judgment on which discretionary dependencies to include. Most teams include no more dependencies than necessary since more dependencies give the project manager fewer choices as the project progresses.

8-6a Leads and Lags

Exhibit 8.6 shows the most common type of logical dependency, **finish-to-start (FS)**, which is "a logical relationship where initiation of work of the successor activity depends upon the completion of work of the predecessor activity."[10] In this example, the *marketing plan* must be completely designed before the *graphics design* starts. However, maybe the *graphics design* could start five workdays before the *marketing campaign design* is complete. This could be modeled as a **lead**, which is "a modification of a logical relationship that allows an acceleration of the successor activity."[11] With this lead of five workdays, the arrow connecting *design marketing campaign* and *design graphics* would still represent a finish-to-start relationship, only with a five-day overlap during which time people could work on both activities. Leads are helpful if a project needs to be completed quickly since they show how a successor activity can be overlapped with its predecessor instead of waiting until the predecessor is completely finished.

Perhaps in the example, the salespeople are more effective if the *design graphics* are completed 10 days before they start *performing sales calls* so they have extra time to better understand the graphics. This could be shown by a **lag**, "a modification of a logical relationship that directs a delay in the successor activity."[12] In this example, the arrow connecting *design graphics* and *perform sales calls* would still represent a finish-to-start relationship, only with a 10-day gap during which no one could work on either activity.

8-6b Alternative Dependencies

Other types of relationships exist besides finish-to-start, including the following:

- **Finish-to-finish (FF)** is "the logical relationship where completion of work of the successor activity cannot finish until the completion of work of the predecessor activity."[13] For example, perhaps the graphics could be designed while the *marketing campaign* is being designed, but could not be completed until the *marketing campaign* is completed.
- **Start-to-start (SS)** is "a logical relationship where initiation of the work of the successor schedule activity depends upon the initiation of the work of the predecessor schedule activity."[14] For example, perhaps the *graphics design* could not start until the *design marketing campaign* started.
- **Start-to-finish (SF)** is "the logical relationship where completion of the successor schedule activity is dependent upon the initiation of the predecessor schedule activity."[15] This is the least used relationship. An example is for a project to replace an old system where the new capability must be started before the old one is completely discontinued.

 On Agile projects, the sequencing is performed at a high level for the entire project or for the product release (often three to six months). Then for each iteration, the team develops the sequence by which the detailed activities of that sequence need to be completed.

8-7 Estimate Activity Duration

You can begin **estimating activity durations** once the activities have been defined and sequenced. Estimating activity durations is the process of approximating the number of work periods needed to complete individual activities with estimated resources. **Duration** is "the total number of work periods (not including holidays or other nonwork periods) required to complete a schedule activity … usually expressed as workdays or workweeks."[16]

It makes sense to identify the people who will work on each activity as soon as possible since they often have the most knowledge about how to actually do the work and how long it will take. Also, the length of time to perform an activity is often dependent upon who will do that work. We discuss resource assignments in Chapter 9.

When estimating how long activities are expected to take, each activity should be evaluated independently. All assumptions and constraints made when estimating should be documented since a change in one of these assumptions could change the estimate. For the first estimate of each activity, a normal level of labor and equipment and a normal workweek should be assumed. If overtime is planned right from the start, the project manager is unlikely to have much flexibility if the schedule needs to be accelerated. For each activity, the output to be created and the skill level required to perform the work should be identified. Any predetermined completion date can be disregarded at this point. Negotiation with a customer or supplier may be necessary, but the project manager needs to understand what is reasonable under normal circumstances before entering those negotiations. When a past project is being used as a guide, it is preferable to use actual time to perform the activities and not the estimated or planned time. Additional suggestions for creating good estimates include the following:

- Ensure the WBS is complete.
- Do not include anything outside the WBS in the estimate.
- Clearly identify each activity.
- Include appropriate contingencies.
- Use relevant and sufficient data.
- Include all relevant stakeholders in making estimates.

EXHIBIT 8.7

ACTIVITY DURATION ESTIMATE EXAMPLE	
TIME ESTIMATE IN WORKDAYS	ACTIVITY NAME
5	Determine new product features
20	Acquire prototype materials
10	Produce prototype
10	Design marketing campaign
10	Design graphics
30	Conduct marketing
25	Perform sales calls

- Conduct an independent review.
- Revise the estimate if there is a major project change.[17]

Exhibit 8.7 is a continuation of the product upgrade example with the times estimated for individual activities. Note that the estimated times in this example are in workdays. It is important to keep time estimates in the same unit of measure, be it hours, days, weeks, or another increment of time. Exhibit 8.8 includes suggestions for creating realistic time estimates.

When using the actual time from a previous project, adjust the estimate up or down based upon size, familiarity, and complexity differences.

8-7a Problems and Remedies in Duration Estimating

Many factors can impact the accuracy of activity duration estimates. A list of potential problems, remedies for those problems, and the chapter in which each is discussed is

EXHIBIT 8.8

SUGGESTIONS FOR CREATING REALISTIC TIME ESTIMATES

1. Verify all time estimations with the people doing the work. Or, even better, have the people doing the work provide the initial estimates of the activity completion time.
2. Estimate times of completion of work without initial reference to a calendar. Just consider how long you believe each activity will take under normal working conditions.
3. Make sure all time units are identical: workdays, work weeks, months (consider time off for company holidays), or another measure.
4. Some people tend to estimate optimistically. Keep in mind the following time constraints:
   - Unexpected meetings
   - Learning curves
   - Competing priorities
   - Vacation
   - Resources or information not available on time
   - Inaccuracy in work instructions
   - Interruptions
   - Emergencies and illness
   - Rework
5. Contrary to point 4, some people estimate pessimistically in order to look good when they bring their project or activities in under budget and under schedule. Try to develop an understanding of the estimator's experience along with their optimistic or pessimistic tendencies and try to encourage balance in estimates.
6. Don't initially worry about *who* is going to do the work, and don't worry about the mandatory deadline. Figure out a realistic estimate first, and then figure out what to cut later.

EXHIBIT 8.9

ACTIVITY DURATION ESTIMATING PROBLEMS AND REMEDIES		
POTENTIAL ACTIVITY DURATION ESTIMATING PROBLEM	REMEDY	CHAPTER
Omissions	Refining scope and WBS	7
	Checklists, templates, devil'sadvocate	8
	Lessons learned	15
General uncertainty in estimate	Rolling wave planning	7
	Reverse phase schedule	9
	Learning curve	8
	Identify and reduce sources of uncertainty	11, 12
	Manage schedule aggressively	14
Special cause variation	Risk analysis	3, 11
	Resolve risk events	14
Common cause variation	PERTMonte Carlo	8
	Project buffer	8
		9
Merging (multiple predecessors)	Milestones	3, 8
	Reverse phase schedule	9
	Feeding buffer	9
	Manage float	14
Queuing	Staggering project start dates	2
	Resource leveling	9
	Resource buffer	9
Multitasking	Prioritizing projects	2
	Carefully authorize start of noncritical activities	9, 14
Student syndrome (starting late)	Float	8
	Critical path meetings	14
Not reporting early completion of rework	Project culture	4
	Project communications	6
	Contract incentives	13
	Project leadership	5
	Progress reporting	14

Source: Adapted from Larry Leach, "Schedule and Cost Buffer Sizing: How to Account for the Bias between Project Performance and Your Model," *Project Management Journal* 34 (2) (June 2003): 44.

shown in Exhibit 8.9. These techniques are not mutually exclusive. Many organizations use several of them; however, few organizations use them all. It is important for business students to be aware of these techniques and their potential benefits, since some companies use each. Many companies customize the mechanics of how they use these techniques.

8-7b Learning Curves

The concept behind learning curves is simple: The more times a person performs an activity, the better and faster he or she becomes. This concept can be utilized for activity duration estimating, as the rate of improvement can be studied and predicted. Therefore, on types of projects where certain activities are performed many times, a project planner can predict how long it will take each time to perform the activity. The rate of improvement can vary widely depending on many factors, such as:

- How much the culture of the organization stresses continual improvement
- How much skill is involved in the activity
- How complex that activity is
- How much of the activity is dependent on the worker versus dictated by the pace of a machine
- If there is frequent job rotation

The amount of time necessary to perform an activity is calculated based upon a rate of improvement that occurs every time the number of repetitions doubles. For example, if the learning rate is 80 percent and the first time the activity was performed (by producing the first unit), it took 100 minutes, then after doubling the number of units produced, the second unit would require 80 minutes. To double the repetitions again, the fourth unit would require 64 minutes. The time estimates for each time the activity is performed can be found in learning curve tables such as the one shown in Exhibit 8.10. Notice that the rate of learning is very important since more rapid learning leads to much faster performance times for successive times an activity is performed.

For consumers, one result is rapidly declining prices when an industry has a steep learning curve. People expect prices to decline for new electronics and other consumer items. As a project manager, you also need to plan for the amount of learning that may take place. Further, as a project manager, you need to create and sustain the environment that encourages and expects rapid learning so you can always become more competitive.

On Agile projects, duration estimates improve with each iteration and as early iterations are completed. Armed with more specific knowledge of how long certain activities take, later iterations can be estimated more accurately. Project managers can use velocity of progress to estimate how much work will be accomplished in each iteration. **Velocity** is "the sum of the estimates of delivered (i.e., accepted) features per iteration … measured in the same units as feature estimates, whether this is story points, days, ideal days, or hours that the team delivers."[18]

EXHIBIT 8.10

LEARNING CURVE TABLE				
ACTIVITY	60%	70%	80%	90%
1	100	100	100	100
2	60	70	80	90
4	36	49	64	81
8	21.6	34.3	51.2	72.9

8-8 Develop Project Schedules

All the scheduling processes discussed thus far must be completed even if you use Microsoft Project or another scheduling tool. At this point, you have defined, sequenced, and estimated the duration for all the schedule activities. Now is the time to use all of this information to develop a project schedule. Once the schedule is developed based upon this information, resource needs and availability and cash flow constraints often extend the proposed schedule, while imposed date constraints often suggest the need for schedule compression.

The first major task in developing the project schedule is to identify the **critical path**, which is "the sequence of schedule activities determining the duration of the project. Generally, it is the longest path through the project."[19] Because it is the longest sequence of activities, the critical path determines the earliest possible end date of the project. Any time change to an activity on the critical path changes the end date of the entire project. If the project manager changes an activity on the critical path to start at a later date, then the whole project will end at a later date. If the amount of work for an activity on the critical path is increased, then the project will be delayed and it will end at a later date. If, on the other hand, an activity on the critical path is performed faster than planned, the entire project could be completed sooner. The critical path gets its name not because it is the most critical in terms of cost, technical risk, or any other factor, but because it is most critical in terms of time. Since virtually everyone wants to complete projects at the promised time, the critical path gets a great deal of attention.

The two methods for determining the critical path are the two-pass and enumeration methods. Each uses the same activity identification, duration estimate, and activity sequencing data but processes the data in a different manner. While both determine the critical path, each also determines other useful information.

8-8a Two-Pass Method

The two-pass method is used to determine the amount of slack or float each activity has. To perform this method, two logical passes should be made through the network. The first pass is called the forward pass. The **forward pass** is "the calculation of the early start and early finish dates for the uncompleted portions of all network activities."[20] On the forward pass, the project team starts at the beginning of the project and asks how soon each activity can begin and end. If the project is being scheduled with software, actual calendar dates are used. Often, when calculating the schedule by hand, a team starts at date zero. In other words, the first activity can begin after zero days. To envision this, consider Exhibit 8.11, where all of the previously determined information has been displayed.

A legend is shown in the lower-right corner of Exhibit 8.11. This explains each bit of information that is displayed for each activity. For example, the first activity name is "Determine new product features." The estimated duration for this activity is five days. This activity is coded with the letter A. The four corners of each block display four important times for each activity:

- **Early start date (ES)**—"the **earliest** possible point in time on which uncompleted portions of a schedule activity can **start**, based upon the schedule network logic, the data date, and any schedule constraints."[21]
- **Early finish date (EF)**—"the **earliest** possible point in time on which uncompleted portions of a schedule activity can **finish**, based upon the schedule network logic, the data date, and any schedule constraints."[22]

EXHIBIT 8.11

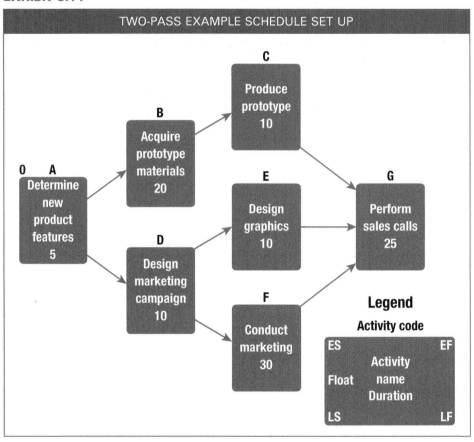

TWO-PASS EXAMPLE SCHEDULE SET UP

- **Late start date (LS)**—"the **latest** possible point in time that a schedule activity can **start**, based upon the schedule network logic, the project completion date, and any schedule constraints."[23]
- **Late finish date (LF)**—"the **latest** possible point in time when a schedule activity can **finish** based upon the network logic, the project completion date, and any constraints."[24]

"Determine new product features," for example, has an early start time of zero since it can begin as soon as the project is authorized.

FIRST OR FORWARD PASS   The first pass is then used to calculate the early finish, which is the early start plus the estimated duration (**ES + Duration = EF**). In this case, 0 + 5 = 5 means the activity "Determine new product features" can be completed after five days. (The zero for the first activity means it can start after zero days—meaning at the beginning of the first day.) Each activity that is a successor can start as soon as its predecessor activity is complete. Therefore, the next two activities can each start after five days. (That means at the start of the sixth day.) To calculate the early finish for each of these activities, add its duration to the early start of 5, for early completion times of 25 and 15, respectively. The difficult part of calculating the first pass comes when an activity has more than one predecessor. For example, "Perform sales calls" cannot begin until *all three preceding activities* ("Produce prototypes," "Design graphics," and "Conduct

EXHIBIT 8.12

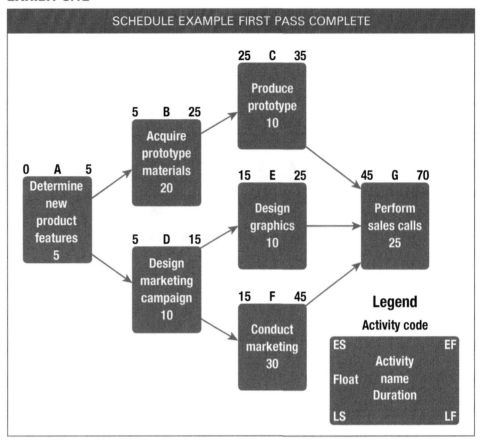

SCHEDULE EXAMPLE FIRST PASS COMPLETE

Legend

Activity code

ES		EF
	Activity	
Float	name	
	Duration	
LS		LF

marketing") are complete. Therefore, its early start is 45. This is true even though "Produce prototypes" and "Design graphics" have earlier finish times, because "Conduct marketing" cannot be completed until day 45. The later time is always taken. The results of the first pass are shown in Exhibit 8.12. Note that the earliest the entire project can be completed is 70 workdays.

SECOND OR BACKWARD PASS   The second pass is sometimes called the backward pass. The **backward pass** is "the calculation of late finish dates and late start dates for the uncompleted portions of all schedule activities. Determined by working backward through the schedule network logic from the project's end date."[25] When performing the backward pass, teams start at the end and work backward, asking, "How late can each activity be finished and started?" Unless there is an imposed date, the late finish for the last activity during planning is the same as the early finish date. In our example, we know the earliest we can finish the entire project is 70 days, so we will use that as the late finish date for the last activity. If the activity "Perform sales calls" must end no later than 70 and it takes 25 days, then it must start no later than day 45. In other words, calculate the late start by subtracting the duration from the late finish (**LF – duration = LS**). The confusing part of calculating the second pass is when there is more than one successor. In Exhibit 8.13, one place this occurs is at the first activity, "Determine new product features," since two activities are immediate successors. Enough time must be left for all of the successors, so whichever one must start soonest dictates the late finish

EXHIBIT 8.13

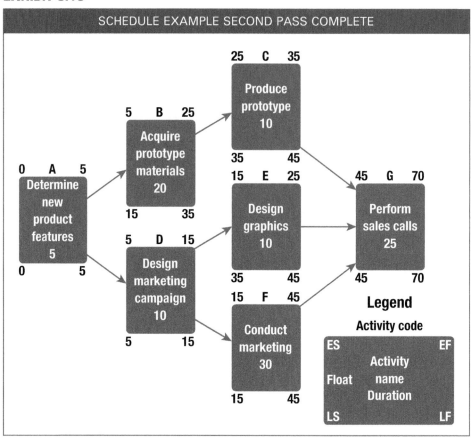

SCHEDULE EXAMPLE SECOND PASS COMPLETE

date of the predecessor. In this example, "Design marketing campaign" must start no later than after day 5; therefore, five days is the late finish for the first activity.

FLOAT AND THE CRITICAL PATH   Once both passes are complete, the early and late start dates for every activity and the amount of time the entire project will take to complete are known. However, the team also wants to know the critical path. This is calculated easily by first determining each activity's float (sometimes float is called slack). Float can be **total float**, which is "the amount of time a schedule activity may be delayed from its early start date without delaying the project end date"[26] or **free float**, which is "the amount of time a schedule activity can be delayed without delaying the early start of immediately following schedule activities."[27] A project manager wants to know how much float each activity has in order to determine where to spend her time and attention. Activities with a great deal of float can be scheduled in a flexible manner and do not cause a manager much concern. Activities with no float or very little float, on the other hand, need to be scheduled and managed very carefully.

Float is calculated by the equation Float = Late start – Early start (**Float = LS – ES**). The critical path is the sequence of activities from start to finish in the network that have no float. In Exhibit 8.14, activities A, D, F, and G have no float and, therefore, create the critical path. It is typical to mark the critical path in red and/or in boldface to call attention to it. Activities B, C, and E each have float and are not on the critical path. If

EXHIBIT 8.14

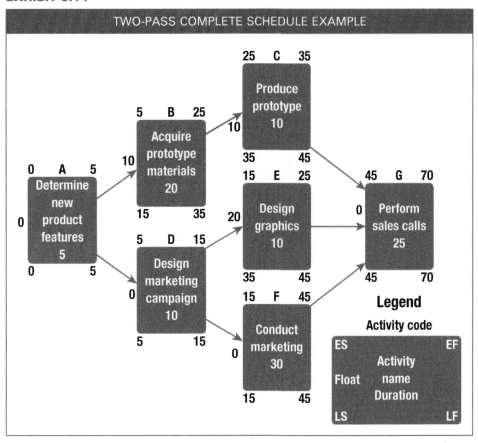

TWO-PASS COMPLETE SCHEDULE EXAMPLE

activity B is delayed, it will delay the start of activity C; therefore, activity B has total float. While activity B can be delayed up to 10 days without delaying the entire project, any delay to activity B would delay the start of activity C. On the other hand, activities C and E can be delayed by 10 and 20 days, respectively, without causing any other activity to be delayed. Therefore, their float is free float—impacting neither the overall project nor any activity in it.

Project managers carefully monitor the critical path activities. They also closely watch activities with little float—think of these as "near-critical" activities. A project with many activities that have little float is not very stable. Even small delays on near-critical activities can change the critical path. Project managers can sometimes "borrow" resources from an activity with plenty of float to use first on an activity that is either already critical or nearly critical. Chapter 9 discusses resource scheduling in detail.

8-8b Enumeration Method

The second method of determining the critical path is the enumeration method. To complete this, we list or enumerate all of the paths through the network. The advantage of this method is that since all of the paths are identified and timed, if a team needs to compress the project schedule, they will know both the critical path and the other paths that may be nearly critical (or those with very little float). It is imperative to keep track of both critical and near-critical paths when compressing a schedule. In Exhibit 8.15, three paths are

EXHIBIT 8.15

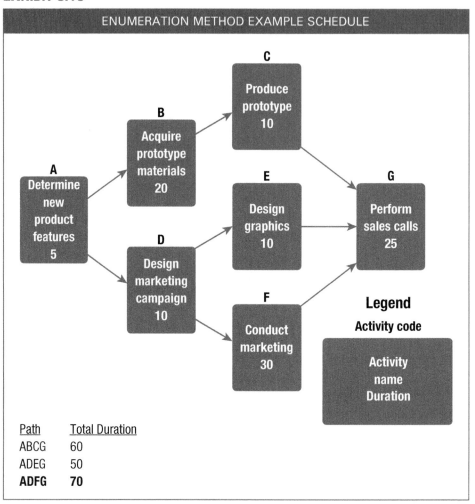

ENUMERATION METHOD EXAMPLE SCHEDULE

Path	Total Duration
ABCG	60
ADEG	50
ADFG	**70**

identified, and the total duration for each is calculated. ADFG is the critical path with an expected duration of 70 days, just as was determined with the two-pass method. Now, however, we also know that path ABCG is expected to take 60 days (10 fewer than the critical path), and path ADEG is expected to take 50 days (20 fewer than the critical path).

8-9 Uncertainty in Project Schedules

On some projects, it is easy to estimate durations of activities with confidence. On others, so many uncertainties exist that managers have far less confidence in their ability to accurately estimate. However, project managers still need to tell sponsors and clients how long they believe a project will take and then be held accountable for meeting those dates. One common strategy for handling this potential problem is to construct the best schedule possible and then manage the project very closely. A different strategy is to estimate a range of possible times each individual activity may take and then see what impact that has on the entire schedule. PERT and Monte Carlo are two methods sometimes used for this strategy.

8-9a Program Evaluation and Review Technique

Program evaluation and review technique (PERT) was developed during the 1950s to better understand how variability in the individual activity durations impacts the entire project schedule. To use PERT, a project team starts by sequencing the activities into a network, as described in Section 8.6 earlier in this chapter. However, instead of creating one time estimate to complete each activity, they create three estimates: optimistic, most likely, and pessimistic. For example, the first activity, "Determine new product features," will most likely take five days, but it could take as little as four days if everything works well and as long as 12 days if a variety of things interfere. The person scheduling the project then calculates the estimated time to perform each activity as shown in Exhibit 8.16 using the following equation:

$$\textbf{Estimated time} = \frac{\textbf{Optimistic} + 4(\textbf{Most likely}) + \textbf{Pessimistic}}{6}$$

$$\textbf{Therefore, for the first activity, the estimated time} = \frac{4 + 4(5) + 12}{6} = 6$$

The primary advantage of PERT is that it helps everyone realize how much uncertainty exists in the project schedule. When people use single time estimates, sometimes there is a tendency to believe that the estimates foretell exactly what will happen. On many projects, a great deal of uncertainty exists, and PERT helps to make it visible. In addition to making the overall uncertainty more visible, calculations often show that the expected time is actually longer than the most likely time; if many things go very well on an activity, generally only a little time can be saved, but if many things go terribly wrong, a great deal of time can be lost.

However, using PERT involves difficulties. First, it is often hard enough to create *one* estimate of how long an activity will take, so it takes even more effort (and therefore money) to create *three* estimates. Second, there is no guarantee of how good any of the three estimates are. In other words, it is not necessarily the case that a three-point estimate of an activity would be more accurate than a single duration estimate. Third, PERT can underestimate the risk of a schedule running long because it does not accurately address when two or more activities need to be completed before a third one can begin.[28]

EXHIBIT 8.16

PERT TIME ESTIMATE EXAMPLE				
ACTIVITY	OPTIMISTIC	MOST LIKELY	PESSIMISTIC	EXPECTED
Determine new product features	4	5	12	6
Acquire prototype materials	16	20	30	21
Produce prototype	8	10	12	10
Design marketing campaign	9	10	14	10.5
Design graphics	6	10	20	11
Conduct marketing	28	30	50	33
Perform sales calls	20	25	30	25

Since PERT highlights uncertainty in project duration, its logic is useful to project managers. However, since it has some problems, only a few project managers actually use it to calculate and monitor project schedules. Some project managers informally use three time estimates for a few key activities on the critical path to get a sense for the amount of uncertainty and to better understand the activities that need close monitoring. Other project managers who want to understand the potential variation use Monte Carlo simulation. Students of project management need to be aware that both PERT and Monte Carlo simulations are sometimes used to help understand uncertainty in project schedules.

8-9b Monte Carlo Simulation

Monte Carlo simulation is "a computerized mathematical technique that allows people to account for risk in quantitative analysis and decision making that furnishes the decision maker with a range of possible outcomes and the probabilities with which they will occur."[29] Monte Carlo is more flexible than PERT, in that an entire range of possible time estimates can be used for any activity or the project itself. The project schedule is calculated many times (perhaps 1,000 or more), and each time, the estimate for a particular activity is generated based upon the likelihood of that time as determined by the project manager. For example, suppose a project manager estimated that for a particular activity, there was a 10 percent chance of taking five days, a 30 percent chance of taking six days, a 40 percent chance of taking seven days, and the remaining 20 percent chance of taking eight days. Then, for each 100 times the computer generated a project schedule, when it came to that activity, 10 times it would choose five days, 30 times it would choose six days, 40 times it would choose seven days, and 20 times it would choose eight days. The output from the computer would include a distribution of how often the project would be expected to take each possible length of time. Many other possible outputs can also be generated from Monte Carlo simulations.

One advantage of Monte Carlo analysis is the flexibility it provides. This allows more realistic estimates. Another advantage is the extent of information it can provide regarding individual activities, the overall project, and different paths through the project that may become critical.

A disadvantage of Monte Carlo is the amount of time necessary to estimate not just a most likely duration for each activity, but an entire range of possible outcomes. Another disadvantage is that special software and skill are necessary to effectively use Monte Carlo. This disadvantage is not as large as it once was because more software is available and most students are learning at least the fundamentals of simulation in statistics or operations courses.

A project manager needs to decide when some of the more specialized techniques are worth the extra effort for a project. The old saying that a person should spend $100 to save $1,000, but should not spend $1,000 to save $100, applies. If the savings on a project from using techniques such as learning curves, PERT, or Monte Carlo are significant, project managers should consider using one of them. If not, they should create the best estimates possible without the specialized techniques, incorporate risk management by carefully identifying and planning for specific risks as discussed in Chapter 11, and manage the project schedule very carefully as discussed in Chapter 14.

These specialized techniques are sometimes used in research and development (R&D) projects. However, some R&D projects do not need this level of sophistication. Exhibit 8.17 shows an actual R&D project schedule used by D. D. Williamson of Louisville, Kentucky, when a Chinese customer asked it to develop a new product somewhat different from any it had previously developed. Once D. D. Williamson decided to take the job, it developed

EXHIBIT 8.17

NEW PRODUCT DEVELOPMENT SCHEDULE IN CHINA EXAMPLE

Week one—Request is received from the customer for a product that is darker than anything we have in our current offering. Our sales manager forwards the request to our VP sales and our R&D department. A quick review of the potential price versus cost of materials is completed by the VP sales (with finance input), and the product is deemed saleable at an acceptable margin.

Week two—A trial cook in our "baby cooker" is conducted by our R&D department. Within two attempts, a product that is within the customer-requested specs is produced. An additional trial is conducted to quickly check repeatability. The trial product is express shipped to the customer and to our China facility for comparison purposes.

Week three—The formulation and related instructions for cooking are communicated to our China operations with a "red sheet" process. China has anticipated the receipt of this red sheet and is able to schedule time in production within a week.

Week four—The initial red sheet production is successful and passes the specification tests in China and in Louisville.

Week five—Customer confirms purchase order and the first shipment is sent. The product contributes significantly to the revenues and profitability of the China facility. Success!

Key factors—Strong communication between all the players and a clear understanding of the customer expectations up front.

Source: Elaine Gravatte, D. D. Williamson.

and communicated the project schedule to all stakeholders both in its company and the customer's company within the first week.

Australian researchers have discovered that two primary causes of late delivery of IT projects are variance in time to complete individual work activities and multiple dependencies for some activities. Suggestions for overcoming these two problems are shown in Exhibit 8.18.

EXHIBIT 8.18

INITIATIVES TO IMPROVE ON-TIME SCHEDULE DELIVERY		
CAUSE OF LATE DELIVERY	INITIATIVE	EXPLANATION
Activity variance	Increase activity transparency	Allows for better planning
	Increase user participation	Ensures that the product delivered meets the user needs
	Reduce project size	Ensures that estimates for tasks are more accurate
	Manage expectations, e.g., set realistic goals by drawing from "outside views"	Mitigates optimism bias and misrepresentation
	Use packaged software	Provides a standard within which to develop the system
Activity dependence	De-scope	Reduces the number of dependencies
	Improve requirements definition	**Ensures that there is no confusion over what is to be developed and when** If activity links are reduced, then dependencies exert less influence
	Reduce activity coupling	
	Stage projects (incremental development or iterative development)	Reduces delay bias by minimizing multitasking, merging, queuing (i.e., reduces the dependencies)

Source: Vlasic, Anthony and Li Liu, "Why Information Systems Projects Are Always Late," *Proceedings Project Management Institute Research and Education Conference 2010* (Oxon Hill, MD, July 2010).

8-10 Show the Project Schedule on a Gantt Chart

The discussion in this chapter so far has been how to determine the project schedule. While this is necessary, it can be confusing to show people a network diagram. A tool for communicating a project schedule that is much easier to understand is a Gantt or bar chart. A **Gantt chart** is a horizontal bar chart that shows each work activity on a separate line with the bar placed from the early start date to the early finish date for each activity on a timescale. It is not uncommon to use Gantt chart for small projects.

The simplest Gantt charts show a bar for each activity stretched out over a time line. Many stakeholders also want to see which activities are critical and the amount of float noncritical activities have. Therefore, critical activities are normally shown in red or bold-face, noncritical activities are normally shown in blue or normal face, and the amount of float is shown in a muted or thin line out to the late finish of each noncritical activity. The units of time are the units the project team used in creating the schedule, whether that is hours, days, weeks, or another unit of measure. A Gantt chart is shown in Exhibit 8.19. It is easy to understand when each activity should be performed. However, the basic Gantt chart does not show other useful information such as predecessor–successor relationships, late start dates, and so forth. These can all be easily displayed on a Gantt chart that is developed using scheduling software such as Microsoft Project. The instructions for using MS Project to create and print Gantt charts are covered in the following section.

8-11 Using Microsoft Project for Critical Path Schedules

As you begin to work with schedules, remember there are five major elements affecting project completion: logical order (or sequence) of project tasks, duration of each task, the number of resources available when needed to complete those tasks, imposed dates, and cash flow. When building schedules in MS Project, you will find it helpful to keep these limitations in order. In the following tutorial, we'll determine the sequence of tasks before coming up with durations for them. Since the bottom line for many stakeholders is often "How long is this going to take and how much will it cost me?" you may find more success if you allow decision makers to focus on determining the sequencing order of tasks *first*, rather than how long each activity will take.

Keep in mind that we are continuing with the Suburban Parks Home project from the tutorial in Chapter 7 (if you have not completed that tutorial, this one will not make

EXHIBIT 8.19

GANTT CHART EXAMPLE															
Activity	Time in workdays														
	0	5	10	15	20	25	30	35	40	45	50	55	60	65	70
Determine new product features															
Acquire prototype materials															
Produce prototype															
Design marketing campaign															
Design graphics															
Conduct marketing															
Perform sales calls															

much sense). First, we will inspect the project calendar to make any adjustments necessary. Next, steps to develop the network diagram will be explained. Finally, the critical path will be discussed as well as how to view and manage the developing schedule.

8-11a Set up the Project Schedule

Setting up the project schedule begins with ensuring the correct start date for the project is set, and then defining your organization's working days, hours, and holidays.

SET (OR UPDATE) THE PROJECT START DATE   In the Chapter 3 tutorial, we set the start date for the project. Often that time can change once planning begins and needs to be updated. To do that:

1. Click **Project Tab>>Project Information**
2. Set the start date to **12/4/17**
3. Click **OK**

DEFINE YOUR ORGANIZATION'S WORKING AND NONWORKING TIMES   MS Project's calendar system defines working and nonworking time. The calendar system consists of a default **project calendar** and a **resource calendar** for each resource. The project calendar refers to what you think of as a normal calendar: the working and nonworking dates for a project, including holidays. The resource calendar pertains to the resources of a project—that is, the *people, equipment, space,* or *materials* used in a project. In this tutorial, we are focused on the project calendar (the resource calendar will be addressed in a future tutorial).

To avoid unrealistic project schedules, you must ensure your organization's working and nonworking times are defined in the project calendar (as well as resource vacations in resource calendars). The default project calendar has all days, except Saturday and Sunday, defined as eight-hour working days. The working hours during the day are 8:00 to 12:00 and 1:00 to 5:00. By default, **no holidays are defined** and must be defined as nonworking days. All project calendar content is copied into all resource calendars. Resource calendars are used to block out vacation days and other *resource-specific* nonworking days. Resource calendars are then used to determine when a resource assignment can be scheduled. If there are no resource assignments, the project calendar is used to determine scheduling.

Use the following steps to change a working day to nonworking in the Suburban Parks Home project, as shown in Exhibit 8.20. The legend explains the different shadings on the calendar days. To open the project calendar:

1. Click **Project Tab>>Change Working Time**
2. Make sure "**Standard (Project Calendar)**" is selected in the "For calendar:" box
3. Use the scroll bar to the right of the calendar to find the date you want to edit
4. Click on the date you want to edit
5. Click the **Exceptions Tab** in the table below the calendar, then click an empty row
6. Enter a description for the nonworking day in the Name column
7. Click another cell in the same row (or **Tab**) to review the results
8. Repeat these steps until all nonworking days are defined as in Exhibit 8.20
   a.   You can also type your nonworking days into the table and set the Start and Finish dates without clicking on them in the calendar
9. Deleting a row restores the default working hours for that day
10. Click **OK** to close the project calendar options

EXHIBIT 8.20

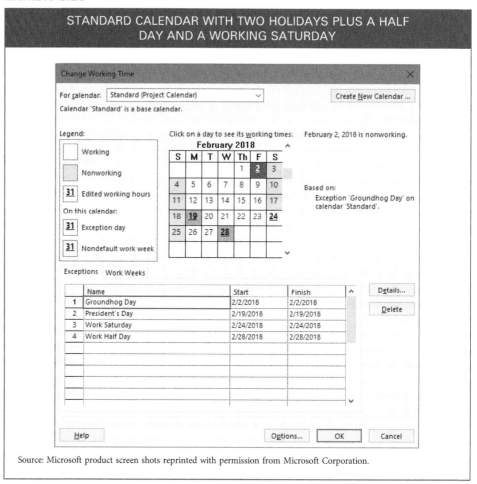

STANDARD CALENDAR WITH TWO HOLIDAYS PLUS A HALF DAY AND A WORKING SATURDAY

Source: Microsoft product screen shots reprinted with permission from Microsoft Corporation.

To change the working time for a day, as shown in Exhibit 8.21:

1. Select the day and enter a description in the table below the calendar
2. Click the **Tab** key to fill the Start and Finish dates
3. Click Details...
4. Choose the "**Working Time**" radio button and modify the "**From:**" and "**To:**" values in the table
5. To eliminate one set of work times (such as afternoon), select those times and click the delete key so only morning times are working
6. Click **OK** twice

8-11b Build the Network Diagram and Identify the Critical Path

We will now begin to build the network diagram for the Suburban Parks Home project. The steps to create a network diagram in MS Project are as follows:

1. Enter tasks and milestones
2. Edit the timescale
3. Understand and define task dependencies
4. Assign task duration estimates

EXHIBIT 8.21

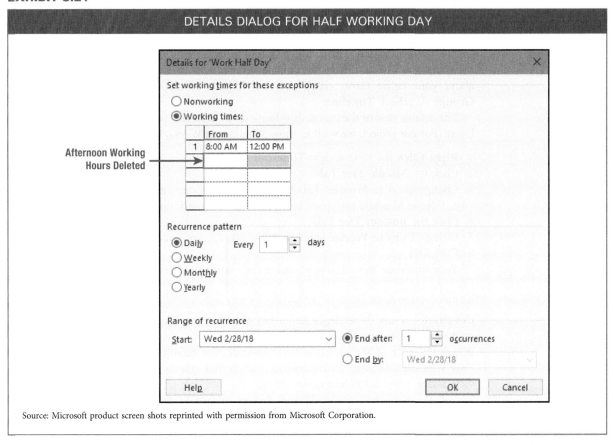

DETAILS DIALOG FOR HALF WORKING DAY

Afternoon Working
Hours Deleted →

Source: Microsoft product screen shots reprinted with permission from Microsoft Corporation.

5. Identify the critical path
6. Understand the network diagram view

STEP 1: ENTER TASKS AND MILESTONES   In the Chapter 7 tutorial, you populated the Gantt chart's table with project tasks and used the milestones from the Suburban Parks Home project as WBS deliverables (summary tasks). We will now add two milestone tasks so they will show graphically (as a diamond) on the Gantt chart.

To add a milestone task, do the following:

1. Click on the intermediate summary task "Foundation Work" (WBS ID 2.4) to select it
2. Click **Task Tab>>Insert Group>>Milestone**
3. You will see a new milestone added to the task list; name it "**Construction Begins**"
4. Tab over to the **Start** date column, and type in the date **1/10/18**
   a. Note since a milestone typically has zero days of duration, MS Project automatically populates the **Finish** column with the same date
5. On the Gantt chart's right side, you should see a diamond appear along with a date
6. Repeat this step for the summary task "County clearance" (WBS ID 5) and type "**Construction Complete**"
7. To show the name of the milestone (instead of the date) on the Gantt chart's graphical side, do the following:
   a. **Format Tab>>Format>>Bar Styles**
   b. Select **Milestone** from the list; click the **Text Tab**

    c.   In the "**Right**" field of the table, change to **Name**

    d.   Click **OK**

    e.   The milestone name should replace the date on the right side

STEP 2: EDIT THE TIMESCALE   Along the top of the right side of the Gantt chart is the timescale. This is different from the Timeline *view*. If the Timeline view is showing above your entire Gantt chart, you can hide it by clicking **View Tab>>Split View Group>>Uncheck Timeline**

The default view of the timescale is likely set to show the Year and Quarter in a "two-tier" layout. For our project, we want to show Months and Weeks. To change the timescale:

1. **Right-Click** the time scale>>**Timescale…**
2. Click the **Middle Tier Tab**
3. Change Units to **Months**; Label to **January**; set Count to **1**; set Size to **55**
   a.   Note: Size sets the space between each tick mark on the timescale for that item
4. Click the **Bottom Tier Tab**
5. Change Units to **Weeks**; Label to **1/25, 2/1, …**; set Count to **1**; set Size to **55**
6. Click **OK**
7. Your timescale should now resemble the one in the Preview window of Exhibit 8.22

STEP 3: UNDERSTAND AND DEFINE TASK DEPENDENCIES   As related earlier in this chapter, a task dependency definition includes both a logical link type (finish-to-start, start-to-start, finish-to-finish, or start-to-finish) and any associated lead or lag value. The default link type in MS Project is finish-to-start. The default lead or lag value is zero days. Task dependencies may be established and viewed graphically in the Network Diagram view and in several different Gantt views.

For the Suburban Parks Home project example, determining dependencies and sequencing is fairly straightforward. Most deliverables in this example must be

EXHIBIT 8.22

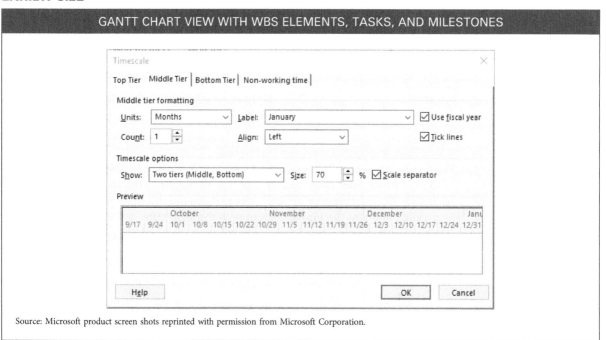

Source: Microsoft product screen shots reprinted with permission from Microsoft Corporation.

completed before the next one can be started. Subtasks of each deliverable likely need some sequencing, and it is helpful to think about what tasks could be done in parallel or where there could be overlap. Sequencing decisions are usually made with the input of the project manager, the sponsor, and other key project stakeholders. Projects of any real size are rarely as straightforward as this example.

Before defining dependencies, ensure the "Start", "Finish", and "Predecessors" columns are visible. You can show more columns on the Gantt chart to the right of the "Duration" column by sliding the view divider to the right. The "Predecessors" column shows the Task ID number (not the WBS code) for predecessor tasks.

Dependencies can be defined using the following steps:

1. Click on the **Task Name** field to select the predecessor task row
2. Press and hold **Ctrl** while selecting the successor task
3. Release **Ctrl** after you click your selection
4. Click the **Task Tab>>Schedule Group>>Link Tasks** (chain icon)
   a. Delete a dependency definition by again selecting both tasks, and then clicking on **Unlink Tasks** (broken chain icon)
5. Adding (or deleting) Task ID numbers in the "Predecessor" column is another way you can define task dependencies

A series of dependencies can also be defined or deleted in a similar manner:

1. Select all of the tasks to be linked in a series
   a. Click and drag with the mouse or **Shift-Click** the first and last task in the series
2. Click the **Task Tab>>Schedule Group>> Link Tasks or Unlink Tasks**

As you start defining task dependencies, you will notice the durations and the start/finish dates change as MS Project begins to build the schedule. The right side of the Gantt chart also begins to take shape. Task relationship arrows show finish-to-start links. Using the **Predecessors** column as a guide, update your task dependencies to match those in Exhibit 8.23.

STEP 4: ASSIGN TASK DURATION ESTIMATES   Once the logical sequence of project tasks is established, it is time to assign duration estimates to those tasks so the critical path can be identified and the actual working schedule can be determined. This is accomplished by first assigning duration estimates and then by instructing MS Project to identify the critical path.

The first principle to keep in mind is to *use the same unit of time for each task*. Mixing up hours, days, or weeks will create confusion. The default time unit is days, so this tutorial uses days. The second principle is to *only assign duration estimates to subtasks, not their summaries*. MS Project calculates the duration for WBS summaries based on the durations selected for the tasks that comprise each summary.

To assign duration to a task:

1. Click the **Duration** cell of the task and enter the duration value
   a. If days are being used, an adjustment can be made up or down with the arrows
   b. A number can also be deleted and then another number typed in the cell
2. MS Project will automatically determine the duration for each summary task as you adjust subtask durations
3. Assign durations to your project using Exhibit 8.23 as a guide

STEP 5: IDENTIFY THE CRITICAL PATH   In most graphical task views, MS Project can mark Gantt bars of critical path tasks and network diagram task nodes in red.

EXHIBIT 8.23

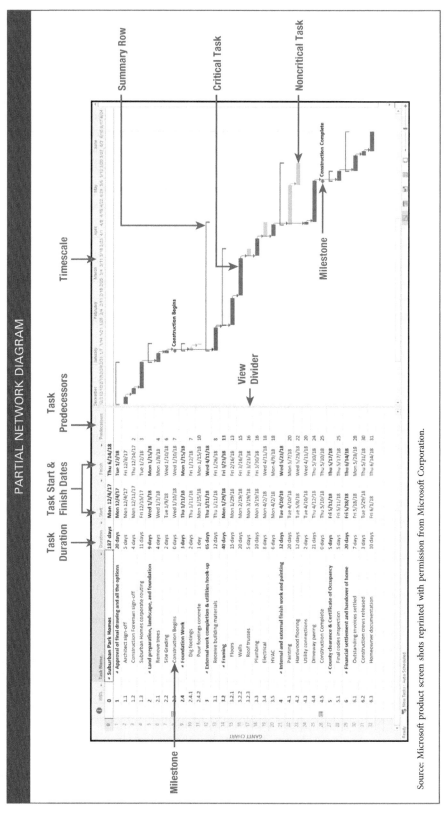

PARTIAL NETWORK DIAGRAM

Source: Microsoft product screen shots reprinted with permission from Microsoft Corporation.

EXHIBIT 8.24

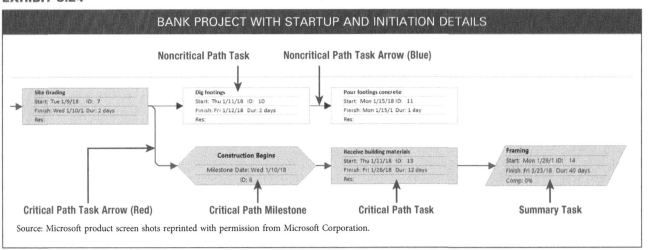

BANK PROJECT WITH STARTUP AND INITIATION DETAILS

Source: Microsoft product screen shots reprinted with permission from Microsoft Corporation.

Unfortunately, this is not the default behavior. To enable this visual cue, do the following:

1. Click the **Task Tab>>Format Tab>>Bar Styles Group>>**check **Critical Tasks**
2. You should now see all your critical tasks shown in red (as in Exhibit 8.23)

STEP 6: UNDERSTAND THE NETWORK DIAGRAM VIEW   The Network Diagram view shows all tasks, summary tasks, and milestones as shown in Exhibit 8.24. The network diagram can be used to verify the logical flow of the project, find tasks with no predecessor or successor, spot opportunities to complete tasks in parallel or overlap, and see the critical path across the project. Again, the Suburban Parks Home project is a straightforward example, so the network diagram is not as useful as it could be in more complex projects.

Although they can be printed, network diagrams in MS Project are best viewed on the computer as they can become quite large. Printing the entire diagram usefully requires piecing multiple sheets of paper or a large-format printer. Network diagrams in MS Project can be unwieldy and difficult to work with, but there are a few ways to make them slightly more user-friendly:

1. Click the **View Tab>>Task Views Group>>Network Diagram**
   a. The network diagram appears
   b. Logical links between tasks can be seen as link lines in blue (noncritical path) and red (critical path)
2. Zoom the view out using the zoom slider at the bottom right of the screen (or **Ctrl-Scroll**)
3. Click the **Format Tab>>**uncheck **Summary Tasks**
4. Click the **Format Tab>>Format Group>>Layout>>**uncheck "**Show page breaks**" and check "**Hide all fields except ID**" (tasks are denoted by Task ID)
5. Click **OK**
6. Zoom in to see the simplified network diagram as in Exhibit 8.25

PMP/CAPM Study Ideas

The scheduling portion of Project Management has been around for decades and is well established. It is also easier to quantify than some of the other knowledge areas, so you should expect to see several questions like the ones in the Exercises above. Be prepared

EXHIBIT 8.25

BANK PROJECT WITH EXECUTING AND CLOSING ACTIVITIES

Source: Microsoft product screen shots reprinted with permission from Microsoft Corporation.

to make calculations based on a variety of information, including Start and Finish times, activity durations, and logical dependencies. Make your decisions and calculations with an eye toward maintaining the critical path above all else, since delays in the critical path will put your entire project behind schedule.

Summary

Project schedules are created by listing all of the activities that need to be performed. This information should be derived from the work packages at the lowest level of the work breakdown structure. Each work package may require one or more activities to be completed to create the required deliverable. Each activity needs to be defined in enough detail that it can be assigned to one person who can accurately determine how it will be accomplished and by whom, estimate how long it will take and how much it will cost, and then be held accountable to ensure it is accomplished.

Once all of the activities have been defined, they need to be sequenced—that is, the team must determine which activities must go first (predecessors) and which activities depend on others to be accomplished before they can start (successors). Many people find that determining these relationships is easiest with Post-it Notes and a large work space.

A person on the planning team needs to estimate how long each activity will take. This is greatly dependent on who will do the work, which is discussed in the next chapter. Care should be taken when creating the estimates since some people tend to be optimistic and many things can interfere with the ability to work on a specific activity. Other people tend to pessimistically pad their estimates to make sure they can finish early and look good.

The three time-management processes described above—activity definition, activity sequencing, and activity duration estimating—need to be accomplished even if scheduling software will be used, since the scheduling software is only as good as the logic behind it! The next step is schedule development. Some teams use Post-it Notes to develop this schedule manually by making two logical passes through the network to determine both the earliest and latest any activity can be started and ended. However, this requires tedious calculations and is greatly simplified by using software such as MS Project.

Schedule development is an iterative process. Once an initial schedule is developed, it needs to be compared to resource limits, imposed dates, and cash flow. Often, a sponsor or customer wants the project sooner than the original schedule suggests. In these cases, many approaches may be considered to expedite the schedule. These schedule adjustments will be considered in Chapters 9 and 10.

Key Terms Consistent with PMI Standards and Guides

activity, 246
plan schedule management, 246
sequence activities, 246

estimate activity durations, 246
develop schedule, 246
control schedule, 246

Chapter Review Questions

1. When can the first draft of a project schedule be constructed?
2. What is the difference between an activity and a work package?
3. What is another name for *activity on node* diagramming?
4. What purpose do project milestones serve?
5. Describe the relationship between a predecessor activity and a successor activity.
6. Describe the four most common types of logical dependency.
7. One potential problem that can occur with activity duration estimating is having omissions. What are three potential remedies for this problem?
8. What two methods can be used to determine the critical path of a schedule?
9. If an activity on the critical path falls behind schedule, what effect will this have on the entire project?
10. If a painted room must dry for four hours before work can continue, the result is a delay in the successor activity. The wait for the paint to dry is an example of a _____.
11. A professor cannot grade his students' exams until the students have completed taking the test. What kind of relationship is this?
12. What is one advantage and one disadvantage of Monte Carlo analysis for predicting a project schedule?
13. How can a Gantt chart be helpful in project planning?
14. A lead is a change in the logical relationship that results in the _____ of the successor activity.
15. How do you calculate float? What is the difference between free float and total float?

Discussion Questions

1. Describe the five factors that may limit how fast a project can be completed. Give an example of each.
2. Think of one thing you have to do this week. Describe how it does or does not meet all five parts of the definition of an *activity*.
3. Discuss at least four potential problems in creating accurate duration estimates for activities and two methods for dealing with each potential problem.
4. Describe how a WBS and a schedule work together.
5. You are the project manager assigned to build and decorate a model home. What might be an example of a lead you encounter when scheduling work activities? A lag?
6. Describe the process used to calculate *float*. Describe how you can tell if it is *total float* or *free float*.

Exercises

1. Label the box below to create a two-pass schedule legend.

2. If the learning rate is 60 percent and the first time the activity was performed took 200 minutes, the second time performing the activity should take _____ minutes, and the fourth time should take _____ minutes.

3. In the example below, label which activities are predecessors and which activities are successors.

4. Create a logical network using the activities listed below.

    Planting a Flower Bed

    1. Purchase flowers, potting soil, and tools.
    2. Water flowers.
    3. Prepare soil by weeding and adding fertilizer.
    4. Plant flowers.
    5. Dig hole.

5. Calculate early start, early finish, late start, late finish, and float for each of the activities in the network below. The duration of each activity is given.

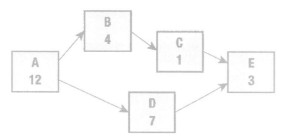

6. Identify the critical path for the network in Exercise 5. How long should the project take?

7. Display the schedule from Exercise 5 on a Gantt chart showing critical activities, noncritical activities, and float.

8. Given the information below, create the project schedule network. Then, using the two-pass method, calculate and show the early and late starts and float for each activity and the critical path. Show the schedule on a Gantt chart showing critical and noncritical activities and float.

ACTIVITY	DAYS	IMMEDIATE PREDECESSOR
A	5	
B	2	A
C	4	A
D	7	A
E	3	B
F	6	B, C
G	8	D, E, F

9. Given the information below, create the project schedule network. Then, using the enumeration method, calculate and show all of the paths through the network. Show how long each path will take. Identify the critical path. Show the schedule on a Gantt chart showing critical and noncritical activities and float.

ACTIVITY	DAYS	IMMEDIATE PREDECESSOR
A	7	B
B	2	-
C	3	A
D	5	A
E	7	B
F	3	C
G	4	D
H	6	E, F
I	5	G, H

10. Using the data below, schedule the problem in MS Project. Display and print the schedule in a Gantt chart showing the critical path and the predecessors.

WBS	ACTIVITY	IMMEDIATE PREDECESSOR	DURATION IN WEEKS
1	**Operational definition**		
1.1	Research literature		3
1.2	Identify and define terms	1.1	1
1.3	Obtain approval of definition	1.2	2
2	**Target Selection**		
2.1	Solicit partners for pilot		2
2.2	Hold brainstorming meeting	2.1	2
2.3	Identify characteristics of targets	2.2, 3.1	1
2.4	Obtain approval of partners	2.3, 1.2, 3.4	1
3	**Question set**		
3.1	Identify process group members		2
3.2	Develop question set	2.3	4
3.3	Prototype and validate question set	3.2	3
3.4	Add partners	3.1, 2.1	3
4	**Pilot process**		
4.1	Schedule with target audience	2.4	2
4.2	Conduct beta test	3.4, 2.4	2
4.3	Process feedback from target audience	4.2	2
4.4	Conduct pilot	4.3	2
4.5	Analyze results	4.4	2

11. Using the data below, schedule the problem in MS Project. Display and print the schedule in a Gantt chart showing the critical path and the predecessors.

	ACTIVITY	IMMEDIATE PREDECESSOR	DURATION IN DAYS
A	Evaluate freezers		2
B	Chart temperatures		6
C	Review service record		2
D	Consult with HVAC engineer	A, B, C	3
E	Develop construction plan	D	10
F	Complete IC assignment	E	2
G	Complete ROI analysis	E	5
H	Conduct regulatory review	E	4
I	Obtain construction approval	F, G, H	2

12. Using the information for Exercise 8.8, input the data into MS Project. Display and print the schedule in Gantt chart format as shown in Exhibit 8.19.

13. Using the information for Exercise 8.9, input the data into MS Project. Display and print the schedule in Gantt chart format as shown in Exhibit 8.19.

PMBOK® Guide Questions

1. The Midlands Company is eager to develop a project schedule. They have already completed the scope statement, work breakdown structure, and schedule management plan. What is the next thing they should do in order to start creating a project schedule?
   a. define activities
   b. nothing; they are ready to proceed
   c. sequence activities
   d. estimate activity durations

2. Which of the following is *not* a characteristic of an activity?
   a. It is a distinct, scheduled portion of work performed during a project.
   b. It has clear starting and ending points.
   c. It is defined using a verb/noun format.
   d. It is one of the deliverables at the lowest level of the WBS.

3. Another term for "activity on node," the most commonly used technique for constructing a schedule model, is:
   a. precedence diagramming method (PDM)
   b. arrow diagramming method (ADM)
   c. activity on arrow (AOA)
   d. activity attribute method (AAM)

4. You are planning the schedule and come to an activity you are unfamiliar with. Your SMEs give you the following time estimates: most likely = 5 hours; optimistic = 2 hours; pessimistic = 14 hours. Using PERT, which activity duration do you use in your plan?
   a. 6 hours
   b. 2 hours
   c. 5 hours
   d. 10 hours

5. A critical path activity has _____ float during the planning process.
   a. the most
   b. zero
   c. negative
   d. positive

6. The Bluestar Creative Agency is developing a new marketing campaign for a client. They have determined that the client's marketing plan must be completed before the graphic design can begin. This situation describes what type of dependency?
   a. start-to-start (SS)
   b. start-to-finish (SF)
   c. finish-to-start (FS)
   d. finish-to-finish (FF)

7. What is an advantage of using Monte Carlo analysis when estimating the duration for an activity?
   a. It uses historical data from a similar activity or project to calculate the duration.
   b. It uses brainstorming techniques to reach a team consensus for the duration.
   c. It can provide a great deal of information about how activity times may vary.
   d. It is less costly and time consuming than other estimating techniques.

8. A Gantt chart represents project schedule information in an easy-to-read, graphical format. Which of these is *not* a component of this type of Gantt chart?
   a. activities
   b. budget data
   c. start and end dates
   d. durations

9. As a project manager, which of the following situations would concern you the most?
   a. a three-day delay on an activity with five days total float
   b. realizing that an activity on your critical path only took two days instead of the four you assigned it using the PERT method
   c. a one-day delay to an activity with 0 total float
   d. a two-day delay to a noncritical path activity with two predecessor activities

10. How do you calculate Late Start, using the two-pass method?
    a. Late Finish – Duration
    b. Duration – Early Start
    c. Early Finish – Early Start
    d. Late Finish – Early Finish

INTEGRATED EXAMPLE PROJECTS
SUBURBAN HOMES CONSTRUCTION PROJECT

Refer to the project charter from Chapter 3 and the WBS in Chapter 7. The initial scope as identified in the project charter is mentioned below:

Building a single-family, partially custom-designed home as required by Mrs. and Mr. John Thomas on Strath Dr., Alpharetta, Georgia. The single-family home will have the following features:

- 3,200 square-feet home with 4 bedrooms and 2.5 bathrooms
- Flooring—hard wood in the first floor, tiles in the kitchen and bathrooms, carpet in bedrooms
- Granite kitchen countertops, GE appliances in the kitchen
- 3-car garage and external landscaping
- Ceiling—10' in first floor and vaulted 9' ceilings in bedrooms

---

In the previous chapter (Chapter 7), you were asked to develop a WBS. If you have not already done so, Suburban Homes is requesting that you complete the WBS to several levels such that the lowest level represents work packages and activities. Also, you need to make sure that no work components are missing to deliver the project outcome: a single-family home. You are asked to exclude the project management part of it and instead focus on the *what* aspect of the project and not on the *how* aspect of the WBS. Once the WBS is completely developed, please perform the following tasks.

Tasks to Complete
- Expand the WBS (Chapter 7) so that work packages or activities are defined at the lowest level.
- Develop a project schedule at the lowest level of WBS work elements after defining logical relations.
- Estimate durations of each element in the network.
- Compute forward pass and backward pass to determine project duration.
- Determine critical path for the project.

CASA DE PAZ DEVELOPMENT PROJECT

This is an example of the five features and the several stories that comprise each feature as developed by the Promotion and Community Relations Working Group. In their next meeting, they created a more detailed list of tasks that need to be accomplished and determined the first few they would accomplish (selected stories from their backlog to accomplish during their first iteration).

Timothy Kloppenborg

Website	Location/Building	Partnerships Sponsors	Communication Materials	Joint Ventures
Key Contact SM Update site	Zoning/Building Permits Insurance	St. Bernard Church Bellarmine Chapel St. Leo's Church St. Carlos Church St. Susana Church Our Savior (PJ)	LOGO	March Visit to Chicago Casa de Paz
Expand Donation Options Example: Room Sponsorship	Remodeling (Security and Safety) Update Bathrooms Basement Laundry Painting Carpet on stairs Locks (doors and windows) Security Cameras	Corporations(Duke Energy, GE, PG, etc.)	Sign	Su Casa YWCA WHW Santa Maria Immigrant Women Phoenix group
Post Progress Updates (Pictures)	Construction Crews Professionals Habitat for Humanity	Health and Education Providers	Brochures	University interns
Calendar Current events	Donation of construction materials Furniture	Local Hispanic Organizations	Social Media Facebook	CFJ/students
Volunteer Opportunities	Recruiting Volunteer	Employment opportunities	Press Release (*C. Telegraph*, etc.)	Service Leaning

Date	Action Steps
March 1–10	Visit St. Bernard Rectory Visit Casa de Paz Chicago SM to get website access from Ashley and start collecting information that needs posting
March 15–30	Contact Phoenix Group (Alejandra, Laura) Support Gill for March 21 presentation List of potential building contractors and volunteers (Alejandra) List of Churches (Tim) List of Education groups (Kathleen) List of Health organizations (Laura
April 1–15	Zoning/Building permits

Semester Project Instructions

Take the WBS you have already developed. Define all of the activities that will be necessary to create each deliverable in your WBS. Create a schedule for your sample project. First, create the schedule by hand using Post-it Notes and then put the information into MS Project. Create a printed copy of the schedule on a Gantt chart with no more than 40 lines per page. Do not use more pages than necessary. Sponsors do not like to flip pages. Be sure to include all of the summary rows (including the first row for the project title) and any key milestones. Make sure the critical path is easy to see.

PROJECT MANAGEMENT *IN ACTION*

Sample Project Schedule for an Iterative/Incremental Software Development Project

This is a typical schedule for an iterative/incremental software development project as used by an African consulting company. It can be easily modified depending on the complexity of the project. The schedule is shown below with notes that follow to explain several sections.

Review and Signoff (Project Charter)

Depending on the organization and the project, the process to review and signoff the project charter may take longer than a few days. The project may be critical in nature and may require a signoff by senior stakeholders in the organization who may not be easily available. This should be considered and

communicated by the project manager during the project kickoff meeting. Should the project manager choose to continue the project before signing off the charter, he/she should identify and communicate relevant risks of doing so to the steering committee.

Onboarding Project Team

The period between signing off the project charter and commencing the analysis of the business requirements should be used to work out a more detailed plan and communicate the project objectives, milestones, deliverables and timelines, as well as roles and responsibilities, with the project team.

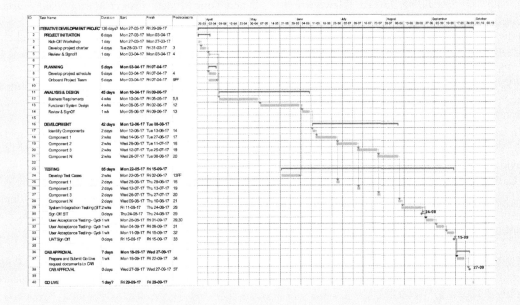

Business Requirements and Functional System Design

At the end of each of these stages in the project, the project manager may want to reassess the development and testing estimates communicated earlier in the project. More detailed information regarding the complexity of the project will be revealed during these project stages.

Development and Component Testing

The development stage is broken down into multiple components that may be developed independently. If a USE CASE approach is followed, these components will represent individual USE CASES. Following the development of each component, a period of time should be set aside to test the component. The project schedule illustrated here shows that the development of the next component commences as soon as the previous component is completed. Depending on the number of resources available and the system being developed, the development and testing of these components may be arranged differently.

Source: Clive Enoch, PhD, PMP, PfMP.

Cab (Change Approval Board)

IT (information technology) departments usually have a committee that meets regularly to assess, approve, or reject any system changes planned for implementation. Such a committee is typically called a Change Approval Board (CAB). One of the criteria assessed by this committee is the UAT (User Acceptance Testing) signoff. The project manager needs to ensure that the correct dates for submission of documents and the sitting of the CAB are plotted correctly on the project schedule. It must be borne in mind that delays in UAT will mean that submission to the CAB will be delayed. Alerting the CAB of delays as soon as possible *or* booking an approval request as close to the end of UAT as possible is advised. You do not want to repetitively change the request for approval dates as this will attract a negative perception of the project management ability on the project.

References

Practice Standard for Project Estimating (Newtown Square, PA: Project Management Institute, 2011).

Practice Standard for Scheduling, 2nd ed. (Newtown Square, PA: Project Management Institute, 2011).

Douglas, Edward E., III, "Schedule Constructability Review," *AACE International Transactions* (2008) PS.16.1–PS.16.6.

Gray, Neal S., "Secrets to Creating the Elusive 'Accurate Estimate,'" *PM Network*, 15 (8) (August 2001): 54–57.

Haugan, Gregory T., *Project Planning and Scheduling* (Vienna, VA: Management Concepts, Inc., 2002).

Hulett, David T., "Project Schedule Risk Analysis: Monte Carlo Simulation or PERT?" *PM Network* 14 (2) (February 2000): 43–47.

Hulett, David T., "Project Schedule Risk Assessment," *Project Management Journal* 26 (1) (March 1995): 21–31.

Kelley, J. F., "Critical Path Planning and Scheduling: Mathematical Basis," *Operations Research* 9 (3) (1961): 296–320.

Leach, Larry, "Schedule and Cost Buffer Sizing: How to Account for the Bias between Project Performance and Your Model," *Project Management Journal* 34 (2) (June 2003): 34–47.

Lukas, Joseph A., "Top Ten Scheduling Mistakes and How to Prevent Them," *AACE International Transactions* (2009): PS.10.1–PS.10.11.

Malcolm, D. G., et al., "Applications of a Technique for R and D Program Evaluation (PERT)," *Operations Research* 1 (5) (1959): 646–669.

McGary, Rudd, *Passing the PMP Exam: How to Take It and Pass It* (Upper Saddle River, NJ: Prentice Hall PTR, 2006).

Moder, Joseph J., "Network Techniques in Project Management," in David I. Cleland and William R. King, eds., *Project Management Handbook*, 2nd ed. (New York: Van Nostrand Reinhold, 1998): 324–373.

Moder, J. J., C. R. Phillips, and E. W. Davis, *Project Management with CPM, PERT, and Precedence*

Diagramming, 3rd ed. (New York: Van Nostrand Reinhold, 1983).

http://www.palisade.com/risk/monte_carlo_simulation. asp, accessed March 2, 2017.

Salem, O., J. Solomon, A. Genaidy, and M. Luegr-ring, "Site Implementation and Assessment of Lean Construction Techniques," *Lean Construction Journal* (2) (October 2005): 1–21.

https://www.versionone.com/agile-101/agile-management-practices/agile-scrum-velocity/, accessed March 2, 2017.

Vlasic, Anthony and Li Liu, "Why Information Systems Projects Are Always Late," *Proceedings Project Management Institute Research and Education Conference 2010* (Oxon Hill, MD, July 2010).

Waterworth, Christopher J., "Relearning the Learning Curve: A Review of the Derivation and Applications of Learning-Curve Theory," *Project Management Journal* 31 (1) (March 2000): 24–31.

Webster, Francis W., Jr., "They Wrote the Book: The Early Literature of Modern Project Management," *PM Network* 13 (8) (August 1999): 59–62.

Endnotes

1. *Practice Standard for Scheduling 2nd ed.*:122.
2. Adapted from Gregory T. Haugan, *Project Planning and Scheduling* (Vienna, VA: Management Concepts, Inc., 2002): 52.
3. *Practice Standard for Project Estimating*: 71
4. *Practice Standard for Project Estimating*: 70.
5. *Practice Standard for Scheduling*: 117.
6. Ibid.
7. *Practice Standard for Scheduling*: 124.
8. *Practice Standard for Scheduling*: 124.
9. *Practice Standard for Scheduling*: 133.
10. *Practice Standard for Scheduling*: 120
11. *Practice Standard for Scheduling*: 121.
12. *Practice Standard for Scheduling*: 121.
13. Ibid.
14. *Practice Standard for Scheduling*: 120.
15. *Practice Standard for Scheduling*: 133.
16. *Practice Standard for Project Estimating*: 71.
17. *Practice Standard for Project Estimating*: 14.
18. https://www.versionone.com/agile-101/agile-management-practices/agile-scrum-velocity/.
19. *Practice Standard for Scheduling*: 117.
20. *Practice Standard for Scheduling*: 120.
21. *Practice Standard for Scheduling*: 131.
22. Ibid.
23. *Practice Standard for Scheduling*: 133.
24. Ibid.
25. *Practice Standard for Scheduling*: 127.
26. *Practice Standard for Scheduling*: 148.
27. *Practice Standard for Scheduling*: 133.
28. David T. Hulett, "Project Schedule Risk Assessment," *Project Management Journal* 26 (1) (March 1995): 21–31; and David T. Hulett, "Project Schedule Risk Analysis: Monte Carlo Simulation or PERT?" *PM Network* 14 (2) (February 2000): 43–47.
29. http://www.palisade.com/risk/monte_carlo_simulation.asp.

Resourcing Projects

CHAPTER OBJECTIVES

After completing this chapter, you should be able to:

CORE OBJECTIVES:
- Show resource assignments on RACI chart, Gantt chart, and resource histogram.
- Develop an effective project schedule, considering resource constraints.
- Describe methods of resolving resource overloads.

BEHAVIORAL OBJECTIVES:
- Create a Resources Management Plan, including role descriptions.
- Assign roles and responsibilities based on strengths.

TECHNICAL OBJECTIVES:
- Compress a project schedule using crashing and fast tracking, and describe the advantages and disadvantages of both.
- Compare various alternative scheduling methods.
- Using MS Project, assign resources, pinpoint overloads, and describe methods of dealing with them.

© Jakub Jirsák/Dreamstime.com

How does a more than fifty-five-year-old prepress company transform its business from that of a manufacturer to a service provider? Schawk, Inc. was founded in 1953 in the basement of a Chicago home by entrepreneur Clarence W. Schawk. The product being manufactured was printing plates. More than fifty years and fifty acquisitions later, Schawk, with offices all over the world, is recognized as a global leader in brand point management.

How did we get here? Schawk capitalized on its knowledge and skills in streamlining processes and managing color. Today, one of the key challenges for product manufacturers is bringing new and/or modified products to market quickly, accurately, and consistently. This is especially challenging in high-growth, emerging markets where additional challenges, such as counterfeiting and trademark infringement, cost manufacturers 10 to 15 percent of their revenue. Being agile enough to respond to evolving consumer demand while demand is high can be key to achieving category leadership and maximizing sales. Being first to market can confer long-lasting benefits to the brands seen as "the original." Ultimately, bringing products to market that help brands win at the shelf—where the consumers vote with their wallets—delivers measurable, long-lasting benefits to brand owners.

Many of the world's most respected organizations struggle with managing projects globally. While their products and marketing strategies may be innovative, their go-to-market processes are often linear, time-consuming, and very inefficient. Their progress toward achieving strategic business goals through the

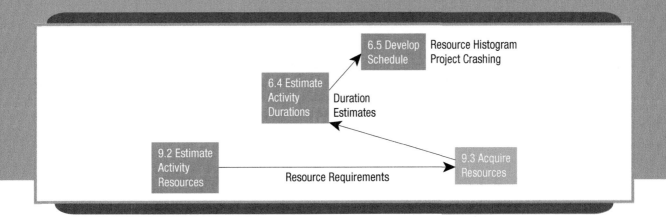

launch of new brands and products is thwarted by many factors, including "silo-ization" and heterogeneous cultures, languages, government regulations, and time zones.

Schawk has adapted by integrating our strategic, creative, and executional capabilities, which are supported by BLUE, our primary brand management tech-nology product. BLUE enables global companies to unite their stakeholders (inter-nal and external), projects, and processes into a single, streamlined workflow management system regardless of geographic boundaries. While workflows are unique to each company, they often combine on-, near-, and off-site project teams around the world.

Increasingly, companies outsource their non-core competencies such as inter-nal design and production departments to Schawk, because that is a core compe-tency of ours, and we can manage these functions more efficiently. This allows the client's project manager to manage a single Schawk point of contact, allow-ing him or her to spend more time focusing on higher-value strategic issues.

We identify and help remove process bottlenecks, offer online collaborative project management tools, and provide knowledgeable human talent to deliver what we call brand point management. Brand point management helps companies create compelling and consistent brand experiences across brand touch points.

—*Patti A. Soldavini, director, Corporate Marketing, Schawk, Inc.*

How do you decide who you need to work on your project? How do you know when you need each project team member? How do you secure the services of those peo-ple? How do you make sure each worker has a steady amount of work to do, but not an overwhelming amount at any time? How do you make sure that each project team mem-ber is challenged to perform at optimum level? How do you make sure your project schedule is realistic, considering who will do the work?

These and many other related questions are answered when you correctly resource a project. Resources include people (human resources), along with machines, space, and other things you need to get the project done. In this chapter, we will primarily discuss human resources.

The total means available to a company for increasing production, service, or profit are considered resources. People, equipment, materials, tools, and licenses are typical resources for any organization. For projects, a resource refers to anything that will cost money to obtain and is necessary for the completion of work. Therefore, money is not a resource, but it is considered a means to acquire resources because it is a common denom-inator for all resources. If required resources are in abundance, managing resources will not be an issue. However, that is not the case in most situations (Anantatmula, 2014).

People management may be the largest deviation from traditional project management that an agile approach embodies. The ideas in this chapter are, in particular, very different from the approach agile takes. In traditional project management (using a plan-driven approach), one needs to reduce uncertainty and then primarily follow the plan. In agile (a change-driven approach), uncertainty is embraced.

9-1 Abilities Needed When Resourcing Projects

Project managers need two types of abilities to resource a project effectively and efficiently. The first type of skill is technical. Various techniques can be used to estimate resource demands, assess competencies required, create a staffing management plan, assign one or more persons for each activity, ensure that each team member's workload is at an optimum level (no less or excess workload), schedule a project with optimum resources, and compress (speed up) a project schedule.

The second type of skill needed is behavioral. As you might guess, many behavioral issues are involved in completing project resourcing tasks, such as:

- Selecting the right people
- Identifying exactly what each person needs to accomplish
- Ensuring that each person has the capability needed (or develops that capability)
- Dealing with difficult individual work schedules
- Getting people to work overtime when there are schedule conflicts
- Making honest and open estimates of the amount of work required
- Assembling an effective team
- Dealing with people from diverse backgrounds
- Deciding where each person will work
- Deciding how a geographically dispersed team can work effectively and virtually

9-1a The Science and Art of Resourcing Projects

The science and art of project resourcing are to perform the technical and behavioral aspects together in a manner that reinforces and complements each aspect. A resource-based schedule that is technically brilliant, but has little acceptance from those who must do the work, has little value. Likewise, an effective project team, whose members have impractical resource assignments, is still likely to struggle. If one needs to choose between the two, a motivated team with poor assignments or very challenging assignments is more likely to be successful. However, when both the technical and behavioral aspects are addressed well, the project will have a much higher probability of achieving good results.

This chapter covers both technical and behavioral aspects of determining and securing effective human resources for a project. While each specific skill and behavioral consideration is introduced separately, keep in mind that people are inclined to support what they have helped to plan. Therefore, when possible, identify your key people as soon as possible and get them engaged in the planning.

9-1b Considerations When Resourcing Projects

As we cover the specific skills and behavioral aspects of resourcing projects, the following ideas should be kept in mind:

- If some of the key people on a project do not have the skills to participate, managers should help them develop those skills.

- Projects always have trade-offs; with respect to resources, trade-offs—time versus human resources versus other costs versus scope—should be considered. Which of these takes precedence on the project you are planning?
- Project managers need to understand resource limitations to prevent overpromising. Often, after activities are tentatively scheduled, as discussed in the previous chapter, it appears that the project can be completed by a specific date. However, the schedule may become unrealistic if required resources are not available at key points in time.
- People are often a large portion of total project cost. This is especially true when a project requires special knowledge.

Of all the resources, managing people is the most challenging aspect of a project. Resource availability, specifically human resources, is a major constraint for projects. Many times, we need these resources for simultaneous execution of project activities to reduce project duration and to utilize resources efficiently. Caution must be exercised to avoid overloading or assigning multiple tasks at the same time.

9-1c Activity- versus Resource-Dominated Schedules

All project schedules are based in part on the individual activities (both the estimates of how long each activity will take and their logical order, as discussed in Chapter 8) and in part on the number of human resources who are available when needed (the topic of this chapter). However, in some circumstances, the schedule is based more on the activities, and in others, it is based more on the resource limits. Exhibit 9.1 lists situations where schedules are based more on activities or more on resources. Some organizations use critical chain (explained in Section 9.8) or agile in situations where the schedule is dominated more by resources.

Agile techniques are often used when the client does not fully understand their needs at the project start, when a rapid rate of scope change will probably occur on the project, and/or when multiple short deliveries are possible. The client and project team can collaborate to reduce the impact of interdependency of activities. Agile project schedules are limited to the amount of work the assigned resources can handle. The team of workers assigned to an agile project should remain on the project for at least each iteration, and preferably for the entire duration. An agile team is a cross-functional team with general

EXHIBIT 9.1

ACTIVITY–VS. RESOURCE-DOMINATED SCHEDULE BASIS COMPARISON		
	MORE ON ACTIVITY	MORE ON RESOURCE
Time in project when scope is determined	Early	Late
Confidence in duration estimates	Great	Little
Rate of resource learning	Small	Extensive
Specialization of resources	Commodity	Unique
Availability of resources	Easily available	Tight availability
Firmness of activity predecessors (order)	Absolute	Optional
Concurrency of activities	Little	Significant

expertise that puts them together on a long-term basis. They develop skills as needed to produce the product needed by the business. The idea is that the work flows to the team and not the other way around.

9-2 Estimate Resource Needs

A starting point in resourcing a project is to estimate how many resources of each type and skill or knowledge level are needed to execute all the activities identified by the WBS. The WBS identifies project activities, yet it includes no estimates of time, resources, or project costs. However, it facilitates the process of integrating project plans for time, resources, and scope.

Estimating activity resources is a process of assessing all types of resources—people, materials, tools, and equipment (along with quantities)—required for each activity to complete it as specified in project scope. This can be accomplished at either a detailed or an overview level. When a project team determines a detailed list of activities that must be performed, it makes sense to ask what type of person (by specific knowledge or skill) is needed to perform each of these activities. However, when a project team does not identify individual activities, they still need to determine how many resources and what knowledge and skill each needs to complete the project. If the team uses rolling wave planning, they probably develop detailed resource requirements for the early part of the project for which they have identified specific activities, and less detailed requirements for later project phases for which the activity-specific details are not developed yet.

When estimating resource needs, the team also must consider support needs such as information systems and other services. Specific constraints are placed on some types of workers as to how they are hired, scheduled, and released. Further, co-located teams and highly skilled resources often require more detailed resource planning. Many issues may be involved in securing specific knowledge or skills. When estimating resource needs, it is wise to include time to communicate between activities as well as time to perform activities. "Handoffs" occur when one person or group passes work on to another group.

9-3 Plan Resource Management

Plan Resource Management is the process of identifying resources and required skills for the project, defining and assigning roles and responsibilities to all the resources, developing a reporting hierarchy, and communicating expectations. Roles and responsibilities for project participants can be documented in role descriptions. These often include title, assigned duties, and limits of authority, as shown in Exhibit 9.2.

A **staffing management plan** is a proposal focused on acquiring, developing, and retaining human resources for as long as you need them on the project. The staffing management plan addresses how to identify potential internal and/or external human resources for the project; determine the availability of each; and decide how to handle timing issues with regard to building up, developing, rewarding, and releasing the project team.

It is important to document roles and responsibilities, authority, responsibility, and the required competency for each role. Then reporting relations can be established using a project organization chart and subsequently, a staff management plan can be developed.

Once the roles and responsibilities of project team members are identified with all the WBS activities, it is captured as a responsibility matrix. It serves as a good staff management plan and helps the project manager to promote teamwork and productivity.

EXHIBIT 9.2

ROLE DESCRIPTION EXAMPLE

ROLE: Project Team Member

ASSIGNED DUTIES:

- Achieves the project objective, working closely with the PM and project team
- Applies Project Management concepts, methodology, and best practices
- Works well with co-located teams, virtual teams, cross-functional teams
- Delivers on commitments, completes tasks on time, communicates clearly

LIMITS OF AUTHORITY:

- Takes action and contributes to decisions within the parameters of the project (cost, schedule, scope, quality)
- Accountable to and reports to the Project Manager

Source: Connie Plowman, PMP, COO (retired), PMI Eric Jenett Project Management Excellence Award Recipient

9-3a Identify Potential Resources

The project manager should plan, estimate, and manage all tasks and their respective resources independent of where the resources reside, administratively or physically. Identifying people who might work on a project differs significantly from one organization to another. Often, many organizations practice a lean approach for staffing and have few people from whom to choose. In a small organization, one particular person may often be the logical choice for certain types of work on a project. However, in larger organizations and in situations where outside resources may be hired, identifying potential people becomes a bigger issue. Whatever the situation, a project manager needs to understand who is potentially available to work on her project. A project manager also keeps in mind the estimated resources needed when identifying the people who could potentially work on the project. This information can include factors such as:

- Work functions (may include job titles and range of responsibilities)
- Professional discipline (may include degrees and professional certifications)
- Skill level (may include experience and performance ratings)
- Physical location (may include willingness to relocate and travel)
- Organizational/administrative unit (may include costs and contractual issues)[1]

Once the required information is identified for the most likely pool of people, a project manager can compare the available people to the estimated resource needs to identify both gaps in specific skills that are needed and gaps in the number of people available versus those needed.

A **resource breakdown structure (RBS)** is defined as grouping all resources into main categories in level one and populating each main category with resources based on either function or skill level. Consistency in the division bases remains a crucial component of the structure. RBS is a very useful tool for developing a staff management plan. Like WBS, in-house resources of the project should be scrutinized and categorized by the creation of the RBS. It classifies and catalogs the resources that are required to meet project objectives. In many ways, the RBS claims advantages in improving communication, integration, planning, and estimating. Similar to the WBS, the RBS provides a consistent framework for dividing the resources into small units for planning, estimating, and managing. Exhibit 9.3 is an example of an RBS.

EXHIBIT 9.3

				UNIT	RATE
RESOURCE BREAKDOWN STRUCTURE EXAMPLE					
1.0	**Personnel**				
	1.1 Management				
		1.1.1	Project Manager	hour	$100.00
		1.1.2	Project Engineer	hour	$ 80.00
	1.2 Design				
		1.2.1	Civil Engineer	hour	$ 80.00
		1.2.2	HVAC Engineer	hour	$ 80.00
	1.3 Construction				
		1.3.1	Foreman	hour	$ 70.00
		1.3.2	Draftsman	hour	$ 50.00
		1.3.2	Electrician	hour	$ 60.00
		1.3.3	Carpenter	hour	$ 40.00
		1.3.4	Mason	hour	$ 35.00
2.0	**Materials**				
	2.1 Civil/Architectural				
		2.1.1	Lumber	each	$ 4.00
		2.1.2	Paint	gallon	$ 20.00
		2.1.3	Drywall $(0.5'' \times 4' \times 8')$	each	$ 8.50
	2.2 Electrical				
		2.2.1	Wire	foot	$ 0.75
		2.2.2	Switches	each	$ 4.75
		2.2.3	Lighting fixtures	each	$ 55.00

If it is clear that more and/or different people are needed, then the project manager needs to look elsewhere. That could mean other departments or divisions of the company, or it could mean looking outside the organization. A project manager, perhaps with help from the sponsor, continues the identification of potential resources until an adequate number and mix of potential people have been identified.

Key people should be identified as early as possible. The project core team is ideally identified and assigned soon enough to participate in chartering the project and defining the scope based on the client's requirements. Beyond the core team, it is helpful to get key subject matter experts (SMEs) on board early if possible, not only to help plan the project, but also to help develop the project culture and get it off to a quick start. People are more likely to be enthusiastic about performing work they helped to plan, and this motivation often comes in handy during difficult stretches in a project.

When possible, create options for people—try not to assign people who are unwilling participants. Experienced project managers understand that the better they take care of people who work with them on one project, the easier it is to recruit capable and enthusiastic people for their next project.

Project managers must make opportunities equally available to qualified candidates. First of all, project managers need to do this both from legal and ethical perspectives. Successful project managers also find many advantages in having diverse teams. It is beneficial to consider different perspectives in making decisions as it may help avoid major risks that a single perspective would not have uncovered. Further, diverse opinions help to consider more creative approaches. More stakeholders are effectively managed since a diverse group of project team members sometimes relate better to various stakeholders.

9-3b Determine Resource Availability

Once the potential resources have been identified and compared to the estimated resource needs, it is necessary to discover if the identified people are available and to secure their commitment. This is necessary even for internal projects because multiple projects often choose resources from the same resource pool. An RBS is very useful in identifying resources that are available for the project. A schedule is preliminary until needed resources are committed to the project.

In terms of resource availability, full- and part-time resources as well as internal and external resources may be available. If the new project is of higher priority than an existing project, resources that were already committed may be freed up. Regarding ability to commit at a very detailed level, some people have individual calendars with specific vacation or other unavailable times. Exhibit 9.4 shows how a consulting company determines resource availability.

EXHIBIT 9.4

MANAGING RESOURCE AVAILABILITY

Under pressure to complete the next phase of a new product being developed, a product development team urgently needed talented manpower. The existing team consisted of mostly technical talent (engineers, designers, and technicians). The product development team performed a review to find potential resources. Potential sources included:

- Existing staff
    - Within their department
    - Within their company but outside their department
- Staff misfit but talented
- Staff burned out and in need of a fresh challenge
- Temporary staff
- External supplier and customer staff

To the team's frustration, requests for additional staff were declined. To their surprise, upon further investigation, multiple opportunities developed:

- Product development staff working on separate projects had some idle time. Staff members thought to be dedicated to only a specific project were available for part-time support due to gaps in their schedule.
- Product development staff disinterested or "burned out" with their current project were eager for a different challenge.
- Underemployed staff members (at large) were found to be eager to step up to the plate. Existing projects did not keep them fully challenged.
- Some of the work required for completion of the next project phase was highly technical, requiring advanced knowledge, computer hardware, and very costly analysis software. To the team's delight, dedicated supplier staff was available to help with development. Advanced computer hardware and software, otherwise unreachable by the core team, were available if potential sales would justify the time investment. A balance was struck where the manufacturer and supplier effectively met each other's needs for mutual benefit. The product development team could overcome their technical hurdles, while the supplier could grow the business through new sales.

Source: Jeff Flynn, ILSCO Corporation.

9-3c Decide Timing Issues When Resourcing Projects

Projects, because of their temporary nature and unique outputs, have timing issues unlike those of ongoing operations. Early in the project, one timing issue is when to bring people on board. Bringing them on before they are needed can be costly. However, if the project manager takes a chance with an important resource and that person is not available, the schedule will probably be delayed. The general solution to the first timing issue is to assign key players as quickly as possible. This helps establish good project planning, effective project culture, and early project progress. Of course, a project manager may need to negotiate not just for who will be assigned to his project, but also when they will be assigned.

As members are brought on board, timing issues involve getting the team functioning effectively and keeping them motivated and on schedule. Team development is covered in Chapter 5.

Near the end of a project, timing issues include rewarding, recognizing, and releasing project team members. How are they rewarded? Under what circumstances are they released from the project, and what provision is made for them to be assigned to new work and/or promoted? These issues are addressed in Chapter 15.

The staffing management plan deals with these three issues: how the project planners identify potential people for the project, how they determine who is available to secure their services, and how to deal with timing issues of building up and then releasing the project workforce.

Estimating resource needs is done quite differently on agile projects. The budget is set at the people level and then the product is produced at the pace the team can maintain. This is a very different approach compared to estimating head count and then delivering a budget for functionality. So, again, we are determining how much investment goes into a particular product.

9-4 Project Team Composition Issues

Project teams are often composed of people from many sources—both within and outside a parent company. Several of these issues, such as who will be on the project and where each will be physically located, are best considered when selecting team members. These issues are introduced here, and the management of teams with these compositions is discussed in Chapter 5.

9-4a Cross-Functional Teams

Projects typically require inputs from multiple disciplines and, therefore, require cross-functional teams. When people representing different disciplines and skills work together, misunderstandings often arise. An engineer may be predisposed to look at an issue one way, while an accountant may look at the same issue a different way. This could be due to different thinking styles and perspectives based on education, experience, culture, and/or personality. A project manager may feel sometimes that she is a translator between various functions that are working on the project. It is useful for project managers to develop the ability to understand and speak effectively with various technical experts. The project manager may not be the expert, but she must understand the experts, communicate with them effectively, and have the experts trust her judgment.

9-4b Co-Located Teams

Another team issue involves *where* everyone physically performs work. Co-located teams are when the members are assigned work spaces near each other or in proximity to each other, such as being in the same building or in another building in the vicinity. Many minor decisions are made every day. Often, a person might not feel that something is important enough to create a document or make a phone call, but he or she might ask the person sitting in the next desk or someone they pass in the hall. Sometimes a person does not want to interrupt her thought process, but would casually ask a person at the next desk a question. Co-location helps to create these opportunities for easy communications, relationship building, and productivity improvement. On some projects, members of a supplier company and/or representatives from the customer may have a desk in the project workspace.

However, project managers and teams can often take advantage of many modern information and communication technologies for communicating remotely and from anywhere on the planet. These methods are used often, especially for larger decisions and global projects.

9-4c Virtual Teams

Due to advances in information and communication technologies, virtual teams are common and represent the opposite approach from co-location. Virtual teams are the norm for global projects and multinational organizations. However, co-located teams sometimes also communicate virtually. Members of virtual teams do not meet face to face very often. Sometimes a project requires the expertise of many people who are geographically dispersed, and it is impractical to have them all work in the same area. These teams require many forms of communications. Many people report that if they have met another person face to face even once, they feel they can relate better to that person. Therefore, even for geographically dispersed teams, it is common to bring people

together for project chartering or project kick-off sessions. Of course, some project managers travel frequently to allow for regularly scheduled face-to-face contact with important team members, customers, and suppliers.

9-4d Outsourcing

Project managers often are faced with the prospect of not finding the necessary talent within their organization. When that is the case, project managers often need to hire expertise from other organizations. This is discussed in Chapter 13. The author remembers one project where he worked for a European consulting firm that was hired to establish project management discipline at the IT headquarters of a large U.S. accounting firm. Although the accounting firm had fired its internal consultants and replaced them with those of the European company, it decided to keep one of its own consultants from each of its Boston and New York offices on the team for political reasons. This was an awkward arrangement as most of the work was outsourced, but two internal consultants were retained. This type of situation occurs often. Outsourcing can allow a project to bring in talent from anywhere in the world, but it can also lead to some tense situations.

Team composition is done at a high level and might include some database experience, some GUI experience, and so forth. Specific skills are not optimized for in this outsourcing model. People are assigned to a long-standing team and they figure out how to get the work done.

9-5 Assign a Resource to Each Activity

Once you have identified the people needed for the project, you will be able to easily get them if your project is a high priority for your organization or if you have already developed a reputation as a project manager with whom many people would like to work. However, it is not a common experience for other projects, and a project manager is unlikely to secure all the necessary highly qualified resources he needs. He is expected to negotiate to obtain the desired people.

Hopefully, the core team was assigned during the initiating stage and participated in chartering the project. Now is the time to ensure that the core team is complete and has no undue overlaps. It is also the time to assign team members to each activity. On small projects, most of these assignments are assigned to core team members. On larger projects, other individuals may be involved as subject matter experts. It is also helpful to specify exactly what each person is responsible for and what authority and responsibility that person has.

9-5a Show Resource Responsibilities on RACI Chart

A **responsibility assignment matrix (RAM)** is "a matrix that shows all the work packages and the resources assigned for various responsibilities regarding each work package." A **RACI chart** is a popular form of RAM that presents roles of key stakeholders and their roles defined as responsible (R), accountable (A), consult (C), and inform (I) for project activities in a matrix form. The first column on the RACI is usually the WBS coding of work packages and activities. The second column includes the names of the work packages and project activities that correspond to the WBS. The remaining columns each represent a person who is involved with the project. A partial RACI chart example is shown in Exhibit 9.5.

In Exhibit 9.5, many activities involve more than one person. For example, for the activity "conduct student surveys," Dan is responsible for completing the work, but the project manager is the one person who is accountable for the results. Dan needs to consult with team member Ben and the students and needs to inform everyone else. In a RACI chart, only one person should have primary accountability for any activity. If more than one person has accountability, it is too easy for them to blame each other when something goes wrong.

RACI charts are extremely useful for assigning activities to project core team members, subject matter experts, and the project manager. They are also useful in managing project communications. They go further than the original communications plan in that they identify every project activity and specify the exact involvement of each stakeholder.

9-5b Show Resource Assignments on Gantt Chart

Once it has been decided who will perform each activity, it is easy to show the assignments on a project schedule. For example, the responsible person for each activity for a portion of a space utilization project is listed right next to the activity in the Gantt chart schedule in Exhibit 9.6. Showing the responsibilities directly on the schedule is a simple, visual way to communicate responsibilities. For simplicity's sake, we are saying either of our two workers can do any activity and each is available full time for this project. In some projects, some people will spend a smaller percentage of their time on a project since they have other responsibilities, and because some activities may require only a small fraction of their time during the activity. Generally, people are available for work on a project less than 100 percent of their time for many reasons. Nevertheless, this demonstrates how to keep track of the time a person spends working on a project. Directions for how to construct each of the exhibits regarding resources in MS Project are given in Section 9.9.

9-5c Summarize Resource Responsibilities by Time Period with Histogram

Once it is clear who is responsible for each activity, it is time to understand how the multiple demands add up on each resource. Are any of the resources overloaded?

EXHIBIT 9.5

				PARTIAL RACI CHART				

WBS	WORK PACKAGES AND ACTIVITIES	SPON-SOR (LYNDA)	PROJECT MANAGER (JOE)	TEAM MEMBER (ALI)	TEAM MEMBER (BEN)	TEAM MEMBER (DAN)	STUDENTS	PARENTS
0.0	**High School Recruitment Plan**							
1.0	**Project Management**							
1.1	Manage Key Stake-holder Expectations	A	R	C	C	C	I	I
1.2	Develop Operating Methods		A	C	R	C		
1.3	Create Communi-cations Plan	I	A	R	R	R		
1.4	Control Progress	I	A	C	C	R		
2.0	**Information Assessment**							
2.1	Conduct Campus Visit	C	A	R	R	R	I	I
2.2	Conduct Students Surveys	I	A	I	C	R	C	I
2.3	Lead Group Discussion	I	A	C	C	C	C	
3.0	**Workshop/ Activities**							
3.1	Develop Ideas	C	A	C	C	R	C	
3.2	Analyze Possible Techniques	C	A	C	C	R	C	C
3.3	Compile Activities/ programs	C	A	C	C	R	C	I
3.4	Respond to Sponsor Feedback	R	A	I	I	I		
3.5	Reassess Activity Plan	C	A	C	C	C	I	I
3.6	Secure Sponsor Approval	R	A	I	I	I	I	I

To answer this question, the demands for each resource at each time period should be added. Note that a resource can be an individual worker such as *Mary*, or a resource could be a class of worker such as *carpenter*. Exhibit 9.7 shows the responsibilities for our resource, who we call *worker* for the various activities.

EXHIBIT 9.6

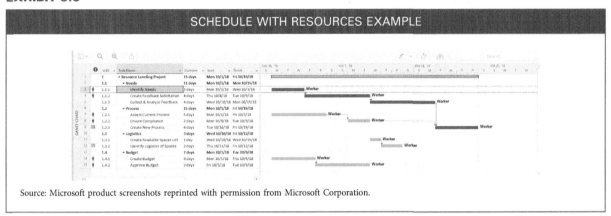

SCHEDULE WITH RESOURCES EXAMPLE

Source: Microsoft product screenshots reprinted with permission from Microsoft Corporation.

Note a couple of things regarding this resource histogram. First, we are using our two workers for whichever activities are needed, so the 100 percent capacity of the resource really means two people working full-time (80 hours per week). If we had only one person working 10 hours per week on our project, the 100 percent line would then be 10 hours per week. Second, we show the amount of work within the resource's capacity in blue and the amount of overload in red. You can see that the worker is overloaded by 50 percent for the first seven workdays. Another thing to note is that we use the same timescale for the resource histogram that we used on the Gantt chart, making it easy to see which activities contribute to the overload.

The team members on an agile project decide among themselves who will do each work activity. The ideal team member on an agile project is described as a generalized specialist, meaning that she can accomplish very specific things, but she can also be quite flexible when needed. Team members pick up the next-highest-priority story when they finish what they have been working on. If they need help, they ask; if they need to learn, they learn.

EXHIBIT 9.7

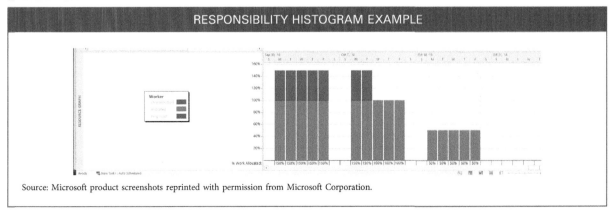

RESPONSIBILITY HISTOGRAM EXAMPLE

Source: Microsoft product screenshots reprinted with permission from Microsoft Corporation.

9-6 Dealing with Resource Overloads

Once it is obvious that a particular person has been overloaded at a given point in time, it is helpful to pinpoint exactly which activities are involved. One easy way to do that is to compare the resource histogram, such as the one in Exhibit 9.7, to the Gantt chart schedule, shown in Exhibit 9.6. It is desirable and helpful to view both charts together using the same timescale, as shown in Exhibit 9.8

Clearly, our workers were scheduled to perform three activities at the same time during the first seven workdays and are overloaded at that time. Project scheduling software helps to deal with resource overloads by pinpointing when the overloads occur for each worker and by identifying which activities that worker is assigned to perform. How should this be resolved? Software greatly assists in identifying and understanding the problem, but it takes management decisions to solve the problem.

9-6a Methods of Resolving Resource Overloads

Once a project manager understands who is overloaded and what activities are involved, she can employ many possible methods to rework the project schedule so the worker is not too overloaded. Some of these methods are as follows:

- Assign certain activities to other workers.
- Sometimes an activity can be split into two activities, with the first part being performed as scheduled and the last part delayed. This is often not an attractive strategy because many activities take more total time when split. It also takes people a little time to remember where they left off when they resume work. However, it would be productive if you split an activity into two activities and then execute them in parallel, but with different resources. We will discuss this later in this chapter.

EXHIBIT 9.8

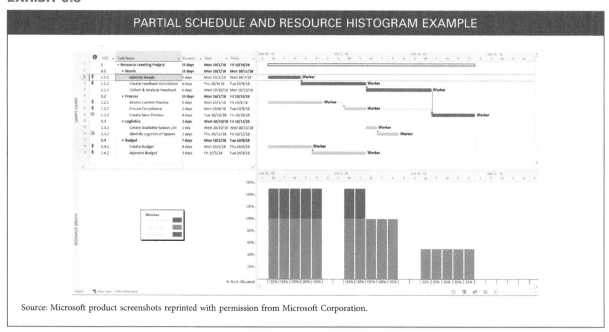

PARTIAL SCHEDULE AND RESOURCE HISTOGRAM EXAMPLE

Source: Microsoft product screenshots reprinted with permission from Microsoft Corporation.

- Another method of resolving the overloads is to reorder the activities. This may include questioning the logic that was used when creating the schedule. One means of reordering activities, *fast tracking*, is covered in Section 9.8 on compressing schedules.
- Sometimes when people understand how badly overloaded a resource is, they realize the need and decide to acquire or borrow additional resources.
- If a resource is impossibly overloaded, perhaps the project scope needs to be reduced or the schedule needs to be extended.
- If there is a severe overload and one of the above strategies needs to be employed, it usually makes sense to inform the sponsor. The project manager needs to understand who is overloaded, when the overload occurs, and what activities cause the overload. Good project managers will then be able to determine possible courses of action. However, it may be up to the sponsor to make the final decision on how to resolve the overload.
- It is often helpful to resource-level the overloaded person's schedule as described below.

Resource leveling is a project execution technique of adjusting the use of resources based on resource availability and the amount of float on activities to accomplish work as soon as possible, given the limited resource availability. The most common form of resource leveling is when activities are delayed so the person does not need to perform as many activities at the same time. Normally, noncritical activities are delayed by an amount no more than their slack period in the hope that the overloads can be resolved without extending the project schedule. However, if none of the alternative strategies discussed above is feasible and delaying the noncritical activities within their slack is not sufficient, the project schedule will slip. Essentially, this delay reduces peak demand and smoothens the period-to-period resource usage. An example follows, starting with Exhibit 9.9.

This is the same example we have been using, but we now put blocks around the amount of time needed for each activity. For example, Activity 1.1.1 (Identify Needs)

EXHIBIT 9.9

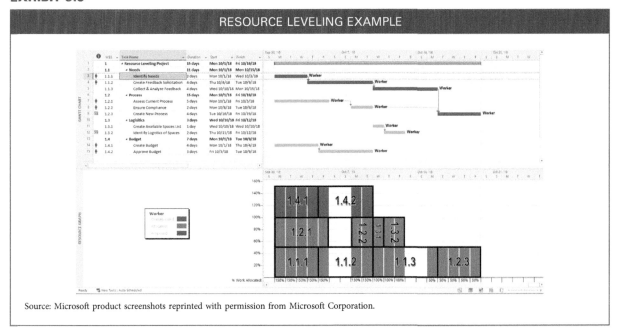

Source: Microsoft product screenshots reprinted with permission from Microsoft Corporation.

takes one worker four days and can start right away, so it is shown during the first four days. The easiest way to understand the work demands and be able to adjust the schedule within the limits of the available work time starts with creating a critical path schedule, as shown in the top portion of Exhibit 9.9. It is helpful to clearly mark the critical path and to "front load" the schedule—that is, to show every activity starting as soon as the activities that precede it are complete. Then, a resource histogram can be built for each person who may be overloaded. Start by placing the critical path activities on the bottom, because those activities need to be completed as scheduled or the entire project will be late. In our example, these critical path activities are 1.1.1, 1.1.2, 1.1.3, and 1.2.3. Next, place all of the noncritical path activities above the critical path activities at the earliest time they can be scheduled. In our example, these are 1.2.1, 1.2.2, 1.3.1, 1.3.2, 1.4.4, and 1.4.2. For example, all of the other activities have some float and can be delayed if needed. With the 100 percent line showing our workers' maximum available time, it is easy to see that they cannot complete everything as scheduled.

To visualize resource leveling, think about the game Tetris. In that game, one tries to fit shapes into spaces. That is exactly what we are doing here. If you can play Tetris, you can resource level. In our initial schedule, we have seven workdays of more work than our workers can handle, as shown by the blocks around activities 1.1.1 and 1.4.2. Note also that we are only working Monday through Friday, so weekends are shown as non-work days. The question is, can we level the demand for our workers without extending the project? In this example, you can see the critical activities on the bottom are still scheduled as originally planned and Activities 1.2.1 and 1.2.2 are both still scheduled as originally planned. All of the other activities have been delayed a bit without violating their constraints. Each has been delayed by no more than the amount of float. The result is that the project is still scheduled to be completed on time, but now instead of seven workdays of overload, there are just two days. Resource leveling often reduces an overload, but it does not always eliminate it entirely.

EXHIBIT 9.10

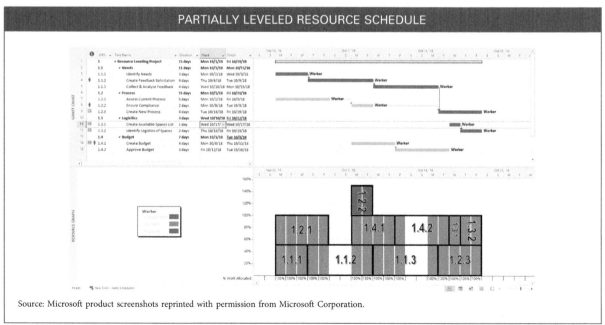

Source: Microsoft product screenshots reprinted with permission from Microsoft Corporation.

If the noncritical activities must be completed at the rate of effort shown in the original schedule, some of them may need to be assigned to another worker. Resource leveling can be as much art as science. The combination of the critical path schedule and resource histogram allows a project manager to understand who is overloaded, at what time, and by what specific activities. Then, the project manager seeks to move some of the noncritical activities within their slack to level the demand for that worker. If enough leveling can be done, the project can proceed as scheduled. If not, some activities must be accomplished by other means, the schedule will slip, or perhaps the scope will need to be reduced.

Resource overloads are not a serious problem in agile since the team is cross-functional and the team commits to get the work done in the iteration. They self-manage the conflicts.

9-7 Compress the Project Schedule

Once the schedule is prepared and loaded with resources, the project manager will know the project duration. Then he can compare it with what the sponsor or customer wants. If the expected time is too long, he will need to reduce the critical path to reduce the total completion time (remember that because the critical path is the longest, it dictates the total project duration). Sometimes, this adjustment must be done when project activities during the initial phase take longer to complete than planned. Also, when the scope of the project is increased but the customer requests the project completion as originally planned, the project manager needs to explore options for schedule compression.

9-7a Actions to Reduce the Critical Path

A variety of actions can be taken to reduce the critical path as follows:

- Reduce the project scope and/or quality.
- Overlap sequential activities using finish-to-finish (FF), start-to-start (SS), or start-to-finish (SF) relationships.
- Partially overlap sequential activities by using time leads.
- Increase the number of work hours per day or workdays per week.
- Schedule activities that are normally in sequence at the same time.
- Shorten activities by assigning more resources.
- Shorten activities that cost the least to speed up.
- Shorten the activity with the least probability of increasing project risk.

The first item, reducing scope and/or quality, normally requires permission from the sponsor and/or customer. Scope reductions are common. Sometimes, the original scope includes features that are nice to have but are not essential, which people are willing to give up when they understand the schedule impact. Quality reductions are far less common and are discussed in Chapter 12.

The next two items, time leads and alternative dependencies, are discussed in Chapter 8. The last four items, on the other hand, describe two well-known techniques to compress schedules, which are generally recognized categories or methods:

- Fast Tracking
- Crashing

Fast tracking is a method to expedite a project by executing activities at the same time that ordinarily would be done one after the other. In a design-to-production project, one way to accomplish this is to overlap the design and production phases. In other words, the design is not complete when construction starts, which is against the conventional approach of completing the design and then moving on to the construction phase. Research has shown that this can be an effective method of expediting.

Crashing is speeding up the critical path, often by adding additional resources or employing existing resources for longer hours and/or more days per week. While this may shorten a schedule, it does so at an additional cost, both in terms of the costs of labor (in terms of overtime pay) and also in lost productivity or efficiency.

One simple way to understand the differences between crashing and fast tracking is to determine what is given up in return for the faster schedule. Crashing almost always costs more money to speed up the schedule. Fast tracking almost always increases the risk to speed up the schedule. Both the approaches result in making the project more difficult to manage since either more activities take place at the same time and/or more activities have workers on overtime. Let us turn to the specifics of each.

9-7b Crashing

When crashing a project schedule, certain activities are performed at a faster-than-normal pace. This often requires overtime pay, but could also require extra charges for expedited deliveries, more expensive machinery, or employing more skilled people who can do the activity faster and better. When deciding which activities to speed up, two questions must be asked: First, which activities are on the critical path? Since the critical path determines how long the project takes, speeding up any activity not on the critical path makes no difference to project duration. Second, which critical path activity costs the least on a per-day basis to speed up? There is no sense in paying more than necessary. We will use the project in Exhibit 9.11 to illustrate crashing.

Note that the enumeration method was used to identify each path and its duration. Path ABEG at 25 days is the critical path. This example is in days, but it works equally well with weeks or any other unit of time. Also note that three small tables of information are included in Exhibit 9.10 to help us keep track of times and costs as we make the crashing decisions. The first table is the list of the paths with duration. Remember, we only want to crash activities on the critical path. Every time we reduce the length of an activity, we record the impact on the affected path(s). As you speed up activities on the critical path, you may find yourself left with a new critical path (or paths), which is now the longest in terms of duration.

The second information table lists each activity along with the normal time and cost (the expected time and cost if this activity is not crashed), the crash cost and time (the fastest the activity could be accomplished and the total cost incurred if it is crashed), and the crash cost per unit of time (in this example, per day). The activities that are on the critical path are identified by a triangle symbol. Two activities, A and C, have the same crash time as normal time. This means they cannot be crashed and are crossed out. We need the information in this table to identify which critical path activities cost the least to speed up.

We use the third small table to keep track of how long the project is, which activity (ies) we choose to speed up, and how much it costs. Using the normal time for all activities, the project is expected to take 25 days. We crash activities one day at a time. Note that path ADFG requires 24 days—only one day less than the critical path.

Activities A, B, E, and G are on the critical path. Activity A cannot be crashed. Some activities are impractical to speed up, even for extra cost. Activity B at $50 is the least expensive of the choices, so that is the one to crash first. Note that activity F only

EXHIBIT 9.11

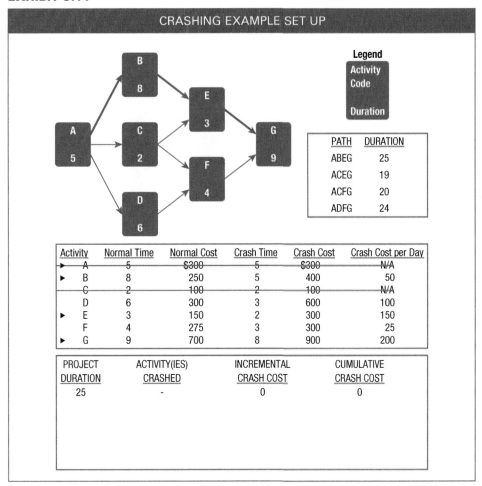

CRASHING EXAMPLE SET UP

PATH	DURATION
ABEG	25
ACEG	19
ACFG	20
ADFG	24

Activity	Normal Time	Normal Cost	Crash Time	Crash Cost	Crash Cost per Day
A	5	$300	5	$300	N/A
B	8	250	5	400	50
C	2	100	2	100	N/A
D	6	300	3	600	100
E	3	150	2	300	150
F	4	275	3	300	25
G	9	700	8	900	200

PROJECT DURATION	ACTIVITY(IES) CRASHED	INCREMENTAL CRASH COST	CUMULATIVE CRASH COST
25	-	0	0

costs $25 to speed up, but it is not on the critical path, so it is not chosen. Once we speed up B by one day, the resulting information is placed into the tables, as shown in Exhibit 9.12.

In the first table, path ABEG has been reduced to 24 days since B is now being crashed. In the second table, activity B is now shown as seven days since it has been crashed one day. In the third table, the duration is now 24 days, B is crashed, the incremental cost is $50, and so is the cumulative cost because that is the only activity crashed so far. Now there are two critical paths of 24 days each. The activities on the second critical path, ADFG, are identified by a circular symbol. To further crash the project, both paths need to be shortened. This could be accomplished by crashing one activity on each critical path, such as B or E on the first path and D or F on the second path. It could also be accomplished by crashing one activity that is on both paths, such as activity G. The least expensive of these alternatives is B and F for a total cost of $75. The results of this are shown in Exhibit 9.13.

After two rounds, both critical paths are 23 days. Note that path ACFG is also reduced, as F is on it and F was crashed. Since F cannot be crashed any further, a line is drawn through it. The cumulative cost of crashing the project two days is $125.

EXHIBIT 9.12

CRASHING EXAMPLE AFTER ONE ROUND

Legend
Activity
Code

Duration

PATH	DURATION
ABEG	2̶5̶ 24
ACEG	19
ACFG	20
ADFG	24

Activity	Normal Time	Normal Cost	Crash Time	Crash Cost	Crash Cost per Day
►• A̶	5̶	$̶3̶0̶0̶	5̶	$̶3̶0̶0̶	N̶/̶A̶
► B	8̶ 7	250	5	400	50
C̶	2̶	1̶0̶0̶	2̶	1̶0̶0̶	N̶/̶A̶
• D	6	300	3	600	100
► E	3	150	2	300	150
• F	4	275	3	300	25
►• G	9	700	8	900	200

PROJECT DURATION	ACTIVITY(IES) CRASHED	INCREMENTAL CRASH COST	CUMULATIVE CRASH COST
25	-	0	0
24	B	$50	$50

Exhibit 9.14 shows the choices of continuing to crash activities until it is no longer worthwhile. That is called an "all-crash" schedule. Note that even in that circumstance, activity D is not reduced the full amount possible since reducing it further would not make a difference in the length of the overall project.

Many questions can be answered with this information, such as the following:

- How fast can the project be completed?
- To crash the project one day, what activity would be crashed, and what would it cost?
- To crash the project two days, what activities would be crashed, and what would it cost in total?
- If there is a bonus of $125 per day for finishing early, what activities would be crashed, and how fast would the project be completed?
- If there is a bonus of $225 per day for finishing early, what activities would be crashed, and how fast would the project be completed?
- Crashing is called swarming in agile; actually, it comes from XP (Extreme Programming—one type of agile). It happens within the iteration when the team falls behind on meeting their commitment. They swarm on a problem to help the team get back on track. In this way, the planning for problems is handled by the team and done almost in real time.

AGILE

EXHIBIT 9.13

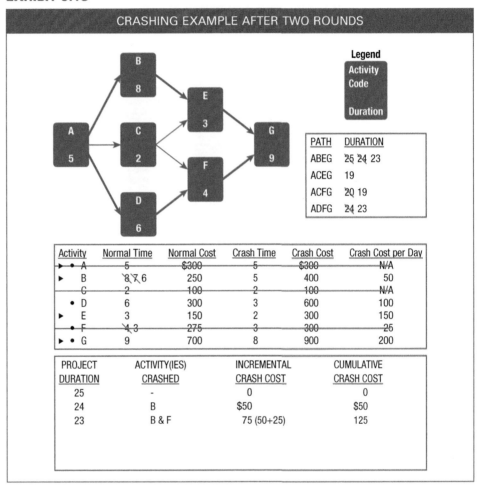

CRASHING EXAMPLE AFTER TWO ROUNDS

Legend

Activity
Code

Duration

PATH	DURATION
ABEG	25 24 23
ACEG	19
ACFG	20 19
ADFG	24 23

Activity	Normal Time	Normal Cost	Crash Time	Crash Cost	Crash Cost per Day
A	5	$300	5	$300	N/A
B	8 7 6	250	5	400	50
C	2	100	2	100	N/A
D	6	300	3	600	100
E	3	150	2	300	150
F	4 3	275	3	300	25
G	9	700	8	900	200

PROJECT DURATION	ACTIVITY(IES) CRASHED	INCREMENTAL CRASH COST	CUMULATIVE CRASH COST
25	-	0	0
24	B	$50	$50
23	B & F	75 (50+25)	125

9-7c Fast Tracking

Fast tracking occurs when activities that are normally performed in series (one after the other) are performed at the same time. In Exhibit 9.15, fast tracking could potentially be accomplished at several points. For example, while A is being done, B could also be performed. This certainly can speed things up as more things can be done at the same time. There is a risk, however. For example, if activity A is to design a part and activity B is to order material for the part, the normal routine would be to wait until the part is designed to be sure to order the correct materials. By performing both at the same time, there is a risk that the design will call for different materials than expected and the materials will need to be reordered. One strategy to gain benefits of fast tracking while attempting to control risk is to use a combination of alternate dependencies with time leads and lags to only partially overlap activities, as described in Chapter 8. Partial activity overlaps entail less risk than full overlaps. Another strategy is to overlap only a few activities so you can manage them closely. One would ordinarily look for long-duration activities on the critical path for this overlapping.

EXHIBIT 9.14

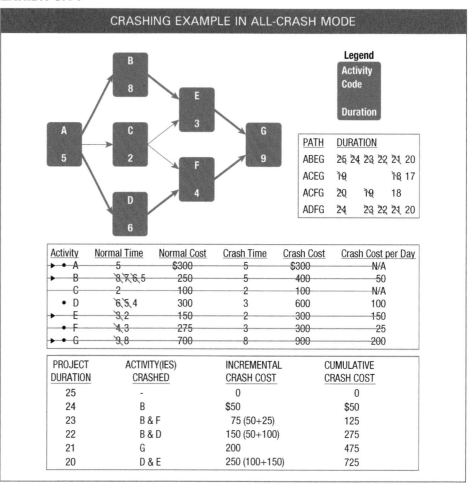

CRASHING EXAMPLE IN ALL-CRASH MODE

Legend
Activity Code

Duration

PATH	DURATION					
ABEG	25	24	23	22	21	20
ACEG	19				18	17
ACFG	20		19	18		
ADFG	24		23	22	21	20

Activity	Normal Time	Normal Cost	Crash Time	Crash Cost	Crash Cost per Day
A	5	$300	5	$300	N/A
B	8 7 6 5	250	5	400	50
C	2	100	2	100	N/A
D	6 5 4	300	3	600	100
E	3 2	150	2	300	150
F	4 3	275	3	300	25
G	9 8	700	8	900	200

PROJECT DURATION	ACTIVITY(IES) CRASHED	INCREMENTAL CRASH COST	CUMULATIVE CRASH COST
25	-	0	0
24	B	$50	$50
23	B & F	75 (50+25)	125
22	B & D	150 (50+100)	275
21	G	200	475
20	D & E	250 (100+150)	725

EXHIBIT 9.15

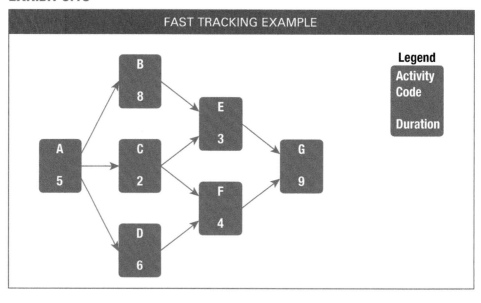

FAST TRACKING EXAMPLE

Legend
Activity Code

Duration

9-8 Alternative Scheduling Methods

Several alternative approaches are used in certain industries or certain situations to create project schedules, including critical chain, reverse phase, agile, auto/manual, and rolling wave scheduling. These approaches are not mutually exclusive—a person can use some of the logic from more than one of these methods on the same project.

9-8a Critical Chain Project Management (CCPM)

There are several problems with scheduling projects in many organizations that traditional critical path scheduling, even with resource leveling, does not always address satisfactorily. Some of these problems are as follows:

- Many people make conservative duration estimates. Often, people are punished for completing work late, so they give themselves plenty of time in their estimates.
- Durations of some activities vary greatly. The part of this variation that is due to specific possible events taking place can be managed by risk management techniques, as discussed in Chapter 11. The other part of the variation, known as common cause or random variation, sometimes is just difficult to accurately estimate.
- Many project team members tend to use all the time available to them. Instead of finishing early and getting the work to the next person, they keep fine-tuning their work and turn it in on time. It is partly due to a belief that if you complete the work early, it may be perceived as poor quality.
- To keep multiple projects moving, many workers are asked to multitask. Up to a point, multitasking is helpful in keeping multiple projects moving and keeping the workers stimulated. However, many people are asked to multitask far beyond that point; by not focusing on a limited number of things, they sometimes cannot give adequate attention to any.
- People in the project team delay the start of an activity (student syndrome), although there is no justifiable reason to postpone the activity.

One approach to address problems such as these is called critical chain project management (CCPM). CCPM is also sometimes known as the critical chain method. The **critical chain method** is an alternate scheduling technique that modifies project schedule by taking resource constraints into account. It makes use of principles of theory of constraints. This method allows the project team to place buffers on any project schedule path to manage constraints associated with limited resources and project uncertainties. Simply put, rather than calculate the critical path based upon predecessor–successor relationships alone, it also incorporates calculations on resource availability. Once the resource that is most in demand is identified, efforts are made to keep that resource appropriately busy on critical chain activities (those critical both because of the predecessor–successor relationships and because of resource shortages) but not overloaded. Other components of the CCPM system include the following:

- Avoiding multitasking
- Estimating aggressively how quickly each activity can be completed
- Putting a feeding buffer of time directly in front of critical chain activities to ensure they will not be delayed
- Putting the time normally reserved for the uncertainty in each individual activity at the end of the project as a total project buffer that the project manager can use as needed
- Finishing activities early if possible and passing the work on to the next worker

Proponents of critical chain say it is a major innovation that helps to overcome some of project management's most difficult scheduling and resourcing problems. Detractors say it is another approach that may work in certain circumstances. It requires a great deal of reeducation and communication on everyone's part to make it successful, and when resources are reallocated from the buffer to a task in trouble, more work may be created.

9-8b Reverse Phase Schedules

Another alternative scheduling method that is sometimes used in the construction industry is called a **reverse phase schedule** or Last Planner System. The reverse phase schedule is developed by the people closest to the work (often either the hands-on workers or the fore-persons who directly supervise work) by starting with the final project deliverables and continually asking what needs to be completed prior to starting work on this deliverable. As each activity is defined, its order is established, and the person proposing it verifies that their company has manpower to complete the activity as shown in the tentative schedule.

Using this method, the team systematically thinks from the end of the project toward the beginning. This is also a good practice to help ensure that all of the project deliverables and the list of activities are both complete because by working backward, missing deliverables and activities tend to be easier to identify. This approach is similar to developing a deliverable WBS—looking at the project from the client's or end user's perspective.

9-8c Rolling Wave Planning

The idea behind **rolling wave planning** is to plan the first part of the project in as much detail as needed and to plan later phases only at a high level. This allows the project team to focus on the near term without ignoring the longer term. It means the project team needs to plan progressively in more detail as information becomes available. Rolling wave planning is illustrated near the end of Chapter 10 by showing a dummy activity for a later project phase. The extreme of rolling wave planning is agile.

9-8d Agile Project Planning

The fundamental ideas behind agile project planning are to use a collaborative approach with the project team and other stakeholders heavily involved in planning; to recognize that while it may be difficult to scope the entire project at the outset, stakeholders do want to have a ballpark idea of total cost, schedule, and functionality before approving a project; and to understand that while uncontrolled change is bad, too strenuous change control often means valid emergent stakeholder wishes are not met. These ideas permeate the contemporary project management approach of this book. They have been introduced in several earlier chapters and identified with margin icons and are explained in more detail in the Project Management in Action example at the conclusion of this chapter.

9-8e Auto/Manual Scheduling

Microsoft Project now includes a feature called manual scheduling to enable users to more closely emulate MS Excel. This may be comforting for users who are more familiar with Excel than Project. When people are chartering a project and want to show the few milestones without committing to dates, manual scheduling may be a good starting point. Also, for projects with few predecessor–successor relationships, manual scheduling may sometimes be useful. However, for the majority of projects, the ability of MS Project to plan and track activities based upon logical relationships is useful and suggests manual scheduling is not enough.

9-9 Using MS Project for Resource Allocation

Up to this point in the Suburban Park Homes project tutorials, you have created a file with a project in MS Project, created the WBS for the project, defined the predecessor–successor relationships among the tasks, entered the expected duration for each task, and shown the critical path. This covers the first two ways in which a project schedule may be constrained—namely the logical order of tasks and the expected duration of each. Now it's time to consider a third way in which a project schedule can be constrained—the number of resources available when needed. Using MS Project to understand resource limitations includes five steps:

1. Defining resources
2. Setting up a resource calendar (as needed)
3. Assigning resources
4. Identifying overallocated resources
5. Dealing with overallocations

While MS Project is well suited to handle the first three, dealing with overallocations requires involvement of the project manager.

9-9a Step 1: Defining Resources

For a resource to be available to a project, it must first be described in MS Project's database. A resource may be a single unit, such as a person, or a resource may be a pool of like units, such as five crane trucks. Resources can include people, materials, supplies, facilities, or office spaces—anything necessary for the completion of a task.

To define your project's resources, do the following:

1. Click the **View Tab>>Resource Views Group>** click **Resource Sheet**
2. In the first blank row, enter the resource name in the **Resource Name** cell
3. In the **Initials** cell, enter the initials of the resource (if different from the auto-generated)
4. Click the **Max Units** cell and enter the resource's maximum availability

Max Units defines the availability of a resource for *project* work. Although the default is 100 percent, people resources are rarely 100 percent available (even if they are working full-time on a project), so availability will typically be something less than eight hours if that is the normal working day. For example, a person assigned primarily to one project may be available about six hours per day (or 75 percent of eight hours) for that project. If so, 75 percent would be the Max Units for that resource. Note in Exhibit 9.16 that Bruce is available up to 75 percent of his time for the project, while Jack is only available 25 percent of his time; none of the resources are available 100 percent of the time.

While MS Project offers many fields to define resources, **Resource Name** and **Max Units** are the only fields that require definition (if costs are to be modeled, then the **Std. Rate**, **Ovt. Rate**, **Cost/Use**, and **Accrue At** values must also be defined). Keep in mind that whatever names you assign to resources will be seen throughout your project data. Make sure resource names are relevant to your project team and other key stakeholders who may interact with your MS Project data. Update your Suburban Park Homes project to match Exhibit 9.16.

EXHIBIT 9.16

		Resource Name ▼	Type ▼	Material ▼	Initials ▼	Group ▼	Max. ▼	Std. Rate ▼	Ovt. Rate ▼	Cost/Use ▼	Accrue At ▼	Base ▼
1		Bruce	Work		BF		75%	$0.00/hr	$0.00/hr	$0.00	Prorated	Standard
2		Jack	Work		JC		25%	$0.00/hr	$0.00/hr	$0.00	Prorated	Standard
3		Brady	Work		BD		75%	$0.00/hr	$0.00/hr	$0.00	Prorated	Standard
4		Anniston	Work		AC		50%	$0.00/hr	$0.00/hr	$0.00	Prorated	Standard
5		Judah	Work		JS		50%	$0.00/hr	$0.00/hr	$0.00	Prorated	Standard
6		Liam	Work		LF		25%	$0.00/hr	$0.00/hr	$0.00	Prorated	Standard
7		Oliver	Work		OL		50%	$0.00/hr	$0.00/hr	$0.00	Prorated	Standard

DEFINING RESOURCES

RESOURCE SHEET

Source: Microsoft product screenshots reprinted with permission from Microsoft Corporation.

9-9b Step 2: Set Up a Resource Calendar

Resource calendars are used to block out vacation days and other *resource-specific* non-working days. Resource calendars inherit project-wide working day definitions from the project calendar (set up in the Chapter 8 tutorial) when the resource is first defined. Resource calendars are used by MS Project to determine when a resource assignment can be scheduled. If a task has no resource assignment, then the project calendar is used to determine task scheduling. To set nonworking days or hours for a specific resource:

1. Click the **View Tab>>Resource Sheet**
2. Double-click the row of the resource whose calendar needs revision to activate the Resource Information dialog (see Exhibit 9.17)
3. On the **General Tab**, confirm the correct resource is chosen in "Resource Name" field
4. Click **Change Working Time…**
5. Make revisions to resource working hours as needed as described in the Chapter 8 tutorial

Update your Suburban Park Homes project so Bruce's vacation dates match exhibit 9.17.

9-9c Step 3: Assigning Resources

During resource assignment, a project manager allocates one or more resources to an activity. MS Project then generates assignment information based on activity information, resource information, software settings, and any overrides. Assigning a resource to an activity with no existing resource assignments (using default settings) includes the following steps and is illustrated in Exhibit 9.18:

1. Click the **Task Tab>>View Group>>Gantt Chart**
2. Right-click in the **Start** column header >>**Insert Column>>** type **Work>>** press **Enter** to add the Work column
3. Click the **View Tab>>Split View Group>>** click **Details>>** choose **Task Form** in the drop-down list
4. Right-click the form in the lower pane and select **Resources and Predecessors**
5. In the upper pane, click the task row needing a resource assignment
6. Click the first blank row in the **Resource Name** column in the lower pane's form
7. Choose the resource name from the drop-down list
8. Repeat Steps 6 and 7 to add additional resources to the assignment list

EXHIBIT 9.17

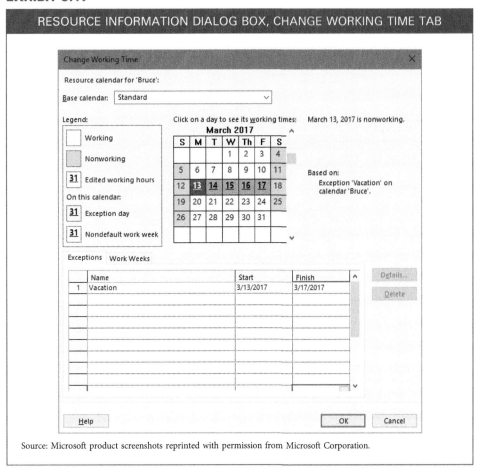

RESOURCE INFORMATION DIALOG BOX, CHANGE WORKING TIME TAB

Source: Microsoft product screenshots reprinted with permission from Microsoft Corporation.

9. Enter a **Units** value if the Max Units value is not correct for any assignment:
   i. If the Max Units entered in the Resource Sheet is correct, you can leave this blank and it will autofill
10. Click the **OK** button (no assignment is made until the OK button is clicked)
11. Note that Work is calculated and the activity duration value did not change

When creating resource assignments, keep the following in mind:

- **Duration** is the number of time units between the activity start and end (the default display value is in days spanning eight work hours).
- **Units** represents the availability of a resource for work each day.
- **Work** (hours assignment) is calculated by multiplying the Duration value (converted to hours) by the Units value.
- **Task type** determines which of three values (duration, units, and work) changes when one of the other two is modified (choices are Fixed Units, Fixed Duration, and Fixed Work).

(*Note:* For the purposes of the rest of this tutorial's screenshots, all resources will be assigned to multiple tasks in the Suburban Park Homes project. You can do the same, but your screenshots may not exactly match the ones in the rest of the tutorial).

EXHIBIT 9.18

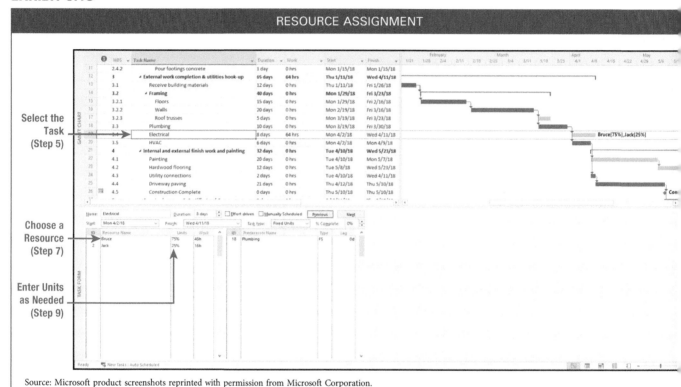

Source: Microsoft product screenshots reprinted with permission from Microsoft Corporation.

BASIC ASSIGNMENT CALCULATION WITH FIXED UNITS SELECTED (DEFAULT SETTINGS)   When an assignment is made, MS Project uses the Duration and Units values to calculate the number of hours a resource will work on the activity. In the Task Usage View (**View Tab>>Task Views>>Task Usage**), the Work field value in an activity row (e.g., *Electrical*) is the sum of the Work field values for resources assigned to that task. In the Resource Usage view (**View Tab>>Resource Views>>Resource Usage**), the Work field value in a resource row (e.g., *Bruce*) is the sum of the Work field values for tasks assigned to that resource. Here are some basic calculations that MS Project makes with resource assignments:

- **Activity with no prior resource assignments**
  - MS Project uses the Duration and Units values to calculate the assignment work value and sums the assignment work values into the activity Work field.
  - The assignment of a 100 percent available resource (Units = 100%) to a two-day-duration activity (eight-hour days) results in 16 hours of resource work across the two-day duration.
    - [(%resource available converted to decimal) × 8(hour workday)× 2(work days) × 1(number of resources)
      = 16(hours of the resource working on the task)]
  - An assignment of two 75 percent available resources (Units = 75%) results in 24 hours of work assigned across the two-day duration.
    - [.75(%resource available converted to decimal) × 8(hour workday)× 2(work days) × 2(number of resources)
      = 24(hours of the resource working on the task)]

- **Activity with one or more resources already assigned**
  - When yet another resource(s) is added, MS Project holds the activity Duration value constant and adjusts the activity Work value.
  - The *addition* of a 100 percent available resource (Units = 100%) to a two-day duration activity that already has a 100 percent available resource assigned results in 32 hours of activity work across the two-day duration activity, with each resource assigned 16 hours of assignment work.
- **Removal of resources works in reverse of the above**
  - Removal of the resource from an activity with one resource assigned results in zero task work.
  - Removal of one resource from an activity with two resources assigned results in the activity duration held constant, work calculated for the remaining resource assignment, and the activity work value the same as the assignment value.

MODIFYING AN ASSIGNMENT   After a resource assignment is made, MS Project maintains the relationships among the Duration, Units, and Work values. To see this behavior in action:

1. Ensure the **Task Form View** is activated in the lower pane
2. Select a task that has resources assigned to it in the upper Gantt chart pane
3. In the Task Form View options, set the "**Task type**" drop-down to **Fixed Units**
   - If you change the Duration and click OK, MS Project changes the assignment work and task work values.
   - If you change the Work and click OK, MS Project changes the duration and assignment work values.
   - If you change Units and click OK, MS Project holds the assignment work value constant and changes the task duration.
   - When modifying resource assignment, keep the following in mind:
   - If you don't like MS Project adjusting the Duration value as you add and remove resources assignments, an alternative is to switch the "Task type" setting in the Task Form View to **Fixed Work**.
     - Note: If desired, you can make this a *global change* in the MS Project for all new projects in two steps:
       - Click **File Tab>>Options>> Schedule>>** change "Default task type" to **Fixed Work**
     - Change "Scheduling options for this project" to **All New Projects**
   - Since trying different resource assignments on an activity makes it easy to lose the original duration value, you may find saving the original estimated duration value helpful:
   - Click the **Task Tab>>Gantt Chart>>** right-click **Duration column heading>> Insert column>>**enter **Duration 1**
   - Right-click the **Duration 1 heading>>Field Settings>>** enter **Estimated Duration** in the Title box to name the column
   - You can now enter the duration of any task you want to play with and not lose the original duration

9-9d Step 4: Finding Overallocated Resources

Resource overallocation usually occurs when a resource is assigned to two or more activities whose start and finish dates overlap, or if an assignment Units value is greater than the resource's Max Units value. The Gantt chart's "**Indicators**" field (first column with "i" icon) will display a red stick figure if an assigned resource is overallocated.

MS Project can find and understand resource overallocation to help project managers determine solutions; however, most solutions cannot be automatically implemented. For instance, you can level resources to resolve most overallocations by delaying the start of all but one of the conflicting activity assignments by clicking the **Resource Tab>>Level Resource**. While powerful and quick, it may produce an unacceptably lengthened schedule. This automated tool is just one of many solution options that the project manager must evaluate.

RESOURCE ALLOCATION VIEW   With slight modification, the Resource Allocation View is very helpful to find and analyze resource overallocation. The Detail Gantt marks the critical path (red) and graphically displays free slack following each activity (how much the activity can be delayed before creating a new, longer critical path). In addition, you also will be able to see the total assignment hours for each resource in the upper pane. To do so, make the following changes:

1. Click the **Task Tab>>View Group>>Gantt Chart** drop-down menu >>click **More Views...**
2. On the **More Views dialog**>> scroll to **Resource Allocation**>> click **Edit**
3. On the **View Definition dialog**>> click **Details Pane** drop-down >> choose **Detail Gantt**
4. Click the **Show in menu** checkbox
5. Click **OK>>** click **Apply**
6. In the upper pane, right-click the **Work column header>>Insert Column**
7. Enter **Max Units>>** click **Enter**
8. In the lower pane, right-click the **Leveling Delay column header>>Insert Column**
9. Enter **Work>>** click **Enter**
10. In the upper pane, click the empty box to the left of the Indicators icon to select all rows
11. Click the **View Tab>>Data Group>>Outline>>** click **Hide Subtasks**

The results of these steps can be seen in Exhibit 9.19.

The **Resource Allocation View** is a combination view with the Resource Usage view in the upper pane and the Detail Gantt view in the lower pane. The timescale in the upper pane is synchronized with the Gantt graphic in the lower pane, and adjusting the zoom affects both panes. Once you have adjusted settings in the steps above, you can quickly reach this view by clicking the **View Tab>>Resource Views Group>>Resource Usage>>Resource Allocation**.

The Gantt bars in the lower pane represent the duration of the work hours displayed in the upper pane. Selecting a resource in the upper pane's table displays the assignments of that resource in the lower pane. If the resource data in the upper pane's table is red, that resource is overallocated (you will also see a red stick figure in the Indicators column). In Exhibit 9.19, Bruce, Liam, and Oliver are all overallocated.

A straightforward method to analyze overallocated resources in this view is as follows:

1. Set the timescale to the start of the schedule.
2. Slowly scroll the timescale toward the end of the schedule.
3. Analyze each instance of cell values displayed in red for cause and severity.

9-9e Step 5: Dealing with Overallocations

Once overallocations are identified, the project manager has many options. In this tutorial, MS Project is a tool only. It is helpful in identifying overallocations, but the project manager is responsible for deciding what to do with them. Remember, each action will have associated risks, and often one change can "break" something down the line, so be sure to protect your critical path. Below are a few choices:

EXHIBIT 9.19

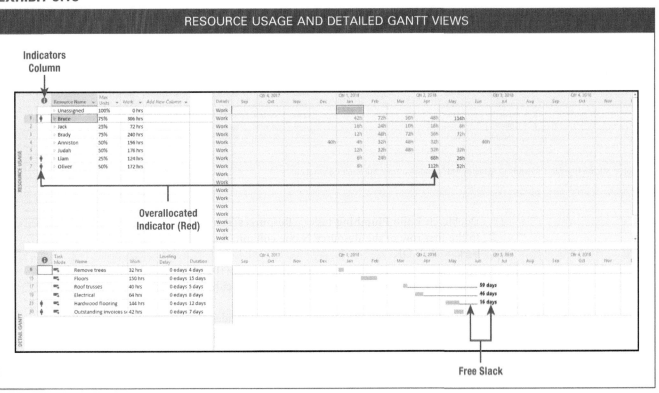

RESOURCE USAGE AND DETAILED GANTT VIEWS

- Replace an overallocated resource with one that has time for the assignment.
- Reduce the Units assignment, extending the activity duration (this could affect the finish date of the project).
- Lessen the scope of one or more activities.
- Ignore the overload if the resource impact is temporary.
- Try **Resource Tab>>Level Group>>Level Resource** or **Level All** and see what happens to your timeline (remember, the Undo command is **Ctrl-Z**).

9-9f Crashing a Critical Path Activity

If your overall project duration needs to be shortened, one way to accomplish it is to "crash" an activity on the critical path. Crashing is simply adding resources to a task in order to shorten the time it takes to complete it.

For this example, we will add three Plumbers to our Resource Sheet and then add them to the Plumbing task to crash the activity and shorten the overall project length:

1. Click the **View Tab>>Split View>>** uncheck **Details**
2. Click the **View Tab>>Resource Sheet**
3. In the next available row, type "**Plumbers**" in the **Resource Name** column
4. In the **Initials** cell, enter the initials of the resource (if different from the auto-generated)
5. Click the **Max Units** cell and enter the resource's maximum availability as 300% (This means the project has three plumbers who can work 100% of the time on the project.)
6. Your Resource Sheet should now look like Exhibit 9.20
7. Click the **View Tab>>Task Views>>Gantt Chart** (Readjust timescale and column views as needed; ensure you can see the Start and Finish columns.)

EXHIBIT 9.20

DEFINING RESOURCES

	ⓘ	Resource Name	Type	Material	Initials	Group	Max.	Std. Rate	Ovt. Rate	Cost/Use	Accrue At	Base
1	👤	Bruce	Work		BF		75%	$0.00/hr	$0.00/hr	$0.00	Prorated	Standard
2	👤	Jack	Work		JC		25%	$0.00/hr	$0.00/hr	$0.00	Prorated	Standard
3		Brady	Work		BD		75%	$0.00/hr	$0.00/hr	$0.00	Prorated	Standard
4		Anniston	Work		AC		50%	$0.00/hr	$0.00/hr	$0.00	Prorated	Standard
5		Judah	Work		JS		50%	$0.00/hr	$0.00/hr	$0.00	Prorated	Standard
6	👤	Liam	Work		LF		25%	$0.00/hr	$0.00/hr	$0.00	Prorated	Standard
7	👤	Oliver	Work		OL		50%	$0.00/hr	$0.00/hr	$0.00	Prorated	Standard
8		Plumbers	Work		P		300%	$0.00/hr	$0.00/hr	$0.00	Prorated	Standard

Source: Microsoft product screenshots reprinted with permission from Microsoft Corporation.

8. Double-click the **Plumbing** task>> **Resources Tab**
9. In the first row of the Resource Name column, drop-down menu and choose **Plumbers**>> click **OK**
10. This assigns one plumber to work on this task (100%)
11. You will notice work hours are added, but neither the critical path nor project's duration has changed
    Now assume that the project manager decides the Plumbing task needs to be completed more quickly, and the decision to crash that task is made.
12. Double-click on the **Plumbing** task >>**Resources Tab** again
13. Change the Units from 100% to 300% (This will assign three plumbers to the task.)
14. Click **OK** (See Exhibit 9.21.)
15. You will now see that the critical path Gantt bar has shortened, the duration of the task has shortened, and the overall project finish date has shifted back (because Plumbing was a critical path activity).
16. Good job! You just got the plumbing done sooner!

EXHIBIT 9.21

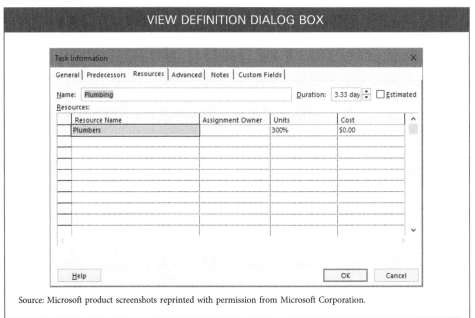

VIEW DEFINITION DIALOG BOX

Source: Microsoft product screenshots reprinted with permission from Microsoft Corporation.

Remember that you only want to crash tasks on the critical path because they will be the only tasks to shorten the overall project. Also keep in mind that crashing is simply one option available to the project manager. Sometimes throwing more resources at a task isn't always the best option. For simplicity's sake, we added more plumbers in this example. However, sometimes adding more people resources can actually end up increasing the time it takes to complete a task. Not every resource may be as qualified or up to speed as the next, and time-consuming spin up or training might be required before they can be effective helpers on a task. Also as noted earlier, rarely can a resource be available 100 percent of the time. When an activity is crashed, the project manager still has to worry about overallocation of resources and the consequences of removing resources from one task to put them on another.

PMP/CAPM Study Ideas

Keep in mind how resourcing a project ties in to the other project work you have completed so far. When resourcing your project, a good starting place is to take the WBS you created and use it to identify resources needed (human and other). Make sure you are very familiar with all steps of *Plan Resource Management,* as well as two important deliverables: the staffing management plan and resource breakdown structure (RBS).

As is the case with scheduling and budgeting, resourcing projects is a hands-on skill, and you should anticipate that the majority of resource questions you may see will be exercises, such as those given above. Since the critical path determines the project's duration, you will need to know all things pertaining to it—especially how to calculate it and how, if required, to reduce the critical path (fast tracking or crashing).

Summary

Resourcing projects goes hand in hand with scheduling (Chapter 8) and budgeting (Chapter 10). To ensure that adequate human and other resources are assigned to a project, first the project manager needs to look at the listed activities and estimate the resources needed to perform each. Potential resources need to be identified, and their availability needs to be confirmed. The project manager may need to negotiate to secure the services of the needed people. Usually, some people assigned to the project are ready to go, while others need training and/or mentoring. Project teams sometimes need to rely on co-located and/or outsourced team members.

Several tools are useful in identifying and scheduling people. A human resource management plan with role descriptions and a staffing management plan as components helps the team plan. Resource assignments are often posted directly on a Gantt chart schedule. RACI charts are matrices that depict work activities on the vertical scale (often in the form of a WBS) and the various people who are involved on the horizontal scale. Work responsibilities are shown by code in the cells. Once workers have been assigned, responsibility histograms can be developed for each worker to determine whether he or she is overloaded at any point.

The combination of the critical path schedule with resource assignments and the resource histogram allows project planners to determine who is overloaded, at what time, and by what activities. Resource leveling is the method of using this information to reduce the peak demands for workers by postponing some of the noncritical activities within the amount of available slack. Sometimes this solves the problem. If not, some work might be assigned to a different person, the schedule might be delayed, the project scope might be reduced, and/or other methods might be employed. Often, the sponsor will want to be involved in making these decisions.

Once the project schedule is established and resources are assigned, it sometimes appears that the hoped-for completion date is not attainable. In these cases, it is common to look for methods of accelerating (or compressing) the project schedule. One frequently used method is crashing, in which a decision is made to pay extra money (often in the form of overtime pay) to speed up certain activities on the critical path. Another frequently used method is fast tracking, whereby activities that are normally conducted in sequence are either overlapped or performed in parallel. Fast tracking can lead to faster schedules. However, the risk is increased because the activity that normally is a successor depends on the output of its predecessor, and if that output is not as expected, the successor activity may need to be reworked.

Several alternative methods of scheduling can be used alone or combined with traditional scheduling and resourcing. These methods include critical chain, reverse phase, rolling wave, agile, and auto/manual scheduling. Experienced project managers attempt to use the best ideas from several of these alternative approaches.

Project scheduling software such as Microsoft Project is extremely useful when determining the resources for a project. This software helps pinpoint exactly when each worker is needed, for what activity, and where there are overloads. Despite the power of these scheduling systems, they do not make all of the decisions for a project. The project manager needs to understand the output of the software and be able to ask a number of what-if questions. Ultimately, the project manager needs to make the decisions—often in conjunction with the sponsor.

Key Terms Consistent with PMI Standards and Guides

estimate activity resources, 290
plan resource management, 290
staffing management plan, 290
resource breakdown structure, 291
responsibility assignment matrix, 297
RACI chart, 297

resource leveling, 301
fast tracking, 303
crashing, 304
critical chain method, 309
reverse phase schedule, 310
rolling wave planning, 311

Chapter Review Questions

1. In addition to technical skills, what other skills must a project manager have in order to successfully resource a project?
2. Why is it important to involve workers in the planning phase of a project when possible?
3. What does a staffing management plan address?
4. What are the three "r" activities that take place near the end of a project, regarding team members and timing issues?
5. What does RAM stand for, and what is its purpose?
6. What does each column of a RACI chart depict?
7. Why is it necessary to have only one person assigned primary accountability for an activity?
8. What can a project manager use to help determine if workers are overloaded?

9. Whom should the project manager consult when performing resource leveling?
10. What will happen to a project's schedule if an activity on the critical path is delayed?
11. In regard to resource leveling, why are noncritical path activities generally the first to be delayed?
12. What are two techniques used to compress a project schedule?
13. When crashing a project, what two criteria are considered when deciding which activities to speed up?
14. In addition to predecessor–successor relationships, what does critical chain project management (CCPM) factor into its scheduling?
15. Who develops the schedule when using Reverse Phase Scheduling?

Discussion Questions

1. Identify three examples of when a project manager uses technical skills and three examples of when she uses behavioral skills.
2. Compare a project you've worked on that was limited mostly by activities with another project you've worked on that was limited mostly by resources. Which did you find more challenging? Why?
3. List at least four factors a project manager should consider when identifying individuals to work on a project. Why is each important?

4. Describe a potential timing issue that can occur early in a project and a potential timing issue that can occur at the end of a project. How would you address each of these issues in your project?
5. Describe two ways a project manager can resolve resource overloads. Under what circumstances should each be used?
6. Describe how to perform resource leveling.
7. Give an example of what is given up in a project when it is crashed and when it is fast-tracked and an appropriate time to use each.

8. Cite problems with traditional project scheduling techniques and why some organizations might opt to use critical chain project management.

9. List three common problems that can occur when traditional critical path scheduling is used. How would you address each?

PMBOK® *Guide* Questions

1. Crashing the following activity chains would save time and cost extra money as follows:

   AGJQ—2 days $300

   CDIL—3 days $400

   Which sequence of activities would you, as a project manager, choose to crash?
   a. AGJQ
   b. CDIL
   c. neither AGJQ nor CDIL
   d. depends on which, if either, is on the critical path

2. A _____ addresses when and how project team members will be acquired and how long they will be needed.
   a. resource histogram
   b. staffing management plan
   c. project organization chart
   d. responsibility matrix

3. The process "Estimate Activity Resources" involves identification of the _____ and _____ of resources required for each activity within a work package.
   a. types; quantities
   b. costs; quantities
   c. names; locations
   d. types; costs

4. Recognition and rewards _____ .
   a. should be used on rare occasions, for exceptional performance
   b. are the responsibility of the functional manager
   c. should be included in the project's Staffing Management Plan
   d. are perquisites reserved for the project manager and project sponsor

5. A "schedule compression technique in which activities or phases normally done in sequence are performed in parallel for at least a portion of their duration" is referred to as _____ .
   a. critical path
   b. critical chain
   c. crashing
   d. fast tracking

10. As a project manager, how can you ensure that your activity and resource estimates are as accurate as possible?

11. Give an example of a project on which you might expect to see Reverse Phase Scheduling.

6. In RACI chart, the single individual who will have to provide an explanation if something goes wrong is indicated with a(n) _____ .
   a. R—Responsible
   b. A—Accountable
   c. C—Consult
   d. I—Inform

7. The "process of identifying and documenting project roles, responsibilities, required skills, reporting relationships, and creating a staffing management plan" is called _____ .
   a. Identify Stakeholders
   b. Create Stakeholder Management Strategy
   c. Plan Resource Management
   d. Acquire Project Team

8. After creating a Staffing Management Plan, the project manager and team might create a chart that provides a visual representation of project resource needs by type of resource and time period (weeks, months, etc.) This chart is called a(n) _____ .
   a. project Gantt chart
   b. resource histogram
   c. network diagram
   d. organization chart

9. An iterative planning technique where "the work to be accomplished in the near term is planned in detail, while the work in the future is planned at a higher level" is referred to as _____ .
   a. three-point estimating
   b. rolling wave planning
   c. parametric estimating
   d. analogous estimating

10. When the demand for resources is greater than the available supply, the project manager can use a scheduling method that adjusts the start and finish dates of activities in order to address resource limits or constraints. This technique is called _____ .
    a. fast tracking
    b. crashing
    c. resource leveling
    d. critical path method

Exercises

1. A certain project has three activities on its critical path. Activity A's normal completion time is five days. It can be crashed to three days at a cost of $500. Activity B's normal completion time is six days, and it can be crashed to four days at a cost of $50. Activity C's normal completion time is eight days. It can be crashed to three days at a cost of $1,000. Which activity should the project manager crash and by how many days? How much will it cost?

2. Using the data below, create the project schedule using normal times. Determine the order in which you would crash the project one day, two days, and so on until it is in an all-crash mode. Identify how much it would cost for each day you crash the schedule.

Activity	Predecessor	Normal Time	Normal Cost	Crash Time	Crash Cost	Crash Cost per Day
A	–	12	200	9	350	
B	A	8	300	8	300	
C	A	9	250	7	450	
D	B	6	400	5	600	
E	B, C	5	150	4	225	
F	C	10	500	9	650	
G	D, E, F	8	400	6	900	

3. Using the data below, create the project schedule using normal times. Determine the order in which you would crash the project one day, two days, and so on until it is in an all-crash mode. Identify how much it would cost for each day you crash the schedule.

Activity	Predecessor	Normal Time	Normal Cost	Crash Time	Crash Cost	Crash Cost per Day
A	B	5	200	4	350	
B		8	220	8	220	
C	B	6	250	4	650	
D	A	9	500	5	600	
E	A, C	10	150	9	500	
F	E	10	500	9	650	
G	D, F	8	400	6	900	

4. Using the data below, create the project schedule in MS Project. Be sure to use both the predecessor relationships and the resource assignments. Use a split screen to show both the Gantt chart with critical path and resource assignments with overloads.

WBS	Activity	Immediate Predecessor	Duration in Weeks	Resource
1	**Operational definition**			
1.1	Research literature		3	Becky
1.2	Identify and define terms	1.1	1	Ann

WBS	Activity	Immediate Predecessor	Duration in Weeks	Resource
1.3	Obtain approval of definition	1.2	2	Clive
2	**Target Selection**			
2.1	Solicit partners for pilot		2	Ann
2.2	Hold brainstorming meeting	2.1	2	Becky
2.3	Identify characteristics of targets	2.2, 3.1	1	Ann
2.4	Obtain approval of partners	2.3, 1.2, 3.4	1	Clive
3	**Question set**			
3.1	Identify process group members		2	Clive
3.2	Develop question set	2.3	4	Ann
3.3	Prototype and validate question set	3.2	3	Becky
3.4	Add partners	3.1, 2.1	3	Becky
4	**Pilot process**			
4.1	Schedule with target audience	2.4	2	Becky
4.2	Conduct beta test	3.4, 2.4	2	Clive
4.3	Process feedback from target audience	4.2	2	Ann
4.4	Conduct pilot	4.3	2	Clive
4.5	Analyze results	4.4	2	Clive

5. Using the data below, create the project schedule in MS Project. Be sure to use both the predecessor relationships and the resource assignments. Use a split screen to show both the Gantt chart with critical path and resource assignments with overloads.

	Activity	Immediate Predecessor	Duration in Days	Resource
A	Evaluate freezers		2	Alcides
B	Chart temperatures		6	Joan
C	Review service record		2	Alcides
D	Consult with HVAC engineer	A, B, C	3	Alcides
E	Develop construction plan	D	10	Joan
F	Complete IC assignment	E	2	Alcides
G	Complete ROI analysis	E	5	Joan
H	Conduct regulatory review	E	4	Joan
I	Obtain construction approval	F, G, H	2	Alcides

SUBURBAN HOMES CONSTRUCTION PROJECT

Refer to the project charter from Chapter 3, WBS in Chapter 7, and the project schedule in Chapter 8. The initial scope as identified in the project charter is mentioned below:

Building a single-family, partially custom-designed home as required by Mrs. and Mr. John Thomas on Strath Dr., Alpharetta, Georgia. The single-family home will have the following features:

- 3,200 square-feet home with 4 bedrooms and 2.5 bathrooms
- Flooring—hard wood in the first floor, tiles in the kitchen and bathrooms, carpet in bedrooms
- Granite kitchen countertops, GE appliances in the kitchen
- 3-car garage and external landscaping
- Ceiling—10' in first floor and vaulted 9' ceilings in bedrooms

After developing the WBS and the project schedule using the CPM method, you were asked to identify resources for all the activities identified in the schedule. To begin, you need to identify all the available resources in-house and resources required externally. One of the promising practices is to develop a resource breakdown structure (RBS). Once the RBS is completely developed, please perform the following tasks:

Tasks to Complete

- Identify resources (people, materials, equipment, etc.) required for each element in the schedule.
- Analyze resource constraints (the same resource may be required for two or more activities at the same time) based on resource availability.
- Develop a responsibility assignment matrix (RAM) and RACI table.
- Develop a resource histogram for the entire project.
- Identify resource overloads and propose resolutions to address them by resource leveling.
- Estimate time required to complete each work element by considering resource constraints.
- If required, calculate the project schedule again. Compute forward pass and backward pass to determine project duration. Determine the critical path for the project.
- If the new project duration exceeds the commitment deadline, develop schedule-compression strategies to complete the project on time.
- Develop a resource calendar.
- As a part of this exercise, update the WBS and project schedule, if required.

CASA DE PAZ DEVELOPMENT PROJECT

Based on the scope and the schedule, the team discussed how this would be very challenging. Members of the team are volunteers, and most work full time and have family commitments. Given both this challenge and the partnerships Casa de Paz has started with various organizations, what suggestions do you have for reducing the risk of the project being late because the workers who are volunteers are overloaded? Note that because this project is being conducted in an agile fashion, rather than look at details of exactly who is scheduled to perform a particular activity at a particular time, the planners use judgment to "eyeball" the amount of work needed and then determine if more resources are needed, if the project schedule can be delayed, or if less work can be completed and the project still be finished adequately.

Semester Project Instructions

For your example project, create the following:

1. A Human Resource Management plan, including role descriptions and staffing management plan
2. RACI chart
3. Gantt chart with resource assignments
4. Histogram of demands on each key participant's time
5. Plan for resolving resource overloads

PROJECT MANAGEMENT *IN ACTION*

Managing Software Development with Agile Methods and Scrum

The Scrum process was described for use in agile software development by Ken Schwaber and Mike Beedle. Exhibit 9.22 illustrates the Scrum process.

In practice, many agile methods and variations are utilized, but they all share a basis in iterative development, extensive verbal communication, team interaction, and the reduction of resource-intensive intermediate products. Agile software development methods attempt to minimize risk via short time boxes called iterations or *Sprints*. Typically, the time boxes are from one to a maximum of four weeks and usually include numerous subtasks. Each Sprint is frequently like a software development project in and of itself and includes planning, requirements analysis, design, coding, testing, documentation, and validation of deliverables. Some iterations may generate new

products or capabilities, but most are integrated into larger groups to be released as new products. Scalability is one of the benefits of the approach, and another is the opportunity to reevaluate priorities in an incremental fashion. This technique, therefore, can be used effectively for software maintenance and enhancements, as well as new product development.

Scrum is facilitated by a *scrum master*, who organizes the project like any good project manager. This person has the primary task of removing impediments to the ability of the team to deliver the Sprint goal and project objectives. The scrum master is not necessarily the leader of the team in the traditional formal sense (as the teams are self-organizing), but acts as a productivity buffer between the team and any destabilizing influences. This encourages the emergence of

EXHIBIT 9.22

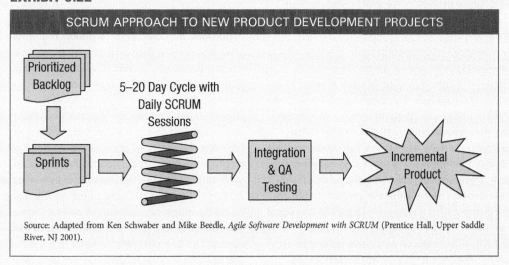

Source: Adapted from Ken Schwaber and Mike Beedle, *Agile Software Development with SCRUM* (Prentice Hall, Upper Saddle River, NJ 2001).

informal leadership and team cohesiveness. Scrum includes the following elements, which define the process:

- A dynamic backlog of prioritized work to be accomplished
- The use of short iterations or Sprints
- A brief daily meeting or Scrum session during which progress is explained, upcoming work is described, and impediments are identified and, if possible, immediately resolved
- A brief planning session during which the prioritized backlog of items for the Sprint is identified and further defined by the team
- A brief retrospective during which all team members reflect about the past Sprint and any design or other influences on future Sprints or objectives

This approach keeps everyone on the team engaged and focused. It works very well when everyone is co-located to facilitate verbal communications, but has been shown to work well in virtual teams or geographically dispersed teams as well. The emphasis on verbal communications has proven to be particularly useful for international teams where written communications alone may not be clearly understood. The use of video conferencing and virtual development environments is also beneficial in these situations.

Agile software development teams include all resources necessary to accomplish the tasks and finish the software product. This includes designers, architects, analysts, testers, technical writers, managers, and customers (the people who define the final product).

The primary metric for progress in this environment is working software based on the scope as identified in the Sprints. Schedules and other resources are based on accomplishing the Sprints and removing impediments. With their preference for verbal communications, agile methods produce little written documentation relative to other methods. That is not to say that the team produces no documentation, as it is important to have requirements, design, and other aspects of the software product documented to facilitate maintenance and support and in some cases to meet industry regulatory compliance requirements. This reduced emphasis on documentation has resulted in criticism of agile methods as

undisciplined or, as some have called it, "cowboy coding." As a rule, this does not seem to be the case in practice because, if properly implemented, the requirements are documented in the prioritized backlog; the design is documented in the Sprints and Scrum sessions; and the testing, user, and technical documents complete the documentation set. It is important to note that the use of a scribe during Scrum sessions, planning, or retrospective sessions is vital to capture what is transpiring, since the sessions tend to be short and intense by nature.

Many companies have now embraced the agile methods to reduce development time, foster innovation, and reduce development risk. One example is a Seattle-based company that has utilized Scrum to shorten development cycle time and improve quality for software deliveries to its clients. It uses Sprints to group similar requirements and provide a two-week window of work for its developers. Daily Scrum sessions help it stay focused and deal immediately with impediments. This works ideally, in that it keeps task scope to a minimum for the developers, and everyone on the team is aware of what is transpiring throughout the development process. This has shortened development time and led to more rapid release of products and enhancements to the clients, thus reducing development costs and improving margins.

Another example is an Ohio company that utilizes agile methods and Scrum for software development for clients in the highly regulated pharmaceutical, biotech, and medical device industries. A recent software system developed to be used in manufacturing data acquisition and control for products requiring complete traceability, including raw materials and processes, was designed and developed in five months to beta delivery. The software will ultimately track and control all of the company's production when fully implemented. The system was put into a pilot manufacturing line. It was working within thirty minutes of software installation and processed product through the pilot production facility the same day without a glitch. The system was delivered essentially bug free. This was unheard of previously using traditional development methods and would have taken a year or more to get to beta delivery, with many more issues. The company accounts for this success due to the use of the agile process, Scrum, and thorough quality testing. The requirements in this regulated environment were developed in a traditional manner; however, once the requirements were approved by the client management, the Scrum approach was used, which represented a departure from the traditional waterfall approach. Each module of the system was developed separately using the Scrum approach by focusing on developing a few design elements at a time rather than trying to focus on the entire system design at once. In this way, the development team could focus and accomplish a few things at a time and leave the big picture design and architecture to the scrum master and development management. Use of this approach exceeded all expectations.

Source: Warren A. Opfer, CCP, PMP®.

References

A *Guide to the Project Management Body of Knowledge (PMBOK® Guide)*, 5th ed. (Newtown Square, PA: Project Management Institute, 2013).

Anantatmula, V. (2014). "Managing Resources," in Turner, R. (Ed.). Gower Handbook of Project Management, 5th Edition. Hardback edition: ISBN: 9781472422965 (Farnham, UK: Gower Publishing).

Brown, David, "Top 10 Steps to Schedule Management," *Electrical Construction and Maintenance* (March 2008): C22–C28.

Butler, Charles W., and Gary L.Richardson, "A Variable Time Project Planning and Control Model," *Journal of Management Policy and Practice* 12 (6) (2011): 11–19.

Gagnon, Michel, "A Method of Integrating Personnel into the Project Schedule," *Proceedings, PMI Research Conference 2006* (Montreal, July 2006).

Grant, Kevin P., and Michael R.Baumann, "Leveraging Project Team Expertise for Better Project Solutions," Proceedings, *PMI Research Conference 2006* (Montreal, July 2006).

Haugan, Gregory T., Project Planning and Scheduling (Vienna, VA: Management Concepts, Inc., 2002).

Leach, Larry P., "Critical Chain Project Management Improves Project Performance," *Project Management Journal* 30 (2) (June 1999): 39–51.

Piney, Crispin, "Critical Path or Critical Chain: Combining the Best of Both," *PM Network* 14 (12) (December 2000): 51–55.

"PMI Code of Ethics and Professional Conduct," PMI Today (December 2006): 12–13.

Rad, Parviz, and Vittal Anantatmula, Project Planning Techniques (Vienna, VA: Management Concepts, Inc., 2005).

Trietsch, Dan, "Why a Critical Path by Any Other Name Would Smell Less Sweet?" *Project Management Journal* 36 (1) (March 2005): 27–36.

Tsou, Chi-Ming, "On the Project Management Scheduling Based on Agent Technology and Theory of Constraint," *International Journal of Electronic Business Management* 10 (4) (2012): 286–295.

www.ambysoft.com/essays/agileProjectPlanning.html, accessed May 22, 2013.

www.youtube.com/watch?v=IExA5fuWFgg, accessed May 22, 2013.

http://jbep.blogspot.com/2010/01/rolling-wave-planning-or-sliding.html, accessed August 3, 2010.

www.brighthub.com/office/project-management/articles/8717.aspx, accessed August 3, 2010.

http://office.microsoft.com/en-us/project-help/fast-track-tasks-to-shorten-your-project-schedule-HA010036399.aspx, accessed August 3, 2010.

http://en.wikipedia.org/wiki/Critical_Chain_Project_Management, accessed August 3, 2010.

Endnote

1. Adapted from Rad, Parviz, and Vittal Anantatmula, *Project Planning Techniques* (Vienna, VA: Management Concepts, Inc., 2005): 68–72.

Budgeting Projects

CHAPTER OBJECTIVES

After completing this chapter, you should be able to:

CORE OBJECTIVES:

- Define project cost terms and tell how each is used in estimating project cost.
- Compare and contrast analogous, parametric, and bottom-up methods of estimating cost.
- Create a time-phased, bottom-up budget for a project.

TECHNICAL OBJECTIVES:

- Show both summary and bottom-up project budget information with cumulative costs using MS Project.

BEHAVIORAL OBJECTIVES:

- Describe issues in project cost estimating and how to deal with each.

I sold escalators and elevators for my first job out of business school. As part of my training, before I was sent to the field, I would look over the estimates made by the sales staff. This served to double-check their math so the company had confidence in their estimates. It also served to teach me many of the little nuances that more experienced estimators used. I had my training manuals, lists of standards, main methods of calculation, and so forth, but learning from others' experience instead of making all my own mistakes helped.

One of the last parts in my training was to spend eight weeks at the Denver branch to get seasoned a little bit. Construction was booming in Denver during the late 1970s. In fact, some days I needed to bid more than one job. The first part of putting together a bid was to go the office where the requests for proposals, plans, specifications, and the like were stored. Then, armed with that information, I would put together an estimate. Finally, the actual bidding took place—usually over the phone. The problem was that creating a detailed estimate would generally take at least half a day. If that was my only duty (it was not), I would still have had a hard time when multiple jobs were let for bid on the same day. Something had to give.

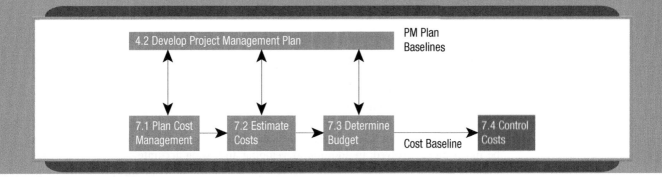

Every morning around 10 A.M., I met the construction superintendent for coffee. We would discuss each bid that was due. What other job was it like? How was it bigger or smaller than a recently completed job? What features did it include more or less than a previous job? Did we make money on that job? We used these questions to compare an upcoming job to other recently completed jobs. We would also ask, "What do we think our competition will bid?" By the end of the conversation, we had determined our strategy for bidding the job. If we won the bid, we would complete a detailed cost estimate to see if we were close.

After my training, I was transferred to Kansas City. Kansas City had less construction than Denver. I had enough time to perform detailed cost estimates before I submitted bids. Therefore, we were more certain that if we got the bid, we would have a good chance of making money.

I worked for the same company in both cities. However, we used two very different methods of estimating cost. Both made sense where they were used. In Denver, if we wanted to bid every job (and you cannot win the job if you do not bid on it), we needed a fast method. In Kansas City, we had the time to develop detailed cost estimates, and so we took the time. There are many methods of estimating project costs and each has its place.

—*Timothy J. Kloppenborg*

10-1 Plan Cost Management

This chapter starts with estimating project costs. Once the overall cost is estimated, the next step is to develop the budget by aggregating the costs and determining the project's cash flow needs. Project managers also need to establish a system to report and control project costs. The final section of the chapter deals with how to use Microsoft Project to aid in cost management activities.

Cost and schedule are closely related. Sometimes, the two move in the same direction. The schedule is maintained by the use of resources, and resources expend parts of the budget. For example, when a schedule calls for materials to be delivered, or for workers to perform, money must be available to pay for the materials or workers. Sometimes, they move in opposite directions. For example, if a project needs to be completed earlier than planned, more money probably will need to be found to pay for overtime.

Plan cost management is the process to determine how to plan, estimate, and control project costs. Cost planning entails developing a cost management plan for your project.

The **cost management plan** is "a continuous activity which requires reforecasting and refinement of the cost estimates throughout the project."[1] The cost management plan defines the cost baseline, modifies it whenever necessary, and uses it for monitoring and controlling costs. On small projects, this can be as simple as ensuring accurate estimates are made, securing the funding, and developing cost reporting procedures to ensure that the money is spent correctly. On large projects, each of these processes can be much more involved; in addition, developing and using accurate cash flow estimates become critical. A project cost management plan includes descriptions, procedures, and responsibilities for the following:

- Costs included (such as internal and external, contingency, etc.)
- Activity resource estimating
- Cost estimating
- Cost baseline
- Budget determination
- Cost control, including metrics, reporting, and change approvals

A project cost management plan needs to be consistent with the methods of the parent organization. In many organizations, project managers are provided with specific guidance on setting up their cost management plan. The plan provides guidelines to the project manager and other stakeholders to serve several purposes:

- First and most fundamentally, it shows how to develop and share relevant, accurate, and timely information on cost that the project manager, sponsor, and other stakeholders can use to make intelligent and ethical decisions.
- It provides feedback, thereby showing how the project's success is linked to the business objectives for which it was undertaken.
- It provides information at a detailed level for those who need details and at appropriate summary levels for those who need that.
- It helps all project stakeholders focus appropriately on schedule and cost performance.[2]

10-2 Estimate Cost

Estimate cost is "the process of developing an approximation of monetary resources needed to complete project activities."[3] Cost estimating is linked closely with scope, schedule, and resource planning. To understand cost implications completely, a project manager needs to understand what the work of the project includes, what schedule demands exist, and what people and other resources can be used. When more of these details are available, the cost estimates can be more precise.

The first principle in dealing with project costs is for the project manager to never lie to himself. Many times, in dealing with project costs, the project manager will need to negotiate with sponsors, customers, and other stakeholders. If he does not understand what the project costs really are, he is just trading meaningless numbers. That is neither an effective nor an ethical method of establishing and committing to sensible budgets.

The second principle in dealing with project costs is for the project manager to never lie to anyone else. Since sponsors, customers, and other stakeholders can often drive hard bargains, it is sometimes tempting to shade the truth to secure necessary funding. This is wrong on two counts: First, it is ethically wrong. Second, as a practical matter, a project manager's reputation goes a long way for good or for bad. People are more inclined to work with project managers who are viewed as being honest and trustworthy.

To estimate project costs accurately, the project manager must understand the various types of costs, the timing and accuracy of cost estimates, the different methods that can be employed to estimate costs, and a variety of cost-estimating issues.

10-2a Types of Cost

Costs can be better understood by considering various types of classifications such as those shown in Exhibit 10.1.

FIXED VERSUS VARIABLE COSTS   Costs can first be classified as either being fixed or variable. **Fixed costs** are those that remain the same regardless of the size or volume of work. For example, if you need to buy a computer for your project, the cost is the same regardless of how much you use it. **Variable costs** are those that vary directly with the volume of use. For example, if you were building a cement wall, the cost of the cement would vary directly with the size of the wall. To understand the importance of fixed versus variable costs, a project manager ideally structures costs and the impact of changes on those costs. When a project manager understands how big a project is likely to be, she will try to determine how to complete all of the project work at the lowest possible cost. On many projects, there are choices of how to perform certain activities. Some of these choices reflect a high-fixed-cost and low-variable-cost alternative such as buying an expensive machine that can make parts with low variable costs versus a more manual process of inexpensive machines but high labor costs. These choices require both some fixed and some variable costs. Ideally, the cost curve for the expected project volume appears as shown in Exhibit 10.2. This reflects the lowest possible total cost at the size the project is expected to be. Unfortunately, problems may occur if the volume of the project work is substantially larger or smaller than first expected. If the volume drops a little bit, the total costs may drop very little. If the volume expands a little, the costs may go up significantly. Therefore, when considering fixed and variable cost choices, it is important to understand the project scope.

DIRECT VERSUS INDIRECT COSTS   A second classification divides project costs into direct and indirect costs. **Direct costs** are those that only occur because of the project and are often classified as either direct labor or other direct costs. For example, direct

EXHIBIT 10.1

COMPARISON OF COST TERMS	
Fixed	Variable
Direct	Indirect
Recurring	Nonrecurring
Regular	Expedited
Internal	External
Lease	Purchase
Labor	Material
Estimate	Reserve

Source: Adapted from Kim LaScola Needy and Kimberly Sarnowski, "Keeping the Lid on Project Costs," in David I. Cleland, ed., *Field Guide to Project Management*, 2nd ed. (Hoboken, NJ: John Wiley & Sons, 2004): 145–147.

EXHIBIT 10.2

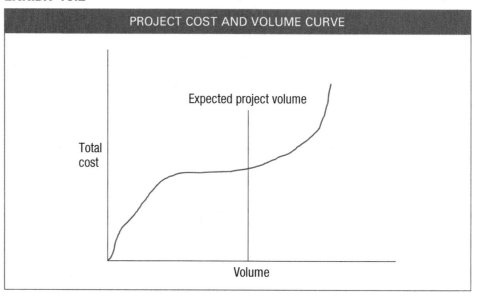

PROJECT COST AND VOLUME CURVE

labor includes workers who are hired specifically to work on the project and who will be either assigned to a new project or released when the project is complete. Other direct costs may include such items as materials, travel, consultants, subcontracts, purchased parts, and computer time.

Indirect costs are those that are necessary to keep the organization running, but are not associated with one specific project. The salaries of the company executives and the cost of company buildings, utilities, insurance, and clerical assistance are examples. These costs are allocated among all of the projects and other organizational and internal work that benefit from these resources. The methods of allocating these costs have evolved in recent years thanks to activity-based costing, as described in the cost estimating issues section. Exhibit 10.3 shows both direct and indirect costs for a work package.

RECURRING VERSUS NONRECURRING COSTS   The third cost comparison is recurring versus nonrecurring costs. **Recurring costs** are those that repeat as the project work continues, such as the cost of writing code or laying bricks. **Nonrecurring costs** are those that happen only once during a project, such as developing a design that, once approved, guides the project team. Nonrecurring costs tend to occur more often during project planning and closing, while recurring costs tend to occur more often during project execution.

REGULAR VERSUS EXPEDITED COSTS   A fourth cost comparison is regular or expedited. Regular costs are preferred and occur when progress can be made by normal work hours and purchasing agreements. Expedited costs occur when the project must be conducted faster than normal and overtime for workers and/or extra charges for rapid delivery from suppliers are necessary. The comparison of these costs shows why it is vital to understand schedule pressures and resource demands as costs are estimated.

OTHER COST CLASSIFICATIONS   The next several cost comparisons require little explanation. They are helpful to understand both in structuring the cost estimates and as checklists to help remember items that may be forgotten. One comparison is costs internal

EXHIBIT 10.3

DIRECT AND INDIRECT COSTS IN A WORK PACKAGE		

PROJECT: ACCOUNTS PAYABLE REFINEMENT	WORK PACKAGE: INSTALL MODULE 1	
Description: Install accounts payable refinement application and related hardware.	**Deliverable(s):** Installed and functioning accounts payable module.	
Cost Categories	Quantity	Total
Direct Labor		
Programmer	120 hrs @ $ 75/hr	9,000
Systems Analyst	40 hrs @ $ 100/hr	4,000
Systems Architect	20 hrs @ $ 120/hr	2,400
Other Direct		
Hardware		20,000
Software		8,400
Consultant Services		12,000
Indirect Costs (.6 * DL)		**9,240**
	Total	**65,040**

Source: Kevin P. Grant, University of Texas, San Antonio. Adapted with permission.

to the parent organization versus those external to it. Major external cost items such as equipment can be either leased or purchased. Direct cost items are often employees or materials.

Estimate versus reserve costs form the next comparison. The **estimate** is "a quantified assessment of the likely amount. ... It should always include an indication of accuracy."[4] The **reserve** is extra money in the project budget to be used if necessary—usually if a risk event occurs. Reserves are often classified more specifically as a management reserve or contingency reserve. **Management reserve** is money assigned to the project for unknown possible costs and money that senior management controls. By contrast, **contingency reserve** is money assigned to the project and allocated for identified risks for which contingent responses are developed.

Just as uncertainly exists when estimating how long an activity will take, there is uncertainty regarding how much an activity will cost. Some activities are easy to estimate with higher levels of accuracy. Other less familiar activities have many uncertainties, and estimating their cost is more like guessing. If one were to estimate conservatively on each uncertain activity, the total estimate for the project would likely be too high to be approved. To overcome this problem, project managers are sometimes encouraged to estimate at least a bit more aggressively. That means some activities will run over their estimates, while others will cost less. Project managers frequently add a contingency reserve to cover the activities that run over their aggressive estimates. In any event, one must remember the two principles of ethical estimating discussed earlier in the chapter (not to lie to yourself and to others).

10-2b Accuracy and Timing of Cost Estimates

Project managers need to understand when cost estimates should be developed, how accurate they need to be, and how they will be used. During project initiation, many project managers need to develop cost estimates to have their project charters approved. At this point, very little detail is understood regarding the project, so the estimates are only approximate. However, as the scope becomes well defined in the work breakdown structure (WBS), schedules are planned, and specific resources are assigned, the project manager knows much more and can estimate costs associated with each work package more precisely. Many organizations have specific names and guidance for their estimates and these vary widely. Normally, estimates should be documented, and the level of confidence in the estimate should be described. Exhibit 10.4 shows several points regarding different types of project cost estimates.

ORDER OF MAGNITUDE ESTIMATES　Several things should be noted from these comparisons. First, estimates go by several different names. For example, **order of magnitude estimates** that are often used to seek initial charter approval are also sometimes called *ballpark, conceptual, initial,* or *level-one* estimates. These early estimates are often created during the project initiating stage when very little information is available about the project. At this point, a very rough order of magnitude estimate could underestimate the project by as much as 100 percent (that is, the final cost could be double the initial estimate). And it may be the only possible estimate. There is no way to really know how accurate an estimate is until the project has been completed, but with less detailed knowledge concerning the project in the initiating stage, there is likely to be a larger margin of error. Order of magnitude cost estimates and the parallel high-level views in

EXHIBIT 10.4

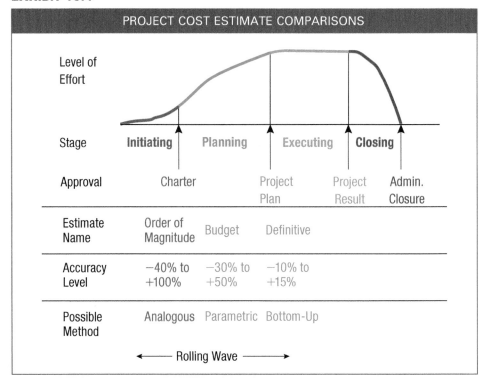

PROJECT COST ESTIMATE COMPARISONS			
Level of Effort			
Stage	**Initiating**	Planning	Executing	**Closing**
Approval	Charter	Project Plan	Project Result	Admin. Closure
Estimate Name	Order of Magnitude	Budget	Definitive	
Accuracy Level	−40% to +100%	−30% to +50%	−10% to +15%	
Possible Method	Analogous	Parametric	Bottom-Up	

◄──── Rolling Wave ────►

each of the other planning areas can quickly give enough information to approve the project charter and begin to invest time and money into detailed planning.

A concept of progressive elaboration applies here. Progressive elaboration is "Continuously improving and detailing a plan as more detailed and specific information and more accurate estimates become available as the project progresses, thereby producing more accurate and complete plans that result from the successive iterations of the planning process."[5]

BUDGET AND DEFINITIVE ESTIMATES   Once a project plan enters into the more detailed planning stage, it is generally possible to create a more accurate cost estimate. This is the same thought that goes into creating a more detailed project schedule, resource estimates, risk profiles, quality plans, and communications plans. Depending on the complexity and size of their projects and organizational norms, some project managers can proceed directly to definitive cost estimates at this point. Others may still need to look at one or more intermediate levels of detail before they have enough detailed knowledge to create cost estimates with accuracy. At the end of project planning, cost estimates should have a small enough margin of error that they can be used to create a project budget, show cash flow needs, and be used as a basis for controlling the project. Most project organizations prefer an accuracy level of no more than plus or minus 10 to 15 percent, and some require considerably better, such as plus or minus 5 percent.

On agile projects, project managers may use rolling wave planning to estimate costs. They do this by creating a definitive estimate for the first iteration of the project (and committing to it) and an order of magnitude estimate for the remainder of the project. As the work on the first iteration nears an end, the project manager, equipped with detailed information about scope for the next iteration, then creates a definitive estimate for the second iteration and reevaluates the order of magnitude estimate for the remainder of the project. At each stage, the project manager has more information than at the preceding stage and can create more accurate estimates.

10-2c Methods of Estimating Costs

Many methods can be used for estimating project costs. Most are variations of one of the methods discussed in this section. While these methods can sometimes also be used to estimate project scope or duration, the discussion in this chapter centers on using them to estimate project cost. Exhibit 10.4 indicates that as more details of a project are known as planning progresses, more detailed estimating methods may be used. However, Exhibit 10.5 shows that even at the end of project planning, a project manager may sometimes use a combination of cost estimating methods. If the organization has established accurate analogous and parametric estimating methods and capable estimators, sometimes parts of a project can be estimated by those methods instead of the more detailed (and time-consuming) bottom-up methods. The method chosen for cost estimation should account for the extent of complexity, risk, interdependencies, work force specialization, and site-specific issues of the project.[6]

ANALOGOUS ESTIMATING   **Analogous estimating** is "an estimating technique that uses the values of parameters on a scale, such as scope, cost, budget, and duration or measures of scale such as size, weight, and complexity from a previous and similar activity or project as the basis for estimating the same parameter or measure for a future activity or project respectively."[7] Analogous estimating was the technique used in Denver in this chapter's opening vignette. To create a bid for a project—in this case, the installation of elevators—a similar project was considered as the starting point. Immediately,

EXHIBIT 10.5

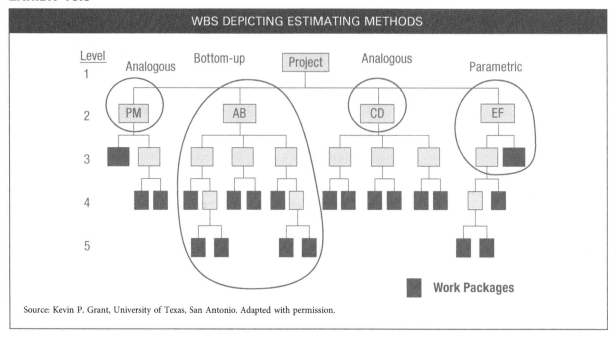

WBS DEPICTING ESTIMATING METHODS

Level 1

Analogous   Bottom-up   Project   Analogous   Parametric

PM   AB   CD   EF

■ **Work Packages**

Source: Kevin P. Grant, University of Texas, San Antonio. Adapted with permission.

questions were asked regarding how this job compared in size and complexity with the previous job.

Several things need to be in place for analogous estimates to be effective. First, the organization needs to have experience in performing similar projects and know actual costs of each of those projects (not just what they were estimated to cost). Second, the estimator needs to know how and to what extent the proposed project differs from the previous project. Third, the estimator needs to have experience with the methods and processes by which the project will be performed. In the Denver example, sales and construction people jointly discussed how much the project would cost.

PARAMETRIC ESTIMATING **Parametric estimating** is "an estimating technique that uses a statistical relationship between historical data and other variables (e.g., square footage in construction, lines of code in software development) to calculate an estimate for ... scope, cost, and duration."[8] Parametric estimating can be used to determine the impact of key variables on project costs. A bit more information is needed to complete a parametric cost estimate as compared to an analogous estimate. Exhibit 10.5 shows this graphically by suggesting that another level of detail in the WBS might be used. In the chapter opener example of estimating the cost of elevator installation projects, parametric estimates might involve finding a bit more information regarding the project. For example, one might want to know how tall the elevator was, how fast it needed to travel, how large the platform would be, the trim level, the complexity of the controls, and the like. Each of those factors would have an impact on the elevator installation cost. For example, the cost per foot traveled might be calculated (this would cover the cost of providing and installing guide rails, wiring, etc.). Another cost might be associated with speed because faster elevators require bigger motors, more stability, stronger brakes, and so on.

BOTTOM-UP ESTIMATING **Bottom-up estimating** is "a method of estimating ... what is needed to meet the requirements of each of the lower, more detailed pieces of work, preferably the lowest level of WBS work elements, and these estimates are then aggregated into a total quantity."[9] For a bottom-up estimate, the WBS needs to be broken down to the most detailed level, and the specifications need to be very clear. In the elevator example, bottom-up estimates were created in Kansas City. Details to be estimated included exactly how many buttons the control panel had, exactly what kind of light fixtures were mounted in the ceiling, what kind of finish was requested, and so on. The cost was estimated for each item. For example, for the process of installing the guide rail, first there was a small amount of time, such as one hour, to set up or get everything in place to do this step. Then, it took a certain fraction of an hour of labor to secure each foot of the rail into position. A material charge was incurred for the guide rails themselves and the fasteners that held them in place. The cost of supervision was charged for the foreperson, who ensured the work was scheduled and performed properly. Finally, overhead costs (indirect costs) were allocated to each dollar of fixed costs.

Bottom-up estimating is the most detailed, time-consuming, and potentially the most accurate way to estimate. Many projects use this method eventually to serve as a basis for estimating cash flow needs and for controlling the project. One important caution on bottom-up estimating is to ensure that every item is included. If a portion of the project is left out, that portion is underestimated by 100 percent! A WBS detailing all deliverables is best suited for bottom-up estimating. Some organizations first create a bottom-up estimate and then compare it to a top-down view to consider adjusting it if the top-down view yields a much higher number. Exhibit 10.6 summarizes differences in cost estimating methods.

EXHIBIT 10.6

COST ESTIMATING METHOD COMPARISON			
	ANALOGOUS	PARAMETRIC	BOTTOM-UP
Amount of Information Required	Least	Middle	Most
Amount of Time Required	Least	Middle	Most
Accuracy Obtained	Lowest	Middle	Highest

10-2d Project Cost Estimating Issues

Regardless of what method is used to estimate project costs, several issues need to be considered. Some of these issues are pertinent to all projects; others pertain only to certain projects. These issues are shown in Exhibit 10.7.

SUPPORTING DETAIL   Supporting detail for project cost estimates includes describing the scope, method used to create the estimate, assumptions, constraints, and range of possible outcomes. The project scope tends to be the least well defined at the project outset and becomes increasingly well defined throughout project planning. Each estimate should state exactly what scope it is based on. Version control is critical for this purpose.

The method used might be analogous, parametric, or bottom-up. The name of the method and exactly how the method is used should be described.

When creating an estimate, many assumptions and constraints are considered. Assumptions should be outlined because two different people coming from two different backgrounds may view a situation differently and assume that two different things will happen. Even if everyone involved with planning a project assumes the same thing, it still may not happen. Assumptions that are not true often cause more work or other problems for a project such as changes in scope, cost, and schedule. As more details are available, a project manager may review assumptions with an eye toward uncovering assumptions that have now proven to be false. When this happens, the project manager can investigate any impact this may have on the project budget (and schedule and scope). Examples of assumptions that may arise when estimating the cost of direct labor might include the following:

- Workers will be paid at the prevailing wage rate of $14 per hour.
- Workers are already familiar in general with the technology being used on the project.
- Workers will be paid for 40 hours per week whether there is always that much work for them or not.

EXHIBIT 10.7

ISSUES IN PROJECT COST ESTIMATING	
Supporting detail	Activity-based costing
Causes of variation	Life cycle costing
Vendor bid analysis	Time value of money
Value engineering	International currency fluctuations

- Overtime will never be authorized.
- The project schedule can be delayed if the only alternative is to pay overtime.

Constraints are also important since they often dictate the methods available for performing the project work. Examples of constraints include:

- Only in-house workers will be used.
- No extra space will be provided.
- No extra budget will be allowed.
- The current version of the XYZ software will be incorporated into the design.

The range of possible outcomes should always be stated with a project cost estimate. If the range is not stated, people may lock onto the first number they hear and remember it. If the actual project costs could be 100 percent higher than the order of magnitude estimate, the project manager had better state that accuracy level loud and clear, or she may find herself continually explaining why she is grossly over budget. In fact, many estimators resist giving an order of magnitude estimate because they fear they will be held to it. A natural tension exists between managers who try to effectively manage their departments by establishing budgets as soon as possible and project managers who try to provide budget estimates as late as possible (once they know more about the project).

CAUSES OF VARIATION   There are many causes for project costs to vary. On routine projects using proven technology, with fewer uncertainties, and an experienced and well-known project team, the causes may be relatively few and easy to categorize. On other projects where some of these factors are not true, more causes of uncertainty in project costs may exist, and some of those may be from unknown sources. Statisticians classify variation as coming from either normal or special causes, as shown in Exhibit 10.8.

Variation occurs in all work processes. The more routine a process is and the more work is driven by machines, the less variation occurs. Projects, however, tend to have novel work and high human interaction, so there are many opportunities for variation. Normal variation comes from many small causes that are inherent in a work process. For

EXHIBIT 10.8

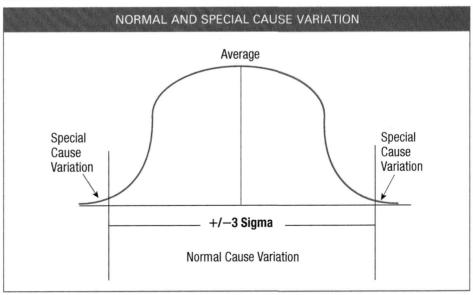

instance, the variation in the productivity of a programmer writing code could be from phone calls, instant messages, and in-person interruptions that occur each day. Special cause variation, on the other hand, is when something out of the ordinary occurs. For example, a lightning strike could cause such a large power surge that it overwhelms the normal protectors and destroys some of the computers. Most causes of variation are of the normal variety, and improving work methods (as discussed in Chapter 12) can help to reduce this type of variation. Special causes, however, are handled more as risks, as discussed in Chapter 11. Both types of variation add to project costs and need to be considered.

VENDOR BID ANALYSIS   On some projects, most or all of the cost is internal to the parent organization. On other projects, a substantial portion of the budget goes to securing services and supplies from vendors and external sources. Vendor bid analysis is used to determine whether the price being asked by the vendors appears to be reasonable. If several vendors compete for the work, it is reasonable to believe that the lowest responsible offer is fair. In the absence of competition, however, other methods may be needed to ensure a fair price. On some items, prices are determined in the marketplace and reported in business papers and websites for anyone to read. On specialized services and products, one often must negotiate with a vendor. In the absence of any other method, for an expensive item, a project manager may need to develop a sound cost estimate. That is, try to determine how much effort the vendor may need to expend, and then add a fair profit margin to arrive at the price you believe the vendor should charge.

VALUE ENGINEERING   **Value engineering** is "a formal, structured process to ensure projects meet or exceed cost objectives without compromising quality … divides the total project scope into components, examining each individual component for alternatives that offer benefits."[10] It is aimed at increasing the value or productivity of a work element while minimizing the cost. In other words, it is a ratio of function to the cost associated with the product or service. Value engineering can be a very powerful method of double-checking all of the chosen methods for accomplishing work and the features of the project deliverable. Frequently, stakeholders find that a feature in the specifications costs more than they wish to pay.

In a project to update an older church, the liturgical committee proposed many controls for special lighting that would be used only on special occasions. The general contractor suggested simplifying the controls, while retaining all the new lights, at a savings of $100,000! While the liturgical committee was disappointed, the church council readily agreed. Value engineering is so common in some industries that a separate stage is incorporated late in the project planning to ensure that time is spent for this purpose to reduce project cost and/or time and to improve project quality and/or usefulness.

ACTIVITY-BASED COSTING (ABC)   Another issue project managers need to understand when estimating costs is what type of accounting system the organization employs. Historically, most companies used functional-based accounting systems. When using these systems, overhead (indirect) costs are assigned to a cost pool, which is often allocated to direct costs based on volume. When direct costs were a large percentage of total costs, this made sense. In more contemporary times, indirect costs form a much larger percentage of total costs, so careful allocation of them is necessary both for selecting the projects that truly will contribute the most profit and for ensuring a focus on controlling the highest costs. ABC is another accounting approach, by which indirect costs are allocated to fixed costs based upon four different types of drivers. The cost drivers are number of units produced (frequently, the only method used in functional-based accounting), number of batches run, number of product variations, and amount of facility utilized. ABC requires more involved methods for allocating indirect costs, but yields more accurate cost information. By furnishing more specific information on cost drivers, ABC also helps to support process improvement and justify spending money on expensive equipment. Project managers need to understand how costs are allocated in their organization so they can accurately estimate the amount of indirect costs that will be assigned to their projects.

LIFE CYCLE COSTING   **Life cycle costing** is another concept project managers need to understand when estimating their project costs. Many project selection decisions are made based upon the total costs of both creating the project and of using the result of the project during its useful life. This total cost is called the life cycle cost, in which life cycle denotes the life of the product or deliverable of the project. Many times, trade-off decisions are considered that might involve spending more during the project to create a product that costs less to operate during its useful life. In an age in which environmental concerns are appropriately being considered more heavily, to calculate total life cycle costs, a project manager may also need to consider disposal costs of the product after its useful life is complete. This can entail designing more recyclable parts (even at a higher cost) into the product and adopting sustainable approaches for project execution that would reduce the project cost in the long run.

TIME VALUE OF MONEY AND INTERNATIONAL CURRENCY FLUCTUATIONS
When considering future costs and revenues, project managers must know how to calculate the time value of money. One dollar today is presumably worth more than one dollar next year. Discounting the value of future revenue and cost streams enables better project decisions. Often, the finance department at a company tells the project manager what rate to use as a discount factor. The rate depends upon the prevailing inflation rate plus the cost of capital. On international projects, it can also depend upon international currency fluctuations.

10-3 Determine Budget

Once the project costs have been estimated, it is time to establish the project budget. **Determine budget** is "the process of aggregating the estimated costs of individual activities or work packages to establish an authorized cost baseline."[11] To develop the budget, the project manager starts by aggregating all the costs. Once those are totaled, it is time to determine how much money is required for reserve funds. Finally, the project manager must understand cash flow—both in terms of funding and requirements to meet costs for activities on a day-to-day basis.

10-3a Aggregating Costs

When the entire project costs, both direct and indirect, have been added up, the result is a **cost baseline,** which is "that part of the project baseline that handles the amount of money the project is predicted to cost and on the other side when that money will be spent. It is an approved budget usually in a time distribution format used to estimate, monitor, and control the overall cost performance of the project."[12]

The work packages of a WBS not only take time, but also cost money. The project budget can be aggregated from the work packages. Exhibit 10.9 shows how six work packages appear on a Gantt chart with the cost of each work package listed on a monthly basis. The total cost for the month is shown and the cumulative cost for the project shown below that. Finally, a graph appears at the bottom that shows the cumulative cost of the project at each point in time. This represents the time-phased project budget. This will be used for control purposes as the project progresses. Note the cumulative cost curve approximates an "S" shape with slow expenditures (and progress) early in the project, rapid in the middle, and gradual late in the project. This is normal as projects often require much planning during the early phases of a project and have fewer activities to finish at the end.

10-3b Analyzing Reserve Needs

Another view of project cost variation is to consider how well it is understood and how each type is handled. This is displayed in Exhibit 10.10.

Variation in project costs (and schedules) can be partially explained by the presence of certain events associated with a project. These events are classified as known knowns, known unknowns, or unknown unknowns, depending on the extent to which they are understood and predicted. Known knowns are discovered during planning and can be estimated directly. An example could be that when a construction crew takes soil samples, they discover that extra pilings are required to stabilize the new building, and they add the cost into the project estimate to cover that expense.

Known unknowns are events discovered during risk identification that may or may not occur. An example could be snowstorms that cause traffic problems for three days at a critical time, preventing workers from getting to their jobs. In the next chapter on risk, methods for calculating costs associated with known unknowns are discussed. They will appear as contingency reserves.

Finally, sometimes things happen that are totally unexpected and can cause an increase in cost and/or schedule. For example, a very dependable supplier goes out of business perhaps due to the sudden death of the owner. These unknown unknowns (commonly called *unk unks*) also need to be covered in the project budget. The money used to cover them is frequently called management reserve and is usually authorized by company executives.

EXHIBIT 10.9

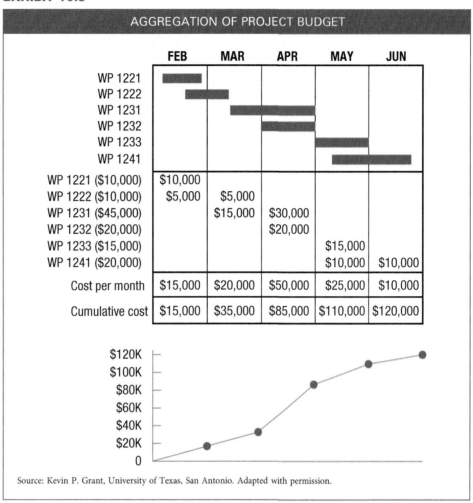

AGGREGATION OF PROJECT BUDGET					

Source: Kevin P. Grant, University of Texas, San Antonio. Adapted with permission.

EXHIBIT 10.10

ESTIMATING COSTS OF PROJECT VARIATION			
HOW VARIATION IS UNDERSTOOD	KNOWN KNOWNS	KNOWN UNKNOWNS	UNKNOWN UNKNOWNS
How It Is Discovered	Scope definition Create WBS	Risk identification	Situation occurs
Stage When It Is Usually Uncovered	Initiating or planning	Initiating or planning	Executing
Method of Estimating Costs	Estimate directly	Contingency reserves	Management reserves

The amount placed into contingency reserve is calculated during risk analysis. The amount placed into management reserve is determined by how much uncertainty management feels exists in the project. Typical ranges are from 5 percent of project costs for well-understood, routine projects to 30 percent or more of project costs for poorly understood, unusual projects. These costs are not to be used to overcome poor estimating or project execution.

Once the cost baseline is determined along with both contingency and management reserves, it is time to determine if sufficient funds are available. On many potential projects, a funding limit exists. The project sponsor for internal projects and the customer for external projects need to be very clear if the necessary funds exceed the limit of what is available. If enough funds are not available, this is the time to look hard at all the estimates, schedule, and scope to determine what changes need to be made before the project management plan is accepted. It does no good for anyone to deliberately start a project with insufficient funds.

10-3c Determining Cash Flow

Projects require cash to make progress with the work. Suppliers and workers need to be paid in a timely fashion. A common difficulty is that the project's customer may not pay for the work until it is completed—often months after project bills were supposed to be paid. Therefore, the timing of cash inflow and outflow for a project is just as important as the amount of money required.

Just as the demands on individual workers can be applied to individual activities in the project schedule to determine where overloads may occur, expenses can be applied to individual activities in the schedule to see when cash is needed. Revenue can also be tracked to interim deliverables in the project schedule to show when revenue can be expected. If a project is internal to a company, the timing of cash availability is also important to understand. While workers may work every day and suppliers may deliver frequently, cash may be supplied through organizational budgets only on a periodic basis. A project manager needs to ensure that the cumulative amount of cash coming into the project either from internal budgeting or from customer payments meets or exceeds the demands for paying cash out. This cash flow is shown in Exhibit 10.11 where incoming cash is in large increments, yet outgoing cash is almost continuous. The cumulative revenue at project completion minus the cumulative cost at project completion equals the profit (or surplus) generated by the project.

EXHIBIT 10.11

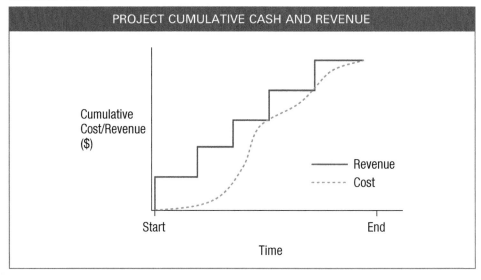

10-4 Establishing Cost Control

The approved project budget with contingency reserves (and any amount of management reserve that has already been approved) serves as a baseline for project control. The budget shows both how much progress is expected and how much funding is required at each point in time. These are used for establishing project control. **Control cost** is the process of monitoring the project costs and managing changes to the cost baseline. Cost control is discussed in Chapter 14.

When establishing cost control, a typical measuring point is a milestone. Major milestones are often identified in the milestone schedule in the project charter, and additional milestones may be identified while developing the project schedule. Project managers can use the cash flow projections they have made to determine how much funding they expect to need to reach each milestone. This can then be used for determining how well the project is progressing. The sponsor and project manager often jointly determine how many milestones to use. They would like to have enough milestones to keep track of progress, but not so many that they become an administrative burden. Microsoft Project and other software can be used to automate the cost reporting.

10-5 Using MS Project for Project Budgets

MS Project supports both bottom-up and summary level cost modeling. Bottom-up cost modeling is primarily based on the cost of each resource assignment to WBS tasks. Assignment costs can be seen in the related task's Cost field (when shown) in the Gantt chart and other views. Task costs are summarized at the parent WBS levels (summary tasks).

Summary costs allow the project manager to make a "summary level" estimate of the cost of the project. Often when the complete details of later stages of the project are not known, placeholder or "dummy" tasks are added to the schedule and costs are estimated. Using summary cost estimates, a projected duration and cost estimate of the entire project can be provided to project stakeholders.

The following examples will continue to use the Suburban Park Homes project from previous chapters' examples.

10-5a Developing a Bottom-Up Project Budget Estimate

To develop a bottom-up project budget estimate, a project manager needs to understand the assignment and task costs for each task of the project. MS Project allows the user to view costs from different perspectives in order to better understand where costs are coming from and which tasks are cost centers for the project. We will now look at assignment and task costs in more detail.

ASSIGNMENT COSTS   The following data are used to compute each assignment's cost value:

- **Assignment work hours** (calculated when the work assignment is made)
- **Resource standard rate**
- **Resource overtime rate** (only if modeling overtime)

An assignment cost value is the total number of assignment hours multiplied by the standard rate (cost) of that resource (e.g., $50 an hour). Each resource has a standard rate; some may have an overtime rate as well. Cost rates can be assigned when defining

EXHIBIT 10.12

		ⓘ	Resource Name ▾	Type ▾	Material ▾	Initials ▾	Group ▾	Max. ▾	Std. Rate ▾	Ovt. Rate ▾	Cost/Use ▾	Accrue At ▾	Base ▾
1		⚥	Bruce	Work		BF		75%	$55.00/hr	$0.00/hr	$0.00	Prorated	Standard
2		⚥	Jack	Work		JC		25%	$50.00/hr	$0.00/hr	$0.00	Prorated	Standard
3			Brady	Work		BD		75%	$40.00/hr	$0.00/hr	$0.00	Prorated	Standard
4			Anniston	Work		AC		50%	$40.00/hr	$0.00/hr	$0.00	Prorated	Standard
5			Judah	Work		JS		50%	$35.00/hr	$0.00/hr	$0.00	Prorated	Standard
6		⚥	Liam	Work		LF		25%	$50.00/hr	$0.00/hr	$0.00	Prorated	Standard
7		⚥	Oliver	Work		OL		50%	$25.00/hr	$0.00/hr	$0.00	Prorated	Standard
8			Plumbers	Work		P		300%	$30.00/hr	$0.00/hr	$0.00	Prorated	Standard

ASSIGN COST RATES

Resource Name — Standard Rate (Cost) Assignment — Overtime Rate (Cost) Assignment

RESOURCE SHEET

Source: Microsoft product screenshots reprinted with permission from Microsoft Corporation.

the resource in the Resource Sheet (**View Tab**>>**Resources Sheet**), as described in Chapter 9, or assigned later when costs are known. Exhibit 10.12 shows the Resource Sheet with standard rates assigned to the project resources.

TASK COSTS   The task cost value is the sum of all *assignment* cost values, plus any task's fixed cost value (e.g., a building permit). Exhibit 10.13 displays the **Task Usage View** in the top pane (with the **Cost** column inserted) and the **Task Form View** in the lower pane. To generate this view:

1. Click the **Task Tab**>>**View Group**>> click **Task Usage**
2. Click the **View Tab**>>**Split View Group**>> click **Details**>> choose **Task Form**
3. Right-click in the form in the lower pane and choose "**Work**"
4. In the upper pane, right-click the **Start** column header >>**Insert Column**>> type "**Cost**"
5. Your screen should now look like Exhibit 10.13 (with adjustment of view dividers)

In Exhibit 10.13, rows 1, 5, 9, and 12 are summary tasks; rows 2, 3, 4, 6, 7, 8, 10, and 11 are subtasks. The unnumbered rows are resource assignments. Two resources are assigned to the task "Remove Trees" (Row 6). Bruce is assigned to work 24 hours on the task, and Jack is assigned eight hours. Reviewing the Resource Sheet reveals their standard cost rates are $55 and $50 per hour, respectively. Their individual costs to the task are calculated in the cost column cells at $1,320 and $400. Since they are the only two resources assigned to the task "Remove Trees," summing the two values provides the total cost of the task. Therefore, the task of removing the trees from the lot will cost the project $1,720 as calculated $[(24 \times \$55) + (8 \times \$50) = \$1,720]$, and shown in the summary row's Cost column cell. The assignment Units and Work values for the "Remove Trees" task are shown in the Task Form View in the lower pane.

VIEW COSTS FROM A DIFFERENT PERSPECTIVE   The preceding discussion has been from the view of the WBS, or task perspective. Cost data may also be viewed

HIBIT 10.13

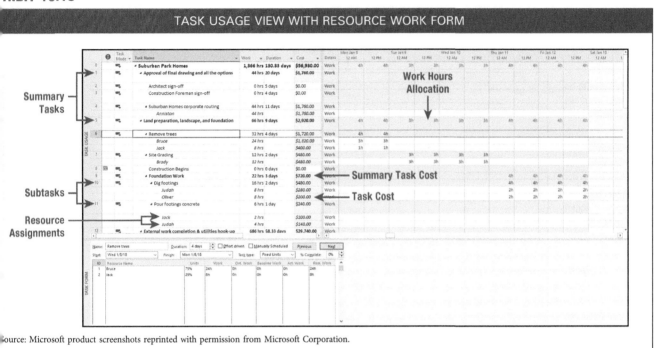

TASK USAGE VIEW WITH RESOURCE WORK FORM

Source: Microsoft product screenshots reprinted with permission from Microsoft Corporation.

from a resource perspective using the **Resource Usage View**. In this view, assignment costs are summarized at the resource level (as seen in Exhibit 10.14). To activate this view:

1. Click the **View Tab>>Split View>>** uncheck **Details**
2. Click the **View Tab>>Resource Views Group>>Resource Usage**
3. Insert a **Cost** column in the left pane (if one is not already showing)
4. In the right pane, right-click >> choose **Cost**
   a. **Work** is the default view in the Details column; this adds **Cost** to Details

In Exhibit 10.14, the most indented rows are tasks. The "Unassigned" set represents tasks with no assigned resources. If a resource has no show/hide control, then it has not been assigned.

10-5b Develop Summary Project Budget

Once duration and costs have been determined for project tasks, a simple summation of all summary row durations and costs gives the project manager an overall estimate of the project's total duration and cost. However, as discussed earlier, details of later project phases may not be completely identified in earlier stages of the project. In other words, there may be tasks later in the project whose details cannot be known early in the project.

Regardless of project unknowns, stakeholders will want ongoing estimates of the completion date and cost of the project. One way the project manager can manage these unknowns and still provide estimates is to add "dummy tasks" under any summary task where there is not enough information to plan in detail. A dummy task is simply a

EXHIBIT 10.14

RESOURCE USAGE VIEW

Work/Cost Details Column

Tasks With No Assigned Resources

Unassigned Resource (no show/hide triangle)

Task Name

Assigned Resource

	❶	Resource Name	Max. Units	Work	Cost	Details	Qtr 1, 2018 Jan	Feb	Mar	Qtr 2, 2018 Apr	May
		⊿ Unassigned	100%	80 hrs	$0.00	Work					
						Cost					
		Architect sign-off		0 hrs	$0.00	Work					
						Cost					
		Construction Foreman sign-off		0 hrs	$0.00	Work					
						Cost					
		Construction Begins		0 hrs	$0.00	Work					
						Cost					
		Receive building materials		0 hrs	$0.00	Work					
						Cost					
		Construction Complete		0 hrs	$0.00	Work					
						Cost					
		Final codes inspection		0 hrs	$0.00	Work					
						Cost					
		Codes rework		80 hrs	$0.00	Work					
						Cost					
		Suburban Homes Legal Counsel	100%	0 hrs	$0.00	Work					
2	♦	▷ Bruce	75%	308 hrs	$16,830.00	Work	42h	72h	70h	16h	
						Cost	$2,310.00	$3,960.00	$3,850.00	$990.00	
3	♦	▷ Jack	25%	72 hrs	$3,600.00	Work	16h	24h	23.33h	2.67h	
						Cost	$800.00	$1,200.00	$1,166.67	$133.33	
4		⊿ Brady	75%	240 hrs	$9,600.00	Work	12h	48h	108h	10h	
						Cost	$480.00	$1,920.00	$4,320.00	$400.00	
		Site Grading		12 hrs	$480.00	Work	12h				
						Cost	$480.00				
		Walls		120 hrs	$4,800.00	Work		48h	72h		
						Cost		$1,920.00	$2,880.00		
		HVAC		36 hrs	$1,440.00	Work			36h		
						Cost			$1,440.00		
		Hardwood flooring		72 hrs	$2,880.00	Work				10h	
						Cost				$400.00	
5		▷ Anniston	50%	198 hrs	$7,840.00	Work	4h	32h	74.67h	5.33h	
						Cost	$160.00	$1,280.00	$2,986.67	$213.33	
6		▷ Judah	50%	176 hrs	$6,160.00	Work	12h	32h	48h	78.67h	
						Cost	$420.00	$1,120.00	$1,680.00	$2,753.33	
7	♦	▷ Liam	25%	124 hrs	$6,200.00	Work	8h	24h	13.33h	78h	
						Cost	$300.00	$1,200.00	$666.67	$3,900.00	
8	♦	▷ Oliver	50%	172 hrs	$4,300.00	Work	8h		2.67h	156h	
						Cost	$200.00		$66.67	$3,900.00	
9		⊿ Plumbers	300%	80 hrs	$2,400.00	Work			80h		

Source: Microsoft product screenshots reprinted with permission from Microsoft Corporation.

placeholder for future project work. When creating a dummy task, the project manager estimates both duration and cost of the task. This estimate becomes part of the overall project summary cost and duration estimate. As details of later project phases emerge, dummy tasks can be replaced with actual task data. Each update further sharpens overall project duration and cost estimates.

A dummy task example can be seen in Exhibit 10.15. The "County clearance & Certificate of Occupancy" summary row has the dummy task "Codes rework" added. Since the project manager cannot know if rework on the house will be necessary due to a failed codes inspection (the inspection will happen after the project is almost completed), codes rework makes for a useful dummy task. No resources are assigned to the task yet, but a cost and duration estimate are assigned, allowing the project manager to factor this task into project estimates. Dummy tasks should not be carelessly added to the project since they affect project timelines and cost estimates. With experience and good planning, the project manager can judiciously add dummy tasks that will serve both the project and the stakeholders.

 Agile projects commonly use dummy tasks to summarize the work for future project iterations that have not yet been defined. Since the number of workers is often known and the length of the iteration is known, the amount of cost can usually be established. However, the exact task activities are only determined during iteration planning.

EXHIBIT 10.15

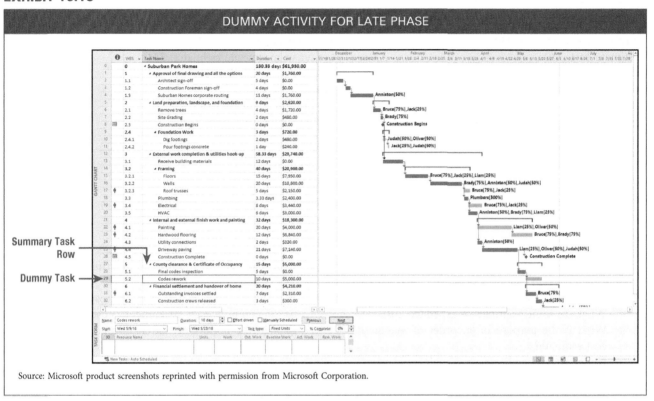

DUMMY ACTIVITY FOR LATE PHASE

Summary Task Row

Dummy Task

Source: Microsoft product screenshots reprinted with permission from Microsoft Corporation.

PMP/CAPM Study Ideas

Whether you are sitting for your CAPM or PMP exam, you are likely to see at least a couple questions pertaining to methods of cost estimating. Be able to identify parametric, analogous, and bottom-up estimating by description or via an example. Make sure you know the relative benefits and weaknesses of using each.

While budgeting occurs in countless domains, budgeting for projects is different in several ways from budgeting for ongoing operations. Specifically, you will need to familiarize yourself with the "S curve" of project expenditures and predict and answer questions about cash-flow problems that may result. Also, make sure you know the difference between contingency and management reserves and who controls each.

Summary

The cost management plan outlines how to structure and control project costs. On a small project, it can be very simple. On a large, complex project, it may need more structure. It guides the project manager during the project.

Cost estimating can be challenging because some activities may have a great deal of variation. Many methods are available to assist in cost estimating. Use a simple method if it will suffice, and use more rigorous methods, if necessary. Generally as project planning identifies more specifics, more detailed and accurate cost estimates can be made.

Cost budgeting includes aggregating individual costs, analyzing needs for cost reserves where uncertainty exists, and determining cash inflow and outflow. Establishing cost controls includes establishing cost reporting systems. MS Project can assist in developing either bottom-up project budgets or summary project budgets.

Key Terms Consistent with PMI Standards and Guides

Chapter Review Questions

1. What type of cost does not depend on the size of a project?
2. During which phase of a project do recurring costs typically occur?
3. What are some examples of expedited costs?
4. What is the purpose of an order of magnitude cost estimate?
5. Under which conditions can analogous estimating be effective?
6. Which method of estimating can produce the most accurate estimate: parametric or bottom-up?
7. What are some examples of supporting detail pertaining to cost estimates?
8. Is it possible to completely avoid variation in a project? Why or why not?
9. What can be used to determine whether a vendor's bid is reasonable?
10. Define value engineering.
11. What is the "time value of money," and why is it relevant to project management?
12. For a routine project, what is a typical percentage of total project costs that should be placed into contingency reserves? For an unusual project?
13. What is used to compare actual project spending with planned expenditures to determine if corrective action is needed?
14. What three types of data does Microsoft Project use to compute each assignment's cost value?
15. Explain the importance of creating a cost management plan.
16. Why is it important for project managers to understand the fixed and variable costs of a project?
17. Describe the difference between direct and indirect project costs.
18. During which phase(s) of a project do nonrecurring costs typically occur? Give an example of a nonrecurring cost.
19. The project manager at a software company predicts her project's costs based on previous projects she has worked on that were similar. (She takes into account the differences between her current and previous projects, as well.) What type of cost estimating is she using?
20. Why is it important for assumptions to be listed in the cost estimate?

Discussion Questions

1. A rockslide closes down a major highway on your delivery route and leads to unforeseen costs. Does the extra money needed come from contingency reserves, management reserves, or elsewhere? Why?
2. You are the project manager in charge of construction of a new school building. Give one possible example each of a known known, known unknown, and unknown unknown you might encounter.
3. Using the same project described in question 2, what are a few examples of milestones at which you might measure cost control?
4. Using the same project described in questions 2 and 3, which method(s) of estimating cost would you use in order to establish a baseline budget? Why?
5. Give an example of how a project manager could run into problems with cash flow, even when he is within budget on the overall project.

6. Describe a few normal causes and special causes of variation on a project you have worked on. How did you address these variations?

7. What is the purpose of dummy tasks, and on what types of project would you use them for budgeting purposes?

8. The order of magnitude budget estimate you created during chartering is deemed by your sponsor to cost far more than your organization is willing to spend on your project. What are your options as a project manager?

PMBOK® Guide Questions

1. The "process that establishes the policies, procedures, and documentation for planning, managing, expending, and controlling project costs" is referred to as:
   a. determine budget
   b. estimate costs
   c. plan cost management
   d. control costs

2. Activity cost estimates, the basis of estimates and other supporting detail, are outputs of which process?
   a. determine budget
   b. estimate costs
   c. plan cost management
   d. control costs

3. As the project progresses from initiation through planning and executing, and additional detail is gathered, the range of values for the project cost estimate will:
   a. broaden
   b. stay the same
   c. narrow
   d. be replaced with a single number

4. _____ is "the process of aggregating the estimated costs of individual activities or work packages to establish an authorized time-phased project budget or cost baseline."
   a. Determine cash flow
   b. Determine budget
   c. Determine cost estimates
   d. Determine funding requirements

5. A(n) _____ is used to compare actual project spending with planned expenditures over time to determine if corrective action is needed.
   a. cost baseline
   b. funding limit reconciliation
   c. reserve analysis
   d. activity resource estimate

6. Jason, a project manager, is working with his team to estimate the total cost of developing a web-based CRM system. After reviewing the planned scope of work with Jason, his sponsor suggests that Jason use the budget from a previous, similar project as the basis for his project budget. The estimating process that Jason's sponsor is using is called _____ .
   a. three-point estimating
   b. parametric estimating
   c. analogous estimating
   d. single-point estimating

7. One of the principle benefits of creating a bottom-up estimate during planning is that the estimate:
   a. can be created quickly
   b. is very accurate
   c. matches the high level estimate in the project charter
   d. will not change once the project is in flight

8. The amount of project budget reserved for unforeseen project work that addresses the "unknown unknowns" that can affect a project is the _____ .
   a. project buffer
   b. funding limit
   c. contingency reserve
   d. management reserve

9. Ellen is estimating how much it will cost to recarpet the executive conference room. After selecting the grade and pattern of carpet, Ellen multiplies the carpet price per square yard times the number of square yards in the conference room to derive the total price of the material. This estimating method is called _____ .
   a. expert judgment
   b. analogous estimating
   c. parametric estimating
   d. three-point estimating

10. The budget within the cost baseline that is allocated for identified risks, for which mitigating responses are developed, is called the _____ .
    a. contingency reserve
    b. management reserve
    c. control account
    d. activity cost estimate

Exercises

1. A baker has a contract to bake three dozen chocolate chip cookies for a customer's party. Create a bottom-up estimate that includes both items needed for the project and the cost. According to your estimate, how much should the baker charge for the cookies?

2. Using the data below, create a time-phased budget for the project. Show how much the daily and cumulative costs for the project are, just as the monthly and cumulative costs are shown in Exhibit 10.9.

	Activity	Immediate Predecessor	Duration in Days	Resource	Hourly Cost	Work Hours per Day
A	Evaluate freezers		2	Alcides	$45	6
B	Chart temperatures		6	Joan	$50	4
C	Review service record		2	Alcides		
D	Consult with HVAC engineer	A, B, C	3	Alcides		
E	Develop construction plan	D	10	Joan		
F	Complete IC assignment	E	2	Alcides		
G	Complete ROI analysis	E	5	Joan		
H	Conduct regulatory review	E	4	Joan		
I	Obtain construction approval	F, G, H	2	Alcides		

3. Using the data below, create a time-phased budget for the project. Show how much the daily and cumulative costs for the project are, just as the monthly and cumulative costs are shown in Exhibit 10.9.

WBS	Activity	Immediate Predecessor	Duration in Weeks	Resource	Hourly Cost	Hours per Week
1	Operational definition					
1.1	Research literature		3	Becky	$35	30
1.2	Identify and define terms	1.1	1	Ann	$60	30
1.3	Obtain approval of definition	1.2	2	Clive	$50	20
2	Target Selection					
2.1	Solicit partners for pilot		2	Ann		
2.2	Hold brainstorming meeting	2.1	2	Becky		
2.3	Identify characteristics of targets	2.2, 3.1	1	Ann		
2.4	Obtain approval of partners	2.3, 1.2, 3.4	1	Clive		
3	Question set					
3.1	Identify process group members		2	Clive		
3.2	Develop question set	2.3	4	Ann		
3.3	Prototype and validate question set	3.2	3	Becky		
3.4	Add partners	3.1, 2.1	3	Becky		

WBS	Activity	Immediate Predecessor	Duration in Weeks	Resource	Hourly Cost	Hours per Week
4	Pilot process					
4.1	Schedule with target audience	2.4	2	Becky		
4.2	Conduct beta test	3.4, 2.4	2	Clive		
4.3	Process feedback from target audience	4.2	2	Ann		
4.4	Conduct pilot	4.3	2	Clive		
4.5	Analyze results	4.4	2	Clive		

INTEGRATED EXAMPLE PROJECTS
SUBURBAN HOMES CONSTRUCTION PROJECT

You developed the WBS of multiple levels, including work packages, at the lowest level based on the initial project requirements below, which were further elaborated. Also, you were asked to identify all the available resources in-house and resources required externally in Chapter 9 for this case study. If not developed, it is important now to develop a resource breakdown structure (RBS) to estimate the total budget of the project.

Building a single-family, partially custom-designed home as required by Mrs. and Mr. John Thomas on Strath Dr., Alpharetta, Georgia. The single-family home will have the following features:

- 3,200 square-feet home with 4 bedrooms and 2.5 bathrooms
- Flooring—hard wood in the first floor, tiles in the kitchen and bathrooms, carpet in bedrooms
- Granite kitchen countertops, GE appliances in the kitchen
- 3-car garage and external landscaping
- Ceiling—10′ in first floor and vaulted 9′ ceilings in bedrooms
- 7-year warranty for structure and 2-year warranty for finishing components

Using the WBS and RBS, you were asked to develop a bottom-up cost estimate. This approach will require you to identify resources required for each lowest-level WBS activity. Once resources are identified, you will estimate the effort required for each resource. The cost estimate is derived from the resource effort required.

This approach tends to be more stable because, when estimating, errors have a chance to balance out. However, it requires more preparation effort than top-down estimates. In essence, the estimate is based on a more detailed understanding of the project

Tasks to Complete
- The resource expenditure of each lowest-level WBS activity is estimated.
- Resource effort (duration and cost) in monetary terms is estimated for all the resources.
- Costs for all the activities under the same WBS element at the next higher level are rolled up.
- This process is continued for all the WBS elements to determine the overall project estimate.

CASA DE PAZ DEVELOPMENT PROJECT

We received a donation of $20,000 from a personal friend who wants to remain anonymous.

We will need a total of 12 (instead of 8) donations at the $5,000.00 level for a total of $60,000, for start-up funds.

An annual event, a list of corporations as sponsors, and grant seeking are still developing.

Our choice of building will have major budget ramifications.

The list of repairs considered necessary for our second considered building (Saint Bernard) is complex and totals somewhere between $100,000 and $150,000.

Two other possible buildings are Mitchell Avenue, estimated at $50,000.00, and Virginia Avenue, estimated at $74,000.

Semester Project Instructions

Create a time-phased budget for your example project using bottom-up estimating. To the extent that your sponsor supplies rates for workers, use those. Use approximate rates for ones you cannot get. Ask your sponsor how they treat indirect costs. Be sure to include direct labor costs for yourself and your teammates. Budget your costs at the starting salary you expect to receive when you graduate (or your current salary, if you are employed). Divide your annual salary by 2,080 hours and add 20 percent for fringe. State all assumptions and constraints you have used when creating your budget. State how confident you are in your estimates and what would make you more confident. Give examples of known knowns and known unknowns on your project. Tell how you have budgeted for both of them as well as how you have budgeted for unknown unknowns.

PROJECT MANAGEMENT *IN ACTION*
The Value of Budget Optimization

At a major midwestern electric utility, budgeting for the ongoing capital expansion of the electric power system represents a process at the core of the organization's strategy and operations. During extensive annual planning efforts, a three-year capital project portfolio is developed for implementation and budgeted. The budgeting process is used to ensure that available capital is carefully scrutinized by management and applied judiciously to those projects providing the greatest strategic value on a schedule minimizing overall risk. Maintaining the forecasted budget and completing projects as planned ensures the integrity of the electrical system and the financial strength of the business.

The budgeting process itself is actually conducted year-round as planners, engineers, project managers, and financial experts endeavor to balance multiple competing objectives into a rational, achievable, and ongoing capital spending plan. There is little margin for error. Annual spending for major capital projects is typically over $250 million, representing approximately 500 projects to be completed across a five-state area. Underbudgeting means that projects potentially critical to the reliability of the electrical network may not be completed. Overbudgeting could result in investment dollars not yielding a return and reducing earnings.

As with any enterprise, the electric utility capital budget is restricted by annual spending targets necessary to maintain prudent financial ratios. In the case of capital spending, one key element involves maintaining a targeted debt-to-equity ratio. For this reason, judgments need to be made about the cost versus the value of projects considered for investment and the risks associated with potentially postponing projects to maintain favorable financial ratios.

To enable this entire process to work continuously and effectively, the utility adopted a project portfolio optimization process to create, analyze, and refine the budget for the project portfolio. This process involves executive management in creating a strategic value and risk scoring methodology that is applied during the planning phase for each project. The method assigns a value and risk score based on each individual project's forecasted impact in five critical strategic areas: financial, reliability, customer, regulatory, and system operations. A computer-based mathematical algorithm is used to optimize all possible spending portfolios to maximize value and minimize risk at specified budget levels. Within hours, the utility can analyze multiple optimized budget scenarios at various annual spending levels involving thousands of projects and nearly $1 billion of investment.

This methodology has several key benefits for the electric utility that can be applied to any organization attempting to make budgeting decisions for complex project portfolios.

- **Budget strategy well understood and communicated through the organization**—The process starts with an annual review by executive management of the strategy categories to which value and risk assessments will be applied. These categories and relative importance weightings can be adjusted to match the organization's current strategic emphasis. These categories and their relative weightings are published, communicated, and used throughout the organization.
- **Budget optimized for strategic objectives**—The scores of value and risk for each project are applied to the strategy categories and optimized to provide maximum value and minimum risk for the capital spending available. Computer software allows instant scenario changes and what-if options to be analyzed. The outcome provides management with consistent and well-understood decision-making information.

- **Consistent organizational strategy ensured**—Projects are submitted for budget consideration in the capital portfolio from throughout the utility's five-state operating area. There is a diverse array of business and financial reasons for each project to be evaluated. The use of a single enterprise-wide tool allows all projects to be analyzed on an equal basis, providing assurance that the organizational strategy is universally applied.
- **Risk thresholds and tolerance understood**—Postponing projects to conserve capital brings with it certain risks. The budget optimization process provides detailed risk analysis information on all deferred projects. Widespread communication of these risks and expert analysis of the consequences and probability allow management to make calculated and carefully considered decisions. Importantly, management gains recognition of its own risk tolerance and risk threshold levels as a result.
- **Planning horizon and purchasing power expanded**—The most significant result of the budget optimization process is the certainty with which implementation (the project execution phase) of the budget plan can be approached. The high levels of up-front management scrutiny leave little doubt about executive support for the plan going forward. This enables the planning horizon to be significantly expanded into future years and brings with it an enormous level of labor and material purchasing power in the market.
- **Project dynamics accounted for**—Although the three-year budget plan is updated annually, there are still elements of uncertainty associated with implementation of a large project portfolio. These changes might be items such as significant shifts in public policy or regulations, fundamental changes to the business model, unexpected weather events, and so on. These midstream shifts can be dealt with readily, if needed, by changing project scoring criteria, reoptimizing the project mix, and reevaluating the resulting information for options going forward.

Source: Paul R. Kling, PE, PMP, director of project management and controls, Duke Energy.

References

A *Guide to the Project Management Body of Knowledge (PMBOK® Guide)*, 6th ed. (Newtown Square, PA: Project Management Institute, 2017).

Practice Standard for Project Estimating (Newtown Square, PA: Project Management Institute, 2011).

Good, Gordon K., "Project Development and Cost Estimating: A Business Perspective," *AACE International Transactions* (2009) TCM.01.01–TCM 01.14.

Goodpasture, John C., *Project Management the Agile Way: Making It Work in the Enterprise* (Fort Lauderdale, FL: J. Ross Publishing, 2010).

Hansen, Don R., and Maryanne M. Mowen, *Managerial Accounting*, 9th ed. (Mason, OH: Cengage South-Western, 2010).

Kim, Byung-Cheol, and Kenneth F. Reinschmidt, "Combination of Project Cost Forecasts in Earned Value Management," *Journal of Construction Engineering and Management* 137 (11) (November 1, 2011): 958–966.

Kim, Yong-Woo, et al. "A Case Study of Activity-Based Costing in Allocating Rebar Fabrication Costs to Projects," *Construction Management and Economics* 29 (May 2011): 449–461.

Kinsella, Steven M., "Activity-Based Costing: Does It Warrant Inclusion in *A Guide to the Project Management Body of Knowledge (PMBOK® Guide)?*" *Project Management Journal* 33 (2) (June 2002): 49–56.

Kwak, Young Hoon, and Rudy J. Watson, "Conceptual Estimating Tool for Technology Driven Projects: Exploring Parametric Estimating Techniques," *Technovation* 25 (12) (2005): 1430–1436.

Li, Huimin, et al. "Factors That Affect Transaction Costs in Construction Projects," *Journal of Construction Engineering and Management* 139 (1) (January 1, 2013): 60–67.

Madden, Debbie, "Your Agile Project Needs a Budget, Not an Estimate," *Harvard Business Review*, https://hbr.org/2014/12/your-agile-project-needs-a-budget-not-an-estimate, accessed April 10, 2017.

Milosevic, Dragan Z., *Project Management Toolbox: Tools and Techniques for the Practicing Project Manager* (New York: John Wiley & Sons, 2003).

Needy, Kim LaScola, and Kimberly Sarnowski, "Keeping the Lid on Project Costs," in David I. Cleland, ed., *Field Guide to Project Management*, 2nd ed. (Hoboken, NJ: John Wiley & Sons, 2004).

Rad, Parviz F., *Project Estimating and Cost Management* (Vienna, VA: Management Concepts, Inc., 2002).

Rad, Parviz F., and Vittal S. Anantatmula, *Project Planning Techniques* (Vienna, VA: Management Concepts, Inc., 2005).

Tichacek, Robert L., "Effective Cost Management: Back to Basics," *Cost Engineering* 48 (3) (March 2006): 27–33.

Todd, Greg, "Five Considerations to Improve Project Estimates," *Information Management* (November/December 2009): 45–47.

Uppal, Kul B., "Cost Estimating, Project Performance and Life Cycle," *AACE International Transactions* (2009): TCM.03.01–TCM.03.09.

http://www.fluor.com/services/engineering/pages/value-engineering.aspx, accessed April 10, 2017.

http://www.rationalplan.com/projectmanagementblog/creating-budget-or-cost-baselines-for-projects/, accessed April 10, 2017.

Endnotes

1. *Practice Standard for Project Estimating*, 18.
2. Adapted from Kim LaScola Needy and Kimberly Sarnowski, "Keeping the Lid on Project Costs," in David I. Cleland, ed., *Field Guide to Project Management*, 2nd ed. (Hoboken, NJ: John Wiley & Sons, 2004): 150.
3. *Practice Standard for Project Estimating*, 83.
4. Ibid.
5. *Practice Standard for Project Estimating*, 85.
6. Greg Todd, "Five Considerations to Improve Project Estimates," Information Management (November/December 2009): 47.

7. *Practice Standard for Project Estimating*, 81.
8. *Practice Standard for Project Estimating*, 84.
9. *Practice Standard for Project Estimating*, 82.
10. http://www.fluor.com/services/engineering/ pages/value-engineering.aspx, accessed April 10, 2017.

11. *Practice Standard for Project Estimating*, 82.
12. http://www.rationalplan.com/projectmanage- mentblog/creating-budget-or-cost-baselines-for- projects/, accessed April 10, 2017.

CHAPTER 11

Project Risk Planning

David R. Frazier Photolibrary, Inc./Alamy Stock Photo

The Texas Medical Center (TMC) is composed of forty-nine not-for-profit institutions that are dedicated to the highest standards of patient care, research, and education. These institutions include thirteen renowned hospitals and two specialty institutions, two medical schools, four nursing schools, and schools of dentistry, public health, pharmacy, and virtually all health-related careers. People come from all walks of life and from all over the world to have access to the best healthcare anywhere. Member institutions specialize in every imaginable aspect of healthcare, including care for children and cancer patients, heart care, organ transplantation, terminal illness, mental health, and wellness and prevention.

Currently, 11 major construction projects are underway, including the Texas Children's Hospital's 407,000-square-foot Neurological Research Institute and 720,000-square-foot Maternity Center, along with a 12-story, 27,000-square-foot concrete-frame addition to the M. D. Anderson Cancer Center of the University of Texas Medical Center. Collectively, these major projects will add facilities that will be staffed by up to 27,000 additional employees. When complete, TMC will have 40 million square feet of occupied space. If you consider downtown business space, by itself it forms the seventh-largest downtown business district in the United States.

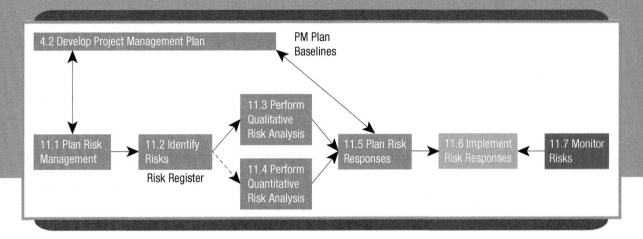

With hurricane season approaching, TMC held a conference for over 100 contractors to review how to prepare for a potential hurricane. Contractors must have a plan in place detailing how they are going to secure their construction sites and keep materials from becoming airborne missiles in the event of a hurricane. Conference attendees were given a handout describing TMC's hurricane guidelines. These guidelines call for storm preparations to be completed 24 hours before tropical storm winds are predicted to hit land. Examples of storm preparations include dismantling scaffolds and privacy screens, securing giant cranes, emptying and weighting down dumpsters, photographing all buildings and assets, and unblocking all streets for emergency access.

While project managers cannot prevent hurricanes, through careful risk planning, actions can be taken to greatly mitigate the impact.

—Rhonda Wendler, Texas Medical Center News

I magine you are asked to plan for risks on two different projects. One is a major construction project at TMC with hurricane season approaching. The other is planning a small fund-raising event for charity. Would you handle the risks on these two projects the same way? Would you invest the same level of time and energy into planning these two projects? The answers are yes and no. Yes, you would approach the risks in the same way. But you would not spend the same amount of time planning for risk on both projects. You would spend considerably more time and money on risk management planning for the major construction project that is vulnerable to a hurricane than for the small fund-raiser project. Just as in other types of project planning, there is an approach to planning for risks that all projects follow; however, the depth of planning depends greatly on the potential project risks and consequences if some of these risks are not managed. In other words, a smart project manager gladly spends $100 in risk planning to save $1,000 in expected consequences, but does not gladly spend $1,000 to save $100.

The purpose of risk management is to reduce the overall project risk to a level that is acceptable to the project sponsor and other key stakeholders. The methods that project managers use in risk management start with identifying as many risks as possible. Once the risks are identified, each risk is analyzed in terms of its likelihood of occurrence and impact on project goals if it occurs. Using this analysis, the project team can concentrate their attention on the most critical risks. Analysis always consists of a qualitative or judgmental approach for all the identified risks and sometimes also includes a quantitative approach for the critical risks. In the final risk management process, the project team decides how to respond to each potential risk. Once all the risk management planning has initially been accomplished, the response plans are incorporated into the overall project management plan. Changes may need to be made to the schedule, budget, scope, or communication plans to account for certain risks. These risk management planning processes are covered in this chapter. Risk management also includes monitoring and controlling the risks according to plan. These are covered, along with ongoing risk planning, in Chapter 14: Determining Project Progress and Results.

Agile projects are similar to other projects in regard to developing early risk planning, assessment, and response planning at a high level. However, more detailed and timely risk management occurs in planning each subsequent iteration, in daily stand-up meetings, and in retrospectives at the end of each iteration.

11-1 Plan Risk Management

Plan risk management is "the process of defining how to conduct risk management activities for a project."[1] A future event is considered a project risk if it threatens the successful accomplishment of a project goal. Obviously, a project manager must first understand the project's objectives to plan for project risks. A project manager develops this understanding initially by realizing what project success in general is and then by understanding the specific priorities of the most important project stakeholders, as discussed in Chapter 6. Exhibit 11.1 summarizes current project success research results.

The first set of general project success measures is meeting various agreements associated with a project. This includes meeting the project requirements while not going over the cost and schedule agreements. The second set of project success measures focuses on the project's customers, specifically addressing questions such as the following: *Did the project results or outcomes meet the customers' needs? Did the customers use the project result? Did it enhance the customers' satisfaction?* The third set deals with the future of the performing organization, the one that manages the project. The specific measures vary, but essentially, they focus on whether the project helped the performing organization. The **performing organization** is an enterprise whose employees have a direct involvement in executing and completing the project. Typical project success measures for the performing organization include market share, new markets and/or technologies, and commercial success of the project output. The final set of project success measures deals with the project team, for example: *Did they become better and more dedicated*

EXHIBIT 11.1

PROJECT SUCCESS MEASURES
• **Meeting Agreements** Cost, schedule, and specifications met • **Customer's Success** Needs met, deliverables used, customer satisfied • **Performing Organization's Success** Market share, new products, new technology • **Project Team's Success** Loyalty, development, satisfaction

Source: Kloppenborg, Timothy J., Debbie Tesch, and Broderick King, "21st Century Project Success Measures: Evolution, Interpretation, and Direction," *Proceedings, Project Management Institute Research and Education Conference,* July 2012, Limerick, Ireland.

EXHIBIT 11.2

SPECIFIC PROJECT STAKEHOLDER PRIORITIES			
	IMPROVE	KEEP	
Scope		X	
Quality		X	
Time			≤ 1 month to save $5,000
Cost	Want to save		
Contribution to Organization		X	
Contribution to Society		X	

Source: Adapted from Timothy J. Kloppenborg and Joseph A. Petrick, *Managing Project Quality* (Vienna, VA: Management Concepts, Inc., 2002), 46.

employees? Did they meet professional and personal aspirations and personal development goals?

The specific priorities of the project's most important stakeholders can be summarized in a table such as Exhibit 11.2. In general, the unspoken expectations from the project team are to complete the project sooner and below the budget while delivering the agreed-upon scope and quality. A project manager and the project team need to understand not only what the project plans call for but also what area(s) the most important stakeholders would like to improve and what area(s) they are willing to sacrifice to enable those improvements. For example, consider a project that calls for building a four-bedroom house of 2,800 square feet. Perhaps the homeowner (the most important stakeholder) insists on keeping the size at 2,800 square feet and insists on the normal quality (no leaks, square walls, etc.), but would like to improve on the cost (pay less money). To improve on the cost objective, one of the other objectives probably needs to be sacrificed. Perhaps the homeowner would be willing to move in a month late if the savings were $5,000.

Once the project team understands the project success measures and priorities, attention is turned to understanding the project risks. All projects have some risk, and the more unique a project is, the more risk there will be. Uniqueness of a project is usually associated with uncertainties and unknowns, which contribute to project risks. It is impossible to remove all sources of risk. It is undesirable to even try to remove all risks because that means the organization is not trying anything new. Without risk, there is no gain or progress.

A **project risk** is anything that may impact the project team's ability to achieve the general project success measures and the specific project stakeholders' priorities. This impact can be something that poses a **threat**, which is "a condition or situation unfavorable to the project that presents a negative set of circumstances or events or consequences. A threat also is a risk that will have a negative impact on a project objective if it occurs."[2]

The impact of a threat, on the other hand, could be something that poses an **opportunity** or "a condition or situation favorable to the project, a positive set of circumstances, a positive set of events, a risk that will have a positive impact on project objectives."[3]

Wise project managers strive to develop a **risk management plan**, an important plan that is integral to the comprehensive project management plan that describes how risks

EXHIBIT 11.3

RISK MANAGEMENT PLAN GUIDANCE FOR AN IT CONSULTING COMPANY

Risk management includes guidance on how to perform three risk management activities:

1. Decide what level of risk premium to charge for the project. The team must rate factors such as project size, complexity, technology, and type. The combined ratings dictate that a risk premium of 0, 10, or 20 percent be added to the estimated project cost or, for very risky projects, that executive approval is mandated.
2. Mitigate risk external to the firm through contract clauses and risk internal to the firm through agreements.
3. Manage the risk very carefully through specifically designed weekly conference call meetings and reports.

Source: Rachana Thariani, PMP®

are prioritized, monitored for changing priorities, and how prioritized risk management activities will be planned and performed. Usually, a risk management plan develops a mitigation strategy for all the prioritized risks before these risk events occur. By documenting risk information in a proactive manner, a project manager can eliminate or reduce the impact of some threats and capitalize on some opportunities. The risk management plan is also useful for communicating with the various project stakeholders and for later analysis to determine what worked well and may be good practice to use on future projects, as well as what went poorly and should be avoided on future projects.

Some risk management plans include all the topics in this chapter. Others are smaller. For example, a risk management plan template for an IT consulting company is shown in Exhibit 11.3.

11-1a Roles and Responsibilities

It is a good practice to encourage wide participation in risk management activities. One reason is that everyone brings a different perspective, and the more perspectives that are considered, the more likely it is that important risks will be uncovered early. Another good reason is that people often resist when they are told what to do but work with great enthusiasm if they participated in the planning. The surest way to get the various project stakeholders to buy into a risk management approach is to involve them in risk management planning right from the beginning. Potential critics can be turned into allies if their concerns are included.

The risk management plan should define who is responsible for each risk management activity. On small projects, often the project manager or a core team member is responsible for most risk activities. On larger projects, the plan can be more elaborate and subject matter experts may be involved at many points.

11-1b Categories and Definitions

Most projects have many types of possible risks. Therefore, it is helpful to look at risks in a systematic manner so as to consider as many types of risks as possible. One way to look at risk is by considering when it occurs in the project life cycle. For example:

- Certain types of risks, such as a customer not agreeing on the price, may occur during project initiation.
- Others, such as not finding a capable supplier, may occur during project planning.
- Risks, such as delivery difficulties from a supplier, may occur during project execution.

- Omission of some of the essential activities in the WBS may also be realized during the project execution.
- Risks, such as the project deliverable not actually working properly, may even appear near the project conclusion.

The number and costs of project risks over a project life cycle are graphed in Exhibit 11.4. More project risks are typically uncovered early in the life of a project. However, the cost per risk discovered early is often less since there will be an opportunity and time to make changes to the project plan. Risks discovered late in a project can prove to be very expensive. Experienced project managers work hard to uncover risks as early in the project as feasible. Usually, some risks are uncovered when chartering the project. On small or simple projects, this may be the biggest risk identification push, but on other projects, a great deal of time and effort may also be expended during project planning.

In addition to being categorized by when they might occur in a project, risks can also be categorized by what project objective they may impact, such as cost, schedule, scope, and/or quality. Risks can also be classified as external to the performing organization and internal to it, or by whether they are operational or strategic. Many organizations have developed lists of risks for certain types of projects they routinely perform. In addition, many writers have created general lists of risk factors for certain types of projects. For example, recent research has shown the largest risks on megaprojects include risks from nine causes:

1. Design
2. Legal and political
3. Contractual

EXHIBIT 11.4

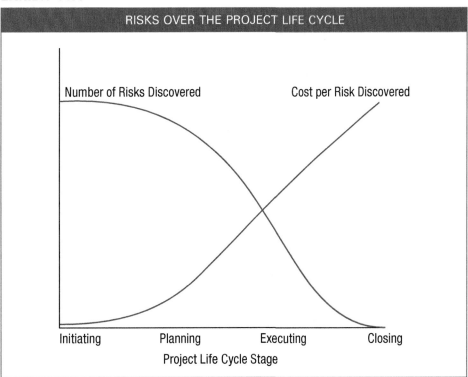

RISKS OVER THE PROJECT LIFE CYCLE

Number of Risks Discovered   Cost per Risk Discovered

Initiating   Planning   Executing   Closing

Project Life Cycle Stage

4. Construction
5. Operation and maintenance
6. Labor
7. Customer/user/society
8. Financial
9. Force majeure (an unforeseen event that prevents a contract from being fulfilled)[4]

Another recent study found that green retrofit projects classify their biggest risks as coming from eight areas:

1. Post-tenants' cooperation
2. Regulatory
3. Industry
4. Financial
5. Pre-retrofit tenant's cooperation
6. Varying concerns from different stakeholders
7. Material supply and availability
8. Quality[5]

For a few further examples, Exhibit 11.5 shows the biggest 14 risks on the Panama Canal expansion (which might be similar to those of other major construction projects). Exhibit 11.6 shows major risk categories for international projects generally, and Exhibit 11.7 shows common risks for information systems projects. Any of these categorizations can be shown as a **risk breakdown structure**, which presents a hierarchical organization of risks based on categories such as operational, strategic, finance, external, and project management. A Risk Breakdown Structure is similar to a WBS or a resource breakdown structure (RBS) in its hierarchical representation. It can be presented in graphic or table format.

Yet another method to classify project risk is by what is known and what is not known about each risk. Something that is a known known can be planned and managed with certainty; therefore, it is not a risk. An example is that cement will harden. The next level is known unknowns, which are risks that can be identified as risk but the likelihood of them is not known. In other words, a known unknown may or may not happen. These risks should be identified, and an analysis (qualitative for sure and quantitative if

EXHIBIT 11.5

FOURTEEN MOST IMPORTANT RISKS IN PANAMA CANAL EXPANSION	
Changes in design and quantities	Extreme bad weather
General inflation	Inadequate claims administration
Ineffective contracting process	Inefficient planning
Insufficient revenues	Lack of controls
Lack of skilled and local labor	Local labor strikes
Material, equipment, and labor cost	Organizational risks
Owner-driven changes	Referendum delays

Source: Alarcon, Luis F., et al., "Risk Planning and Management for the Panama Canal Expansion Program," *Journal of Construction Engineering and Management* (October 2011): 762–770.

EXHIBIT 11.6

TOP RISKS IN EACH FACTOR FOR INTERNATONAL PROJECTS	
CULTURAL	VIRTUAL
Number of languages	Communication issues
Trust level	Number of countries
Economic culture	Management experience
Number of religions	Number of time zones
POLITICAL	REGIONAL
Government desire for project	Crime rate
Government unrest	Climate/weather
Laws and regulations	Housing availability
Relationship with government	Safety issues and procedures

Source: Steffey, Robert W., and Vittal S. Anantatmula, "International Projects Proposal Analysis: Risk Assessment Using Radial Maps," *Project Management Journal* (April 2011): 62–70.

EXHIBIT 11.7

TOP RISKS IN EACH FACTOR FOR SOFTWARE PROJECTS	
EXECUTION MANAGEMENT	USER COORDINATION
Configuration management system	User evaluation of progress
Formality of status reports	User understanding of complexity
Specification approval process	Care in user manual preparation
Post-project audits	Coordination with user
Regularity of technical reviews	Informal communication channels
HUMAN RESOURCE MANAGEMENT	PROJECT PLANNING
Flexibility of working hours	Frequency of software reuse
Individual performance incentives	Planning tools used
Technical assistance availability	Minimum cost software design
Recognition for extra work	Removal of unnecessary requirements
Enforced attendance system	Individual accountability

Source: Thomas, Sam, and M. Bhasi, "A Structural Model for Software Project Risk Management," *Journal of Management* (March 2011): 71–84.

helpful) must be made to identify a mitigation strategy before a contingency reserve is established to pay for them. An example on a long construction project is that bad weather will probably happen at some points, but no one knows exactly when or how bad it will be. The final level is for the true uncertainties. These are called unknown unknowns (or unk unks by people who must deal with them). Since they cannot even be envisioned, it is hard to know how much reserve time and money are needed to cover them. They are usually covered by a management reserve, and the amount of this reserve is often negotiated based upon the confidence level the project manager and key stakeholders have regarding how well they understand the project. An example could be a 100-year flood that covers a construction site that everyone thought was on high enough ground to stay dry—an event so rare it is expected to happen only once a century. The tsunami that devastated a part of Japan in March 2011 was completely unexpected and an unknown risk that many projects in that region did not anticipate.

Savvy organizations are now often encouraging their project managers to reduce the number of unk unks by learning more about them so they can be known unknowns. They learn more by a combination of design approaches such as analyzing scenarios, using checklists, considering weak signals that might have been previously ignored, and mining big data. They also use behavioral approaches such as frequent and effective communication and creating incentives for discovery.[6]

11-2 Identify Risks

Once the risk management planning is in place, it is time to begin identifying specific risks. **Identify risks** is "the process of determining which risks may affect the project and documenting their characteristics."[7] Project managers are ultimately responsible for identifying all risks, but often they rely upon subject matter experts to take a lead in identifying certain technical risks.

11-2a Information Gathering

A large part of the risk identification process is gathering information. The categories shown in Exhibits 11.5, 11.6, and 11.7 and/or project stages can be a good starting point in this information gathering. The project manager either needs to act as a facilitator or get another person to serve as facilitator for information gathering. This is essentially a brainstorming technique, during which time the question "What could go wrong?" is repeatedly asked of everyone who is present for every activity identified in the WBS. It is helpful to use Post-it Notes and write one risk per note to prepare for further processing the risks during risk analysis.

Classic rules for brainstorming are used. For example, every idea is treated as a useful idea. The risks will be assessed next. Even if a suggested risk does not prove to be important, it is preferable to keep it on the list. Also, sometimes a risk that is obviously not important—or is even humorous—may cause another person to think of an additional risk they would not have considered otherwise.

While it is helpful to have as many stakeholders together as possible to "piggyback" on each other's ideas, with the information technology available today, much of the same interaction can be achieved by global and virtual teams; it just takes more careful planning. Variations, combinations, and extensions of possible risks can help a project team to identify additional risks.

Several other techniques are also used in risk identification. The project team members may choose to interview stakeholders, specifically when a project is big, complex, and is associated with many uncertainties. In certain cases, **SWOT analysis**, which is a detailed analysis of the project's and project management's strengths, weaknesses, opportunities, and threats, might be used. Remember, risks can be both threats to overcome and opportunities to exploit. Yet another method of identifying risks is the **Delphi technique**, an information gathering technique used as a way to reach a consensus among experts on a subject, with the experts participating anonymously in order to avoid groupthink and prejudice. Responses are summarized and recirculated for further comments and improvements. Finally, a team can use a structured review to identify risks.

11-2b Reviews

A project manager and team can review a variety of project documents to uncover possible risks. Exhibit 11.8 lists some of the documents a project manager may use and typical questions he or she would ask for each. Project teams can often identify risks from each type of review shown in the exhibit. Of these, assumptions and the WBS are especially important sources for identifying risks. Every wrong assumption becomes a project risk. We initially develop a list of assumptions and constraints in the project charter. However, the list needs to be updated during the project planning phase and must be critically examined during the risk management planning to assess if all these assumptions are correct. Likewise, each work package in the WBS must be examined to identify risks associated with it. It is important to maintain balance between the extent of the reviews and the amount of useful information for identifying risks. As with the brainstorming mentioned previously, it is better to identify many possible risks and later determine that some of them are not major, rather than to *not* identify what *does* turn out to be a big risk.

EXHIBIT 11.8

PROJECT RISK REVIEWS	
TYPE OF REVIEW	QUESTION
Charter	Is there clarity and common understanding in each section?
Stakeholder register	What could upset any of them?
Communication plan	Where could poor communications cause trouble?
Assumptions	Can you verify that each assumption is correct?
Constraints	How does each constraint make the project more difficult?
WBS	What risks can you find going through the WBS item by item?
Schedule	What milestones and other merge points might be troublesome?
Resource demands	At what points are certain people overloaded?
Touch points	What difficulties may arise when some project work is handed off from one person to another?
Literature	What problems and opportunities have been published concerning similar projects?
Previous projects	What projects and opportunities have similar projects in your own organization experienced?
Peers	Can your peers identify any additional risks?
Senior management	Can senior management identify any additional risks?

11-2c Understanding Relationships

Project managers can also seek to identify risks by learning the cause-and-effect relationships of risk events. One useful technique is a flow chart that shows how people, money, data, or materials flow from one person or location to another. This is essentially what the team does when it reviews the project schedule, provided it looks at the arrows that show which activities must precede others. By studying the flows, a person can consider which "handoffs" (when one person or team passes deliverables to another) might be risky.

A second method of understanding risk relationships is to ask why a certain risk event may happen. This can be accomplished through **root cause analysis**, which is an analytical technique to ascertain the fundamental or causal reason or reasons that affect one or more variances, defects, or risks. A simple approach to root cause analysis is to simply consider each risk one at a time and ask, "Why might this happen?" At this point, since many potential risks have probably been identified, project teams do not spend a large amount of time on any single risk. If necessary, the project team can perform more detailed root cause analysis of the few risks that have been designated as major risks during risk analysis.

One more type of relationship project managers like to understand is **trigger conditions**, or a "circumstance under which a risk strategy or risk action will be invoked."[8] A trigger can be specific to an individual risk, such as when a key supplier stops returning phone calls, which may jeopardize their delivery of materials.

11-2d Risk Register

The primary output of risk identification is the risk register. When complete, the **risk register** is "the document containing the results of the qualitative risk analysis, quantitative risk analysis, and risk response planning. It details all identified risks, including description, category, cause, probability of occurring, impact(s) on objectives, proposed responses, owners, and current status."[9] At this point (the end of risk identification), the risk register includes only the risk categories, identified risks, potential causes, and potential responses. The other items are developed during the remainder of risk planning. An example of a partial risk register is shown in Exhibit 11.9.

The risk register is a living document. As a risk is identified, it is added. More information regarding a risk can be added when it is discovered. It is normal to identify more risks during all the phases of the project. As risks are addressed, they can be removed from the risk register because they no longer are of the same level of concern. On smaller projects, a spreadsheet works fine for a risk register. On larger, more complex projects, some organizations use databases.

11-3 Risk Analysis

Every project team must consider risks diligently. If a project team is serious about risk identification, they will uncover quite a few risks. Next, the team needs to decide which risks are major and need to be managed carefully, as opposed to those minor risks that can be handled more casually. The project team should determine how well they understand each risk and whether they have the necessary reliable data. Ultimately, they must be able to report the major risks to decision makers.

11-3a Perform Qualitative Risk Analysis

Perform qualitative risk analysis is "the process of prioritizing risks for further analysis or action by assessing and combining their probability of occurrence and impact."[10] All project teams should perform this analysis. If the project team understands enough about the risks at this point, it can proceed directly to risk response planning for the major risks. If not, they use more quantitative techniques to help them understand the risks better. The risk factor of a risk is the product of probability and consequence. Risks with higher risk factors are considered for quantitative analysis.

DIFFERENTIATING BETWEEN MAJOR AND MINOR RISKS Project teams use two primary questions in qualitative risk analysis: How likely is this risk to happen? If it does happen, how big will the impact be? This was shown in Exhibit 3.8 (see page 74). A somewhat more involved example is shown in Exhibit 11.9. Note that for each dimension—probability and impact—in Exhibit 11.10, a scale of 1 to 5 is used with descriptions. The scale used does not matter, as long as it is applied consistently and is easy for everyone to understand. Note also the dark line. This line separates the major and catastrophic risks that need either further analysis and/or specific contingency plans from minor and moderate risks that can just be listed and informally monitored. Without making a distinction like this, project teams may be tempted to either ignore all risks or to make contingency plans for all risks. Ignoring all risks is not desirable because it almost warrants that the project has problems. Making contingency plans for even minor risks is a terrible waste of time and draws focus away from the critical risks.

Some people choose to make a finer distinction in their risk analysis by coding the biggest risks red, moderate ones yellow, and smaller ones green like stoplights. This

Teams should assess potential risks and predict possible outcomes involved in a project.

Paul Hennessy/Alamy Stock Photo

EXHIBIT 11.9

PARTIAL RISK REGISTER

RISK DESCRIPTION (EVENT)	IMPACT	CATEGORY	PROB	IMPACT	SCORE	MITIGATION STRATEGY-RESOLUTION
Incomplete requirements were identified in the RFP and Exhibits (see Risk 7).	Greater possibility of gaps in functionality. Greater possibility of missing State specific functionality. Greater possibility of "Scope Creep." Greater possibility of delay in finalizing requirements. Greater possibility of rework in subsequent phases.	Business Requirements	5	4	20	MAXIMUS will begin conducting the detailed BA sessions 09/20/2012. Additional requirements will be gathered in those sessions and documented in subsequent versions of the Requirements Validation Documentation. A schedule of future Business Architecture and Technical sessions is being developed. State will provide closure and decisions regarding requirements and system scope.
Since there are various vendor products (IBM/Curam, Connecture), each with its own rules engines, it is not clear which rules engine takes precedence.	Potential duplication of rules or conflicting rules that lead to different outcomes.	Technology	3	4	12	Engage Point will provide an explanation of how to mitigate this risk. (See Risk Response Plan for resolution.)
Difficulty integrating to States end- to-end Infrastructure.	Potential difficulty integrating new technology into existing infrastructure.	Technology	4	4	16	Work with the State to define infrastructure requirements and ensure we are providing any necessary information to the MN-IT staff.
Going through hierarchical reporting structure will impact real-time decision making.	Potential bottlenecks in document reviews and decision making may affect task completion according to the Project Schedule.	Communications	4	4	16	Identifying a Point-of-Contact for each functional area from vendor and state to eliminate bottlenecks.
State functional POCs may have competing priorities that will hinder their ability to response in a timely manner.	Secondary risk—related to Risk 6.	Communications	4	4	16	Identifying multiple Points-of-Contact for each functional area from vendor and state to eliminate bottlenecks.
Delays in procurement process may negatively impact project schedule.	Inability to acquire resources in a timely manner may negatively impact related activities in the Project Schedule.	Procurement	2	5	10	Add lead time as early as possible. Evaluate procurement requirements during the change order process. Make sure Commerce procurement staff are engaged in the PO development process.

Source: http://mn.gov/hix/images/BC9-1-IT AttachmentN.pdf, accessed April 26, 2013.

EXHIBIT 11.10

QUALITATIVE RISK ASSESSMENT					
PROBABILITY		IMPACT			
	INSIGNIFICANT (1)	MINOR (2)	MODERATE (3)	MAJOR (4)	CATASTROPHIC (5)
Almost certain (>90% chance)	High	High	Extreme	Extreme	Extreme
Likely (50–90%)	Moderate	High	High	Extreme	Extreme
Moderate (10–50%)	Low	Moderate	High	Extreme	Extreme
Unlikely (3–10%)	Low	Low	Moderate	High	Extreme
Rare (<3%)	Low	Low	Moderate	High	High

may be good practice on bigger, more complex projects. The important point is to make sure to have specific plans for big risks while not overreacting to small ones.

Project teams must ask, regarding each risk: When it is likely to occur in the project lifecycle? This can be useful because those risks that are likely to occur earlier often need to be assigned a higher priority. Teams may also inquire how easy it is to notice and correctly interpret the trigger condition. Risks with triggers that are difficult to notice or interpret often are assigned a higher priority.

CAUSE-AND-EFFECT RELATIONSHIPS   One additional type of qualitative risk analysis is to determine cause-and-effect relationships. This is part of root cause analysis, which was described in the previous section on understanding relationships. While effects are often more visible, it is easier to change the effect by changing the underlying cause. For example, assume that a construction worker is not laying stones evenly for a patio (the effect). Perhaps the easiest way to ensure that future stones are placed evenly is to understand why the worker is having problems. The cause may turn out to be inconsistent stone size, incorrectly prepared ground, the cement for holding the stones having bigger gravel than normal, or an improperly functioning leveling tool. Once the causes are understood, they can serve as trigger conditions to identify that a risk event may be about to happen. This knowledge is useful when developing responses to risks.

CAUSE-AND-EFFECT DIAGRAM   A tool that is useful in this analysis is the cause-and-effect diagram. Many project teams use this diagram to identify possible causes for a risk event. An example is shown in Exhibit 11.11.

The cause-and-effect diagram is also known as the fishbone diagram because its many lines make it look like the skeleton of a dead fish. To construct the cause-and-effect diagram, the project team first lists the risk as the effect in a box at the head of the fish. In this example, it is late delivery. The more specifically the risk is stated, the more likely it is that the team can uncover its real causes. The next step is to name the big bones. In this case, there are four big bones named *people, machines, methods,* and *materials.* There can be any number of big bones, and they can be named whatever makes sense to the team constructing the diagram. Team members are then encouraged to keep asking the question "Why?" For example: Why could people be a cause? Two reasons are shown: they are not trained properly or they are overallocated. Often, a team proposes

EXHIBIT 11.11

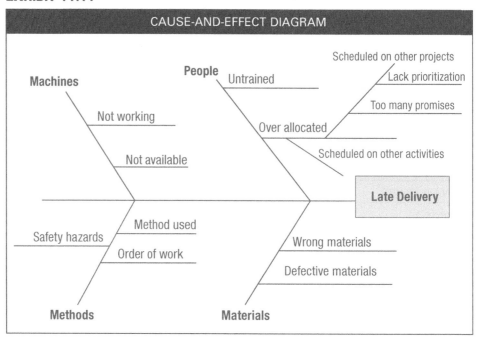

CAUSE-AND-EFFECT DIAGRAM

many possible reasons. The team continues to break down the reasons—that is, asking "why" until it no longer makes sense to ask why. Cause-and-effect diagrams are frequently much fuller than this small example (Exhibit 11.11), with dozens of potential causes. Once the team no longer can think of possible causes, they need to determine which of the many possible causes are true causes. Selecting a few likely causes and then testing them can determine this.

11-3b Perform Quantitative Risk Analysis

Perform quantitative risk analysis is "the process of numerically analyzing the effect of identified risks on overall project objectives."[11] While all projects use qualitative risk analysis, quantitative risk analysis is used only when necessary and only on selected risks. Bigger, more complex, riskier, and more expensive projects often can benefit from the additional rigor of these more structured techniques. Quantitative risk analysis is often used when predicting with confidence the probability of completing a project on time, on budget, and with the agreed-upon scope and/or when the agreed-upon quality is critical. Some of the more frequently used quantitative techniques follow:

- **Decision tree analysis:** a graphic tool depicting alternative choices as branches, multiple options for each alternative, and evaluating potential outcomes in terms of uncertainty and monetary value.
- **Expected monetary value (EMV) analysis:** a statistical technique to calculate present value of future outcomes to choose the best alternative. It is generally used for engineering economics and cost-benefit analysis.
- **Failure mode and effect analysis (FMEA):** "a step-by-step approach for identifying all possible failures in a design, a manufacturing or assembly process, or a product or service."[12]

- **Sensitivity analysis:** a quantitative what-if risk analysis technique that presents comparative analyses of various desirable outcomes with respect to a financial measure or uncertainty. It can be used to determine which risks have the most impact on the project outcomes or goals.

  Tornado diagrams are often used to represent this analysis. A **tornado diagram** is a special type of bar chart and data where project goals are listed vertically and risk uncertainties are depicted horizontally as probability. The order of presenting the categories is that that the largest bar appears on the top and the smallest bar appears at the bottom.
- **Simulation:** a technique that mimics real situations using uncertainties and assessing their impact on project objectives. In the context of projects, the simulation technique called Monte Carlo analysis develops probability distribution of risks and their impact on project goals such as cost and time.

Criteria to help select a suitable quantitative risk technique or methodology should do the following:

- Use explicit knowledge of the project team members.
- Allow quick response.
- Help determine project cost and schedule contingency.
- Foster clear communication.
- Be easy to learn and use.

11-3c Risk Register Updates

The probability of each risk occurring and the impact if it does happen are added to the register for each risk. The priority for each risk is also listed. Some organizations use a "Top 10" list to call attention to the highest-priority risks. In addition, some organizations choose to place higher priority on risks that are likely to happen soon. Some organizations want to call attention to risks that are difficult to detect—that is, risks with obscure trigger conditions. Any of these means of calling attention to certain risks are also listed in the risk register. If the project team performed any quantitative risk analysis, the results are also documented in the risk register.

11-4 Plan Risk Responses

Once risks have been identified and analyzed, the project team decides how they will handle each risk. **Plan risk responses** is "the process of developing options and actions to enhance opportunities and to reduce threats to project objectives."[13] This is often a creative time for project teams as they decide how they will respond to each major risk. Sometimes a team develops multiple strategies for a single risk because they do not believe one strategy will reduce the threat or exploit the opportunity as much as the stakeholders would like. The team may decide that it is not worth the effort to eliminate a threat completely. In those cases, the goal is to reduce the threat to a level that the sponsor and other stakeholders deem acceptable.

11-4a Strategies for Responding to Risks

Because so many possible strategies can be developed for dealing with project risks, it helps to classify the strategies. Common risk strategies are shown in Exhibit 11.12.

Leo/Shutterstock.com

AVOID RISK   Many people prefer to avoid a risk if possible, and often, that is the best strategy. Sometimes, a project plan can be altered to avoid a risk by deleting the risky section or work element. For example, if the local police tell the organizers of a parade that traffic patterns on one section of their route are very difficult to control, perhaps they may alter the route. Project risk response strategy decisions often must be made with a thorough understanding of the key stakeholders' priorities of cost, schedule, scope, and quality. In this example, if no powerful stakeholder had a strong interest in the exact route, the change might be easily made. However, project managers need to understand that every decision they make regarding risk response strategies may impact something else.

Another avoidance strategy is to ensure communications are good, especially concerning risky issues. Many risks can be more easily addressed with prompt and accurate information. The ultimate avoidance strategy is to not perform the project at all. This choice is sometimes made when the risks posed by the project are deemed unacceptably large compared to the potential benefits. Before a decision is made not to perform a project at all, normally each of the other strategies is considered.

TRANSFER RISK   Sometimes, a decision is made to transfer a part of or an entire project risk to another organization. One common means to do so is through insurance. Project insurance works like any other type of insurance: a premium is paid to another organization, which will assume a level of risk. Higher premiums need to be paid for more risk to be assumed (think of lower deductibles). Therefore, using insurance as a risk transfer strategy is a two-part decision: Do we transfer risk, and, if so, how much risk do we transfer? The answer generally is "enough so the overall risk is acceptable to key stakeholders."

A second transfer strategy deals with the type of contract used. An owner wishing to transfer risk to a developer will want to use a fixed-price contract. The developer who

EXHIBIT 11.12

COMMON PROJECT RISK STRATEGIES		
STRATEGY	TYPE OF RISK	EXAMPLES
Avoid	Threat	1. Change project plan and/or scope 2. Improve project communications 3. Decide not to perform project
Transfer	Threat	1. Insurance 2. Fixed-price contract 3. Hire expert
Mitigate	Threat	1. Lower probability and/or impact of threat 2. Build in redundancy 3. Use more reliable methods
Accept	Threat and opportunity	1. Deal with it if and when it happens 2. Establish triggers and update frequently 3. Establish time and/or cost contingencies
Research	Threat and opportunity	1. Get more and/or better information 2. Verify assumptions 3. Use prototype
Exploit	Opportunity	1. Assign talented resources to project 2. Give more emphasis to project
Share	Opportunity	1. Allocate partial ownership to third party 2. Form joint venture
Enhance	Opportunity	1. Increase probability and/or positive impact 2. Identify and maximize key drivers 3. Add more resources

Source: Adapted from *A Guide to the Project Management Body of Knowledge (PMBOK® Guide)* (Newtown Square, PA: Project Management Institute, 2008): 261–263; Paul S. Royer, *Project Risk Management: A Proactive Approach* (Vienna, VA: Management Concepts, Inc., 2002): 35; and Eric Verzuh, *The Fast Forward MBA in Project Management,* 2nd ed. (Hoboken, NJ: John Wiley & Sons, 2005): 100–103.

accepts the risk would insist on a higher price to cover her uncertainty. A fixed-price contract can be used when the scope is well defined. A developer who wishes to transfer risk to an owner would prefer a cost-plus contract under which she is compensated for her cost plus a certain amount of profit. The owner, in turn, would prefer to drive for a low cost in such an arrangement because he is assuming the risk. This risk transfer strategy of using contracts is employed when the scope cannot be defined completely. Other types of contracts can be written so that both parties share the project risk.

A third risk transfer strategy is to hire an expert to perform the risk and to hold that person accountable. None of the transfer strategies eliminate risk; they just transfer the risk and let someone else assume it.

MITIGATE RISK   Mitigation strategies are those in which an effort is made to lower risk. In general, this means either reducing the probability of a risk event happening and/or reducing the impact if it does happen. For example, a major risk could be that a key resource may not be available. To reduce the probability of that happening, perhaps the person could be hired well in advance of the project and then not be assigned to work on any other projects. To reduce the impact if this person were not available, perhaps the project team would like to use the second mitigation strategy of building redundancy. They could train another team member to do the work of the key resource. Redundancy is a way of life in systems projects. An example is building a redundant system when developing an aircraft to increase reliability and safety. However, we must be judicious in selecting redundancy because the weight of the aircraft would increase and could become prohibitive in cost. In such cases, a third mitigation strategy is often utilized: use more reliable methods. If the primary way of performing a key activity is highly reliable, there is less need for other mitigation strategies.

ACCEPT RISK   A fourth risk response strategy is to accept the risk. This is often used for risks that are deemed to be minor. The project team deals with them if and when they happen. If the risks are deemed to be minor, most of them will not happen, and when they do, most will not cause major disruptions. However, some risks can have significant impact on the project if left untended. Therefore, project teams often define a trigger condition for some of these accepted risks. The trigger condition marks the dividing point where, instead of just monitoring the risk, the team starts to deal with it.

For fruit and vegetable growers in California, the trigger condition may be a weather report predicting cold temperatures. Armed with that knowledge, the growers enact strategies to protect their crops to the extent possible. The growers are willing to accept the risk of cold weather occasionally because they make enough money at other times to compensate for the loss. If they were in a climate with more cold weather, they may choose not to grow sensitive crops during the cold season. One other acceptance strategy is to put contingencies of time and/or money into the project plan to cover the risks that transpire. Each of these acceptance strategies can also be used to take advantage of opportunities. All the strategies—establishing trigger conditions to notify the team when an opportunity is present, dealing with it as it happens, and having a little extra time and money to alter the project plans to reap the potential benefits—make sense. An example of these three strategies applied to an opportunity could be when a company develops a new style of hat, a celebrity wears it on TV, and then the demand takes off. By using more money to advertise to the unexpected customers, the company may generate many additional sales.

RESEARCH RISK   In certain instances, the best way to handle a risk is to learn more about it. The first research strategy, therefore, is to secure better and/or more information so the project team understands what they are dealing with. Projects often are conducted in a rapidly changing environment in which decisions need to be made quickly, often based upon imperfect and incomplete information. It is unusual to gather and verify all the information desired, and we may not be able to do so; however, at times it is useful to gather as much information as possible.

Another research strategy is to verify assumptions that have been made. Assumptions that prove to be false become risks. Yet another research strategy is to perform the project on a small scale first to see if it works. This can include developing a prototype, test marketing a new product, running new software in one department first, and so on. Project teams can often learn a great deal from trying their ideas on a small scale first. These research strategies work well for both reducing threats and capitalizing on opportunities.

EXPLOIT OPPORTUNITY   One strategy that is aimed exclusively at opportunities is exploitation. A project manager may identify trigger conditions that, if reached, will allow her to go to her sponsor to request that the project be assigned a higher priority. If the organization wants to exploit opportunities, they can assign more or better resources to the project, remove barriers, and give it more visibility in management reviews.

SHARE OPPORTUNITY   One additional exploitation strategy deals with the results of the project. Perhaps the project team can develop a new product or service so revolutionary that the parent organization is not capable of fully exploiting it. In a case like this, the parent organization may spin off a nimble subsidiary, form a joint venture with another firm, or sell the rights to the product.

ENHANCE OPPORTUNITY   Essentially, a project team wants to either maximize the probability that an opportunity will occur and/or maximize the benefit if it does. The project manager wants to identify key drivers of these positive impacts and develop strategies to capitalize upon them. Certainly, adding more or better resources is one way to enhance opportunities.

11-4b Risk Register Updates

The project manager sees that the risk register is updated with the results of the response planning. For each risk, the response strategy is noted. It also means that a single person is assigned as the "owner" of each risk, and that person is responsible for understanding the trigger and for implementing the strategy. Finally, any changes that need to be made to the project schedule, budget, resource assignments, and communications plan should be included.

Risks associated with agile projects are often associated with development process conflicts, business process conflicts, and people conflicts. Development process conflicts relate to functionality and short and focused iterations. They are different from traditional projects that aim at optimizing development. Business process conflicts in agile projects are due to higher ambiguity and uncertainty that compel us to focus on short-term results and long-term haziness. Further, the WBS is developed incrementally.

On the other hand, agile projects demand that the product owner remain closely involved throughout the project. This focus can reduce risk because many details are handled as they arise. Also, since something of value needs to be delivered at each iteration with a test to confirm that it works, risks tend to be uncovered quickly, before they become too significant.

PMP/CAPM Study Ideas

As a project manager, your goal is to complete your project on time, on budget, at an agreed-upon level of quality, and to the satisfaction of your client and other stakeholders. Risks are anything that could impede—*or help*—you in this goal. Remember that, according to the Project Management Institute, project risks can be negative or positive. The strategies for dealing with negative risks, or threats, are as follows: avoid, transfer, mitigate, research, and accept. Conversely, the strategies for dealing with positive threats, or opportunities are the following: exploit, enhance, share, research, and accept.

In creating a risk management plan, the first step is to identify all possible risks. While it may seem counterintuitive (and, therefore, you may see a question or two about it on your CAPM or PMP test), you do not want to plan for all risks. That is why your next step is to categorize them based on both probability of occurrence and potential impact. Only the risks that emerge as "major" based on these two criteria are actively planned for. All projects make use of qualitative planning, and larger projects often proceed to quantitative planning (if may help you to remember that the "l" in *qualitative* comes alphabetically before the "n" in *quantitative*). You won't need to be an expert, but you should be familiar with the most common quantitative assessments.

Summary

All projects have some risks. More unique projects have more uncertainties and unknowns and, therefore, more risks. A project manager needs to use an appropriate level of detail in risk planning—enough to plan for major risks, yet not so much that a great deal of time is spent on minor risks.

Risk management planning starts with understanding what constitutes success for the upcoming project. This may require understanding the trade-off decisions that key stakeholders are willing to make among the project scope, cost, time, and quality. Risk management planning is part of the overall project management plan and may be performed concurrently with other project planning components.

Identifying risks includes gathering information on potential risks. This can be accomplished by having the project core team and selected subject matter experts brainstorm all of the possible risks. Many times, a core team can review documents such as the project charter, WBS, communication plan, or schedule to help identify risks. The core project team can look beyond project documents for external risks using reviews of literature and consulting with external experts. Once risks have been identified, the core team creates the risk register with each risk categorized. Sometimes, a team also lists potential causes for each risk and potential responses.

The next major activity is to analyze the risks. At a minimum, this involves determining which risks are major—at least from the standpoints of how likely each risk event is to occur and how big of an impact it will have if it does occur. Sometimes, more sophisticated analysis is performed to identify the root causes of risks, to identify the trigger conditions that signify the risk event is about to happen, or to consider more complex relationships among risks. Quantitative techniques are sometimes used to determine which risks are major in terms of probability to occur and potential to impact project goals.

Risk response planning involves determining in advance how to respond to each major risk. Minor risks are handled by simply being aware of their potential and dealing with them if they occur. Eight types of risk response strategies that can be applied to major risks are avoid, transfer, mitigate, accept, research, exploit, share, and enhance. A project manager may decide to use multiple strategies on a large and critical risk. Armed with proper risk planning, a project manager can confidently begin even a risky project.

Key Terms Consistent with PMI Standards and Guides

plan risk management, 360
performing organization, 360
project risk, 361
threat, 361
opportunity, 361
risk management plan, 361
risk breakdown structure, 364
identify risks, 366
SWOT analysis, 366
Delphi technique, 367
root cause analysis, 368

trigger condition, 368
risk register, 368
perform qualitative risk analysis, 368
perform quantitative risk analysis, 372
decision tree analysis, 372
expected monetary value (EMV) analysis, 372
failure mode and effect analysis (FEMA), 372
sensitivity analysis, 373
tornado diagram, 373
simulation, 373
plan risk responses, 373

Chapter Review Questions

1. A negative impact is known as a(n) _____, while a positive impact is known as a(n) _____.
2. Who should be involved in identifying potential risks for the project?
3. List and describe the four different categories of project success measures.
4. During which stage of a project are most risks typically uncovered?
5. Relative to the project's life cycle, when is the cost per risk discovered typically highest?
6. When a project manager is gathering information about risks, is it a good idea for her to set a limit on the number of risks that will be considered? Why or why not?
7. What does a SWOT analysis examine?
8. What is a root cause analysis?
9. Name three different ways to categorize project risks.
10. A key supplier for your project has not been returning your calls or responding to your e-mails. This is an example of a(n) _____, which indicates that a risk is likely to occur.
11. What two main criteria are used when evaluating risks during qualitative risk analysis?
12. Should every risk, no matter how major or minor, have a contingency plan created to address it? Why or why not?
13. Are both qualitative and quantitative risk analyses used on all projects? Why or why not?
14. What is an example of transferring risk?
15. Describe the various types of information that are often contained in the risk register. Why is each included?
16. In the risk register, why should only one person be assigned "owner" of a risk?
17. Which three risk strategies are used specifically for dealing with opportunities?

Discussion Questions

1. Give one example each of a known known, known unknown, and unknown unknown you have encountered on previous projects.
2. Describe trade-offs that may need to be made among project stakeholders' priorities. How would you address these trade-offs as a project manager?
3. List three methods that can be used for categorizing project risks. For a fund-raising project, give examples of risk using each categorizing method.
4. To help identify risks, what are some questions a project manager could ask when reviewing the project charter and WBS?
5. You are hosting a large dinner party. What are two possible risks you would encounter? Identify at least one trigger condition for each.
6. What is the difference between a major risk and a minor risk? How do you determine which risks are major versus minor?
7. List and describe at least three common quantitative risk analysis techniques. Under what circumstances would you find each one useful?
8. Name the eight common risk responses that are used and describe how you might use two or three of them together on a project.
9. You are the project manager of a construction project for a large organization and will be relying mostly on independent contractors to execute the project work. Which type of contract would you prefer to use to procure their services? Why?
10. Give an example of a risk you have chosen to accept on a previous project. How did you make the decision to accept it? In retrospect, was that the right decision to make?

PMBOK® Guide Questions

1. A SWOT analysis is an information-gathering tool that helps increase the range of identified risks by examining strengths, weaknesses, _____, and threats to a project.
   a. opportunities
   b. options
   c. origins
   d. organizations

2. The _____ is a living document in which the results of risk analysis and risk response planning are recorded.
   a. root cause analysis
   b. risk register
   c. risk management plan
   d. cause-and-effect diagram

3. While all projects use _____ risk analysis, _____ risk analysis is used only when it is needed and there is sufficient data to develop appropriate models.
   a. quantitative, qualitative
   b. quantitative, opportunity
   c. opportunity, qualitative
   d. qualitative, quantitative

4. A team's attempt to list, on individual sticky notes, all of the possible threats and opportunities that could occur to an upcoming project might be used during the _____ process.
   a. plan risk responses
   b. perform qualitative risk analysis
   c. identify risks
   d. perform quantitative risk analysis

5. Avoid risk, mitigate risk, accept risk, and _____ are all strategies for responding to negative risks, also known as threats.
   a. enhance risk
   b. prevent risk
   c. transfer risk
   d. share risk

6. An analytical technique used to determine the basic underlying source of a variance, a defect, or a risk is called _____.
   a. qualitative risk analysis
   b. Monte Carlo analysis
   c. SWOT analysis
   d. root cause analysis

7. The Risk Management Plan describes the methodology, roles and responsibilities, budgeting, timing, and risk categories for potential causes of risk. These risk categories can be structured into a hierarchical representation called a(n):
   a. organizational breakdown structure (OBS)
   b. risk breakdown structure (RBS)
   c. work breakdown structure (WBS)
   d. threats breakdown structure (TBS)

8. Risks that have been identified and may or may not happen are referred to as known unknowns, and a _____ should be established to cover them if they are triggered.
   a. contingency reserve
   b. management reserve
   c. funding reserve
   d. risk buffer

9. _____ is a quantitative risk analysis modeling technique used to help determine which risks have the most powerful impact on the project. Using a tool such as a tornado diagram, it "examines the extent to which the uncertainty of each project element affects the objective being studied when all other uncertain elements are held at their baseline values."
   a. Fishbone diagram
   b. Monte Carlo technique
   c. Expected monetary value analysis
   d. Sensitivity analysis

10. Expected monetary value (EMV) is commonly used within this type of analysis:
    a. root cause
    b. decision tree
    c. Monte Carlo
    d. cost/benefit

Exercises

1. For a project in which you are planning a campus event with a well-known speaker, identify and quantify risks and develop contingency plans for the major risks.

2. For the same campus event project, perform a literature review to identify risks.

3. Engage another student team to perform a peer review of project risks for your project. In turn, you perform a peer review for theirs.

4. For one of the risks identified in Exercises 1 through 3 above, construct a cause-and-effect diagram to determine possible root causes. Determine which of the possible root causes are probable. Describe how you would test each probable root cause to determine if it really is a root cause.

5. For the risks identified in Exercises 1 through 3 above, identify trigger conditions that indicate each risk may be about to happen.

6. Brainstorm and group at least twelve risk factors (as shown in Exhibits 11.5, 11.6, and 11.7) for risks in one of the following types of projects:

- Research and development projects
- Organizational change projects
- Quality improvement projects

INTEGRATED EXAMPLE PROJECTS
SUBURBAN HOMES CONSTRUCTION PROJECT

Refer to the project WBS from Chapter 7. You developed the WBS of multiple levels, including work packages at the lowest level based on the initial project requirements below, which were further elaborated.

Building a single-family, partially custom-designed home as required by Mrs. and Mr. John Thomas on Strath Dr., Alpharetta, Georgia. The single-family home will have the following features:

- 3,200 square-feet home with 4 bedrooms and 2.5 bathrooms
- Flooring—hard wood in the first floor, tiles in the kitchen and bathrooms, carpet in bedrooms
- Granite kitchen countertops, GE appliances in the kitchen
- 3-car garage and external landscaping
- Ceiling—10' in first floor and vaulted 9' ceilings in bedrooms

---

High-level Assumptions and Constraints

- The list of options is limited and the cost of the house would vary based on options selected.
- The client must choose one from among the models offered.

- 7-year warranty for structure and 2-year warranty for finishing components

After the WBS was developed, it is necessary to identify risks associated with the project and include prioritized risks in revising cost and schedule estimates. For this purpose, you were asked to develop a comprehensive risk management plan.

Tasks to Complete

- Identify all the risks. To do so, you will use a WBS and ask yourself, "What can go wrong with this work package?" for each work package identified at the lowest level of the WBS. Also, you can identify more risks by challenging all the assumptions listed in your project plan.
- Develop a risk register as discussed throughout the chapter.
- Develop a risk breakdown structure.
- Perform qualitative assessment to prioritize risks.
- Develop risk response strategies for the top ten risks in the prioritized list of risks.
- Choose a critical risk and develop a greater understanding of the risk using quantitative risk assessment.

CASA DE PAZ DEVELOPMENT PROJECT

Questions for students to answer first for the project overall and then for each iteration in turn at a smaller scale are the following:

1. Brainstorm all of the risks you can imagine.
2. Assess the risks to determine which you believe are big.

3. Create response plans for the big risks, including who owns each and what the triggers are that indicate they may happen soon.
4. Which of the risks do you feel are showstoppers?

Semester Project Instructions

Create a risk register for your example project. Categorize each risk, list potential causes, and list potential responses for each cause, as shown in Exhibit 11.9.

Describe what each project success measure (from Exhibit 11.1) looks like on your example project. Identify at least three risks to each success measure, determine which are major risks, and for each major risk, develop one or more contingency plans. Identify whether the contingency plan is an avoidance plan (reducing the probability of the risk

event), a mitigation plan (reducing the impact of the event), or both.

Facilitate a discussion with the sponsor and other key stakeholders of your project. Have them determine the relative importance of their priorities and document them, as shown in Exhibit 11.2.

Perform a risk review for your example project. Use at least three types of review, as shown in Exhibit 11.8. Which of these types gave you the most useful information? Why?

PROJECT MANAGEMENT *IN ACTION*

Risk Management on a Satellite Development Project

Introduction

Proactive risk management is definitely one of the key advantages in implementing and using standardized project management practices today. We always have the balancing act of managing the triple constraints of cost, time, and scope, and on top of that, we need to effectively assure project quality and that we have enough resources to do the job. In this age, we are continuously asked to optimize our performance and "be more efficient; often, this is because we simply have too much work and not enough people to do it. So, in practice, we work with risks every day—from the risk of not spending enough time planning to the risk of not having enough supplies, or even the risk of not running a thorough enough risk management program.

Some time ago, I worked on a satellite development project that involved a lot of research technologies. There were many unknowns, with variables in the manufacture of components, integration of systems, working with subcontractors, tests, and other areas that made the project full of risk. Additionally, we were on a tight timeline for production and had only limited budget reserves available to handle cost overruns. Thus, we needed a practical way to manage and deal with the risks of the project. By systematically working with the risks of the project, we were better able to prepare responses to the risks if and when they occurred.

Planning

For our project, it was essential to have an integrated system and mechanism for risk management. Thus, at the outset of the project, during the planning phase, we developed our risk management plan and established with the team the process for dealing with not only risk but also any subsequent changes that could occur with the project as a result of the risk. This was done during a daylong clinic where we exclusively worked on developing this risk plan, as we knew our project was high risk and we wanted to make sure we could work with the plan. We developed criteria for evaluating probabilities of occurrence and impact for the risk and also for prioritizing risks. Furthermore, we researched and compared our methods to industry standards for risk management such as those from SEI®.[14]

Execution

Once we had a solid approach for risk management in this project, we then went forward with the processes of identifying our project risks, analyzing the risks, developing potential responses for the risks, and deciding upon next steps for the risks. Our approach to all this was an integrated one, using a risk management database tool we developed as its cornerstone. This tool allowed for anyone in the project team to view the risks, enter new risks, and provide input for potential risk responses. An

EXHIBIT 11.13

RISK MANAGEMENT WORKSHEET

Risk Management Worksheet

ID | **Risk Name**
1 | Reduced Testing

Description
Reductions in hardware tests for structural integrity of the integrated unit, including shortening the timeframe for acoustical and thermal tests, can affect the overall program's schedule if fixes are needed.

Timeframe | **Probability** | **Degree of Impact** | **Impact Area**
Mid Term | 25.0% | 100.0% | Schedule

Action
Monitor unit-level testing and recommend additional inspections and verifications. Consider reallocation of contingency reserve for additional testing if needed. |

Risk Review Date
3/1/2003

Source: Microsoft product screenshot(s) reprinted with permission from Microsoft Corporation.

example of a similar type of tool is shown in 11.13, where each risk is logged as a record in the database. The database allowed the team to have a single repository for recording and logging all the risks for the project, which was critically important because the risks in satellite development were constantly changing.

Every other month, the project team would hold a risk management review, in which each risk would be discussed and any decisions on actions would be made. Typically, we would meet and review the risks logged in the database in this group setting, and the risk's assigned owner would talk about the background of the risk, things that occurred since the risk was first logged (or since the last risk review), and what he or she felt the next steps needed to be. Project team members brought up other areas of the project that might have been impacted by the risk or new risks that resulted from the occurrence of the risk, or provided potential ideas for deferring, transferring, mitigating, or accepting the risk. The team also determined whether the risk decision needed to be elevated.

Another reason we held risk management reviews was to make sure that the team was up to date with the overall project's risks. Based on the criteria we defined in developing the risk management plan, the

database tool provided us a prioritized report of all the project's risks. That risk report was used by the group to make decisions about the project and look at mitigation strategies for the project as a whole. The risk management review provided us with an avenue through which we could work together to resolve the high-priority risks of the project. Often, the high-priority risks were related to overall project drivers, and it was essential to be as proactive as possible in managing those risks. Moreover, by examining and analyzing the project risks in this manner, potential risks for other related projects, in this case other satellite development projects, were also identified.

The level of risk management necessary for a project can vary greatly. On the satellite development project, it was necessary to have a comprehensive program to address risk because there were many unknowns. We performed all our duties with the notion of understanding risk, and thus the risk management program addressed both the daily needs of logging and updating risks and the long-term strategic needs of understanding risk implications. However, for a smaller or more well-defined project, having such a detailed level of risk management may be unwieldy and difficult to manage. The key is finding the appropriate level for the project at hand.

Source: Lydia Lavigne, PMP, Ball Aerospace Co. Reprinted with permission.

References

A Guide to the Project Management Body of Knowledge (PMBOK® Guide), 6th ed. (Newtown Square, PA: Project Management Institute, 2017).

Alarcon, Luis F., et al., "Risk Planning and Management for the Panama Canal Expansion Program," *Journal of Construction Engineering and Management,* October 2011: 762–770.

http://asq.org/learn-about-quality/process-analysis-tools/overview/fmea.html, accessed March 28, 2017.

Browning, Tyson R. and Ranga V. Ramasesh, "Reducing Unwelcome Surprises in Project Management," *MIT Sloan Management Review,* Spring 2015: 53–62.

Hwang, Bon-Gang, Yi Lin See, and Yun Zhong, "Addressing Risks in Green Retrofit Projects: The Case of Singapore," *Project Management Journal,* August/September 2015: 76–89.

Kloppenborg, Timothy J., Arthur Shriberg, and Jayashree Venkatraman, *Project Leadership* (Vienna, VA: Management Concepts, Inc., 2003).

Kloppenborg, Timothy J., Debbie Tesch, and Broderick King, "21st Century Project Success Measures: Evolution, Interpretation, and Direction," Proceedings, PMI Research and Education Conference 2012 (Dublin, Ireland, July 2012).

Kloppenborg, Timothy J. and Deborah Tesch, "Using a Project Leadership Framework to Avoid and Mitigate Information Technology Project Risks," in Dennis P. Slevin, David I. Cleland, and Jeffrey K. Pinto, eds., *Innovations: Project Management Research 2004* (Newtown Square, PA: Project Management Institute, 2004).

Kloppenborg, Timothy J., and Joseph A. Petrick, *Managing Project Quality* (Vienna, VA: Management Concepts, Inc., 2002).

Krane, Hans Peter, et al., "How Project Manager-Project Owners Interaction Can Work Within and Influence Project Risk Management," *Project Management Journal,* April 2012: 54–67.

Lehtiranta, Liisa, "Relational Risk Management in Construction Projects: Modeling the Complexity," *Leadership and Management in Engineering,* April 2011:141–154.

Mbachu, Jasper, "Sources of Contractor's Payment Risks and Cash Flow Problems in New Zealand Construction Industry: Project Team's Perceptions of Risks and Mitigation Measures," *Construction Management and Economics* (October 2011) 29: 1027–1041.

Papadopoulos, Thanos, et al., "The Criticality of Risk Factors in Customer Relationship Projects," *Project Management Journal* (February 2012): 65–76.

Practice Standard for Project Risk Management (Newtown Square, PA: Project Management Institute), 2009.

Royer, Paul S., *Project Risk Management: A Proactive Approach* (Vienna, VA: Management Concepts, Inc., 2002).

Sanchez-Cazorla, Alvaro, Rafael Alfalla-Luque, and Ana Isabel Irima-Dieguez, "Risk Identification in Megaprojects as a Crucial Phase of Risk Management: A Literature Review," *Project Management Journal* (December/January 2017): 75–93.

Steffey, Robert W., and Vittal S. Anantatmula, "International Projects Proposal Analysis: Risk Assessment Using Radial Maps," *Project Management Journal* (April 2011): 62–70.

Thomas, Sam, and M. Bhasi, "A Structural Model for Software Project Risk Management," *Journal of Management* (March 2011): 71–84.

Yeh, Chung, et al. "Risk Assessment and Action Selection in Preliminary Design," *International Journal of Innovation and Technology Management* 8 (1) (2011): 77–94.

Endnotes

1. *Practice Standard for Project Risk Management,* 122.
2. *Practice Standard for Project Risk Management,* 124.
3. *Practice Standard for Project Risk Management,* 122.
4. Sanchez-Cazorla, 2017: 85–86.
5. Hwang, 2015: 82.
6. Browning and Ramasesh, 2015: 59.
7. *Practice Standard for Project Risk Management,* 121.
8. *Practice Standardfor Project Risk Management,* 124.

9. *Practice Standard for Project Risk Management,* 124.

10. *Practice Standard for Project Risk Management,* 122.

11. *Practice Standard for Project Risk Management,* 122.

12. http://asq.org/learn-about-quality/process-analysis-tools/overview/fmea.html accessed May 23, 2017.

13. *Practice Standard for Project Risk Management,* 122.

14. www.sei.cmu.edu/risk/ Accessed May 23, 2017.

CHAPTER 12

Project Quality Planning and Project Kickoff

After completing this chapter, you should be able to:

CORE OBJECTIVES:

- Define each core project quality concept and explain why each is vital in planning and managing projects.
- Explain what may be included in a project quality management plan.
- Compile a complete project management plan, including all parts covered in the last several chapters.

TECHNICAL OBJECTIVES:

- Baseline your complete project plan in Microsoft Project.

BEHAVIORAL OBJECTIVES:

- Describe the major contributions to contemporary project quality made by each of the quality gurus and by TQM, ISO, and Six Sigma.
- Kick off a project with effective premeeting preparation, a kickoff meeting, and documentation.
- Develop a quality-conscious approach to managing project activities and decisions.

Bettmann/Getty Images

Founded in 1947, General Tool Company is a Cincinnati-based contract manufacturer of highly engineered defense and aerospace hardware. GTC's Fortune 500 customers include Lockheed Martin, General Electric, General Dynamics, Raytheon, Boeing, and others.

Performing to the exacting standards of such a demanding clientele is an entry barrier that few contract manufacturers can overcome. A failure to provide objective quality evidence of sound and auditable project, risk, and quality planning systems can (and usually does) exclude would-be subcontractors from the bid and proposal process. For example, most major manufacturers of flight safety hardware are required to adhere to AS 9100c, which incorporates the well-known ISO 9001:2000 quality management system standards. In short, for GTC, proper quality planning is more than good project management—it is a matter of survival!

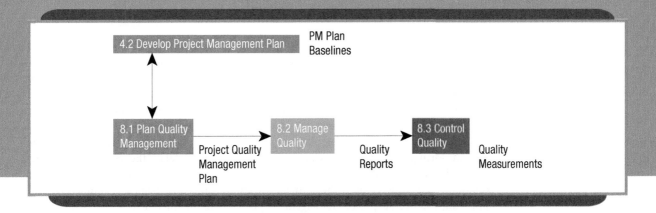

Quality and Risk

As if manufacturing highly complex, tight-tolerance aerospace and defense hardware is not challenging enough, the majority of related contracts transfer risk to the subcontractor through firm-fixed-price arrangements. Under such arrangements, the subcontractor agrees to manufacture hardware at an agreed-upon fixed price, assuming all risks associated with schedule and cost overruns (unless otherwise specified through an approved change order process).

In such an environment, it is imperative for the subcontractor to understand all quality and technical performance requirements *prior to beginning the manufacturing process.* Within GTC's quality planning system, vendor selection requires special investigation to ensure the following criteria can be met:

- The vendor is on the GTC "Approved Vendor" list.
- The vendor is capable of providing the service in the required timeframe and has available capacity to meet the demand.
- The vendor can meet all the procedural requirements and provide the required certifications for traceability and part pedigree.

Failing to "flow-down" all quality requirements at the start of a project can create significant, if not irreversible, challenges to part delivery. This makes the quality planning process especially important to companies operating within the firm-fixed-price environments, like GTC.

Few knowledge areas are more important than project quality management; and this is especially true where the safety of aviation and defense personnel are involved.

—Brad Brezinski, Jim Stewart, Korey Bischoff, and
Mark Butorac of General Tool Corporation

Perhaps the best way to understand the contemporary approach to project management is to learn how the contemporary approach to project quality management developed. Many people have influenced the modern approaches to quality, and their contributions have largely been meshed together to give project managers a full understanding of project quality demands, processes, and tools. With this understanding, project managers are ready to perform project quality management—all the necessary work to ensure that project deliverables satisfy their intended purpose. This chapter includes the first part of project quality management, namely **plan quality management**, which is "the process of identifying quality requirements and/or standards for the project and its deliverables, and documenting how the project will demonstrate compliance."[1] The remaining parts of quality management are covered in Chapter 14.

This is the final chapter dealing with project planning. Quality planning is often performed simultaneously with other aspects of project planning. In certain ways, quality of the project deliverable is integrated with scope planning as requirements are translated into specification with clearly defined qualitative and quantitative parameters based on standards and industry practices.

Once the various aspects of planning are complete, the project manager leads the team in sorting out any inconsistencies. The team then takes the completed project plan to the sponsor and other stakeholders for approval. Once the plan is accepted, it is communicated widely, and the project execution formally begins. Completing and approving the overall project management plan in this manner demonstrates how contemporary project management is integrative, iterative, and collaborative.

12-1 Development of Contemporary Quality Concepts

The contemporary approach to quality management has evolved first from the teachings of several quality "gurus" from the 1950s through the 1980s and then through various frameworks popularized during the last 25 years.

12-1a Quality Gurus

Arguably the most influential thought leader in quality was W. Edwards Deming. One concise way to summarize his ideas is his four-part Profound Knowledge System, shown in Exhibit 12.1. Deming started as a statistician and initially preached that understanding variation was essential to improving quality. By the time he had fully developed this system, he also stated that it is important to understand how companies operate as systems; that managers need insight in order to accurately predict the future; and that leaders need to understand individual motivations.

Joseph Juran, who was a contemporary of Deming, also wrote and lectured prolifically for decades. Juran is perhaps best known for his Quality Trilogy of quality planning, quality control, and quality improvement, as shown in Exhibit 12.2. The *PMBOK®* *Guide* coverage of quality largely mirrors Juran's approach.

Many other pioneers in quality, particularly Japanese and American, have added to the body of quality concepts and tools. Several of the most influential thought leaders and their contributions that apply specifically to project quality are shown in Exhibit 12.3.

Much of the work of these pioneers and many others has been incorporated into three popular frameworks that many organizations use to define and organize their

EXHIBIT 12.1

DEMING'S PROFOUND KNOWLEDGE SYSTEM	
Systems	Interactions occur among parts of a system, and parts cannot be managed in isolation.
Variation	Managers need to understand common and special causes of variation and then work to reduce both.
Knowledge	Managers need to learn from the past and understand cause-and-effect relationships to predict future behavior.
Psychology	Leaders need to understand what motivates each individual and how different people and groups interact.

Source: Adapted from James R. Evans and William M. Lindsay, *The Management and Control of Quality*, 8th ed. (Mason, OH: Cengage Learning South-Western, 2011): 94–99.

EXHIBIT 12.2

JURAN'S QUALITY TRILOGY	
Quality Planning	Identify all customers and their needs, develop requirements based upon those needs, and develop the methods to satisfy those requirements.
Quality Control	Determine what to control, establish measurement systems, establish standards, compare performance to standards, and act on differences.
Quality Improvement	Select and support improvement projects, prove causes, select and implement solutions, and maintain control of improved processes.

Source: Adapted from James R. Evans and William M. Lindsay, *The Management and Control of Quality*, 8th ed. (Mason, OH: Cengage Learning South-Western, 2011): 104–106.

quality initiatives. These frameworks are Total Quality Management (TQM), the International Organization for Standardization (ISO), and Six Sigma.

12-1b Total Quality Management/Malcolm Baldrige

TQM came into vogue during the late 1980s when it was becoming more widely apparent that the old way of trying to catch quality problems by inspection was not adequate. Many early advocates of TQM used slightly different ways of describing it. What they had in common was implied by the first word in the name: *total*. Most serious practitioners included several components in their TQM system. In the United States, government, business, consulting, and academic specialists in quality worked together to develop a common means of describing TQM. This description forms the key areas of the Malcolm Baldrige National Quality Award, as shown in Exhibit 12.4.

EXHIBIT 12.3

OTHER PROJECT QUALITY PIONEERS	
THOUGHT LEADER	ADDITIONAL KEY PROJECT QUALITY CONTRIBUTIONS
Clifton	High-quality organizations encourage individuals to develop their strengths.
Crosby	Quality is meeting requirements, not exceeding them. The burden of quality falls on those who do the work. Quality costs least when work is done correctly the first time. Quality improves more by preventing defects rather than fixing them.
Harrington	Business processes can be improved using a systematic method.
Ishikawa	Quality outputs start with understanding customers and their desires. Work to identify and remove root causes, not just symptoms. All workers at all levels must engage to improve quality. Most quality problems can be solved by using simple tools.
Senge	Team learning is necessary to improve quality.
Shiba	Societal networking accelerates quality improvement. When continual improvement is not enough, a breakthrough is needed.
Taguchi	Reducing variation saves money. Project deliverables will be better with a focus on improving methods.
Zeithaml	Services pose different challenges from manufacturing when improving quality.

EXHIBIT 12.4

MALCOLM BALDRIGE NATIONAL QUALITY AWARD KEY AREAS AND SPECIFIC CRITERIA	
KEY AREA	SPECIFIC CRITERIA
1. Leadership	Senior leaders' personal ethical behavior and integrity Organization governance system
2. Strategic Planning	Develop strategic objectives and action plans Deploy strategic objectives and action plans Measure progress
3. Customer Focus	Engage customers Build customer-focused culture Listen to voice of customer and use this information to improve
4. Measurement, Analysis, and Knowledge Management	Select, gather, analyze, manage, and improve data, information, and knowledge assets Manage information technology Reviews and uses reviews for performance improvement
5. Workforce Focus	Engage, manage, and develop workforce; assess workforce capability and capacity; build workforce environment conducive to high performance
6. Operations Focus	Design, manage, and improve work systems Design, manage, and improve key processes Prepare for emergencies
7. Results	Performance and improvement in all focus areas Performance levels relative to competitors

Source: Adapted from https://www.nist.gov/sites/default/files/documents/baldrige/publications/Baldrige_20_20.pdf, accessed April 10, 2017.

12-1c ISO 9001:2008

While the Baldrige Award is a framework developed in the United States, ISO represents a framework developed in Europe. The International Organization for Standardization has developed many technical standards since 1947. ISO 9001 is the quality management standard, and the 2015 designation is the latest revision of the standard. When the standards first appeared, they focused largely on documenting work processes. However, over the years, the standards have evolved, and the current seven quality management areas with specific requirements are shown in Exhibit 12.5. Notice that they contain many of the same ideas as the current Baldrige Award key areas and specific responsibilities.

12-1d Lean Six Sigma

Lean evolved from lean manufacturing ideas of eliminating as much waste as possible from work processes. *Sigma* stands for *standard deviation*—a statistical term for the amount of variation in data. Six Sigma quality literally means quality problems are measured in parts per million opportunities. Many projects have few routine activities and many unusual and nonroutine activities, so the rigor of the statistics in Six Sigma is not always applicable. However, the ideas behind Six Sigma provide a meaningful framework for project quality. As of this writing, Six Sigma is a popular approach to quality as Motorola, General Electric, and many other companies have promoted its application and usage. General Electric,

EXHIBIT 12.5

ISO 9001: 2015 AREAS AND SPECIFIC RESPONSIBILITIES	
AREA	SPECIFIC REQUIREMENT
Context	Understand your organization and its unique context Clarify the needs and expectations of interested parties Define the scope of your quality management system (QMS)
Leadership	Focus on quality and customers Establish a suitable quality policy Define roles and responsibilities
Planning	Define actions to manage risks and address opportunities Set quality objectives and develop plans Plan changes to your QMS
Support	Provide the necessary resources Ensure that people are competent and know how to help Manage your communications and documentation
Operations	Develop, implement, and control your operational processes Determine and document product and service requirements Control product and service release Control nonconforming outputs and document actions taken
Evaluation	Monitor, measure, analyze, and evaluate QMS performance Use internal audits to examine conformance and performance Carry out management reviews and document your results
Improvement	Determine improvement opportunities and make them Control nonconformities and take corrective action Enhance the effectiveness of your QMS

Source: Adapted ISO 9001 2015 Translated into Plain English, http://www.praxiom.com/iso-9001.htm and ISO/DIS Quality Management Systems–Guidelines for quality management on projects, https://www.iso.org/obp/ui/#iso:std:iso:10006:dis:ed-3:v1:en, accessed April 10, 2017.

in particular, expanded the focus of Six Sigma to include many service processes that people had previously said were too difficult to measure.

Six Sigma uses a disciplined process called the define, measure, analyze, improve, and control (DMAIC) process to plan and manage improvement projects. The DMAIC methodology is a 15-step process broken up into five project phases: define, measure, analyze, improve, and control, as shown in Exhibit 12.6. The DMAIC process is illustrated to show objectives within each of the five key stages. It is shown as a continuous, circular flow because DMAIC is typically used as a method of implementing continuous improvement and thus can be practiced repeatedly. Lean Six Sigma uses DMAIC and waste elimination together to improve performance.

On agile projects, quality is planned at a high level for the entire project at the outset and at a detailed level just before the start of each iteration. Therefore, you might envision conducting the equivalent of a small kickoff meeting and plan for each iteration rather than a large one for the entire project.

All of the gurus and approaches described above have a general characteristic in common. They all build upon established technical approaches with an increased emphasis on human behavior. Agile does the same in terms of project management. While some

EXHIBIT 12.6

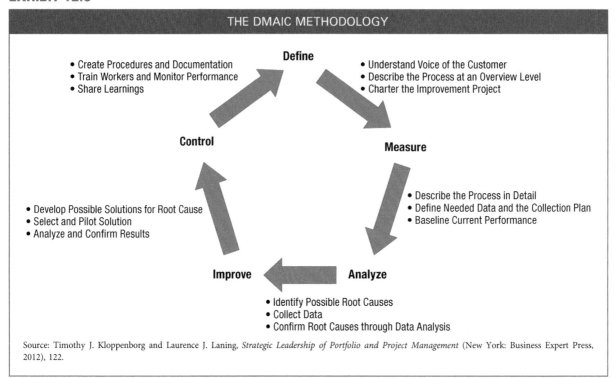

THE DMAIC METHODOLOGY

Define
- Create Procedures and Documentation
- Train Workers and Monitor Performance
- Share Learnings

- Understand Voice of the Customer
- Describe the Process at an Overview Level
- Charter the Improvement Project

Control

Measure
- Describe the Process in Detail
- Define Needed Data and the Collection Plan
- Baseline Current Performance

- Develop Possible Solutions for Root Cause
- Select and Pilot Solution
- Analyze and Confirm Results

Improve   **Analyze**
- Identify Possible Root Causes
- Collect Data
- Confirm Root Causes through Data Analysis

Source: Timothy J. Kloppenborg and Laurence J. Laning, *Strategic Leadership of Portfolio and Project Management* (New York: Business Expert Press, 2012), 122.

agile proponents deemphasize many project management techniques, essentially, agile builds upon good project practice and much of what is added emphasizes behavioral possibilities. Just as total quality dramatically changed general management in the 1990s, agile is dramatically changing project management in the 2010s.

In agile projects, the conditions of acceptance are the proxy for quality. We have general quality requirements for all stories, like it must run on this set of web browsers. We must have unit test coverage above 90 percent, and so forth.

As an agile thought exercise, consider what the quality expectations are for an e-mail. This similar to the discussion that the Product Owner and team may have while they are refining a story in the backlog.

12-2 Core Project Quality Concepts

Each of the quality gurus and frameworks provides input into the contemporary understanding of project quality. When defining quality, a number of perspectives should be considered, including:

- Product—the presence of desired attributes
- Value—the ratio of benefits to price
- Manufacturing—consistency in goods and services
- Customers—ability to satisfy given needs and expectations[2]

We condense these ideas, as stated in Chapter 1, into a simple definition of **project quality**: "the characteristics of a product or service that bear on its ability to satisfy stated or implied needs." Remembering that customer satisfaction is the most important goal on most projects, this emphasis on satisfying needs is critical to project success. However, to fully understand both the meaning of this definition and how to achieve it, one needs to understand the four contemporary core project quality concepts that have evolved from the sources above:

1. Stakeholder satisfaction
2. Process management
3. Fact-based management
4. Empowered performance

12-2a Stakeholder Satisfaction

Stakeholder satisfaction consists of identifying all stakeholders and understanding the stakeholders' ultimate quality goals using a structured process to determine relevant quality standards. External stakeholders may include customers, suppliers, the public, and other groups. Internal stakeholders may include shareholders and workers at all levels and all functions within the organization.

DEVELOPING QUALITY STANDARDS BASED UPON STAKEHOLDER REQUIREMENTS   The decision process for developing relevant quality standards on a project consists of the following steps:

1. Identify all stakeholders.
2. Prioritize among the stakeholders.
3. Understand the prioritized stakeholders' requirements.
4. Develop standards to ensure the requirements are met.
5. Make trade-off decisions.

Some stakeholders actively participate in the process of developing quality standards. Therefore, they make judgments about the quality of a process based on what they see. Thus, the quality both of project work processes and of deliverables is monitored and judged. When making trade-off decisions, the project manager often facilitates the process, and the stakeholders actually make the decisions. Stakeholders frequently need to be reminded that the relative importance of cost, schedule, scope, and quality can be very helpful in determining sensible standards. Often, quality costs money and requires more time. Sacrificing quality may save money and time, but the stakeholder satisfaction could be in jeopardy.

STAKEHOLDER SATISFACTION SAYINGS   When satisfying stakeholders, it is helpful to remember a few sayings. One is the old carpenters' advice of "measure twice, cut once." This careful planning tends to yield less variation, less cost, and faster delivery—all of which satisfy stakeholders. Another saying is "meet requirements, but exceed expectations." Contractually, a project must meet the agreed-upon specifications, but if stakeholders see excellent work processes and experience clear communications, their expectations will be exceeded, and they will be even happier. This point regarding meeting requirements while exceeding expectations comes from two sources. Good project management practice is to meet requirements without spending extra money or time. Good quality practice is to not only satisfy but also to delight customers. The third saying is "a smart project manager develops capable customers." That means the customer is able to use the project deliverables to do his or her job better. This often results in opportunities for additional revenue streams by partnering, training, and supporting the customer.

12-2b Process Management

A **process** is "a sequence of linked activities that is intended to achieve some result, such as producing a good or service for a customer."[3] To effectively manage project processes, project managers need to understand, control, and improve them.

PROCESS UNDERSTANDING WITH A SIPOC MODEL   The first part of understanding a project is to demonstrate that all work flows from suppliers, through the project, to customers. A useful way to envision this is a tool called a supplier-input-process-output-customer (SIPOC) model, as shown in Exhibit 12.7.

In Exhibit 12.7, the process boundaries are clearly defined. This prevents future scope creep from occurring by eliminating previous or later steps in the process. The SIPOC above also begins to identify key stakeholders who both provide inputs into the process (suppliers) and receive benefits from the process (customers) and shows feedback loops that provide useful information.

One way to interpret the SIPOC is to think backward from the project's customers. As described previously in the stakeholder satisfaction section, it is helpful for a project manager to identify all the customers for his or her project and their desired outputs. Since that is usually a far-reaching list, prioritization decisions need to be made. At that point, the project manager can work with the project core team to define the work processes necessary to create those outputs. Then they can identify the inputs to accomplish those activities and determine who will supply them.

Once the supplier-customer view is understood, it is time to determine whether the process is capable of creating the project deliverables. This discussion should be initiated when the project charter is developed. As people discuss the milestone schedule, risks,

EXHIBIT 12.7

PDE DELIVERABLE ANALYSIS FUNCTIONAL MODEL

PDE Deliverable Analysis Functional Model

Input Adjustment Feedback

Resources
- Labor/Skill Sets
- Materials/Equipment
- Vendors
- Applications

Deliverable Process

Supplier
- Upstream Functional Interface

Input
- Qualities
- Characteristics
- Standards
- Localized Items
- Timing
- Conditional Needs

Deliverable

Customer
- Downstream Functional Interface
- Qualities
- Characteristics
- Standards
- Localized Items
- Timing
- Conditional Needs

Deliverable Adjustment Feedback

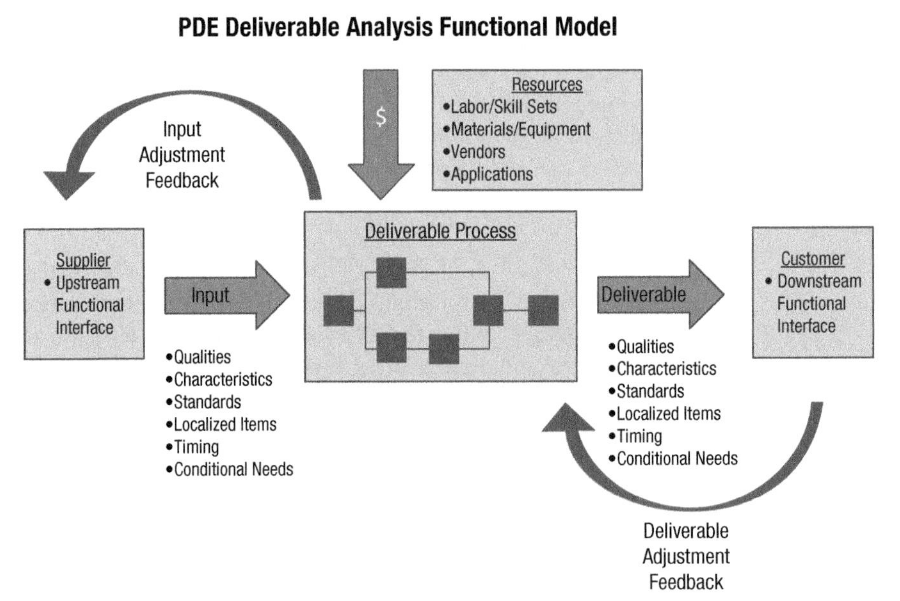

Source: Paul Kling, PMP.

and constraints, any serious doubts people have should be raised. On some small projects, that may be enough to determine if the proposed methods of creating the project deliverables will work. On others, more detailed analysis of schedule, resources, and risks may yield further insight. When considering if a project process is capable, the project manager needs to understand the conditions in which the project may operate and ensure that the methods can be flexible enough to handle various contingencies that might develop.

Experienced project managers understand that it is far better to design quality into their processes than to find problems only upon inspection. In the first place, it costs more to make junk and then remake to obtain good outputs. Second, having to rework anything aggravates time pressure that already exists on many projects. Finally, even the best inspectors do not find every mistake, and some of the mistakes are likely to reach customers.

PROCESS CONTROL   The second aspect of process management is process control. **Control** is "the activity of ensuring conformance to the requirements and taking corrective action when necessary to correct problems and maintain stable performance."[4] The purpose of process control is to have confidence that outputs are predictable. Process control is covered in Chapter 14. If the outputs are not predictable—or if they are predictable but not satisfactory—then a project manager needs to use the third aspect of process management: process improvement.

PROCESS IMPROVEMENT WITH A PDCA MODEL   Processes can be improved in either a continuous or a breakthrough fashion. All project core team members and subject matter experts (SMEs) should be thinking of little ways they can improve at any time. Slow and steady improvement is a good foundation. However, sometimes substantial improvement is necessary, and a breakthrough is in order. Regardless of the size of improvement desired, many models exist to guide the effort. Improvement models such as DMAIC are usually based upon the plan-do-check-act (PDCA) improvement cycle, as displayed in Exhibit 12.8.

EXHIBIT 12.8

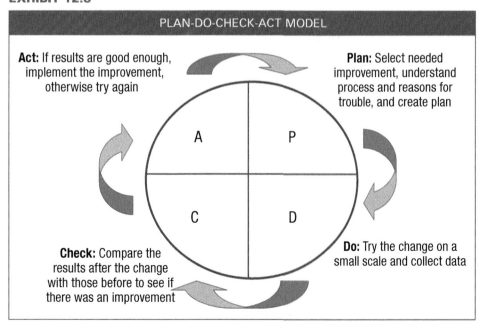

PLAN-DO-CHECK-ACT MODEL

Act: If results are good enough, implement the improvement, otherwise try again

Plan: Select needed improvement, understand process and reasons for trouble, and create plan

A   P

C   D

Check: Compare the results after the change with those before to see if there was an improvement

Do: Try the change on a small scale and collect data

Even with good inspectors, somemistakes will reach customers if poor quality exists in project processes.

When project managers are considering process improvements, they often involve suppliers and/or customers in a partnering arrangement. Often, they need to forecast changes in their work environment, technology, or customer desires. Organizations that take a balanced view of long-term improvement and short-term results create a culture in which project process improvement can thrive. Organizations that focus almost exclusively on short-term results make it hard for project managers to devote much energy to process improvement.

12-2c Fact-Based Management

One challenge many project managers face is making decisions based upon facts. Making decisions using facts sounds like an obvious thing to do, yet it is difficult because:

- Opinions get in the way.
- It is hard to know what data need to be collected.
- Projects often operate with so much time pressure that decisions need to be made quickly.

Four aspects of fact-based management are understanding variation, deciding what to measure, working correctly with data, and using the resulting information appropriately.

UNDERSTANDING VARIATION   Project decision makers need to understand the difference between two types of variation. A common cause is variation that is a result of the product design and the method of making it and is exhibited by a random pattern within predictable limits. On the other hand, a special cause is variation that comes from external sources that are not inherent in the process and can be quite unpredictable. It is important to determine when there is variation on a project whether it is within the range of what can be expected for that particular work activity or deliverable (common cause) or whether something unusual is happening (special cause). If the variation is due to a common cause, but the results are still not acceptable, some change needs to be made to the system—the way in which the work is accomplished. However, if the change is due to a particular cause, then the way to improve is to change that particular cause and not the entire system. Many quality proponents estimate that a large majority of variation is due to common causes, yet many managers are quick to try to find a person or issue to blame (special cause). The problem is often compounded when a cause is really part of the system, yet individuals are blamed. The problem does not go away, and people become fearful. Management by facts requires an understanding that variation can be due to either common or special causes, a determination to discover which type, and the resolve to act appropriately upon that discovery.

DETERMINING WHAT TO MEASURE   A project manager wants to avoid the extreme of not measuring anything since he or she is in a hurry and there is not enough time and the other extreme of measuring many things just to be sure. As project managers become more experienced, they develop an understanding of how many data are useful to collect and when they need to move into action regardless of the data they have.

A **quality metric** is "a measurement used to ensure customers receive acceptable products or deliverables."[5] Measures may include project attributes such as on-time or on-budget performance or product attributes such as defect frequency. A milestone schedule, in a good project charter, with acceptance criteria for each milestone can provide useful measures. Project teams often can seek useful measures when they study lessons learned from previous projects. Many lessons state either what worked well and should be repeated on future projects or what worked poorly and should be avoided on future projects. Both of these aspects can provide ideas for useful measures. The project manager and sponsor should agree on what measures will be taken, when they will be taken, and under what circumstances. While many sponsors can be quite busy, the more specific this agreement becomes, the more useful the data collected are likely to be.

WORKING CORRECTLY WITH DATA   A third aspect of management by facts is how the identified data are collected, handled, and stored. **Data** is information in a raw or unorganized form that refer to, or represent, conditions, ideas, or objects.[6] Generally, the persons closest to the situation are best for collecting data. Efforts should be made to ensure that the data are complete, without errors, and timely. Many project teams either use templates from their organization or create their own forms for collecting data. When more than one person is involved, consistency must be ensured. Once the data are collected, they should be analyzed. A great deal can be learned by using simple tools to look for patterns and trends in data. On larger, more complex projects and sophisticated Six Sigma projects, more detailed statistical analysis is often used. The analysis should turn the raw data into information for decision making.

USING THE RESULTING INFORMATION APPROPRIATELY   The final aspect of making fact-based decisions is how the information is used. **Information** is data that is (1) accurate and timely, (2) specific and organized for a purpose, (3) presented within a context that gives meaning and relevance, and (4) can lead to an increase in understanding and decrease in uncertainty.[7] Project communications plans often spell out how the information is disseminated. The best project cultures encourage facts and transparency in communication—even when it is inconvenient. People are encouraged to use information to challenge opinions and decisions. Making decisions based upon facts often requires courage. It also requires judgment because challenges that are of a factual nature are helpful; yet, if the challenges become personal and are not fact based, they can be destructive and demotivating.

12-2d Fact-Based Project Management Example

A rapidly growing, fast, casual restaurant chain was experiencing growing pains that were manifest in delays for restaurant openings. SWOT analysis revealed a number of broad issues that were threats to opening the restaurants on time, but the issues needed to be quantified for improvement. The company had been keeping records on the time required to open a restaurant after breaking ground. Exhibit 12.9 shows that 80 percent of the restaurants opened within 160 days or fewer, but some of the others took much longer. At $5,000 lost revenue per day for the franchisee and a 4 percent loss for the franchisor, it was in the interest of all stakeholders to dissect the facts and determine the causes for delayed openings. With the anticipation of expanding to an additional 500 restaurants in the next two to three years, every improvement of one day would result in a $0.5 M increase to revenue, assuming the same 20 percent of the troubled projects were lagging the average for the 80 percent of excellent or healthy performing projects. The corporate franchising organization needed to determine the root cause of the delays.

Exhibit 12.10 is a Pareto chart showing the frequency of causes in the troubled projects. Seven causes for delays were identified for the troubled projects. The top four causes were found in 80 percent of the troubled projects. This led to a focus on improving projects by better managing the risks associated with each cause or by making

EXHIBIT 12.9

DAYS FROM BREAKING GROUND TO OPENING		
DAYS	FREQUENCY	CUMULATIVE %
60	0	0%
80	1	1%
100	8	10%
120	26	41%
140	23	67%
160	11	80%
180	8	90%
200	5	95%
220	2	98%
240	1	99%
260	1	100%
280	0	100%
More	0	100%
Total	86	

Source: Scott C Wright, PhD, P.E., PMP (University of Wisconsin–Platteville)

EXHIBIT 12.10

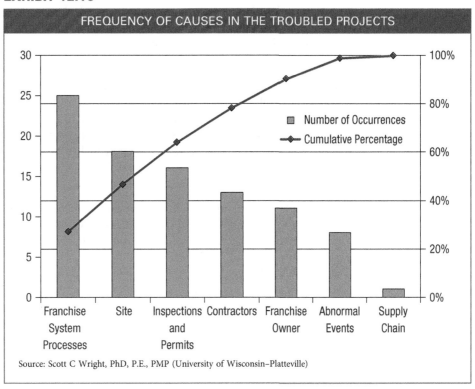

FREQUENCY OF CAUSES IN THE TROUBLED PROJECTS

Source: Scott C Wright, PhD, P.E., PMP (University of Wisconsin–Platteville)

changes to management processes that were negatively impacting the project's time objective. Based on root cause information, a risk breakdown structure was used to categorize threats causing delays and develop appropriate responses to avoid or mitigate the risks for future openings.

12-2e Empowered Performance

The fourth and final core project quality concept is empowered performance. The goal of empowered performance is to have capable and willing workers at every level and every function within a company. Corporate leaders set the stage for this by developing the organizational culture. Project sponsors and managers, in turn, develop the project culture. Remember from Chapter 4 that organizational culture includes the formal and informal practices utilized, along with the values shared by members of an organization. Part of an empowered performance culture is setting an expectation for managers to encourage their associates to take appropriate risks and to treat risk events as learning opportunities, not as a time to punish. Part of it is training and equipping workers so they are willing to take risks. Part is getting managers to let go of some decision-making authority so those lower in the organization can make some decisions. Yet another aspect of empowered performance is helping to develop specialists who can aid anyone in the organization. For example, a person trained as a Black Belt in a Six Sigma organization can become an expert in guiding process improvement projects, or an internal coach/mentor in an organization that is adopting agile can observe the team and provide suggestions.

RECOGNIZE INDIVIDUALITY   One essential understanding in creating capable and willing workers is to recognize everyone's individuality and diversity. Leaders at all levels must promote inclusiveness and recognize that diversity is not only to be accepted, but it is also very helpful as projects develop.

CAPITALIZE ON INDIVIDUAL STRENGTHS   Outstanding project managers not only want to recruit people with unique skills and develop a strong project team, but they also want to capitalize on each person's strengths. Every team member feels validated when he uses his unique skills and gets an opportunity to improve them. When a person feels his boss understands him and works to create opportunities for him to do both what he most wants to do and what he has the potential to be best at doing, he is motivated to perform at the highest level.

EMPHASIZE INDIVIDUAL RESPONSIBILITIES   Empowered performance requires that people understand and accept their responsibilities. Much of the responsibility falls upon the project manager and core team. However, SMEs are responsible for their individual activities. Functional managers, who are the technical supervisors of the SMEs, are responsible for work methods in their functional areas. Sponsors share a high-level responsibility for project completion with project managers. Customer representatives are responsible for understanding the impact of directives they may give a project manager. Ultimately, everyone must understand what they need to do, realize how it fits in the bigger picture, and then commit to both completing their work correctly and accepting the consequences of their decisions.

USE APPROPRIATE COLLABORATION   Finally, appropriate collaboration is a key to developing empowered performance. This is true both within and beyond the organizational boundaries. Cross-functional teams perform a great deal of project work and are most effective when individual, team, and organizational learning flourishes. One effective method of encouraging this learning in projects is to develop lessons learned at the completion of project milestones and at project closure. These lessons then need to be shared openly with other project teams. Collaboration and learning accelerate when people share information outside their parent organization. Of course, some things such as information that provides a competitive advantage cannot be shared, but a surprising number of things can be shared. When the recipients of those lessons reciprocate, the first team learns something new. This type of external sharing can take place through conferences, company exchanges, or other means. An example of a unique project challenge that required empowered performance to be successful is the vintage aircraft-shipping project in Exhibit 12.11.

12-2f Summary of Core Concepts

A summary of project quality core concepts is shown in Exhibit 12.12.

Advice given on agile projects is to communicate often (maybe daily) with the owner and other stakeholders. This is good advice for any project. This approach provides shorter faster feedback loops. Everything in this section applies to agile. It is a discussion of how much of these tools you need for the product of the project.

As such, an agile project deliverable often goes through routine quality checks and tests to confirm desired performance and these checks are used as feedback to modify project management processes and plans. Customer involvement throughout the project execution presents the unique advantage of quality audit and control.

EXHIBIT 12.11

VINTAGE AIRCRAFT SHIPPING PROJECT

Global Shipping Company (GSC) was approached by an individual who was interested in selling and shipping an antique $1 million 1942 Staggered-Wing Beech aircraft from Cincinnati to a buyer in Australia. Since the aircraft was fragile, a plan needed to be developed for moving it as economically as possible while avoiding damage.

One challenge was handling the entire project in-house using only the company's staff, equipment, and resources, and the other was devising a custom solution for moving this unusual piece of cargo.

GSC has an organizational culture that encourages cross-training, collaboration among departments, risk-taking, and designing creative approaches to problem solving while minimizing cost. Because of the size and fragility of the aircraft, a strategy was devised to dismantle it and ship via containerized ocean freight. The project was broken down into five distinct segments: pickup, dismantling, packing, loading, and shipping.

To pick up the entire aircraft, the equipment, permits, and escorts had to be arranged to get the aircraft intact from the airport and move it to the warehouse down a major street on the back of a flatbed truck. In order to fit in a standard ocean container, the aircraft had to be dismantled—under the supervision of the FAA—and documented to meet FAA regulations. To avoid damage, each piece had to be individually packaged. Different types of cloth and foam had to be tested and selected in order to prevent scratching the aircraft. Due to the height restrictions, the warehouse personnel had to design and build a custom gurney to allow the body of the plane to be wheeled into the container and secured. Once packaged, the individual pieces were then loaded, blocked, and braced into the container to prevent damage while in transit; then the aircraft was shipped. The dismantling, documentation, and packing process was designed in a way that the new owner of the aircraft could replicate it in order to move the plane for air shows and events.

The Classic 1942 Beech Staggerwing D17S

© Danny McKee

The project's success was achieved by having the courage to take on the project in the first place, the ability to use the company's resources creatively and efficiently, and the ability to adapt the plan when unexpected events occurred. The result was a project that was successfully completed, meeting all FAA standards, exceeding stakeholder expectations, and developing a shipping process that can be replicated.

Source: Danny McKee, Global Shipping Company.

12-3 Plan Quality Management

The **quality management plan** "defines the acceptable level of quality, which is typically defined by the customer, and describes how the project will ensure this level of quality in its deliverables and work processes."[8] Therefore, a logical place to start is by understanding what a quality policy is and how it governs the actions of a project manager and team. The remainder of this section discusses the components of a project quality management plan and process improvement plan.

12-3a Quality Policy

The top management of an organization normally writes a concise statement to guide their company's quality efforts. This policy reflects top management's principles of achieving quality and the benefits they hope to achieve with good quality. Project

EXHIBIT 12.12

SUMMARY OF PROJECT QUALITY CORE CONCEPTS	
CONCEPT	SPECIFIC GUIDANCE
Stakeholder Satisfaction	Identify all internal and external stakeholders. Prioritize among the stakeholders. Understand the prioritized stakeholders' requirements. Develop standards to ensure the requirements are met. Make trade-off decisions. Realize stakeholders will judge quality both of work processes and deliverables. Measure twice, cut once. (Plan and check the plan.) Meet requirements, but exceed expectations. Develop capable customers.
Process Improvement	Learn about process with the supplier-input-process-output-customer model. Realize designing a quality process is far better than merely trying to find mistakes. Ensure project processes are capable and flexible. Control project processes to make them predictable. Improve project processes using a model based upon the plan-do-check-act concept.
Fact-Based Management	Understand the difference between common and special causes of variation. Select a few key well-defined items to measure. Carefully collect data and use appropriate analysis techniques to create useful information. Encourage truthful, transparent, and challenging communication when making decisions.
Empowered Performance	Develop capable and willing workers at every level and every function. Develop a risk-taking project culture. Understand each person is an individual. To the extent possible, let everyone do what they will enjoy doing and what their strengths support. Ensure everyone understands and accepts their responsibilities. Share lessons learned and other information as widely as possible.

managers normally first consider using the quality policy of their parent company—if it is a good fit. If not, or if the project is a partnership between organizations, the project manager may need to combine and/or supplement the quality policies. However, the project's quality policy should never violate the intent of the quality policies of either the parent company or of a major customer.

A study of 25 organizational quality policies in 2017 found that they vary widely. Some are fewer than 30 words, while others are over 100 words. The content and style can be quite different. The frequency of terms that interest project managers is shown in Exhibit 12.13.

Several interesting patterns can easily be found. First, the most frequent terms are *customers* and *improving processes*. Many include *satisfying requirements*, but very few include *exceeding requirements*. This means that, for most companies, quality is measured by how well requirements are met, not surpassed. A large percentage of policies mention both products and services—a reminder to project managers that services and information are frequently needed along with products to satisfy a customer's needs.

EXHIBIT 12.13

EVOLUTION OF TERMS IN QUALITY POLICIES 2013 TO 2017		
TERM	PERCENT OF POLICIES IN 2013	PERCENT OF POLICIES IN 2017
Customer	92	80
Improve Process	84	80
Satisfy Requirements/Meet Standards or Laws	68	72
Sustainable/Reliable/Dependable	36	64
Employee	44	60
Commitment/Leadership	40	52
Product	72	48
Best/Excellent/High Quality/Exceed Requirements	44	44
Service	64	36
Value/Cost	56	28
Communication	*	28
Suppliers	16	24
Safety/Risk	16	20

*Communication did not appear on any of the 25 quality policies surveyed in 2013.

What is interesting is that five concepts now appear in a higher percentage of quality policies than a few years ago:

1. Sustainability
2. Employee engagement
3. Leadership and commitment
4. Communication
5. Suppliers

This shows that more organizational leaders are concerned both with sustainability and with a variety of behavioral aspects of great project leadership. Remember, many of these policies are very short and only include a few key thoughts. They are meant to set direction, not plan detail.

12-3b Quality Management Plan Contents

In addition to the quality policy, most project quality management plans describe which quality standards the project will use and how the project team will implement them. The quality management plan may include a description of the quality baseline by which the project will be judged, along with methods for quality assurance and control.

The quality management plan is a portion of the overall project management plan. On many small, simple projects, the quality planning is performed concurrently with other planning, and the quality plan is seamlessly incorporated into the project plan. On some large, complex, or unusual projects, the quality planning is handled separately, and the plan, while a portion of the overall project plan, appears as an additional plan document.

A project quality management plan should describe how to identify some or all of the following:

- Quality objectives
- Key project deliverables and processes to be reviewed for satisfactory quality level
- Quality standards
- Quality control and assurance activities
- Quality roles and responsibilities
- Quality tools
- Plan for reporting quality control and assurance problems[9]

12-3c Quality Baseline

At the point of developing the quality baseline, the project work should be clearly defined in a scope statement and/or a work breakdown structure. Appropriate quality standards are selected for the materials and other inputs, work activities, documentation, and project deliverables. These standards might be industry norms, customer-specific standards, or government regulations. The project manager is ultimately responsible for selecting appropriate standards and developing additional standards that may be needed. However, project managers normally take their cues from functional managers and SMEs for many standards dealing with methods and from customers on standards dealing with documentation and deliverables.

The quality baseline reflects the agreed-upon quality objectives. It can include metrics that define exactly what will be measured, how each will be measured, and the target value of each.

12-3d Process Improvement Plan

A **process improvement plan** is "a subsidiary plan of the project management plan. It documents the steps for analyzing processes with the purpose of improvement. It considers process boundaries, process configuration, process metrics, and targets for improved performance."[10] Process improvement was discussed earlier in the process management core concept.

 On agile projects, a definition of done (completion) is explicitly stated. This includes acceptance criteria of features, agreement of what done is for each iteration, and a demonstration to prove the deliverables work as intended.

Quality is what happens to the product in agile. It normally is not focused on other aspects or ideas. So when we think about agile projects and quality, it is worth maintaining this focus. For all other areas, it is about continual improvement.

12-4 Manage Quality

Manage quality is the process of using the quality plan and policy to perform tasks that will most likely lead to creating project outputs to customers' satisfaction. A key part of managing quality is the forward-looking quality assurance. **Perform quality assurance** is "an executing process that is primarily concerned with overall process improvements to ensure that each time a deliverable is produced it is error free."[11] Quality assurance ensures that proper methods and standards are used. It consists of a broad set of proactive management activities designed to give key stakeholders confidence that sensible methods and capable people are working on the project. This hopefully yields good project deliverables and documentation. Quality assurance is one way to simultaneously improve quality and manage stakeholder relations.

Perhaps quality assurance is best understood by considering two of its primary methods: the quality audit and process analysis. A **quality audit** is "a key tool used in quality assurance. Quality audits enable us to review the project to evaluate which activities taking place in the project should be improved and which meets the quality standards. Quality audits have dual objectives in improving acceptance of the product, identifying areas of improvement, and improving the overall cost of quality."[12] A quality audit is used to determine what methods are being used (hopefully the methods determined in the quality baseline) and whether they are effective. For audits to be effective, people need to be convinced that the real purpose is to improve work methods and not to punish individuals.

Quality audits sometimes show the need to request changes. These requests may include recommendations for:

- **Preventive actions**—"steps taken when the project is trending away from the planned scope, schedule, cost, or quality requirements. Preventive actions are proactive in nature, based on a variance and trend analysis."[13] Preventive actions are taken to ensure future performance is acceptable.
- **Corrective actions**—"steps taken when the project has deviated from the planned scope, schedule, cost, or quality requirements. Corrective actions are reactive in nature and are intended to bring the project's performance back into alignment with the agreed-upon project baselines."[14]
- **Defect repair**—"steps taken when the product or deliverable does not meet the documented quality requirements."[15] Not all defects can be repaired, so judgment is required to decide if the output is repairable or if it needs to be scrapped and a new output will be created.

Process analysis is "a step-by-step breakdown of the phases of a process, used to determine the inputs, outputs, and operations that take place during each phase. A process analysis can be used to improve understanding of how the process operates, and to determine potential targets for process improvement through eliminating waste and increasing efficiency."[16] It can follow an improvement model such as the DMAIC method shown in Exhibit 12.6 or the PDCA model shown in Exhibit 12.8. Process improvement is used to improve both quality and productivity. It can be of a continuous nature, in which many incremental improvements are made over time, or of a breakthrough nature, in which a substantial change is planned and implemented at once.

Processes can be measured for both efficiency and effectiveness. Efficiency is the ratio of outputs to inputs. A more efficient process uses fewer inputs to create the same number of outputs. This could equate to fewer work hours or less money spent to create the same project deliverable. Effectiveness is the extent to which a process is creating the desired deliverables. A more effective process is one that creates higher-quality deliverables and better pleases the stakeholders. Process improvement can deal with both efficiency and effectiveness and is akin to the concept of value engineering for products and services.

There are many avenues for improving project processes. One is to interpret the results of quality control measurements with an eye toward process improvement. Feedback from customers, suppliers, work associates, and other stakeholders can often lead to suggestions for improving processes. These suggestions might pinpoint opportunities to improve both the inputs into a process and the actions within the process.

Another useful method of process improvement is benchmarking. Benchmarking is a structured consideration of how another organization performs a process with an eye toward determining how to improve one's own performance. It is not directly copying the methods. Benchmarking consists of 10 steps:

1. Determine a process that needs dramatic improvement.
2. Identify another organization that performs that process very well.
3. Make a deal with that organization to learn from them (they might require payment or the sharing of one of the observer's best practices with them).
4. Determine what needs to be observed and what questions need to be asked.
5. Make a site visit to observe and question the other organization.
6. Decide which observed methods will help the organization.
7. Adapt the methods to fit the organization's culture and situation.
8. Try the new methods on a small scale.
9. Evaluate the results.
10. If the methods are good enough, adopt them.

Quality assurance is a continuous process in each iteration and provides incremental progress toward higher product or service quality for the customer.

12-5 Control Quality

Control quality is "the activities … used to verify that deliverables are of acceptable quality and that they are complete and correct. Examples of quality control activities include inspection, deliverable peer reviews, and the testing process."[17] This detailed set of reactive technical activities verifies whether specific project deliverables meet their quality standards. The purposes of quality control on projects are to reduce the number of defects and inefficiencies, as well as to improve the project process and outputs. Quality control consists of the following:

- Monitoring the project to ensure that everything is proceeding according to plan
- Identifying when things are different enough from the plan to warrant preventive or corrective actions
- Repairing defects
- Determining and eliminating root causes of problems
- Providing specific measurements for quality assurance
- Providing recommendations for corrective and preventive actions
- Implementing approved changes as directed by the project's integrated change control system.

MONITOR THE PROJECT QUALITY   Project managers use quality control focus on project inputs, processes, and outputs. When considering inputs, a project manager wants to ensure that the assigned people can do their work. He also works with suppliers to ensure that materials, information, and other inputs meet the required specifications and perform satisfactorily. When considering the project processes, the manager wants to minimize rework because it wastes time, effort, and money, which are in short supply on most projects. Rework also often has negative impacts on both worker morale and stakeholder relations because it is very discouraging to make and/or receive an inferior product, even if it is fixed eventually. When considering outputs, a project manager may first use internal inspection to ensure the deliverables work before they are sent to the customer. External inspection may also be required to convince the customer that the deliverables are developed to meet the desired performance.

While the specifics vary greatly from project to project, there are some useful general lessons regarding the timing and types of project inspections, including the following:

- Conduct an inspection before a critical or expensive process to make sure the inputs are good before spending a large amount of money or time on them.
- Process stages in which one worker hands off work to another worker are good times for both the workers to conduct inspections.
- Milestones identified in the project charter provide good inspection points.
- As practiced in software development, think of an inspection in terms of units (individual components), integration (how components work together), and the system (how the deliverable performs).

QUALITY CONTROL TERMS   Many terms with specific meanings are used in project quality control. Exhibit 12.14 shows pairs of terms that are sometimes confused, and the differences between each pair are described in the following paragraphs. While few projects repeat processes enough times to formally use statistical quality control, the concepts are still quite useful in making good decisions.

- **Prevention versus Inspection** Prevention is keeping errors out of a process, while inspection is trying to find errors after they occur to correct these errors before they reach the customer. Preventing a problem in the first place is preferred over trying to use an inspection to find it. Prevention is a cheaper alternative. Inspection does not guarantee that a problem is detected. Inspection should be practiced, but every effort should be made to prevent problems from happening in the first place.
- **Sample versus Population** Sample and population are the factors considered for determining the scope of inspection. A population is all of the possible items in a set, such as all the students in a class. It is often costly, difficult, or even impossible to inspect an entire population. Instead, a sample or subset is inspected. Three

EXHIBIT 12.14

PAIRS OF PROJECT QUALITY CONTROL TERMS	
TERM:	SOMETIMES CONFUSED WITH:
Prevention	Inspection
Sample	Population
Attribute	Variable
Precision	Accuracy
Tolerance	Control limit
Capable	In-control
Special cause	Common cause
Preventive action	Corrective action

students, picked randomly, would be a sample. The key is to use a big enough sample to be representative of the population, but a small enough sample that it is cost and time effective.

- **Attribute versus Variable** Quality is measured either as an attribute or a variable. An attribute is determined with a yes-or-no test, while a variable is something that can be measured. Either one may be chosen. For example, if one of the goals of a project was to teach all the people in a client's company, an attribute for each employee might be, "Did that person pass the test?" A variable might be, "How many questions did each employee score correctly?" Attributes are usually quicker (and cheaper) to observe, but may not yield as much detailed information. Project managers make a trade-off between more information and more cost when they decide if they will count or measure.

- **Precision versus Accuracy** A process is precise when the outputs are consistently very similar, such as shooting three shots at a target that all land in a cluster near each other. A process is accurate when, on the average, it produces what the customer wants. Ideally, a process is both precise and accurate.

- **Tolerance versus Control Limit** A tolerance limit is what the customer will accept and is sometimes called the voice of the customer. This could be if the customer wants a 1-inch bolt, perhaps they are willing to accept bolts ranging from a lower tolerance limit of 0.99 inches to an upper tolerance limit of 1.01 inches. A control limit reflects what the process can consistently deliver when things are behaving normally and is sometimes called the voice of the process. The upper and lower control limits are often statistically calculated to be three standard deviations above or below the process average.

- **Capable versus In Control** A process is determined to be in control when the outputs are all within the control limits. A process is considered capable when control limits are within the tolerance limits so that customers can remain satisfied with project performance even when the performance is outside its tolerance. Project managers try to ensure that their processes are both in control and capable of consistently delivering acceptable quality.

- **Special versus Common Cause** Special causes are statistically unlikely events that usually mean something is different from normal. Common causes are normal or random variations that are considered part of operating the system at its current capability. Special causes are identified by individual points outside the control limits or by unusual patterns within the limits. Common causes need systematic change for improvement—perhaps new methods or better training or tools that would allow workers to more consistently produce excellent quality. Special causes, on the other hand, require specific interventions that include identifying the root causes and making changes so those same root causes do not happen again.

- **Preventive versus Corrective Action** Preventive action is a proactive approach of making a change because a problem may occur otherwise. Corrective action is a reactive approach of making a change to fix a problem that has occurred.

 Agile creates and measures quality in small batch sizes and as small chunks of work. This is often different in larger integrated systems where the components are dependent on other components to demonstrate they are of quality.

There is not as much focus on the quality process in agile projects because agile projects tend to allow more variability for the sake of speed to market. The concept of Minimum Viable Product (MVP) has emerged in the agile community to indicate the least amount of value that could be perceived by the customer. This does not mean that MVP delivered is not of the appropriate quality.

12-6 Cost of Quality

Even with good inspectors, some mistakes will reach customers if poor quality exists in project processes. **Cost of quality** is a sum of the cost of conformance of quality and cost of nonconformance of quality. Quality decisions should be based on costs associated with all the factors listed in Exhibit 12.15.

12-7 Develop Project Management Plan

Chapters 5 through 11 have all dealt with aspects of project planning. On small and simple projects, the various portions of this planning may already be combined to a large extent. On larger, more complex projects, specific methods are often used to plan the various project aspects separately, such as cost, schedule, resources, communications, risk, and quality. If they have not been planned together, they need to be compiled into a unified project management plan. Conflicts need to be resolved. A configuration management system needs to be selected or developed. The project manager should apply a sanity test to all project plans. There is often a formal project kickoff of some sort, and after everything is agreed, the scope, schedule, budget, and so forth are baselined, and the baseline becomes part of the project management plan.

12-7a Resolve Conflicts

Sometimes, when all parts of the plan come together, it becomes obvious that the overall plan is impractical. If this occurs, the key stakeholders may need to determine their priorities and trade-offs.

- What do they really most want and need from the project?
- Are all of the quality standards truly mandatory, or can one of them be relaxed a bit?
- Is the imposed deadline really critical, or, considering the impact it poses for costs and risks, can it be relaxed a bit?
- Is the budget a true maximum, or can it be adjusted to secure the desired features?

EXHIBIT 12.15

COSTS OF QUALITY	
COST OF CONFORMANCE	COST OF NONCONFORMANCE
• Planning	• Scrap
• Training	• Rework and repair
• Process control and validation	• Additional material
• Product design validation	• Inventory
• Test and evaluation	• Warranty repairs and service
• Quality audits	• Compliant handling
• Maintenance and calibration	• Liability judgments
• Inspection	• Product recalls
• Field testing	• Field service
	• Expediting

These questions and others like them have probably been asked all along, but now they take on added urgency because once the project plan is approved, it may be more difficult to make these changes.

12-7b Establish Configuration Management

Project planning can be hard work. Once the plan is in place, it still takes a lot of hard work to control the project. One last part of planning is to create a configuration management system to aid project control. A **configuration management system** has four parts:

1. Process for identifying and uniquely naming items that need to be controlled
2. Activity of managing the project deliverables and documentation
3. Recording and reporting all changes
4. Verifying the correctness of all deliverables and components of them[18]

12-7c Apply Sanity Tests to All Project Plans

A common saying is appropriate to consider here: "can't see the forest for the trees." This means that sometimes a person is so concerned with details that they forget the big picture. During the initial stage of a project (initiating), the team creates the primary deliverable, a project charter. The charter is a high-level view of a project, so seeing the big picture is easy. During the more detailed planning stage, however, the team looks in great detail at scope, schedule, resources, cost, communications, risks, and quality. Now they need to step back a bit and ask if all these elements work well together. The project manager and core team should apply a sanity test to their project plans by asking one another questions to ensure that the comprehensive project plan makes sense. Some of these questions could be as follows:

- Does the critical path look reasonable?
- Do the milestones look achievable?
- Are some resources overallocated?
- Does everyone understand what they are supposed to do?
- Do we really understand our customers?
- Are the customers' desires likely to change?
- How well do we understand the standards we will be judged against?
- Are the methods for completing our work really sensible?
- Are we confident we can gather and analyze the data we need to control the plan?

On agile projects, the overall plan for the project (called the release plan) is only at a high level, while the detailed plans for each iteration are baselined right before each iteration starts. The idea is to allow as much flexibility as possible, up until the last responsible minute to respond as quickly as possible to the changing needs of the customer.

12-8 Kickoff Project

Project kickoff meetings are conducted for many reasons. First, everyone should express their legitimate needs and desires and should strive to understand the desires of all the other stakeholders. If the leader, charged with accomplishing the project, does not have the full authority to direct all the project work activities, she needs to use her influence to get everyone excited about the project, to feel pride in their participation, to feel they share in the risks and rewards the project offers, and to be motivated to self-manage as much as possible. Many people may have helped with some parts of the project

Monkey Business Images/Shutterstock.com

planning. This is their chance to see how all the parts fit together. Since many projects fail because of "touchpoints" where one person hands off work to another, it is critical for all parties to understand these potential trouble spots. Kickoff meetings are also helpful in convincing all the project stakeholders that the project leaders (sponsor, project manager, and core team) will be good stewards of the customer's and the parent organization's assets. Answering any remaining questions and overcoming lingering concerns helps to accomplish this. Finally, all interested parties (outside customers, top management, functional managers, frontline workers, and any others) should be eager to commit to the project and get on with the work!

12-8a Preconditions to Meeting Success

Several preconditions must be met for project kickoff meetings to be successful:

- The sponsor and project manager need to set clear direction during the planning.
- The core team needs to commit to the project first—it is hard for them to convince others if they do not believe in it themselves.
- Everyone should contribute to setting up an atmosphere of trust and relationship building.
- Project leaders need to practice active listening to uncover potential problems.
- As many people as possible should be included in parts of the planning to enhance chances that they will buy in to the resulting project plan.

12-8b Meeting Activities

The formality of a kickoff meeting can vary considerably depending on the size and type of project. Typical activities that might be included in the kickoff meeting are the following:

- The sponsor and project manager describing the importance of the project

- The customer(s) describing their acceptance standards, sense of urgency, and budget concerns
- The project manager outlining the project goals
- The project manager and the core team describing work expectations
- The project manager unfolding the project plan and its current status (if work has commenced)
- The core team explaining the communications, risk, and quality plans
- Everyone asking questions and making suggestions
- The project manager authorizing appropriate changes to the project plan
- Everyone concurring with the overall plan and to his or her individual action items

On small, simple projects, presenting the charter and signing can take the place of a kickoff meeting. However, on many projects, the team needs to perform much more detailed planning after the charter is signed. Project kickoff meetings are vital for communications and commitment on these projects. Exhibit 12.16 is an example of how the

EXHIBIT 12.16

IS&T PROJECT LAUNCH ASSESSMENT AGENDA

Purpose: The Project Manager is to illustrate to an executive audience the chartered IS&T project's readiness to successfully launch. Upon conclusion of the Project Manager's presentation, the executive audience will determine and document the actions required for the project to launch.

Prerequisite: The Project Manager is required to complete the Project Deliverable Review and receive documented approval from the Project Deliverable Review Board in order to proceed to the Project Launch Assessment.

Standard Participants

- Core Group (CG) (CIO and IS&T Director) PMO Manager
- Project Manager
- Functional Manager PMO Consult
- Quality Consult
- Security Consult (Optional)
- Test Coordinator
- Sponsor

Required Documents: The Project Manager is required to present the PLA materials online. If a paper copy is needed, it should be printed double-sided.

- Project Charter PMO Risk Forms
- Project Financial Worksheet
- Master Test Plan
- Progress Report—PDR

Project Launch Assessment Agenda: The Project Manager is required to present all of the listed deliverables in the provided order, focusing on specifically the identified components and content specified.

1. Project Charter—Discuss Business Need, Purpose, Logical Scope: In-Scope, Out-of-Scope, and Assumptions.
2. Master Test Plan—Discuss Sections 1.3—Test Levels, Objectives, and Deliverables; 3—Test Timeline and Key Events; and 5—Define System Characteristics, Relative Importance, and Subsystems.
3. Privacy and Security—Discuss the Security and HIPAA Template for PMO Projects.
4. Risk Forms—Discuss all populated and scored forms created to date.
5. Project Financial Worksheet—Discuss populated spreadsheet.
6. Progress Report (PDR)—Speak to the current status of all actions provided for each deliverable.

Source: Nancy D'Quila, PMP.

information systems and technology division of a major healthcare company kicks off a project.

In scaled agile models, there is a large meeting every planning cycle that behaves much like a kickoff meeting.

12-9 Baseline and Communicate Project Management Plan

Once the project plan is complete and accepted by the stakeholders, the plan is baselined. A baseline is the approved plan. Many project plans are developed iteratively as more information comes to light. A project plan is considered to be in draft form until enough information is available for the key stakeholders to commit to all of the details and baseline the plan. At that point, it becomes official, and any changes in the future need to be formally approved and documented.

This is a time of great joy because this marks the transition between planning and executing the project. In reality, on many projects, some activities that are on the critical path or nearly critical paths are started before the official project kickoff. Planning also continues in the form of replanning to adjust to changing circumstances. However, the majority of planning is done, and the majority of executing is just starting.

The project management plan needs to be communicated in accordance with the communications plan requirements. Hopefully, many of the key stakeholders are able to attend the kickoff meeting. Regardless of who is present, proper communication needs to be sent to all stakeholders.

12-10 Using MS Project for Project Baselines

MS Project can be used as a tool to automate and communicate many facets of a project. A key job of the project manager is monitoring and controlling the project. MS Project can assist the project manager in this effort by creating a project baseline to measure against as the project is executed. Before a baseline is created with MS Project, the project manager needs to verify that the following items have been incorporated in the planning (you'll probably note some of these are glaringly omitted in our running Suburban Park Homes tutorial):

* Quality assurance and quality control activities are included.
* Risk response plan activities (or duration compensation) are included.
* Performance posting activities are included.
* All "hard" date constraints are incorporated.
* A realistic start date has been chosen.
* Organizational holidays and resource vacations are entered.
* Resource allocations are realistic and overloads are addressed.
* Management and contingency reserves are in the schedule.
* Time and cost trade-offs are applied to the schedule.

12-10a Baseline the Project Plan

Once the project plan has been completed as above and agreed on by the key stakeholders, it is important to "lock in" the plan, or baseline it. Baselining is important so the project manager can track and measure how well actual project performance matches the original plan (the baseline). Tracking and measuring these variances is one way the project manager monitors and controls the project.

Up to this point, the project manager has inputted start, finish, and duration data into MS Project, along with resources, their costs, and assignments. These values, together with project quality and scope targets, are what the stakeholders agreed to, approved, and expect as key measures of project success. Collectively, these values and targets, along with the risk and communications plans, form the project management plan.

However, once work begins on the project (execution), the *actual* value of the inputs will begin to vary from the *planned* value for most if not all of these inputs (unless the project is executed *exactly to plan,* which is unlikely). When the baseline is created, MS Project makes a project plan snapshot of all planned input values (i.e., duration, start, stop, resources). With this snapshot, MS Project begins to track the variance between baseline and actual values as the project is executed. The project manager can use MS Project to compare the baseline with actual schedule, work, and cost variance values and display these graphically and in tables. This comparison can be used to know where the project is doing well, and where it may need help. Baseline variance can also help predict future impacts to time and cost targets. With these bits of information, project managers can take action to get the project back on track where needed, and reduce or eliminate undesirable future impacts to the project.

12-10b Create the First Time Baseline

Once key stakeholders agree to the project plan, the baseline is created by:

1. Click the **Project Tab>>Schedule Group**>>click **Set Baseline**>>click **Set Baseline…**
2. The defaults should be accepted as shown in Exhibit 12.17, click **OK**

12-10c Subsequent Baselines

For any number of reasons, it may not be useful to continue to manage to the present baseline. Reasons to change the baseline might include changes to the project scope, project delay, or unavailability of planned resources (among a host of other reasons). If

EXHIBIT 12.17

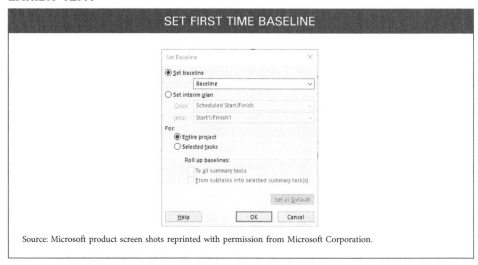

Source: Microsoft product screen shots reprinted with permission from Microsoft Corporation.

a change is approved, the changed tasks must be re-baselined, as well as the WBS parents of the new or changed tasks (Step 3 below):

1. Select the changed or added activities, milestones, and WBS elements
2. Click the **Project Tab>>Schedule Group>>**click **Set Baseline>>**click **Set Baseline...**
3. Ensure the original baseline is selected in the drop-down menu under "**Set baseline**"
4. Click **Selected tasks>>**check **To all summary tasks**
5. Click **OK**

Instead of re-baselining as above, you may wish to create an entirely new baseline. MS Project supports up to 11 baselines. Some project managers like to save a baseline for each iteration of planning to compare different values, while others like creating a new baseline as each phase or milestone of a project is reached. Steps for creating additional baselines match those of creating the original baseline, only the drop-down menu under "**Set baseline**" needs to be changed to **Baseline 1** (or Baseline 2, 3, 4, etc., whichever number of baseline the project happens to be on).

12-10d Viewing Baselines and Variances

The Gantt Chart view can be formatted to show "baseline bars," which provide a graphical view of differences between the planned and actual schedule of each task. To display baseline bars in the Gantt view:

1. Click the **View Tab>>Task Views>>Gantt Chart**
2. Click the **Format Tab>>Bar Styles Group>>Baseline>>**click the **Baseline you want to view**

A good way to view the difference between a task's baseline value versus its actual value is side by side. This is easily accomplished in MS Project using the Variance table:

1. Click the **View Tab>>Task Views>>**click **Other Views>>Task Sheet**
2. In the **Data Group>>Tables>>Variance**

The variance table appears and shows you several columns as in Exhibit 12.18. Once the project has entered the execution phase, many of your start and finish dates will likely be different from what was originally planned (baselined). The variance table shows you the Start and Finish dates (the actual dates you executed on) and the baselined Start and Finish dates (the dates you planned to execute on). It also shows you the Start and Finish variance (the difference between the planned and the actual date).

As you can see in Exhibit 12.18, a date change in the project has been made to the task "Architect sign-off." The original plan was for this task to start on Monday 12/4/17 (the Baseline Start). However, the actual start was on Wednesday 12/6/17 as seen in the Start column. This change shows up in the Start and Finish Variance columns as a two-day variance. If you go back to the Gantt view (**View Tab>>Task Views>>Gantt Chart**), you will notice that the baseline bars have been revealed more prominently as the task bars have shifted to the right.

As other project tasks shift, variances will ripple down through the project and give the project manager an idea of how the schedule will shift on the project. This is just another tool the project manager can use to examine critical path activities and plan to crash or make other adjustments to the schedule as necessary.

- Agile embraces the idea of building quality into the product at the smallest batch size.
- There is not a separate step for quality.

EXHIBIT 12.18

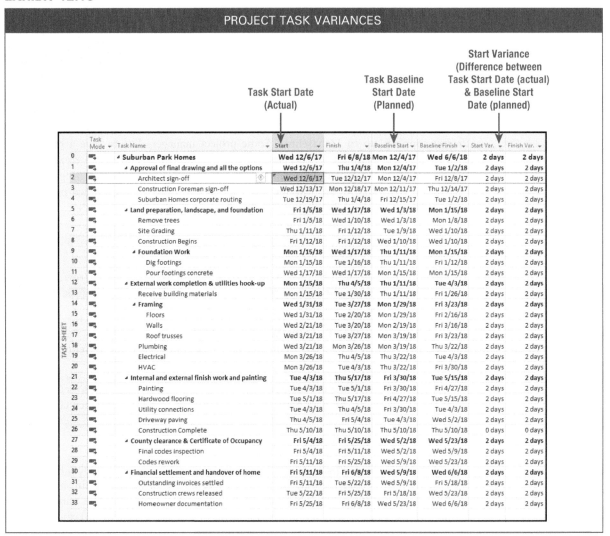

	Task Mode	Task Name	Start	Finish	Baseline Start	Baseline Finish	Start Var.	Finish Var.
0		⊿ Suburban Park Homes	Wed 12/6/17	Fri 6/8/18	Mon 12/4/17	Wed 6/6/18	2 days	2 days
1		⊿ Approval of final drawing and all the options	Wed 12/6/17	Thu 1/4/18	Mon 12/4/17	Tue 1/2/18	2 days	2 days
2		Architect sign-off	Wed 12/6/17	Tue 12/12/17	Mon 12/4/17	Fri 12/8/17	2 days	2 days
3		Construction Foreman sign-off	Wed 12/13/17	Mon 12/18/17	Mon 12/11/17	Thu 12/14/17	2 days	2 days
4		Suburban Homes corporate routing	Tue 12/19/17	Thu 1/4/18	Fri 12/15/17	Tue 1/2/18	2 days	2 days
5		⊿ Land preparation, landscape, and foundation	Fri 1/5/18	Wed 1/17/18	Wed 1/3/18	Mon 1/15/18	2 days	2 days
6		Remove trees	Fri 1/5/18	Wed 1/10/18	Wed 1/3/18	Mon 1/8/18	2 days	2 days
7		Site Grading	Thu 1/11/18	Fri 1/12/18	Tue 1/9/18	Wed 1/10/18	2 days	2 days
8		Construction Begins	Fri 1/12/18	Fri 1/12/18	Wed 1/10/18	Wed 1/10/18	2 days	2 days
9		⊿ Foundation Work	Mon 1/15/18	Wed 1/17/18	Thu 1/11/18	Mon 1/15/18	2 days	2 days
10		Dig footings	Mon 1/15/18	Tue 1/16/18	Thu 1/11/18	Fri 1/12/18	2 days	2 days
11		Pour footings concrete	Wed 1/17/18	Wed 1/17/18	Mon 1/15/18	Mon 1/15/18	2 days	2 days
12		⊿ External work completion & utilities hook-up	Mon 1/15/18	Thu 4/5/18	Thu 1/11/18	Tue 4/3/18	2 days	2 days
13		Receive building materials	Mon 1/15/18	Tue 1/30/18	Thu 1/11/18	Fri 1/26/18	2 days	2 days
14		⊿ Framing	Wed 1/31/18	Tue 3/27/18	Mon 1/29/18	Fri 3/23/18	2 days	2 days
15		Floors	Wed 1/31/18	Tue 2/20/18	Mon 1/29/18	Fri 2/16/18	2 days	2 days
16		Walls	Wed 2/21/18	Tue 3/20/18	Mon 2/19/18	Fri 3/16/18	2 days	2 days
17		Roof trusses	Wed 3/21/18	Tue 3/27/18	Mon 3/19/18	Fri 3/23/18	2 days	2 days
18		Plumbing	Wed 3/21/18	Mon 3/26/18	Mon 3/19/18	Thu 3/22/18	2 days	2 days
19		Electrical	Mon 3/26/18	Thu 4/5/18	Thu 3/22/18	Tue 4/3/18	2 days	2 days
20		HVAC	Mon 3/26/18	Tue 4/3/18	Thu 3/22/18	Fri 3/30/18	2 days	2 days
21		⊿ Internal and external finish work and painting	Tue 4/3/18	Thu 5/17/18	Fri 3/30/18	Tue 5/15/18	2 days	2 days
22		Painting	Tue 4/3/18	Tue 5/1/18	Fri 3/30/18	Fri 4/27/18	2 days	2 days
23		Hardwood flooring	Tue 5/1/18	Thu 5/17/18	Fri 4/27/18	Tue 5/15/18	2 days	2 days
24		Utility connections	Tue 4/3/18	Thu 4/5/18	Fri 3/30/18	Tue 4/3/18	2 days	2 days
25		Driveway paving	Thu 4/5/18	Fri 5/4/18	Tue 4/3/18	Wed 5/2/18	2 days	2 days
26		Construction Complete	Thu 5/10/18	Thu 5/10/18	Thu 5/10/18	Thu 5/10/18	0 days	0 days
27		⊿ County clearance & Certificate of Occupancy	Fri 5/4/18	Fri 5/25/18	Wed 5/2/18	Wed 5/23/18	2 days	2 days
28		Final codes inspection	Fri 5/4/18	Fri 5/11/18	Wed 5/2/18	Wed 5/9/18	2 days	2 days
29		Codes rework	Fri 5/11/18	Fri 5/25/18	Wed 5/9/18	Wed 5/23/18	2 days	2 days
30		⊿ Financial settlement and handover of home	Fri 5/11/18	Fri 6/8/18	Wed 5/9/18	Wed 6/6/18	2 days	2 days
31		Outstanding invoices settled	Fri 5/11/18	Tue 5/22/18	Wed 5/9/18	Fri 5/18/18	2 days	2 days
32		Construction crews released	Tue 5/22/18	Fri 5/25/18	Fri 5/18/18	Wed 5/23/18	2 days	2 days
33		Homeowner documentation	Fri 5/25/18	Fri 6/8/18	Wed 5/23/18	Wed 6/6/18	2 days	2 days

- The saying that helps us remember this is: aim small miss small.
- There is little planning for quality, other than the team owns quality, and the Condition of Acceptance for each story is the definition acceptable to the customer.
- Architectural runway is an aspect of quality in more agile environments and this speaks to how the infrastructure where the software will run needs to prepared. When this is done as a critical path activity, the product quality is higher.
- While agile has been predominately used in software and product development environments, much of what agile does with regard to quality could work in other areas as well.

PMP/CAPM Study Ideas

You are likely to see a few elements from this chapter on either a CAPM or PMP test. One of the paramount things to remember is the difference between quality assurance (forward-looking/preventative) and quality control (inspection) and how a quality policy or plan can integrate the two.

Understand how to follow an improvement model such as PDCA or DMAIC and know the difference between common causes and special causes of variation. Be familiar with the contributions of some of the thought leaders in the field of quality—especially Deming and Juran. Finally, know what **Six Sigma** means and why it is relevant and be prepared to use its standard deviation formula to determine whether a process is in control or out of control. We will delve into more specific quality tools in Chapter 14.

Summary

Deming, Juran, and many other people have contributed to the modern approaches to quality. The Malcolm Baldrige Award, ISO certification, and Six Sigma each present a framework with many good points. The contemporary approach to project quality draws upon all of these sources.

The first concept in contemporary project quality management is stakeholder satisfaction. It is critical to understand project stakeholders, prioritize their needs, manage toward those needs, keep the relationships strong, and always strive to ensure that the customer is capable of using the project deliverables. The second concept is process management. This includes understanding both continual and breakthrough forms of improvement, seeking the root cause of problems, and using an appropriate model such as DMAIC to guide improvement efforts. The third concept is fact-based management. This entails understanding variation, making good decisions regarding what to measure, capturing and analyzing data correctly, and using the information in an open and honest decision-making manner. The final concept is empowered performance. Project managers want to have capable and willing workers throughout their project and should treat each person as an individual, ensure people accept responsibility, and strive to get more done through collaboration.

When project managers perform quality management planning, the first thing they need to do is either adopt the quality policy of their parent organization or supplement it. The policy should broadly guide their efforts. The quality plan should include the quality baseline defining performance expectations. It should also include instructions for how the quality assurance and quality control will be handled.

Many quality tools have been developed over the years, and quite a few of them work well on projects. Many of these tools can be used in additional project management activities.

Once the quality management plan and all of the other subsidiary plans have been developed, it is time to iron out any inconsistencies among the various plans. The overall project management plan needs to make sense. Quality, cost, schedule, human resources, risk, and communications may have been planned somewhat independently on a large project, and now is the time to make sure they all work well together.

The project core team usually asks themselves a number of questions concerning the practicality of the overall plan and then holds a kickoff meeting with all of the project stakeholders. Hopefully, the outcome of the meeting is commitment and excitement all around. Now, the project officially moves into execution. While some of the project activities may already be under way (or even complete), the approval of the project plan signals the change from primarily planning to primarily execution. Ongoing planning and replanning still occur, but managing the performance of project activities and communicating with various stakeholders consume much of the project manager's time from this point forward.

Key Terms Consistent with PMI Standards and Guides

plan quality management, 387
project quality, 392
stakeholder satisfaction, 393
process, 394
control, 395
four aspects of fact-based management, 396

quality metrics, 397
data, 397
information, 397
quality management plan, 401
process improvement plan, 404
manage quality, 404

Chapter Review Questions

1. What is the name of the process that identifies which quality standards are relevant to the project and how to comply with them?

2. Who was the influential thought leader in the area of quality who created the Profound Knowledge System?

3. Who is best known for creating the Quality Trilogy?

4. What does the acronym TQM stand for? How does it apply to project management?

5. What does the name *Six Sigma* refer to?

6. Define the term *project quality*.

7. Give some examples of external stakeholders.

8. What are the four core project quality concepts?

9. What are three main reasons it is better to design quality into a process than to find problems upon inspection?

10. Identify and describe the steps of the PDAC model.

11. What is the difference between common and special causes of variation?

12. Define quality assurance and the primary methods that can be used to achieve it.

13. Define quality control and the primary methods that can be used to achieve it.

14. What activities are typically included in a project kickoff meeting?

15. What marks the transition between the planning and executing project phases?

Discussion Questions

1. What did Deming mean when he said that organizations operate as systems? Give examples.

2. Identify similarities and differences among TQM, ISO, and Six Sigma. What strengths and weaknesses are inherent in each of these approaches?

3. Rank the seven quality management areas of ISO from most to least important. What rationale is your list based upon?

4. Describe the process of achieving stakeholder satisfaction. How would you address a situation in which two stakeholders have mutually exclusive goals for the project?

5. Give examples of how a single company might use continuous process improvement and/or breakthrough process improvement.

6. Give some examples of common and special cause variation that you have witnessed. Which

of these causes of variation can be addressed through continuous improvement?

7. Discuss the four areas of fact-based decision making. In your opinion, what is the greatest obstacle to using fact-based decision making?

8. Discuss the costs of conformance versus nonconformance and how they both factor into the overall cost of quality. What percent of your budget would you put toward conformance-related tasks compared to nonconformance-related tasks? Why?

9. In your own experience, have you seen companies integrate quality within their project planning processes? If so, how and when have they done so? If not, do you think it would have been more beneficial to address quality in one area of the overall project plan or continuously throughout the plan?

PMBOK® Guide Questions

1. An important input to the Plan Quality Management process is requirements documentation. This is because:

   a. the organization will have a uniform set of specific quality requirements that every project must adhere to.

b. requirements include the schedule and cost information that must be balanced against quality needs for the project.

c. requirements documentation captures the stakeholder expectations that the project should meet.

d. the sponsor's directives for the project's level of quality are expressed in the requirements.

2. Which of the following is part of a Configuration Management System?

a. process for identifying and uniquely naming items that need to be controlled

b. recording and reporting all changes

c. verifying the correctness of all deliverables and components of them

d. all of the above

3. What cycle is the basis for Six Sigma quality planning and improvement?

a. DMAIC

b. PDCA

c. DOE

d. TQM

4. All of these are components of a work flow diagram called the SIPOC model *except*:

a. customer

b. process

c. input

d. support

5. The PMBOK® Guide defines quality as:

a. exceeding customer expectations by delivering more than they requested.

b. achieving the highest-possible level of value using objective measures.

c. the degree to which a set of inherent characteristics fulfills requirements.

d. a category used to distinguish items that have the same functional use.

6. During quality management planning, the project manager and team determine what will be measured during the Control Quality process. Project or product attributes such as on-time performance, defect frequency, and costs versus budget are known as _____ .

a. quality metrics

b. quality thresholds

c. quality tolerances

d. quality boundaries

7. Preventive action _____ .

a. is primarily addressed in the Control Quality process

b. realigns the performance of the project work with the project management plan

c. seeks to ensure the future performance of the project work is aligned with the project management plan

d. modifies a nonconforming product or product subcomponent

8. According to the PMBOK, which of the following is *not* a quality management process?

a. Plan Quality Management

b. Monitor Quality

c. Perform Quality Assurance

d. Control Quality

9. Once the project management plan is complete and accepted by the stakeholders, the approved plan is _____ .

a. reviewed

b. baselined

c. followed

d. documented

10. Who came up with the four-part Profound Knowledge System?

a. Deming

b. Juran

c. Maslow

d. Ford

Exercises

1. Create a SIPOC for an everyday activity (i.e., paying bills, parallel parking, or making cookies).

2. Identify key quality project plan steps that you feel should be included within a typical overall project plan. Be sure to include quality items throughout the project plan life cycle.

3. Create a SIPOC model for a project where your university is modernizing its student center to include space for on-campus, student-run businesses. Be sure to include all relevant stakeholder groups. Describe how you would use this information to design quality into your project.

4. Improve a work process using either the DMAIC or the PDCA model to guide your actions. What project quality tools did you use, and why did you select each?

5. Identify the quality policy for a local company. Speculate how the policy focuses the efforts on a project in that company. Find a project manager at that company and ask his or her opinion of the quality policy's impact.

INTEGRATED EXAMPLE PROJECTS
SUBURBAN HOMES CONSTRUCTION PROJECT

Suburban Homes realized that its ambitious plan of expanding its business to several Southern States in the United States is possible if it is known for its high-quality homes that meet local, state, and federal standards as well as exceed industrial standards for quality.

Even though Suburban Homes did not place a strong emphasis on quality but focused on meeting industrial standards, the company has realized that it must exceed all the quality standards to expand its business successfully. Although Adam Smith worked for several years in the construction industry, he is not specifically trained in quality management and he is not well versed with quality management tools and techniques. He is actively seeking help internally and externally.

In the previous chapters, you have developed a scope plan (WBS), schedule network, cost estimation along RBS, and risk assessments for the project described. Now, the quality management plan needs to be added to make the project plan comprehensive project.

Adam's primary task is to develop a quality management plan. Further, he realized that employee turnover and the expansion of the business in the southern states has led to Suburban Homes developing a centralized quality management team. You are hired as a consultant to develop a comprehensive quality management plan.

Tasks to Complete

- Assess quality expectations of a typical home buyer who is the primary stakeholder and other key stakeholders to develop a plan for stakeholder satisfaction.
- Identify relevant standards of quality.
- Develop quality measures for monitoring project performance.
- Develop a quality management plan as described in this chapter.
- Perform a qualitative assessment to prioritize risks.
- Develop a quality policy.
- Develop a process improvement plan.
- Define a quality assurance approach.

CASA DE PAZ DEVELOPMENT PROJECT

Some of the quality implications the team needs to address include the following:

Zoning and building codes

Professional standards for various programs (nursing, ESL, career readiness, etc.)

Credentialed staff

Semester Project Instructions

Talk with your sponsor to determine if the organization for which you are planning your example project has a quality policy. If it does, determine whether you will adopt it as is or ask to augment it. Tell why you wish to either accept or modify it.

With your sponsor, determine the quality baseline for your project. What standards will you use?

Perform a stakeholder analysis. After completing the tool, are there any stakeholders that you didn't think of before? Are there any who are opponents? What actions could you take to try to change those who are opponents into enthusiasts?

Create a SIPOC for your project. What did you learn that surprised you? How will your project plan be different because of what you learned?

Create an agenda for a kickoff meeting for your project. Conduct the kickoff meeting and capture minutes for it. Tell what went as you expected and what went differently from what you expected.

Baseline your project management plan with the activity baseline start, activity baseline finish, activity baseline duration, activity baseline cost, and activity baseline work shown in MS Project. Also show in your project management plan the agreed-upon quality and scope targets, risk, and communications plans.

Pick one work process related to your example project. Use the DMAIC model to improve the process. Perform the define and measure steps. Tell what you learned. Identify what project quality tools you expect to use on the remaining steps and tell why you will use them.

PROJECT MANAGEMENT *IN ACTION*
Quality Planning at GTC

Every customer-facing project performed by General Tool Company (GTC) has an associated Quality Plan Requirements (QPR) document. The QPR is an output of the technical review process and is performed by the Quality Engineer (QE) during the preliminary planning stages of the project. The QPR is derived from various source documents, including the Purchase Order Agreement, Statement of Work, technical publications, customer flow-down requirements, and drawing notes. Familiarity with the customer's quality system requirements is an essential element of the review process. It is not uncommon for a customer to mistakenly leave out critical quality requirements when issuing a purchase order or request-for-proposal. However, by being familiar with the customer's quality systems and manufacturing needs, GTC is able to work with the customer to correct any deficiencies prior to beginning the manufacturing process.

Through the QPR process, the QE may (and often does) uncover project risks previously unknown to the team. Such risks may impact cost, schedule, scope, or any combination thereof. At a minimum, identified risk must be investigated by the project manager so as to

EXHIBIT 12.19

SUPPLIER SCORECARD

Supplier Rating:

Quarter 1, 2, 3 & 4 of 2012

General Tool Company

Suppliers will be categorized into one of four tiers; A, B, C or D.

A) An A tier supplier has a rating of 85 – 100.

B) A B tier supplier has a rating of 75 – 84.

C) A C tier supplier has a rating of 65 – 74.

D) A D tier supplier has a rating of 64 or less.

Below are the charts and graphs that represent **GTC's** performance in the last 4 quarters.

Overall Rating: A Tier.

On Time Delivery:
Delivery issues due to Quality misses in 3rd Quarter. Process improvements have restored highest rating.

Quality List of defects:
Cert accuracy – missing information/incomplete documents delayed product receipt.
Machining failure caused decrease in 3rd Quarter Quality rating. GTC implemented Corrective Actions.
Reference GTC Quality Action Plan.

Source: Brad Brezinski, Jim Stewart, Korey Bischoff, and Mark Butorac of General Tool Corporation.

ensure there are no changes to the scope of work as originally proposed. While many tools exist to identify and address quality-related risks (DMIAC, Ishikawa Diagram, 5 Whys, etc.), GTC utilizes the Quality Improvement Action Plan for planning and in-process management of project risks.

Of course, not all risks are uncovered during the planning phase. Unsuspecting performance issues can arise at any point during the project's lifecycle and must be dealt with appropriately to ensure cost, schedule, and performance objectives are met. In the example on the following pages, GTC identified, by way of the supplier scorecard in Exhibit 12.19, delivery issues associated with a particular aerospace project. The scorecard led the project team down the continuous improvement path, in an effort to bolster the supplier rating. The relationship between the supplier scorecard and the Quality Improvement Action Plan is clearly indicated (as

well as the marked improvement in the subsequent quarter).

By working closely with the customer and the QE, the project manager ensures that the project's quality and technical requirements are properly identified and integrated into the project plan. In addition, the QPR process provides an opportunity to validate the team's underlying assumptions from the bid process. Any incongruences can be addressed before the manufacturing process begins, thus giving the project the best opportunity for a successful outcome. Further, it is often during the quality planning process that the customer comes to realize the significant costs associated with heightened quality and technical requirements. In a firm-fixed-price environment, this is the best time for the subcontractor to negotiate any associated cost impact, as the risk is squarely on the shoulders of the subcontractor once the purchase order agreement is accepted.

References

A Guide to the Project Management Body of Knowledge (PMBOK® Guide), 6th ed. Exposure Draft (Newtown Square, PA: Project Management Institute, 2013).

Baldrige National Quality Program, "Criteria for Performance Excellence," https://www.nist.gov/sites/default/files/documents/baldrige/publications/Baldrige_20_20.pdf, accessed April 10, 2017.

Business Dictionary, http://www.businessdictionary.com/definition/data.html, accessed April 10, 2017.

Crawford, Lynn, and Jeanne Dorie, "Quality First," *PM Network* 20 (5) (May 2006): 42–47.

Deep Fried Brain PM Certification Blog, http://www.deepfriedbrainproject.com/2010/05/activities-configuration-management.html, accessed April 11, 2017.

Diffin Compare Anything, Quality Assurance vs. Quality Control, http://www.diffen.com/difference/Quality_Assurance_vs_Quality_Control, accessed April 11, 2017.

DoIT Project Management Advisor, https://pma.doit.wisc.edu/plan/3-2/what.html, accessed April 10, 2017.

Evans, James R., and William M. Lindsay, *An Introduction to Six Sigma & Process Improvement,* 1st ed. (Mason, OH: Thomson South-Western, 2005).

Evans, James R., and William M. Lindsay, *The Management and Control of Quality and Performance* (Mason, OH: Cengage Learning, 2015): 6–8.

International Organization for Standardization, "Quality Management Principles," https://www.iso.org/obp/ui/#iso:std:iso:10006:dis:ed-3:v1:en, accessed April 10, 2017.

ISO 9001 2015 Translated into Plain English, http://www.praxiom.com/iso-9001.htm, accessed April 10, 2017.

ISO/DIS Quality Management Systems–Guidelines for quality management on projects, https://www.iso.org/standard/70376.html accessed May 24, 2017.

Juran, Joseph M., *A History of Managing for Quality: The Evolution, Trends, and Future Directions of Managing for Quality* (Madison, WI: ASQC Quality Press, 1995).

Kloppenborg, Timothy J., and Joseph A. Petrick, *Managing Project Quality* (Vienna, VA: Management Concepts, Inc., 2002).

Kwak, Young Hoon, John J. Wetter, and Frank T. Anbari, "Business Process Best Practices: Project Management or Six Sigma?" *Proceedings, PM1 Research Conference 2006: New Directions in Project Management* (Montreal, Canada, 2006).

Neuendorf, Steve, *Six Sigma for Project Managers* (Vienna, VA: Management Concepts, Inc., 2004).

Passionate Project Management, https://www.passionatepm.com/blog/corrective-versus-preventive-actions-versus-defect-repairs-pmp-concept-38, accessed April 11, 2017.

PMI Code of Ethics and Professional Responsibility, http://www.pmi.org/About-Us/Ethics/~/media/PDF/Ethics/ap_pmicodeofethics.ashx, accessed May 3, 2013.

Project Management Docs, http://www.projectmanagementdocs.com/project-documents/quality-metrics.html#axzz4dse9892h, accessed April 10, 2010.

Project Management Docs, http://www.projectmanagementdocs.com/project-planning-templates/process-improvement-plan.html#axzz4dse9892h, accessed April 11, 2017.

Shiba, Shoji, and David Walden, *Breakthrough Management* (New Delhi, India: Confederation of Indian Industry, 2006).

Simplilearn, https://www.simplilearn.com/project-quality-management-article, accessed April 11, 2017.

Stevens, James D., Timothy J. Kloppenborg, and Charles R. Glagola, *Quality Performance Measurements of the EPC Process: The Blueprint* (Austin, TX: Construction Industry Institute, 1994).

Svensson, Richard Berntsson, et al. "Quality Requirements in Industrial Practice—An Extended Interview Study at Eleven Companies," *IEEE Transactions on Software Engineering* 38 (4) (July–August 2012): 923–936.

Swanson, Sandra A, "Winning Pair: Integrating Six Sigma and *PMBOK® Guide* at an Organizational Level," *PMNetwork* 25 (7) July 2011: 54–58.

Wagner, Rodd, and James K. Harter, *12: The Elements of Great Managing* (New York: Gallup Press, 2006).

Zhang, Weiyong, and Xiaobo Xu, "Six Sigma and Information Systems Project Management: A Revised Theoretical Model," *Project Management Journal* 39 (3) (2008): 59–74.

http://www.pma.doit.wisc.edu/plan/3-2/print.html, accessed May 3, 2013.

Endnotes

1. *PMBOK® Guide 6th Edition Exposure Draft* 20.
2. Adapted from James R. Evans and William M. Lindsay, *Management for Quality and Performance* (Mason, OH: Cengage Learning, 2015): 6–8.
3. Evans. James R., and William M. Lindsay, *Management for Quality and Performance* 205.
4. Evans, James R., and William M. Lindsay, *Management for Quality and Performance* 222.
5. http://www.projectmanagementdocs.com/project-documents/quality-metrics.html#axzz4dse9892h, accessed April 10, 2017.
6. http://www.businessdictionary.com/definition/data.html, accessed April 10, 2017.
7. http://www.businessdictionary.com/definition/information.html, accessed April 10, 2017.
8. https://pma.doit.wisc.edu/plan/3-2/what.html, accessed April 10, 2017.
9. Adapted from http://www.pma.doit.wisc.edu/plan/3-2/what.html, accessed April 10, 2017.
10. http://www.projectmanagementdocs.com/project-planning-templates/process-improvement-plan.html#axzz4dse9892h, accessed April 11, 2017.
11. https://www.simplilearn.com/project-quality-management-article, accessed April 11, 2017.
12. Ibid.
13. https://www.passionatepm.com/blog/corrective-versus-preventive-actions-versus-defect-repairs-pmp-concept-38, accessed April 11, 2017.
14. Ibid.
15. Ibid.
16. http://www.businessdictionary.com/definition/process-analysis.html, accessed April 11, 2017.
17. http://www.diffen.com/difference/Quality_Assurance_vs_Quality_Control, accessed April 11, 2017.
18. Adapted from http://www.deepfriedbrainproject.com/2010/05/activities-configuration-management.html, accessed April 11, 2017.

PART 4

PERFORMING PROJECTS

ORGANIZE   LEAD   PLAN   **PERFORM**

Performing a project includes leading, managing, and controlling all of the various knowledge areas of the *PMBOK® Guide* simultaneously so as to ensure progress is being made and results will be delivered. Chapter 13 deals with the procurements area, including all work with suppliers and partners in the supply chain. Chapter 14 includes the ongoing work concerning scope, schedule, cost, quality, communications, risks, and stakeholders. Chapter 15 wraps up the project, showing how to successfully close a project and reap the benefits.

Project Supply Chain Management

Mark Herreid/Shutterstock.com

The Challenge—As an independent inventor, IP owner, and entrepreneur, the greatest challenge is the need to muster the required organizational support, critical capital, and project management input while staying agile and responsive to developing conditions. Project management adds crucial skills you need to generate cooperation from your resources without implicit or granted hierarchal authority.

Background—This story was born when I encountered a challenge on a landscaping project. The solution to the previous project became a significant independent project called Super Absorbent Polymer Turf (SAPTURF). The problem is that synthetic turf systems generate extreme heat of 50 to 60 degrees above the ambient temperature on the surface, which is unpleasant and even dangerous. As a small, independent individual, I developed and patented a polymer that solves this problem in many situations.

Initially, I chose a large multinational based in Europe to partner with on the next step in commercializing SAPTURF. I chose this international partner because they are the market leaders. I still controlled the intellectual property (IP) and entered into an agreement to further test my technology to calibrate the value.

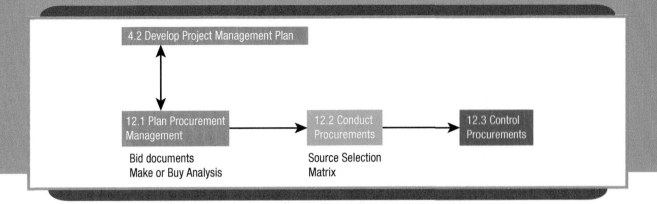

PMBOK® GUIDE

Topics:

- Plan procurement management
- Conduct procurements
- Control procurements

CHAPTER OUTPUTS

- Make or buy analysis
- Bid documents
- Source selection matrix

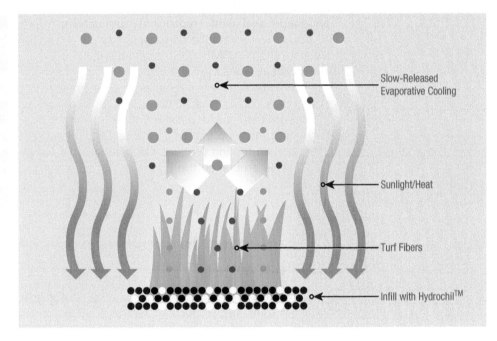

Stay Agile—After the trial process, I ended up choosing a different firm in the synthetic turf industry as a long-term partner and licensee. I chose Shaw Industry, a Berkshire Hathaway company. Shaw Industries operates three synthetic turf divisions. Shaw's experience as the largest flooring manufacturer in the United States and its financial stability as a Berkshire Hathaway company were additional reasons I selected them as a long-term partner. I also developed confidence that they would respect both my knowledge and my intellectual property.

I entered into a long-term license agreement with Shaw Industries and they trademarked my technology "HydroChill." HydroChill is being commercialized worldwide.

In addition to my license agreement, I provide consultancy services to Shaw Industries and some of their affiliates on an ongoing basis, which allows me to stay close to the *"shop floor"* and facilitates ongoing implementation and improvement of the HydroChill technology. This also allows me to share some of my tacit knowledge to increase probabilities that applications are successful.

The Product—Our technology is applied to a field where components react and form a coating on the infill. The field is watered to activate HydroChill, and then energy from sunlight drives out water, removing heat from the surface.

The cooling effect of HydroChill after watering can last two to three days. Watering alone can result in some cooling, but temperatures can rise and quickly exceed uncomfortable levels of heat. HydroChill creates a substantial and sustained temperature difference.

Applications—HydroChill projects have been executed in the categories of large-scale athletic fields, parks, roof gardens, and residential lawns throughout the world. One of the most recent and notable HydroChill projects is a complete par three golf course in the French Riviera town of Grimaud. A few of the other applications include:

Athletic field HydroChill application, http://www.shawsportsturf.com/, http://www.shawhydrochill.com/

Landscape and Golf HydroChill application, http://www.southwestgreens.com/, https://www.youtube.com/watch?v=m8As-rUnOZA, https://www.youtube.com/watch?v=ZR-B68MBdJY, http://hydrochill.cool

And the Beat Goes On ...

Our flexible contracts for licensing the technology and for supporting further development allow us to continue our first love—developing exciting new projects. My son and I are developing other applications outside the synthetic turf industry under the Taro Inc. flag. One application we are currently commercializing is Equestrian footing product. Operators in the dressage, jumper, and rodeo categories have embraced the Equestrian footing application.

—Chris Tetrault, owner and founder, SAPTURF

13-1 Introduction to Project Supply Chain Management

Can you provide a project example that is fully completed by the project organization itself, without using any products or services from outside suppliers? Most likely, the answer is no. As the opening case illustrates, in-house personnel complete almost no serious projects from scratch anymore. In fact, outsourcing part of project tasks has been a well-established practice in various industries for a long time. In many cases, companies have to rely on external suppliers for acquiring many of the unique resources they need. In this chapter, we consider the interorganizational purchasing-related issues (hereafter referred to as supply chain management) in the context of project management.

A supply chain consists of all parties involved, directly or indirectly, in fulfilling a customer request. In project management, this request can be made by the project team in order to acquire some specific product or service required for completing various stages of the project. The customer can also make the request. As a result, supply chain operations require managerial processes that span functional areas within individual organizations and link trading partners and customers across organizational boundaries.

In recent years, the topic of supply chain management has evolved into a systematic approach for managing all material, service, monetary, and information flows across supply chain partners. With its broader coverage and profound impact, project supply chain management has become a challenge to many firms. Because the ultimate goal of serving project customers hinges on the systematic and coordinated performance of all partners (suppliers, transporters, and so forth), supply chain management becomes a critical project management activity. However, many companies traditionally have been concerned with purchasing and procurement, where the goal was to obtain necessary goods and services at the lowest possible price. In this chapter, we cover not only traditional procurement and contractual management topics but also supplier partnership and collaboration issues.

We define project **supply chain management** as a system's approach to managing the entire flows of physical products, information, and funds from suppliers and producers, through resellers, and finally through the project organization for creating customer satisfaction. A sample project supply chain is shown in Exhibit 13.1.

The traditional purchasing perspective is only concerned with the relationship between the project team and its supplier(s)—those who supply the project organization directly. At its most extensive, supply chain management involves strategic and operational issues concerned with all organizational partners involved in projects. Doubtless, all supply chain parties need to work together to complete the project faster, better, and/or cheaper. They all need to remember that the key project stakeholders determine the trade-offs for better results in achieving project outcomes.

In traditional project procurement management literature, *purchasing, supply chain management,* and *procurement* are usually used interchangeably to refer to the integration of related functions to purchase or acquire the needed materials and services for the project team. Thus, procurement management is concerned with more than the standard steps in the purchasing process, such as recognizing needs, translating needs into commercially equivalent descriptions, and searching for suppliers. Further responsibilities of a project supply chain may also include receiving, inspection, storage, inbound and outbound transportation, and disposal. Project procurement management can also be extended to cover various stages of the supply chain for providing the necessary goods or services (e.g., the supplier's supplier). It is helpful to think in terms of the following:

- **Owner**—the "person or entity that owns the product of the project and to whom that product will be handed over at the time of its completion"[1]
- **General contractor**—a person or agency that "does not specialize in one kind of work; often used to refer to the primary contractor who employs specialty subcontractors"[2]
- **Subcontractor**—a "contractor who is holding a contract with a prime contractor (also referred to as a first-tier subcontractor) or is holding a contract with a subcontractor to the prime contractor (i.e., lower-tier subcontractor)"[3]

Though supply chain management (SCM) and project management (PM) are traditionally separate business areas, we find that integrating SCM into PM can significantly enhance the effectiveness of project management. We also discuss project procurement management. The last section of the chapter covers how to improve project supply chain performance.

EXHIBIT 13.1

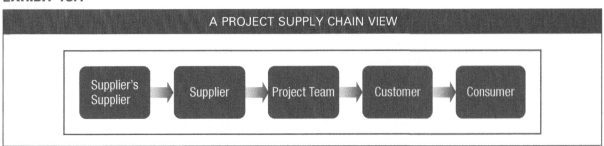

A PROJECT SUPPLY CHAIN VIEW

Supplier's Supplier → Supplier → Project Team → Customer → Consumer

13-1a SCM Components

In particular, this chapter focuses on the following project supply chain management components:

- **Make-or-buy decisions**—These are "the act of choosing between manufacturing a product in-house or purchasing it from an external supplier."[4]
- Contract types—We introduce the contact types and compare their advantages and disadvantages in case a buy decision is warranted.
- Collaboration and cooperation—As different firms take care of their own interests, it is essential to coordinate their project activities to ensure the deliverables are produced as scheduled. The project at hand should become the common goal of all the parties concerned.
- System integration—This concerns the trade-offs among project goals such as time, cost, and quality.

13-1b SCM Factors

Generally, supply chain management is more important to projects in which a large portion of the work is being subcontracted and more collaboration is needed. Other factors include the following:

- The value of the outsourced products or services relative to the total value of the project
- The timing of the work being purchased
- The capability of the project team
- The role of the outsourced work in the entire project
- The number of suppliers required
- The structure of the procurement supply chain (the number of stages in the supply chain and the nature of the intercompany relationship)

As noted earlier, it is common for a significant part of the value of a project to come from various external suppliers. It is also increasingly common for some organizations to exist only as coordinators of activities, without having their own capability of producing and offering the project deliverables. In the meantime, not only do large companies outsource project tasks, but many small businesses also outsource. In fact, small firms tend to rely more on outside resources as they may not have the special capability of in-house execution for certain project activities or the working capital to own and employ resources.

13-1c SCM Decisions

Some of the major project supply chain management decisions are:

- Distribution network configuration
- Inventory control in a supply chain
- Logistics
- Supply contracts
- Distribution strategies
- Supply chain integration and strategic partnering
- Outsourcing and procurement strategies
- Product design
- Information technology and decision-support systems
- Matching internal inadequacies with external expertise

In practice, these decisions often involve quantitative analysis. All of these decisions can play an important role in managing a complex project. The implication is that project managers must be aware of these methodologies for ensuring project completion in a timely and cost-effective way.

13-1d Project Procurement Management Processes

Project procurement management includes the following three processes.

1. Plan procurement management
2. Conduct procurements
3. Control procurements

13-2 Plan Procurement Management

Plan procurement management is determining how project procurement decisions, approach, and dealing with sellers will be accomplished and documented. It identifies those project needs that can be met by acquiring products or services from outside suppliers, determines what to purchase or acquire, and finalizes when and how to do so. On some projects, a portion of the services or materials may be sourced from another company; on other projects, the bulk or even all of the work may be performed by an external company. A client company needs to plan for purchasing and acquisition, whether it is for part or all of a project. The needs of the parent organization should be considered as well as those of the project when deciding how to acquire necessary items because it may be better for the parent organization to buy an item rather than to rent it for the current project and then rent it again for a future project.

To effectively plan for purchasing and acquisition of materials and services, a project team typically finishes identifying customer requirements and most of the project planning to understand what are the true project needs. At a minimum, the project team requires knowing the project scope, which was defined in Chapter 1 as the entirety of what will and will not be done to meet the specified requirements. Once the requirements are identified, a project manager should be able to determine whether or not to buy and if buying, what to buy and the quantity to buy.

13-2a Outputs of Planning

One primary output of this planning is a **procurement management plan,** which is the portion of the project management plan that describes how a project team will acquire goods and services they choose to purchase. The procurement management plan can include guidance for types of contracts to be used, risk management issues, and how to select potential suppliers. This plan guides the client company's efforts through all activities dealing with the acquisition of all the necessary materials and services to complete the project. Another major output is the **procurement statement of work,** which documents the portion of work to be purchased, described in enough detail so potential suppliers can decide if they feel they are capable of and interested in providing it. This document should ensure that both the contractor and the client companies clearly understand the work that is being requested; for example, the document should provide information such as specifications, quantity desired, quality standards, performance data, work requirements, schedules, inspections, and other needs.

13-2b Make-or-Buy Decisions

Project procurement can be considered from the view of the buyer–seller interface. Depending on the application areas, the seller can be called a supplier, supplier's supplier, or contractor. Depending on the buyer's position in the project acquisition cycle, the buyer can be called an owner, a customer, a service requestor, or a purchaser. The seller can be viewed during the contract life cycle first as a bidder and then as the contracted supplier or vendor.

For any products or services needed in a project, during the purchase planning phase, the project team determines which project needs can best be met by purchasing or acquiring products and services from an outside provider and which project needs can be accomplished by the project team. Buying from an outside supplier to meet project needs is a well-established practice. For example, many firms outsource information technology requirements, accounting work, legal functions, logistics, and so on.

REASONS TO BUY OR SELL   The make-or-buy decision is not trivial. It involves intricate issues such as a project organization's competitive analysis and demand analysis. The project team also needs to evaluate the advantages and disadvantages of outsourcing from the viewpoint of time, cost, and performance control. The analysis should also include both direct and indirect costs so that the final decision is based on equal comparisons. The project personnel evaluate alternative suppliers and provide current, accurate, and complete data that are relevant to the buy alternative. Exhibit 13.2 lists a variety of considerations for make-or-buy decisions.

Most firms begin conducting a strategic outsourcing analysis by identifying their major strengths and then building on them. A firm's competitive advantage is often defined as lower cost, product differentiation (better quality), and/or responsiveness (fast delivery). To project teams, these have different levels of importance, depending on the wishes of the customer and the progress the project is making at the moment. Project time-cost analysis often helps generate insights about making efficient procurement decisions. For example, a noncritical activity may be outsourced with a focus on minimizing cost but not necessarily receiving the fastest delivery. However, during different stages of a project, a noncritical task can become a critical task, which raises the importance of timing and shifting priorities. Factors like this can hold quite different implications for a make-or-buy decision in different phases of project execution.

While make-or-buy investigations usually begin with a cost analysis, various qualitative factors frequently portend more far-reaching consequences than does the cost analysis. A thorough investigation is clearly complicated by the dynamics and uncertainties of various project activities.

EXHIBIT 13.2

REASONS TO MAKE OR BUY	
REASONS TO MAKE	REASONS TO BUY
1. Lower production cost 2. More control over quality and time 3. Lack of suitable suppliers 4. Obtain a customized item 5. Utilize project team's expertise and time 6. Protect proprietary design or knowledge	1. Frees project team to deal with other important activities 2. Ability to utilize specialized suppliers 3. Flexibility in procurement 4. Inadequate managerial or technical resources 5. Inadequate capacity 6. Small volume requirements

OUTSOURCING ISSUES   While outsourcing has gained in popularity, there are potential issues related to outsourcing. Some of these are relatively important with regard to the goal of projects:

- Loss of time control for completing project activities
- Lack of cost control for outsourced activities
- Gradual loss of special skills for doing some specific activities
- Loss of project focus and a potential conflict of interest
- Ineffective management as a result of complicated business interactions
- Loss of confidentiality and double outsourcing when a third party is used
- Sharing of proprietary knowledge that impacts competitive advantage

The concepts and techniques of project supply chain management possess strategic importance because of these potential issues related to outsourcing. Purchasing can contribute to the achievement of benefits such as higher product quality, shorter lead times, and lower costs. Project procurement strategies can change often and differ from corporate procurement strategies because of constraints, availability of critical resources, and specific project requirements that change dynamically. After making the make-or-buy decision, the project team proceeds to the next step of project outsourcing for selecting the right supplier and negotiating the contract.

The outputs of procurement planning also include documents and criteria for selecting a supplier, if a buy decision has been made. When multiple suppliers are available, selection standards such as total cost of ownership and risk also need to be developed.

When a buy decision is made, the client company is attempting to create a situation in which prospective contractor companies have the capability and motivation to provide useful and complete proposals that are easy to evaluate in order to determine which one best suits the client company's needs. The client company typically uses **procurement documents,** which are documents that define the requirements and contractual relationship between suppliers and customers of services and products used on a project.

Project procurement personnel need to understand the differences between types of requests so they use the correct one.

- **Request for Information (RFI)** is "a proposal requested from a potential seller or a service provider to determine what products and services are potentially available in the marketplace to meet a buyer's needs and to know the capability of a seller in terms of offerings and strengths of the seller."[5] An RFI is used to learn about the potential sellers and/or the products or services.
- **Request for Quotation (RFQ)** is a type of procurement document "used when discussions with bidders are not required (mainly when the specifications of a product or service are already known) and when price is the main or only factor in selecting the successful bidder."[6] An RFQ is used to compare prices from various vendors of standard items.
- **Request for Proposal (RFP)** is a type of procurement document used at "an early stage in a procurement process issuing an invitation for suppliers, often through a bidding process, to submit a proposal on a specific commodity or service."[7] An RFP is often used to compare different approaches for nonstandard items.

The client company creates evaluation criteria to define how they will evaluate and rank the proposals. Armed with these documents, the client company is now prepared to conduct the procurement.

13-3 Conduct Procurements

The second project procurement management process is to **conduct procurements,** which includes receiving seller responses, selecting a seller, and awarding a contract. Client firms need to decide which potential contractor companies they wish to solicit and then make sure those companies know about the potential project. Sometimes, firms develop a qualified sellers list and only allow listed companies to submit a proposal on the upcoming project. Other times, they advertise widely in hopes of attracting new contractors' interest. In either event, a formal request is normally sent out with hopes that competent firms will compete for the right to perform the project.

One Singapore company describes its project procurement process in Exhibit 13.3. The first part of the procurement process encompasses gathering of market intelligence, developing a procurement strategy, and developing a contract.

The *intelligence gathering* phase includes defining the scope for the procurement, analyzing the needs of the end user, and the articulation of upstream and downstream market forces. It is important to question whether the procurer has leverage or is beholden to the tight supply situation. A *strategy* is then developed and some parts are shared with "partner vendors" so that there is a clear understanding of the needs, available supply, and the satisfaction criteria of procurement. After understanding the total cost of procurement, a *Go to Market* position needs to be developed. The procurer needs to be armed with the best alternatives. The culmination of the strategy phase is to obtain clear mandates to negotiate. A *contract* is then developed. The contract should articulate clearly, without contradictory clauses, the legal aspects, technical requirements, and commercial terms.

These developments are the result of continuous dialogue between the procurer and prospective suppliers.

13-3a Sources for Potential Suppliers

Based on the nature of what is being requested in early procurement stages, the project team usually starts the selection process by establishing a robust list of potential suppliers. The following information sources are frequently used to identify these potential suppliers:

- Supplier websites
- Supplier information files
- Supplier catalogs

EXHIBIT 13.3

PROCURER, PROSPECTS, AND THE PROJECT MANAGER		
INTELLIGENCE	STRATEGY	CONTRACTING
Scope	Statement	Legal
Needs	Analyses	Technical
Market forces	Go to Market direction	Commercial
	Alternatives	
	Mandates	

Source: Raji Sivaraman, M.S., PMI-ACP, PMP-2017

- Trade journals
- Phone directories
- Sales personnel
- Trade shows
- Professional organizations and conferences
- Electronic search engines
- Published information by local, state, and federal governments

13-3b Approaches Used When Evaluating Prospective Suppliers

Once potential contractors submit bids or proposals, the client company applies previously defined selection criteria to select one or more sellers who are qualified to perform the work and are acceptable as sellers. On some projects in which the services or materials are commodities, the selection decision is made mostly or entirely on price. On other projects, the client chooses the contractor on the basis of life cycle cost—that is, the cost to both purchase the item and use it for the entirety of its useful life. On still other projects, price is one of multiple considerations. With more complex projects, the client company may very well decide that one company is more capable than another on technical, managerial, financial, or experiential grounds. The evaluation criteria developed during the plan procurement process should guide this decision.

For example, a research study in the Middle East involving a range of public sector contracting agencies revealed that when a client selects a design-build contractor (one who supervises both the design and construction for a project with many other companies involved), several tangible and intangible selection factors are considered, as shown in Exhibit 13.4. In essence, the selection of a design-build contractor is chiefly guided by clients' business needs, functional requirements, and expectations of the outcome of the design-build process. Clients look for a sound business partner who is capable of and committed to delivering the design-build promise of producing better projects faster and at a reduced cost. The design-build contractor selection process is indeed twofold: one is process-related, focusing on project outcomes, and the other is organization-related, focusing on the actual abilities and qualities of the design-build contractor's organization.

After developing a comprehensive list of potential suppliers, the project team needs to evaluate each prospective supplier individually. The approaches and analyses can include the following:

- Supplier surveys that provide sufficient knowledge of the supplier to make a decision to include or exclude the firm from further consideration
- Financial condition analysis that reveals whether a supplier is clearly incapable of performing satisfactorily
- Third-party evaluators such as Dun and Bradstreet that can be hired for obtaining relevant information
- Facility visits to allow the project team to obtain firsthand information concerning the adequacy of the firm's technological capabilities, manufacturing or distribution capabilities, and managerial orientation
- Quality ability analysis that examines the potential supplier's quality capability
- Delivery ability analysis that estimates the supplier's capability to deliver the required product or services on time; backup solutions can also be considered

The analyses listed above should not necessarily be limited to potential first-tier suppliers. In some cases when second- or even third-tier suppliers are involved, the project team needs to evaluate all these suppliers as well. This proactive screening process

EXHIBIT 13.4

FACTORS TO CONSIDER WHEN SELECTING A DESIGN-BUILD CONTRACTOR

Component A: Process-related design-build contractor selection factors:

PRIORITY	FACTOR	DEFINITION
I	Shorten Duration	To reduce the overall project delivery time as compared to other project delivery methods
II	Reduce Cost	To reduce the overall project delivery cost as compared to other project delivery methods
III	Reduce Claims	To eliminate claims raised by contractors due to design errors or shortcomings
IV	Establish Cost	To fix project budget early on, long before completing detailed designs and specifications
V	Establish Schedule	To fix schedule of project benefits long before completing detailed designs and specifications
VI	Innovation	To benefit from the innovation opportunity created by designers and builders' interaction
VII	Reduce Coordination	To reduce client risk and effort of coordinating between contractors and designers

Component B: Organization-related design-build contractor selection factors:

TECHNICAL	MANAGERIAL	FINANCIAL	EXPERIENTIAL
Know-how	Brand	Financial strength	Design-build similar projects
Expertise	Culture	Marketability	
Plant/equipment	Trust/integrity	Stability	Diversity
Specialism	Methodology	Audit reports	Resources
Design capacity	Organization	Turnover	Reputation

Source: Adapted from Dr. Sherif Hashem, "*The Power of Design-Build: A Guide to Effective Design-Build Project Delivery Using the SAFEDB-Methodology*" (Business Expert Press: USA, August 2014).

usually generates a handful of potential suppliers with good standing. If the organization has a list of current qualified sellers, it can form the basis for new projects.

13-3c Supplier Selection

After one or more potential suppliers have passed the evaluation process, the selection process must begin. The project team now invites potential suppliers to submit bids or proposals. Procurement documents are used to solicit proposals from various vendors. The most common procurement document is the request for proposal (RFP). The RFP can be a foundation for the future working relationship between the buyer and the supplier. In fact, the proposal prepared by the vendor often becomes a part of the final contract, as an addendum or exhibit, between the supplier and the vendor. A request for proposal usually includes the following items:

- Purchasing overview
- Basic supplier requirements

- Technical requirements
- Managerial requirements
- Pricing information
- Appendices

The basic supplier selection decision is a classic decision tree problem. This is a choice between alternatives under uncertainty. The outcome is concerned with both price and performance, including delivery time. Does the decision maker wish to trade a higher price against supply assurance under all circumstances? The difficulty in quantifying all consequences reinforces the need for sound judgment in key decisions.

Evaluation criteria are used to rate proposals and other supplier characteristics. The criteria can be objective or subjective, and they are often provided in the RFP. Typically, the most important evaluation criterion is price. Other important criteria include the vendor's technical capability, reputation, and so on. Exhibit 13.5 shows factors in addition to price that can be used in assessing suppliers.

The project team selects one or more sellers who are both qualified and acceptable as sellers. Many tools and techniques, including the following, can be used in the seller selection decision process:

- Weighting system
- Independent estimates
- Screening system
- Seller rating system
- Expert judgment
- Proposal evaluation techniques

The goal of selecting suppliers is to award a contract. A **contract** is "a mutually binding legal relationship obligating the seller to furnish supplies or services and the buyer to

EXHIBIT 13.5

FACTORS USED IN ASSESSING POTENTIAL SUPPLIERS

- Replenishment lead time: This is the lead time between placing an order and receiving the order, which can be translated into the required responsiveness for purchasing.
- On-time performance: This affects the variability of the lead time.
- Supply flexibility: It is the amount of variation in order quantity that a supplier can tolerate without letting other performance factors deteriorate.
- Delivery frequency and minimum lot size, which affect the size of each replenishment lot ordered by a firm.
- Supply quality: A worsening of supply quality increases the variability of the supply of components available to the firm.
- Inbound transportation cost: The total cost of using a supplier includes the inbound transportation cost of bringing materials in from the supplier.
- Information coordination capability affects the ability of a firm to match supply and demand.
- Design collaboration capability.
- Exchange rates, taxes, and duties can be quite significant for a firm with a global manufacturing and supply base.
- Supplier viability is the likelihood that the supplier will be around to fulfill the promises it makes. This consideration can be especially important if the supplier is providing mission-critical products for which it would be difficult to find a replacement. If a supplier has two key people who can each perform the necessary work, the second worker is sometimes considered to be "truck insurance" in case the first worker gets run over by a truck.

provide consideration for them."[8] A contract establishes a legal relationship between parties, and it is subject to remedy in the court system. The project organization can be a seller in dealing with the project owner or customer and a buyer in a more prevalent procurement setting. In many project management scenarios, the project manager must be aware of how a wide range of contracts is developed and executed. A procurement contract is awarded to each selected seller. The contract can be in the form of simple purchase order or a complex document detailing generic and specific conditions of the contract. The major components in a contract document generally include the following:

- Statement of work
- Schedule baseline
- Period of performance
- Roles and responsibility
- Pricing
- Payment terms
- Place of delivery
- Limitation of liability
- Incentives
- Penalties

13-4 Contract Types

Different types of contracts can be used as tools in planning acquisitions specified in the make-or-buy decision. Contracts differ by type with regard to how the risk is distributed and how the project is performed. The seven most common types of project procurement contracts are shown in Exhibit 13.6.

EXHIBIT 13.6

TYPES OF CONTRACTS		
CONTRACT TYPE	COST RISK ABSORBED BY	APPROPRIATE WHEN
Firm-fixed-price	Seller	Costs are well known
Fixed-price-incentive-fee	Mostly seller	Costs are well known and buyer wants to maximize some performance aspect
Fixed-price-economic-price-adjustment	Both	Project may be long duration and inflation and commodity prices may fluctuate
Cost-plus-incentive-fee	Mostly buyer	Costs are not well known and buyer wants to maximize some performance aspect
Cost-plus-award-fee	Mostly buyer	Both parties agree most of fee is based upon buyer's opinion of seller performance on stated criteria
Cost-plus-fixed-fee	Buyer	Costs not well known
Time and material	Buyer	Cost rates known, volumes are unknown

13-4a Fixed-Price Contracts

A **fixed-price contract** is an agreement that binds the seller to perform the agreed-upon work for the agreed-upon money. The contract may also include an agreed-upon date for completion. The most common types of fixed-price contracts are firm-fixed-price (FFP), fixed-price-incentive-fee (FPIFD), and fixed-price-economic-price-adjustment (FP-EPA).

FIRM-FIXED-PRICE (FFP) CONTRACT   The **firm-fixed-price contract** is a contract in which the seller has to complete the job for the agreed-upon amount of money regardless of the actual cost incurred. Any cost increase due to adverse performance is the responsibility of the seller, who is obligated to complete the effort. A simple form of a firm-fixed-price contract is a procurement order for a specified item to be delivered by a certain date for a specified price, such as a truckload of mulch delivered on the job site of 3110 Elm Street on May 15 for $300.

FIXED-PRICE-INCENTIVE-FEE (FPIF) CONTRACT   The **fixed-price-incentive-fee contract** is a contract in which the price is fixed as defined by the contract, but the seller can earn an additional amount as incentive if the seller meets defined project metrics. An example is a contract for rebuilding a bridge for a fixed price of $1,250,000 with an incentive of an extra $3,000 for every day it is complete before the scheduled date of September 15. The buyer would like to have use of the bridge sooner, and the seller would like to earn a higher fee, so both have an incentive to finish the project early. Performance incentives can also include bonuses for better quality, more features, or anything else that the buyer wishes to maximize and is willing to pay for.

FIXED-PRICE-ECONOMIC-PRICE-ADJUSTMENT (FP-EPA) CONTRACT   The **fixed-price-economic-price-adjustment contract** is a fixed-price contract with a clause to protect the seller from conditions such as inflation or commodity cost increases. An example is a contract that states the contractor will receive $400,000 to supply all of the gravel for a project, but the price may be adjusted based upon market price for gravel at the dates when it is delivered.

Fixed-price contracts provide low risk for the buyer, since the buyer does not pay more than the fixed price regardless of how much the project actually costs the seller. Consequently, a seller bidding on a fixed-price project must develop accurate and complete cost estimates and include sufficient contingency costs. Certainly, overpricing should be avoided, as a competing contractor with a lower price might be selected. In case the seller does not have a clear understanding about the project scope, the next type of contract should be considered as an alternative.

Cost-reimbursable contracts, unlike fixed-price contracts, provide lower risk for the seller and higher risk for the buyer. They are generally more appropriate when it is difficult to estimate the project cost.

13-4b Cost-Reimbursable Contracts

Cost-reimbursable contracts are a type of contract in which the seller is reimbursed for the actual approved costs of completed work, plus a fee typically representing profit. The three variations of commonly used cost-reimbursement contracts are cost-plus-fixed-fee, cost-plus-award-fee, and cost-plus-incentive-fee.

COST-PLUS-FIXED-FEE (CPFF) CONTRACT   The **cost-plus-fixed-fee contract** is a type of contract in which the buyer reimburses the seller for all of the seller's allowable costs plus a fixed amount of profit (fee). An example is a research project in which all scientist hours spent on the project are paid along with a fee of $5,000 regardless of how many hours the scientist spent.

COST-PLUS-AWARD-FEE (CPAF) CONTRACT   The **cost-plus-award-fee contract** is a type of contract that involves payments to the seller for all allowed costs incurred for completed work, plus an award fee based on satisfying certain subjective performance objectives. An example is a development contract that pays the contractor $3,000,000 plus puts in escrow an award fee pool of $210,000, and an executive in the customer's organization has sole discretion regarding how much of the award fee pool is given based upon customer satisfaction criteria.

COST-PLUS-INCENTIVE-FEE (CPIF) CONTRACT   The **cost-plus-incentive-fee contract** is a type of contract in which the buyer reimburses the seller for the seller's allowable costs and pays the seller a fee if it meets defined performance criteria. These criteria can be for schedule, cost, and/or performance. An example of a schedule criterion is a contract for constructing a college dormitory that calls for completion by August 15 so it is ready for the fall semester. A cost criteria example is the buyer of a small house negotiating a total project cost of $150,000. A performance criteria example is when an auto company enters a contract with a supplier to develop a battery that can get 55 miles per gallon in a 3,000-pound car. In each of these cases, the contract can call for the seller to receive a bonus if it does better than the agreed-upon target and/or a penalty if it does worse. Both the buyer and the seller can benefit if performance criteria are met.

13-4c Time and Material (T&M) Contracts

Time and material contracts are hybrid contracts containing aspects of both cost-reimbursement and fixed-price contracts generally used when the deliverable is labor hours and/or amounts of materials. In this type of contract, the unit rate for each hour of labor or pound of material is set in the contract as it is practiced in a fixed-price contract. However, the amount of work is not set, so the value of the contract can grow like a cost-reimbursement contract. The seller simply charges for the work to produce the product or service in the contract. This can be problematic if the time scheduled for production is greatly underestimated. This type of contract is used when the scope of the project work is ambiguous.

In choosing the right type of contract, the nature of the outsourced project activity influences the decision. The requirements that a buyer imposes on a seller, along with other planning considerations such as the degree of market competition and degree of risk, also determine which type of contract is used. The following items are frequently considered when selecting the right type of contract:

- Overall degree of cost and schedule risk
- Clarity about the scope of work
- Type and complexity of requirements
- Extent of price competition
- Cost and price analysis
- Urgency of the requirements
- Performance period
- Contractor's responsibility
- Contractor's accounting system
- Extent of subcontracting

One of the important factors to consider is the degree of risk for the seller and the buyer that each type of contract presents. Each of the contract types has risk attached to it. When considering different contracts, it must be clear who assumes the most risk—the buyer or the seller. Under normal conditions, the greatest risk to the buyer is when the cost-plus-fixed-fee contract is chosen. The contract with the greatest risk to the seller is the firm-fixed-price contract. Generally, the buyer and seller negotiate details of the contract risks and benefits that both parties can accept.

One risk management technique that is rapidly becoming popular for insuring large projects is the use of wrap-ups. A wrap-up, or owner-controlled insurance program (OCIP), is a single insurance policy providing coverage for all project participants, including the owner and all contractors and subcontractors. An OCIP can potentially reduce an owner's total project cost by 1 to 2 percent compared to traditional fragmented programs. Its major advantages include broader coverage, volume discounts, and reduced claims due to comprehensive loss-control programs. The type and complexity of the agreements may also necessitate assistance from legal specialists, buyers, and contracting experts.

13-5 Control Procurements

Control procurements include managing relationships between sellers and customers, monitoring contract performance, and making changes and corrections if needed. Both buyers and sellers administer contracts to make sure that the obligations set forth in the contract are met and to make sure neither party has any legal liability. Both must perform according to the contract terms. The seller creates performance reports, and the buyer reviews these reports to ensure that the performance of the seller satisfies the obligations of the contract.

13-6 Improving Project Supply Chains

Project supply chain performance can be improved by careful and innovative use of partnering, third-party involvement, lean purchasing, sourcing, logistics, and information.

13-6a Project Partnering and Collaboration

Companies are constantly in need of outsourcing or contracting significant segments of project work to other companies. The trend for the future suggests that more and more projects will involve working with people from different organizations in a partnering relationship. **Partnering** is "a long-term relationship between an owner and a contractor in which the contractor acts as a part of the owner's organization for certain functions."[9]

Research also finds that through strategic partnering, companies are more likely to access advanced technology, share risks, and improve project-based performance and relative competitiveness. This section extends the previous discussion of project procurement and contracting by focusing specifically on issues surrounding working with different suppliers to complete a project. The term *partnering* is used to describe this process. Partnering is a method for transforming contractual arrangements into a cohesive, collaborative project team with a single set of goals and established procedures for resolving disputes in a timely and cost-efficient manner. The single set of goals takes care of the customer requirements and the entire project instead of each individual organization. Exhibit 13.7 presents an excellent example of project partnering and collaboration in the international airport industry.

SOURCES OF CONFLICT DURING PROJECT PURCHASING   In the procurement and purchasing environment, conflicts are inevitable. For example, many people envision the purchasing process as a type of zero-sum game, meaning what one party loses is what the other party gains. (The most common type of conflict is this: lower price means cost reduction for the buyer, but it also means revenue loss to the seller.) In

EXHIBIT 13.7

JORGE CHAVEZ INTERNATIONAL AIRPORT, LIMA, PERU

The location of Lima in the center of the west coast of South America presents an extended area of attraction, making the airport into a natural international hub. The proximity of Jorge Chavez International Airport (JCIA) to Port Callao, the principal port of Peru, offers the possibility of developing a sea/air plan in favor of external commerce.

LIMA AIRPORT PARTNERS

Fraport-Bechtel-Cosapi Consortium won the international public tender for the concession of the JCIA. With an equity contribution of $30 million, the consortium founded Lima Airport Partners (LAP). The three consortium partners each have impressive track records. Fraport AG operates the Frankfurt Airport, considered one of the largest in continental Europe. Fraport also provides other airport services such as handling and other commercial services. Fraport participates in more than 50 projects around the world. Bechtel is a private construction company founded in 1898. It has participated in more than 1,000 projects in 67 countries, of which 80 have been airport projects. Cosapi is a local construction company founded in 1960 with projects in South America. Currently, LAP's shareholders are Fraport AG, the International Finance Corporation (IFC), and the Fund for Investment in Infrastructure, Utilities and Natural Resources, managed by AC Capitales SAFI S.A.

LAP's objectives are to improve both facilities and operation of JCIA. The improved facilities will be transferred to the State of Peru. The concession term is 30 years with an option for a 10-year extension.

Source: Patricia Quiroz, Professor of Pontificia Universidad Catolica del Peru.

---

fact, many types of interest conflicts arise among different companies. For example, delays in construction are common and expensive, and litigation related to design and construction is rising.

Obvious conflicts of interest predispose owners and contractors to be suspicious of one another's motives and actions. Suspicion and mistrust prevent effective problem solving throughout the process. In taking care of each party's own interests, mistakes and problems are often hidden. When conflicts emerge, they often create costly delays as well as questionable responses simply because the information transferred may be distorted many times before it reaches the decision maker. The consequences, however, are avoidable from the beginning.

RESOLVING PROJECT PURCHASING CONFLICTS   One approach to resolving conflict is to use project partnering as an effective way to engage both the project owner and contractors. Project partnering naturally developed as people began to realize that the traditional win/lose adversarial relationship between owner and contractor degenerates into a costly lose/lose situation for all the parties involved. The systematic project supply chain management view goes beyond this traditional view to increase the baseline of trust and collaboration.

Ten key elements for effective project partnerships are shown in Exhibit 13.8.

MUTUAL GOALS IN PROJECT PARTNERSHIPS   Some common goals warrant a more supportive relationship. For example, both the buyer and seller would like to complete the project on time and safely. Both parties would prefer to avoid costly and time-consuming litigation. On the other hand, once the specified project can be finished on a faster and less-expensive basis, either party is in a better position of getting better operational rewards. Some of the many advantages for establishing a project partnership are shown in Exhibit 13.9.

EXHIBIT 13.8

Ten key elements of a successful partnership:

1. Recognition of the need for a partnership
2. Clear and agreed purpose and objectives
3. Commitment and ownership
4. Trust between partners
5. Create clear and robust partnership arrangements
6. Good communication with all partners
7. Mutual benefits for all partners
8. Conflict resolution and mediation
9. Systems to monitor, measure and learn
10. Outcomes that live on beyond the life of the partnership

Source: Sustainability Learning Guide: Successful Partnerships: https://www.lgnsw.org.au/files/imce-uploads/35/SLG_successful_partnerships.pdf, accessed April 24, 2017.

For example, Procter & Gamble (P&G) started using the Web to share information and streamline purchasing a few years ago. Ford used 900 virtual workspaces to design cars and hold meetings. In one project, Ford used digital conference rooms from eRoom to manage the formation of the auto industry e-marketplace Covisint.

EXHIBIT 13.9

ADVANTAGES OF PROJECT PARTNERSHIPS		
ADVANTAGES TO BOTH PARTIES	ADVANTAGES TO CLIENTS	ADVANTAGES TO VENDORS
Shared motivation	More effectively managed risks	Clearly stated expected outcome
Flexibility	Reduced up-front project cost	Greater potential profit
Reduced administration of frequent bids	Potential of lower cost	More dependable stream of work
Improved project execution	Ability to focus on core capabilities	Opportunity to prove oneself
Ability to explore new technologies		
Improved communication		
Ability to make better decisions		
Improved resource utilization		

Source: Adapted from Tom Chaudhuri and Leigh Hardy, "Successful Management of Vendors in IT Projects," *PM Network* 15 (6) (June 2001): 48; and He Zhang and Peter C. Flynn, "Effectiveness of Alliances Between Operating Companies and Engineering Companies," *Project Management Journal* 34 (3) (September 2003): 49.

EXHIBIT 13.10

EFFECTIVE PROJECT PARTNERING APPROACHES

Organization-wide willingness to:

- Use long-term perspective
- Share power with partner
- Trust partner
- Adapt to partner
- Go beyond contractual obligations

Mutual commitment to:

- Quality
- Continuous improvement
- Clearly understand partner
- Ongoing relationship with partner

Effective methods:

- Openly share information
- Develop contractual relationships
- Develop interpersonal relationships
- Resolve conflict

Lawyers from law firms and three automakers shared virtual rooms to haggle over contracts.

EFFECTIVE PROJECT PARTNERING APPROACHES   Many differences exist between the way traditional project procurement unfolds and the way contemporary project procurement takes place in a partnering mode. Exhibit 13.10 lists some of the requirements of effective project partnering.

Many large Japanese manufacturers have found a middle ground between purchasing from a few suppliers and vertical integration. These manufacturers are often financial supporters of suppliers through ownership or loans. The supplier then becomes part of a company coalition known as a *keiretsu*. Members of the *keiretsu* are assured long-term relationships and are therefore expected to function as partners, providing technical expertise and stable quality production to the manufacturer. Members of the *keiretsu* can also have suppliers farther down the chain, making second- and even third-tier suppliers part of the coalition. Most partners value their membership and work hard to do their part. In the rare instance in which a partner consistently takes advantage of the situation, the partner is eventually dropped.

Companies can use different purchasing modes for specific purchasing items when dealing with large projects. For example, one major Chinese petroleum company used five purchasing models for multiple projects, which include purchasing mechanisms for strategic materials, full competitive products, limited resource products, nonstandard products, and existing long-term collaboration suppliers. Third-party inspection companies were hired to conduct on-site assessment and quality approval for the incoming materials of multiple projects at the same time. The integrated on-site warehousing management system streamlined the management process, reduced unnecessary inventory to almost zero, and minimized the total investment of the projects.

SECURING COMMITMENT TO PARTNERING   When developing a project supply chain partnership, a project manager may want to consider contractors with a mutual interest and expertise in partnerships. At the beginning, the owner needs to get the commitment of the top management of all firms involved. All the benefits of the partnership and how the partnership would work need to be described in detail. Team building is an effective approach for involving all the key players from different firms. Separate training sessions and workshops are offered to promote a collaborative spirit. One of the major goals of the team-building sessions is to establish a "we" as opposed to an "us and them" attitude among the different participants. A second objective of the sessions is to establish a mechanism in advance designed to ensure that this collaborative spirit is able to withstand the problems and setbacks that will invariably occur on the project. Some of the most significant mechanisms are as follows:

- Problem resolution—Solving problems at the lowest level of organizations and having an agreed-upon escalation procedure
- Continuous improvement—Endless process of waste elimination and cost reduction
- Joint assessment—Reviewing the partnering process jointly
- Persistent leadership—Displaying a collaborative response consistently

More project organizations are pursuing partnering relationships with each other. Project partnering represents a proactive way for managing many of the challenges associated with working with different organizations. The process usually starts with some agreed-upon procedures and provisions for dealing with problems and issues before they happen. One way is to design a contract with specific incentives and penalties. On the other hand, partnering is not just about relationship contracting. For example, although many companies may wish to develop company-wide policies and procedures for inter-firm conflict resolution, this method is less effective since each project and each company different. The partnering approach has to be dynamic to unite a wide variety of suppliers and contractors for some common goals that everyone cares about. Although the project purchasing relationship has been moved from short-term arrangements based on contracts to long-term relationships based on trust, this change is by no means universally applicable.

Partnering fosters a strong desire to contain costs when changes are necessary and leads to a team approach in resolving any financial and time consequences. In the next section, we discuss the integrated project supply chain management approach.

Partnering seeks to recast relations between actors in projects by promoting the use of collaborative, more open relationships. The integrated supply chain perspective further shifts traditional channel arrangements from loosely linked groups of independent businesses that buy and sell products or services to each other toward a managerially coordinated initiative to increase collaboration, customer satisfaction, overall efficiency, continuous improvement, and competitiveness. For example, in the construction industry, the construction supply chain (CSC) consists of all the construction partners such as client, designer, general contractor, subcontractor, supplier, and consultant. In fact, the CSC itself represents a concept of systematic coordination of relevant business activities within the supply chain.

13-6b Third Parties

In general, third parties can increase the supply chain performance effectively if they are able to aggregate supply chain assets or flows to a higher level than a firm can by itself. Third parties can use various mechanisms to grow the supply chain performance (e.g., reducing delivery time and cost), by aggregating:

- Capacity
- Inventory
- Transportation
- Warehousing
- Information
- Receivables
- Relationships

13-6c Lean Purchasing

Lean purchasing refers primarily to a manufacturing context and implementation of just-in-time (JIT) tools and techniques to ensure every step in the supply process adds value while various costs are kept at the minimum level. By reducing ordering cost for placing orders (e.g., the fixed part of the shipping cost), project organizations can use JIT for eliminating waste in ordering time and cost, which eventually results in timely completion of projects and customer satisfaction.

Doubtlessly, integrating SCM into project management helps project managers create win/win situations for all parties involved in the project supply chain as they become more efficient and effective. The specific supply chain techniques can help project managers make better trade-offs between project costs and time to create better customer satisfaction.

13-6d Sourcing

Sourcing encompasses all processes required for a firm to purchase goods from suppliers. Effective sourcing decisions thus have a significant impact on project performance. Good project sourcing decisions can improve project performance by aggregating orders, making procurement transactions more efficient, achieving design collaboration with suppliers, facilitating coordinated forecasting and planning with suppliers, and improving customer satisfaction.

13-6e Logistics

Logistics, in contrast to supply chain management, is the work required to move and position inventory throughout a supply chain. Supply chains use a combination of the following modes of transportation:

- Air
- Package carrier
- Truck
- Rail
- Water
- Pipeline
- Intermodal

The transportation cost a supply chain incurs is closely linked to the degree of responsiveness the supply chain aims to provide. Thus, decision makers must consider the trade-off between responsiveness and transportation cost when making the relevant logistics decisions. Moreover, the necessity of shipping speed needs to be considered, as noncritical project activities tend to have some slack.

13-6f Information

Information is also key to the success of project supply chain management because it enables management to make decisions over a broad scope that crosses both functions and firms. For instance, information sharing in many cases can allow the project supply chain to shorten the delivery time and, at the same time, offer better-quality products or services to meet the dynamic demand of a project. Information must have the following characteristics to be useful when making supply chain decisions:

- Accurate
- Accessible in a timely manner
- Of the right kind

Information is a key ingredient not just at each stage of the project supply chain but also within each phase of supply chain decision making. This is where IT comes into play. IT consists of the hardware, software, and people throughout a project supply chain that gather, analyze, and execute procurement actions based on information. In today's business world, IT-based information management is crucial to the performance of project supply chains simply because it provides the basis of decision making, which has profound impacts for every aspect of project management.

PMP/CAPM Study Ideas

Some of the questions you will see on the material covered in this chapter will be at least partly based on vocabulary. For example, there are several types of contracts, and some of their names are similar, but you need to completely understand the difference between terms such as *cost-plus-award-fee* and *cost-plus-incentive-fee*, as well as when each type of contract may be used and how each type of contract divides risk between buyer and seller.

Likewise, similar terms are used in the seller selection process, and you will need to know the difference between a Request for Information (RFI), Request for Quotation (RFQ), and Request for Proposal (RFP) and to apply that knowledge to a variety of questions/problems.

Summary

More and more companies are seeking cooperative relationships with each other to compete in today's demanding marketplace. Project supply chain management represents a set of proactive responses to many challenges created by people from different organizations working together on one-time projects. By identifying the project needs and wants, project organizations start with assessing the need to outsource part of the project work. Contracting is commonly used to specify and manage supplier–buyer relationships.

Purchasing details such as scope, deliverables, and quality expectations are legally enforced in the contract. As such, project teams take great care in selecting a specific and attainable contract to meet customer delivery expectations and internal profitability goals. However, project supply chain management is not just about contracting. Partnering and coordinating purchasing across all supplier stages allow a firm to maximize economies of scale in purchasing and also to reduce transaction costs.

Key Terms Consistent with PMI Standards and Guides

supply chain management, 427

owner, 427

general contractor, 427

subcontractor, 427

make-or-buy decisions, 428

plan procurement management, 429

procurement management plan, 429

procurement statements of work, 429

procurement documents, 431

request for information, 431

request for quotation, 431

request for proposal, 431

conduct procurements, 432

contract, 437

fixed-price contracts, 437

firm-fixed-price contracts, 437

fixed-price-incentive-fee contracts, 437

fixed-price-economic-price-adjustment contracts, 437

cost-reimbursable contracts, 438

cost-plus-fixed-fee contract, 438

cost-plus-award-fee contracts, 438

cost-plus-incentive-fee contract, 438

time and material contracts, 438

control procurements, 439

partnering, 440

lean purchasing, 445

sourcing, 445

logistics, 445

Chapter Review Questions

1. Do small businesses often outsource project work? Why or why not?
2. Name the three processes that make up project procurement management.
3. In supply chain management, what are some other names for the seller? What are some other names for the buyer?
4. List three functional areas that are frequently outsourced by business organizations.
5. What is the difference between a request for quotation (RFQ) and a request for proposal (RFP)?
6. After an organization has developed a list of potential suppliers, how should the organization evaluate each supplier individually?
7. What are four potential information sources that organizations can use to identify potential sellers?
8. Describe two methods that can be used to evaluate potential suppliers.
9. What items are generally included in a request for proposal?
10. In a fixed-price contract, who assumes the greatest level of risk?
11. What type of contract is good to use if it is necessary for both parties to share the risk?
12. In what type of contract does the buyer assume the greatest level of risk?
13. What is the name of a single insurance policy that is used to provide coverage for all project participants?
14. What is meant by *logistics* and how does it relate to project management?
15. _____ is a method for transforming contractual arrangements into a cohesive, collaborative project team with a single set of goals and established procedures for resolving disputes.

Discussion Questions

1. Why does the project team require a project scope statement prior to planning procurements?
2. List three reasons an organization might choose to make a product or service in-house and three reasons why an organization might choose to buy or outsource the work.
3. Should activities on the critical path be outsourced? Why or why not?
4. Which of the three competitive advantages do you think companies are most willing to outsource for? List any examples you can think of.
5. Your company is hoping to outsource some of its work constructing a new development of condominiums. What would you use as selection criteria to narrow down your list of potential sellers?

6. You decide to board your dog at the vet's office while you are on vacation and sign papers saying you will pay $25 per day plus $15 for a bath every third day. What type of contract have you entered into?

7. What would be your top two considerations when selecting a type of contract to enter into?

8. Describe three differences between a partnering relationship and a traditional seller–buyer arrangement.

9. What are some potential issues related to outsourcing? How could you mitigate these issues?

10. You are the project manager in charge of renovating a large apartment building, and your team has decided to outsource the installation of a new septic system. Do you put out an RFQ or RFP to interested contractors? Why?

PMBOK® *Guide* Questions

1. The Project Procurement Knowledge Area includes all of the following processes *except*:
    a. plan procurement management
    b. conduct procurements
    c. close procurements
    d. control procurements

2. In order to plan for procurements, the project team uses a project document that includes a list of deliverables, acceptance criteria, project assumptions and constraints, and a description of the product, service or result. This document is called the _____ .
    a. work breakdown structure (WBS)
    b. project charter
    c. project contract
    d. project scope statement

3. One output of the Plan Procurement Management process is the _____, a document that describes the item to be procured "in sufficient detail to allow prospective sellers to determine if they are capable of providing the products, services, or results."
    a. request for proposal
    b. procurement statement of work
    c. scope statement
    d. procurement management plan

4. Which of the following contracts is riskiest for a buyer?
    a. time and material
    b. cost reimbursable
    c. firm-fixed-price
    d. fixed-price-economic-price-adjustment

5. A _____ analysis is a technique that results in a decision about whether particular work can best be accomplished by the project team or should be purchased from external sources.

    a. make-or-buy
    b. SWOT
    c. sensitivity
    d. vendor

6. Which contract type puts the most risk on the seller?
    a. time and material
    b. cost reimbursable
    c. firm-fixed-price
    d. fixed-price-economic-price-adjustment

7. What is a hybrid type of contract that is often used for staff augmentation or any outside support in which a precise statement of work cannot be defined, and which often includes a not-to-exceed value and time limit to prevent unlimited cost growth?
    a. time and material
    b. cost reimbursable
    c. fixed price
    d. incentive fee

8. The type of procurement document that might be used to request prices for standard products or services is called a(n) _____ .
    a. request for proposal (RFP)
    b. request for information (RFI)
    c. invitation for negotiation (IFN)
    d. request for quotation (RFQ)

9. During which of the following processes is evaluation criteria developed, in order to evaluate potential sellers?
    a. plan procurement
    b. conduct procurement
    c. control procurement
    d. plan communication management

10. Procurement performance reviews, contract change control system, payment systems, and

performance reporting are all tools and techniques for which procurement process?

a. plan procurement management

b. conduct procurements
c. close project
d. control procurements

Exercises

Find a story in your local newspaper about a project that is about to start. For that project, answer each of the following questions and justify your answers:

1. Using the ideas in Exhibit 13.2, speculate on what activities, supplies, or services could be contracted out.
2. Create a request for information for one portion of the project work that could be contracted out.
3. Using ideas from Exhibits 13.4 and 13.5, determine criteria you would use to select sellers for the portion of contract work under consideration.
4. Determine what type of contract you would use for this work and explain why.
5. Describe the extent to which any partnering makes sense for this project. What are the challenges and benefits to this partnering? What would prevent any further partnering?

INTEGRATED EXAMPLE PROJECTS
SUBURBAN HOMES CONSTRUCTION PROJECT

A well-known aspect of the construction industry is that it is a fragmented industry with a large share of working people engaged with it. Due to its nature of operations and fluctuations in demand, the construction industry thrives on hiring contractors and subcontractors on an as-needed basis. Likewise, one can find multiple sources of suppliers nationwide for all the hardware items such as windows, doors, drywall, doorknobs, and HVAC equipment. Suburban Homes, as an organization, realizes the importance of long-term partnership with various suppliers and contractors and the many benefits of such a partnership. Suburban Homes is planning to revisit their existing partnerships with various suppliers and contractors because competition is rising and profit margins are declining. Suburban Homes is looking for partners and suppliers to improve profits and increase customer satisfaction. Suburban Homes developed a set of criteria to select partners for construction work and supply of materials:

- Collaboration
- Reliability
- Value engineering (higher quality at a competitive price)
- Performance

- Trust
- Transparency in commercial deals and communication

With its ambitious plan of expanding its business to several southern states and its vision to deliver high-quality construction that adheres to local, state, and federal standards as well as exceed industrial standards for quality, Suburban Homes is willing to identify, negotiate, and partner with competent and reliable suppliers and contractors. Adam Smith entrusted you with the task to develop a procurement and supply chain management plan. For this purpose, you were asked to do the following tasks:

Tasks to Complete
- Assess the current market situation.
- Identify prospective partners for supply of materials and construction work.
- Select an appropriate type of contract for each supplier (it may not be same for everyone).
- Assess risks associated with each contract.
- Develop contract terms and conditions.
- Perform qualitative assessment to prioritize risks.
- Develop a procurement policy.

CASA DE PAZ DEVELOPMENT PROJECT

Casa de Paz has multiple supply chain issues. Some questions to answer include the following:

1. Will Casa de Paz rent or buy a building? If renting, how much can they help pay for needed upgrades? How can they partner with a potential landlord for the best long-term goals of each?

2. What kind of organizations can Casa de Paz partner with for professional services such as nursing, English as a Second Language, occupational readiness, counseling, and so forth?

3. What kind of partnership can they establish in the religious and nonprofit communities? What should they look for in potential partners?

Semester Project Instructions

Using the ideas in Exhibit 13.2, determine what activities, supplies, or services needed on your example project could be contracted out. Create a request for information for one portion of the project work that could be contracted out. Using ideas from Exhibits 13.4 and 13.5, determine criteria you would use to select sellers for the portion of contract work under consideration. Determine what type of contract you would use for this work and tell why. Describe the extent to which you are partnering on your example project. Describe the extent to which any other person or group may be partnering on the project. What are the challenges and benefits to any partnering that is occurring? What is preventing any further partnering?

PROJECT MANAGEMENT *IN ACTION*

Implications for Project Management in a Networked Organization Model

What Is a Networked Organization?

In a small organization, it is quickly recognized that you cannot do it all. You need to develop a business model where you leverage the strengths and expertise of your core team, while partnering and networking with specialized organizations and experts where you build trusted alliances and long-term relationships.

Our company is a project management training and consulting firm. We have seven people on our core team. These individuals are critical to the success of the company. They perform the "essential functions" required to run the business—primarily operations such as accounting, legal, contracting, sales, and project management. Functions we do not have to do ourselves are outsourced to experts such as human resources (we have seven employees), information technology (we had seven computers), fulfillment

(packing and shipping training materials), marketing (branding and social media), and independent contractors (hired as expert trainers and consultants under contract with the firm

As a seven-person company, we must have a high-performance team and a solid network of business partners who are considered part of our team, but not part of our payroll.

The Challenges

Running a business with a number of external partners has its challenges. Do they understand our business to be a key contributor? Will they have time for our projects while they are working with other organizations? Will they be working with competitors while they are servicing us?

In addition, so that we could better service our worldwide clients with local providers, we decided to globalize the company. This added another element of complexity—time zones, language and cultural differences, and in-country laws for contracting their services.

Our Approach

1. Establish a common PM Methodology—Since our company uses PMI's *Guide to the Project Management Body of Knowledge* (PMBOK® Guide) as a foundation, our global partners also use the PMBOK Guide, translated in their local language. This created a common terminology for all of us, which helped discussions and accelerated problem solving.

2. Have a central point of contact—Communications is key. As the chief operating officer (COO), my role is to be the "go-to" person for all business partners. It is crucial to establish an element of trust and transparency, especially when negotiating and executing contracts.

3. Establish a Quality Management System—We became ISO 9001 certified. This enables us to help our business partners be accountable for the delivering of our products and services under our brand name. To accelerate doing business together, one of the ISO processes is establishing and documenting "shared expectations" with each business partner. Not only does this include the specific details about services being delivered, but also the financial aspects of procurement, payments, and fulfilling various types of contracts. ISO also gives us a competitive advantage in the marketplace.

4. Invite strategic partners into the business—In our networked organization, we call our outside experts "business partners" or "strategic alliances." They are not vendors. They are critical to the success of our business and are invited to attend our strategic planning sessions and business planning meetings. If they are involved in a project, they attend the project status meetings and participate on project teams. They are key to our success.

It is amazing what seven people in an organization can do. With the right partners, the right resources, the right contracts, and the right relationships, we can make an international footprint as a leading project management training and consulting firm.

Source: Connie Plowman, PMP, Chief Operating Officer (retired), PMI Eric Jenett, Project Management Excellence Award Recipient.

References

A Guide to the Project Management Body of Knowledge (PMBOK® Guide), 6th ed. (Newtown Square, PA: Project Management Institute, 2017).

Alderman, N., and C. Ivory, "Partnering in Major Contracts: Paradox and Metaphor," *International Journal of Project Management* 25 (2007): 386–393.

Benton, W. C, *Purchasing and Supply Management* (New York: McGraw-Hill, 2007).

Bowersox, D. J., D. J. Closs, and M. B. Cooper, *Supply Chain Logistics Management*, 3rd ed. (McGraw-Hill, 2010).

Bozarth, Cecil C., and Robert B. Handfield, *Introduction to Operations and Supply Chain Management*, 2nd ed. (Upper Saddle River, NJ: Pearson Prentice Hall, 2008).

Chaudhuri, Tom, and Leigh Hardy, "Successful Management of Vendors in IT Projects," *PM Network* 15 (6) (June 2001): 45–48.

Chen, Wei Tong, and Tung-Tsan Chen, "Critical Success Factors for Construction Partnering in Taiwan," *International Journal of Project Management* 25 (5) (July 2007): 475–484.

Chopra, S., and P. Meindl, *Supply Chain Management: Strategy, Planning and Operations*, 4th ed. (Upper Saddle River, NY: Prentice Hall, 2009).

Construction Extension to the PMBOK® Guide (Newtown Square, PA: Project Management Institute, 2016).

Haried, Peter, and K. Ramamurthy, "Evaluating the Success in International Sourcing of Information Technology Projects: The Need for a Relational Client-Vendor Approach," *Project Management Journal* 40 (3) (September 2009): 56–71.

Hashem, Sherif, *The Power of Design-Build: A Guide to Effective Design-Build Project Delivery Using the SAFEDB-Methodology* (New York: Business Expert Press, 2014).

Huston, Larry, and Nabil Sakkab, "Connect and Develop: Inside Procter & Gamble's New Model for Innovation," *Harvard Business Review* 84 (3) (March 2006): 58–66.

Investopedia, http://www.investopedia.com/terms/m/make-or-buy-decision.asp, accessed April 21, 2017.

Leenders, M. R., P. F. Johnson, A. E. Flynn, and H. E. Fearon, *Purchasing and Supply Management: With 50 Supply Chain Cases,* 13th ed. (New York: McGraw-Hill, 2006).

Love, Peter E. D., Dina Mistry, and Peter R. Davis, "Price Competitive Alliance Projects: Identification of Success Factors for Public Clients," *Journal of Construction Engineering & Management* 136 (9) (2010): 947–956.

Lu, S. K., and H. Yan, "An Empirical Study on Incentives of Strategic Partnering in China: Views from Construction Companies," *International Journal of Project Management* 25 (2007): 241–249.

Martinsuo, Miia, and Tuomas Ahola, "Supplier Integration in Complex Delivery Projects: Comparison Between Different Buyer-Supplier Relationships," *International Journal of Project Management* 28 (2) (2010): 107–116.

National Contract Management Association: The Contract Management Standard Final Edition Version 1.0, http://www.ncmahq.org/docs/default-source/default-document-library/pdfs/the-contract-management-standard.pdf?sfvrsn=4, accessed April 24, 2017.

PM Study Circle Types of Procurement Contracts used in Project Management, https://pmstudycircle.com/2013/12/types-of-procurement-contracts-used-in-project-management/, accessed April 24, 2017.

Shane, Jennifer S., et al., "A Multidimensional Model of Project Leadership," *Leadership and Management in Engineering* (April 2011): 162–168.

Simchi-Levi, David, et al, *Designing & Managing the Supply Chain* (New York: McGraw-Hill, 2009).

Sustainability Learning Guide: Successful Partnerships, https://www.lgnsw.org.au/files/imce-uploads/35/SLG_successful_partnerships.pdf, accessed April 24, 2017.

Tutorialspoint, https://www.tutorialspoint.com/management_concepts/procurement_documents.htm, accessed April 24, 2017.

Wang, Fang, "Standardization of Modes of Project Purchase Management," *Journal of Sinopec Management Institute* 10 (3) (2008): 72–74.

Zhang, He, and Peter C. Flynn, "Effectiveness of Alliances Between Operating Companies and Engineering Companies," *Project Management Journal* 34 (3) (September 2003): 48–52.

Endnotes

1. *Construction Extension to the PMBOK® Guide* 220.
2. *Construction Extension to the PMBOK® Guide* 220.
3. *Construction Extension to the PMBOK® Guide* 221.
4. http://www.investopedia.com/terms/m/make-or-buy-decision.asp, accessed April 21, 2017.
5. https://www.tutorialspoint.com/management_concepts/procurement_documents.htm, accessed April 24, 2017.
6. https://www.tutorialspoint.com/management_concepts/procurement_documents.htm, accessed April 24, 2017.

7. https://www.tutorialspoint.com/management_concepts/procurement_documents.htm, accessed April 24, 2017.

8. http://www.ncmahq.org/docs/default-source/default-document-library/pdfs/the-contract-management-standard.pdf?sfvrsn=4, accessed April 24, 2017.

9. *Construction Extension to the PMBOK® Guide* 220.

CHAPTER **14**

Determining Project Progress and Results

CHAPTER OBJECTIVES

After completing this chapter, you should be able to:

CORE OBJECTIVES:

- Develop and demonstrate use of a change control system.
- Demonstrate how to monitor and control project risks with various resolution strategies.
- Create and present a project progress report.

BEHAVIORAL OBJECTIVES:

- Describe the importance of formal reporting and communications.
- Demonstrate negotiating skills.
- Manage conflicts during the project execution

TECHNICAL OBJECTIVES:

- Describe project quality control tools, including how and when to use each.
- Calculate current project schedule and budget progress, and predict future progress, using earned value analysis.
- Document project progress using MS Project.

Wavebreakmedia/Shutterstock.com

The fundamental reason for determining project progress and results comes down to one thing—*presenting actionable, decision-making information to project leaders.*

A major U.S. electric utility company is continuously faced with the daunting task of managing over 1,200 simultaneous projects in all phases of planning, execution, and completion over a geographic area consisting of five states. These projects are supported by over 40 departments within the utility and hundreds of external contractors and equipment suppliers. Over 85 percent of these projects take place over multiple years. There are over 15,000 activities tracked for active projects every month. Today, many of these projects are related to Smart-Grid efforts to fundamentally change the way the electric utility system delivers power to homes, schools, and businesses.

This utility regularly sets the standard for its industry each year by completing over 90 percent of its projects on time and utilizing its annual project budget within just a few percentage points. How is this accomplished?

By identifying and collecting just the right amount of financial, scheduling, resource, and risk management data, and by focusing intently on turning raw data into actionable information for the groups leading and supporting the

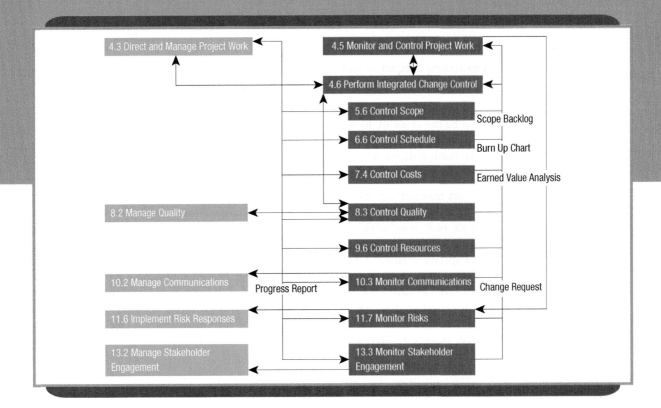

projects, the utility's project controls staff can continuously find and highlight the information that requires leadership attention and project team action.

With the large number of projects being managed, the focus on individual projects decreases and management of the entire group of projects as a portfolio becomes paramount. The actionable information presented highlights significant issues for individual projects, but more important, forecasts trends over the entire portfolio and extended spans of time, helping turn earned-value statistics into meaningful strategies.

Presenting valuable decision-making data to the multiple resource and leadership groups required to support a project provides the critical linkage between the feedback of raw data and the ability to successfully control a single project or an entire multiyear portfolio. Project data collection and management present the opportunity to simultaneously manage an organization's "profit, people, and planet" objectives in an optimal way.

As you move forward with this chapter and your own projects, consider the use and impact of the project information that needs to be collected. What are the key factors for your project—financial, environmental, resource management, scheduling, risk identification, stakeholder management, or others? Who needs the project progress data, and exactly what do they need to know to make good decisions and successfully achieve organizational objectives?

Identifying, collecting, managing, and presenting data that allow you to control critical aspects of your projects are fundamental elements of project success.

—Paul Kling, director—project management and controls,
Power Delivery Engineering, Duke Energy

The word *determine* in the context of "determine project progress and results" has multiple meanings. While each offers a slightly different perspective, collectively, they help a project manager understand what she needs to do to ensure that her project is progressing adequately and will yield the intended results in the end. *Determine* can mean the following:

- To give direction to or decide the course of
- To be the cause of, to influence, or to regulate
- To limit in scope
- To reach a decision
- To come to a conclusion or resolution[1]

Project managers, in the course of planning, give direction to a project. Many projects also require replanning due to any number of causes. Project managers sometimes can influence only how work is accomplished (when people do not report to them), but they may be able to regulate or demand the work to be accomplished at a certain time or in a specific manner. To be successful in influencing and regulating project work, the project manager needs to consider the stakeholder priorities and communications needs, as discovered in Chapter 6, and use those to design the monitoring and control mechanisms described in this chapter. Many stakeholders on projects attempt to persuade the project manager and team to deliver more scope, but one important role of the project manager is to jealously guard the agreed-upon scope. Throughout a project, decisions will be made. In such instances, the project manager can do one of the following:

- Personally make these decisions
- Be part of a group that makes decisions
- Delegate decisions to others
- Facilitate the process by which each decision is made

Often, project managers need to follow up to ensure that decisions are made and then carried out. Finally, the project manager is responsible for making sure that the project is satisfactorily completed.

14-1 Project Balanced Scorecard Approach

To successfully accomplish all five aspects of project determination (direct, regulate, limit, decide, and conclude) in managing project progress, a project manager can think in terms of a balanced scorecard approach. The concept behind a balanced scorecard is that an organization needs to be evaluated from the perspectives of customer, internal business, financial, and growth and innovation. If one considers a project as a temporary organization, the same perspectives make sense when monitoring and controlling a project. Exhibit 14.1 shows a project balanced scorecard approach to project determination.

When a project manager seeks to monitor and control a project, different critical aspects are often interrelated, and thus, their impacts on each other must be considered. For example, a proposed change may impact the scope, quality, schedule, and/or cost. However, to understand project control, one must consider each aspect individually before assessing the impact on all other factors. This chapter begins with the project manager controlling internal project issues. The next major section of this chapter deals with the customer-related issues of quality and scope. The final sections deal with the financial issues of resources, schedule, and cost. The project manager can utilize a number of tools to manage schedule overloads and conflicts and to reprioritize the work. Earned value and project scheduling software such as MS Project can prove to be useful to manage these issues. Growth and innovation include issues of participant development covered in Chapter 5 and managing project knowledge covered in Chapter 15.

EXHIBIT 14.1

BALANCED SCORECARD APPROACH TO PROJECT DETERMINATION		
INTERNAL PROJECT	CUSTOMER	FINANCIAL
Direct and manage project work	Manage quality	Control resources
Monitor and control project work	Control quality	Control schedule
Perform integrated change control	Control scope	Control costs
Implement risk responses		
Monitor risks		
Manage communication		
Monitor communication		

Source: Adapted from Kevin Devine, Timothy J. Kloppenborg, and Priscilla O'Clock, "Project Measurement and Success: A Balanced Scorecard Approach," *Journal of Healthcare Finance* 36 (4) (2010): 38–50.

14-2 Internal Project Issues

While all aspects of a project are important and interrelated when determining progress and results, a logical starting place is with the project work that needs to be accomplished. Closely related are the risks that may impede the work and adequate communication. Collectively, these form the project's internal issues. These issues can be envisioned as the project's nerve center. Problems in any of them travel to all other project areas just as nerves in a body carry information throughout. When dealing with this project nerve center, project managers direct and manage project work; monitor and control the project work; perform integrated change control; implement risk responses monitor project risks; and manage and monitor communications.

14-2a Direct and Manage Project Work

Directing and managing project work is performing the work as defined in various components of the project management plan, including approved changes with an intent to accomplish project objectives. When project managers authorize project work, they should empower others to the extent possible, yet control them to the extent necessary. It should be clear who is allowed to authorize each portion of work to commence. The project management plan identifies work to be accomplished, but the project manager or her appointee must tell someone when it is time to perform the work. Often, spending limits are intertwined with work authorization (e.g., *"Please perform this activity and do not spend more than $X on it. Report back to me for approval if you need to spend more."*).

The work to be performed can come from one of several sources. The primary source is the work package level of the work breakdown structure. However, approved corrective actions, preventive actions, and defect repairs may also trigger work to be authorized.

When directing project work, trade-offs are often present both between projects and other work within the project itself. Organizations often have many projects and a variety of other work that must all be accomplished. Some work is of higher priority than other work. A project manager needs to understand where her work fits in the priority. If her project is relatively low in priority, she may have trouble getting people and resources to perform the project-related activities as per the planned schedule. In a case like that, the project manager and sponsor should have open and transparent communications so the sponsor can either help the project manager secure the resources needed or understand that the project could be delayed.

Projects often are resource-constrained or time-constrained. In resource-constrained projects, the project is limited by budget constraints. In this case, the project schedule gets extended. When a project is time-constrained or its completion date is nonnegotiable, organizations may have to expend more resources to complete the project, and project cost is likely to exceed the planned cost. In both the resource- and time-constrained projects, project scope is often not compromised. However, one should remember that the project manager should have some leeway with one of the three constraints. If all the three constraints (cost, time, and scope) are fixed, it is unlikely that the project manager and the team will be successful in completing the project within time, on budget, and with the promised scope and acceptable quality.

As the project progresses, are there changing priorities that impact project importance? Remember, any proposed change to the project scope, quality, schedule, or budget needs to be processed through the integrated change control system described later in this chapter.

Projects are undertaken with scope goals and with constraints on cost, schedule, and quality. Exhibit 14.2 gives an example of Tatro, Inc., dealing with project trade-offs.

Well-developed project charters, effective stakeholder management, and clear communications help the project manager make sensible trade-off decisions. Sometimes, an owner representative works closely with the project manager to make these decisions. Skills an owner representative can use when working closely with a project manager to make these trade-off decisions effectively are shown in Exhibit 14.3.

14-2b Monitor and Control Project Work

Monitoring and controlling project work includes a series of activities such as identifying work packages for tracking, reviewing, and documenting the progress to ensure that the project execution meets performance objectives as defined in the project plan. The term **monitor** refers to reviewing the progress and capturing project performance data with reference to the project plan; developing performance measures; and communicating performance information. **Control** means assessing actual performance obtained from monitoring a work element and comparing it with planned performance, determining variances, analyzing trends to identify and implement process improvements, evaluating possible alternatives, and finally, recommending appropriate corrective action as needed.

A **variance** is a measurable departure from a planned baseline or expected value. Variance is often measured in quantitative terms, but qualitative measures cannot be

EXHIBIT 14.2

PROJECT TRADE-OFF DECISIONS AT TATRO, INC.

Tatro, Inc., is a company that describes itself as a designer, builder, and caretaker of fine landscaping. It has both commercial and private (homeowner) clients. Landscaping projects for private homes often cost well over $100,000. Homeowners who contract for landscaping projects of this magnitude are ultra-successful people who will not change their mind once they decide they want something special. These clients tend to focus closely on the process of a project. They wish to have polite, skilled workers with no interruptions. The reason they wish to have the project completed is to create a "wow factor." Therefore, they will rarely compromise at all on either scope or quality, but they will often compromise on the necessary cost and schedule.

Source: Chris Tetrault, president, Tatro, Inc. Reprinted with permission.

EXHIBIT 14.3

USEFUL OWNER REPRESENTATIVE SKILLS IN PROJECT TRADE-OFF DECISION MAKING	
Partnership	Building trust
	Improving relations
	Collaborating
	Creating alliances
	Assuring quality
Management	Planning
	Managing change
	Aligning resources
Leadership	Communicating
	Team building
Technical	Project management
	Knowledge of criteria

Source: Adapted from Denis R. Petersen and E. Lile Murphree, Jr., "The Impact of Owner Representatives in a Design-Build Construction Environment," *Project Management Journal* 35 (3) (September 2004): 35–36.

ruled out. Monitoring and controlling activities allow a project manager to keep an eye on many project activities that can indicate how well the project performance is progressing. This prepares her to act if necessary to get the project back on track. The most difficult part of monitoring and controlling is figuring out what metrics to keep, what to measure, and how to report the results to various decision makers as necessary.

Monitoring and controlling are not activities that are done only once. Monitoring and controlling activities occur along with project execution. Monitoring and controlling are a continuous, overarching part of an entire project's life cycle, from project initiation through project closing. Since the purpose of monitoring and controlling project work is to be able to take corrective action, these activities need to be timely. In fact, the reverse of an old adage is in order. Instead of shooting the messenger when there is bad news, reward the messenger if the message is delivered quickly enough to bring the project back into control and at low cost.

To the extent possible, letting people self-control their work adds to their enthusiasm. In other words, make them responsible and accountable by empowering people and delegating the work. That said, the project manager is ultimately accountable for all of the project results and needs to develop a sense for how much control is necessary, given the work and the person performing it.

TYPES OF PROJECT CONTROL   While this section deals with monitoring and controlling project work, the remainder of this chapter deals with monitoring and controlling each of the other project management knowledge areas. Two types of control are used extensively on projects and both compare actual performance against the project plan. One type is steering control, in which the work is compared to the plan on a continual basis to see if progress is equal to, better than, or worse than the project plan. Adjustments can be made as often as necessary. The second type of control is go/no-go control. Go/no-go control requires a project manager to receive approval to continue.

EXHIBIT 14.4

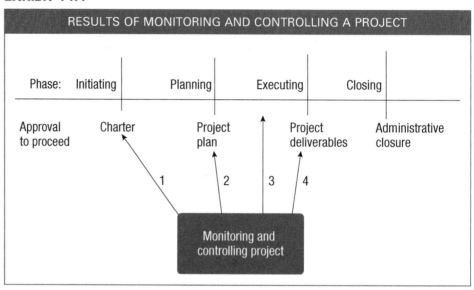

| RESULTS OF MONITORING AND CONTROLLING A PROJECT |

Phase: Initiating   Planning   Executing   Closing

Approval   Charter   Project   Project   Administrative
to proceed   plan   deliverables   closure

                          1   2   3   4

Monitoring and
controlling project

This control is often used at milestones (such as those developed in the project charter) or when someone needs to determine if a key deliverable is acceptable or not. If it is acceptable, the project continues as planned. If not, either the work needs to be redone or the project could even be cancelled. For both types of control, resulting change requests can include corrective actions, preventive actions, or defect repair.

The results of monitoring and controlling project work, schedule, budget, risks, or anything else can range from minor to major, depending on how close the actual progress is to the plan. This can be seen in Exhibit 14.4.

Depending on the extent to which actual progress performance varies from planned performance, the results of monitoring and controlling activities can suggest anything from modifying the charter to transferring project deliverables as planned. Some of the monitoring and controlling decisions are listed below:

1. If the actual progress is very different from the original intent, perhaps the project charter needs to be revisited to ensure that the project still makes sense.
2. If progress is somewhat different from what was planned but the charter is still a good guide, perhaps the project plan needs to be adjusted.
3. If the project plan is still a useful guide, perhaps minor adjustments need to be made in day-to-day instructions within the project executing stage.
4. Finally, if the results indicate the customer is ready to accept the project deliverables, perhaps it is time to proceed into the project closing stage.

PERFORM INTEGRATED CHANGE CONTROL   George and John are new project managers fresh out of college. Both are approached by internal customers of their projects (managers of departments where the project deliverables will be used). Their customers tell them what a fantastic job the two of them are doing. The customers then say, "This is great! Could you add these couple of little improvements to it? Then it would be even more valuable to me." George, wanting to please his customer, says, "Yes, we can add that little bit." John's immediate answer is, "Let's see what impact that might have on the schedule, budget, quality, and project team. I will be happy to consider it, but

I want to be sure to deliver the project results we promised on time and on budget." George, in his eagerness to please the customer, made a classic mistake. Many great projects have been derailed because someone stroked the ego of a project manager who then agreed to changes without understanding their impact.

Perform integrated change control is reviewing all change proposals, estimating their impact on project goals wherever appropriate, approving or declining changes, and managing changes to deliverables, schedules, budgets, and the project management plan. **Change control** is a process wherein change proposals to various project planning elements are acknowledged, formally documented, and either approved or declined after review. Change control includes considering the impact of any change, deciding whether to agree to the change, and then documenting and managing that change. An observant project manager will ensure that changes that were not approved are not somehow slipped in anyway by a stakeholder who does not take no for an answer. Proposed changes are documented in a change request such as the one shown in Exhibit 7.14.

The decision to approve the proposed change needs to be made by the appropriate person or group responsible for it. Generally, if the proposed change requires a modification to the project charter (or contract for an external project), then the sponsor and/ or customer would decide. If the change does not rise to that level, often a project manager is empowered to make the decision. Some organizations use a **change control board**, which consists of a formal group authorized and responsible for reviewing, evaluating, approving, delaying, or rejecting any changes to any aspect of the project plan by following a formal communication method of documenting the decision process. The change control board often consists of the project manager, sponsor, project core team, and perhaps other key stakeholders. Since some changes have far-reaching impacts, it is often wise to include people with diverse knowledge and skills on the change review board.

Change is a reality on virtually all projects. While we cannot predict or plan what changes will occur, we can plan for how we will deal with those changes. Some projects are easier than others to plan, especially the later phases of the project. If the planning team can plan most details at the outset, change control may be the primary method they use for handling change. On other projects, where it is difficult to plan the later phases or parts in detail until results from the early parts of the project are known, change control is still used, but it is not enough. What is also used in these cases is the rolling wave planning described in Chapter 9. The early parts of the project are planned in detail, and the later parts are planned in less detail until later when additional detail is added. Often, a detailed plan for the following section of the project is required before being allowed to proceed. Agile projects are planned in a rolling wave fashion.

14-2c Monitoring Project Risk

During project planning, the project team normally develops a risk management plan that is used to guide risk monitoring and response activities. They also normally create a risk register to record each identified risk, its priority, potential causes, and potential responses. The risk management plan and risk register are used to monitor and implement responses to project risks and to resolve them when they occur.

Monitor risks is the process of adhering to the risk response plan of tracking identified risks, identifying new risks, monitoring residual risks, and evaluating the effectiveness of the risk response process throughout the project. On some projects, the majority of risk events that materialize are ones that the project team has previously identified. Efforts needed on these risks largely include tracking the identified risks, executing the response plans, and evaluating their effectiveness. Project managers know it is wise to consider multiple responses to a given risk. This is true both because some risks cannot be fully handled with just one strategy and because the first strategy may not always be the best strategy.

On other projects, however, many unanticipated risks may materialize. This could be partly due to poor or incomplete risk planning. It could also be partly due to events that would have been so unlikely that the team could not have been expected to plan for them. In either event, specific contingency plans may not be in place to deal with these risks. Identifying these new risks is vital—and the sooner the better. Two categories of project management methods can help to deal with previously unidentified risks. First, the project team in planning may recognize that unknown risks may surface, and they may add a contingency reserve of time, budget, and/or other resources to cover these unknowns. Good project management practice suggests a need for this. The amount of cost and budget reserves that are included can vary extensively based upon the customer's perception of risk and the type of project that is involved. Competitive pressures often dictate a lower limit on reserves than project managers may prefer.

The second category of project management methods includes a number of good practices that project managers often employ anyway. These practices can be classified according to whether the project team has full, partial, or no control over the events, as shown in Exhibit 14.5. Note especially the second column, which deals with risks partially within a project manager's control. A project manager cannot completely control many situations, but by using good leadership and ethics, the project manager can certainly help create a situation in which others want to help the project.

14-2d Implement Risk Responses

Implement risk responses is the process where when a risk event occurs or is quite likely to occur soon, the person assigned to that risk executes the strategy identified in

EXHIBIT 14.5

RISK EVENT RESOLUTION STRATEGIES		
RISKS WITHIN PROJECT CONTROL	RISKS PARTIALLY WITHIN PROJECT CONTROL	RISKS OUTSIDE PROJECT CONTROL
Understand and control WBS	Establish limits to customer expectations	Understand project context and environment
Closely monitor and control activity progress	Build relationships by understanding project from client's perspective	Actively monitor project environment
Closely manage all project changes	Use honesty in managing client expectations	Understand willingness or reluctance of stakeholders to agree to changes
Document all change requests	Work with client to reprioritize cost, schedule, scope, and/or quality	
Increase overtime to stay on schedule	Carefully escalate problems	
Isolate problems and reschedule other activities	Build team commitment and enthusiasm	
Research challenging issues early		

Source: Adapted from Hazel Taylor, "Risk Management and Problem Resolution Strategies for IT Projects: Prescription and Practice," *Project Management Journal* 37 (5) (December 2006): 55–60.

the risk management plan. Exhibit 11.12 outlines the most typical strategies with examples of each. One core team member should be assigned to each risk. That person should be alert to any trigger condition that suggests the risk event may happen and be prepared to implement the response strategy quickly. Possible outcomes of implementing a risk response include updates to the risk register, approved change orders, and perhaps lessons learned so that both this project and future projects may avoid that same risk event in the future.

14-2e Manage Communications

Manage communications as defined in Chapter 6 is all the work connected with the project communications plan, starting with planning for it; generating it; organizing and sharing it; and, finally, storing and disposing of it. This includes determining project information needs and establishing an information system as described in Chapter 6. Then, while the project is under way, the project manager and team need to determine any additional information needs that were not already uncovered, collect information on executed work and work in progress, and then report progress to all stakeholders.

COLLECT INFORMATION ON EXECUTED WORK AND WORK IN PROGRESS   Project managers gather data on the work they have authorized so they can understand the progress being made. This information is necessary for scheduling additional work, for understanding how the project is doing with respect to the schedule, and for quality purposes. A project manager may try to gather data to answer the following typical questions:

- How well is this particular activity proceeding in terms of time and budget?
- How well is the entire project proceeding in terms of time and budget?
- How much more money will need to be spent to finish?
- To what extent does the quality of this work meet requirements?
- How many hours of human resources have we used to complete this activity, compared to how much we estimated?
- What methods have we used that are worth repeating?
- What methods have we used that need to be improved before we do that type of work again?
- What evidence supports the answers to the above questions?

REPORT PERFORMANCE   Performance reporting includes gathering **work performance data** and using it to create work performance information and reports. Work performance data are the actual and raw observations and measurements during execution of project activities. **Work performance information** is the performance data collected from these processes, analyzed in context, and then integrated, considering relations across areas. **Work performance reports** are the compilation of work performance information in some physical or electronic form that are presented as project documents intended to generate awareness, discussions, decision making or other suitable actions.

Performance can be reported either at fixed time intervals or at key project milestones. Detailed progress can be reported informally but frequently within the project team and to functional managers who control resources—perhaps weekly or even daily on a project with critical time pressure. More general progress may be reported formally but on a less frequent basis to sponsors, senior management, and clients—perhaps semiweekly or monthly. If regular reports and meetings already exist within the parent organization that can serve for performance reporting vehicles for a project, they can

substitute for these reports. On the other hand, if your project needs additional or different meetings and reports, then develop and use those as well.

Progress reporting within the project team and to functional managers who control resources is often done in the form of meetings. The emphasis should be on specifics. Each team member can report for each deliverable for which he is responsible: the target date, status, and what other work or information on which progress depends. Once all the deliverables have been reported, the project team can update the risk register and issues log. Recommended changes that are within the project manager's discretion are either approved or rejected and then documented. Recommended changes beyond the project manager's discretion are formally sent to the sponsor or change control board for consideration. Approved changes become part of the project plan with activities, responsibilities, and timing assigned. Consequently, the project baseline will be updated. Finally, progress reporting meetings are a great time to capture lessons learned.

Performance reporting to sponsors, management, and clients can be in the form of either meetings or reports. Think in terms of three time horizons, as shown in Exhibit 14.6. It is often helpful to establish an agenda for progress report meetings based upon what sponsors wish to know concerning each of these three time horizons.

1. Past time period—The first time horizon is the immediate period between your last report and now. When looking back like this, it is important to be able to state what was planned to be accomplished during that time and what actually was accomplished. Any variance or difference between the approved plan and actual performance, along with reasons for the variance, should also be part of the retrospective portion of performance reporting.

2. Current time period—The second time horizon is from now until the next performance report is due: What work is to be accomplished during this time period (current plan)? What risks and issues are foreseen? Finally, what changes need to be approved?

EXHIBIT 14.6

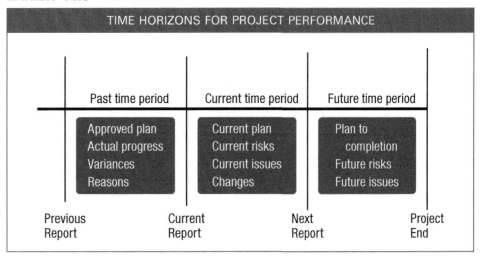

TIME HORIZONS FOR PROJECT PERFORMANCE

Past time period	Current time period	Future time period
Approved plan Actual progress Variances Reasons	Current plan Current risks Current issues Changes	Plan to completion Future risks Future issues

Previous Report   Current Report   Next Report   Project End

3. Future time period—The third time horizon is after the next reporting period. Sponsors especially want to know what future risks and issues are envisioned because they may be able to head some problems off before they grow. Remember the concept of rolling wave planning—the plan for the later part of the project might still be evolving, but what is known about it right now?

14-2f Monitor Communications

Monitor communications is monitoring and controlling communications throughout the project life cycle to make certain that the information needs of all the project stakeholders are met. The project manager and core team often discuss whether the project communications are following the plan, how effective they are, and how to improve their effectiveness.

 Self-directed teams on agile projects are largely empowered to decide what work to do and when to do it, consistent with the prioritizing of deliverables by the product owner.

On Agile projects, change is expected, and the only part that is planned in detail at the outset is the first iteration. Subsequent iterations are planned in a rolling wave fashion. Within an iteration, there is great reluctance to change. Conducted well, agile projects may have less risk because communication is so frequent and specific; because during each iteration, the team needs to demonstrate that the project deliverables perform correctly; and because it is common practice to maintain a visible, monitored, prioritized risk list.

Communication is frequent and rapid on agile projects. Often, a directional indicator showing that things are getting better or worse in some manner is more valuable than a more detailed and polished report. Teams generally display highly visible information registers so everyone concerned can tell in a transparent manner how the project is proceeding.

Progress report meetings are held every morning as brief (15 minutes) standup meetings. Each core team member discusses the previous day as the past time period and today as the current time period. The more distant future is generally not discussed in these meetings.

Documentation often starts very tersely and becomes more complete as the deliverables are better understood. Progressively more complete working product is the primary measure of progress.

EXHIBIT 14.7

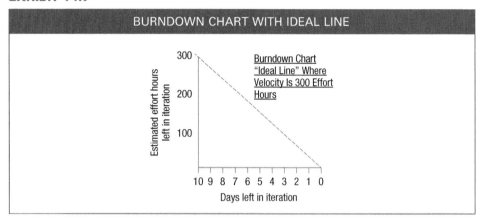

Agile projects often use a Burndown Chart to show the amount of work remaining. A Burndown Chart is useful to Scrum Masters as it projects how close to plan the team is within a given time box—that is, it is a graphical representation of work effort remaining in an iteration (or similar) versus the days left in an iteration.

The vertical axis is typically the number of effort hours remaining in an iteration. The horizontal axis identifies how many days are left in an iteration. Exhibit 14.7 displays a straight line, which is called the ideal line. It depicts a team with a velocity of 300 effort hours and 10 days of iterations.

The way this works is that each day, the members of the Scrum Team let the Scrum Master know how many effort hours of work they have left to complete for the current iteration. Velocity, which is used to draw the ideal line, is determined by tracking the team's historical progress. Exhibit 14.8 displays a Burndown Chart with the team constantly behind schedule.

EXHIBIT 14.8

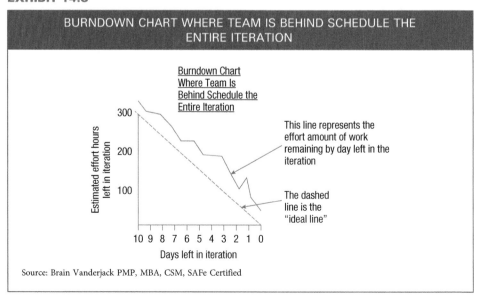

Source: Brain Vanderjack PMP, MBA, CSM, SAFe Certified

14-3 Customer Issues

The second major perspective included in a balanced scorecard approach to project control is that of the customer. Customers need the deliverables of the project. They want the results to be useful (quality) and complete (scope).

14-3a Manage and Control Quality

As previously defined in Chapter 12, **manage quality** is the process of using and improving the quality plan and policy to perform tasks that will most likely lead to creating project outputs to customers' satisfaction. This forward-looking, broad management process (often known as quality assurance), both ensures that work is performed correctly and that key stakeholders are convinced that the work is performed correctly.

Also as previously defined in Chapter 12, **control quality** is "the activities … used to verify that deliverables are of acceptable quality and that they are complete and correct. Examples of quality control activities include inspection, deliverable peer reviews, and the testing process."[2] This backward-looking, detailed set of reactive technical activities verifies whether specific project deliverables meet their quality standards.

QUALITY MANAGEMENT AND CONTROL TOOLS   A variety of quality management and control tools can be used effectively on projects. Some of the most common tools and their primary uses on projects are shown in Exhibit 14.9.

The following discussion presents a small example of a project process that is used to demonstrate a few of the project quality tools. A straightforward presentation of each tool is demonstrated. Multiple variations exist for some of the tools, and an interested student can find more detailed examples and instructions in a statistics or quality textbook.

Flow Chart   A flow chart is a tool that project managers use as they begin to control quality. Flow charts can be used to show any level of detail from the overall flow of an entire project (such as a network diagram of the project schedule) down to very specific details of a critical process. Flow charts show clearly where a process starts and ends. A box shows each step in the process. Arrows show the direction in which information, money, or physical things flow. Exhibit 14.10 is a flow chart of the process of estimating project cost.

This is a high-level flow chart of the process. Perhaps the project team looks at this and realizes labor cost estimates are unreliable. They might decide they need more detailed understanding of this step. One method would be to create a more detailed flow chart of just that step. Another method is to gather some data using a check sheet such as the one shown in Exhibit 14.11.

Check Sheet   Check sheets are customized for each application. Decide exactly what data will be useful in understanding, controlling, and improving a process, and create a form to collect that information. It is helpful to also collect the date or time when each event happened and notes regarding the impact or any special circumstances. When creating categories on a check sheet, it is wise to have a category titled "other" because many times, a problem comes from an unexpected source.

Pareto Chart   Once a check sheet is used, the gathered data can be displayed on an analysis tool such as the Pareto chart shown in Exhibit 14.12. The purpose of the Pareto chart is to quickly understand the primary sources of a problem using the 80/20 rule, wherein 80 percent of defects often come from only about 20 percent of all the sources.

EXHIBIT 14.9

PROJECT MANAGEMENT AND QUALITY TOOLS		
TOOL	CHAPTER	DESCRIPTION
Charter	3	High-level agreement to start project describing authority, scope, expectations, and resources
Lesson learned	3 and 15	Knowledge from experience captured and shared
Stakeholder analysis	6	Identification and prioritization of stakeholder desires
Communication management plan	6	Document that guides and assigns responsibility for communication with stakeholders
Voice of the customer	7	Captured desired benefits and features in customer's own words
Brainstorming	7	Quick generation of many ideas to identify gaps, issues, roadblocks, or potential solutions
Quality metrics	7	Crisp definition of what and how to measure specific performance
Project risk review	11	Thorough document review to uncover risks
Root cause analysis	11	Technique to discover underlying reason for problem
Cause and effect diagram	11	A visual outline, often resembling a fish skeleton, used to identify and organize possible causes of a stated outcome
Supplier, input, process, output, customer (SIPOC)	12	High-level view of process and stakeholders
Quality audit	12	Structured process to ensure project activities comply with organizational policies
Benchmarking	12	Identifying and analyzing best practices for improvement ideas
Flow chart	14	A visual model used to show inputs, flow of work, and outputs and to identify possible data collection points for process improvement
Check sheet	14	A simple, structured form used to gather and organize data for analysis
Pareto chart	14	A vertical bar graph used to identify and plot problems or defects in descending order of frequency or cost
Histogram	14	A vertical bar chart used to show the average, extent of variation, and shape of measurements recorded for a process variable
Run chart	14	A special type of scatter diagram in which one variable is time, used to see how the other variable changes over time
Control chart	14	A run chart with process average and control limits used to distinguish between common and special causes of variation

Note that, in this example, the error of using an incorrect scope shows the highest cost impact by far. Therefore, that is probably the first place the project team looks for improvements.

Cause-and-Effect Diagram   Exhibit 14.13 shows how the largest bar on the Pareto chart often becomes the head of the fish on the cause-and-effect diagram—the result that the project team tries to improve.

EXHIBIT 14.10

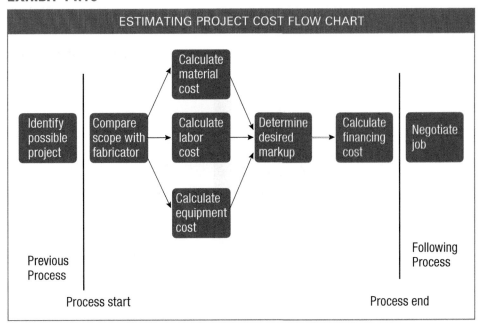

The cause-and-effect diagram (also commonly known as the fishbone diagram, because it resembles a fish skeleton, and the Ishikawa diagram, named after its developer) is constructed with each "big bone" representing a category of possible causes. For example, in Exhibit 14.13, one of the possible categories is "deliverable design," meaning that maybe something about the design of the project's deliverables contributed to problems with the "head of the fish"—in this case, using incorrect scope to estimate the labor cost. Once categories of possible causes are identified, the project team brainstorms ideas with the goal of identifying as many potential causes as possible. Once the

EXHIBIT 14.11

CHECK SHEET FOR LABOR COST ESTIMATING			
LABOR COST ISSUE	DOLLAR IMPACT	DATE DISCOVERED	ACTION TAKEN
Incorrect scope used			
Category of labor			
Quantity of labor			
Hourly rate			
Pace of labor learning			
Unexpected experience level			
Mathematical error			
Other (be specific)			

EXHIBIT 14.12

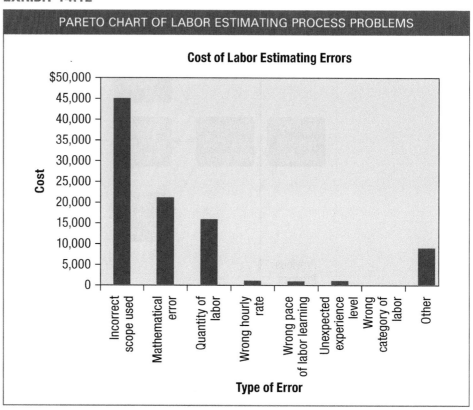

PARETO CHART OF LABOR ESTIMATING PROCESS PROBLEMS

team can think of no additional possible causes, they decide to test one or more possible causes to see if they actually have an impact. Testing can be done by gathering more data on the project as it is currently operating. Alternatively, a project team can test a new method and then collect data on it.

EXHIBIT 14.13

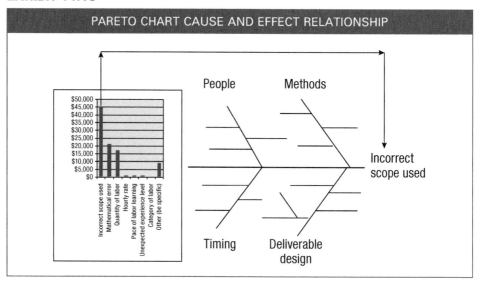

PARETO CHART CAUSE AND EFFECT RELATIONSHIP

EXHIBIT 14.14

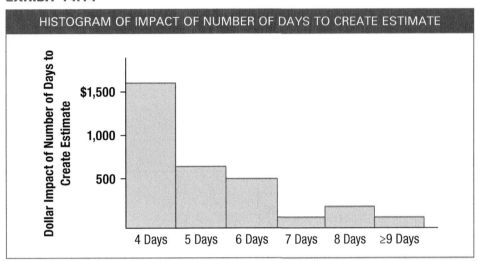

HISTOGRAM OF IMPACT OF NUMBER OF DAYS TO CREATE ESTIMATE

Histogram Once the additional data are gathered, they can be analyzed using a histogram, run chart, and/or control chart. For example, if one of the potential causes of using incorrect scope is that the client demands the cost estimate within four days of job notification (that is, within the timing category), perhaps the charts would appear as shown in Exhibit 14.14, Exhibit 14.15, or Exhibit 14.16.

A project manager can interpret several things from a histogram such as the one shown in Exhibit 14.14. First, if nothing unusual is happening, a normal or bell-shaped

EXHIBIT 14.15

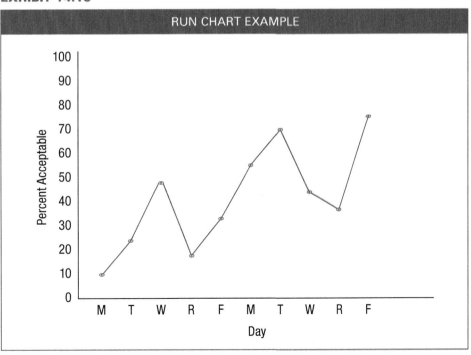

RUN CHART EXAMPLE

EXHIBIT 14.16

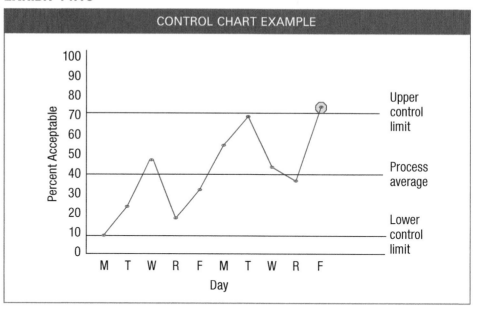

curve might be expected. However, this histogram is highly skewed, with much more impact happening when the client demands an estimate within four days. When the client demands the estimate in four days, the impact is approximately $1,600. When comparing that to the total impact of about $15,000 for using the wrong scope, this error appears to explain only a bit more than 10 percent of the total problem. It might be worth changing this, but most of the problem will still exist. Therefore, changing this factor alone does not solve the entire problem.

Run Chart   Perhaps the project team wants to see how one specific aspect of the work process may change over time. If they collect data for two weeks on a daily basis and show them on a run chart such as the one in Exhibit 14.15, they could determine trends in how the process is changing over time.

The team could look for three types of variation. First, is there a trend either up or down? In this example, there is an upward trend. Second, is there a repeating pattern, such as a low every Monday or a high every Wednesday? In this case, it is too early to tell. Both Tuesdays are up from Mondays, and both Thursdays are low, but day of week does not seem like the major source of variation. The third type of variation is abrupt changes, such as either a single point far higher or lower than the others or all of the points suddenly being much higher or lower than previous points. The question teams ask when trying to find this variation is: "How big of a change is big enough to count?"

Control Chart   Quality control charts are helpful in answering this question. Exhibit 14.16 displays the same data on a control chart with a process average and control limits shown. This chart shows the final point above the upper control limit. This means the variation is enough that it is not likely to have happened purely by chance. Something is causing the variation—some sort of special cause.

When considering any of these quality control tools, remember that it is easy to get lost in the details, but the purpose of quality control is to make sure the agreed-upon scope and quality are met per the project charter.

Dmitry Kalinovsky/Shutterstock.com

14-3b Control Scope

Control scope is the act of closely monitoring the project and product scope status and only allowing necessary changes to the scope baseline. Ideally, project managers and teams practice scope control proactively. They attempt to understand what might cause changes to either the product scope (the features of the project deliverables) or the project scope (the work that must be done to create the deliverables). Once a project team discovers something that may cause a need to change the scope, their first effort is typically to head it off. It is easiest if the stakeholders can still be satisfied and project objectives can be met without changing the scope. However, many times, it may be necessary to make a scope change. A **scope change** is any change to the project work activities or deliverable. When the scope changes, the project cost and/or schedule also need to change. For this reason, proposed scope changes are processed through the integrated change control system to determine what impact each might have on other critical aspects of the project goals. Some scope changes start as proposed changes to cost or schedule, just as some changes to cost or schedule start as proposed scope changes.

As with any type of proposed change, one must have a scope baseline in order to understand scope changes; that is, the approved scope definition and work breakdown structure must be clearly understood. Only then can the project team determine how big a proposed scope change is, what impact it will have, and how to best manage it.

Variance analysis is the process of determining both the cause and the amount of difference between planned and actual performance. Variance analysis includes determining how large the difference is between the actual and planned scope (or schedule or budget), the reasons for the difference, and whether any action is necessary to resolve it. For scope variances, the action can include updating the scope definition and work breakdown structure.

Quality is enhanced on agile projects by having the appropriate team members resolve issues quickly. Success of the product is predicted by having team members, including the product owner, use the product before users do.

14-4 Financial Issues

Cost control is obviously a financial issue. Cost, schedule, and scope are often so closely intertwined that they are monitored and controlled simultaneously, and a change in one of them impacts the others. The amount of resources of all kinds needed to perform the project has a direct impact on cost, so we also cover controlling resources here.

14-4a Control Resources

Control resources is a process by which all of the physical resources needed to perform the project are planned and monitored, and changes are made if needed. This occurs throughout the life of the project. Obviously, if needed resources are late, the project can be delayed. If needed resources are in short supply, the cost and schedule might both be impacted unfavorably. Project managers need to look ahead at potential trends, be willing to proactively solve problems, and work cooperatively with a myriad of stakeholders to ensure the needed resources are available when required.

14-4b Control Schedule and Costs

Schedule and cost control are very similar in concept to control. The project manager should start with the approved cost and schedule baseline. Next, the current status of the schedule and cost should be determined.

If the schedule or budget has changed by at least a previously agreed amount, changes should be formally recommended and managed through the integrated change control system to ensure that any impacts on other areas are considered. Cost control often has one additional consideration—that is, ensuring that no more money is spent than the authorized amount. This may force other changes on the project, such as delaying the schedule or reducing part of the project scope. While many methods exist for controlling cost and schedule, the two discussed in this chapter are two of the most common: earned value management and project scheduling software such as MS Project.

Very often, the project manager must work with his or her company's finance department or CFO to get the proper data on accounts payable, accounts receivable, and other information. The project may require the help of someone skilled at financial software. If the project manager is not personally adept at using such software, the finance department representative might be included in the project team either as a core team member or in SME capacity.

14-4c Earned Value Management for Controlling Schedule and Costs

Earned value management is "a disciplined, structured, objective, and quantitative method to integrate technical work scope, cost, and schedule objectives into a single cohesive contract baseline plan called a Performance Measurement Baseline for tracking contract performance."[3] Earned value allows a project team to understand the project's progress in terms of cost and schedule as well as to make predictions concerning the project's schedule and cost control until the project's conclusion. Earned value is used as a decision-making tool. The project manager can quickly assess how the project is doing according to the baseline plan and whether the project will end without major cost and/or schedule overruns. The earned value data presents a snapshot of the status of his or her project at a given point in time. It is valid only for the day that the cost and schedule progresses are measured.

When interpreting earned value management, cost and schedule must be considered independently. A project can be either ahead or behind the planned schedule and either over or under the planned budget. Second, all earned value terms deal with one of two time frames. Each represents either status as of the last date that project data were gathered or a prediction for the end of the project. Exhibit 14.17 lists 11 questions and answers that introduce all of the earned value management terms.

Exhibit 14.18 uses an example to show each of the earned value management terms. Currently known values for the example are stated, followed by their definitions. Variances, indexes, and estimates are next defined, and calculations for the example are shown.

CURRENTLY KNOWN VALUES   In this example, the first several items are provided:

$$PV = \$250,000, \ EV = \$200,000, \ AC = \$400,000, \ \text{and} \ BAC = \$750,000$$

Each of these terms also has a formal definition.

Planned value (PV) is "the approved value of the work to be completed in a given time. It is the value that should have been earned as per the schedule."[4] In our example, we expected to spend $250,000 for the work we planned to have accomplished by now.

EXHIBIT 14.17

EARNED VALUE MANAGEMENT TERMS			
QUESTION	TIMING	ANSWER	ACRONYM
How much work *should be done?*	Now	Planned value	**PV**
How much work *is* done?	Now	Earned value	**EV**
How much did *the* "is done" work cost?	Now	Actual cost	**AC**
How much was the total project *supposed to* cost?	**End**	Budget at completion	BAC
How much *is* the project schedule ahead or behind?	Now	Schedule variance	**SV**
How much *is* the project over or under budget?	Now	Cost variance	**CV**
How efficient is the project *so far* with its schedule?	Now	Schedule performance index	SPI
How efficient is the project *so far* with its budget?	Now	Cost performance index	CPI
How much more do we expect to spend to finish the project?	**End**	Estimate to complete	**ETC**
What do we now think the total project will cost?	**End**	Estimate at completion	EAC
How efficient do we need to be to finish on budget?	**End**	To-complete performance index	TCPI

EXHIBIT 14.18

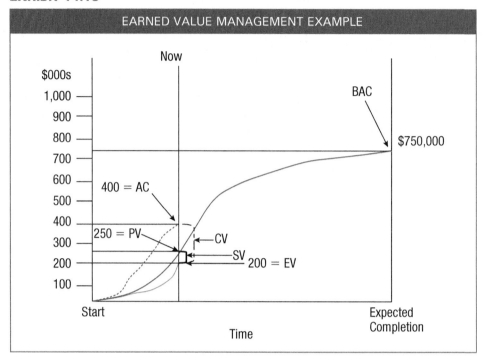

EARNED VALUE MANAGEMENT EXAMPLE

Earned value (EV) is the value of the work actually completed to date. In our example, the work that has been completed is worth $200,000.

Actual cost (AC) is the total of costs incurred in accomplishing work on the activity during a given period. In our example, we owe $400,000 for the work that has been completed.

Budget at completion (BAC) is the total amount budgeted for the entire project. In this example, our approved budget for the entire project is $750,000. Now that we know these four pieces of information, we can calculate answers to all of the remaining questions listed in Exhibit 14.16.

VARIANCES   **Schedule variance (SV)** is the difference between the earned value (EV) and the planned value (PV), and it denotes schedule performance. In our example, it is calculated as $200,000 − $250,000 = −$50,000. We know we are behind schedule because the variation is negative (unfavorable):

$$SV = EV - PV$$

Cost variance (CV) is the difference between earned value (EV) and actual cost (AC), which reflects cost performance. In our example, it is calculated as $200,000 − $400,000 = −$200,000. We know we are over budget because the variation is negative (unfavorable):

$$CV = EV - AC$$

The two variances help us understand, in dollar terms, how poorly or well we are performing on cost and schedule. In this example, we are performing poorly in terms of both cost and schedule. These are commonly used indicators. However, some people prefer to use efficiency measures to understand in percentage terms how well or poorly the project is performing.

INDEXES **Schedule performance index (SPI)** is a schedule performance measure expressed as the ratio of earned value (EV) to planned value (PV). In our example, it is calculated by $200,000/$250,000 = 80%. We know our project is behind schedule because we only accomplished 80 percent of what we planned:

$$\textbf{SPI} = \textbf{EV/PV}$$

With performance indexes, 100 percent means right on plan, less than 100 percent means less efficient than planned, and over 100 percent means more efficient than planned.

Cost performance index (CPI) is a cost performance measure expressed as the ratio of earned value (EV) to actual cost (AC). In our example, it is calculated by $200,000/$400,000 = 50%. We know our project is over budget because we have only received $0.50 worth of results for every dollar we have spent:

$$\textbf{CPI} = \textbf{EV/AC}$$

Now that we understand how we have performed so far (poorly in our example), it is time to forecast how we will perform for the remainder of the project. The simplest way to estimate future performance is to predict that the past performance trend will continue. The following calculations are based upon that assumption. There are projects, however, that may have unusual circumstances in the early stages that are not likely to be repeated later. In those instances, the project manager and sponsor need to use judgment to determine if the original estimates for the remaining work or some other method of estimating it are better predictors. In each case, an estimate is made for the remaining work and added to the actual cost of work completed to provide the overall estimate. We will use the two most common methods of estimating the remaining work.

ESTIMATES **Estimate to complete (ETC)** is the expected budget required to complete all the remaining project work. In our example, if we predict that our future performance will have the same efficiency as our past performance, it is calculated by:
(BAC − EV)/CPI = ($750,000 − $200,000)/50% = $1,100,000:

First method (Work to date is good estimate of future) ETC = (BAC − EV)/CPI

Unless we improve upon our efficiency, we can expect to pay more for the remaining project work than we originally expected to pay for the entire project!

The second method of calculating the ETC is to believe that the original plan is a better predictor than the work to date (maybe because of unusual circumstances that are unlikely to continue). This method is calculated by budget at completion (BAC) − EV = $750,000 − 200,000 = $550,000:

Second method (original plan is good estimate of future) ETC = BAC − EV

Estimate at completion (EAC) is the total cost of completing all the project work expressed as the sum of actual cost to date and the estimate to complete. In our example, if we believe our efficiency to date is a good predictor of the future, it is calculated by $400,000 + $1,100,000 = $1,500,000. On the other hand, if we believe what happened so far will not be repeated and our original plan is good for the remaining work, it is calculated by $400,000 + $550,000 = $950,000:

$$EAC = AC + ETC$$

Because our cost efficiency is only half of our plan (as we learned from our CPI), unless we become more efficient, we can expect to pay double our original estimate! Even if we match our original plan for the rest of the project, we will still be over the budget in the end. Perhaps our sponsor still wants to know what it would take for us to finish on budget.

The **to-complete performance index (TCPI)** is a measure of the cost performance required to complete the remaining project work within the remaining budget. This is the ratio of the remaining work to the remaining budget and on our example is calculated as ($750,000 − $200,000)/($750,000 − $400,000) = 157%. That means that so far, our cost efficiency as measured by our CPI is 50% and we need to suddenly raise it to 157% for the remainder of the project to complete on budget!

$$TCPI = (BAC - EV)/(BAC - AC)$$

Each term in earned value management helps project managers understand a bit more about their project's performance. Collectively, the earned value management terms give project managers insight for monitoring and controlling project cost and schedule. In addition to and often in conjunction with earned value management, many project managers use scheduling software to help control their projects.

14-5 Using MS Project to Monitor and Control Projects

When used to its fullest, MS Project can be a powerful tool for monitoring and controlling the project schedule, cost, and resources. Once a project has entered into the execution phase, the job of the project manager shifts primarily to tracking the project to see if it is executing according to plan. To understand how MS Project assists in this regard, it is helpful for the project manager to understand the following:

1. What makes a schedule useful
2. How MS Project recalculates the schedule based upon reported and inputted actuals
3. The current and future impacts of time and cost variances

Once these concepts are understood, the project manager can use MS Project to update the schedule in a step-by-step fashion.

14-5a What Makes a Schedule Useful?

To properly control a project, the project manager must provide useful status reports, produce accurate assignment dates, take timely corrective actions, and make other necessary management decisions. This is difficult or impossible to do well without a sufficiently useful schedule. To be useful, three sets of schedule data must exist for comparison purposes. Each set includes dates, duration, work, and cost (along with any approved changes). The three sets are as follows:

1. The Baseline Set (sometimes called the planned schedule)
   a. This set is the original stakeholder-approved scheduled values (as discussed in Chapter 12).
   b. Data includes the *Baseline Start, Baseline Finish, Baseline Duration, Baseline Work*, and *Baseline Cost*.

2. The Actual Set (sometimes called the performance data)
   a. This set is what actually happens during project execution as reported by the resources assigned to project tasks.
   b. Data includes the *Actual Start, Actual Finish, Actual Duration, Actual Work*, and *Actual Cost.*
3. The Scheduled Set
   a. This set is the future estimated time and costs and is calculated by MS Project.
   b. Data includes the *Start, Finish, Duration, Work*, and *Cost.*
   c. Values are continuously recalculated during project execution as tasks and estimates are entered, as the project network is defined, as resources are assigned and balanced, and as actual execution data is entered.

14-5b How MS Project Recalculates the Schedule Based on Reported Actuals

As actual data is entered into a task's *Actual* field, MS Project copies that data into the task's *Scheduled* field, replacing the estimated values. MS Project then recalculates the schedule for future tasks based on a combination of what actually happened and the estimates of the remaining tasks.

14-5c Current and Future Impacts of Time and Cost Variance

With the three sets of data, comparisons can be made between any two of the sets. This is useful in understanding future impacts of various issues, such as:

- Time and cost performance variances from baseline
- Critical path changes
- Resource allocation issues
- Emerging risks
- Remaining contingency and management reserves
- The impacts of proposed changes

14-5d Define the Performance Update Process

The performance update process is simply the project manager updating actual project data as the project is executed. The update process is defined by the project manager informing the project team on who needs to report, what information is needed in each report, and when each report needs to be submitted. The following guidelines will help the project manager keep the schedule updated and accurate.

WHO REPORTS?   All team members and suppliers assigned to tasks that were scheduled during the past reporting period need to report. Also, any resource wanting to change the estimate of a soon-to-be-starting task needs to report the new estimate.

WHAT IS REPORTED?   Actual Start, Actual Finish, Actual Duration Complete, and Estimated Remaining Duration are reported. The sooner the project manager learns of variances from estimates, the sooner he or she can take corrective action, making Estimated Remaining Duration and Actual Finish among the most important values to update accurately.

WHEN TO REPORT?   The project manager determines what day of the week resources will report performance ("Status Date" or "As of Date"), as well as the frequency. The Status Date is usually driven by the date of stakeholder review meetings and the time needed to make adjustments before that meeting. The project manager wants to walk into that meeting with the most accurate and up-to-date status information as possible.

14-5e Steps to Update the Project Schedule

The process of updating the project schedule in MS Project includes six steps as described below. Please note: for the purposes of this chapter's tutorial, a simplified version of the running Suburban Park Homes example has been used.

STEP 1: ACQUIRE THE PERFORMANCE DATA   Performance data is duration-based data. From each resource assignment, collect the date when the task started, how much duration has been completed, how much duration remains, and the actual finish date (if the task has been finished).

STEP 2: SET THE STATUS DATE (AS OF)   The Status Date, or "as of" date, is the date the project manager sets for the team to report on the progress of the project. To be useful, the Status Date must be updated every time the project manager requires performance data reported.

1. Click the **Project Tab>>Properties Group>>Project Information**
2. Click the "**Status date**" drop-down
3. Set status date to **12/7/17** (as shown in Exhibit 14.19)
4. Click **OK**

STEP 3: DISPLAY THE STATUS DATE LINE ON THE GANTT CHART   Displaying a Status Date line on the Gantt chart provides a visual cue as to how much of the work has been completed for each task (once the update data is entered).

1. Click the **Task Tab>>View Group>>Gantt Chart**
2. **Right-click** on the right pane>>select **Gridlines**

EXHIBIT 14.19

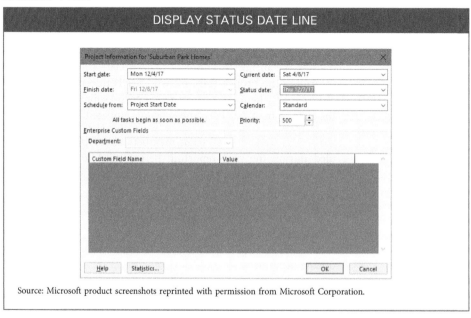

Source: Microsoft product screenshots reprinted with permission from Microsoft Corporation.

EXHIBIT 14.20

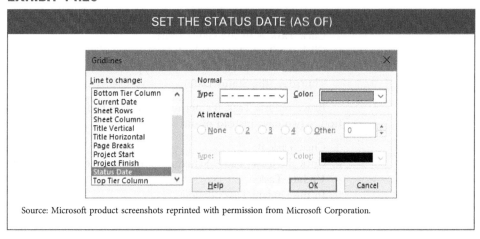

Source: Microsoft product screenshots reprinted with permission from Microsoft Corporation.

3. In the "Line to change list", select **Status Date** (as shown in Exhibit 14.20)
4. In the "Normal" box, choose **dashed dotted line**; choose **Green** for the color
5. Click **OK**

STEP 4: ENTER THE DURATION-BASED PERFORMANCE DATA   Exhibit 14.21 shows a simplified Suburban Park Homes project schedule in the Gantt Chart View with resource assigned tasks A–F (Task IDs two through seven) and beginning and end milestones (Task IDs one and eight). To the right of the Task Name column, a user-defined text column has been inserted (**Right click>>Insert Column>>type a heading name**) to record the performance report from the assigned resource(s). The Status Date is end of day on Thursday December 7, 2017 (denoted by the vertical dashed line in the right side pane of the Gantt view). Resources have been assigned to each task and are denoted by the resource name in the right-side pane. Updating reported performance data for each task is demonstrated in the next steps.

EXHIBIT 14.21

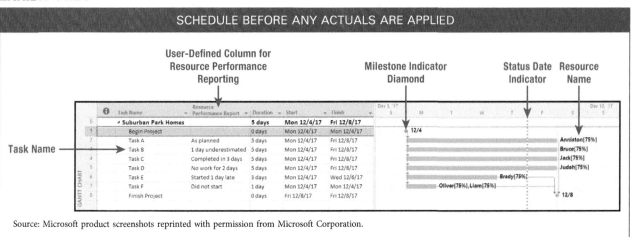

Source: Microsoft product screenshots reprinted with permission from Microsoft Corporation.

Anniston reports Task A's performance was as scheduled through the end of day on Thursday (remember that Thursday, December 7 is the Status Date).

1. Click **Task A** in the Gantt chart
2. Click the **Task Tab>>Schedule Group>>**click **Mark on Track**
3. Notice a dark progress bar line appears in the Gantt bar through the end of day on Thursday (the Status Date)

Bruce reports Task B's performance as scheduled, but the estimated remaining duration is two days instead of one.

1. Click **Task B**
2. Click the **Task Tab>>Schedule Group>>**click the **Mark on Track drop-down>>**click **Update Tasks**
3. In the Update Tasks dialog:
   a. Actual dur: **enter "4d"**
   b. Remaining dur: **enter "2d"** as shown in Exhibit 14.22.
4. Click **OK**
5. Notice Task B's duration has updated to six days and extends through the end of day Monday, as shown in Exhibit 14.23

Jack reports that Task C finished two days early.

1. Click Task C
2. Click the **Task Tab>>Schedule Group>>**click the **Mark on Track drop-down>>**click **Update Tasks**
3. In the Update Tasks dialog:
   a. Actual dur: **enter "3d"**
   b. Remaining dur: **enter "0d"**
4. Click **OK**
5. Notice in Exhibit 14.24 that Task C's duration is now three days and the activity is marked complete (as denoted by a checkmark in the Indicators column)

EXHIBIT 14.22

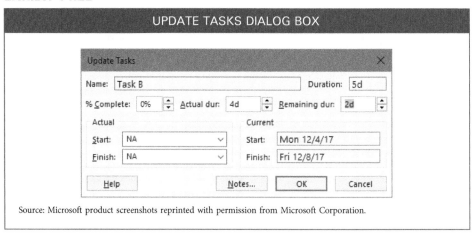

Source: Microsoft product screenshots reprinted with permission from Microsoft Corporation.

EXHIBIT 14.23

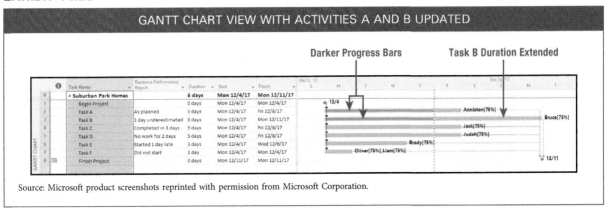

GANTT CHART VIEW WITH ACTIVITIES A AND B UPDATED

Source: Microsoft product screenshots reprinted with permission from Microsoft Corporation.

Judah reports that no work was done for two of the five days on Task D.

1. Click Task D
2. Click the **Task Tab>>Schedule Group>>**click the **Mark on Track drop-down>>**click **Update Tasks**
3. In the Update Tasks dialog:
   a. Actual dur: **enter "2d"**
   b. Remaining dur: **enter "3d"**
4. Click **OK**
5. Notice Task D's dark progress bar indicates there is still work scheduled for Wednesday and Thursday

Brady reports that Task E started one day late.

1. Click Task E
2. Click the **Task Tab>>Schedule Group>>**click the **Mark on Track drop-down>>**click **Update Tasks**

EXHIBIT 14.24

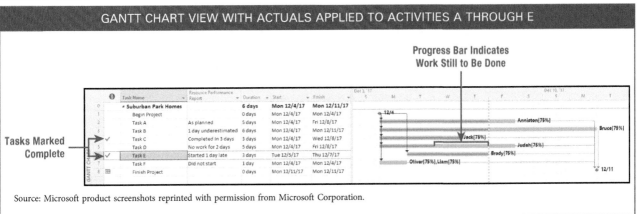

GANTT CHART VIEW WITH ACTUALS APPLIED TO ACTIVITIES A THROUGH E

Source: Microsoft product screenshots reprinted with permission from Microsoft Corporation.

3. In the Update Tasks dialog:
   a. Actual Start: **enter "12/5/17"**
   b. Actual dur: **enter "3d"**
   c. Remaining dur: **enter "0d"**
4. Click **OK**
5. Notice that Task E is marked complete

Oliver and Liam report that no work was done on Task F. This update will be addressed in the next step.

STEP 5: RESCHEDULE REMAINING WORK   Both tasks D and F still have work scheduled for dates prior to the Status date. This work must be moved to start no earlier than the day following the Status Date.

1. Click Task D
2. Click the **Project Tab>>Status Group>>**click **Update Project**
3. In the Update Project dialog, click "**Reschedule uncompleted work to start after:**"
4. Enter the Status Date if not already entered as shown in Exhibit 14.25
5. Click on **Selected tasks**
6. Click **OK**
7. Repeat these steps for Task F

As seen in Exhibit 14.26, Task D is now split with the completed work showing on Monday and Tuesday, and the remaining work rescheduled to resume on Friday. If a more likely date to resume work is not Friday, the Gantt bar can be dragged to the likely date.

Task F is also scheduled to resume on Friday. When all of a task is rescheduled, a "start-no-earlier" constraint is automatically applied. That constraint can be modified to select a more likely resume date. Ignoring unfinished work that is scheduled earlier than the Status Date is a risky practice.

STEP 6: REVISE FUTURE ESTIMATES   The most accurate estimates are made just before a task gets started. Therefore, at any status meeting, it's a good practice to ask project team members if they believe the estimates for any of their upcoming tasks need updating.

EXHIBIT 14.25

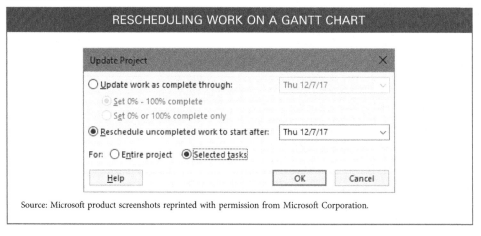

Source: Microsoft product screenshots reprinted with permission from Microsoft Corporation.

EXHIBIT 14.26

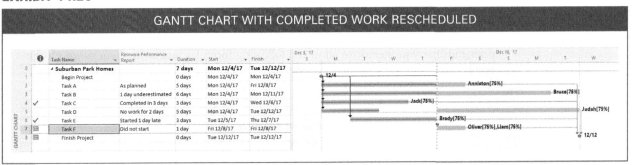

GANTT CHART WITH COMPLETED WORK RESCHEDULED

14-6 Replanning If Necessary

Sometimes it becomes necessary to replan a project. The project manager can use the integrated change control system to understand the impact the proposed changes may have and to secure approval to make the change. The changes are then reflected in a revised plan. The schedule, cost, and resource changes can be shown on an updated MS Project schedule. Other changes can be reflected in risk register updates or issues log updates. Two questions still exist regarding replanning: "What kinds of changes might be made in response to the problems?" and "Does the approval for a change need to be escalated to higher management?"

Changes a project manager may need to recommend include reassigning activities to different workers, splitting activities so at least some work can get started, reordering activities so they may be accomplished sooner, borrowing or acquiring additional resources, reducing scope, and so on. Many of these types of change can help a project get back on track; however, make sure the appropriate stakeholders agree with the changes because many times, a change that improves one aspect of a project degrades another.

Consider that people at each level in an organization have the ability to make specific decisions and are generally allowed a certain amount of time to deal with a problem before notifying a superior. Whoever makes the decision is still expected to document it appropriately. If a very minor problem occurs on a project, perhaps a team member can make the decision regarding how to handle it. A bit larger problem may fall in the domain of the project manager. Large decisions may go to the sponsor, and really critical decisions may be sent to the leadership of the parent organization. Escalation answers the question of what kinds of decisions are submitted to a higher level and how much time the lower-level person gets before raising the problem. A person who escalates minor decisions, or even major decisions very quickly, gives the impression of being weak and indecisive. However, a person who does not escalate important decisions or who takes so long to escalate them that the problem has worsened, exhibits poor judgment.

 AGILE

Replanning is conducted for each release and each iteration in agile. Within an iteration, once the replanning is complete, very little additional change is allowed.

PMP/CAPM Study Ideas

You can expect to see several questions using Earned Value Management (EVM) on either the CAPM or PMP, and you will not be provided with the formulas. We recommend that you memorize all of the following formulas and write them down on the blank paper you are provided as soon as you enter the testing room so you can refer to them throughout the test:

$$\textbf{CV (cost variance)} = \textbf{EV} - \textbf{AC}$$
$$\textbf{SV (schedule variance)} = \textbf{EV} - \textbf{PV}$$
$$\textbf{CPI (cost performance index)} = \textbf{EV/AC}$$
$$\textbf{SPI (schedule performance index)} = \textbf{EV/PV}$$
$$\textbf{ETC (estimate to complete)} = (\textbf{BAC} - \textbf{EV})/\textbf{CPI} = \textbf{BAC} - \textbf{EV}$$
$$\textbf{EAC (estimate at completion)} = \textbf{AC} + \textbf{ETC}$$
$$\textbf{TCPI (To} - \textbf{complete performance index)} = (\textbf{BAC} - \textbf{EV})/(\textbf{BAC} - \textbf{AC})$$

You will need to apply these formulas for the test, so refer back to section 14-4c of this book to review abbreviations, when to use each formula, and how to interpret the results. In addition to EVM, you can expect at least a few questions pertaining to the *Integrated Change Control* process. Remember that once the project management plan is approved and you have a baseline, any proposed change to schedule, budget, or scope needs to go through the change control process.

Summary

For a project manager to effectively determine that the desired project progress is being made and results are being delivered, a multitude of things need to be monitored and controlled. Many of these are interdependent, so a project manager needs to understand how changes in one area might impact another area.

Project managers need to monitor and control the actual work of the project or the activities. This entails observing the work as it is executed and making adjustments as needed. Any adjustments that may have a sizable impact must be processed through the project's integrated change control process. Each potential change is proposed, approved or disapproved, and documented, and the approved changes are implemented. A risk register is maintained to keep track of active risks, whether the risk events transpire, and how they are handled. New risks are added as they are discovered, and no-longer-relevant risks are retired.

Project managers also need to control the various aspects of the project that are subject to potential trade-offs—namely, scope, quality, cost, and schedule. When controlling these, the project manager looks for variances—that is, any difference between what was planned and what has actually happened. The project manager also seeks to understand how a change in any one area will impact the others. Several tools exist for helping project managers with this control. Many quality tools are widely used when seeking to understand what the quality level is, where problems may exist, what the root causes are for problems, and how to improve project processes so the problems do not reoccur. Sponsors and other stakeholders want to understand progress made on the project, current plans, and what might derail the project. Regular progress meetings and reports serve this purpose. Earned value management and MS Project are both quite helpful in understanding, documenting, and improving upon cost and schedule progress.

Key Terms Consistent with PMI Standards and Guides

direct and manage project work, 459
monitor and control project work, 460

monitor, 460
control, 460

Chapter Review Questions

1. What five aspects of project success are evaluated in the balanced scorecard approach?
2. Give three categories of internal project issues and an example of each.
3. In addition to the WBS, what might trigger project work to be authorized and performed?
4. What is an advantage of letting workers self-control their work?
5. What are two types of control frequently used on projects?
6. What members of the project team should serve on the change control board?
7. What is the difference between work performance data and work performance information?
8. Which time periods are discussed in Agile project progress meetings?
9. What three sets of data should a project manager have after completing a project audit?
10. Give some examples of times in the project lifecycle when an inspection might be especially useful.
11. Why is prevention preferable to inspection?
12. What is the difference between an attribute and a variable?
13. The highest bar on a Pareto chart often becomes the "head of the fish" in the _____.
14. What three types of variation should one look for in a Run Chart?
15. How does one calculate schedule variance?
16. What does cost performance index (CPI) measure?
17. What should your initial response be if a customer asks for a change to your project?
18. What is the main purpose of monitoring and controlling a project?
19. Describe the purpose of using an integrated change control system.
20. Describe the three time horizons for project performance reporting, what should be reported in each, and why.

Discussion Questions

1. Describe how a project manager can determine project progress for each element in the project balanced scorecard.
2. In your opinion, under what conditions should the sponsor approve a project change, and when is it okay for the project manager to authorize a change? Give an example of each.
3. Give specific examples of risks on a project that are within the team's control, partially within the team's control, and outside the team's control. Tell how you would deal with each.
4. As project manager, what would be your reaction to learning that, as of the last audit, your project's SPI was and your CPI was Why?

5. What is the difference between efficiency and effectiveness? Give an example of something that is one but not the other.

6. In your own words, what is the difference between Manage Quality and Control Quality on a project?

7. List and give an example of when to use each of the seven project quality control tools described in this chapter.

8. Give an example of a common cause and a special cause, and describe how you would address each.

9. If you were sponsoring a project, would you want to be updated in terms of cost and schedule variance or cost and schedule performance indexes? Why?

10. When it comes to monitoring progress, which parts of Microsoft Project schedule do you find most useful? Why?

PMBOK® *Guide* Questions

1. In regard to Project Work, which activity refers to "reviewing the progress and capturing project performance data with reference to the project plan, developing performance measures, and communicating performance information?"
   a. controlling
   b. monitoring
   c. executing
   d. managing

2. Juan is a project manager for a project that has been baselined and is now under way. When a customer approaches Juan and asks him to increase the project's scope, Juan's response should be to _____ .
   a. comply with the customer's request if it seems reasonable
   b. determine the schedule performance index (SPI)
   c. perform integrated change control
   d. calculate the Estimate to Complete (ETC)

3. Which of the following formulas represents the schedule performance index (SPI)?
   a. EV/PV
   b. EV − PV
   c. EV − AC
   d. EV/AC

4. If your sponsor asks for an estimate as to how much more money your team needs to complete all project work as scheduled, which of the following formulas might you use?
   a. BAC − EAC
   b. EV/PV
   c. (BAC − EV)/CPI
   d. (BAC − EV)/(EAC − AC)

5. What is the final step in the *Perform Integrated Change Control* process?
   a. Review Change Proposals

   b. Manage changes to deliverables and Project Management Plan
   c. Estimate impact of proposed changes on project goals
   d. Approve or Decline change requests

6. Which quality control tool is a special type of vertical bar chart that is used to identify the primary (vital few) sources that are responsible for causing most of a problem's effects, often referred to as the 80/20 rule?
   a. Ishikawa diagram
   b. Pareto diagram
   c. Control chart
   d. Force field analysis

7. Which quality control tool is sometimes referred to as a "fishbone diagram" because it places a problem statement at the head of the fishbone and uses each "big bone" in the fish's skeleton as a category of probable cause, in order to determine the root cause of the problem?
   a. Ishikawa diagram
   b. Pareto diagram
   c. Control chart
   d. Force field analysis

8. Good project management practice suggests a need to include a _____ within the cost baseline in order to cover identified risks that are accepted, and for which responses have been developed.
   a. contingency reserve
   b. project buffer
   c. control account
   d. management reserve

9. The "methodology that combines scope, schedule, and resource measurements to assess project performance and progress" is called _____.
   a. cost management (CM)

b. funding limit reconciliation
c. triple constraint management
d. earned value management (EVM)

10. The "ToComplete Performance Index" (TCPI) is a measure of the cost performance required in order to finish the outstanding work within the remaining budget. The formula for this index is _____.
a. BAC − EAC
b. AC + BAC − EV
c. EV/AC
d. (BAC − EV)/(BAC − AC)

Exercises

1. Use the following information to answer parts a through h. Describe what the results of each calculation mean to you as a project manager. What do you propose to do?

$$PV = \$500,000$$
$$EV = \$350,000$$
$$AC = \$550,000$$
$$BAC = \$1,200,000$$

   a. Schedule variance (SV)
   b. Cost variance (CV)
   c. Schedule performance index (SPI)
   d. Cost performance index (CPI)
   e. Estimate to complete (ETC—first method)
   f. Estimate to complete (ETC—second method)
   g. Estimate at completion (EAC)
   h. To-complete performance index (TCPI)

2. Use the following information to answer parts a through h. Describe what the results of each calculation mean to you as a project manager. What do you propose to do?

$$PV = \$25,000$$
$$EV = \$30,000$$
$$AC = \$29,000$$
$$BAC = \$1,000,000$$

   a. Schedule variance (SV)
   b. Cost variance (CV)
   c. Schedule performance index (SPI)
   d. Cost performance index (CPI)
   e. Estimate to complete (ETC—first method)
   f. Estimate to complete (ETC—second method)
   g. Estimate at completion (EAC)
   h. To-complete performance index (TCPI)

3. A project manager has just learned that the schedule performance index (SPI) for his project is 85 percent. The calculation of the cost performance index (CPI) is 107 percent. How would you describe this project both in terms of budget and schedule?

4. Document the flow of a project work process. Be sure to identify the starting and ending points.

5. Create a check sheet to gather data regarding a step in the process flow chart you constructed in Exercise 4 above.

6. For a cost savings project, you have captured data that show the following costs: delays between operations = $900; broken/missing tools = $1,200; water losses = $3,700; poor seals = $1,500; other = $2,000. Construct a Pareto chart. What would your next course of action be?

7. For a productivity improvement project, you discover the most frequent cause of delays in receiving payment is incorrect invoices. Construct a fishbone diagram to identify possible reasons for this problem. What action do you recommend with the results of your fishbone diagram?

8. Using the data below, construct a run chart to visualize how the number of customer complaints is changing over time. Describe what you find in terms of trends, repeating patterns, and/or outliers.

Date	Day	Complaints
1	Mon	14
2	Tue	17
3	Wed	11
4	Thu	12
5	Fri	21
8	Mon	15
9	Tue	21
10	Wed	19
11	Thu	22
12	Fri	23

Date	Day	Complaints
15	Mon	27
16	Tue	11
17	Wed	29
18	Thu	31
19	Fri	35

9. Using the data below, construct a schedule in MS Project. Show where the project is ahead and/or behind schedule. Be specific. Which activities did the best? Which had the most problems?

Planned Start	Planned Finish	Actual Start	Actual Finish
8/31	9/5	8/31	9/5
8/25	9/8	8/25	9/8
9/5	9/8	9/5	9/8
8/25	9/2	8/26	9/3
8/26	8/27	8/28	8/29
8/25	9/8	8/28	9/8
8/25	9/6	8/29	9/6
8/25	9/1	8/29	9/6
9/1	9/2	9/5	9/11
9/1	9/6	9/5	9/11
9/1	9/8	9/6	9/14

Planned Start	Planned Finish	Actual Start	Actual Finish
9/8	9/15	9/13	9/22
8/25	10/26	8/31	10/31
8/25	9/16	8/31	9/23
9/16	9/29	9/23	10/9
9/16	9/19	9/23	9/25
9/20	9/28	9/30	10/6
9/20	9/21	9/30	10/21
9/22	9/28	10/3	10/28
9/16	9/27	9/26	10/27
9/16	9/20	9/27	10/10
9/21	9/26	10/6	10/16
9/28	10/6	10/15	11/6
9/28	10/5	10/22	11/5
10/7	10/10	11/7	11/20

10. Find a company (or other organization) that has a reputation for excellence in some aspect of project work. Benchmark their methods and determine how you can use the results to help your team improve.

11. Create a process improvement plan using the DMAIC model in Exhibit 4.9 to improve a project work process either for your own project or for another one.

INTEGRATED EXAMPLE PROJECTS
SUBURBAN HOMES CONSTRUCTION PROJECT

The project monitoring and controlling phase is where most of the resources are employed for project execution, and it is essential that the project execution happen strictly according to the project plan. Projects often experience changes during the execution because everything cannot be anticipated. However, Suburban Homes has an excellent track record of completing projects on time and within the budget and delivering its products to the customer's satisfaction.

With its plans to expand operations to other states, Suburban Homes is acutely aware of its inadequacies in new working environments and with new stakeholders. Specifically, it is more concerned with risk management, change management, quality expectations, and communication issues.

Suburban Homes has requested to review and modify its existing project management practices and processes. They want to use your comprehensive understanding of the importance of project baselines for scope, cost, and schedule. They also want to use your knowledge of project control, progress reports—including earned value analysis—the importance of communications, and change control. Specifically, you are requested to develop templates and checklists to do the following:

- Develop a communication (formal and informal) plan with details about frequency, intended receivers, and medium of communication

- Review and modify the change management plan
- Monitor risks and develop a risk response plan
- Revise the quality assurance plan and incorporate new quality control tools and techniques

---

CASA DE PAZ DEVELOPMENT PROJECT

As with many development projects managed in a largely agile fashion, Casa de Paz has proceeded in unexpected ways. The board voted to negotiate a one-year lease on the target building without a commitment to do substantial work on it. The negotiated agreement included an option to extend the lease for up to five years with a negotiated agreement on the amount of money spent on upgrades that Casa de Paz would pay and what the owner would pay. This allows for the further development of the community for the target population that Casa de Paz will ultimately serve, without sinking large amounts of cash into a building that may not be suitable. It means that Casa de Paz will continue with most other aspects of the project, including developments such as the following:

- Programs
- Strategic partnerships

- Community building
- Website
- Fundraising
- Volunteers

This approach lessens risk because large commitments are not being made until more people are engaged and more is understood. It also allows for further board and working group development so the people side of the infrastructure will be able to communicate effectively and handle the increased demands when the building opens. It also recognizes that the primary goal is to help abused Latina women and their children develop self-sufficiency. Meetings and outreach can serve many more families than the few who can be served more intensively through the residency program.

Semester Project Instructions

For your semester project, complete the following at a minimum:

1. Document the change requests and their disposition (if you have had any changes proposed to your project).
2. Identify any changes to your risk register with new risks added and/or old ones removed.
3. Show any quality tools you have used and explain how you interpret and act upon the results from them.
4. Show your progress updates on MS Project.

5. If you are tracking cost on your project, show the most current status of the 10 earned value management terms.
6. Create one key deliverable for your project. This should be one deliverable that your sponsor asked your team to create when you wrote the charter. Gather information regarding your process of creating the deliverable.
7. Describe trade-off issues on your project. These can include trade-offs between the needs of your sponsor's organization, the project, and your project

team. The trade-offs can also be within the project objectives and constraints of scope, quality, time, cost, other resources, and stakeholder satisfaction.

8. Show the information you have collected using the information retrieval and distribution system you set up (introduced in Chapter 6).

PROJECT MANAGEMENT *IN ACTION*

Controlling, Monitoring, and Reporting Projects at a Major Medical Center

The Emergency Medicine Division of Cincinnati Children's Hospital Medical Center typically has a large number of active quality improvement projects that require effective control, monitoring, and reporting. Division leadership aims for three levels of effective monitoring and control and reporting:

1. Team-level monitoring: Self-monitoring progress against process and outcome measures at daily, weekly, or monthly intervals.
2. Division-level monitoring: Main outcome and select process measures reported to division leaders who can then guide and support teams as needed.
3. Institutional-level monitoring: Main outcome measure progress followed and presented along with other projects to institutional leadership and other stakeholder groups.

An essential part of effective monitoring is the development of a well-defined aim. Each aim is associated with a primary outcome measure and is supported by process measures. For the division's strategic flow project, the primary aim was a reduction in the length of stay for patients and was supported by process measures representing specific intervals of this time, such as time from arrival in the department to being seen by a physician and time from being able to leave the department to actually leaving.

Team-Level Monitoring

Team-level monitoring functions in slightly different ways from those of the other two levels. On the ground, the feedback loop for evaluating tests needs to be nimble and timely. Rather than using a single outcome measure to gauge progress, teams utilize a number of process measures, the collection of which typically represents the main identified outcome measure of a given project. Process measures are tracked frequently as the teams conduct tests within the system and during the course of a project are often displayed in daily, weekly, and monthly formats. Ad hoc analysis supplements these measures, particularly for tests that are run for discrete periods of time.

At this level, changes are tested for short periods of time. Individual tests are evaluated using process measures; often, the daily variants of the measure or ad hoc analysis are employed, particularly in the first three to six months of a project or during intensive periods of testing. Teams meet weekly and discuss tests, adapting, adopting, or abandoning tests as they are evaluated. Weekly charts are used to minimize the noise of day-to-day variance, and teams monitor these over time. Monthly charts are used to view larger trends over time and are more important in months six through twelve as changes are implemented and systems experience this change for longer periods of time. An example measure used by a team is shown in Exhibit 14.27.

Division-Level Monitoring

Individual teams organize work into 90-day blocks for planning, execution, and reporting purposes. Teams formally report after each 90-day cycle to a group of senior leaders using a preestablished reporting template. Team presentations typically last 20 minutes and include data reporting in the form of annotated run charts for all key performance measures. Teams share special challenges and seek guidance on issues blocking progress. Teams also share goals, work plans, and predictions of key

EXHIBIT 14.27

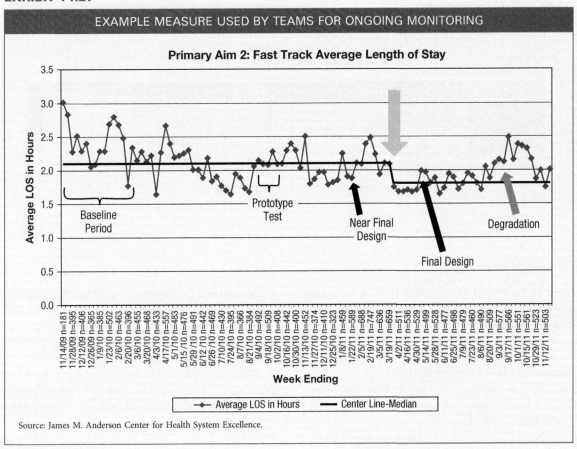

EXAMPLE MEASURE USED BY TEAMS FOR ONGOING MONITORING

Primary Aim 2: Fast Track Average Length of Stay

Baseline Period

Prototype Test

Near Final Design

Final Design

Degradation

Week Ending

→ Average LOS in Hours   — Center Line-Median

Source: James M. Anderson Center for Health System Excellence.

measure progress for the next 90-day cycle. A formal leadership letter follows each team presentation summarizing key discussion points and action items.

High-Level Reporting Structure and Management (Macro)

At the highest level, individual team progress is displayed on a department-wide dashboard. Aggregating each individual measure across all projects, this dashboard is designed to provide visibility to department leads, institutional stakeholders, and hospital leadership on the progress of projects. Historical data

for measures, along with current performance, yearly goals, and immediate past quarterly performance, are indicated. High-level trend lines are provided, and links to individual charts are embedded within the dashboard itself. A dashboard example is shown in Exhibit 14.28.

The intent of this dashboard is to provide hospital leadership with a high-level view of recent progress on individual projects. Reporting at this level occurs monthly to department leadership and three times a year to institutional leadership. Feedback from these groups is given to teams depending on progress.

EXHIBIT 14.28

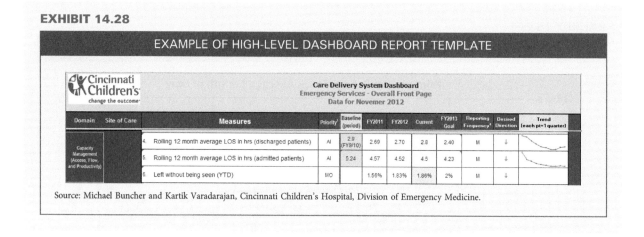

Source: Michael Buncher and Kartik Varadarajan, Cincinnati Children's Hospital, Division of Emergency Medicine.

References

A Guide to the Project Management Body of Knowledge (PMBOK® Guide), 6th ed. (Newtown Square, PA: Project Management Institute, 2017).

Anbari, Frank T., Earned Value Project Management Methods and Extensions, *Project Management Journal* 34 (4) (December 2003): 12–23.

Cerpa, Narciso, and June M. Verner, Why Did Your Project Fail? *Communications of the ACM* 52 (12) (December 2009): 130–134.

Devine, Kevin, Timothy J. Kloppenborg, and Priscilla O'Clock, Project Measurement and Success: A Balanced Scorecard Approach, *Journal of Health Care Finance* 36 (4) (2010): 38–50.

Evans, James R., and William M. Lindsay, *The Management and Control of Quality and Performance*, 10th ed. (Mason, OH: South-Western Cengage Learning, 2015).

Howard, Dale, and Gary Chefetz, *What's New Study Guide Microsoft Project 2010* (New York: Chefetz LLC dba MSProjectExperts, 2010).

Kloppenborg, Timothy J., Arthur Shriberg, and Jayashree Venkatraman, *Project Leadership* (Vienna, VA: Management Concepts, Inc., 2003).

Kloppenborg, Timothy J., and Joseph A. Petrick, *Managing Project Quality* (Vienna, VA: Management Concepts, Inc., 2002).

Meier, Steven R., Causal Inference of the Cost Overruns and Schedule Delays of Large-Scale U.S. Federal Defense and Intelligence Acquisition Programs, *Project Management Journal* 41 (1) (March 2010): 28–39.

Norie, James, and Derek H. T. Walker, A Balanced Score-card Approach to Project Management Leadership, *Project Management Journal* 35 (4) (December 2004): 47–56.

Office of the Assistant Secretary of Defense for Acquisition, http://www.acq.osd.mil/evm/, accessed April 28, 2017.

PM Study Circle: A PMP Exam Preparation Blog, https://pmstudycircle.com/2012/05/planned-value-pv-earned-value-ev-actual-cost-ac-analysis-in-project-cost-management-2/, accessed April 28, 2017.

Paquette, Paul, and Milan Frankl, *Agile Project Management for Business Transformation Success* (New York: Business Expert Press, 2016).

Rozenes, Shai, Gad Vitner, and Stuart Spraggett, Project Control: Literature Review, *Project Management Journal* 37 (4) (September 2006): 5–14.

Sharma, V. K., Earned Value Management: A Tool for Project Performance, *Advances in Management* 6 (5) (May 2003): 37–42.

Stewart, Wendy E., Balanced Scorecard for Projects, *Project Management Journal* 32 (1) (March 2001): 38–53.

Taylor, Hazel, Risk Management and Problem Resolution Strategies for IT Projects: Prescription and Practice, *Project Management Journal* 37 (5) (December 2006): 49–63.

Vanderjack, Brian, *The Agile Edge: Managing Projects Effectively Using Agile Scrum* (New York: Business Expert Press, 2015).

Yosua, David, Karen R. J. White, and Lydia Lavigne, Project Controls: How to Keep a Healthy Pulse on Your Projects, *PMI Global Congress Proceedings 2006*, Seattle, WA.

Endnotes

1. Adapted from http://www.merriam-webster.com/dictionary/determine and http://dictionary.reference.com/browse/determine?s=t, accessed May 18, 2013.
2. https://www.coursehero.com/file/pp9dfj/Quality-Control-is-the-ongoing-effort-to-maintain-the-integrity-of-a-Quality/, accessed May 24, 2017.
3. http://www.acq.osd.mil/evm/, accessed April 28, 2017.
4. https://pmstudycircle.com/2012/05/planned-value-pv-earned-value-ev-actual-cost-ac-analysis-in-project-cost-management-2/, accessed April 28, 2017.

CHAPTER 15

Finishing the Project and Realizing the Benefits

After completing this chapter, you should be able to:

CORE OBJECTIVES:

- Describe how to determine when a project should be terminated early and the process for terminating a project in normal completion time.
- Describe the importance of the project closing activities and how to perform them.
- Create and present a transition plan for the project, including a plan for ongoing support and sharing lessons learned.
- Capture and share project lessons learned.

BEHAVIORAL OBJECTIVES:

- Secure customer feedback and acceptance of the project.
- Assist senior management in managing talent and managing resources for upcoming projects.

TECHNICAL OBJECTIVES:

- Close your projects administratively using MS Project.

Lilyana Vynogradova/Shutterstock.com

After managing a number of projects to successful completion, it wasn't until I was overseeing a project in Trinidad and Tobago that I fully realized the importance of the project team celebrating its success.

Trinidad and Tobago is the southernmost Caribbean island, seven miles off the coast of Venezuela. The client company, Trinmar Limited, was formed as a joint venture between Texaco and Petrotrin, wholly owned by the government. Texaco had recently sold its equity share in Trinmar, leaving state-owned Petrotrin to produce 35,000 to 40,000 barrels of oil per day.

Many of the rigs Trinmar inherited were over 25 years old and declining in production. In addition to building a new organization and strategy, Trinmar faced the difficult decision of whether to upgrade the existing rigs or invest in building new rigs.

Our consulting team quickly identified over 80 potential projects. Working closely with the executive team, we were able to facilitate a portfolio optimization process to establish the strategic criteria and help Trinmar evaluate, prioritize, and make decisions regarding each project. The company invested in only a few new capital projects, while focusing on monthly well output and proactive preventative maintenance, resulting in an overall increase in production.

PMBOK® GUIDE

Topics:

- Validate scope
- Close project or phase

CHAPTER OUTPUTS

- Customer feedback
- Transition plan
- Closure documents
- Benefits analysis

Flying in from Miami to discuss the final steps of the project closing process, I was greeted at the airport by the company driver offering a gift bag. Inside was a polo shirt with a company logo and a card.

The day was spent in semiformal meetings with company executives and the portfolio team. We presented and discussed the culmination of customer reviews that had been conducted throughout the project—customer feedback, areas for improvement, lessons learned, project results, and approval of the final deliverables.

The evening had a much different tone, with live music, local delicacies, and drinks flowing freely. All company executives and their spouses were joined by everyone associated with the project. Several team members brought relatives, including cousins. Partway into the evening, the CEO stood and made an announcement, describing the project success and complimenting our partnership. He personally recognized everyone associated with the project. Each team member received an award of accomplishment and had their picture taken with the CEO Before he left, the CEO pulled me aside and said, "Mr. Miller, on behalf of our company and country, we sincerely thank you for hosting us with this generous celebration."

When I arrived back at the hotel early the next morning after settling the evening's bill, I saw the gift bag and finally opened the card. It read "Mr. Bruce Miller cordially invites you and your guest to join us in a celebration of our project success."

It was only later that I was sheepishly advised by one of my fellow consultants that he had offered to have our company sponsor the celebration and did not have the chance to tell me in advance. But the true impact of the celebration—reflected in the sincere joy and pride of the project team members as they received the sincere thanks of their CEO—had already proven the value of the event.

—Bruce Miller, PMP, managing partner, Xavier
Leadership Center, Xavier University

Projects are often started with great enthusiasm. They serve as vehicles to accomplish important organizational objectives. Many things happen during the course of a project that may impact its success. Regardless of the level of success achieved by the project, going out on a strong note is good for everyone involved.

When purchasing a new home, buyers and a builder's representative do a "walkthrough" to inspect the finished product and discuss mechanical functions and features of the home.

Project completion is either pleasant and predictable or unpleasant and unexpected. In the first case, the project team successfully meets project goals. In the second case, reasons could be different: performance is inadequate, the project deliverable may no longer be needed, or project constraints such as time or cost prevent the team from completing the project.

Blend Images/Superstock

A project moves into the closing stage when its customers validate that the scope is complete and accept the project deliverables. A project can close as planned or be terminated early. In either event, closing activities include securing customer feedback and approval, planning and conducting a smooth transition of project deliverables to a client or into ongoing operations, capturing and sharing lessons learned, performing administrative closure, celebrating success, and providing ongoing support.

15-1 Validate Scope

Validate scope is formally accepting the completed project deliverables. Stakeholders validate that scope is complete with interim deliverables throughout the project and with final deliverables near the end. When the stakeholders formally accept the final project deliverables, the project completes the executing stage and proceeds into the closing and realizing stages. To illustrate, imagine you have contracted with a construction company to build a new home. Before you close on the house, you want to make sure the house has been properly finished and a certification of occupancy is obtained. Therefore, the common practice is to have a "walk-through," where as a customer you literally walk through the house with a representative from the building company. The representative points out features and describes how things work. You try light switches, look at the finish, and consider all of the things you wanted (and agreed to pay for) in the house. Often, a few little things are not yet finished, and these can form a "punch list" of items to complete. The **punch list** is the list of "work items that are identified during a final inspection that need to be completed."

If the punch list is small enough, as a customer you agree to formally take possession of the house subject to the contractor finishing the punch list items. Once you formally agree the work is complete and agree to take possession, the house becomes an accepted deliverable.

However, if there are major concerns and/or a long punch list, you may decide not to formally accept the house until certain things are complete. Most projects are like this: The customer only formally accepts the deliverables once he or she is convinced they will work as planned. At that point, the buyer provides the seller with a formal written acceptance, and the project transitions from the executing stage to the closing stage.

Project managers need to ensure that all work on their project has been successfully completed. They can refer to the charter, scope statement, WBS, schedule, and all communications plans to verify that everything they committed to do is actually done. Many organizations also use project closeout checklists that itemize typical project activities and/or deliverables. These can be used to assign responsibility to each item concerning project closeout. An example of a project closeout checklist is shown in Exhibit 15.1.

15-2 Terminate Projects Early

Ideally, all projects continue until successful conclusion, with all deliverables meeting specifications and pleasing customers. However, this is not always the case. Sometimes, a project is terminated before its normal completion. Early termination can be the result of mutual agreement between the contractor and buyer, because one of the parties has defaulted (for cause), or for convenience of the buyer.

MUTUAL AGREEMENTS On some projects, by closeout, not all of the deliverables are completed. Remaining deliverables need to be integrated into another project, stopped altogether, or continued as a lesser project or a further phase of the finishing project. If both parties agree to stop the project before its planned completion, a negotiated settlement may take place. If some of the deliverables or documentation is not completed, the project manager may need to negotiate with the customer. Perhaps the customer would rather have most of the capability now rather than all of it later. The project team may have made a larger-than-expected breakthrough in one area and can negotiate with the customer to deliver more in that area and less in another. Ideally, both parties agree what deliverables or partial deliverables go to the buyer and what compensation goes to the seller, and any outstanding issues are resolved. If agreement cannot be reached by direct negotiations, either courts or alternative dispute resolution can be used to reach a settlement. Perhaps it is in all parties' best interest to finish the project as is and part as friends.

TERMINATIONS FOR DEFAULT Terminations for default occur for projects executed externally and often result from a problem with the project's cost, schedule, or performance. A buyer can also decide to terminate a project early because he or she has lost confidence in the contractor who is performing the project. Good project management practices consistently applied throughout the project can lessen the chance of early termination for cause by managing stakeholder expectations and by delivering what customers want on spec, on time, and on budget.

TERMINATIONS FOR CONVENIENCE OF BUYER Projects can also be cancelled for the convenience of the buyer. This can happen through no fault of the contractor. Sometimes, the buyer faces unexpected difficulties or changing priorities. If a customer's needs change, it might decide that the resources assigned to a project could be more profitably applied to a different project. If a customer decides to terminate a project for

EXHIBIT 15.1

EXAMPLE PROJECT CLOSEOUT CHECKLIST			

Project Name: Closeout Date:

Project Team:

Project Manager:
Sponsor:

Item	Who	Target Date	Completion Date
Final Certificate of Occupancy			
Punch List Complete			
Notice of Punch List Completion			
Certificate of Substantial Completion			
Utilities Transferred to Owner			
Notice to Owner on Insurance			
Facility Manual			
As-Built Drawings			
Attach Job Files to Database			
Update Projects Database			
Final Retainage Billing			
Release of Subcontractor Retainage			
Complete Subcontractor Evaluations			
Team Close-Out Meeting			
Send Out Owner Survey			
Bond Release			
Estimating Feedback Cost Report			

Approved for Closeout:

_____   _____   _____

Project Manager   Sponsor   Vice President–Construction

convenience, it invokes a contract clause. This clause normally stipulates that the contractor is reimbursed for the money it has spent up to that point and the customer takes ownership of the deliverables in whatever form they currently exist. Internal projects can also be terminated if organizational priorities change.

Project managers can pursue two avenues to possibly head off early termination. First, a project manager who has been serious about managing stakeholder relationships may be able to find other stakeholders in the customer organization or elsewhere who can provide some funds to keep the project viable—even if the scope has to be reduced. Second, the project manager can look internally to find ways of continuing with the project, but at lower cost.

Project managers serve as the strongest advocates for their projects throughout the project's life. Considering that most projects face many challenges, this unwavering support is often critical to project success. However, when a project is no longer needed or no longer viable, project managers owe honest and timely communication to their parent organization. Project managers need to present the facts of project progress and make recommendations for early termination if they feel it is warranted.

If a decision is made to terminate a project early, the project manager is obligated to communicate this decision to his or her team quickly and honestly. Let the team know as soon as possible and tell them exactly why the decision was made. Care must be taken to ensure that no unjust blame is placed on anyone. It is absolutely unethical to have reputations and careers suffer for a termination in which the impacted party was not at fault. Once a decision is made and communicated to terminate a project early, much of the remaining work is similar to that of a project that is completed as planned.

15-3 Close Project

As stated in Chapter 1, closing a project entails finalizing all activities needed to finish the project. The remainder of this chapter details what a project team does when finishing a project on time. Customers are asked both to accept the project deliverables and to provide feedback. Lessons learned are captured and shared. Contracts are closed. Participants are reassigned and rewarded. Reports are created and archived. Success is celebrated, and the project team ensures that customers receive the ongoing support they need to successfully use the project deliverables.

A few key challenges arise at the end of projects. One is to keep the right workers engaged until project completion. Some of the final activities are administrative. Often, new projects are starting up that are more exciting and cause distraction.

15-3a Write Transition Plan

A project manager may decide to create a **transition plan** to help the customer to use the project deliverables successfully. Project transition plans are a sort of instruction manual on how the customer should use the project deliverables once the project team has completed its work.

The reason a project is performed is that some person or organization needs the resulting deliverables. Some project deliverables are created by one group and turned over to another group. Sometimes the group performing the project also uses the results or deliverables. In either case, a transition plan can ensure that all responsibilities are considered and all deliverables—whether complete or not—are handed over with appropriate documentation to the people who will use them. If any activities remain incomplete when the deliverables are transitioned, they should be itemized, and responsibility for each should be clearly identified. For example, if a home buyer wanted to close on a house before everything is complete, a punch list of remaining items would be determined, and the contractor would agree to complete them. A transition plan helps to ensure the following:

- Quality problems are avoided during the transition.
- The project deliverables transition into their service or operational role.
- The needed maintenance, upgrades, and training take place.

15-3b Knowledge Management

The fourth area identified in using the balanced scorecard approach to controlling and improving projects is growth and innovation. While the portion of this pertaining to team development is covered in Chapter 5, the portion concerning knowledge management is covered here. Knowledge management should occur throughout the project life, but it may become most apparent as a project comes to an end. Project customers, whether internal or external to a company, can provide valuable feedback concerning both the project process and results. Ask them what they think! Exhibit 15.2 is a simple form for asking project customers for their opinions.

CAPTURE LESSONS LEARNED　**Lessons learned** are the useful knowledge gained by project team members as they perform a project and then reflect on both the process of

EXHIBIT 15.2

PROJECT CUSTOMER FEEDBACK FORM

Customer: _____　　　Date: _____

Rating　　Importance (Rank order 1= most important)

1. How would you rate the quality of our deliverables?
   1 Poor　Avg.　5 Excellent

2. How well did we control schedule?
   1 Poor　Avg.　5 Excellent

3. How well did we control budget?
   1 Poor　Avg.　5 Excellent

4. How would you rate stakeholder relationships?
   1 Poor　Avg.　5 Excellent

5. How effective were our communications?
   1 Poor　Avg.　5 Excellent

6. Overall, how would you rate your satisfaction?
   1 Poor　Avg.　5 Excellent

7. How can we improve?　_____

doing the work and the results that transpired. Lessons can include what worked well that the project team members think should be copied and/or adapted for use on future work. Lessons can also include areas for which a different method may yield better results. Furthermore, information about mistakes and what went wrong should be captured to avoid repeating them again. The project meeting Plus-Delta evaluation template shown in Exhibit 6.14 is an example of capturing lessons learned at the end of a project meeting. Lessons can also be captured at milestones and at the end of a project. On long-duration projects, it is often better to capture lessons frequently because people may not remember clearly what happened months previously. Therefore, the best project managers capture lessons learned early and often. A project manager may wish to capture lessons learned first from the core project team and then from all of the stakeholders.

The first step in capturing end-of-the-project lessons learned is for the project manager to send an e-mail asking the participants to identify major project issues. Then, the actual meeting begins with each participant writing his or her top issues on a flip chart or other workspace where everyone can see them. Once all participants have listed their top issues, the entire group can vote on the top five (or perhaps top ten on a large project). Then the project manager can go through one top issue at a time by asking leading questions to determine what went wrong and how it might be avoided in future projects.

Likewise, the participants can list significant successes on the project and discuss factors that contributed to each. They can then ask what practices can be used to re-create similar successes on future projects.

Some organizations use a standard form for capturing project lessons learned, such as the one shown in Exhibit 15.3.

DISSEMINATE AND USE LESSONS LEARNED   The process of capturing and discussing lessons learned is valuable learning for the participants. However, for the remainder of the organization to capitalize on those lessons, a method must be established for documenting and sharing the lessons. More organizations effectively collect lessons learned than effectively disseminate and use them. One problem is deciding how to store the lessons so all workers in a company can easily access them. Some companies have created databases, shared folders, or wikis for this purpose. Many companies that do a good job with lessons learned have one person assigned to "own" and be responsible for designing and maintaining the lessons-learned database. Every project team that collects lessons then sends the new lessons to this "owner," who compares the new lessons with existing lessons and decides whether to modify, combine, or add the lessons and to possibly remove an old lesson. Thus, the database only grows when unique and useful new lessons are added. Another idea some companies use is to have the person who submitted each lesson list her cell phone number and e-mail so another person considering the lesson can contact her to ask questions. This is especially helpful because it is hard to document all tacit knowledge, and even if a person did so, the lessons would be so long, many people would not take the time to read them.

Coding each lesson by factors such as the type of project, stage in project life cycle or project phase, issue it concerns, and project knowledge area helps future project teams when they search for new lessons to apply. Many organizations find that it is helpful to have a limited number of categories and have each lesson stored according to the category in which it is best suited. The ten *PMBOK® Guide* knowledge areas can be a useful starting point when determining useful categories. Exhibit 15.4 shows thirteen categories used by a company along with two or three lessons in each category.

Another problem is that most people are busy and do not seek lessons learned just for fun. One way to overcome this is for sponsors to sign charters only if lessons from other recently completed projects are included. That forces project teams to consider what lessons they can use.

EXHIBIT 15.3

LESSONS-LEARNED PROJECT CLOSING DOCUMENT

PROJECT CLOSING DOCUMENT:

Project Number:
Closing Date:

As your project comes to a close, please capture continuous improvements, lessons learned and issues to consider for future projects. Please focus on the positive aspects that would help other teams in the future and you would like to see done again (+) and on things that could be changed/improved upon in the future (Δ). These learnings will be entered into a database for future reference to help all associates.

Criteria	Plan	Actual	Learnings (+/Δ)
Outcome • Future state achieved? • Success measure (attach graph/data)			
Schedule • Milestones • Completion			
Cost (Cap Ex)			
Hours required: • Project Manager • Sponsor • Core team members • SMEs			

Risks and Countermeasures	
Anticipated	**Unanticipated**

Communication Plan Implementation	
What worked well (+)	**What did not work (Δ)**

Other Learnings	
What worked well (+)	**What did not work (Δ)**

Source: Elaine Gravatte, D. D. Williamson.

Another effective way to transfer lessons is to assign roles to people. One person in the organization can serve as process owner with responsibility to continue to improve that particular work process regardless of what project it is performed on. Also, every project team member can have an additional role as improvement team member.

One of the challenges in using lessons-learned information is that most people are busy. One way to overcome this issue is for sponsors to sign the project charter only if lessons

EXHIBIT 15.4

LESSONS-LEARNED EXAMPLE	
ACCOUNTABILITY:	Use formal accountability and measurement systems down to the individual performance level.
	Ensure all team members have clearly defined roles and responsibilities.
BUY-IN AND COMMITMENT:	It is helpful when directors attend project meetings.
	Be sure sponsor secures buy-in from other executives.
	Involve people with decision-making authority early in the project.
COMMUNICATION:	Develop and follow a communications management plan to develop trust.
	Communication about change needs to be ongoing.
	Communication needs to be early and ongoing with all key audiences and stakeholders.
COMPLEXITY:	Many projects are multifaceted and involve numerous trade-offs that need to be managed.
	Project manager should attend some client meetings and sponsor should attend some team meetings to ensure integration.
CULTURE AND CHANGE:	Lean concepts challenge the organization's culture for data collection and transparency.
	Commitment to transparency and change is needed prior to project initiation.
	Educating leaders in change management strategies helps them deal with resistance.
EXPECTATIONS:	Set and state clear expectations.
	Define and stay within scope.
	Manage expectations of sponsor, stakeholders, customers, and project team.
MEETINGS:	Team members will be prepared with previous meeting minutes, agenda, and project updates.
	End a meeting with clear action items and due dates for each team member.
	Plan meetings in advance to make them more efficient.
PLANNING:	Have well-defined roles and responsibilities.
	Scale planning at the appropriate level of detail.
	Expect many revisions.
PROCESS IMPROVEMENT:	Always discuss what we could have done better.
	Keep working to sustain results on completed projects.
	Investigate feedback provided to assure it is understood and utilized as appropriate.
PROJECT TEAM:	Listen to and respect input from all team members.
	Let each team member be responsible for setting his or her own timetable to the extent possible.
	Determine in advance how project team will make decisions.
SCOPE:	Define success early.
	Be specific about scope.
	Manage scope creep.
SPONSOR SUPPORT:	Sponsors and other leaders need to publicly endorse the project and remove barriers.
	Speak candidly and informally to your sponsor in addition to formal reports.
	Obtain sponsor's signature on charter before proceeding.
STAKEHOLDERS:	Invite key stakeholders to specific meetings.
	Be sensitive to the political climate within your client's organization.
	Be open to constructive criticism and other input from stakeholders.

from other recently completed projects are considered and relevant aspects are included. Some lessons learned are more effectively transferred by informal means such as conversations, unscheduled meetings, or having a project team member also serve as a team member on another project. An organization that seriously uses a lessons-learned process makes continual improvements in its project management processes and develops an organizational learning culture. The best lessons learned are only of value if they are used!

Closure of a project entails ensuring that all work has been accomplished, all resources have been reassigned, and all documentation is complete. The project manager and team can review the project charter, WBS, and schedule to make sure that everything that was promised was delivered. They can review the issues log and risk register to ensure all items on both of them have been addressed. They can review the communications plan to check that all documentation was created. The customer feedback and scope verification should also be reviewed to verify that the customers thought everything was accomplished.

However, closure activities can take place during the project execution as well. Many of the quality assurance activities fall in that category. Also, the project team can review the communications plan to check that all documentation was created and used as mandated, which brings a closure to the project communication plan.

15-3c Create the Closeout Report

Many organizations have formal procedures for closeout reports and archiving project records. The **closeout report** usually includes a summary status of the project that can be gleaned from progress reports. The closeout report also normally includes lessons learned. Finally, the closeout report often contains a review of the project's original justification. Did the project accomplish what it was originally approved to do? This is an important question because many projects change along the line. The exact timing, costs, and deliverables may have changed, but did the project still accomplish its goals? Finally, the project manager needs to ensure that the records are in a workable format and stored in a manner that will allow others in the organization easy access for lessons learned, financial audits, or other uses.

Organizations often create templates for closeout reports such as the one in Exhibit 15.5. See the Project Management in Action feature at the end of this chapter for more ideas on how to effectively capture, share, and use lessons learned.

EXHIBIT 15.5

CLOSEOUT REPORT TEMPLATE			
This deliverable, required for each small project, contains the project charter, the original work breakdown structure, summary of weekly progress reports, and client feedback summary.			

PROJECT SUMMARY REPORT FOR PROJECT _____			
TASK OR ITEM DESCRIPTION	SATISFACTORY	UNSATISFACTORY	COMMENTS
A. Project charter updated and included			
B. Original WBS included			
C. Weekly progress report summary included			
D. Client feedback summary included			

Knowledge management is hugely important on agile projects. At the end of every two- to four-week iteration, a ceremony (meeting) called a retrospective is held to determine what worked well and what can be improved with an eye toward improving the current project, not just future projects. As with many organizations, if asked what worked well and what did not, many team members initially do not have much to offer. Therefore, many scrum masters (project managers) will use gimmicks and jokes to liven the mood and truly get team members to share and even joke about what happened. That way, not only do good ideas surface but because most team members discussed them, there also is widespread buy-in.

15-4 Post-Project Activities

15-4a Reassign Workers

Project managers owe the members of their team timely updates for their personnel records, honest recommendations, help securing their next assignments, and rapid notification of any issues. Wise project managers know it is not only ethical to treat their members well, but if a project manager also develops a reputation for taking good care of team members, it becomes much easier to recruit team members for future projects. Helping good workers secure follow-on work is one of the most important things a project manager must do near the end of a project. Many of these workers will be eager to work again for that project manager and will share their good experience with others in the organization.

It is important to understand aspirations and recognize individual strengths of all the project team members to recommend future project assignments. Ideally, it would be immensely beneficial for organizations when individual aspirations and professional goals are aligned with project objectives. The project manager plays an important role in advising senior management and support in meeting this issue of strategic importance.

15-4b Celebrate Success and Reward Participants

The successful conclusion of a project should be celebrated for many reasons. Perhaps one way to understand the many reasons is to utilize a play on the very word *celebrate*:

Challenge

Energize

Limit

Exert

Believe

Recognize

Acknowledge

Transition

Ease Stress

When people are reminded of their recent accomplishments, they realize they just met a large **challenge** and are motivated to undertake new challenges. The team members are frequently **energized** to finish the last few administrative chores so they can move on to another project. By recognizing their accomplishments, they are now ready to say "the project is over; we will **limit** any additional work on this project." The team members exert themselves to finish the last few items. Celebrations can persuade members to believe they can do just a bit more than they might otherwise think is possible.

racom/Shutterstock.com

Celebrations are excellent times to **recognize** and **acknowledge** both effort and results. Celebrations mark **transition** points as people leave one project and move on to another. Finally, celebrations of success **ease** the stress of working hard for a prolonged period of time trying to accomplish a project.

When a primary project deliverable is quite visible, such as a new building, celebrating right at the project site makes sense. People feel success partly just by observing the deliverable. When the project deliverables are less visible, project managers can still create ceremonial deliverables to demonstrate the project results. Project managers may be able to use specially packaged software, oversized checks, posters of thanks from customers, or other creative means of visualizing project results.

15-4c Provide Ongoing Support

Ultimately, a project manager should ensure that customers can effectively use the project deliverables. This may include providing ongoing support in the forms of training, change management, and/or other services. A transition plan can guide this support. Project managers aim to create useful project deliverables on time and on budget. They want to turn those deliverables over to capable, satisfied customers who will directly provide more project work in the future and who will enthusiastically tell others how pleased they are.

15-4d Ensure Project Benefits Are Realized

Many organizations insist that project managers follow up with customers weeks or months after the project deliverables are in use. One of the most important measures of project success is how well the customers can use the project deliverables. When considering the full impact of the project results, project managers are encouraged to consider use by direct customers and other stakeholders (people), and also how the results contribute to the other parts of the triple bottom line—profit for the parent company and sustainability of the planet.

15-5 Using MS Project for Project Closure

15-5a Creating Project Progress Reports

As your project executes and eventually enters into the closing phase, there are likely to be multiple occasions where you must generate project reports to share with stakeholders. Often, organizations have existing templates, web portals, or other specific methods they want used to report project data. If not, you can quickly create customized or prebuilt (canned) reports within MS Project to share with project stakeholders. Using the simplified Suburban Park Homes project from Chapter 14, the following will demonstrate how to create a canned project report. However, you can easily create these reports with any MS Project file.

CREATE A CUSTOMIZABLE CANNED REPORT   Although the **Report Tab** gives the project manager the option to create a new report from scratch (**Report Tab>>View Reports Group>>New Report**), it also contains a variety of canned reports from which to choose, including Resources, Costs, and In-Progress reports. There are also several Dashboard style reports that provide overviews of the project, for example, the "Project Overview" in Exhibit 15.6 and "Cost Overview" in Exhibit 15.7. The variety of canned reports, and the ability to customize them once generated, greatly reduces the need for the project manager to struggle with creating a new report from scratch. To create a Project Overview report like the one in Exhibit 15.6, do the following:

1. Click the **Report Tab>>View Reports Group>>Dashboards>>Project Overview**

Once generated, the elements of the report can be manipulated and customized. Element position can be changed by clicking and dragging to different areas of the report, and fonts, colors, shading, and effects can be altered by double-clicking elements to open

EXHIBIT 15.6

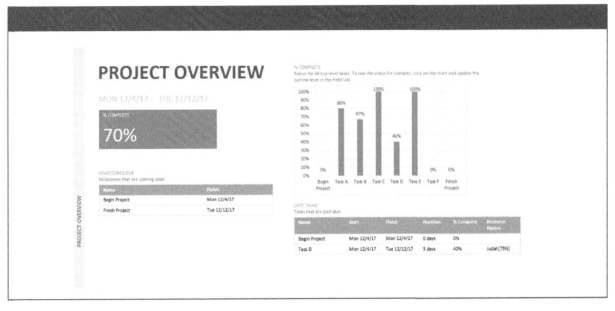

EXHIBIT 15.7

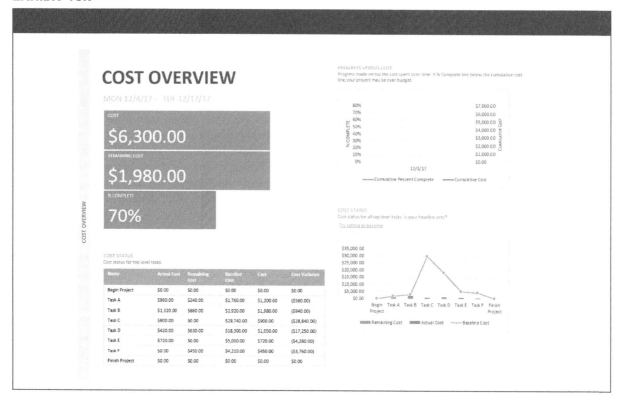

formatting panels. In addition, images from a file can be added to the report if desired. Formatting techniques and image insertion follow the same conventions as other Microsoft Office applications. Many of the controls for formatting can also be accessed from the **Design Tab** once the report is active on-screen.

SHARING REPORTS   Once the report is formatted to your specification, it can be printed or saved as a PDF and published to e-mail, a web portal, or other location. MS Project has native support for sharing to e-mail or MS SharePoint in the **File>>Share** menu options, as seen in Exhibit 15.8.

EXPORT A REPORT TO MS EXCEL   MS Project can also export a variety of reports to MS Excel. The following steps will create a customizable report, as seen in Exhibit 15.9:

1. Click the **Report Tab>>Export Group >>Visual Reports**
2. Click the **Resource Summary Tab**>> select **Resource Remaining Work Report**
3. Click **View**
4. The report will build and then open in MS Excel (where is can be customized and distributed)
5. Click **Close** to close the Visual Reports dialog (Exhibit 15.10) in MS Project

15-5b Archiving Project Work

Just as software such as MS Project can be useful in planning, managing, and reporting on a project, it also can be useful when closing out a project and leveraging the benefits

EXHIBIT 15.8

EXHIBIT 15.9

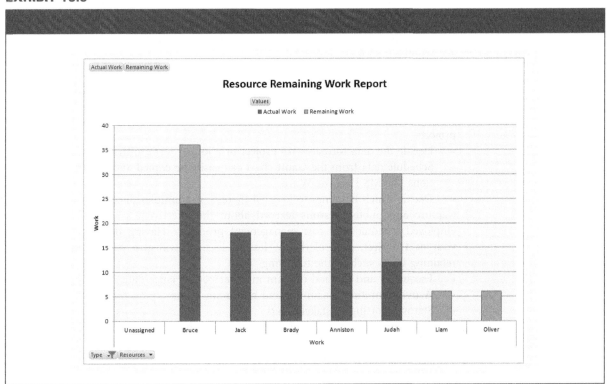

EXHIBIT 15.10

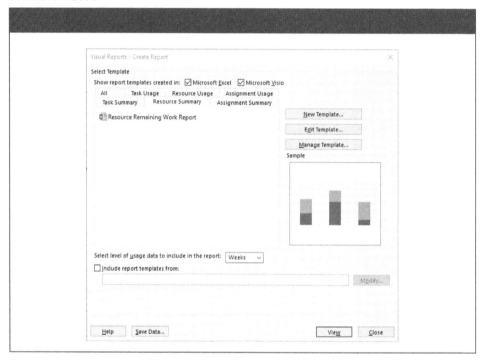

for future projects. Specifically, it is helpful to complete and archive the schedule and to capture lessons learned from to the scheduling process:

1. Complete the schedule to maximize its future usefulness. This includes the following:
   • Applying performance data
   • Applying approved changes
   • Ensuring all activities are complete
2. Archive the schedule for use as a template or "starter" file. A good way to start a new project, particularly if it is similar in nature, is to reference or build from the last project:
   • Decide the data format—MS Project or a longer-term format.
   • Schedule data from the Gantt chart can easily be copied and pasted into applications like MS Excel or Word.
   • Decide which baselines to keep (if there were multiples due to changes).
3. Capture and publish lessons learned about the effectiveness and efficiency of the employed schedule and cost management processes. Having this data as you start your next project, particularly the lessons learned, will give you an edge. Consider retaining items such as the following:
   • Frequency and method of team member performance data collection
   • Activity duration maximum and minimum limits
   • Status reporting to stakeholders
   • Communication technologies employed and their effectiveness
   • Schedule and cost estimate accuracy
   • Max Units value—maximum availability of a resource for work
   • WBS structure

PMP/CAPM Study Ideas

Fewer than 10 percent of the PMP test questions concern the Closing Process Group. That said, there are no formulas and only a handful of processes associated with closing, so you should do well if you can remember a few important things.

First, be sure that you are studying from the most current (6th) edition, since there have been substantial changes made within the Closing Process Group. Most notably, there used to be a *Close Procurements* process, but it has been removed in the *PMBOK*'s 6th edition, and its activities have been reassigned to either *Control Procurements* or *Close Project or Phase*. In other words, all closing activities—whether contractual, administrative, or other—now fall under the *Close Project or Phase* process.

Second, PMI likes to stress knowledge management, so remember the importance of capturing, storing, and disseminating lessons learned (this can and should happen throughout the project but is especially important at a project's end). This needs to take place whether or not the project reaches a successful conclusion.

Third, *Close Project or Phase* is the very last step of a project. It cannot be completed until *everything else* has taken place. *Close Project or Phase* is also known as the Administrative Close, since it involves gathering and storing lessons learned, writing reports, and updating project documents. Whether or not a project reaches a successful conclusion, recognize that the project manager often has limited authority and that the sponsor should be involved in the *Close Project*.

Summary

Hopefully, most projects will be successfully completed. However, some projects are terminated early either because the customer is dissatisfied or wishes to invest their time and money in a different way. Regardless of whether a project was terminated early or on time, a variety of closeout procedures are required. All activities must be completed, money paid and accounted for, documentation completed and distributed, workers reassigned and rewarded, *lessons learned* recorded, and success celebrated. A project manager would like to end a project with team members eager to work for her again and satisfied customers who will either hire the project manager again or direct other potential customers her way by their enthusiastic singing of her praises.

Key Terms Consistent with PMI Standards and Guides

validate scope, 500
punch list, 501
transition plan, 503

lessons learned, 504
closure of a project, 508
closeout report, 508

Chapter Review Questions

1. When does a project move into the closing stage?
2. What is *validate scope*?
3. What is the purpose of a "punch list"?
4. What should a project manager refer back to in order to make sure that all planned work has, in fact, been completed?
5. Under what conditions can a project be terminated early?
6. If both parties agree to stop the project before its planned completion but cannot reach an agreement via direct negotiation, what can be done?
7. Terminations for default often result from a problem with the project's _____, _____, or _____.
8. When might a contract clause be invoked?
9. During project closing, customers are asked both to accept the project deliverables and to _____.

10. What should be done with any activities that remain incomplete at the time of project closure?

11. What is the first step in capturing lessons learned at the end of a project?

12. How is a project transition plan similar to an instruction manual?

13. What does a typical closeout report include?

14. How can Microsoft Project be useful during the closing stage of a project?

Discussion Questions

1. Give two examples of why a project might be terminated early for cause and two examples of why a project might be terminated early for convenience.

2. How can a project manager help to prevent a project from being terminated early?

3. If an early termination of his project seems likely, what two avenues can a project manager explore to increase the likelihood of being able to continue the project?

4. A project manager is in the finishing stage of her project. It is apparent that one of the project's deliverables will not be completed before the project is wrapped up. What options does the project manager have for this uncompleted deliverable?

5. Provide an example of how poor escalation of a project problem can create additional problems.

6. How does celebrating the completion of a project benefit the project manager?

7. Why is it important to go through the process of closing, even for projects that are terminated early?

8. Why is it important as a project manager to help your team members secure follow-up work toward the end of your project?

9. Imagine you are creating a lessons-learned database for a recent project you have completed. What would you list as your top issues? Your top successes?

10. The sponsor of a large multiphased project you are managing suddenly decides to terminate the project early. How do you respond? How and when do you notify your team members?

PMBOK® Guide Questions

1. The process of meeting with customers and/or key stakeholders to formalize acceptance of completed project deliverables is called _____.
   a. validate scope
   b. control scope
   c. close procurements
   d. manage stakeholders

2. During which project management process would a company auditor verify that all contracts have been completed and all required purchasing standards and methodologies have been followed for the project?
   a. Validate scope
   b. Close contracts
   c. Close project or phase
   d. Conduct procurements

3. Terminations for _____ often result from a problem with the project's cost, schedule, or performance.
   a. convenience
   b. completion

   c. default
   d. confidence

4. At the end of the project or phase, lessons learned are finalized and transferred to the company knowledge base for future use. These lessons learned can include all of the following *except*:
   a. project issues log
   b. individual performance reviews
   c. project risk register
   d. which techniques did and did not work well

5. If the buyer decides to terminate a project early, his or her responsibilities to the contractor are laid out in the project's _____.
   a. work breakdown structure (WBS)
   b. communications plan
   c. scope statement
   d. procurement agreement

6. During the "close project or phase" process, the team and project manager may wish to review the _____.
   a. project charter
   b. WBS

c. risk register

d. all of the above

7. What key input is required before a project or project phase can move to the closing stage?
   a. Accepted deliverables
   b. Change Requests
   c. Updated Issues Log
   d. Work Performance Reviews

8. The new management team at a large company has reevaluated ongoing initiatives and has identified new goals and objectives for the year. They direct that all contracts in progress be terminated immediately. This is an example of _____.
   a. management by objectives
   b. termination for cause

c. termination for convenience

d. termination by consensus

9. What serves as an instruction manual in order to help the customer use the project deliverables as intended?
   a. lessons-learned database
   b. transition plan
   c. executed work contract
   d. issues log

10. Contracts can be terminated early for any of the following reasons *except*:
    a. default
    b. mutual agreement
    c. convenience of buyer
    d. convenience of seller

Exercise

1. Utilizing the ideas in Exhibits 15.1 and 15.3, create a project closeout checklist for a project of one of the following types:

   • Information systems

   • Research and development
   • Quality improvement
   • Organizational change

INTEGRATED EXAMPLE PROJECTS
SUBURBAN HOMES CONSTRUCTION PROJECT

The closeout phase is often assigned less importance because project-executing organizations are in a hurry to assign resources to new projects as quickly as possible while the project is still in the closing phase. The construction industry is no different. As soon as the construction work is complete, the resources are assigned to new projects and the closeout phase is often managed by only a few people responsible for tying up any loose ends. This is often the source of customer dissatisfaction.

Project closeout consists of two important activities. First, it is about formalizing acceptance of the project or phase and bringing it to an orderly end, and second, closing the contract after ensuring its completion and then settlement of the contract.

Suburban Homes realizes that there is a scope to improve its existing closeout processes and practices for both scheduled completion and unexpected termination of projects. The existing closeout process includes the following:

• Take stock of entire project.
• Tie up loose ends.

• Write the final report.
• Ensure that documentation is in good order.
• Account for and reassign resources.
• Meet with customers to ensure their needs are addressed
• Prepare for the handover with warranty documentation.

To improve customer satisfaction, Suburban Homes is planning to redefine its closeout process. Adam Smith has requested that you develop a checklist for closing the project. The closeout process must address the following:

• Improve morale and a sense of achievement for the project team.
• Enhance customer satisfaction.
• Close the contract properly to avoid future legal implications.
• Provide Suburban Homes with a detailed project cost.
• Capture lessons learned for easy retrieval and use them to improve the performance of future projects.

CASA DE PAZ DEVELOPMENT PROJECT

Since the primary Casa de Paz project vision is to enable Latinas and their children to be able to live independently and achieve success in work and school, it is critical for those women to take a very active role in running Casa de Paz.

What would you include in the transition plan to help them be successful? How would you capture lessons learned? Who would you share these lessons with? (*Hint:* Think about the partnerships developed in this project.)

Semester Project Instructions

For your example project, complete the following:

1. Capture customer feedback concerning your project using the questions from Exhibit 15.2 or other questions of your choice.
2. Capture lessons learned from your project to date using the questions from Exhibit 15.2 or other questions of your choice. Show how you will use these lessons both to improve the remainder of your

project and for the next project on which you may work. Organize the lessons into categories such as *PMBOK* knowledge areas, ideas from Exhibit 15.4, or your own ideas.
3. Create a transition plan so that the recipients of your project deliverables will be capable and enthusiastic users. Secure client acceptance of your project.

PROJECT MANAGEMENT *IN ACTION*

The Power of Lessons Learned

Projects are discrete. They have a beginning and an end, at which time the project team disbands and moves on to other things. Despite the fact there has inevitably been significant tacit learning during the project, there is often only a limited capture of this into a sharable form for future reuse. Too often, as the project team dissolves, the learning fades into the memories of individuals' minds. This makes it extremely difficult for others to benefit in the future from the insights learned. The usual excuses for this loss echoing through the corridors include "just too hard," "not enough time," "team disbanded before we had the chance," and many more. The key error here is the incorrect assumption that learning during or from projects is an "added bonus" or a "nice-to-have luxury." This is not the case in best practice environments.

Those fortunate enough to work on a well-led project will have observed how learning is just part of how we work together. Experienced and

knowledgeable project leaders understand the value in capturing **lessons learned**, as an embedded part of normal daily activities. They engage the team to deliberately harness knowledge and highlight lessons throughout the project to provide insights and enhance performance (during the project and beyond). The value of doing this greatly outweighs the costs of implementation when it is done well and there is a culture of trust and collaboration. This capture of learning at each stage builds the capabilities of those involved and can form a knowledge base to be used by the team or by others in future stages and future projects. In some cases, this knowledge base remains only in the heads of those involved because there is no attempt to capture it in explicit form. This is a mistake because it is difficult to transfer this knowledge beyond the immediate team (although it can be to some extent if there is a culture of story-telling and low staff turnover).

There are many barriers to developing an effective lessons-learned knowledge base, and culture is often

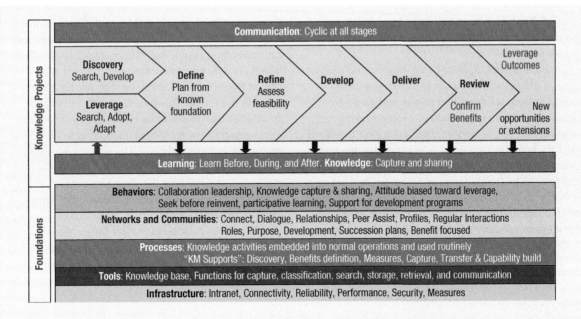

the primary villain. If people involved in the project are not reflective and not willing to invest a little time to capture and share their insights, the lessons are not captured. Equally, culture influences the motivation to look at what has been learned through the discovery process *before* the project starts.

Good projects start with more questions than answers:

Has this been done before?

Did it work? I so, why? If not, why?

What has changed since the last time? (Something that did not work before might now—*if* the context is different.)

If we did it the same, would it still work, or do we need to adapt it?

These questions can be effectively answered only *if* there is some access to what was learned previously and those seeking answers can find it in a convenient and trusted way. This is why talking to someone you know and trust, who was actually involved in the prior project, is always the preferred option. However, in modern organizations, this is becoming increasingly difficult to achieve because of challenges such as high use of contracted team members, high employee mobility, regular restructures, incomplete records in lessons-learned systems (which may be poorly

designed), and the fast change of supporting technologies. So what other good options exist?

Some organizations (including NASA and the U.S. military) have developed quite sophisticated lessons-learned databases. These are usually supported by processes that require people to submit comments into the project systems that will help other people in the future. Over time, these *"what we know"*–based systems build a large volume of data that can be interrogated to provide relevant insights when you need them (hopefully proactively to avert a potential risk becoming an issue, rather than reactively when the issue has occurred). These systems work best when people make it part of their normal work activities to record *both* errors and their solutions as well as what went right and why. Insights of both types are essential to ongoing success. The danger of rigid processes and systems is that people do not see the value in recording something that they believe is for the benefit of unknown others in the future and will not help them (but costs them precious time). So they either just don't do it, or they record only very basic, nonspecific information that will not be particularly helpful for someone in a future context. Some organizations have a "stick" approach and link recording of quality lessons learned to performance reviews or project sign-offs. Others take a "carrot" approach and reward those who record effective lessons learned as judged by other people who found and applied the lessons.

Another approach used by an international project management organization is to combine a content-based system (as described above) and an understanding of *"who knows what."* People seeking insights can ring a "service desk" with their questions and the (experienced) employee answering the phone discusses what it is they need to find out. The service person can be from a range of backgrounds, such as a librarian, a semiretired employee with a long history of the organization's projects, a specialist, or a nominated representative of an internal group such as a technical committee or community of practice.

Sometimes these people will know the answer, but if they do not, they can find a person or document that can guide the seeker. This PM organization records all questions asked and the relevant resources that helped the seeker in a database that can be interrogated in the future. This hybrid of tacit and explicit knowledge was found to be highly effective for fast discovery of ideas. It enabled good ideas to be quickly applied elsewhere and helped to prevent reinvention of ideas already developed in other parts of the organization. It also enabled the discovery process at the beginning of projects to reduce repeating of errors from earlier experiences.

"Successful people learn from Their mistakes AND the mistakes of OTHERS." —Sir John Templeton

Source: Arthur Shelley, http://www.organizationalzoo.com/about/arthur_shelley.

References

A *Guide to the Project Management Body of Knowledge (PMBOK® Guide)*, 6th ed. (Newtown Square, PA: Project Management Institute, 2017).

Barclay, Corlane, Knowledge Management Practices in IT Projects: An Exploratory Assessment of the State of Affairs in the Caribbean, *Proceedings, Project Management Institute Research and Education Conference 2010.*

Carrillo, Patricia, et al., Knowledge Discovery from Post-project Reviews, *Construction Management and Economics* 29 (July 2011): 713–723.

Construction Extension to the PMBOK® Guide (Newtown Square, PA: Project Management Institute, 2016.

Chroneer, Diana, and Fredrik Backlund, A Holistic View on Learning in Project-Based Organizations, *Project Management Journal* 46 (3) (June/July 2015): 61–74.

Daft, Richard L., *Management*, 9th ed. (Mason, OH: South-Western Cengage Learning, 2010).

Dobson, Michael S., and Ted Leemann, *Creative Project Management* (New York: McGraw-Hill Company, 2010).

Kloppenborg, Timothy J., and Joseph A. Petrick, *Managing Project Quality* (Vienna, VA: Management Concepts, Inc., 2002).

Kloppenborg, Timothy J., Arthur Shriberg, and Jayashree Venkatraman, Project Leadership (Vienna, VA: Management Concepts, Inc., 2003).

Knutson, Joan, Transition Plans, *PMNetwork* 18 (4) (April 2004): 64.

Lussier, Robert N., and Christopher F. Achua, *Leadership: Theory, Application, Skill Development*, 4th. ed. (Mason, OH: South-Western Cengage Learning, 2010).

Meyer, Werner G., Early Termination of Failing Projects: Literature Review and Research Framework, *Proceedings, Project Management Institute Research and Education Conference 2012*, Limerick, Ireland.

Milosevic, Dragan Z., *Project Management Toolbox: Tools and Techniques for the Practicing Project Manager* (Hoboken, NJ: John Wiley & Sons, 2003).

Pritchard, Carl L., Project Termination: The Good, the Bad and the Ugly, in David I. Cleland, ed., *Field Guide to Project Management*, 2nd ed. (Hoboken, NJ: John Wiley & Sons, 2004), 503–520.

Reich, Blaize Horner, Andrew Gemino, and Chris Sauer, Modeling the Knowledge Perspective of IT Projects, *Project Management Journal* 39 (2) (2008): S4–S14.

Wang, Xiaojin, and Lonnie Pacelli, Pull the Plug, *PMNetwork* 20 (6) (June 2006): 38–44.

Whitten, Neil, Celebrate, *PMNetwork* 19 (8) (August 2005): 21.

Wiewiora, Anna, et al., Uncovering the Impact of Organizational Culture Types on the Willingness to Share Knowledge Between Projects, *Proceedings, Project Management Institute Research and Education Conference 2012*, Limerick, Ireland.

Wiewiora, Anna, Liang Chen, and Bambang Trigunarsyah, Inter- and Intra-Project Knowledge Transfer: Analysis of Knowledge Transfer Techniques, *Proceedings, Project Management Institute Research and Education Conference 2010*, Washington, DC.

Endnotes

1. *Construction Extension to the PMBOK®* Guide 221.

2. Dobson, Michael S., and Ted Leemann, *Creative Project Management* (New York: McGraw-Hill Company, 2010), 216.

3. Chroneer, Diana and Fredrik Backlund, "A Holistic View on Learning in Project-Based Organizations", *Project Management Journal* 46 (3) (June/July 2015): 70.

PMP and CAPM Exam Prep Suggestions

Introduction

The Project Management Professional (PMP) and Certified Associate in Project Management (CAPM) are globally recognized professional certifications administered by the leading global project management professional group—Project Management Institute (PMI). CAPM is appropriate for an undergraduate with limited work experience, and PMP is appropriate for either a nontraditional undergraduate or an MBA with three or more years of full-time project management experience or its equivalent. Both test detailed knowledge of the *Guide to the Project Management Body of Knowledge, Sixth Edition (PMBOK® Guide 6e).*

Study Aids in *Contemporary Project Management, Fourth Edition (CPM4e)*

Several features of this text have been designed to help you study for and pass the CAPM and PMP exams. These features include the following:

- Inside front cover spreadsheet showing **PMBOK® Guide 6e** *knowledge areas, process groups, and processes*
- Partial flowchart of **PMBOK ® Guide 6e** *processes and major outputs (color coded by process group) and flows covered in each chapter at start of chapter*
- Lists of **PMBOK® Guide 6e** *processes and major outputs covered in each chapter at start of chapter*
- All terms defined in chapters consistent with both **PMBOK® Guide 6e** *and the latest versions of 15 more in-depth PMI standards, practice guides, and extensions to the* **PMBOK® Guide 6e**
- Chapter-specific study suggestions at the end of each chapter
- Ten practice questions at the end of each chapter
- Glossary of terms consistent with **PMBOK® Guide 6e** *and PMI standards, practice guides, and extensions*

- Detailed color-coded flowchart of all **PMBOK® Guide 6e** *processes with major outputs and most common flows depicting work and information*

General Guidance

You need to read through the *PMBOK® Guide 6e* very carefully—every single page. Look up words you do not know because some questions are vocabulary and the correct answers are from the *PMBOK® Guide* Glossary.

Put a Post-it note on page 61 of the *PMBOK® Guide*. The inside front cover of **Contemporary Project Management, Fourth Edition (CPM4e)** shows the exact pages in which each PMBOK process is covered. It is a map mirroring page 61 of the *PMBOK® Guide 6e*. Every time you study a new process, note carefully what process group and knowledge area it falls in. As you study each process, note the inputs, tools and techniques, and outputs. Many of the questions are scenario questions that deal with timing (what would you do first in a situation?). Since the output of one process is often the input to another process, noting inputs and outputs will help you identify what goes first or last.

We encourage you to use *CPM 4e* in conjunction with the *PMBOK® Guide 6e*. The *PMBOK® Guide* is the "what" of project management (essentially a 700-page encyclopedia of project management) and *CPM* is the "how" with examples. For many people, the explanation of "how" along with examples make it much easier to remember all the detailed "what" that will be tested. Few people are good at memorizing encyclopedias.

Detailed suggestions of how to understand the *PMBOK® Guide 6e* material that is covered in each chapter of *CPM 4e* is briefly described at the end of each chapter. Right after those suggestions, ten example questions, typical of those seen on the actual exams, are given on the chapter material with the answers, rationale, and page references in the instructor's manual. This appendix offers general suggestions for study that you can combine with the chapter-by-chapter suggestions to form a comprehensive study plan.

Many people find it useful to go through the *PMBOK® Guide* one chapter at a time, very carefully comparing the "what" from the *PMBOK® Guide* to the "how "with examples from *CPM*. We encourage you to make sure you understand each chapter well before you continue, but go fairly quickly so you do not forget the first chapters by the time you take the exam. The first two chapters are the project management framework. They correspond to the first three chapters in *CPM*.

Always answer questions according to the PMI standard process, not the way you would necessarily do it in your industry or the way an emotional appeal suggests. If one answer is a general category and other answers are specific examples, often the correct answer is the more general one. Choose the answer that is most correct most of the time, not one that is sometimes correct in certain circumstances.

PMBOK® Guide 6e is the latest update on the body of knowledge that began with leading project manager thought leaders expressing a need for some sort of standard over 30 years ago. During most of the intervening time, most project management was conducted in a plan-driven mode, meaning one planned the project and then managed it closely, including tight change-control procedures. In recent years, a growing number of projects are being managed in an agile fashion. *PMBOK® Guide 6e* calls this adaptive project management—where one plans at a high level only at the start and then in more detail as work progresses. While *PMBOK® Guide 6e* recognizes agile or adaptive projects, most of the *PMBOK® Guide 6e* structure and most of the exam questions still reflect a plan-driven approach. The primary exception to this occurs in section 1.2.5 Tailoring, of the *PMBOK® Guide 6e,* where advice is given on how to determine how much plan-driven and how much adaptive methodology should be used for a given project situation.

Test Format

There are ten knowledge areas and five process groups in the *PMBOK® Guide 6e,* with a total of 49 individual processes. Know these well!

We suggest you either make a note sheet or flash cards to study each process. You will not be able to bring a note sheet to the exam, but you can study it right up to the moment you begin the exam. You will be given paper for notes and you may write as many formulas as you can remember before you start with

the questions. Many people write down formulas they have a hard time memorizing so they can study them just before the exam starts.

At any place in the *PMBOK® Guide* where you find a list of three, the question might ask which of the following is *not.* … Therefore, when studying inputs, tools, and techniques, or outputs of a particular process, try to remember anytime there is a list of three items.

If a question is long, read the last sentence first. That is the question and the rest is the background.

All questions are multiple choice with four possible answers. Answer all questions because the only thing that is scored is correct answers. When in doubt—guess instead of leaving it blank. For each question, you can answer it and move on, answer it and mark it to return, or not answer it. We suggest that you never return to the questions you feel confident enough to answer without marking. You have four hours for the PMP and three hours for the CAPM. In both cases, it should be more than enough time. You are allowed to go to a restroom, but the clock keeps going.

PMBOK® Guide

All ten knowledge areas include at least one planning process in the planning process group. Several include one managing process in the executing group, and all include at least one process in the monitoring and controlling process group. Make sure you understand the subtle differences between the monitoring and controlling processes in groups that include both. The key to understanding the difference is there are some things the project manager can directly control, but there are plenty of other things the project manager can only influence.

Many processes occur in parallel with other processes and/or are repetitive. However, some processes clearly occur before others. Know the order! The partial flowcharts at the start of each chapter and the comprehensive flowchart in the inside back cover help one to visualize the order.

Most knowledge areas include quite a bit of vocabulary. You not only want to remember the official *PMBOK® Guide* definition but also what each really means when it is applied. *CPM* helps with the application. All definitions in the *CPM* glossary are either taken directly from a PMI guide, standard, or extension or are written in plain terms consistent with the intent of the definition in the PMI document that we thought was more difficult to understand directly.

Several knowledge areas refer to audits. In this context, an audit is meant to improve the way work is performed. Following are a few specific suggestions for each knowledge area.

The *PMBOK® Guide* often uses the term *register* for a repository of information. For example, the stakeholder register is the recorded information about project stakeholders—who they are, what they want, how they are prioritized, and so forth. Risks are recorded in a risk register in a similar fashion. The repository for issues, on the other hand, is called an *issue log*. In yet another repository example, requirements are often stored in a requirements traceability matrix. In each case, think of these repositories as living documents that change with project progress and additional information. Know the types of information that each may include.

Project Integration Management

Integration describes how decisions in one aspect of a project often impact another area, such as when a change is proposed, it may impact cost, schedule (time), and scope. In fact, if a question deals with one of those three items (such as cost), the correct answer may include the other two. One way to consider integration is to imagine a very large project in which different people plan portions and integration is used to make sure the entire plan makes sense. The last integration process—closing the project—ends with capturing lessons learned. Develop project charter is the integration process that occurs during initiating. Chapter 3 of *CPM* is all about writing and approving the charter.

The first process overall is Develop Project Charter, and the last process overall is Close Project or Phase—both are integration processes. Capturing lessons learned and archiving or distributing them are both part of an executing process called manage project knowledge and last activity (Close Project or Phase) to be performed as part of project closure.

There may be multiple questions on the project management plan. This is the umbrella plan with many subsidiary plans such as budget and schedule. You can note two-headed arrows between the process of developing the project management plan and planning all of the subsidiary portions of the plan. You will also note arrows from developing the project management plan into many of the executing processes. A plan is baselined at the end of planning when all parties agree on the scope, schedule, and budget. Any changes after that time should go through an integrated change control process. Of course, if using agile, the overall scope is only confirmed at a high level and the scope for a given iteration is confirmed just prior to the start of that iteration. Change is greatly resisted within an iteration.

Project Scope Management

Scope is defined by what is and what is not included in the project. Product scope is the features and functions of the project deliverables (products, services, or results). Project scope is the work performed to deliver the product, service, or result with the specific features and functions.

A work breakdown structure (WBS) is like the outline of the project. It includes all of the project deliverables, including interim and detailed deliverables—everything that needs to be produced. It does *not* include the work activities needed to create those deliverables. Defining activities is considered a schedule management process. The work package is the lowest level on the WBS.

Scope, time, and cost are all highly interrelated. All have multiple planning processes and one monitoring and controlling process. If a question contains two of the three knowledge areas of scope, schedule, and cost, the answer very well may be the third one.

Project Schedule Management

Rolling wave planning is a form of progressive elaboration in which the near term is planned in great detail, while the latter parts of the project are planned in a much more general fashion with intent to plan them more carefully when the time draws nearer. Agile is a form of rolling wave planning that is gaining popularity. Agile notes are included in many sections of this book.

Be able to schedule using activity on node (AON) (also called precedence diagramming method or PDM). Also know how to use alternative dependencies of SS, FF, and SF and lead and lag. Know the difference between free float (no other activity is impacted) and total float (the entire project is not impacted, but the next activity in line is). Be able to compute the critical path using the two-pass method so you can answer questions regarding float. Also be able to compute the enumeration method so you can more quickly answer what-if questions, such as what will happen if an activity now takes five days instead of eight.

Crashing speeds up the schedule by performing certain critical path activities faster than normal, but it usually costs more money. Fast tracking speeds up the schedule by performing activities concurrently that are normally performed in sequence. This often adds risk to the project.

Resource optimization techniques include resource leveling and resource smoothing. Know the difference! Resource leveling postpones certain noncritical activities so a resource is not overloaded, but this often requires more time to complete the project. Resource smoothing also reduces the demand for overloaded resources, but not beyond the point where the project schedule would need to be lengthened.

Network diagrams, Gantt (bar) charts, and milestone schedules are all approved means of showing project schedules.

Project Cost Management

Know how to construct a time-phased, bottom-up project budget and the difference between various means of estimating costs and needed reserves, as shown on *CPM* page 335–337. Know how to calculate earned value and the definitions of all of the terms on *CPM* pages 477–480. Be prepared that you may see questions that ask you to calculate estimates to complete in different ways depending on whether the work to date is deemed to be representative of future work or not. Know common financial terms such as those in *CPM*, Exhibits 2.8 and 10.1.

Project Quality Management

Manage quality is a forward-looking, executing process and gives stakeholders confidence the project team can do the work correctly. It is proactive and includes management systems and audits to ensure people are working correctly. Control quality, a monitoring and controlling process, is technically looking at deliverables and asking if they pass specific standards. It looks backward to determine if the outputs are good enough. Both manage quality and control quality are needed. In addition to what is in the *PMBOK® Guide*, know the quality tools on pages 469–474 of *CPM* and the quality control terms on pages 405–408 of *CPM*. The project manager has ultimate responsibility for quality (and almost everything else). In addition, each person has primary responsibility for their own work. Prevention keeps errors out of the process, while inspection keeps errors away from the customer.

Project Resources Management

All of Chapter 5 in *CPM* and parts of Chapter 9 apply to Project Resources Management. There are multiple lists in this knowledge area, so try to understand the differences between items dealing with topics such as teams, power, conflict, and negotiation, as shown in the exhibits in *CPM*.

Know the differences among functional, matrix, and projectized forms of organization. A simple summary is on *CPM* page 107. Make sure you understand the differences between various roles, as described in Chapter 4 of *CPM*. While roles can be shown on an organizational chart or described in a document as text, they are often also shown in a matrix. A matrix may be called a RAM or RACI. Know the stage of team development, such as on *CPM* page 143. Scenario questions are often used to distinguish stages. Know forms of power, as shown on page 157 of *CPM* and conflict resolution, as shown on page 164 of *CPM*.

Project Communications Management

According to PMI, project managers spend about 90 percent of their time on communication in one way or another. Know how to calculate the number of communication channels based upon the formula channels = $(n^2 - n)/2$, when n is the number of people on a team. Authorization to perform work is always a formal communication, but it need not be written. Communication can be more complex in a matrix organization. A war room is a single location where the project team can keep their stuff and use it for any purpose. Exhibit 14.6 in *CPM* is an easy visual to help understand performance reporting.

Project Risk Management

The purpose of project risk management is to reduce the risk to a level acceptable to decision makers. It is *not* to eliminate all risks. Consider both positive risk (opportunity) and negative risk (threat). The most risks occur at the start of the project life cycle, but each risk costs the most money if identified late in the life cycle after decisions are already in place. In charters, risks are identified, qualitative analysis is performed by asking the probability and impact of each, and response planning is conducted for major risks. Qualitative analysis is performed on every project. If that is not enough, quantitative analysis is also performed. All risk management processes occur throughout the project life cycle.

Project Procurement Management

Procurement in the sixth edition of the *PMBOK® Guide* includes only three processes of plan, conduct, and control procurements. Understand contracts, both in general and each specific type. Understand the differences between various procurement documents. The RFI is *not* used to solicit an offer, while the others are. Sole source is when only one vendor is available, but single source is when a decision is made to select a specific vendor.

Project Stakeholder Management

The *PMBOK® Guide* process of identify stakeholders includes identifying each potential stakeholder, determining what interest each has in the project, and prioritizing the long list of stakeholders so more attention can be paid to the most powerful and important stakeholders. This occurs very early as part of the initiating process group. Most projects have multiple stakeholders with conflicting desires, and the increased focus created by establishing stakeholder management as a distinct process group reflects this.

Ethics

Know the code of Ethics and Professional Responsibility very well! There are more questions per page on this short document than on any other topic. You may download this document from http://www.pmi.org/about/ethics/code for free. It has aspirational standards as ideal goals and mandatory standards as bare minimums in the four areas of responsibility, respect, fairness, and honesty.

Ending Suggestions

Do not underestimate either the CAPM or the PMP exam! The first-time pass rate typically is between 50 and 70 percent and that includes many people who have taken exam-prep courses. However, we have taught many of these prep courses and many of our students have successfully passed both exams using these suggestions. We are repeatedly told that by comparing the "what" from *PMBOK® Guide* with the "how" and examples from this book (*Contemporary Project Management*), people felt very well prepared. Good luck and let us know how you did!

Timothy J. Kloppenborg, PMP, PhD,
kloppenborgt@xavier.edu

Vittal Anantatmula, PMP, PdD,
vittal@email.wcu.edu

Kathryn N. Wells, PMP, MEd,
katenoelwells@gmail.com

Agile Differences Covered

The points listed in this appendix are described in more depth in the chapters indicated. Some represent methods and behaviors that are completely different on Agile projects; others are methods and behaviors that are emphasized more or in a different manner on Agile projects. Many behaviors emphasized in Agile also can help traditional project managers. Many of these points have far-reaching impacts, but they are listed here in the order of their first appearance.

Chapter 1: Introduction to Project Management

The Agile Manifesto stresses four values:

- Value individuals more than processes.
- Value working software more than documentation.
- Value customer collaboration more than negotiation.
- Value response to change over following a plan.

- Adaptive or change-driven project life cycle
- In a given iteration, resources (including cost) and schedule are considered fixed and what can vary is value to the customer.
- Most of the same work still needs to be accomplished in organizations using Agile. Different people perform some of the work.
- Agile emphasizes empowering teams.
- Some work is performed later in a project with Agile because requirements and scope emerge gradually.
- Collaborative effort and communication specifically with the client are common features.
- The most essential role is the customer representative—sometimes called the product owner.
- The customer representative does much of what a sponsor might in traditional projects.
- There may also be a designated sponsor (sometimes known as a product manager).
- A portfolio team often performs much of the work of a traditional steering team.
- The scrum master serves and leads in a facilitating and collaborative manner.

- This is a more limited, yet more empowering role than the traditional project manager.
- Many organizations using Agile also have a coach—acting as a facilitator and trainer.
- The team members in Agile projects are assigned full time as much as possible.
- The teams are self-governing.
- Teams are often small and co-located and they work closely together.

Chapter 3: Chartering Projects

- Something of value will be delivered at each iteration.
- An agreement is reached during iteration planning on the "definition of done."
- This is comparable to deliverables with acceptance criteria for each milestone.
- The first iteration is planned as a milestone with acceptance criteria.
- Subsequent milestones and acceptance criteria are determined just in time (JIT).
- Ensure common understanding of success criteria and value.
- Determine minimum acceptable output to fulfill project vision and have a working output.
- Project vision is developed and shared early.
- Establish a shared vision.
- Align project and team goals through vision sharing.

Chapter 4: Organizational Capability: Structure, Culture, and Roles

- Practice servant leadership acting as guides and coaches.
- Give teams the environment and support they need to be self-organizing.
- Organizational culture needs to foster cooperation among many stakeholders and at many levels.
- Transparency must be valued within the organizational culture.

- Create a feeling of safety and allow quick failure with constructive feedback.
- Used in information systems and some other projects; allows for incremental plans and benefits.
- These approaches have been variously called iterative, incremental, adaptive, or change-driven.
- While *Agile* is the umbrella name, some of the specific approaches are called *SCRUM, XP, Crystal, EVO, phased delivery, rapid prototyping,* and *evolutionary.*
- While these models may start like other project life cycle models, they provide short bursts of planning and delivery of benefits in multiple increments during project execution.
- Agile is a form of adaptive or change-driven project management largely reacting to what has happened in the early stages of a project rather than planning everything in detail from the start.
- Documentation is minimal early in the project but becomes progressively more complete.
- A project vision is developed and shared early.
- Project teams plan in short bursts (generally of one to four weeks), often called sprints or iterations.
- The details are planned for the upcoming iteration and very little change is allowed during it.
- Products are defined and delivered one iteration at a time with an output that has business value successfully finished in each iteration.
- The mindset is empowering, engaging, and openly communicating.
- If the scope is hard to define early in the project and/or when much change is expected, an Agile approach often works better.
- The Agile mindset includes four key ideas:
  1. Satisfy the customer by placing emphasis on outputs that fulfill their needs.
  2. Engage all participants through empowerment, cooperation, and knowledge sharing.
  3. Facilitate that engagement through servant leadership and visible and continual communication.
  4. Keep things simple with a sustainable pace or cadence and emphasis on process improvement.
- All Agile roles are more collaborative than confrontational.
- The scrum master facilitates and removes obstacles.
- The teams are self-governing, so the team now accomplishes many of the planning and coordinating activities a project manager would typically perform.
- Often the first iteration is used to determine the product to be built and prioritize the most valuable work for the next iteration.

- Agile projects use four types of meetings (often called ceremonies):
  1. **Iteration planning meetings** have the product owner share the highest value-added output he or she would like the team to work on next, along with a definition of what is "done." The project team commits to how much work they can do in the iteration.
  2. **Daily stand-up meetings** are often held for 15 minutes early in the morning, and each team member shares the previous day's accomplishments, the plans for the current day, and any issues.
  3. **Demonstration meetings** are held at least once per iteration where the team demonstrates usable product.
  4. **Retrospective meetings** are held at the end of each iteration where the project team, scrum master, product owner, and possibly other key stakeholders openly share what worked well and what could work better.
- **Experienced and motivated team members** are needed.
- A key stakeholder, often called the **product owner or customer, needs to commit** to frequent and detailed meetings.
- **Trust** between the client and contractor (or user and developer) is needed because the details of the requirements and scope are initially unknown.

Chapter 5: Leading and Managing Project Teams

- Agile teams are often described as being self-managed, focused on project goals, strong communicators, able to decide quickly, more responsible, and willing to trust their instincts once they understand their sponsor.
- Build teams around motivated individuals.
- Agile project teams typically employ co-located teams to manage rapid changes and increments. Seven desirable habits of Agile teams are:
  1. Question everything.
  2. Associate with innovation.
  3. Fail your way to success.
  4. Communicate thoughts and ideas.
  5. Deliver value frequently.
  6. Change incrementally.
  7. Connect with your purpose.

- The Agile project team members are also responsible to check for deviations regularly and should be capable of detecting aspects that violate the specifications.
- The best solutions arise from self-organizing teams.
- Trust teams to get things done.
- Teams cooperatively devise ground rules.
- Co-locate teams and/or use collaborative tools.
- Discover team and individual motivators.
- Reduce distractions.
- Team members break down barriers and become experts on the product they are creating.
- Team members must develop a sense of ownership of the product and commitment to the team.
- All team members act as leaders when needed.
- Team members resolve issues.
- Promote knowledge sharing.

Chapter 6: Stakeholder Analysis and Communication Planning

- Relationships with stakeholders are based upon collaboration, communication, and trust.
- Client interaction needs to be continuous throughout the project life cycle.
- Stakeholders need to be educated about their roles, alerted in advance concerning changes, and request early and continuous feedback.
- The highest priority is to satisfy the customer through early and continuous delivery of valuable product.
- Change is harnessed to the customer's competitive advantage.
- Face-to-face communication is used when possible, with visualization.
- Solicit stakeholder feedback early and often.
- Form working agreements.
- Design for customer to evaluate deliverables and receive feedback from users.
- The emphasis needs to be on effective rather than efficient communication.
- Conflict must be facilitated, not ignored.

Chapter 7: Scope Planning

- Agile focuses more on the product than the process—even when the customer does not know what they want.
- The documentation in Agile of the requirement is normally much less formal.
- Agile leverages the progressive elaboration mindset.

- The Product Owner is the interface to the product stakeholders and is responsible for aligning stakeholders to priorities and capabilities.
- Agile focuses on delivering value to the customer quickly, so feedback can get to the development team quickly.
- Agile assumes that the people doing the work know how to do the work.
- At every iteration, the delivered product should be able to be used.
- The goal is not to be right; it is to get feedback.
- There is only the judgment of how well the product works.
- The customer ideally would not get involved in how the product is created.
- Creating a model or prototype on many kinds of projects other than software is analogous to Agile delivering working software every few weeks to get feedback.
- The requirements are captured in a product backlog.
- The product manager prioritizes them on an ongoing basis.
- They are delivered in short iterations and reviewed with the stakeholders on a normal cadence.
- Smaller iterations are used to get feedback.
- The team is challenged with conflicting aspirations between finalizing the scope specifications and maintaining flexibility.
- Scope at the outset is not clear to either the project team or the client and is described only at a high level.
- The project team must demonstrate greater adaptability to frequently changing scope and employ iterative or phased planning of scope.
- Scope definition starts with large chunks of work.
- Large features will be broken down into stories and prioritized later.
- The team creates "personas," which are fictional people who represent user types.
- User stories define scope and functionality.
- Acceptance tests will also be agreed upon during the scope definition phase by describing the way project deliverables will be tested and how they should prove workable.
- The customer representative prioritizes the scope based upon business need, value, cost, and risk.
- The team commits to the amount of work they can perform in the first iteration.
- Determine the minimum acceptable number of product features by asking what are the three to

five most important things needed for our customer to use our deliverables.

- Embrace changing requirements, even late in the process.
- Reprioritize as conditions change.
- Engage an empowered business stakeholder.
- Prioritize collaboratively.

Chapter 8: Scheduling Projects

- Ceremonies like sprint retrospectives naturally become milestones in the project schedule, on cadences familiar to the folks doing the work.
- Schedules are created by first considering the product backlog to be accomplished.
- The overall project schedule may initially be developed only at a high level.
- Within an iteration, the team will consider how much uncertainty and complexity exist in the outputs they plan to create.
- The number of team members as resources is often the primary limitation to the schedule, but logical order may also be considered.
- Typically, the product owner and the team agree on what work will be completed in an iteration.
- The team then identifies all of the work activities for that iteration.
- The team commits to the body of work for the iteration, without having the how worked out in detail yet.
- Sequencing is performed at a high level for the entire project or for the product release (often three to six months).
- Then, for each iteration, the team develops the sequence by which the detailed activities of that sequence need to be completed.
- Duration estimates improve with each iteration and as early iterations are completed.
- Teams can use velocity of progress to estimate how much work will be accomplished in each iteration.

Chapter 9: Resourcing Projects

- Agile techniques are often used when the client does not fully understand their needs at the project start, a rapid rate of scope change will probably occur on the project, and/or multiple short deliveries are possible.
- The client and project team can collaborate to reduce the impact of interdependency of activities.

- Schedules are limited to the amount of work the assigned resources can handle.
- The team of workers assigned to an Agile project should remain on the project for at least each iteration, and preferably for the entire duration.
- An Agile team is a cross-functional team with general expertise that puts them together on a long-term basis.
- The budget is set at the people level and then the product is produced at the pace the team can produce.
- Team composition is done at a high level.
- People are assigned to a long-running team and they figure out how to get the work done.
- The team members on an Agile project decide among themselves who will do each work activity.
- Team members pick up the next-highest-priority story when they finish what they have been working on.
- Resource overloads are not a serious problem in Agile since the team is cross functional and the team commits to get the work done in the iteration. They self-manage the conflicts.
- If a team member needs help, he will ask; if he needs to learn, he learns.
- The fundamental ideas behind Agile project planning are to use a collaborative approach with the project team and other stakeholders heavily involved in planning.
- Teams recognize that while it may be difficult to scope the entire project at the outset, stakeholders do want to have a ballpark idea of total cost, schedule, and functionality before approving a project.
- While uncontrolled change is bad, too strenuous change control often means valid emergent stakeholder wishes are not met.

Chapter 10: Budgeting Projects

- Teams may use rolling wave planning to estimate costs.
- They create a definitive estimate for the first iteration of the project (and commit to it) and an order of magnitude estimate for the remainder of the project.
- As the work on the first iteration nears an end, the team then creates a definitive estimate for the second iteration and reevaluates the order of magnitude estimate for the remainder of the project.
- Dummy tasks are often used to summarize the work for future project iterations that have not yet

been defined. Since the number of workers is often known and the length of the iteration is known, the amount of cost can usually be established.

Chapter 11: Project Risk Planning

- Agile projects develop early risk planning, assessment, and response planning at a high level.
- More detailed and timely risk management occurs in planning each subsequent iteration, in daily stand-up meetings, and in retrospectives at the end of each iteration.
- Development process risks relate to functionality and short and focused iterations.
- Business process risks are due to higher ambiguity and uncertainty that compel us to focus on the short-term result and long-term haziness.
- The product owner must remain closely involved throughout the project. This focus can reduce risk because many details are handled as they arise.
- Since something of value needs to be delivered at each iteration with a test to confirm it works, risks tend to be uncovered quickly, before they become large.

Chapter 12: Project Quality Planning and Project Kickoff

- Quality is planned at a high level for the entire project at the outset and at a detailed level just before the start of each iteration.
- Agile builds upon established technical approaches with an increased emphasis on human behavior.
- Advice given on Agile projects is to communicate often (maybe daily) with the owner and other stakeholders.
- On Agile projects, a definition of done is explicitly stated. This includes acceptance criteria of features; agreement of what done is for each iteration, and a demonstration to prove the deliverables work.
- Teams use retrospectives to improve both methods and quality.
- Identifying dependencies and need for coordination helps reduce potential quality problems.
- The better a team is able to plan a sustainable pace and cadence, the better is the quality that should emerge.

- Teams plan for continuous improvement and reflection rather than optimizing a process.
- On Agile projects, the overall plan for the project (called the release plan) is only at a high level, while the detailed plans for each iteration are baselined right before each iteration starts.

Chapter 13: Project Supply Chain Management

- Customer collaboration is preferable to contract negotiation.
- Everyone must work together regularly throughout the process.
- Encourage collaboration.

Chapter 14: Determining Project Progress and Results

- Self-directed teams are largely empowered to decide what work to do and when to do it, consistent with the prioritizing of deliverables by the product owner.
- Change is expected, and the only part that is planned in detail at the outset is the first iteration.
- Subsequent iterations are planned in a rolling wave fashion.
- Within an iteration, there is great reluctance to change.
- Risk is reduced due to frequent and specific communication, demonstration of working product at each iteration, and use of a visible, monitored, prioritized risk list.
- Simple directional indicators updated frequently guide project teams.
- Progress report meetings as stated above are held every morning as brief (15 minutes) stand-up meetings.
- Each team member discusses yesterday as the past time period and today as the current time period.
- Documentation becomes more complete.
- Working product is the primary measure of progress.
- Agile projects often use a burndown chart to show the amount of work remaining.
- People doing the work should be able to maintain a sustainable pace, and cadence is monitored.
- Maintain highly visible information registers.

Answers to Selected Exercises

Note: Some chapters have only behavioral material and do not have exercises.

Chapter 2

2-1 Select Project A first since Project A scored considerably higher than all others (A=78 vs. B=54, C=56, and D=44). The second project to be selected is Project B, but Project C is in a virtual tie, so we would prefer to discuss the relative merits of each, perhaps considering additional *tiebreaking* criteria, before making the final selection.

2-3 Answers vary. The criteria developed would apply to projects that are either starting with a new compound (entirely new drug that may take a long time to get to market), a variation on a compound that is already partially studied (getting a variation of a drug to market sooner), or the purchase of a drug another company has fully or partially developed (perhaps getting the drug to market much quicker). Some criteria might include: speed in getting a new pharmaceutical to market, probability of success, cost of the project, and similarity with the company's existing products (alignment). The weightings can also vary, but students should be prepared to explain the logic behind why they chose the weights they did. Speed in getting a drug to market should be one of the highly rated criteria.

Chapter 3

3-1 Answers vary depending on the assignment. There should be a clear description of exactly *what* the team will do and *why* it is important. Each of those statements should be one to four complete sentences and should be easy to understand.

3-3 Answers vary. Use the four-column format of Exhibit 3.6. Both the current and future state descriptions should be very brief—about three or four words. The future state is likely to be something like "satisfying, profitable picnic." The milestones need to make sense and enable a stakeholder to judge each with easily measurable acceptance criteria that would accompany each.

Chapter 4

4-1 Answers vary depending on the scenario. Use rationale for the chosen structure. An example scenario might be an R&D organization that started many projects and canceled many early, but the remaining projects typically grew to be very large. In this situation, you might suggest a matrix structure. Tell why—such as resource-sharing needs among the many start-ups, yet need for specific attention to the large projects that survive.

4-3 Answers vary. You need to detail specific behaviors and determine which category from Exhibit 4.17 each represents.

Chapter 7

7-3 Answers vary. Here is a typical WBS:
1 Campus Event
  1.1 Site
    1.1.1 Selection
    1.1.2 Environment
    1.1.3 Neighbors
    1.1.4 Preparation
    1.1.5 Cleaning after
    1.1.6 Handover
  1.2 Promotion
    1.2.1 Campus newspapers
    1.2.2 Internet
    1.2.3 Other
  1.3 Finance
    1.3.1 Sponsorship
    1.3.2 Tickets
    1.3.3 Budget
    1.3.4 Audit
  1.4 Human Resources
    1.4.1 Marketing
    1.4.2 Security
    1.4.3 Ticket sales
    1.4.4 Management

1.5 Entertainment

1.6 Staging

Chapter 8

8-1

ES		EF
	Activity Name	
Slack		
	Duration	
LS		LF

8-3 A and B are predecessors, while C is a successor.

8-5

	A	B	C	D	E
Early start	0	12	16	12	19
Early finish	12	16	17	19	22
Late start	0	14	18	12	19
Late finish	12	18	19	19	22
Slack	0	2	2	0	0

8-8

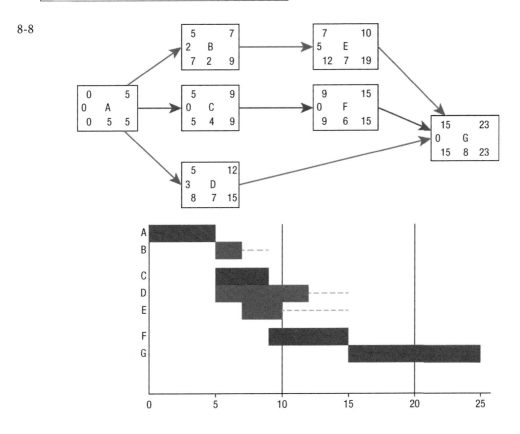

Activity	Days	Immediate Predecessor	ES	LS	EF	LF	Slack	CP?
A	5		0	0	5	5	0	yes
B	2	A	5	7	7	9	2	no
C	4	A	5	5	9	9	0	yes
D	7	A	5	8	12	15	3	no
E	3	B	7	12	10	15	5	no
F	6	B,C	9	9	15	15	0	yes
G	8	D,E,F	15	15	23	23	0	yes

Chapter 9

9-3

Duration	Activity(ies) Crashed	Incremental Crash Cost	Cumulative Crash Cost
42 (normal)			
41	F	150	150
40	C	200	350
39	G	250	600
38	G	250	850
37	A&C	350	1200
36	E	400	1600

Chapter 10

10-2 You can calculate the answers to this on MS Project, on Excel, or by hand. You first need to create the project schedule, create resource assignments, assign costs to each resource, and assign resources to each task. You will discover Alcides has a conflict right away, but one of the activities can be delayed within its slack. Joan has a conflict late that will force the noncritical task to be delayed, which will delay the entire project. The cumulative costs for the entire project are $7970. In the Gantt chart and budget aggregation table below, it may be noted that the final task, conduct regulatory review, was delayed since it conflicted with the previous task, conduct ROI analysis. The total budget for the project remains unchanged, but the project is now scheduled to take a bit longer, and the cash flow corresponds to the schedule.

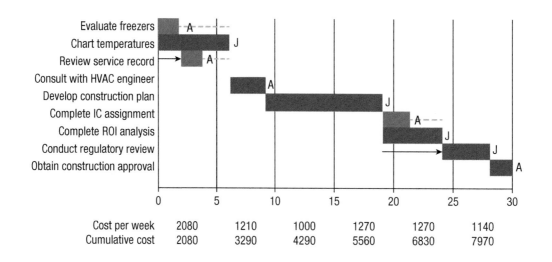

Chapter 11

11-1 Answers vary. An example follows.

Major Risks	Counter Measures
1. No back-up plan	1. Write a back-up plan
2. Security	2. Continuous internal communication w/security
3. Presidential candidate unavailable	3. Refer to back-up plan
4. Date not available	4. Find different venue/ renegotiate contract
5. Important donor not invited	5. Ensure update accurate list
6. Low attendance	6. Invitations/Adv./PR in timely manner
7. No or low media interest	7. Have and execute media plan
8. Issue with speaker	8. Establish crisis plan
9. Loss of money	9. Budget/forecasting
10. Over extending staff and resources	10. Set realistic expectations and stick to them

11-5 Answers vary. Show logical relationships and triggers that should be something easily observable that occurs before the risk event. For example, major risk 6 in exercise 1 above (low attendance) could have a trigger in low response to RSVPs that are sent out two weeks before the event.

Chapter 12

12-2 Within a quality management plan, some or all of the following topics should be addressed with the supporting documentation and definitions:

- The mission and quality policy of the organization
- Roles and responsibilities of management and staff with respect to audit and/or quality activities
- Quality system description
- Personnel qualifications and training; implementation of work processes
- Corrective actions procedures
- Standard operating procedures
- Quality improvement description
- Procurement of items and services
- Documentation and records
- Computer hardware and software

12-5 Answers vary. Include the entire quality policy because it is likely to be short. Articulate specifically some ways the policy will guide the project. An example from Colgate follows:

Colgate Quality Policy: *Our goal is to provide consumers with the highest-quality products by assuring their performance, consistency, safety, and value. This commitment is rooted in our corporate values and is essential to our continued growth and success. We will meet our comprehensive "Global Colgate Quality Standards" in the design, manufacturing, and distribution of our products as well as meet or exceed all government requirements and consumer expectations worldwide. We will maintain these high-quality standards as we design and manufacture our products by the most efficient means possible to ensure they are affordable to the greatest number of consumers throughout the world. Our commitment to quality is vital to all we do.*

Performance, consistency, and safety are all dimensions of quality that are stressed. Value is also mentioned. Time is not. This would suggest that quality is the most important variable for their projects, followed by cost. Schedule then might take a backseat.

Chapter 14

14-1

a. Schedule variance (SV). EV − PV = −$150,000. This project is behind schedule.
b. Cost variance (CV). EV − AC = −$200,000. This project is over budget.
c. Schedule performance index (SPI). EV/PV = 70%
d. Cost performance index (CPI). EV/AC = 64%
e. Estimate to complete (ETC—first method). (BAC − EV)/CPI = $1,328,125
f. Estimate to complete (ETC—second method). BAC − EV = $850,000
g. Estimate at completion (EAC). AC + ETC = $1,878,125
h. To-complete performance index (TCPI) = (BAC − EV)/(BAC − AC) = 131%

14-6

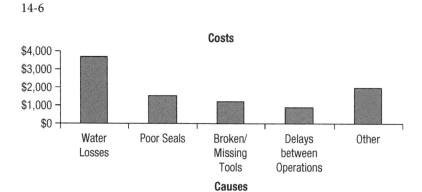

The next course of action would be to investigate the top issue—water losses.

14-8

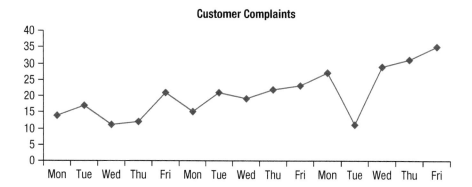

There is an upward trend. Tuesday of the final week appears to be an outlier (it is considerably below others near it). There does not appear to be a strong repeating pattern.

Project Deliverables

PROJECT DELIVERABLE	Type of Objective	Chapter(s)	PMBOK® Process	PMBOK® Knowledge Area (or section)	PMBOK® Process Group
Customer Trade-Off Matrix	behavioral	1		1.2 Foundational Elements	
Project Success Definition	core	1		1.2 Foundational Elements	
Elevator Pitch	core	2		1.2 Foundational Elements	
Project Selection and Prioritization Matrix	technical	2		Selecting Projects	
Project Resource Assignment Matrix	technical	2		Selecting Projects	
Project Charter	core	3	Develop Project Charter	Integration	Initiating
Assumptions Log	behavioral	3	Develop Project Charter	Integration	Initiating
Life Cycle and Development Approach	behavioral	4	Develop Project Management Plan	Integration	Planning
Leader Roles and Responsibilities	behavioral	4		3.4 Project Management Competencies	
Team Charter	behavioral	5	Plan Resource Management	Resources	Planning
Team Assessments	behavioral	5	Develop Team	Resources	Executing
Stakeholder Engagement Assessment Matrix	core	6	Plan Stakeholder Engagement	Stakeholder	Planning
Communication Matrix	core	6	Plan Communications Management	Communications	Planning
Meeting Agenda	behavioral	6	Manage Communications	Communications	Executing
Meeting Minutes	behavioral	6	Manage Communications	Communications	Executing
Issues Log	behavioral	6	Manage Communications	Communications	Executing
Meeting Evaluation	behavioral	6	Manage Communications	Communications	Executing
Requirements Traceability Matrix	core	7	Collect Requirements	Scope	Planning
Scope Statement	core	7	Define Scope	Scope	Planning
Scope Baseline with WBS	technical	7	Create WBS	Scope	Planning
Activity List	core	8	Define Activities	Schedule	Planning

PROJECT DELIVERABLE	Type of Objective	Chapter(s)	PMBOK® Process	PMBOK® Knowledge Area (or section)	PMBOK® Process Group
Milestone List	core	8	Define Activities	Schedule	Planning
Network	core	8	Sequence Activities	Schedule	Planning
Duration Estimates	core	8	Estimate Activity Durations	Schedule	Planning
Schedule Baseline	core	8	Develop Schedule	Schedule	Planning
RACI Chart	core	9	Plan Resource Management	Resources	Planning
Resource Histogram	core	9	Develop Schedule	Schedule	Planning
Project Crashing	technical	9	Develop Schedule	Schedule	Planning
Cost Baseline	core	10	Determine Budget	Cost	Planning
Risk Register	core	11	Identify Risks	Risk	Planning
Project Management Plan Baseline	technical	12	Develop Project Management Plan	Integration	Planning
Bid Documents	technical	13	Plan Procurement Management	Procurement	Planning
Make or Buy Analysis	technical	13	Plan Procurement Management	Procurement	Planning
Contract Type Justification	technical	13	Plan Procurement Management	Procurement	Planning
Source Selection Matrix	technical	13	Conduct Procurements	Procurement	Executing
Change Request	core	14	Perform Integrated Change Control	Integration	Monitoring & Controlling
Progress Report	core	14	Monitor Communications	Communications	Monitoring & Controlling
Earned Value Analysis	technical	14	Control Costs	Cost	Monitoring & Controlling

Index

Terms from the PMBOK® Guide are set in **bold** in this index.

Section
1.2 Foundational Elements

2.4 Organizational Systems
3.3 The Project Manager's Sphere of Influence
3.4 Project Manager Competencies
Selecting Projects

Deliverable
Project Customer Tradeoff Matrix
Project Success Definition
Life Cycle and Development Approach
Elevator Pitch

Leader Roles and Responsibilities
Project Selection and Prioritization Matrix
Project Resource Assignment Matrix

Flowchart of PMBOK F

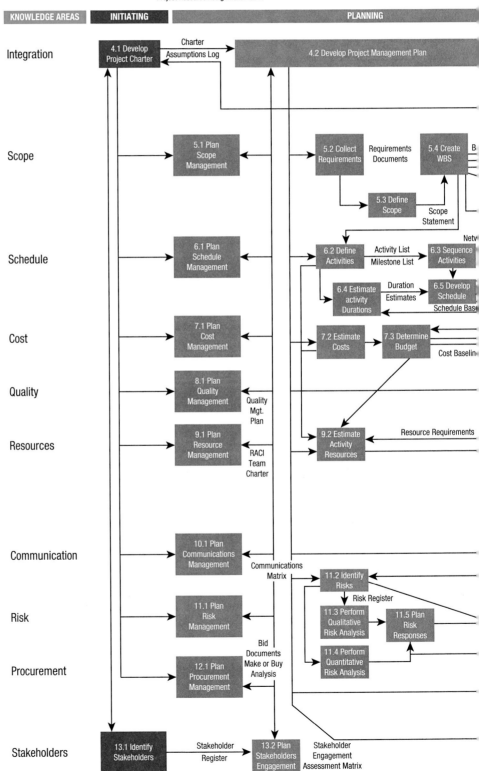